BUSINESS ENVIRONMENT
Indian and Global Perspective

Second Edition

FAISAL AHMED
Associate Professor
International Business Area
FORE School of Management
New Delhi

M. ABSAR ALAM
Assistant Professor
Department of Economics
M.K.S. College
L.N. Mithila University, Darbhanga, Bihar

PHI Learning Private Limited
Delhi-110092
2020

₹ 550.00

BUSINESS ENVIRONMENT: Indian and Global Perspective, Second Edition
Faisal Ahmed and M. Absar Alam

ISBN-978-81-203-5333-6

Third Printing (Second Edition) ... ... **January, 2020**

Published by Asoke K. Ghosh, PHI Learning Private Limited, Rimjhim House, 111, Patparganj Industrial Estate, Delhi-110092 and Printed by Syndicate Binders, A-20, Hosiery Complex, Noida, Phase-II Extension, Noida-201305 (N.C.R. Delhi).

To
my late maternal grandparents
Saira and Hassan Shahid

—FAISAL AHMED

To
my parents
Rabiah and Fazle Alam

—M. ABSAR ALAM

CONTENTS

List of Boxes ... *xv*

List of Figures ... *xvii*

List of Tables ... *xix*

Preface ... *xxiii*

Acknowledgements ... *xxvii*

1. Concepts ... 1–16

Learning Outcomes ... 1

Opening Case: Pravasi Bharatiya Divas ... 1

1.1 Business Environment and Strategic Management ... 2

1.2 Economic and Non-economic Environment ... 3

1.2.1 Economic Environment ... 4

1.2.2 Non-economic Environment ... 5

1.3 Technological Environment ... 9

1.4 Startups: An Emerging Phenomenon ... 13

Closing Case: World Economic Forum at Davos, Switzerland ... 15

Case Questions ... 15

Review Questions ... 16

Suggested Readings ... 16

2. Contemporary Perspectives ... 17–42

Learning Outcomes ... 17

Opening Case: Best Practices in CSR—GAIL (India) Limited ... 17

2.1 Global Business Environment ... 18

2.1.1 Global Economic Scenario ... 20

2.1.2 Indian Economic Scenario ... 21

2.2 Public Policy ... 23

2.3 Corporate Social Responsibility ... 25

2.4 Consumerism 28
2.5 Inclusive Growth 31
2.6 Trade, Growth and Poverty 35
2.7 Sustainable Development 37
Closing Case: Universal Climate Agreement (2020) 39
Case Questions 41
Review Questions 41
Suggested Readings 42

3. Environmental Scanning 43–51

Learning Outcomes 43
Opening Case: Scanning Makes Sense—Instances from Syria and Iran 43
3.1 Meaning and Scope 44
3.2 Types of Research 45
3.3 Research Process 46
3.4 Data Scanning and Quantitative Analysis 46
3.5 SWOT Analysis 47
3.6 PEST Analysis 48
Closing Case: Role of EPCs and Market Intelligence 50
Case Questions 51
Review Questions 51
Suggested Readings 51

4. Economic Systems 52–70

Learning Outcomes 52
Opening Case: From African Socialism to Free Market Economy 52
4.1 Introduction 53
4.2 What is an Economic System? 54
4.3 Evolution of Economic Ideas 56
4.4 Mercantilism 60
4.5 Capitalism 61
4.6 Communist System 63
4.7 Socialist System 63
4.8 Market Economy 64
4.9 Planned Economy 66
4.10 Mixed Economy 66
Closing Case: Think Twice Before You Google in China! 68
Case Questions 70
Review Questions 70
Suggested Readings 70

5. Planning and Reform 71–94

Learning Outcomes 71
Opening Case: Direct Benefit (Cash) Transfer 71
5.1 Introduction 73

5.2 Pre-Independence Period 75
5.3 National Development Council 76
5.4 Five Year Plans 77
5.5 Beginning of New Phase of Planning 82
5.6 Land Reforms 84
5.7 Green Revolution 85
5.8 Evolution of Public Sector in India 89
5.9 Economic Reforms 91

Closing Case: Housing Sector Reforms in India 91
Case Questions 93
Review Questions 93
Suggested Readings 94

6. Macroeconomic Indicators 95–125

Learning Outcomes 95
Opening Case: Onion Price Rise in Delhi 95

6.1 Introduction 96
6.2 National Income 97
 6.2.1 National Income Accounting 97
 6.2.2 National Income and the Economic Environment 101
 6.2.3 National Income Accounting in India 105
 6.2.4 National Income Accounting: Gross Value Added Approach of Government of India 106
6.3 Consumption and Investment 109
 6.3.1 Consumption 109
 6.3.2 Investment 112
6.4 Inflation 113
 6.4.1 Measurement of Inflation 114
 6.4.2 Types of Inflation 115
6.5 Business Cycle 117
 6.5.1 Stages of Business Cycle 118
6.6 Socio-economic Indicators: Poverty, Inequality and Unemployment 119
 6.6.1 Poverty 119
 6.6.2 Inequality 121
 6.6.3 Unemployment 123

Closing Case: Poverty Alleviation—A Continuing Challenge 124
Case Questions 125
Review Questions 125
Suggested Readings 125

7. Industrial Policies 126–158

Learning Outcomes 126
Opening Case: The 'Made in India' Tag? 126

7.1 Introduction 128
 7.1.1 Manufacturing in Defence Sector 128

7.2 Industrial Policy Resolution, 1948 131
7.3 Industrial Policy Resolution, 1956 132
  7.3.1 Objectives of Industrial Policy Resolution, 1956 133
  7.3.2 Characteristics of Industrial Policy, 1956 134
  7.3.3 Outcome of the Policy 135
7.4 Monopolies Inquiry Commission, 1964 137
7.5 Industrial Policy Statement, 1973 138
7.6 Industrial Policy Statement, 1977 138
7.7 Industrial Policy Statement, 1980 139
7.8 Review of Industrial Policy Measures before 1991 139
7.9 Industrial Policy Statement, 1991 140
  7.9.1 Objectives of the 1991 Policy 141
  7.9.2 Features of Industrial Policy Statement, 1991 141
  7.9.3 Micro, Small and Medium Industries and Policies 142
7.10 India's Industrial Progress after 1991 144
7.11 Performance of Small and Medium Scale Industry (SME) Sector 150
7.12 Review of Economic Environment in Industrial Sector 151
7.13 Policies on Foreign Direct Investment in India 153
7.14 Foreign Exchange Regulation Act 155
7.15 Industrial Policy Resolution, 1991 155

Closing Case: Industrial Policy Post-2015—The Global Concern 155

Case Questions 158
Review Questions 158
Suggested Readings 158

8. Fiscal Policy 159–193

Learning Outcomes 159

Opening Case: Right to Food 159

8.1 Introduction 160
8.2 Public Revenue 162
8.3 Tax Revenues 163
  8.3.1 Direct and Indirect Tax Revenue 164
8.4 Non-Tax Revenues 170
8.5 Capital Receipts 170
8.6 Public Expenditures 170
8.7 Fiscal Deficit 172
  8.7.1 Types of Deficits 173
8.8 Objectives of Fiscal Policy 174
8.9 Fiscal Instruments 175
8.10 Guiding Principle of Tax Policies 175
8.11 Burden of Taxation and Incidence of Taxation 176
8.12 Effect of Taxation 177
8.13 Public Debt 177
8.14 Development Activities Financed by Public Expenditure 180

8.15 The Union Budget 2017–2018 181
8.16 The Union Budgets of 2014–2015 and 2016–2017 185
8.16.1 The Union Budget 2014–2015 185
8.16.2 The Union Budget 2016–2017 188
8.17 Finance Commission 190
Closing Case: MGNREGA—What is it Doing? 191
Case Questions 193
Review Questions 193
Suggested Readings 193

9. Monetary Policy 194–214

Learning Outcomes 194
Opening Case: Rupee versus Dollar and the RBI 194
9.1 Introduction 196
9.2 Objectives of Monetary Policies 196
9.3 Types of Monetary Policies 198
9.4 Demand and Supply of Money 198
9.5 Instruments of Monetary Policy 201
9.6 Central Banking in India: RBI 205
9.7 Institutional Frameworks 208
9.8 Recent Trends in Monetary Policy 209
Closing Case: RBI's Crucial Role! 211
Case Questions 214
Review Questions 214
Suggested Readings 214

10. Balance of Payments 215–233

Learning Outcomes 215
Opening Case: India's BoP Challenges and the Business Environment 215
10.1 Introduction 216
10.2 Balance of Payments 217
10.3 Components of Balance of Payments and Its Accounting 217
10.4 Structure of BoP in India 220
10.5 Key Indicators of Balance of Payments 225
10.6 Trends of Balance of Payments in India 230
Closing Case: India's Strategies to Reduce Trade Deficit 231
Case Questions 233
Review Questions 233
Suggested Readings 233

11. Money and Capital Markets 234–253

Learning Outcomes 234
Opening Case: Repo Rate kept Unchanged 234
11.1 Structure of Indian Financial System 235
11.2 Money Market 237

11.3 Capital Market 243
11.4 Recent Developments in Stock Exchanges 246
11.5 Securities and Exchange Board of India (SEBI) 251
Closing Case: Banking Sector Reforms 252
Case Questions 253
Review Questions 253
Suggested Readings 253

12. Legal Framework 254–268

Learning Outcomes 254
Opening Case: Dial 1800-11-4000! 254
12.1 Legal Procedure 256
12.2 Sick Industrial Companies Act (Special Provisions), 1985 256
12.3 Board for Industrial and Financial Reconstruction (BIFR) 257
12.4 Consumer Protection Act, 1986 258
12.5 Companies Act, 1956 and 2013 260
12.6 Monopolies and Restrictive Trade Practices (MRTP) Act, 1969 and Competition Act, 2002 261
12.7 Foreign Exchange Regulation Act (FERA) and Foreign Exchange Management Act (FEMA) 262
12.8 Government's Reform Agenda and Regulatory Bills 264
12.8.1 The Right to Fair Compensation and Transparency in Land Acquisition, Rehabilitation and Resettlement Act, 2013 264
12.8.2 Goods and Service Tax (GST) Bill 265
Closing Case: Can DCHL be Declared Sick under BIFR Provisions? 266
Case Questions 267
Review Questions 268
Suggested Readings 268

13. Principles of International Law for Business 269–278

Learning Outcomes 269
Opening Case: GIPC Index and India–US Legal Dispute 269
13.1 Sources of International Law 270
13.2 Principles of International Law 271
13.3 Scope of International Trade Law 272
13.4 Some other International Conventions Promoting Trade and Commerce 274
13.4.1 Revised Kyoto Convention 274
13.4.2 TIR Convention 275
13.4.3 Convention Concerning International Carriage by Rail (COTIF) 276
13.4.4 The United Nations Framework Convention on Climate Change (UNFCCC)... 276
Closing Case: Supreme Court of India Judgement on Sovereign Immunity 277
Case Questions 278
Review Questions 278
Suggested Readings 278

14. International Organisations 279–303

Learning Outcomes 279

Opening Case: Business Partners with the UN 279

14.1 Introduction..281
14.2 The United Nations 282
14.3 United Nations Conference on Trade and Development (UNCTAD) 285
14.4 United Nations Commission on International Trade Law (UNCITRAL) 287
14.5 United Nations Development Programme (UNDP) 289
14.6 World Food Programme (WFP)..291
14.7 International Labour Organisation (ILO) 292
14.8 International Monetary Fund (IMF)..295
14.9 World Bank 296
14.10 World Trade Organisation (WTO)..298

Closing Case: Dispute on China's Rare Earth Elements in WTO 302

Case Questions 302
Review Questions 302
Suggested Readings 303

15. Models and Frameworks of International Trade 304–321

Learning Outcomes 304

Opening Case: China—The World's Factory 304

15.1 Trade and Its Relevance 305
15.2 Theory of Absolute Advantage 307
15.3 Theory of Comparative Advantage 309
15.4 Factor Endowment Theory..311
15.5 Leontief Paradox 312
15.6 New Trade Theory 312

15.6.1 Revealed Comparative Advantage (RCA)..313
15.6.2 Trade Complementarity Index (TCI)..314
15.6.3 Intra-Industry Trade (IIT) Model..314
15.6.4 Gravity Model of Trade 315

15.7 Evolving World Trade..316

Closing Case: Global Value Chains 319

Case Questions 320
Review Questions 321
Suggested Readings 322

16. Internationalisation of Firms 322–329

Learning Outcomes 322

Opening Case: Domestic Airlines Industry—Moving Beyond Indian Airspace! 322

16.1 Why Companies Cross Borders? 324
16.2 Modes of Entry into a Foreign Market..324
16.3 Porter's Diamond..326

16.4 Multinational Corporations (MNCs) 327
16.4.1 Classification of MNCs 328
Closing Case: Unilever in the Indian Subcontinent—Hindustan Unilever Limited (HUL), Unilever Nepal, Unilever Sri Lanka 328
Case Questions 329
Review Questions 329
Suggested Readings 329

17. Foreign Direct Investment (FDI) 330–353

Learning Outcomes 330
Opening Case: FDI in Multi-brand Retail 330
17.1 Meaning of FDI 331
17.2 Types of FDI 333
17.3 Theories of FDI 334
17.4 Global Trends in FDI Flows 336
17.5 Geographical Distribution of World FDI 336
17.6 Importance of FDI in World Economy 341
17.7 FDI Regime in India: Trends and Pattern 343
17.8 Sources of FDI in India 349
Closing Case: Investment Regimes in Nepal and Bhutan 351
Case Questions 353
Review Questions 353
Suggested Readings 353

18. Trends in Global Trade and Economic Integration 354–371

Learning Outcomes 354
Opening Case: IOR-ARC—Integrating the Boundaries of the Indian Ocean! 354
18.1 Direction of World Trade 355
18.2 Multilateralism and the Multilateral Trading System 358
18.3 Levels of Economic Integration 359
18.4 Regional Integration 363
Closing Case: RCEP—Redefining Integration 370
Case Questions 371
Review Questions 371
Suggested Readings 371

19. The WTO Regime 372–393

Learning Outcomes 372
Opening Case: Russia's Accession to the WTO—Wait and Watch! 372
19.1 General Agreement on Tariffs and Trade (GATT) 374
19.2 The Uruguay Round and the Marrakesh Declaration 375
19.3 Aims, Objectives and Functions of WTO 377

19.4 Principles of the Trading System (WTO)....378
19.5 General Agreement on Tariffs and Trade (GATT)....380
19.6 General Agreement on Trade in Services (GATS)....380
19.7 Trade-Related Aspects of Intellectual Property Rights (TRIPS)....382
19.8 Trade-Related Investment Measures (TRIMs)....385
19.9 Trade Policy Review Mechanism (TPRM)....386
19.10 Dispute Settlement System....387
19.11 Thrust Areas of the WTO....389

Closing Case: Best Practices in Aid for Trade (AfT)....391

Case Questions....393
Review Questions....393
Suggested Readings....393

20. Major Provisions under WTO....394–414

Learning Outcomes....394

Opening Case: India Challenges EU's Ban on Indian Mangoes on SPS Issue....394

20.1 Agreement on Agriculture (AoA)....395
20.2 Sanitary and Phytosanitary Measures (SPS)....399
20.3 Agreement on Textiles and Clothing (ATC)....402
20.4 Rules of Origin (ROO or RoO)....403
20.5 Provisions for LDCs....405
20.6 Tariff and Non-Tariff Barriers....407
20.7 Anti-Dumping Agreement....410
20.8 Subsidies and Countervailing Measures....412

Closing Case: US Imposes Countervailing Duty on Shrimps from India....413

Case Questions....414
Review Questions....414
Suggested Readings....414

21. Cross-cutting Issues in International Environment....415–422

Learning Outcomes....415

Opening Case: India's Solar Power Policy and Dispute with the United States....415

21.1 Cross-cutting Issues....416
21.2 Trade and Climate Change....416
21.3 Trade and Food Security....417
21.4 Trade and Finance....419
21.5 Trade and Geopolitics....419

Closing Case: ONGC Videsh Limited in South China Sea Geopolitics....421

Case Questions....422
Review Questions....422
Suggested Readings....422

22. Foreign Exchange Risk and Exposures 423–428

Learning Outcomes 423

Opening Case: Tax Havens! 423

22.1 Global Cash Flow 424
22.2 Foreign Exchange Exposure 425
22.3 Managing Risks 426

Closing Case: Forex Risk for MSMEs 426

Case Questions 427
Review Questions 428
Suggested Readings 428

23. Country Risk and Political Risk Analysis 429–436

Learning Outcomes 429

Opening Case: Syrian Political Unrest and Country Analysis 429

23.1 Risk Analysis 431
23.2 Country Risk Analysis 431

23.2.1 Evaluation and Diagnosis of Risk 432

23.3 Political Risk Analysis 433

23.3.1 Importance of Political Risk Analysis 433
23.3.2 Valuing Political Risk 434

Closing Case: India's Business in Afghanistan 435

Case Questions 436
Review Questions 436
Suggested Readings 436

24. Doing Business in Select Markets 437–459

Learning Outcomes 437

Opening Case: Doing Business in Afghanistan 437

24.1 Emerging Markets Scenario 439
24.2 Regional Comparison of Doing Business 440
24.3 Doing Business in BRICS, ASEAN, ECOWAS 446

Closing Case: Reforms, Growth and Business Climate 457

Case Questions 458
Review Questions 459
Suggested Readings 459

Index* *461–467

LIST OF BOXES

Box 1.1 Holcim–Lafarge Merger, ***3***
Box 1.2 Demographic Dividend in India, ***7***
Box 1.3 Bicameral and Unicameral Legislatures, ***8***
Box 1.4 Apple's Strategies in India Market, ***9***
Box 1.5 Startup India, Standup India Scheme, ***9***
Box 1.6 Digital India, ***11***
Box 1.7 Startup India Action Plan—Compliance Regime Based on Self-Certification, ***14***
Box 2.1 DBT and Public Policy Doctrine, ***24***
Box 2.2 UNIDO and CSR, ***26***
Box 2.3 Sluggish Exports and Resilient Domestic Demand in Asia and the Pacific, ***28***
Box 2.4 Jan-Dhan Yojana Towards Financial Inclusion, ***32***
Box 2.5 Sastainable Development Goals (SDGs), ***38***
Box 4.1 Mill's Idea of Environment, ***58***
Box 4.2 Monetarist Policies, ***60***
Box 4.3 A Note on Mercantilist Policy, ***61***
Box 4.4 Idea of Capitalism, ***62***
Box 4.5 State Capitalism in Europe, ***63***
Box 4.6 Free Market Economy and the Private Sector, ***64***
Box 4.7 Recent Move Towards Mixed Economies, ***67***
Box 4.8 Eurozone Crisis: The Case of Greece, ***67***
Box 5.1 Main Functions of Planning Commission, ***74***
Box 5.2 Performance of Central Public Sector Enterprises, ***90***
Box 6.1 Illustration based on United Nations System of National Accounts, ***105***
Box 7.1 From Delicensing to Make in India, ***129***
Box 7.2 Strategies of the First Five Year Plan, ***132***
Box 7.3 Industries under Schedule A and Schedule B, ***134***
Box 7.4 Impact of Industrial Policy, 1956, ***136***
Box 7.5 Bhilai Steel Plant, ***137***
Box 7.6 Reforms in Industrial Sector Post-1991, ***146***
Box 7.7 Industrial Dispute: Maruti at Manesar, ***152***
Box 7.8 Examples of Weak Domestic Standards, ***152***
Box 8.1 Union Budget of India, 2013–2014, ***162***

Box 8.2 Goods and Service Tax (GST) and its Benefits, ***169***

Box 8.3 Constitutional Provisions on Distribution of Revenues between the Union and the States, ***190***

Box 8.4 Revenue Share of Different States as per the Thirteenth Finance Commission, ***190***

Box 9.1 Select Monetary Policy Objectives Post-2007–2008 Crisis, ***197***

Box 9.2 Money Aggregates in India, ***199***

Box 9.3 China uses Open Market Operation to Avoid Liquidity Crunch, ***205***

Box 9.4 First Bimonthly Monetary Policy of RBI, 2016–2017, ***208***

Box 9.5 Demonetisation in India, ***211***

Box 12.1 Restrictive Trade Practices as per Consumer Protection Act, 1986, ***259***

Box 12.2 Coca Cola's Departure from India in 1977, ***263***

Box 12.3 Difference between the Provisions of FERA and FEMA, ***263***

Box 12.4 Justification of GST, ***266***

Box 14.1 Preamble of the United Nations, ***283***

Box 14.2 Purpose of the United Nations, ***283***

Box 14.3 Major Outcome of Ministerial Meeting of UNCTAD in Doha, 2012 (UNCTAD XIII), ***287***

Box 14.4 Mandate of United Nations Commission on International Trade Law, ***288***

Box 14.5 Healthcare Waste Management: A Case from India, ***290***

Box 14.6 Purpose of IMF, ***295***

Box 14.7 Sale of Gold by IMF, ***296***

Box 17.1 Financial Instruments Related to FDI, ***332***

Box 18.1 Belarus–Kazakhstan–Russia Customs Union, ***361***

Box 18.2 Common Market for Eastern and Southern Africa (COMESA), ***362***

Box 18.3 EU as Economic Union, ***362***

Box 18.4 BREXIT, ***364***

Box 18.5 Maldives No Longer an LDC, ***366***

Box 18.6 India–ASEAN FTA in Goods and Services, ***368***

Box 19.1 The 15 Original Uruguay Round Subjects, ***376***

Box 19.2 MFN Status: India and Pakistan, ***379***

Box 19.3 Panama–Argentina—Financial Services Dispute, ***382***

Box 19.4 First Trade Policy Review of Myanmar, ***387***

Box 19.5 Trade Capacity Building through CAFTA-DR in Africa, ***390***

Box 19.6 Streamlining Aid for Trade with APRM, ***391***

Box 20.1 List of General Services: Bali Round, ***398***

Box 20.2 Differences between SPS and TBT Measures, ***401***

Box 20.3 Measures Related to Import of Agricultural Products by India, ***402***

Box 20.4 Principles of Harmonised Rules of Origin (HRO), ***405***

Box 20.5 LDC Package at WTO Bali Round 2013, ***407***

Box 24.1 Measures Undertaken by BRICS Countries to Ease Doing Business, ***448***

Box 24.2 Measures Undertaken by ASEAN Countries to Ease Doing Business, ***451***

LIST OF FIGURES

Figure 2.1 Growth in the volume of world merchandise exports and production, 2010–2014, ***19***
Figure 2.2 Benefits of CSR, ***27***
Figure 2.3 Region-wide GDP growth (%), ***33***
Figure 2.4 GDP per capita, PPP (constant 2005 US$), ***34***
Figure 2.5 Trend of GDP growth and trade (%), ***36***
Figure 4.1 Agents of an economic system, ***55***
Figure 4.2 Interactions in an economic system, ***55***
Figure 4.3 Classification of economic systems, ***56***
Figure 5.1 Objectives of land reforms, ***85***
Figure 5.2 Changing share of employment in agriculture sector, ***86***
Figure 5.3 Average production during planning period, ***87***
Figure 6.1 Circular flow of income generation in a realistic economy, ***97***
Figure 6.2 Calculation of national expenditure, ***100***
Figure 6.3 Quarterly projection of growth in GVA at basic prices (year-on-year), ***103***
Figure 6.4 A linear consumption function, ***110***
Figure 6.5 Savings function: Graphical representation, ***111***
Figure 6.6 Investment function: Graphical representation, ***113***
Figure 6.7 Demand pull inflation, ***116***
Figure 6.8 Cost push inflation, ***117***
Figure 6.9 Stages of business cycle, ***118***
Figure 6.10 GDP growth of India and the world: Depicting stages of business cycle, ***119***
Figure 6.11 Poverty headcount ratio (%) in 2008 and 2010, ***121***
Figure 6.12 Percentage point change in the Gini coefficient of household market and disposable incomes, ***122***
Figure 6.13 Lorenz curve, ***122***
Figure 6.14 Gini coefficient, ***123***
Figure 7.1 Index number of industrial production (1950–1951 = 100), ***136***
Figure 7.2 Growth in industrial production and growth in GDP, ***149***
Figure 7.3 Need for foreign direct investment, ***153***
Figure 8.1 Share of components of revenues of central government, ***164***
Figure 8.2 Share of direct and indirect tax in total tax revenue, ***165***
Figure 8.3 Share of income tax and corporation tax in total direct tax revenues, ***167***

Figure 8.4 Share of excise duty and customs duty in total indirect tax revenues, ***168***
Figure 8.5 Instruments of government revenue, ***170***
Figure 8.6 Trend of cash deficit of central government, ***173***
Figure 9.1 Use of CRR as an instrument, ***203***
Figure 9.2 Impact of changes in bank rate on credit demand, ***205***
Figure 10.1 Components of balance of payments, ***218***
Figure 10.2 India's total trade deficit, ***226***
Figure 10.3 Net indicators of balance of payments, ***230***
Figure 11.1 Structure of financial market in India, ***236***
Figure 11.2 Structure of organised banking system in the country, ***237***
Figure 11.3 Population (group-wise) number of branches of scheduled commercial banks (in numbers), ***240***
Figure 11.4 Trend of mobilisation of funds through mutual funds, ***249***
Figure 11.5 Monthly BSE 100 index (base year 1983–1984 = 58), ***251***
Figure 13.1 Composition of business laws, ***274***
Figure 14.1 Objectives of World Food Programme, ***292***
Figure 14.2 Structure of ILO, ***293***
Figure 14.3 ILO's Strategic Objectives, ***293***
Figure 15.1 Understanding opportunity cost for Country A, ***309***
Figure 17.1 Growth rates of global GDP, gross fixed capital formation (GFCF), trade, employment and FDI, 2008–2015, ***336***
Figure 17.2 Trend of global FDI inflow, ***337***
Figure 17.3 Share of major economies in world FDI inflows in 2014 and 2015 (%), ***338***
Figure 17.4 Growth of FDI inflows in developing and developed region (%), ***341***
Figure 17.5 Growth of FDI inflows in India, ***348***
Figure 18.1 Levels of economic integration, ***360***
Figure 18.2 India's trade with the world (region-wise), 2014–2015, ***363***
Figure 18.3 European Union's global trade, ***365***
Figure 18.4 Annual growth of exports and imports in EU (%), ***365***
Figure 18.5 SAARC's global trade, ***367***
Figure 18.6 ASEAN's global trade, ***368***
Figure 18.7 MERCOSUR's global trade, ***369***
Figure 21.1 Global food price index, ***418***
Figure 24.1 GDP growth projections, ***441***
Figure 24.2 Sub-Saharan Africa's economic performance, ***442***
Figure 24.3 Region-wise trend of foreign investment, ***443***
Figure 24.4 Number of procedures and documents required in various regions, ***445***
Figure 24.5 Time required for completing various activities across regions, ***446***
Figure 24.6 GDP growth of BRICS economies and projections, ***446***
Figure 24.7 Total investment as percentage of GDP in BRICS, ***447***
Figure 24.8 BRICS ranking on ease of doing business (2013 and 2014), ***447***
Figure 24.9 Economic growth of ASEAN: Performance and projections, ***449***
Figure 24.10 Total investment as percentage of GDP in ASEAN, ***450***
Figure 24.11 Ranking of ASEAN countries on ease of doing business in 2013 and 2014, ***450***
Figure 24.12 Ease of doing business: Ranking of countries from ECOWAS, 2014, 2015 and 2016, ***453***

LIST OF TABLES

Table 1.1 Network Readiness Index, ***12***
Table 2.1 Annual Per Cent Change, ***20***
Table 2.2 Performance of Indian Economy: Growth Rate (%), ***22***
Table 2.3 Contribution of Components to Real GDP Growth, ***23***
Table 2.4 Economies with Higher Share of Household Consumption in GDP (%), ***29***
Table 2.5 Consumerism in the World, 2014, ***30***
Table 2.6 Some Economic Indicators Related to Inclusive Growth, ***34***
Table 2.7 Global Export Share in GDP, ***36***
Table 2.8 Trend of Annual Growth in Per Capital Income (%), ***37***
Table 3.1 SWOT Analysis: Some Pertinent Factors, ***47***
Table 3.2 Factors for PEST Analysis, ***49***
Table 4.1 Comparative Overview of Economic Systems, ***68***
Table 5.1 Share of Countries and Region in World's GDP (0–1950 AD), ***76***
Table 5.2 Growth Rate (Targeted and Actual) During 30 Years of Plan Era, ***80***
Table 5.3 Output of Foodgrains During Early Phase of Green Revolution, ***87***
Table 5.4 Decadal Picture of Agricultural Productivity (kg/ha), ***88***
Table 5.5 Expansion of Public Sector and Investment in the Sector, ***89***
Table 6.1 GDP Growth—Actual and Projected (at constant 2004–2005 prices), ***102***
Table 6.2 Key Indicators, ***104***
Table 6.3 Advance Estimates of National Income and Expenditures of GDP, 2015–2016 at Constant Price (2011–2012), ***108***
Table 6.4 Calculation of Total Consumption, ***109***
Table 6.5 Share of Population Living below Poverty Line (%), ***120***
Table 7.1 Performance of Some Major Industrial Units, ***137***
Table 7.2 Selected Macroeconomic Indicators 1989–2003, ***144***
Table 7.3 Performance of Industrial Sector, ***145***
Table 7.4 Growth in Productivity of Selected Industries During 2007–2015 (%), ***147***
Table 7.5 Index Numbers of Industrial Production: Use-based Classification, ***148***
Table 7.6 Performance of Industrial Sector, ***149***
Table 7.7 Sub-sector-wise Share in Gross Capital Formation in Industrial Sector at 2011–2012 Prices, ***150***
Table 7.8 Contribution of MSME Sector in GDP and Output (at 2004–2005 Prices), ***151***
Table 8.1 Direct and Indirect Tax Revenue, ***164***

Table 8.2 Tax Rates, ***165***
Table 8.3 Slabs for Women Resident in India, ***166***
Table 8.4 Slabs for an Individual of Age 60 Years or More, ***166***
Table 8.5 Slabs for an Individual of Age 80 Years or More, ***166***
Table 8.6 Expenditure of Central Government, ***171***
Table 8.7 Details of Expenditure of Central Government under Non-planned Expenditure, ***171***
Table 8.8 Public Debt and Other Liabilities of the Central Government, ***178***
Table 8.9 Liabilities of the Central and State Governments, ***179***
Table 8.10 Select Debt Indicators of the Central and State Governments (Percentage of GDP), ***179***
Table 8.11 Budget at Glance: 2017–2018, ***184***
Table 8.12 Budget at Glance: 2014–2015, ***187***
Table 8.13 Budget at Glance: 2016–2017, ***189***
Table 9.1 Trend of Types of Money Stock in India: 1950–1951 to 2015–2016, ***200***
Table 9.2 Pre-reform and Post-reform CRR in India, ***202***
Table 9.3 SLR in India (1964–1981), ***203***
Table 9.4 Effective Dates of Bank Rates in India, ***204***
Table 9.5 Current Rates of the RBI Indicators, ***210***
Table 10.1 A Standard BoP Statement, ***220***
Table 10.2 Statement I: Standard Presentation of BoP in India as per the Sixth Edition of IMF's Balance of Payments and International Investment Position Manual (BPM6), ***221***
Table 10.3 Statement II: India's Overall Balance of Payments, ***223***
Table 10.4 Foreign Investment in India, ***227***
Table 10.5 External Assistance Received by India, ***229***
Table 10.6 External Debt of India: By Component, ***229***
Table 10.7 Net Indicators of Balance of Payments, ***231***
Table 11.1 Sectoral Deployment of Non-food Gross Bank Credit–Outstanding, 2007–2016, ***240***
Table 11.2 Industry-wise Industrial Bank Credit During 2007–2013, ***241***
Table 11.3 New Capital Issues by Non-Government Public Limited Companies, ***245***
Table 11.4 Resource Mobilisation in the Private Placement Market, ***245***
Table 11.5 Bonds Issued by Public Sector Undertakings, ***246***
Table 11.6 Resource Mobilisation through the Primary Market, ***247***
Table 11.7 Trend of Net Mobilisation of Funds through Mutual Funds, ***248***
Table 11.8 Monthly and Annual Average Index of BSE (Base 1983–1984 = 58), ***250***
Table 14.1 Declarations Stated by International Labour Conference, ***294***
Table 15.1 Units of Labour (Labour Hour) Required to Produce 1 Unit of Commodities, ***307***
Table 15.2 Units of Commodity Produced by 1 Unit of Labour, ***309***
Table 15.3 Growth in the Volume of World Merchandise Trade by Select Region and Economy, 2010–2014, ***317***
Table 15.4 Leading Exporters and Importers in World Merchandise Trade, 2014, ***317***
Table 15.5 Leading Exporters and Importers in World Trade in Commercial Services, 2012, ***318***
Table 17.1 FDI Inflows in Top 20 Countries (US$ Billion at Current Prices), ***337***
Table 17.2 Region-wise FDI Trend (US$ Billion at Current Prices), ***340***
Table 17.3 Foreign Investment Inflows in India (Direct and Portfolio), ***348***
Table 17.4 FDI Inflows in India: Major Sources, ***350***
Table 17.5 Sectoral Share of FDI Inflows in India During 2000–2012, ***350***

Table 18.1 Trade Openness (1948–1990), ***356***
Table 18.2 Direction of Exports after World War II, ***357***
Table 18.3 Direction of Imports after World War II, ***358***
Table 18.4 Binding Commitments before and after the Uruguay Round, ***359***
Table 19.1 Round-wise Outcome of GATT, ***374***
Table 19.2 Uruguay Round Meetings and Outcomes, ***377***
Table 19.3 Examples of Some GIs Registered in India, ***384***
Table 19.4 Some Disputes under TRIPS, ***385***
Table 19.5 List of Some TRIMS Related Disputes in the WTO, ***386***
Table 19.6 India in the WTO as Complainant: Select Cases, ***389***
Table 19.7 India in the WTO as Respondent: Select Cases, ***389***
Table 20.1 Tariff, Domestic Support and Exports Targets under AoA, ***397***
Table 20.2 LDC Market Access by Developed Countries (2012), ***406***
Table 20.3 Average Applied MFN Tariff, ***408***
Table 20.4 Examples of Some Select NTBs Imposed on Indian Exports, ***409***
Table 20.5 Few Examples of Definitive Anti-dumping Measures in Force by India, ***411***
Table 24.1 Emerging Markets and Developing Economies Scenario, ***440***
Table 24.2 Region-wise Data on Macroeconomic Indicators, 2012, ***441***
Table 24.3 Starting a Business Across Regions in the World, ***444***
Table 24.4 Construction Permits Across Regions of the World, ***445***
Table 24.5 Rank of BRICS Countries on Parameters of Ease of Doing Business (2013 and 2014), ***448***
Table 24.6 GDP Growth in ECOWAS Region: Performance and Projections, ***452***
Table 24.7 Total Investment as Percentage of GDP in ECOWAS, ***452***
Table 24.8 GDP Growth in Select Countries of Asia and the Pacific, ***453***
Table 24.9 Current and Future Investment as Percentage of GDP in Select Countries of Asia Pacific, ***454***
Table 24.10 Reforms in Select Countries in Asia Pacific in 2016, ***455***
Table 24.11 Doing Business Ranking of Countries from South, Southeast Asia and Pacific, ***456***

PREFACE

Business environment is demanding and vibrant, and the text in hand is the revised and enlarged second edition of the book, which reflects this appeal in a holistic, lucid and practical way. Today, the business world strives to develop newer advantages and value chains amid rapidly evolving technologies. Business professionals have to manage their interface with policy frameworks too at various levels—national, bilateral, regional and multilateral. The text presents and discusses both the theoretical as well as practical aspects of the business environment. The chapters have been written in a way that they assimilate national as well as global perspectives to enhance a broader and an in-depth understanding of the concepts and their applications. The text, thus, follows a holistic approach to understand the business environment. This revised and enlarged edition thus covers contemporary and recent events and phenomena like BREXIT, Demonetisation, Union Budget 2017-18, Sustainable Development Goals (SDGs), Digital India, Start-up India, Make in India, and several other pertinent global issues as well.

Approach

We follow a distinct approach to begin and end the discussion in each chapter. We start with an opening case by reflecting on a relevant scenario on the theme so that the learners can practically relate to the theme. In the end of every chapter, the learners also find a closing case, which is an illustration depicting the business environment on the theme related to the chapter. Besides, the chapters provide plethora of knowledge backed by relevant examples of each and every concept, and perspectives that have a bearing on the business environment. This is aimed to enhance the knowledge base, professional expertise, and thus, the employability of the learners in a world, characterised by multinationals and multilateralism.

There are notes and practical insights given as boxes throughout the text, which aim at giving up-to-date examples and application-oriented learning. The boxes would benefit the learners in developing their own formal or informal perspective on the issue. These boxes have been deliberately kept small to make the learning pleasant and relevant.

The Chapters

The book comprises 24 chapters. Chapter 1 begins with an interesting opening case on *Pravasi Bharatiya Divas*. The chapter outlines the basics of the concepts, which the book later discusses in detail. Chapter 2 begins with a case on corporate social responsibility of an Indian firm and highlights the contemporary perspectives of business environment like public policy, social responsibility of business, inclusive growth, sustainable development, etc. The concept and approach of environmental scanning are discussed in Chapter 3. Further, Chapter 4 of the book begins with a case highlighting the movement from African socialism to free market economies. The chapter deals with the concept of economic systems very comprehensively. It brings out both national and global perspective on the theme and also historically examines the emergence of various types of economic systems. It closes with a case on the theme, 'think twice before you Google in China!'

In fact, once we understand the ideas that influence the structure of an economy, we would be able to understand the trajectory of economic planning and reform. In Chapter 5, we discuss about the five year plans, land reforms, green revolution and the role of public sector. India's economic system has been a reflection of the journey from being a planned economy to becoming a free market economy. With this view, we highlight both the aspects of India's economic structure, including India's planning as well as India's acceptance of liberalisation through economic reforms. This chapter closes with a case on housing sector reforms in India. Then, there are chapters that extensively discuss India's macroeconomic indicators (Chapter 6), industrial policy (Chapter 7), fiscal policy (Chapter 8), monetary policy (Chapter 9), balance of payments (Chapter 10), and money and capital markets (Chapter 11). Further, there is a chapter on legal framework (Chapter 12), which discusses the basic laws and regulations governing the business environment of India. It highlights the provisions related to the Consumer Protection Act, 1986; Companies Act, 1956 and 2013; FERA/FEMA regulations, and Competition Act, 2002. This chapter opens with a case on Dial 1800-11-4000! (*Jago Grahak Jago,* i.e., 'wake up consumers' campaign) and closes with the description of a legal case pertaining to an Indian newspaper publisher.

In continuation of the same, Chapter 13 presents a conceptual understanding of the international law. It begins with an opening case on GIPC index and India–US legal dispute, and discusses the sources and principles of international law. It also examines the scope of international trade law. It closes with a case describing the judgement of Supreme Court of India on sovereign immunity in context of an international airline.

Chapter 14 describes major international organisations and their role and mandate, reflecting how they contribute to the business environment. These organisations include the UNO, the UNCTAD, the UNCITRAL, the UNDP, the WFP, the ILO, the World Bank, the IMF and the WTO. Once the learners are familiar with these organisations and their functions, they can understand the global policy framework that also impacts the business decision-making in multinational companies. Chapter 15 presents the models and frameworks of international trade focusing on various trade theories as well as some practical statistical models. In Chapter 16, we discuss the various modes of entry into a foreign market. The chapter begins with a case on domestic airlines industry and its outreach beyond the Indian airspace, and closes with a case on Unilever in the Indian subcontinent. Chapter 17 opens with a case on FDI in multibrand retail in India and discusses about FDI theories and trends. Chapter 18 discusses the trends in global trade and the levels of economic integration, with a focus on trade blocs like EU, ASEAN, SAARC and others. This chapter carries an interesting opening case on integrating the boundaries of the Indian Ocean.

To become more familiar with the aspects of institutional frameworks and legalities of the institutions regulating the businesses, it would be important for the learners to understand the WTO regimes (Chapter 19) and the major provisions under WTO (Chapter 20). In the WTO regime, we discuss the principles of the trading system like MFN, etc. and also about GATT, GATS, TRIPS, TRIMS and even instruments like Aid for Trade. In major provisions, we describe the agreements and provisions related to agriculture, rules of origin, anti-dumping and least developed countries (LDCs), among others. We also discuss about tariff and non-tariff barriers in this chapter.

The level of regional and global integration and pursuits of higher economic progress resulted in global discourses on various cross-cutting and new issues affecting the global businesses. These issues include those which come at the intersection of trade with climate change, food security, finance and geopolitics. Chapter 21, which opens with a case on India's solar power policy and dispute with the United States, discusses each of these aspects in detail. These are significant issues shaping the business environment, and the learners must be able to comprehend them for a better decision-making. Further, there are some useful insights on the evolving business environment, which are explained in Chapter 22 (on foreign exchange risk and exposures) and Chapter 23 (on country risk and political risk analysis). Chapter 22 opens with a case on tax havens and closes with another case on foreign exchange risk for MSMEs in India. In Chapter 24, we discuss about doing business in select markets, with a focus on BRICS, ASEAN and ECOWAS. This chapter closes with a case on the theme 'Reforms, Growth and Business Climate.'

We hope that the learners would benefit from this book in terms of gaining knowledge and developing practical insights. Given our expertise of working in academics and with think tanks, we have provided some incisive insights based on our knowledge and firsthand experiences as well. Besides being a textbook for PGDM/MBA and Executive MBA programmes, the book would also be highly useful for the officials and professionals working in government ministries, embassies in India, Indian missions abroad, chambers of commerce, NGOs and policy think tanks. Also, the book would be a highly useful reading for civil services aspirants and professionals across all functions from corporate houses, industry, SMEs and trading companies.

Faisal Ahmed
M. Absar Alam

ACKNOWLEDGEMENTS

We express our gratitude to our families for their support and cooperation throughout writing of this book. A special thanks to Mahibah Ahmed on her happiness on knowing about the book and her eagerness to see the first edition, when she was only five. And now, when she is eight years old, she has been so keen to see the new edition.

We are also indebted to our respective institutions, i.e., FORE School of Management and Asian Institute of Transport Development. A special thanks to all the students of regular and executive programs across the country for overwhelmingly accepting the first edition of this book.

This book is based not only on our knowledge, expertise and experiences but also on the learning that we have received through our interactions with some distinguished professionals. We are, thus, indebted to R.C. Sharma, President, FORE School of Management; B.B.L. Madhukar, Secretary General, BRICS Chamber of Commerce and Industry; Jitendra K. Das, Director, FORE School of Management; K.L. Thapar, Chairman, Asian Institute of Transport Development; Charan D. Wadhva, Professor Emeritus, Centre for Policy Research; Jagdish Bhagwati, Professor of Economics and Law, Columbia University; Pradeep S. Mehta, Secretary General, CUTS International; Ravi Capoor, Joint Secretary, Ministry of Commerce and Industry, India; Nagesh Kumar, Director, South and Southwest Asia Office, United Nations Economic and Social Commission for Asia and the Pacific (UNESCAP); Anju Kohli, Professor Emeritus, MLSU, Udaipur; Jabir Hasan Khan, Professor, Department of Geography, Aligarh Muslim University; Jaran Maluleem, Professor, Faculty of Political Science and Head, Indian Studies Program, Thammasat University, Thailand; Chintamani Mahapatra, Professor of American Studies, Jawaharlal Nehru University; Rajan S. Ratna, Economic Affairs Officer, UNESCAP, Bangkok; Dilip K. Banerjee, FMR OSD (Planning), Central University of Jharkhand; A.K. Pasha, Professor of Gulf Studies, Jawaharlal Nehru University; Devendra Pathak, Vice Chancellor, Dr. K.N. Modi University, Jaipur; Azhar Kazmi, Professor, King Fahd University of Petroleum and Minerals, Saudi Arabia; Prabhat Pankaj, Director, Jaipuria Institute of Management, Jaipur; K. Rangarajan, Professor and Head, Kolkata Campus, Indian Institute of Foreign Trade; U.M. Amin, Director, Centre for Management, Jamia Millia Islamia; Kanhaiya Singh, FMR Professor, FORE School of Management; Humaid Al-Maani, FMR Oman Ambassador to India; Sajal Mathur, Professor, Centre for WTO Studies, Indian Institute of Foreign Trade; K.R. Kaushik, Head, Corporate Affairs, Gujarat State Fertilizers and Chemicals Limited, New Delhi; A.K. Srivastava, Chairman, Asia-Pacific Institute of Management, New Delhi; M. Venkatesan, Indian

Institute of Foreign Trade; Gong Baihua, Associate President, Shanghai WTO Consultation Centre; Satish Kumar, Department of Political Science, Central University of Jharkhand; and, Gyula Csurgai, Director, Geneva Institute of Geopolitical Studies, Geneva.

We would also like to thank all our friends and colleagues from academia. Special thanks to Vipul Kumar Singh, Pravin Kumar, Arindam Banerjee, Alok Kumar, Shyama Labh, Preeti Mishra, Jitender Bhandari, Harendra Kumar, Mohd. Faheem, Pranav Saraswat, Rakesh Kumar Saini, Ambrien Ahmed, Sankar Thappa, Laxman Lal Salvi, Kailash C. Nayma, D.S. Meghwal, Rajesh Pyngavil, Pradeep Kumar AV, Uma Shanker Singh, Vinay Asthana, and Jamil Ahmad.

Our heartfelt gratitude to all our friends from the industry and corporate houses, who have always been supportive to our academic endeavours. We would especially like to thank our friends Maneesh K. Ahuja, Pushkar Pachori, M. Akhtar Tauhid, Faizul Islam, Rafi Ahmad, Yawar Alamgir, Moazzam E. Siddiqui, Joseph George, Kshitiz Sharma, Rahbre Azam, Arti Bali, Naseer E. Khan, Rais Ahmad, Atiya Rahman, Shakeb Iftekhar, Mona Gupta, Asghar Raza, Anshu Tewary, Kshitij Ojha, Richa Gaur, Prahlad Gupta, Trishant Verma, Koushik Pal, Amit Deb, Sharique Raza, Asif M. Khan, Vikas Kumar, Rajesh Kumar Sinha, and all those who have taken keen interest in our efforts.

Moreover, Malaya R. Parida and Sarvendra K. Singh of PHI Learning deserve a special mention for making this book possible. We are also grateful to the entire editorial and production team of PHI Learning, especially Babita Misra, Ruchira Dash, Monika Kulshrestha, Mini and Lakshmi for their hard work, professionalism and cooperation during the whole process. Our special thanks to Ajai K. Lal Das for preparing this second edition professionally and timely.

Faisal Ahmed
M. Absar Alam

1

CONCEPTS

Learning Outcomes

After reading this chapter, you will

- Understand the basic concepts of business environment
- Appreciate the significance and factors shaping the economic and non-economic environment
- Examine the role of technological environment in business

Opening Case: Pravasi Bharatiya Divas

On 8th January 2017, the Prime Minister, Narendra Modi welcomed Dr. Antonio Costa, the Prime Minister of Portugal in Bengaluru at the inaugural address of the *Pravasi Bhartiya Divas* (PBD) Convention. In fact, the Government of India celebrates *Pravasi Bharatiya Divas* (Non-resident Indian Day) every year from January 7–9. In the year 1915, Mahatma Gandhi returned from South Africa to India on January 9 to participate in the struggle for freedom. In 2015, as per the decision of the government, it will be held every two years, and in the intervening year, a smaller event will be held in New Delhi.

It may not be surprising to note that around 25 million Indians live and work abroad, constituting all segments of labour—unskilled, semi-skilled and skilled. They are referred to as *Indian diaspora*. Some of the preferred destinations include USA, UK, UAE, Saudi Arabia, Canada, Australia, Oman, Kuwait, New Zealand, Qatar, Singapore, Bahrain, Malaysia, and so on. There are many Indian students studying overseas as well. The overseas Indian community has been making a significant contribution in the development of India through personal remittances of approximately US$70 billion (as per Annual Report 2014–15).

The ministry was established in May 2004 as Ministry of Non-resident Indians' Affairs and was later renamed as Ministry of Overseas Indian Affairs (MOIA) in the month of September of the same year. The ministry worked through its four functional services divisions, namely, diaspora services, financial services, emigration services and management services. It aims to connect and build partnerships with the Indian diaspora. Besides, the ministry is responsible for dealing with all matters related to the overseas Indians. Some of the initiatives in which the ministry is engaged with the diaspora include trade and investment promotion, emigration, education, culture, health, and science and technology. The MOIA was, however merged, with the Ministry of External Affairs in January 2016.

In January 2017, the PBD was held in Bengaluru and had the following objectives (as per the web site of PBD):

1. To redefine the engagement with indian diaspora
2. To strengthen diaspora engagement and provide a platform for networking with the diaspora
3. To recognise the diasporas' contribution to india and know their expectations and concerns
4. To deepen engagement with young diasporas, to help them know more about their roots

The first *Pravasi Bharatiya Divas* was celebrated in 2003 in New Delhi, organised by the Ministry of External Affairs, Government of India along with Federation of Indian Chambers of Commerce and Industry (FICCI), an industry chamber.

Pravasi Bharatiya Divas provides opportunities for business meetings as well for exploring business opportunities, with an urge to facilitate the process of engagement of diaspora with the motherland. In 2013, the *Pravasi Bharatiya Divas* was held in Kerala, and in 2015, it was held in Gandhinagar.

Source: This case is written by the authors based on inputs from the following sources:

1. Web site of PBD, https://pbdindia.gov.in/mission
2. Annual Report 2014–2015, Ministry of Overseas Indian Affairs, Government of India
3. Strategic Plan, Ministry of Overseas Indian Affairs, Government of India, http://moia.gov.in/writereaddata/pdf/Strategic_Plan.pdf

1.1 BUSINESS ENVIRONMENT AND STRATEGIC MANAGEMENT

Strategic management is closely linked with the economic and business environment. The economic and business environment depends on the policies devised by governments. In fact, economic policies become a guiding framework for many strategic decisions made by modern organisations. The strategic endeavour of a business entity is not only the response of the firm's capabilities but also the reflection of evolving business environment both at national and global levels. An industry professional or entrepreneur has to devise his or her strategic orientations in accordance with the changing nature of the business environment.

There are three levels of strategy, which are as follows:

1. ***Corporate strategy:*** It includes decisions made at the top-level management of a company and includes decisions like choice of businesses, entry/diversification decisions, exit/divestiture decisions, priorities for growth, dividend decisions, etc.

2. ***Business or competitive strategy:*** It includes decisions made at middle-level management or business units as well as the decisions like market segmentation, distribution, supply chain, plant location, etc.
3. ***Functional or operational strategy:*** It includes decisions made at lower-level management as well as the decisions related to the implementation of corporate and business-level strategies. It also involves operational and functional-level decisions.

Interestingly, business environment shapes the firm's strategic intents and their decision-making at all levels and is also shaped by it. Box 1.1 provides an example of the corporate strategic decisions.

Box 1.1 Holcim-Lafarge Merger

On 7 April 2014, two giants in global cement industry, *viz.* Holcim of Switzerland and Lafarge of France announced their agreement for merger. They termed this merger as a *merger of equals*. This announcement had a direct impact on the global cement businesses. This merger is expected to create the biggest cement-maker firm in the world, with an annual sale of US$44 billion. Holcim shareholder will hold 53% of the new entity. The merger itself is seen as the biggest tie-up ever. The new business, thus, formed after merger would be based in Switzerland and listed in both the countries' stock market. The market value of the merged entity is deemed to be worth US$55 billion.

Interestingly, the merger is anticipated to have an impact on the Indian cement industry also. Renowned names, like ACC and Ambuja Cements are Holcim-controlled cement companies. India has about 40 cement companies and it is envisaged that this merger will make it the biggest cement group in the country constituting 18% of the market share.

Source: Based on 'Holcim, Lafarge agree to merger to create cement giant', *Reuters*, 7 April 2014, http://in.reuters.com/article/2014/04/07/lafarge-holcim-idINDEEA3607P20140407 and Cement companies rally on Holcim–Lafarge merger, *The Economic Times*, 8 April 2014.

1.2 ECONOMIC AND NON-ECONOMIC ENVIRONMENT

Business environment is broadly categorised into economic and non-economic environment. We understand the very fact that the organisational strategic intents are considered as the responses of not only the market dynamics but also the government policies.

Economic environment refers to the effect of economic policies, economic conditions and the structure of an economy on the prospects of business in the economy. On the other hand, *non-economic environment* may be defined as the effect of policies and structure other than the economic factors on the prospects of business. Such factors are technology, political and social systems, legal framework, and demographic and natural environments. These factors too have a bearing on a firm's strategies and their behaviour in this competitive world.

1.2.1 Economic Environment

The economic environment comprises the following three elements:

1. Economic systems
2. Economic conditions
3. Economic policies

These three elements of economic environment are the broad indicators which, among other things, help in assessing whether an economy has a business-friendly environment or not.

Economic systems

Economic systems represent the economic structure of an economy. This is primarily an agglomeration of economic activities and its related governance. Based on the types of governance to economic activities, the world economy may be divided into three types of economic systems, *viz.* capitalist, socialist and mixed economic systems. These systems have been developed over a period of time, with a focus on controlling or decontrolling the production, consumption and distribution systems.

A capitalist system has a market-friendly economic structure, whereas in a socialist economic system, government controls the economic activities and market has the least role to play. On the other hand, some economies have developed a mixed system, which has elements from both capitalist and socialist economic systems. India is an example of this system. A detailed analysis of the economic systems and their characteristics is presented in Chapter 4.

Economic conditions

Economic conditions refer to the overall macroeconomic environment of an economy. They consist of a set of factors which usually have an impact on business environment as well. These factors include macroeconomic variables such as gross domestic products (GDP), per capita income, growth rates, exports and imports, foreign exchange reserves, scenarios in capital and money markets, etc. These indicators help in understanding the economic condition of an economy.

If the GDP is growing, per capita income is high, foreign exchange reserves are growing, capital market are strong, money market has a business-friendly credit system, then there exist strong prospects of business in the economy. (Chapter 6 provides a detailed discussion on macroeconomic indicator, while Chapter 11 describes the money and capital markets.)

Economic policies

Economic policies of government have direct and indirect impact on business activities. In fact, all economic activities including business operations are subject to compliance with government policies. These policies are related to industrial activities called *industrial policies*, investments by foreign investors in various sectors named as *FDI policies*, *monetary policies* to regulate money market and *fiscal policies* for making expenditure and revenue collection decisions, etc.

Generally, government changes policies over a period of time according to the need of the economic conditions. In other words, as per the economic situations, development needs and political aspirations, governments tend to change these policies from time to time. These policy frameworks are designed to regulate businesses in the economy. It is, therefore, important that business houses need to undertake their business activities within the framework of these policies. In fact, these policies also define the nature of an economic system in a country.

Some of the significant economic policies are as follows:

1. ***Industrial policy:*** It deals with all the regulatory, governance, principles and other economic aspects related to industrial activities. For instance, if an industrialist wishes to set up new industries, then he has to comply with the industrial policies of the country in which he or she wants to set up industries. (Chapter 7 deals with the evolution of industrial policy in India and also with its structural transformation from restrictive regimes to liberalisation.)
2. ***Fiscal policy:*** Fiscal policies are related to public expenditure and collection of public revenues. In India, the Ministry of Finance, Government of India deals with fiscal policies. (Chapter 8 presents a detailed discussion on fiscal policies and its instruments. It reflects a close linkage between fiscal policy and the business environment.)
3. ***Monetary policy:*** The governments use monetary policy as an instrument to keep check on money supply and the rate of interest. In other words, monetary policy instruments are used to facilitate economic growth and economic stability. In India, the Reserve Bank of India (RBI) deals with the monetary policies. (For more details, refer to Chapter 9.)
4. ***Investment policy:*** Investment policies deal with the investment environment in an economy. In case of domestic investment, industrial policies of the economy present both policy and regulatory regimes for the sectors in which domestic industrialists are allowed to make investment. In case of foreign investment, the government announces a separate policy. In India, foreign investment policies are the part of FDI policy. (Chapter 17 examines the theoretical frameworks of FDI, foreign investment scenario in India, and the investment regimes.)
5. ***Trade policy:*** Trade policies are also important, considering the export and import business. If a manufacturer produces a commodity, then he or she needs markets for the same. Trade policies, thus, helps a manufacturer in entering into foreign markets and taking the benefits of internationalisation. The WTO regime defines the evolution of multilateral trading system. Trade, integration and global environment have been discussed in various chapters of this book. In case of India, the Ministry of Commerce and Industry deals with the foreign trade policy. It also publishes foreign trade policy, with the objectives of reducing current account deficit by encouraging exports.

1.2.2 Non-economic Environment

The non-economic environment too impacts the business directly and indirectly. There are various indicators considered as the part of non-economic environment. These include socio-cultural environment, demographic structure and its distribution, labour force, health and education, urbanisation and other socio-cultural aspects of the economy such as literacy rates, poverty, access to basic amenities and also those included in the millennium development goals (MDGs), etc. Political and legal environment is also considered as the part of non-economic environment.

Some of the aspects of political environment are provisions of Indian constitutions such as fundamental rights, democratic scenario, bureaucratic control and other political scenarios. The subsequent section discusses the various indicators of non-economic environment.

Socio-cultural environment

Social environment factors including culture, tradition, health, education, etc. are the various factors which affect the business environment in a country. Generally, the socio-cultural aspects of a society tend to define the consumption pattern for its population. In fact, the values that a society inherits from its culture and civilisation significantly influence the economic activities within the society, and therefore, have a substantial impact on business-related activities.

On the other hand, some other aspects of society which are related to education, health and demographic structure also tend to impact business-related activities. For example, if a large section of population is young and there is a tendency of getting more educational facilities, thereby increasing literacy rates among them, then the consumption pattern would be different as compared to a case of older population. Thus, some of the aspects of socio-cultural environment are as follows:

1. Cultural and civilisational values and attitudes help in developing various types of institutions in a society. These institutions include family systems, caste systems, etc. They have a direct impact on the ceremonial activities, which creates certain types of consumption pattern. For instance, in India, marriage ceremony creates market for various products such as luxury automobiles, other electronic and electrical products, opportunities for event management, and nowadays, opportunities for entertainment activities as well.
2. Another important feature of socio-cultural activities is its rapidly changing nature. Culture evolves through time. We have seen the changing pattern of markets due to the change in cultural values in metropolitan cities. These changes include westernisation of individual's attitude, increasing role of entertainment activities, changing nature of work environment and also the changing ceremonial activities such as partying and gathering. These changes attract sophisticated requirements from the consumers such as arranging party for family and friends, which creates new opportunities for small events, creative supply chain and business strategies, etc.
3. Social problems and issues also affect business activities. For instance, if there is less literacy rate in a society and less health-related awareness, then the consumers are less aware of the quality of products. In such a situation, consumption patterns affect the business activities.
4. In a society, the roles of government, civil society and other social institutions are very important in shaping markets. If the government's objective is to give impetus to the private business activities and civil society opposes it, then this will impact the business environment significantly.

5. Also, the Indian diaspora in countries like US, UAE, Japan, UK, etc. plays a pivotal role as a reference group for their relatives and acquaintances in India. For instance, there are more than 6 million Indians working in the Gulf, and is a major source of remittance for India.

Demographic environment

Demography implies the structure and dynamics of population in a society or in a country. It is vital to understand the size, density, rural-urban distribution, growth and aging pattern of the population. These elements constitute demographic environment, which helps in analysing the demand and supply pattern of goods and services. It, therefore, helps in formulating the strategies for business activities. For instance, in case of India, considering demographic compositions, the country has more than 1.2 billion population out of which 50% is below 25 years of age. This positions India as one of the economies having growing youth population and has demographic dividend (see Box 1.2). The trend of urbanisation is also increasing in the country. These indicators are nothing but the factors which provide opportunities for business.

Box 1.2 Demographic Dividend in India

Demographic dividend derives from a sizeable population of the country, being youth and engaged in the economic activities. This also means that there would be less dependency ratio on the population. *Dependency ratio* is the ratio of children and elderly (i.e., non-working population) to the working population. In India, this ratio is declining owing to a significant reduction in the infant mortality rate. The significant part of India's population is the main workforce between 15–64 years of age and stands at 63.4% of the total.

A projection by the United Nations indicates that this trend will continue up to 2050. This is very important in the context of ageing population in the west. Because of its young population, India is bestowed with the advantages of this demographic transition. India can play a vital role in meeting the human capital requirements of the other countries, which are moving towards the ageing population.

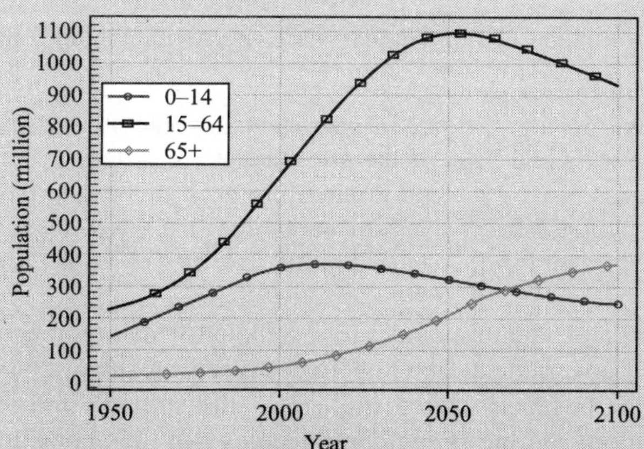

Exhibit 1 Total population by major age groups.

Source: Based on Economic Survey of India and an article in *The Hindu* available at http://www.thehindu.com/news/national/demographic-dividend-at-its-peak/article5102093.ece; and World Population Prospects—The 2012 Revision, Volume II: Demographic Profiles, United Nations, 2013, p. 375.

Political environment

Political environment pertains to political system in a country such as democratic, socialist, kingship, etc. and also political openness to the market forces. Such factors have a substantial impact on the business activities.

The provisions of the Constitution of India in terms of fundamental rights and directive principles of state policies and their implementation by the state machinery have a considerable impact on the business environment. Further, there have been legislations like provision of right to education as a fundamental right. The government has been working in collaboration with the various private sector entities and also with the multilateral organisations to achieve this goal.

Political environment also includes the following:

1. The form of government constitutes the foremost pillar to understand the business environment. The form of government may be republic, democratic republic, socialist republic and/or royal government, and can also have a bicameral and unicameral legislature (see Box 1.3). Every government has its own perspective for market-related business environment.

Box 1.3 Bicameral and Unicameral Legislatures

The forms of government also play a vital role in formulating business-related policies and implementing them. The various layers of government and also centralisation and decentralisation of power have direct impact on the efficiency of policy implementation. A country can have bicameral or unicameral legislature. In a *bicameral legislature*, there are two houses of the Parliament, whereas in case of *unicameral legislature*, the legislative power rests with one house only. For instance, India, which is a parliamentary democracy, has two houses of Parliament—the lower house (Lok Sabha) and the upper house (Rajya Sabha). Same is the case of USA and UK which have two houses—the House of Representatives and Senate in USA, and the House of Commons and the House of Lords in UK. However, many countries have a unicameral legislature as well. Some of these include China, Vatican City, Bulgaria, Finland, South Korea, Kuwait, Nepal, Mauritius, etc.

Moreover, democracy can also be classified as parliamentary and presidential. In a parliamentary democracy, head of the state and head of the government are different. For instance, in case of India, President is the head of the state and Prime Minister is the head of the government. In case of presidential democracy, the head of the state and head of the government remain the same. For instance, in USA, the President is both the head of the state as well as the head of the government.

2. A large number of countries have now adopted democratic form of government. In such a form of government, two important aspects are always taken into account while formulating the business-related strategies—the strength and ideology of the ruling party or coalition, and the strength and ideology of the opposition.
3. In India, the other force which significantly creates an impact is the bureaucracy. In fact, bureaucracy has often been linked to red-tapism. The more the bureaucratic involvement in the process, the adversely it affects the doing business climate of a country. Countries need market-friendly practices to attract investments in various sectors.

4. Finally, political stability is the most important aspect influencing the future prospects of business in a country. A stable government is essential for bringing and sustaining reforms. An unstable government will be highly unpredictable and can have a negative impact on the process of reforms.

Legal environment

This pertains to the laws and regulations of a country and how they influence the business environment. Businesses have to operate within the legal framework of a country. Some of the key legislations which significantly affect the business environment in the country include Companies Act 1956 and 2013, Foreign Exchange Management Act 1999, Competition Act 2002 and others. (Chapter 12 discusses the legal framework in detail.)

1.3 TECHNOLOGICAL ENVIRONMENT

Technological environment is an important aspect to assess the contemporary business environment of a country. The pace at which the technology is evolving is exemplary. We see examples of technological converge like the assimilation of multiple technologies into one device, which can perform multiple functions. An example of this is the mobile phone. An example about Apple is provided in Box 1.4. The use of technological paradigms can also be witnessed in a recent government scheme called the *Startup India*, *Standup India* (see Box 1.5)

Box 1.4 Apple's Strategies in Indian Market

Apple's strategies in India have not been attractive due to its less innovative process of market capturing. However, the firm is looking ahead for new products and innovative processes to capture the market. There are a couple of products due for their launch. In its products, it is said that Apple is likely to use flexible AMOLED display along with 200 mAH–250 mAH battery.

Apple is also likely to introduce smart watch and TV in the market. In addition, it is likely to introduce 64-bit A8 processor, 1GB RAM, LTPS LCD display model in its iPhones that will have optical image stabilisation, Touch ID fingerprint sensor, metal casings and NFC. The next generation iPad will have innovative technological development as Touch ID sensor. Thus, Apple is likely to use multipronged and multiproduct strategies in the Indian market.

Source: Based on article 'Is this Apple's product roadmap for 2014?' The Times of India, 10 April 2014 and http://timesofindia.indiatimes.com/tech/tech-news/Is-this-Apples-product-roadmap-for-2014/articleshow/33562179.cms.

Box 1.5 Startup India, Standup India Scheme

The Prime Minister of India, Mr. Narendra Modi officially launched an ambitious scheme called Startup India, Standup India on 16 January 2016. The scheme aims at helping people who wish to start new business. The main feature of the scheme is the use of information technology to reach out people across the country. A website of the scheme has already been launched with detailed information regarding the scheme. The website contains action plan, related notifications from the government, application process for new startups for "Startup Recognition", and other information, etc. The action plan of the scheme provides for the following:

1. E-registration
2. Self-certification
3. Mobile app and dedicated web portal
4. No inspection during first three years
5. 80% reduction in application fee for new startup patent
6. Easy exit policy
7. Inclusion of credit guarantee fund through a fund of funds corpus
8. Income tax relaxation for first three years
9. Special incentives for female entrepreneurs
10. Atal Innovation Mission for training under the scheme.

Another important feature of the scheme is the projects dedicated to women, particularly those belonging to the scheduled class. The Standup India scheme will facilitate two entrepreneurial projects on an average of one for each category (Women and SC/ST) of entrepreneurs per bank branch. This would mean empowering women entrepreneurship not only through financial inclusion but also through financial support and training programmes.

Source: Action Plan for Startup India available on http://startupindia.gov.in/

Moreover, there is a concept of technological divide also, which is important in terms of understanding the technological penetration. These days the concept of technological divide is also expressed in terms of digital divide. Considering the importance and role of technology to boost business such as those related to cross-border trade and investments, countries are now forming bilateral and regional cooperation frameworks for penetration of new technologies to boost economic activities. The concept of technological divide outlines that how countries have attained technologies or how lack of technologies can act as a barrier to business. It is now a well-known concept used to formulate policies by the governments as well as by the private sector.

Digital divide not only includes the technological advancement but also the skill development of the people of a particular country to adapt to such technology. For example, Afghanistan does not possess extensive railway technologies, and therefore, the country does not have presence of railway personnel. A railway line was in function from Uzbekistan border point, Termez to Hairatan in Afghanistan. This line was operated and maintained by Uzbekistan railways. Now, with the help of Asian Development Bank, Afghanistan is able to extend this line up to its another major city. We can say that there is a decreasing gap in terms of railway technology between Afghanistan and Uzbekistan or other neighbouring countries.

But the other fact is that Afghanistan does not have a trained human capital to run railways. It is in this context, Uzbekistan Railway has been granted a contract to run rail on this line and also to train railway personnel so that in future, Afghanistan would have its own personnel to run rail on the track. This means after some years, the technological divide between these two countries would be reduced in real terms.[1] Thus, the concept of digital or technological divide not only includes the new technologies but also the personnel to adapt to these new technologies. Therefore, capacity development is also taken as an important element.

1. Asian Development Bank (ADB).

However, understanding the role of information technology is important to understand the actual digital divide. This says that availability of technologies is also not related to the strengthening of skill development.

In addition, the technological divide is also measured in terms of connectivity such as transport and communication infrastructure, simplification of business processes such as filling online forms, acceptability of digital signature and documents and so on. The new trade facilitation modules are subject to simplify export and import procedure through digitisation.

In a nutshell, technological advancements in the world play an important role in advancing business opportunities. With this objective, developing countries like India are also pushing for digital economy (see Box 1.6). In fact, it is the technology which creates economies of scale in operations of a business unit. In this rapidly changing world, technological advancements are also required for economic growth, which in turn, would create business opportunities. However, there exists technological divide among various economies. In fact, lack of information and communication technology (ICT) has led several countries loose opportunities of better governance and economic integration.

Box 1.6 Digital India

After the formation of new government in 2014, governance has been the core of the agenda that relates to economic reform. In this regard, the Government of India started several flagship programmes. Digital India is one of the flagship programme of the government, with a vision to transform the country into a digitally empowered society and knowledge economy. Several schemes under Digital India have been initiated. These schemes include digital infrastructure, digital empowerment and on demand government services. These schemes have direct impact on digital divide in the country. They aim at reducing the digital divide and also aim at exploiting the digital dividends available in the country for the betterment of governance. One of the important pillar of the programme is e-governance with a moto of reforming government through technology. The programme is envisaged to reduce leakages in the economy through integration of Adhaar and beneficiaries of other government subsidy-related programmes. Transparency and accountability of flow of funds through technology intervention will bring in the desired educational and health outcomes for the population and pave the way for a healthy and educated India in the near future.

Source: Economic Survey of India, 2016.

The World Economic Forum (WEF) periodically releases Global Information Technology Report (GITR) with the objective to highlight the widening gap between technologically advanced countries and technologically backward nations. It also aims at highlighting the fact how countries are able to reduce the gaps. It provides an analysis in terms of sectors, wherein technological divide between countries exists and how new technologies can be adopted with the help of private sector.

As per GITR 2015, most of the developing economies are not able to create the conditions necessary to reduce the gap in terms of usage of ICT as compared to the developed economies. The report suggests that there exists a clear cut technological gap between the developed and developing economies. The report has also developed an index to identify technological divide. For example, as per the latest report of GITR published in 2015, India is ranked 89th in terms of network readiness among 143 countries, while we know that India is a major player in IT outsourcing business.[2] The index is presented in Table 1.1 for select countries.

Table 1.1 Network Readiness Index

Countries	2015		2014		2013		2012	
	Rank	*Score*	*Rank*	*Score*	*Rank*	*Score*	*Rank*	*Score*
Singapore	1	6.02	2	5.97	2	5.96	2	5.86
Finland	2	6.00	1	6.04	1	5.98	3	5.81
Sweden	3	5.84	3	5.93	3	5.91	1	5.94
Netherlands	4	5.80	4	5.79	4	5.81	6	5.60
Norway	5	5.76	5	5.70	5	5.66	7	5.59
Switzerland	6	5.68	6	5.62	6	5.66	5	5.61
United States	7	5.64	7	5.61	9	5.57	8	5.56
United Kingdom	8	5.62	9	5.54	7	5.64	10	5.50
Denmark	15	5.51	13	5.50	8	5.58	4	5.70
Taiwan, China	18	5.46	14	5.47	10	5.47	11	5.48
Mongolia	61	4.19	61	4.07	59	4.01	63	3.95
China	62	4.16	62	4.05	58	4.03	51	4.11
Sri Lanka	65	4.07	76	3.94	69	3.88	71	3.88
Mexico	69	4.03	79	3.89	63	3.93	76	3.82
South Africa	75	3.99	70	3.98	70	3.87	72	3.87
Brazil	84	3.85	69	3.98	60	3.97	65	3.92
India	89	3.73	83	3.85	68	3.88	69	3.89
Bangladesh	109	3.31	119	3.21	114	3.22	113	3.20
Nepal	118	3.17	123	3.09	126	2.93	128	2.92
Tanzania	123	3.00	125	3.04	127	2.92	123	2.95
Ethiopia	130	2.87	130	2.95	128	2.85	130	2.85
Burkina Faso	132	2.79	136	2.78	130	2.80	135	2.72
Malawi	133	2.78	132	2.90	129	2.83	116	3.05

Source: Global Information Technology Report 2015, World Economic Forum, Geneva.

A comparative statistics for network readiness index is also provided in the table. It indicates that the position of India has been decreasing from 68th in 2013 to 83rd in 2014 and 89th in 2015, a surprise move despite of the efforts like digital India. The GITR report, 2015

2. The Global Information Technology Report 2013: Growth and Jobs in a Hyperconnected World, Beñat Bilbao-Osorio, Soumitra Dutta and Bruno Lanvin (Eds.), World Economic Forum and INSEAD, 2013, http://www3.weforum.org/docs/WEF_GITR_Report_2013.pdf

noted that "despite many clusters of excellence and its knack for frugal innovation, India is not leveraging ICTs for the benefits of its entire population".

The country places in the bottom half of the rankings of seven NRI pillars, and beyond the 100th mark in four. Uptake of ICTs in India is among the lowest in the world. When accounting for multiple SIM-card ownership, approximately one-third of the population owns a mobile phone. Smartphones are the privilege of the very few, with 3 mobile broadband subscriptions for every 100 people. Only 15% of the population uses the Internet. By international standards, technology adoption by businesses remains limited, as it does within the government. Despite its successes and international visibility and recognition, the vibrant IT and business process management industry accounts for only 0.6% of all jobs.

The need for India to embrace technology to power its economy is arguably less pressing than it is for the other, richer BRICS economies, given its stage of development. Yet ICTs could do wonders in improving productivity in agriculture and the services sector, while boosting access to some basic services among the rural population. Furthermore, ICTs could help fulfill India's ambition to become a global manufacturing hub. A most encouraging result amid India's mediocre performance is the country's 1st position in the affordability pillar, as a result of the fierce competition within the vibrant telecommunications sector.

1.4 STARTUPS: AN EMERGING PHENOMENON

Startup is a growing phenomenon across the globe. It became one of the important policy campaigns in the United States of America during Obama Administration. As a "White House initiative", Startup America got momentum and throughout the USA, it inspired people to explore opportunities for new businesses. A public and private partnership was evolved based on the coordinated efforts between these two. In the United States, most startups have been seen in the recent years. This has also been recognised in India. The Government of India recognising the role and importance of fostering entrepreneurship, announced initiative in 2015 called "Startup India". As a key component of this "Startup India" launch, the Government of India organised a global workshop on "Innovation and Startups" on 16 January 2016.

Both "Startup America" and "Startup India" are inspiring the entrepreneurs of the new generation. It is important to note that the USA is the top ranking country in terms of number startups in 2015, and interestingly, startup in India is also getting momentum. As per startups.com, India is ranked second in the number of startups.

The main objective of "Startup America" is to provide expanding access. Eventually, the access to capital has potential to increase the number and scale of new high-growth firms. These firms are the main sources of new economic opportunities as they are creating economic growth, innovation, and quality jobs. They celebrate and honour entrepreneurship as a core American value and the source of competitive advantage; and inspire and empower an ever-greater diversity of communities and individuals to build great American companies.[3] President Obama has called on the academia, business communities and civil society organisations to promote the entrepreneurial spirit and success in the United States. This initiative intends to expand access to capital for high-growth startups, create jobs in America, fund research and

3. Based on the factsheet available at https://www.whitehouse.gov/startup-america-fact-sheet.

development for entrepreneurial development in the country, and remove bottlenecks to high-growth startups, among others.

Likewise, the initiative in India is accompanied by technological penetration. In order to meet the objectives of the initiative, the Government of India announced the Action Plan that addresses all aspects of the Startup ecosystem. This would help the startups in the following aspects and sectoral coverages:

1. In agriculture, manufacturing, social sector, healthcare, education, etc.; and
2. In existing tier-1 cities to tier-2 and tier-3 cities, including semi-urban and rural areas.

The Action Plan is divided across the following areas:

1. Simplification and handholding
2. Funding support and incentives
3. Industry-academia partnership and incubation

Box 1.7 Startup India Action Plan—Compliance Regime Based on Self-Certification

Objective: To reduce the regulatory burden on startups, thereby allowing them to focus on their core business and keep compliance cost low.

Details: Regulatory formalities requiring compliance with various labour and environment laws are time-consuming and difficult in nature. Often, new and small firms are unaware of nuances of the issues and can be subjected to intrusive action by regulatory agencies. In order to make compliance for startups friendly and flexible, simplifications are required in the regulatory regime.

Accordingly, the process of conducting inspections shall be made more meaningful and simple. Startups shall be allowed to self-certify compliance (through the Startup mobile app) with nine labour and environment laws (refer below).

In case of the labour laws, no inspections will be conducted for a period of three years. Startups may be inspected on receipt of credible and verifiable complaint of violation, filed in writing and approved by at least one level senior to the inspecting officer. In case of environment laws, Startups which fall under the "white category" (as defined by the Central Pollution Control Board (CPCB)) would be able to self-certify compliance and only random checks would be carried out in such cases.

Labour laws: These are listed below:

- The Building and Other Constructions Workers' (Regulation of Employment and Conditions of Service) Act, 1996
- The Inter-State Migrant Workmen (Regulation of Employment and Conditions of Service) Act, 1979
- The Payment of Gratuity Act, 1972
- The Contract Labour (Regulation and Abolition) Act, 1970
- The Employees' Provident Funds and Miscellaneous Provisions Act, 1952
- The Employees' State Insurance Act, 1948

Environment laws: These are as follows:

- The Water (Prevention and Control of Pollution) Act, 1974
- The Water (Prevention and Control of Pollution) Cess (Amendment) Act, 2003
- The Air (Prevention and Control of Pollution) Act, 1981

Source: Government of India, Startup Action Plan, available at http://startupindia.gov.in/actionplan.php

Closing Case: World Economic Forum at Davos, Switzerland

The World Economic Forum (WEF) is an international institution which is committed to improve socio-economic prosperity across the globe through public and private cooperation and also through dialogues. It was established in 1971 as a non-for-profit organisation, and is headquartered in Geneva, Switzerland. On various economic and political issues, World Economic Forum engages governments, civil society, entrepreneurs and multilateral institutions, etc. for open dialogues. WEF holds annual meeting every year in Davos Klosters.

In 2012, WEF meeting in Davos was held on the theme 'The Great Transformation' and it touched upon the need for models of employment, innovation, sustainability and technology, which could establish the best practices and be worth replicating.

Also, there was another World Economic Forum on India, which was held in late 2012 and was focused on the theme 'From Deliberation to Transformation'. In fact, modern organisations today need to take lead for capacity building to overcome the problem of jobless growth.

Davos 2013 was based on three pillars—leading through adversity, restoring economic dynamism and strengthening societal resilience. World leaders, academics, NGOs, think tanks and private sector attended this meeting and discussed on several issues. Some of the key issues pertinent to the business environment deliberated during this meeting included those on industry agenda (global competitiveness, innovation, natural resources, etc.) and business agenda (reshaping business models, social technology, science and medicine, etc.).

In 2014, the WEF meeting was held during January 22–25 at Davos. The theme of the conference was 'The Reshaping of the World: Consequences for Society, Politics and Business' and it focused on ensuring pragmatic outcomes to the contemporary and future challenges facing the world.

The WEF also publishes some reports like Global Competitiveness Report, Global Risks Report, Global Gender Gap Report and the Global Enabling Trade Report. The Global Enabling Trade Report 2014 benchmarks the performance of 138 economies in four critical areas—market access, border administration, transport and communications infrastructure, and regulatory and business environment. It helps the economies in integrating with the global value chains and also help companies in making better investment decisions.

Source: This case is written by the authors based on inputs from the following sources:

1. Article 'World Economic Forum 2013 and its Resilient Dynamism' by Faisal Ahmed, published in Diplomatist, February 2013.
2. Introduction to Global Enabling Trade Report, http://www.weforum.org/reports/global-enabling-trade-report-2014.

CASE QUESTIONS

1. Examine the various issues deliberated in Davos 2014.
2. Outline the issues discussed during Davos 2011 and find out their pragmatic outcomes as of now.

REVIEW QUESTIONS

1. What are the three levels of strategy?
2. Describe the Holcim–Lafarge merger case.
3. Explain the elements of the economic environment.
4. Discuss the role of culture in influencing the business environment.
5. What do you understand by diaspora?
6. What do you understand by political environment? Discuss its characteristics.
7. Describe bicameral and unicameral legislatures.
8. Define demographic dividend. Explain its benefits.
9. How does technology influence the business environment?
10. What is Startup India? Explain its features.
11. Examine the impact of World Economic Forum on business environment.

SUGGESTED READINGS

Craig, Tom and Campbell, David, 2012, *Organisations and the Business Environment*, Routledge, Oxford, UK.

Hamilton, Leslie and Webster, Philip, 2012, *International Business Environment*, Oxford University Press, New York.

Sundaram, A.K. and Black, J.S., 1995, *The International Business Environment: Text and Cases*, PHI Learning, Delhi.

World Economic Forum, 2013, Global Information Technology Report 2013, World Economic Forum (WEF), Geneva.

2

CONTEMPORARY PERSPECTIVES

Learning Outcomes

After reading this chapter, you will

- Understand the contemporary perspectives of business environment
- Appreciate the essence of global business environment and public policy in business decisions
- Comprehend key issues and perspectives on contemporary aspects like corporate social responsibility, consumerism, inclusive growth, trade-growth-poverty linkages, and sustainable development and be able to assess their impact on business environment

Opening Case: Best Practices in CSR—GAIL (India) Limited

Gas Authority of India Limited or GAIL (India) Limited has allocated an annual budget of 2% for corporate social responsibility (CSR) activities. The company's total allocation for CSR activities for 2010–2011 stood at ₹57.5 crore. Some of the key areas in which the company contributed include community development, infrastructure, health care, skill development, education, sanitation, and so on. These key areas are shown in Exhibit 1.

GAIL's CSR policy was amended in July 2010. Its objectives, as per the GAIL CSR Policy document, include:[1]

1. To ensure an increased commitment at all levels in the organisation and operate its business in an economically, socially and environmentally sustainable manner while recognising the interests of all its stakeholders
2. To directly or indirectly take up programmes that benefit the communities in and around its workcentres and result over a period of time, in enhancing the quality of life and economic well-being of the local populace
3. To generate, through its CSR initiatives, a community goodwill for GAIL and help in reinforcing a positive and socially responsible image of GAIL as a corporate entity

1. GAIL CSR Policy Document, http://www.gailonline.com/final_site/pdf/final_policy2010.pdf

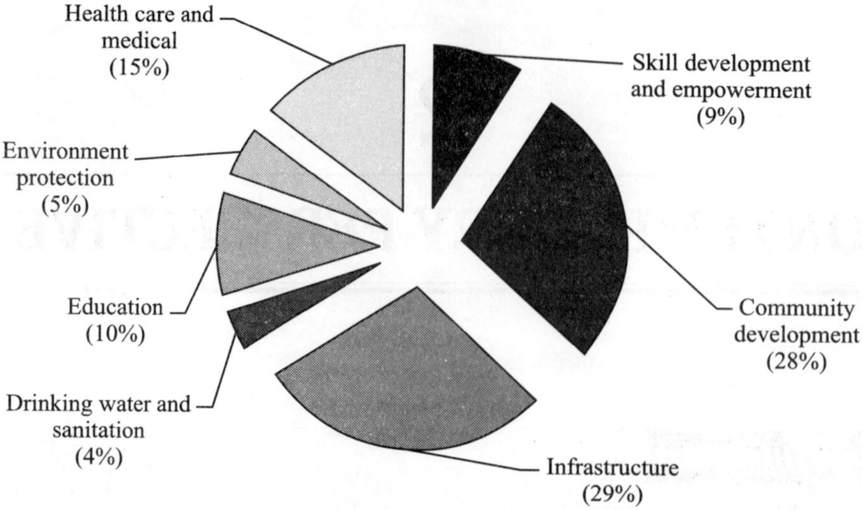

Exhibit 1 CSR fund allocation to various activities in GAIL in 2010–2011.

GAIL India Limited also promotes scholarship programmes to the meritorious students through a scheme launched in 2008–2009. The scholarship covers the following amounts, as shown in Table 1.

Table 1 Recommended Amounts for Scholarship by GAIL India Limited

Class	*Monthly* (₹)	*Yearly* (₹)
VIII	250	3,000
IX to X	300	3,600
XI to XII	350	4,200

GAIL (India) Limited won the Greentech CSR Award 2011 Gold Award category in Oil and Gas sector for outstanding achievement in CSR practices. Moreover, in June 2013, 23 students out of 100 belonging to economically backward strata of the society, who were trained by GAIL under *GAIL Utkarsh programme* got admission to the IITs.

Source: This case is written by the authors based on inputs from the following sources:

1. Website of GAIL
2. GAIL CSR Policy Document
3. http://www.gailonline.com/final_site/pdf/final_policy2010.pdf
4. 23 students of GAIL Utkarsh programme make it to the IITs, GAIL India Ltd. Press Release, http://www.gail.nic.in/final_site/pressrelease_june23_13.html

2.1 GLOBAL BUSINESS ENVIRONMENT

Global business environment is basically conceived with a view to do business in the evolving multilateral trading system. This includes dimensions of international trade in goods and services and also regimes for cross-border investments. Its framework is guided by various agreements that came into existence post the World War II. Thus, the institutions like GATT and later, the

WTO have emerged to regulate the world trade and contribute to the rule-making in international trade in the evolving world order.

The establishment of WTO has been a major achievement of the global community, as it provides a platform for multilateral negotiations on trade issues to all its member countries—developed, developing and least developed countries (LDCs). WTO has 164 members. (Chapter 14 provides a detailed discussion on the establishment and organisation of the WTO. Moreover, further discussion on the WTO regime can be seen in Chapter 19, while Chapter 20 delves into the major provisions under WTO.)

The global business environment has been experiencing a transition since the end of World War II. Based on the commonly agreed multilateral rules, a regime to prevail fair and competitive business practices has been in process. The accession to WTO of a large number of countries compelled them to bring down their tariffs and reduce protectionism. The multilateral trading rules and investment regimes are the main catalyst of market-friendly business environment. Tariff rates on industrial products in most of the developed countries are less than 5%. In developing economies and LDCs, the tariff rates are relatively higher.

Over the years, world trade has been increasing, and in contemporary times, it is significantly affected by shifts in global production network (see Figure 2.1). The changes in production and consumption networks are also creating opportunities for businesses to flourish.

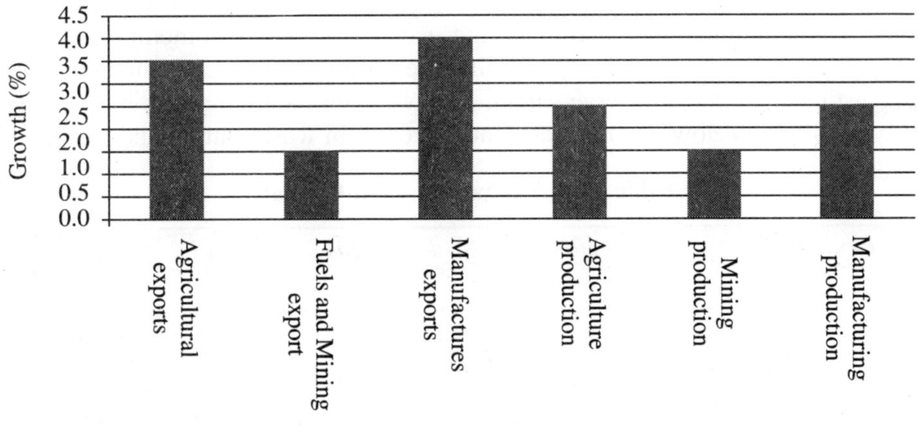

Figure 2.1 Growth in the volume of world merchandise exports and production, 2010–2014.
Source: WTO.

It is well recognised that there is an interlinkage between the multilateral trading system and the businesses. Many smaller countries, which are not the members of the WTO, are already in the process of negotiation and thus, have observer status. In recent years, countries like Russia, Lao PDR and Yemen have acceded to the WTO. In 2015, Kazakhstan and Seychelles became member of the organisation. WTO strives for a freer and transparent trading system. This has also created opportunities for global investment flows.

For instance, Cuba, a socialist government also allowed foreign investments. The Cuban National Assembly voted unanimously in favour of foreign investment law in March 2013. The new law provides incentives and also reductions in the taxes. This market-friendly approach would eventually have a good impact on the business environment of the country.

Today's business environment is governed by both national regulations and multilateral rules. Besides multilateralism, there is regionalism and bilateralism in the international trade as well. The global economic order has also been reshaped by the formation of regional trade agreements (RTAs) or 'trade blocs'. Businesses across the border are also affected by regional blocs. These blocs also assist both regional and global businesses by reducing trade barriers based on the preferential trade for regional stakeholders. However, they may be a stepping stone, but definitely not a substitute to the multilateral trading system, which is rule-based. (Chapter 18 discusses more on regional integration and trade blocs.)

2.1.1 Global Economic Scenario

World Economy has been continuously experiencing shocks and aftershocks. In 2008, financial meltdown led the global economic downturn affecting developed and developing countries. The recovery was seen during 2010 and 2011 but soon crisis in the European Union emerged as the road block to global economic recovery. As per the IMF World Economic Outlook, 2016, the present scenario is that the global recovery continues, but at an everlosing and increasingly fragile pace. The World Bank also indicates that the growth in the global economy in 2015 was not as per the expectations and GDP growth rate was recorded to be 2.4% in 2015 against 2.6% in 2014. The main reason for the performance of global economy is mainly the deceleration of economic activities in developing and emerging economies. The commodity prices are weak and decreasing trend of global capital flows and trade set out the blockages in recovery path. As per the IMF estimates, net non-reserve capital inflows in emerging markets have slowed down considerably. Table 2.1 below summarises annual growth in world output and trade.

Table 2.1 Annual Per Cent Change

Economy	*2010*	*2011*	*2012*	*2013*	*2014*	*2015*
Output						
World	5.4	4.2	3.5	3.3	3.4	3.1
Advanced economies	3.1	1.7	1.2	1.2	1.8	1.9
Emerging economies	7.4	6.3	5.3	4.9	4.6	4.0
Trade in goods and services						
World trade	12.4	7.1	2.8	3.4	3.5	2.8
Exports in advanced economies	12.0	5.9	2.3	3.0	3.5	3.4
Exports in emerging economies	13.3	9.0	4.0	4.4	3.1	1.7
Imports in advanced economies	11.4	5.0	1.1	2.2	3.5	4.3
Imports in emerging economies	14.0	11.4	5.6	5.2	3.7	0.5
Investment as per cent of GDP						
World	24.0	24.7	24.9	24.8	25.1	24.9
Advanced economies	20.8	20.8	20.6	20.8	20.7	20.8
Emerging economies	31.5	31.7	31.5	31.7	31.5	31.5

Source: IMF, World Economic Outlook, 2016.

The annual growth in the year 2010 reflects high rate of change due to recovery from negative growth in 2009 after global financial meltdown. Outputs in both developed economies and emerging economies, including developing countries, have been deteriorating in recent years. The case of trade is also similar. Investment as per cent of GDP indicates a decreasing trend in both advanced countries and developing and emerging countries.

Considering the deteriorating scenario, the IMF has suggested that there is a need for international policy response through identification of appropriate policy options. It recalls enhancing global financial safety net and oversight. It is suggested that in order to secure higher and sustainable growth, the advanced economies would require a three-pronged approach, which could comprise structural reforms, continued monetary policy accommodation, and fiscal support. These are mutually reinforcing methods. These structural changes have the potential to create avenues for higher economic growth in advanced economies. Therefore, these economies could form of growth-friendly fiscal policies as per needs and also pursue fiscal stimulus packages, wherever required. The IMF has also provided policy analysis on supply side of the economies in the world suggesting credible and country-specific structural reforms agenda considering both the short- and medium-term impact of reforms. These were key elements of the comprehensive strategy for advanced economies.[2]

The present world economic outlook suggests that well-defined strategies from policy makers in emerging market and developing economies would be required for sustainable growth, which would reduce macroeconomic and financial vulnerabilities. This can be achieved through elements which could rebuild resilience in the economies of emerging markets and developing countries. Only implementation of structural reforms having potential to enhance productivity in the economy rebuilds resilience.

2.1.2 Indian Economic Scenario

As per the IMF, India along with the other emerging economies like China plays a role in boosting global growth. As per the projection of the IMF, India's GDP is likely to grow at higher rate than that of China in the coming years. Growth in China has been projected to be 6.5% in 2016, whereas in India, it is likely to be 7.5%. India's GDP growth is expected to be influenced by private consumption. This emerging economic scenario in the country is the result of decrease in energy prices and higher real income. India's share in the world's GDP has increased from an average of 4.8% during 2001–2007 to 6.1% during 2008–2013, and further, to an average of 7.0% during 2014–2015 in the current Purchasing Power Parity (PPP) terms.

In 2014–2015, Indian economy registered growth of 7.2% despite the global economic slowdown. The economic growth increased over 2013–2014 of India, whereas as per the IMF, the world output decreased in 2015 as compared to 2014. As per the Economic Survey of India, 2016, the recent Indian growth story appears particularly bright due to the fact that most of the emerging economies are experiencing slowdown, including China. Considering the stable inflationary pressure, it is expected that India's monetary conditions will remain constant in the coming years. However, India's economy is continuously experiencing setback in terms of unfavourable monsoon hampering rural economy and agriculture sector.

2. See the web link: https://www.imf.org/external/pubs/ft/weo/2016/01/pdf/c3.pdf

A sectoral analysis indicates that agriculture sector continuously experiencing low growth on account of shortfall in rain. Agriculture sector grew at –0.2% in 2014–2015 compared to 4.2% in 2013–2014. Foodgrains production was recorded to be 265.0 million tonnes in 2013–2014, which dropped to 252 million tonnes. Industrial sector performance is measured through GVA in industrial sector which indicates that industrial sector is performing well in recent years (Table 2.2).

Service sector performance is still robust despite the experience of moderate growth. A slightly moderated growth in service sector is also compensated by accelerated growth in manufacturing sector in the Indian economy. As indicated in Table 2.2, annual growth in gross value added (GVA) in services is slightly down at 9.5% in 2015–2016 compared to 9.8% in 2014–2015. On the other hand, annual growth in Industrial sector was 5.4% in 2014–2015, which jumped to 7.4% in 2015–2016. The accelerated growth in the gross value added in industrial sector is also a result of the reform agenda being followed by Indian economy showing improvement in manufacturing activity and strength in industrial sector. However, the importance of service sector remains as the main driver of the growth in Indian economy. It is noted that more than half of the contribution in the GDP is from services sector. This sector contributed about 69% of the total growth during 2011–2012 to 2015–2016; and its share in the economy was 49% in 2011–2012 which increased to 53% in 2015-2016 increasing by 4% points.

Table 2.2 Performance of Indian Economy: Growth Rate (%)

Indicators	*2011–12*	*2012–13*	*2013–14*	*2014–15*	*2015–16*
Gross national income	6.9	5.3	6.6	7.3	7.5
GVA in agriculture sector	4.4	1.2	4.0	1.3	2.0
GVA in industrial sector	8.5	4.0	5.3	5.4	7.4
GVA in trade, transport hotel services	4.3	9.7	7.8	9.8	9.5
GVA in financial, insurance and business services	11.3	9.5	10.1	10.6	10.3
Exports of goods	27.2	12.5	15.8	0.2	–
Imports of goods	37.1	14.1	3.1	0.1	–
Foreign direct investment (FDI) inflow	17.1	–5.2	27.1	15.6	–

Source: Economic Survey of India, 2016, revised estimates for 2012–2015 and for 2015–2016 advance estimate.

In terms of external sector, India's exports to the world have been experiencing decline compared to the previous years. The case of imports is also similar. On the other hand, FDI inflows in India reached new heights and increased at more than 15% annual growth during 2014–2015 and 27% during 2013–2014. As per the Economic Survey of India, 2016, the trade and current account deficits moderated due to import restrictions followed by India in 2013–2014 after reaching unsustainably high levels. This moderation in trade and current account deficits continued in 2014–2015.

Such moderation is the result of not only the import restrictions imposed by the government but also the moderate oil prices at global level. It may be noted that the government had withdrawn restrictions from gold imports in 2014–2015. The external sector experienced a robust outcome in 2015–2016, indicating the sustainable and less vulnerable external sector position of the country. This is a promising macroeconomic position in the country, particularly in times when global economy is continuously suffering from slowdown. The prospects of the Indian economy is bright and it is likely to emerge as a fast growing economy in the coming years.

Thus, visible changes are taking place in Indian economy, particularly in aggregate demand. These changes are occurring in the area of private consumption, government consumption expenditure and growth in capital goods. There is considerable improvement in private consumption in the economy and is growing at the rate of more than 6% during 2013–2014 and 2014–2015. Private consumption has strengthened in the current year and expected to grow at 7.6% in 2015–2016. A significant increase in the growth of government consumption expenditure in 2014–2015 was noted, which got corrected in the current year. The growth in government consumption expenditure was recorded to be 12.8% in 2014–2015 over the previous year, which is expected to grow at 3.3% in 2015–2016. The growth of fixed capital formation in Indian economy is an important change that is taking place. More importantly, this growth in fixed capital formation is also due to growth in capital goods. Growth in the fixed capital formation during 2014–2015 was recorded to be 4.9% higher than the growth recorded in 2013–2014. The advance estimates of the Government indicates that growth in fixed capital formation is expected to be increased to 5.3% in 2015–2016, contributing more than 22% in the GDP growth of the economy (see Table 2.3).

Table 2.3 Contribution of Components to Real GDP Growth

Final expenditure	*Share in GDP*		*Growth (%)*			*Contribution to GDP growth (%)*		
	2013–14	*2015–16*	*2013–14*	*2014–15*	*2015–16* (AE)	*2013–14*	*2014–15*	*2015–16* (AE)
Private final consumption	56.2	59.8	6.8	6.2	7.6	57.1	48.3	55.9
Government final consumption	11.1	10.7	0.4	12.8	3.3	0.7	17.6	4.5
Fixed capital formation	34.3	29.4	3.4	4.9	5.3	17.5	22.1	22.4
Change in stock	2.4	1.7	–18.6	20.3	5.5	–6.0	4.6	1.4
Valuables	2.9	1.5	–42.2	15.4	13.3	–17.9	3.2	2.9
Net exports	–6.5	–2.6	70.0	11.7	6.1	67.4	2.9	1.2
GDP at constant market prices	100.0	100.0	6.6	7.2	7.6	100.0	100.0	100.0

Source: Central Statistics Office (CSO).

Note: AE: Advance estimates. Shares/contributions may not add up to 100 due to errors and omissions.

2.2 PUBLIC POLICY

Public policy refers to the study of policies and actions taken by a government, which create a direct or indirect impact on the public life. In fact, the doctrine of public policy has gradually widened across disciplines and these days, the public policy studies socio-economic and political aspects of policies as well as their international dimensions. It helps in formulating the intervention areas of public policies, impact of government actions and also highlights the future requirements and dimensions of policies.

The main idea of public policy is to identify five important aspects of policy formulation and implementation. These aspects include the following:

1. Identification of goals and objectives
2. Development of policies and strengthening of institutional frameworks
3. Strategic analysis and formulation
4. Execution and implementation
5. Impact assessment and grassroots reach out

A major aspect, where the doctrine of public policies looks into, is the impact assessment of these policies. It has been seen in the recent years that several public policy schemes in India like MNREGA, etc. have faced criticism because of their poor implementation. Box 2.1 discusses a government scheme, known as *direct benefit transfer* (*DBT*).

Box 2.1 DBT and Public Policy Doctrine

The Government of India launched an anti-poverty programme on 1 January 2013, called *direct benefit transfer* (*DBT*). The objective of the programme is to transfer benefits of subsidies directly to the beneficiaries. The beneficiaries were identified as the households living below the poverty line. Office of Controller General of Accounts is the agency to regulate transfer of the benefits.

The scheme is being implemented by Central Plan Scheme Monitoring System (CPSMS). Some other projects are also included in this scheme like National Child Labour Project, student scholarships and LPG subsidy. The idea of direct transfer of such benefits also coincides with the idea of financial inclusion of the vulnerable section of the society through a bank account. Until 2013, 11 lakh people have been benefitted from this programme.

The public policy doctrine to this programme is important to know not only its coverage area but also its implementation methodologies and the impact assessment.

Source: *Handbook on Direct Benefit Transfer*, Planning Commission, Government of India.

Need of public policy and issues

Public policy can be categorised in terms of economic policies, political policies, social and institutional policies and frameworks related to governance. Some of the aspects which are covered under public policy include the following:

1. Health
2. Education
3. Poverty alleviation
4. Social security
5. Social inclusion
6. Gender budgeting
7. Food security
8. Water security
9. Democracy and development

10. Trade and development
11. Millennium development goals (MDGs)

Public policy is also closely related to the activities of firms and industries. Particularly, the increasing activities of multinational companies have brought several issues, which need to be taken into account. There is a growing presence of these multinational firms due to increasing adaptability of liberalised economic policy and globalisation. Thus, there is a need to strike a balance between the economic growth and the public policy issues. This is crucial to ensure a sustainable development process.

It is in this context that the United Nations has defined MDGs and the governments across the globe have adopted these goals. Eradication of extreme poverty and hunger, global partnership for development etc. are among the eight goals of MDGs. The target has been set to be achieved by 2015. The UN is already working towards setting the development agenda for a post-2015 world. Public policy is closely linked with these doctrines.

A High-level Plenary Meeting of the UN General Assembly on MDGs was held in 2010. The meeting requested the Secretary-General of the UN to make efforts for setting up a post-2015 development agenda. Moreover, the Rio+20 Conference on Sustainable Development also highlighted the need for sustainable development goals (SDGs). In view of these, the world is in the process of setting up such a global development agenda, considering the need for SDGs. These developments have increased the role of public policy. It is in this context, public policy now also advocates the responsibility of market or corporate sector in achieving sustained and balanced goals. Corporate social responsibility (CSR) has now become a significant factor in public policy discourse.

2.3 CORPORATE SOCIAL RESPONSIBILITY

The policies are formulated to provide economic and social security to the citizens of a country. The government plans are also envisaged to reduce poverty, inequality as well as to provide education and health opportunities. We also know that the government formulates policies to facilitate business-related activities.

However, increasing economic activities also impact the environment inversely. Being a part of the society, the economic activities including business activities done by all the members should share responsibilities towards the society. It is in this context, the concept of shared responsibility by firms operating business-related activities is put under the head of CSR.

As per the United Nations Industrial Development Organisation (UNIDO), *CSR* is a management concept in which each company operating in an economy incorporates and integrates social and environmental concerns in their business-related operations. It is also defined as a way to achieve a balanced economic progress.[3] Also, see Box 2.2.

In fact, over the years, the concept of CSR has been voluntarily adopted by multinational enterprises and domestic companies across the world. However, its presence has not been very strong. Now, this concept has been revived as a much more serious aspect in the market-led economies.

UNIDO launched a Triple Bottom Line (TBL) project in 2001 in four countries, namely,

3. http://www.unido.org/en/what-we-do/trade/csr/what-is-csr.html

India, Pakistan, Sri Lanka and Thailand, with an aim to facilitate market access for developing countries.

Box 2.2 UNIDO and CSR

In order to work towards CSR, UNIDO supports governments to establish public-private partnerships (PPP) through multi-stakeholder consultations by engaging NGOs, industry chambers, academic institutions etc. Its key objectives include:

1. To support small and medium enterprises (SMEs) in examining their key challenges related to CSR
2. To discuss general public policy goals pertaining to poverty alleviation, generation of employment, gender issues, etc.
3. To explore the extent to which SMEs can help in achieving the public policy goals
4. To outline the areas for enhanced cooperation through PPP
5. To find out the ways and means to promote CSR across industrial sectors

Source: UNIDO website.

The TBL implies

1. ***Profit:*** It is related to the economics of social benefits enjoyed by the society which hosts a particular business.
2. ***People:*** It relates to a business practice that creates social inclusion, community development and local capacity building.
3. ***Planet:*** It relates to promoting sustainable livelihoods and a healthier planet by a business, which also intends to create ecological balance by adopting green practices.

In India, the guidelines on CSR and sustainability state that in case of public sector enterprises, CSR should be viewed as a process to conduct business-related activities. The guidelines advocate sustainable business practices and solicit cohesive relationship among the various stakeholders for a common good.[4]

As per the Companies Act 2013 and the notification issued by Ministry of Corporate Affairs, Government of India on 27 February 2014 regarding CSR policy, it is mandatory for every company in India to constitute a CSR committee, and carryout the projects and works under CSR-related activities. The CSR expenditure then includes the contribution to a corpus instituted for CSR activities, as recommended by the said Committee.[5] The Companies Act 2013 has clearly identified the areas and activities, which are included in CSR. Also, the act extensively deals with the policies related to CSR in its section 135.

The main activities included in the Companies Act 2013 are as follows:[6]

1. Eliminating poverty and extreme hunger
2. Promoting education
3. Promoting gender equality and women empowerment
4. Reducing child mortality and improving maternal health

---

4. http://www.dpemou.nic.in/MOUFiles/Revised_CSR_Guidelines.pdf, as stated in the preamble of Guidelines on Corporate Social Responsibility and Sustainability for Central Public Sector Enterprise.
5. http://www.mca.gov.in/Ministry/pdf/CompaniesActNotification2_2014.pdf
6. *Ibid.*

5. Combating human immunodeficiency virus, acquired immune deficiency syndrome, malaria and other diseases
6. Ensuring environmental sustainability
7. Encouraging employment enhancing vocational skills
8. Promoting social business projects
9. Contributing to the Prime Minister's National Relief Fund or any other fund set up by the Central Government or the state governments for socio-economic development and relief, and the funds for the welfare of scheduled castes, scheduled tribes, other backward classes, minorities and women

The Government of India on 28 February 2014 has notified a new CSR regime. Under the new rule, which has come into effect from 1 April 2014, there is a provision for mandatory spending by companies on CSR activities. Companies with at least ₹5 crore net profit or ₹500 crore net worth or ₹1,000 crore turnover need to spend 2% of their 3-year average annual net profit on CSR activities. It also applies to the foreign companies registered in India.[7]

Benefits of CSR activities

CSR activities are based on the idea of sustainable development and inclusive growth. Thus, in its framework ideology, CSR activities bring multifarious benefits to the society and the economy at large. A study conducted by MIT Sloan Management Review and the Boston Consulting Group (BCG) revealed that in the United States, sustainability has now a permanent place in 70% of the corporate agenda.[8] In India also, as per Companies Act 2013, it was obligated and now mandated that at least 2% of the profit after tax would be spent to address CSR issues. Such mandate would certainly lead to social benefits. Even when a company promotes CSR activities, the benefit that society gets out of it is not limited to the beneficiaries of CSR activities only, but also it helps in building brand equity as well. In a survey in the UK, it was found that more than 85% of the consumers or respondent preferred to buy product from those companies which supported CSR activities.[9] Some of the benefits of CSR activities are illustrated in Figure 2.2.

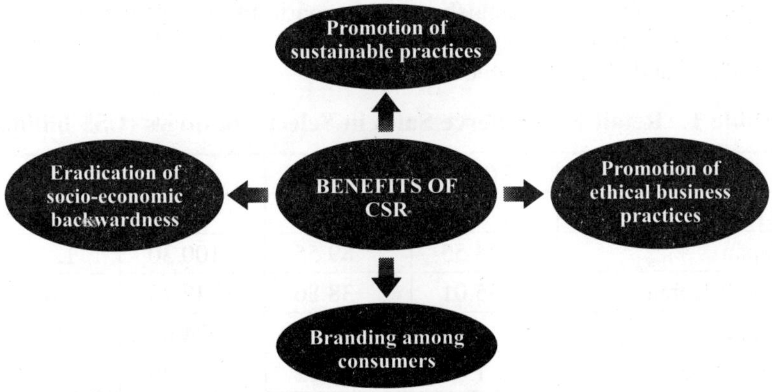

Figure 2.2 Benefits of CSR.

7. Government notifies rules for 2% mandatory CSR spending from profits, PTI, *Business Standard*, 28 February 2014.
8. http://sloanreview.mit.edu/reports/sustainability-strategy/introduction/
9. http://www.simplycsr.co.uk/the-benefits-of-csr.html, Better Business Journey, UK Small Business Consortium.

Thus, the benefits of CSR are not only concentrated on the society and the economy but also help in developing markets for the implementing company. Broadly, the benefits of CSR are as follows:[10]

1. It promotes business accountability across stakeholders.
2. This helps in addressing the environmental concerns.
3. It promotes market-led equitable process of economic development.
4. It helps in complementing the government resources to address environmental challenges.
5. This promotes product safety and quality.

2.4 CONSUMERISM

Consumerism implies encouraging consumption of goods and services in an economy. The doctrine also advocates the development based on the domestic consumption. It is also used to reflect on the protection of consumer rights. However, consumerism is the rise of consumption ability among the population. Higher the income level of population, higher would be the result of consumerism. Broadly, the policies which focus on consumption encourage the economy to rely upon the domestic consumers. Recent years have seen transition in some economies.

The economies in developing and least developed countries have seen higher rate of increase in national expenditure as percentage of GDP. Gross domestic expenditure as a percentage of GDP measures the rate expenditure by household, private sectors and government. This is an important indicator of consumerism in an economy. As percentage of GDP, this indicator is high in developing and least developed countries due to low volume of GDP in these countries.

Box 2.3 Sluggish Exports and Resilient Domestic Demand in Asia and the Pacific

As per the IMF report, the growth of GDP in the fourth quarter of 2015 was relatively moderate in countries of Asia and the Pacific, particularly in China, Japan, Singapore, and other countries of East Asia. In case of countries in Southeast Asia, Indonesia, the Philippines, and Vietnam, economic growth was robust, with sluggish export scenario in most of the economies, in nominal terms, and exports had declined sharply in the second half of 2015. This is reflected in the exports performance of China and Japan in Table 1.

Table 1 Retail E-commerce Sales in Select Countries (US$ billion)

Countries	*2014*	*2015*	*2016*	*2018*
China	472.9	672.01	911.25	1,568.39
Japan	78.55	89.55	100.30	122.46
South Korea	35.01	38.86	42.75	50.55
India	6.10	14.00	24.61	55.26
Indonesia	1.94	3.22	5.29	10.92
Asia and the Pacific	646.92	877.61	1,152.21	1,892.07
World	1,336.16	1,670.99	2,050.36	3,015.15

Source: emarketer.Dec. 2015.

10. http://www.iisd.org/business/issues/sr.aspx

Exports in China and Japan contracted by an average of about 15% in annual terms. However, a rosy scenario is seen in terms of robust domestic demand. Countries like Indonesia and Malaysia have been experiencing underpinning economic growth led by an increase in domestic demand, which is the bright spot in the region in 2015. The healthy domestic demand is reflected in the data of retail sales and private consumption. Consumers' demand for better services and high consumption is also a signal of rising disposable income in the region. Retails sales in Asia and the Pacific was further likely to hit $877 billion in 2015, which was estimated to be 35.7% rise over 2014.

Source: International Monetary Fund and Marketer.com
http://www.emarketer.com/Article/Asia-Pacific-Home-Majority-of-World-Retail-Ecommerce-Market/1013352

Table 2.4 presents some of the economies with higher share in domestic consumption. These countries are mostly developing countries. However, some developed countries (such as Australia) are also included in the table. The data suggests that as economies grow, domestic household expenditure tends to have a reducing share in GDP. In the United States, consumer spending was 62% of GDP during 1980, which was 68.5% in the year 2014.[11]

Table 2.4 Economies with Higher Share of Household Consumption in GDP (%)

Country/Year	*1960*	*1970*	*1980*	*1990*	*2000*	*2010*	*2011*	*2012*	*2013*	*2014*
Lesotho	108.10	118.33	130.25	123.12	123.10	100.03	97.66	94.42	92.54	–
Bangladesh	86.22	79.47	91.81	86.64	75.85	74.43	75.06	74.49	73.71	72.62
Mexico	79.17	71.92	65.07	69.58	66.82	67.45	67.36	66.17	66.96	67.27
Argentina	66.64	64.95	–	77.14	70.67	65.29	64.72	66.14	65.94	64.37
Ghana	72.84	74.37	83.90	85.22	84.27	80.07	69.34	59.78	65.62	64.29
India	80.83	75.37	74.86	64.61	64.22	56.40	57.14	59.12	59.42	59.29
Indonesia	77.19	77.70	51.44	58.89	60.70	56.22	55.48	56.07	57.24	56.57
Israel	68.08	60.33	53.11	55.60	53.36	57.24	57.05	55.47	55.54	55.87
Australia	58.45	54.08	55.23	55.88	58.07	55.44	54.02	53.73	54.83	55.43
Malaysia	53.52	56.31	53.35	51.80	43.75	48.12	47.97	49.65	51.80	52.41

Source: World Development Indicators, World Bank.

A lower share of GDP for national expenditure in developing countries would mean high rate of consumerism due to the fact that in these countries, volume of GDP is multiple times of that of developing and underdeveloped countries. After a slowdown in Europe and the United States during the recent past, countries which were dependent on exports are now shifting towards domestic consumerism. China is one of those countries. The National Bureau of Statistics highlights that in the first three quarters of 2013, consumption contributed over half (55%) of China's growth. In 2014, the final household consumption expenditure experienced annual growth of 13%. This is in contrast with the earlier experience.[12]

11. http://research.stlouisfed.org/fred2/graph/?g=hh3
12. http://www.economist.com/blogs/freeexchange/2012/10/rebalancing-china

In recent years, China's domestic consumption is 36% of the GDP. Data reveals that countries like India, Indonesia, China and Malaysia have been experiencing high growth in domestic consumption expenditure. This has resulted in increase in the share of consumption expenditure to GDP, as depicted in Table 2.5. The final household consumption expenditure in countries like Argentina, Brazil, Venezuela and Paraguay is witnessing slow growth. In 2014, this indicator slowed down in Argentina and Brazil (Table 2.5). The economy of this region is experiencing slowdown. The IMF updated its forecast for the region, i.e., Latin America and the Caribbean Economies to be slower economic growth. The GDP growth projection for the year 2015 is 1.3%, which highlights that the largest economy of the region, i.e., Brazil is likely to be remain stagnant. Most of the economies in this region are dependent on oil prices, which are continuously falling.

Table 2.5 Consumerism in the World, 2014

Country	*Household Consumption Expenditure (% of GDP)*	*Household Consumption Expenditure Annual Growth (%)*
Brazil	62.4	1.3
India	59.3	10.1
Argentina	64.4	–0.5
Indonesia	56.6	6.5
Malaysia	52.4	7.0
Australia	55.4	2.3
US	68.5	2.3
China	36.5	13.1

Source: World Development Indicators, World Bank.

Organised retailing and consumerism

Organised retailing has helped the growth of consumerism. Gradually, countries are now allowing foreign operators in multibrand retailing to achieve domestic consumption-based growth. India has recently enacted this law.

The increasing technological advancements in supply and value chains have helped retail businesses. The retail sector in India is viewed as one of the thriving sectors. It comprises both organised and unorganised retail. The multibrand FDI permission to the sector would increase the organised retail in the country. The quantum of the industry is estimated at US$490 billion.[13]

A modern concept of retailing has been one of the attractive aspects of retail businesses in the country. This has been increasing owing to the surging demand for both national and international brands in the Indian market.

Some of the international giants of multibrand retailing are looking to tap this surging market in India. Cumulative foreign investments in single brand trading during the period April

13. http://www.ibef.org/industry/retail-india.aspx

2000–January 2014 are estimated at US$98.66 million.[14] In view of this changing scenario, the role of innovative supply chain management and value chain has acquired a significance. Several logistics parks are coming up in India which will looks after creating value to the products by facilitating storage, warehousing and distribution.

2.5 INCLUSIVE GROWTH

Inclusive growth is a concept which advocates a balanced growth coupled with the availability of equitable opportunities for all the stakeholders. The concept emerged when the process of economic growth led to an increase in the unequal distribution of the benefits among the citizens. Thus, the idea that highlights the equal and balanced distribution of dividends of economic growth process in an economy to its population came to be known as the *idea of inclusive growth*.

In fact, *inclusiveness* is defined as the process of reducing the degree of socio-economic exclusion in an economy. Thus, the definition of inclusive growth clearly emphasises linking economic growth process with the determinants of equity. As per the ADB's report of the Eminent Persons Group, inclusive growth strategies for a government include the formulation of economic policies, which should address market failures and create avenues for all segments of a society to avail economic opportunities.[15] The report also spells out that the concept of inclusive growth avoids targeting any specific income group for special treatment and instead focuses on facilitating the participation of those less well-off in the increasing market opportunities.[16]

Thus, it is well-accepted among the policy-makers that there is a need for inclusive growth to reduce income inequalities and alleviate poverty. Inclusive growth policy allows the people to actually become a part of the economic progress. It helps the economy in attaining a sustained progress. The Commission on Growth and Development constituted in 2008 states that the concept of inclusiveness encompasses a broad idea of equity, creation of equal opportunities, and protection in market and employment transitions.[17] The commission consists of 19 leaders mostly from the developing countries.

However, the concept of inclusive growth has been defined in various ways by various countries. The inclusiveness has a wide realm which can include various aspects of social and economic discrimination. Governments across the globe adopt it as per their need, and therefore, the definition varies. In a broad form, it is pro-poor growth, which aims at eliminating poverty and reducing inequality.[18]

In order to attain a sustained and long-lasting economic progress, the concept of inclusive growth has, therefore, gained momentum during the recent years, particularly in the developing world. This concept is broadly accepted to formulate policies. In this process, the UN and the Government of Brazil have launched World Poverty Without Poverty Knowledge Initiative in

14. Department of Industrial Policy and Promotion (DIPP), Ministry of Commerce and Industry, Government of India.
15. http://www.adb.org/sites/default/files/pub/2007/new-adb-new-asia-epg-report.pdf (page 14)
16. http://www.adb.org/sites/default/files/pub/2007/new-adb-new-asia-epg-report.pdf
17. http://siteresources.worldbank.org/INTDEBTDEPT/Resources/468980-1218567884549/WhatIsInclusiveGrowth20081230.pdf; Commission on Growth and Development (2008), Growth Report: Strategies for Sustained Growth and Inclusive Development, the World Bank.
18. http://www.worldwewant2015.org/node/350379

2014. The aim of this initiative is to share good practices in order to reduce poverty in low and middle-income countries. The International Policy Centre for Inclusive Growth (IPC-IG) is a UNDP's global forum for policy dialogue and knowledge sharing on innovative development initiatives in the Global South. The centre defines inclusive growth as both an outcome as well as a process.[19]

Box 2.4 Jan-Dhan Yojana towards Financial Inclusion

Economic development needs to be inclusive by involving all sections of society, deprived and marginalised groups like women and children, scheduled tribes, scheduled castes, the differently abled and senior citizens. With the objective to attain inclusive development, it was felt that financial inclusion of those who are deprived needs utmost attention. Accordingly, Jan-Dhan Yojana was launched by the Government of India. There was considerable increase in the opening of basic savings bank deposit accounts (BSBDAs) during the year in view of the government's initiative under the Pradhan Mantri Jan-Dhan Yojana. The BSBDAs reached 441 million for the period ended September 2015 as against 398 million for the year ended March 2015. The total number of banking outlets went up from 5,53,713 as at end-March 2015 to 5,67,530 (5,17,328 branchless modes and 50,202 branches)as at end-September 2015. Business Correspondent–Information and Communication Technology (BC-ICT) transactions in BSBDAs showed steady progress with 359 million transactions during the period of April–September 2015, as against 477 million recorded for the year ended March 2015.

Table 1 Status of Jan-Dhan Yojana as in May 2016

(all figures in crore)

Bank name	*Rural*	*Urban*	*Total*	*No. of rupay cards*	*Aadhaar seeded*	*Balance in accounts*	*Percentage of zero-balance accounts*
Public sector bank	9.58	7.57	17.15	14.48	8.26	29,595.63	26.66
Regional rural bank	3.31	0.54	3.86	2.73	1.23	6,589.83	22.29
Private banks	0.50	0.31	0.81	0.76	0.32	1,431.11	37.88
Total	13.39	8.42	21.81	17.97	9.81	37,616.58	26.30

Jan-Dhan Yojana is further linked with Adhaar and mobile, which is called JAM in abbreviated form. With the combination of digital identification and mobile technology, several developmental programmes have been implemented. One example is LPG subsidy. Through JAM, LPG subsidy had been directly credited to 151 million account holders receiving total of ₹29,000 crore in their bank accounts in 2014–2015. Not only that, schemes like Mahatma Gandhi National Rural Employment Guarantee Scheme (MGNREGA) and others are now linked with JAM Yojana. Such kind of inclusion has direct impact on reducing leakages in the economy.

Source: Economic Survey of India, 2016 and http://pmjdy.gov.in/account

19. http://www.ipc-undp.org/pages/newsite/menu/inclusive/whatisinclusivegrowth.jsp?active=1

Inclusive growth in the world

Poverty and inequality are global phenomena. There is a clear division of the world in terms of Global South and the developed countries. The former term refers to more than 150 developing and least developed countries (LDCs) of the world, whereas the latter implies developed and industrialised economies. This classification itself shows inequality and the presence of an unequal distribution of income across the globe. Also, the World Bank classifies countries as low, middle and high-income economies.

Globally, we see that a larger population is still deprived of the basic amenities. The process of economic growth and development, therefore, need to be redefined. The Human Development Report of the UN states

> Human development is about creating an environment in which people can develop their full potential and lead productive, creative lives in accord with their needs and interests. People are the real wealth of nations.

GDP growth rate and GDP per capita are also taken as the indicators of development. Figure 2.3 shows the region-wide growth rate in the world, while Figure 2.4 indicates the unequal distribution of income across the regions.

The highly populated region in the world, South Asia has a low per capita income, which is just higher than that of the Sub-Saharan Africa (see Figure 2.4). However, this region has been experiencing a higher economic growth. India is the part of the region and it is the largest economy.

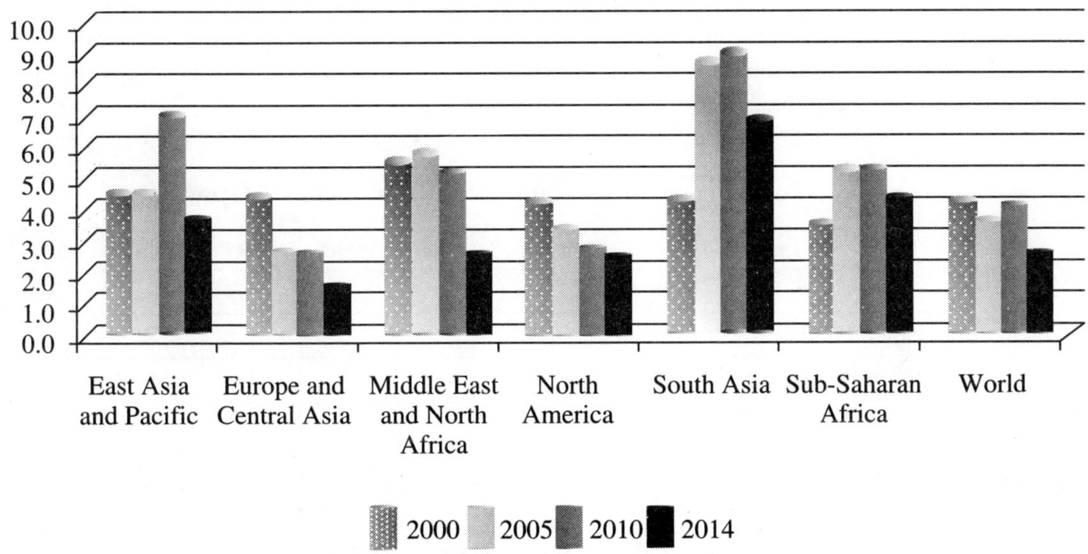

Figure 2.3 Region-wide GDP growth (%).
Source: World Bank.

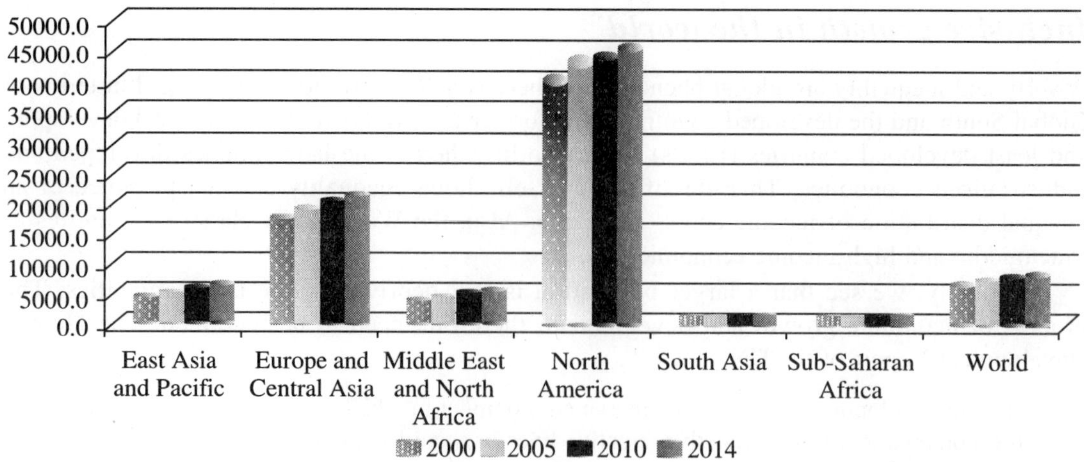

Figure 2.4 GDP per capita, PPP (constant 2005 US$).

Source: World Bank.

India's inclusive growth story

In India, the concept of inclusive growth is linked to the policy planning. The approach paper of the 12th Five Year Plan exclusively mentions about the process of inclusive growth. It mentions the need for faster and inclusive growth. Along with a huge population, the country has also experienced a high growth during the last decade.

The 12th Five Year Plan defines inclusiveness in various ways. It has identified areas which can be targeted while approaching for inclusive growth process in the economy. The areas which are the part of the inclusive growth include not only the elimination of poverty and inequality but also the reduction in regional disparities and gender inequality. Table 2.6 gives an account of the participation of population in the inclusive growth of India over the years.

Table 2.6 Some Economic Indicators Related to Inclusive Growth

Indicators	*2000*	*2005*	*2010*	*2014*
GDP growth	3.8	9.3	10.3	7.3
Growth in per capita GDP	2.1	7.6	8.7	6.0
Population below poverty line*	–	41.64	32.68	
Employers, female (percentage of employment)	0.4	0.5	0.4	-
Employers, male (percentage of employment)	1.1	1.6	1.3	-
Employers, total (percentage of employment)	0.9	1.3	1.1	-
Employment in agriculture (percentage of total employment)	59.9	55.8	51.1	-
Employment in industry (percentage of total employment)	16	19	22.4	-
Employment in services (percentage of total employment)	24	25.2	26.6	-

Continued

Indicators	*2000*	*2005*	*2010*	*2014*
Employment to population ratio, 15+ age, female (%), national	32.9	35.1	27.7	23.8
Employment to population ratio, 15+ age, male (%), national	79.3	79.9	78.1	71.4
Employment to population ratio, 15+ age, total (%), national	56.9	58.2	53.6	49.9
Employment to population ratio, 15–24 age, female (%), ILO	24.2	25.1	17.2	15.6
Employment to population ratio, 15–24 age, male (%), ILO	58.4	58.4	49.1	46.0
Employment to population ratio, 15–24 age, total (%), ILO	42	42.4	33.9	31.5

Source: World Bank. * Economic Survey of India.

As per the document of the 12th Five Year Plan, the inclusive growth has been perceived in the following ways:[20]

1. ***Inclusiveness as poverty reduction:*** The concept of inclusive growth should cover the process of poverty reduction. The benefits of growth should also reach the marginalised sections of the society.
2. ***Inclusiveness as group equality:*** A vital feature of inclusive growth concept is the consideration of social inclusion of the vulnerable sections of the society like scheduled castes (SCs), scheduled tribes (STs), other backward classes (OBCs), minorities and women. Thus, the 12th plan mentions about policies and steps for these groups.
3. ***Inclusiveness as regional balance:*** Inclusive growth is also viewed in terms of regional imbalances in the country. An aim of inclusiveness is to reduce regional disparities among the states.
4. ***Inclusiveness through employment programmes:*** Employment generation is also one of the key objectives of inclusiveness. Inclusive growth policies should be linked to the schemes related to capacity building and generation of employment opportunities.

2.6 TRADE, GROWTH AND POVERTY

International trade is an engine of economic growth and contributes to the socio-economic well-being. The story of world trade depicts that technological advancements and reducing barriers have reduced the distance between the countries.[21] This has eventually led to the reduction of trade cost. The world has witnessed a rapid growth of industrialisation over the centuries, with their nature varying as per the comparative advantages and global competitiveness of the economies. With the advent of the doctrine of globalisation and liberalisation under WTO regime, global trade is seen as a process of achieving economic growth and reducing poverty. Isolated countries are now gradually starting integrating with the world. Countries like Lao PDR have acceded to WTO agreements and become a part of the global economic growth through trade integration. Figure 2.5 depicts the trend of GDP growth vis-à-vis trade.

20. Plan Document, 12th Five Year Plan, Planning Commission, Government of India.
21. http://www.wto.org/english/res_e/booksp_e/wtr13-2b_e.pdf

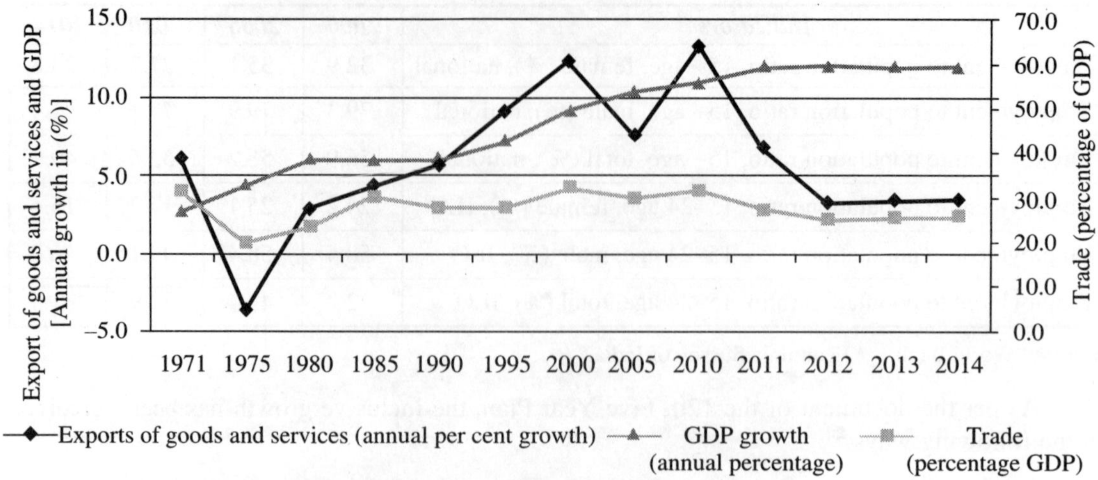

Figure 2.5 Trend of GDP growth and trade (%).

Source: World Bank.

An important phenomenon is that the international trade has grown double the growth of the income of the world. It is evident from Figure 2.6 that the share of trade in world's GDP has also increased over the period of time. It is found that the economy which has more openness towards the trade has achieved higher economic growth.[22]

Also, the share of world trade in GDP has grown during the last century. As per OECD estimates, the share of world exports to the world GDP was merely 4.6% in 1870. The share increased to 7.9% in 1913. However, due to the period of World War, this share reduced to 5.5% but further increased to 17.2% in 1998. As of 2014 calculations, the share of exports of goods and services in GDP was about 29.7% (see Table 2.7).

Table 2.7 Global Export Share in GDP

Year	*Export Share in GDP*
1870	4.6
1913	7.9
1950	5.5
1973	10.5
1998	17.2
2000	26.0
2005	28.0
2011	31.0
2014	29.7

Source: OECD and World Bank.

22. https://www.imf.org/external/pubs/ft/fandd/2001/09/dollar.htm

This increase in trade has resulted in the increase in per capita income in the world (see Table 2.8). The GDP per capita of countries like India, China and Indonesia have grown rapidly during the process of their global economic integration.

Table 2.8 Trend of Annual Growth in Per Capita Income (%)

Country	*1961*	*1970*	*1980*	*1990*	*2000*	*2010*	*2012*	*2014*
China	–26.4	16.1	6.5	2.3	7.5	9.9	7.2	6.7
India	1.7	2.8	4.3	3.4	2.3	9.1	3.7	6.0
Indonesia	3.6	5.4	6.2	7.1	3.4	4.8	4.7	3.7
Malaysia	4.2	3.4	4.9	6.0	6.4	5.3	3.9	4.5
World	2.9	1.1	0.1	1.0	2.9	2.8	1.1	1.3

Source: World Development Indicators, World Bank.

As per Asia–Pacific Trade and Investment Report 2013 published by UNESCAP, trade has led to the decrease in poverty in Asia.[23] The report points out that the services sector is the fastest growing sector of the global economy. It accounts for two-third of the global output and almost 33% of the global employment rests with the sector. Besides accounting for 20% of the global trade, the services sector also contributes more than 50% of the GDP in many developing countries including India. With a focus on manufacturing sector, more employment opportunities can be created.

The report says

> The expansion of trade and investment in the Asia–Pacific has helped in lifting millions of people out of poverty, permitting the global success of halving the poverty five years ahead of the MDG target timeframe. But more than half of the world's poor still live in Asia.

2.7 SUSTAINABLE DEVELOPMENT

In the contemporary business environment, the key objective of businesses is sustainability. Sustainable development was defined by Brundtland Commission in its 1987 report 'Our Common Future'. According to which the concept can be defined as the process of development that meets the needs of the present without compromising the ability of future generations to meet their own needs. Thus, this definition became a benchmark for formulating development policies.

Earlier this concept has been used in economics in terms of sustained process. However, the doctrine of sustainability is closely linked with the environmental degradation. During the Rio+20 Conference in 2012, the countries agreed to adopt a process of sustainable development through setting up sustainable development goals (SDGs). The concept is strongly advocated for post-2015 development agenda.

23. Asia–Pacific Trade and Investment Report 2013, Turning the Tide: towards Inclusive Trade and Investment, http://www.unescap.org/sites/default/files/Full%20Report.pdf

The outcome document of Rio+20 conference states that the member states must adhere to SDGs in the following ways.[24]

1. Be based on Agenda 21 and the Johannesburg Plan of Implementation.
2. Fully respect all the Rio Principles.
3. Be consistent with the international law.
4. Build upon commitments already made.
5. Contribute to the full implementation of the outcomes of all major summits in the economic, social and environmental fields.
6. Focus on the priority areas for the achievement of sustainable development, being guided by the outcome document.
7. Address and incorporate in a balanced way all three dimensions of sustainable development and their interlinkages.
8. Be coherent with and integrated into the United Nations development Agenda beyond 2015.
9. Do not divert focus or effort from the achievement of the millennium development goals.
10. Include active involvement of all relevant stakeholders, as appropriate, in the process.

The concept has a close link with the climate change. The industrialisation process emits carbon dioxide (CO_2), which degrades out the environmental systems. The UN set up an intergovernmental panel to look into this problem. The panel is called Intergovernmental Panel on Climate Change (IPCC) in 1988. Moreover, the organisations like the World Meteorological Organisation (WMO) and the United Nations Environment Programme (UNEP) also work closely with IPCC.

Box 2.5 Sustainable Development Goals (SDGs)

Sustainable development goals (SDGs) as a part of new sustainable development agenda were adopted by the UN General Assembly on 25th September 2015. It set out goals to end poverty, protect earth and ensure prosperity for all. On 1 January 2016, the SDGs of the 2030 agenda for sustainable development came into force and the new goals, which are universally applicable to all the member countries of the UN would need renewed efforts from them. The SDGs have succeeded the millennium development projects (MDGs) after 2015 and are aimed at ending all forms of poverty by 2030. However, SDGs are not legally binding, yet the governments are expected to take initiatives towards achieving the set goals.

There are 17 goals with 169 associated targets, which are integrated within the development agenda. The adoption of the agenda for 2030 recognises the following goals under SDGs:

Goal 1 End poverty in all its forms.

Goal 2 End hunger, achieve food security and improved nutrition and promote sustainable agriculture.

Goal 3 Ensure healthy lives and promote well-being.

Goal 4 Ensure inclusive and equitable quality education and promote lifelong learning opportunities.

24. http://sustainabledevelopment.un.org/index.php?menu=1561

Goal 5	Achieve gender equality and empower all women and girls.
Goal 6	Ensure availability and sustainable management of water and sanitation for all.
Goal 7	Ensure access to affordable, reliable, sustainable and modern energy for all.
Goal 8	Promote sustained, inclusive and sustainable economic growth, full and productive employment and decent work for all.
Goal 9	Build resilient infrastructure, promote inclusive and sustainable industrialization and foster innovation.
Goal 10	Reduce inequality within and among countries.
Goal 11	Make cities and human settlements inclusive, safe, resilient and sustainable.
Goal 12	Ensure sustainable consumption and production patterns.
Goal 13	Take urgent action to combat climate change and its impacts*.
Goal 14	Conserve and sustainably use the oceans, seas and marine resources for sustainable development.
Goal 15	Protect, restore and promote sustainable use of terrestrial ecosystems, sustainably manage forests, combat desertification, and halt and reverse land degradation and halt biodiversity loss.
Goal 16	Promote peaceful and inclusive societies for sustainable development, provide access to justice for all and build effective, accountable and inclusive institutions at all levels.
Goal 17	Strengthen the means of implementation and revitalize the global partnership for sustainable development.

With the above goals and its associated targets, the SDGs aim at eradicating all forms of poverty by 2030 across the globe and fighting inequality and injustice and establish gender equality through concerted efforts by member countries. A high level political forum has been set up in which all the member states of the UN and member state of specialized agencies participates to follow up and review the goals and targets. The next meeting of the high level political forum is to be convened under the auspices of the Economic and Social Council of the UN on 10–19 July 2017, which also includes three-day Ministerial meeting of the forum.

Source: Based on UN Resolution Adopted by General Assembly on 25th September 2015 on Sustainable Development Goals Agenda, http://www.un.org/ga/search/view_doc.asp?symbol=A/RES/70/1&Lang=E

Closing Case: Universal Climate Agreement (2020)

Since the Earth Summit of 1992 that was held in Rio de Janeiro in Brazil, various rounds of deliberations on the issue of sustainable development and climate change adaptation and mitigation have been undertaken under the aegis of the United Nations. The aim is to ensure sustainable livelihoods. Owing to the differences between developed and developing countries over the issue of sustainable development processes, governments have taken the support of unilateral and multilateral frameworks.

The issue of climate change has reached under the ambit of international and multilateral agencies, seeking initiatives from various countries across the globe. *Climate change* and *global warming* refer to an increase in the average global temperature. In fact, an increase in the greenhouse gases (GHGs) like CO_2 leads to global warming. Therefore, GHG emissions, which adversely affect the natural environment, have to be reduced.

In addition to the natural process of gas emissions through the earth system, there are several human activities which also lead to increase in the GHGs through emission. Anthropogenic activities pertaining to industrialisation, transportation, urbanisation, mining, etc. need fossil burning and deforestation, which necessarily contribute to the huge GHG emissions.

Some of the pressing concerns for the international community in respect of climate change are as follows:

1. Global warming
2. Rise in mean sea level
3. Threat of submergence of small island states like Maldives
4. Resource constraints
5. Energy security
6. Mitigation and adaptation strategies
7. Binding commitments

Given the problems associated with the climate change, various institutional frameworks have been developed to govern climate change regulations. These include

1. ***Intergovernmental Panel on Climate Change (IPCC):*** It provides scientific view on contemporary discourses on climate change and also assesses the potential impact of climate change on society and environment.
2. ***United Nations Framework Convention on Climate Change (UNFCCC):*** It is a treaty on global environment which was negotiated during the United Nations Conference on 'Environment and Development' (or the Earth Summit 1992). Its objective is to stabilise the greenhouse gas concentrations in the atmosphere at a level that would prevent dangerous anthropogenic interference with the climate system.[25]
3. ***Kyoto Protocol:*** This protocol, adopted in Kyoto, Japan in 1997 and entered into force in 2005, set binding commitments for the reduction in GHG emissions. It called for an average 5% emission reduction (from the 1990 level) for 37 industrialised countries during the period 2008–2012.[26]
4. ***Bali Action Plan (2007):*** It called for an effective implementation of the provisions of UNFCCC up to 2012 and beyond through cohesive global cooperation. It called for long-term emission reduction goals for mitigating and adapting to climate change.
5. ***Copenhagen Summit (2009):*** This conference of parties (COP) re-asserted the need for reducing carbon emissions, but did not create any binding commitments.
6. ***COP-17 in Durban (2011):*** The Durban conference focused on some issues of critical relevance that come at the intersection of trade policy and climate change issues like unilateral trade measures, climate protectionism, need for climate-friendly technology, role of intellectual property rights (IPRs), carbon labelling, and use of biofuels.[27] It also called for setting universal commitments by 2015.

25. Article 2 of the UNFCCC, http://unfccc.int/essential_background/convention/background/items/1353.php
26. Text of the Kyoto Protocol, UNFCCC, https://unfccc.int/key_documents/kyoto_protocol/items/6445.php
27. It's not Climate versus Trade/The international trade climate change interface is emerging as a 'new issue', by Faisal Ahmed, *The Economic Times*, 27 March 2012, p. 12.

7. ***Warsaw Climate Change Conference (2013)*:** This conference is deemed to be successful in arriving at decisions related to Green Climate Fund and long-term financing. It called all countries to start working on the draft text for a universal climate agreement to be finalised in 2015, and expected to be implemented in 2020.[28]

A multilateral framework is important and the negotiations seem to be going in the right direction. But the real challenge is again to keep a binding commitment like Kyoto Protocol alive, and that too for more number of countries—not merely 37 countries.

Source: This case is written by the authors based on inputs from the following sources:

1. Article 2 of the UNFCCC http://unfccc.int/essential_background/convention/background/items/1353.php
2. Text of the Kyoto Protocol, UNFCCC, https://unfccc.int/key_documents/kyoto_protocol/items/6445.php
3. It's not Climate versus Trade/The international trade climate change interface is emerging as a 'new issue', by Faisal Ahmed, *The Economic Times*, 27 March 2012, p. 12.
4. UN Climate Change Conference in Warsaw keeps governments on a track towards 2015 climate agreement, https://unfccc.int/files/press/news_room/press_releases_and_advisories/application/pdf/131123_pr_closing_cop19.pdf

CASE QUESTIONS

1. Prepare a note on the Universal Climate Agreement. Do you think it is implementable given the North–South divide?
2. Find out the stands of India, China, EU and the US on the issue of binding commitments and compare them.

REVIEW QUESTIONS

1. Outline your general understanding about the global business environment.
2. What is public policy? What are its five important aspects?
3. Give your observation on the Direct Benefit Transfer (DBT) programme.
4. What is corporate social responsibility (CSR)? Examine the role of UNIDO in CSR activities.
5. What do you understand by Triple Bottom Line approach?
6. Outline the main CSR activities included in the Companies Act 2013.
7. Examine the benefits of CSR.
8. What is consumerism? Does organised retailing help in the growth of consumerism?
9. What is the interlinkage among trade, growth and poverty?

28. UN Climate Change Conference in Warsaw keeps governments on a track towards 2015 climate agreement, https://unfccc.int/files/press/news_room/press_releases_and_advisories/application/pdf/131123_pr_closing_cop19.pdf

10. What is inclusive growth? Discuss the provision related to it in the 12th five year plan.

11. Define sustainable development.

12. What are sustainable development goals (SDGs)?

13. Outline the ways and means to attain SDGs as agreed in the Rio+20 Conference.

14. What do you understand by Kyoto Protocol?

15. Describe some features of the Universal Climate Agreement 2020.

SUGGESTED READINGS

Asia-Pacific Trade and Investment Report, 2013, UNESCAP, Bangkok.

Economic Survey of India, 2013–2014, Ministry of Finance, Government of India, New Delhi.

'Inclusive Green Growth: The Pathway to Sustainable Development', 2012, World Bank, Washington DC.

'Preserving Stability and Promoting Growth', *World Bank East Asia Pacific Economic Update*, April 2014, World Bank, Washington DC.

World Development Report, 2014, World Bank, Washington DC.

World Economic Outlook, 2014, IMF, Washington DC.

'World Trade Report: Factors Shaping the Future of World Trade', 2013, WTO, Geneva.

3

ENVIRONMENTAL SCANNING

Learning Outcomes

After reading this chapter, you will

- Understand the essence of environmental scanning
- Comprehend the research process and its need in industry
- Appreciate the importance of PEST and SWOT analyses as instruments of environmental scanning

Opening Case: Scanning Makes Sense—Instances From Syria and Iran

Scanning the environment is integral to understanding the business environment. We have two instances of political turmoil in Syria and Iran, respectively, which impacted Indian businesses also.

Syria

In the mid of 2012, a crisis erupted in Syria when Turkey and Syria entered into a geopolitical conflict. In view of this, Turkey cancelled all its trade and strategic agreements with Syria. This made the situation in the Middle East even more volatile.

In the wake of such development, India's exports to Syria also suffered a decline. It declined from US$536.48 million in 2011–2012 to US$258.77 million in 2012–2013, registering a negative growth of more than 50%. The political instability in Syria already took its toll on the business environment.

The Export Credit Guarantee Corporation of India Limited (ECGC), a Government of India enterprise, which provides export credit insurance for the exporters and banks, classified Syria in the list of restricted cover countries in 2012. This meant that for Indian exports destined to Syria, a tough insurance cover rules would apply.[1]

1. 'Crisis in Syria: Need for Cautious Economic Diplomacy' by Faisal Ahmed, *Diplomatist*, Vol. 4, No. 8, 2012.

Iran

Another example is of India–Iran trade. Owing to US sanctions on the use of US dollar by Iran, India and Iran entered into the rupee–rial arrangement so that India can continue to secure its oil imports from Iran through the arrangement between Halkbank of Turkey and Union Bank of India.[2]

Then, the US Secretary of State Hillary Clinton also visited India and persuaded to cut oil imports from Iran. The state-run refiners in India targeted a cut in oil imports from Iran by around 15%.[3]

Earlier, the European Union (EU) had banned several insurance companies from covering Iranian oil shipments as well. In recent years, this has ultimately led to a decline in India's oil imports from Iran. In January 2014, news about easing of sanctions on Iran was reported, and this helped Iranian oil exports to increase.

Scanning the domestic and international business environment, therefore, makes sense for the businesses and the industry.

Source: This case is written by the authors based on inputs from the following sources:

1. 'Crisis in Syria: Need for Cautious Economic Diplomacy' by Faisal Ahmed, *Diplomatist*, Vol. 4, No. 8, 2012.
2. Faisal Ahmed and M. Absar Alam (2013), 'Bilateral Engagement Amid Geopolitics: A case of India and Iran', *Romanian Economic Journal*, Vol. 16, pp. 55–82.
3. 'India cuts Iran oil imports nearly a fifth in 2013/14', Nidhi Verma, *Live Mint* and the *Wall Street Journal*, 17 April 2014, http://www.livemint.com/Industry/7cSVlLeOXNGdwZKklsoMmK/India-cuts-Iran-oil-imports-nearly-a-fifth-in-201314.html.

3.1 MEANING AND SCOPE

Research is an integral element of managerial work, especially when one is engaged in the process of formulating strategies. It involves making an informed assessment and analysis of the business environment. Such an exercise is called *environmental scanning*. Environmental scanning implies research on both external and internal environment of a firm. It refers to the analysis of economic and non-economic environment affecting a business. For instance, let us assume that a firm wants to internationalise its business from India to South Africa. This would compel its managers to do an environmental scanning. The environmental scanning would consist of the analysis of economic, political and social indicators of the business environment in South Africa in order to ascertain the prospects of business.

Thus, *environmental scanning* may be defined as the analysis and interpretation of the economic and non-economic environment, including the internal environment of a firm. *Environmental analysis* is also considered as one of the important part of the global environmental analysis. It helps in understanding the present global business environment and also enables managers to forecast the future prospects. Here comes the importance of research and analysis as

2. Faisal Ahmed and M. Absar Alam (2013), 'Bilateral Engagement amid geopolitics: A case of India and Iran', *Romanian Economic Journal*, Vol. 16, pp. 55–82.
3. 'India cuts Iran oil imports nearly a fifth in 2013/14', Nidhi Verma, *Live Mint* and the *Wall Street Journal*, 17 April 2014, http://www.livemint.com/Industry/7cSVlLeOXNGdwZKklsoMmK/India-cuts-Iran-oil-imports-nearly-a-fifth-in-201314.html

an integral part of environment scanning. The research needs to be carried out on various aspects of market, industry, firm, demand, supply and competitive landscapes.

The key objectives of environmental scanning include:[4]

1. Situational analysis of a business or sector
2. Ascertaining the factors that cause environmental uncertainty
3. Providing information processing support while devising firm's strategy
4. Enhancing organisational learning and performance

The environmental scanning process depicts the contemporary business environment and has the potential to forecast its future. In this process, environmental scanning also has the potential to assist in policy formulation and outreach. An example of such a research is doing business analysis published by the World Bank and International Finance Corporation (IFC), which comes out in the form of a report every year. This report is known as the *Doing Business Report*. (Chapter 24 discusses the doing business analysis with reference to some selected countries/regions.)

3.2 TYPES OF RESEARCH

Business research is one of the core areas of social science research. Research in social sciences enables us to understand both macro as well as microenvironment. It is applied in diverse fields, including economics, sociology, psychology etc.

The techniques of research in these areas are well-designed and enable the researchers not only to analyse policies but also to assess the behaviour of consumers. There are various kinds of research. Some of these are as follows:

1. ***Exploratory research:*** It is undertaken in a scenario when the problem is not clearly defined. It can also be carried out to explain a phenomenon in which less research is available. This type of research can even be used to generate hypotheses by using case studies and secondary data.
2. ***Descriptive research:*** It is used to describe the characteristic of a population or a phenomenon, delving into its various features. It does not establish any cause and effect relationship between the various variables (or determinants) of a phenomenon. Various types of surveys can be classified as descriptive research.
3. ***Analytical research:*** This process is the extension of descriptive research. It tries to understand the factors which are affecting the population or phenomenon under study, and makes a critical evaluation of the same. This type of research is meant to establish causal relationship among the variables through correlation and regression analysis.
4. ***Predictive research:*** It is used to forecast the likelihood of the occurrence of an event or phenomenon as well as to predict the future. It is based on the analysis of available (historical) data. In most cases, a time series analysis can be carried out to conduct a predictive research.

4. Choo, Chun Wei and Ethel Auster (1993), Environmental Scanning: Acquisition and Use of Information by Managers, in Annual Review of Information Science and Technology, edited by M.E. Williams, Medford, NJ: Learned Information, Inc., for the American Society for Information Science, http://choo.fis.utoronto.ca/fis/respub/chooimreader.pdf

3.3 RESEARCH PROCESS

Understanding the research process is important. The key steps of the research process may include (depending upon the purpose of research) the following:

1. Selecting a theme/identifying a research problem
2. Reviewing literatures on the theme or the problem to ascertain the amount of existing knowledge in that field
3. Identifying a research gap and outlining the rationale of the study
4. Developing the objectives of the study based on the research gap
5. Making research questions and/or hypotheses based on the objectives
6. Identifying the most suitable methodology to answer the research questions or prove the hypothesis in order to meet the objectives of the study. This should include nature of data (primary/secondary), sample size, qualitative analysis (*viz.* developing case studies etc., if applicable), statistical techniques (*viz.* correlation, chi-square test etc., if applicable) and statistical package (*viz.* SPSS, as applicable)
7. Collecting data
8. Applying the methodology and carrying out data analysis and proving the hypothesis (if any)
9. Enlisting the findings and ascertaining that it fulfills the objectives of the study
10. Drawing conclusions and making recommendations based on the findings of the study

3.4 DATA SCANNING AND QUANTITATIVE ANALYSIS

Environmental scanning also requires data analysis to arrive at a defined goal through the use of quantitative techniques. A quantitative analysis could be carried out for business research while doing environmental scanning. These are related to the analysis of macroeconomic indicators. However, in addition to these, the analysis is also carried out for the purpose of effective decision-making. This requires the use of statistical tools as well.

The statistical tools could be employed for the following purposes:

1. Hypothesis testing
2. Forecasting
3. Establishing causal relations
4. Making an empirical analysis

The above techniques and processes help in carrying out the environmental scanning. Environmental scanning can be carried out for improved decision-making in the following broad areas:

1. ***Market information and trend:*** In this process, data scanning requires to collect data on market-related indicators. These indicators include prices of different commodities, consumers demand for commodities, supply scenario, market size and level of competition. These also include policies of government related to doing business. The market scenario can also be analysed based on the secondary data such as trend and growth of macroeconomic indicators, economic reforms etc.

2. ***Market strength and its segmentation:*** The most important indicator for these two things is the growing level of consumption. This is to be analysed based on the trend of per capita income and also through understanding the demographic structure. Data scanning and data analysis are carried out to see the prospects of business on this account.
3. ***Strategic analysis:*** In addition to market analysis, there are other important purposes for data scanning and analysis. These purposes include understanding the overall business environment to enable a better strategy formulation. For this, PEST and SWOT analysis can be used. In addition, customer analysis, risk analysis, product research etc. are the other major purposes for which environmental scanning can be carried out.

3.5 SWOT ANALYSIS

SWOT (*Strengths Weaknesses Opportunities Threats*) analysis is an important technique to analyse the internal and external environment and formulate strategies based on it. It refers to the technique to understand strengths and weaknesses (the internal environment) of a business unit and identify the potential opportunities and possible threats (the external environment). Thus, SWOT analysis is widely used as a tool for analysis and assessment.

The most important feature of the method is its coverage. SWOT analysis covers both the internal and the external environment. The method was originally used by Albert Humphrey. It is now frequently used in corporate planning, strategic management and business policy.

As a method used for formulating strategies, SWOT analysis is used in the form of a matrix in which identification of its core elements are present. Thus, SWOT analysis starts with the identification of strength of a business unit or a firm. Identification of strength covers elements of the internal business environment and some elements of the external environment. On the other hand, it also identifies weaknesses, which are primarily the issues related to a firm's internal environment. It also critically examines the external factors that affect the business environment. A matrix of SWOT analysis incorporating some pertinent factors is given in Table 3.1.

Table 3.1 SWOT Analysis: Some Pertinent Factors

Strengths	*Weaknesses*
• Competent human resources • Core competence • Competitive advantage • Strong cash flows • Innovation, research and development • Geographic advantages • Cost advantages • Robust supply chain • Quality certifications	• Inadequate expertise/human resources • Lack of identifying a core competence • Lack of leadership • Inadequate financials • Inadequate investment in research and development • Locational disadvantage • High production cost • Poorly managed supply chain • Lack of desired certifications

Opportunities	*Threats*
• New market • Ability to innovate • Adequate financial for research and development • Cater to niche segment • Opportunities across geographies • Tie-ups with government and international (intergovernmental) organisations • Memberships of industry chambers, export promotion councils etc.	• Legislative and regulatory changes • Political instability • Changes in trade policies • Pace of technological change • Blurred industry boundaries • Economic health of the host country • Cost of compliance to international environmental requirements • Sustaining the performing in a global supply chain

3.6 PEST ANALYSIS

PEST analysis is another important tool to analyse and understand the market conditions. In other words, it is a method to analyse business environment and formulate strategies for business. PEST is the acronym of *Political, Economic, Social and Technological*. These factors together are responsible for the evolution of business environment in an economy—whether it a market-friendly business environment or otherwise.

As PEST provides a framework to judge and review market situations, it is used to set goals for corporate planning. In addition, experts also use PEST for product diversification in order to cater to the market, as per the market conditions. The method is based on the external factors. Unlike SWOT analysis, it does not use internal factors.

Factors of PEST analysis

1. ***Political factors:*** Political forces are one of the most important factors influencing the business environment. Some of its characteristics are listed below:
   - (i) These allow us to understand the nature of political and economic system.
   - (ii) They also reflect on the degree of intervention by the government in an economy.
   - (iii) They also highlight the economic system adopted by a particular government.
   - (iv) Political interventions are made by the government through various instruments including both fiscal and monetary instruments in addition to some legal instruments.
   - (v) Political factors also include the issue of political instability.

In fact, the prospects of business in an economy are more when it is politically stable. For example, after Arab Spring, in North African region, business prospects have been very low, as the region still continues to be politically unstable.

2. ***Economic factors:*** Economic forces also influence the business environment. Some of its characteristics are as follows:
   - (i) They present a set of macroeconomic indicators to analyse how well a market is doing in terms of its economic situation.
   - (ii) Major macroeconomic indicators like GDP, inflation, exchange rates, per capital income, FDI inflows and international trade, etc. constitute important drivers.

3. ***Social factors:*** Social factors are the constituents of the non-economic environment. Some of its characteristics are given below:
   (i) These include culture, demography, lifestyle, education, etc.
   (ii) Social factors are important to know the consumption pattern of a country or region.
   (iii) Social factors are also important for defining the preferences of consumers.

India has a large young population and demographic dividend. Considering this, the consumption pattern of the country is deemed to be different from a country which has an aging population. Therefore, for businesses, it is important to formulate strategies based on the socio-cultural contexts of the country. PEST analysis can be used as a tool for such analysis.

4. ***Technological factors:*** The importance of technology while formulating strategies can be understood by the fact that if a country is using manual clearance procedure for exports and imports, then the cost of trade for that country would be very high. Moreover, if a country is using new technology such as Electronic Data Interchange (EDI) systems, then it reduces the cost of time and brings efficiency, which is beneficial for the traders and businesses. In other words, technology has been an important factor to facilitate business prospects. Other common examples could be the use of technology in banking or healthcare sectors. It, thus, induces efficiency and reduces the costs associated with doing the business.

We have seen the factors that are being used for PEST analysis. PEST analysis is further extended to PESTEL analysis by incorporating two new factors—'E' for Environmental and 'L' for Legal factors. However, PEST analysis also incorporates these two factors. Yet, we can separately include some of the aspects pertaining to legal and environmental factors like company law, land acquisition, antitrust and competition law, environmental clearance for projects, etc. Table 3.2 highlights some of the factors for PEST analysis.

Table 3.2 Factors for PEST Analysis

Political Factors	*Economic Factors*
• Economic system • Economic policies • Legislations • Regulatory bodies • Trade policies and regimes • Governance • Political stability	• Macroeconomic indicators and trend • Foreign exchange reserves • Taxation-related policies • Money and capital markets • Interest rates • Exchange rates • Institutional framework for development
Social Factors	***Technological Factors***
• Demographic structure • Rural and urban lifestyle • Consumer preferences • Education, health and other aspects • Media and entertainment • Ethnic and cultural factors • Food, health and safety considerations	• Digital connectivity • Automation of business procedures • Research and development • Technology convergence • Innovation and intellectual property rights • Information and Communication Technology (ICT) for development

Closing Case: Role of EPCs and Market Intelligence

Export Promotion Councils (EPCs) have been established across various sectors for the purpose of export promotion. They also work as a bridge between their member exporters and the government for facilitation of schemes such as Market Development Assistance (MDA) and Market Access Initiatives (MAI) run under the aegis of the Ministry of Commerce and Industry, Government of India.

Moreover, some of the functions performed by the EPCs include the following:

1. Export promotion
2. Assisting in availing MDA and MAI schemes
3. Liaison with industry chambers
4. Conducting market research
5. Providing market intelligence
6. Collecting and furnishing market intelligence to the exporters
7. Gathering market intelligence about potential businesses and countries
8. Taking Indian delegations overseas in collaboration with industry chambers
9. Organising trade shows
10. Organising buyer–seller meet
11. Organising conferences and seminars
12. Organising capacity-building and training programmes

Market intelligence, thus, is a crucial function. It is actually a method or a process to understand the behaviour of the market. It helps in environmental scanning as well as in formulating strategies by firms. In this process, it acquires information and data based on both the field surveys and the secondary research through various sources.

Market intelligence is now frequently used in analytics to define the preferences of a consumer as well. It can be gathered through market analysis, competitive analysis and firm's internal analysis. It is helpful in developing scenarios for the future and also in predicting the business environment.

There are several EPCs in India. Some of them are enlisted as follows:

1. Apparel Export Promotion Council (AEPC)
2. Sports Goods Export Promotion Council (SGEPC)
3. Gems and Jewellery Export Promotion Council (GJEPC)
4. Plastics Export Promotion Council (Plexcon)
5. Electronics and Computer Software Export Promotion Council (ESC)
6. Council for Leather Exports (CLE)
7. Pharmaceuticals Export Promotion Council (Pharmexcil)
8. Project Exports Promotion Council of India (PEPC)
9. Wool and Woolens Export Promotion Council (WWEPC)

Source: This case is written by the authors based on inputs from the following sources:

1. Department of Commerce, Ministry of Commerce and Industry, Government of India, http://commerce.nic.in/
2. http://commerce.nic.in/epc.htm

CASE QUESTIONS

1. Find out the market intelligence carried out by AEPC. How does it benefit the exporters?
2. Outline some best practices of market intelligence done by Pharmexcil.

REVIEW QUESTIONS

1. What is environmental scanning?
2. What are the benefits of environmental scanning? Explain the Syria and Iran crisis.
3. Outline the key objectives of environmental scanning.
4. Explain the different types of research.
5. What is a research process?
6. What do you understand by data scanning?
7. What are the broad areas in which environmental scanning can be carried out?
8. Discuss SWOT analysis as a tool of environmental analysis.
9. Explain the four factors of PEST analysis.
10. What is the role of Export Promotion Council (EPC) in environmental scanning?

SUGGESTED READINGS

Aguilar, F.J., 1967, *Scanning the Business Environment*, Macmillan, New York, USA.

Bryman, Alan and Bell, Emma, 2011, *Business Research Methods*, Oxford University Press, Oxford, UK.

Sundaram, A.K. and Black, J.S., 1995, *The International Business Environment: Text and Cases*, PHI Learning, Delhi.

World Economic Outlook, 2014, IMF, Washington DC.

4

ECONOMIC SYSTEMS

Learning Outcomes

After reading this chapter, you will

- Understand the evolution of various economic ideas and how they shaped the development of economic activities and business
- Learn the nature and characteristics of various economic systems
- Appreciate their significance in the contemporary and evolving business environment

Opening Case: From African Socialism to Free Market Economy

The investors are now rushing towards Lagos (Nigeria) and Nairobi (Kenya) to make investments. A higher economic growth has made Sub-Saharan Africa an attractive destination for foreign investors and businesses as well. There is a consistent increase in the foreign direct investment (FDI), which has surged by about 50% since 2005. Earlier, the region was regarded as the one which lacked business opportunities; and doing business there was considered to be a risky game.

But, now the scenario is changing rapidly. Doing business in this region is gradually becoming less risky. For instance, JP Morgan has added Nigeria to its government bond index for the emerging markets. It is predicted that adding Nigerian bonds to its benchmark will lead to an extra US$1.5 billion to the country as per the American Bank, the world's largest underwriter of emerging market debt. New funds are entering into the African markets. Amidst political risks, Africa's GDP is all set to be on a growth trajectory and the employment scenario is also improving. According to an executive from Wall Street firm, salaries for African position has increased by 30% in 2013 in comparison to the salaries offered in 2012.

Since the attainment of freedom, the respective African economies had categorically developed their economic policies. These policies were dominated by the wave of Africanism. In this context, economic policies in African countries were inclined towards socialism to a large extent. However, the idea of African socialism was a new perspective altogether. African socialism was the indigenisation of socialist ideas in the African sub-continent. However, it is claimed that it has its own roots in Africa. On the other hand, the agreed form of African socialism was yet to evolve in Africa when most of the African countries started new economic policy of liberalisation.

Therefore, the distinction with classical socialism was related to the sharing of natural resources of Africa in African ways. Nigeria, Ghana, Tanzania, Kenya, etc. were the main advocates of African Socialism. These economies presently follow mixed economic system. More recently, some of the countries in Africa re-oriented their economic policies towards private sector participation. For instance, in 2000, Nigerian government started privatisation programme. Similarly, Kenya followed inward looking policies with a control on private sector. Due to tight import controls and foreign exchange restrictions, Kenya was less attractive for investments. In 1993, the Government of Kenya started major economic reforms.

In Kenya, the impact of African socialism was clearly evident on its policy planning. The government under its philosophy realised the re-orientation of economic mobilisation and distribution of natural resources. A period of economic slowdown came in Africa during 1970s and 1980s. Since the African countries borrowed heavily, it made the region the most indebted region. As a result of this, West African countries soon adopted privatisation policies.

In the first half of 1980s, 227 firms were privatised in Africa. Between 1988 and 1993, Nigerian government disowned 55 public sector companies. The government gradually eliminated price controls, removed exchange rate restrictions and privatised a range of public sector organisations. This resulted in an increase in both economic growth and investment, particularly the investment from overseas.

The last three decades saw more liberal policy steps in the region, as these regions embrace mixed economic structures with a strong free market orientation. Countries like Nigeria are already well-known as free market economies. The idea of African Union has brought more focus to the concepts of development, trade, integration and the need for an improved business climate.

Source: This case is written by the authors based on inputs from the following sources:

1. Africa's Economy, *The Economist*, 20 October 2012.
2. Nigeria's economy: GDP rebasing to help Nigeria overtake South Africa as Africa's Biggest Economy, *International Business Times*, 13 June 2013.
3. African Socialism and its Application to Planning in Kenya, The World Bank.
4. Privatisation in Africa, African Studies Centre, The Netherlands, http://www.ascleiden.nl/?q=content/webdossiers/privatization-africa.

4.1 INTRODUCTION

Economic activities are pursued everywhere, irrespective of the economic system that a country follows. The same is true for emerging markets as well. Companies have been striving hard to take up the challenges of operating in the emerging markets even when the economic systems are not necessarily the same (for instance, India and China). Yet, the company executives continue to work hard with consistency to diversify their export portfolio by exploring new markets—whether these are BRICS countries or African countries. For instance, in May 2013, Daimler India Commercial Vehicle Private Limited issued a statement to optimise its export markets. This company is an Indian subsidiary of the German Automobile company Daimler AG. It is aimed at reaching out to the emerging markets in Asia and Africa, and has also planned to adopt an Asia Business Model.[1]

Diversification of export market is a strategic initiative, and so, it identifies the right market. Due to various models of economic systems prevalent in different countries, a manager may face difficulties in choosing the right model to enter and work in that market. Therefore, it is crucial that managers who are getting ready for such initiatives are well-versed with the economic systems prevalent in different markets.

Understanding the nature of economic structure (every economic system has its own structure, which makes it different from each other) of an economy is a prerequisite for doing business therein. In fact, economic structure outlines the evolving nature of economic and business environment. For instance, China has socialist structure and South Africa has liberal and capitalist structure. On the other hand, there are several economies in Asian and African continents that are in the mode of transition. For example, Lao PDR is in a transition phase of its economic structure. Generally, transition economies are characterised as those countries which are changing their economic structures from centrally planned to free market economy. The opening case also depicts the rapid transition of some countries. But here, we use transition not only to depict changes in the economic structure but also in the political setup. In most of the countries in Africa, the political setup has also seen changes, which have utmost potential to redefine the economic environment. For instance, a new country called South Sudan has been formed in 2011.

Now, to understand the nature of economic structure of an economy, we need to understand the ideas of economic systems. Most of the economies today follow the ideas that are evolved over a period of time. This chapter discusses the economic systems and their respective characteristics. Such discussion would be helpful for businesses in developing their business models relevant to the business environment in a host country.

4.2 WHAT IS AN ECONOMIC SYSTEM?

An *economic system* is an agglomeration of economic activities and their governance, which broadly includes production, consumption and distribution of goods and services under a defined set of rules and institutions. Therefore, broadly, we have three agents that interact with each other to form an economic system—consumer, producer and government (see Figure 4.1).

A consumer tends to maximise satisfaction by optimal utilisation[2] of limited resources. Therefore, two important factors drive the consumer behaviour—income of the consumer, and available goods and services. It also plays pivotal role in deciding the market patterns. This directly impacts the production of goods and services. The way demand fluctuates, production or supply of goods follows the direction. In some cases, production of goods also plays a role in determining the consumption patterns.

Likewise, the objective of a producer is to maximize its profit by producing more and more goods and services at competitive cost. Thus, the resource constraints of a producer are costs of

1. Daimler's *Asia Business Model* taps into full synergy potential of Mitsubishi Fuso Truck and Bus Corporation (MFTBC) and Daimler India Commercial Vehicles (DICV). This also develops integrated business under the brand Fuso to capture rising Asian markets. *India Today* reports this news on 6 May 2013, Daimler India to roll out FUSO trucks for export markets.
2. Optimal utilisation means maximum possible satisfaction getting out of minimum possible expenditure.

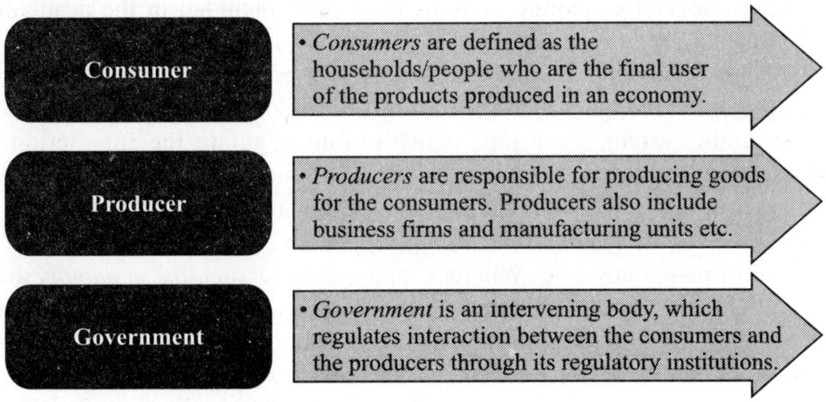

Figure 4.1 Agents of an economic system.

production per unit of a product. Cost of production of a unit product is determined by factors of production.[3]

Thus, economic system is a complex system, which determines the nature of business environment as well. It is a set of bodies and institutions. The complex nature of economic system is presented in a simple diagram (see Figure 4.2). The nature of interaction among the three agents also determines the nature of the market.

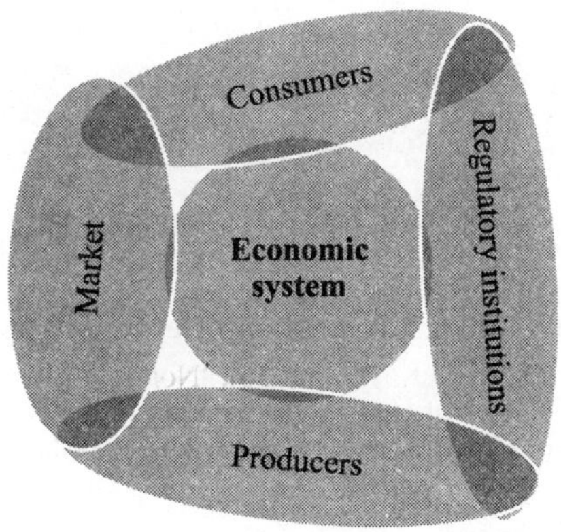

Figure 4.2 Interactions in an economic system.

A significant way to judge the economic system in a country is through finding the answer to a simple question—who owns the resources? In this context, we have two important and contextually significant aspects to look into—one is resource ownership and the other is resource allocation. Based on these two aspects, a broad division of economic systems is studied.

Economists have been studying the economic systems carefully. They have developed ideas, where these agents of economic system can interact optimally. Based on the analysis of

3. Factors of production are the inputs used in producing the products. These include land, labour, capital and entrepreneurship.

various economists, several economic systems have been included in the academic and policy discourses. These include *laissez-faire* (market economy), capitalism, socialism, communism and mixed or planned economy. These systems are still present in the world. Some economies are transforming their economic structure from mixed or socialist to capitalist and liberal.

In an economic system, government institutions regulate the interaction between the consumers/households and the producers/firms. The government also sets objectives, which may have different goals or national development priorities. The role of government, therefore, depends upon the nature of economic system. In a *capitalist economic system*, the market forces (including demand and supply) play a key role. Whereas, in a *mixed or socialist economy*, the government intervenes to regulate the market by setting up standards and also regulates prices. Therefore, for a manager, it is important to understand the nature of economy to operate in a market.

In the subsequent sections, we discuss the characteristics of these economic systems with examples. Before coming to the idea of economic ideas, Figure 4.3 outlines the broad classification of economic system that has evolved over a period of time.

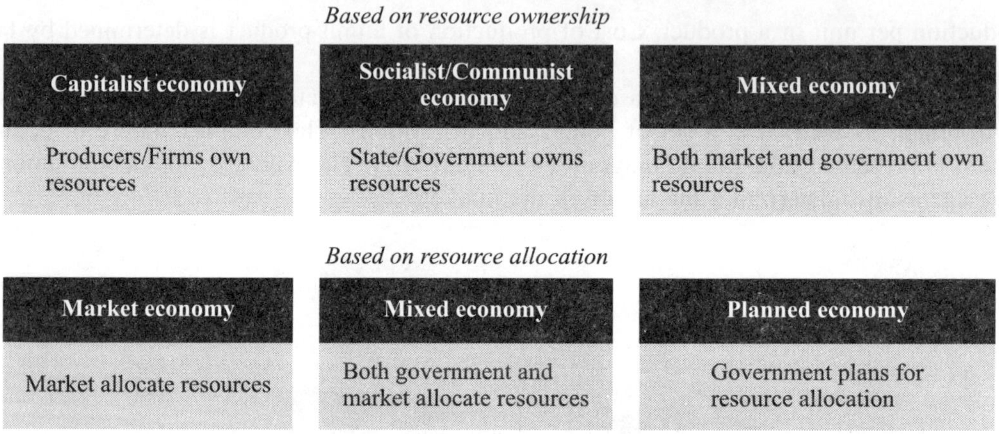

Figure 4.3 Classification of economic systems.

Source: Based on John Maynard Keynes (1936), 'Notes on Mercantilism, the Usury Laws, Stamped Money and the Theories of Under-Consumption', The General Theory of Employment, Interest, and Money, London: Palgrave Macmillan.

4.3 EVOLUTION OF ECONOMIC IDEAS

Economic ideas developed with the evolution of interaction between the consumers and the producers. This dates back to primitive societies when barter system defined an economic system. The essence of economic ideas can also be seen in the works of Aristotle, Plato and Thomas Aquinas.[4] The glimpse of economic ideas of Aristotle was found in his scholarly works *Politics* and *Nicomohaean Ethics*. It is believed that Aristotle published a book on economics as well.[5] Some of the economic historians also consider him as the first economic

4. J.G. Bakhaus (Ed.), *Hand Book of the History of Economic Thought: Insights on the Founders of Modern Economics,* New York: Springer Science + Business Media, 2012.
5. H.D. MacLeod, *History of Economics*, London: Bliss, 1896.

analyst.[6] In his book *Politics*, Aristotle exclusively discussed the financial matters and analysed economics on the ethical principles and referred to the property as a part of household.[7] Aristotle's other book entitled *Nicomohaean Ethics*, whose main theme was justice, highlighted the micro essence of economics including pricing and distribution.[8] Before Aristotle, Plato also highlighted his economic ideas based on the ethical principles.[9] Book II of *Republic* by Plato highlighted an early analysis of the economic systems and the political economy through the participation of individuals. It also gave insight into the concept of division of labour.[10]

However, a systematic study of economic systems starts with Adam Smith's investigation into the wealth of a nation. In 1776, Adam Smith published a treatise *The Wealth of Nations*. With this work, the idea of classical economic system emerged in economics. His idea was built upon the major works of his predecessors such as Francois Quensey (1694–1774) and Anne-Robort-Jcques-Turgot (1727–1781). These two philosophers dominated the movement of physiocracy.[11]

Adam Smith's work appeared on the eve of industrial revolution during the second half of the 18th century. He was a Scottish philosopher and one of the key proponents of Scottish enlightenment.[12]

Smith's works put forth the idea of competition as a system, which was expected to result in the economic prosperity. His successors like Thomas Malthus (1764–1834), David Ricardo (1772–1823) and J.S. Mill (1806–1073) further refined the classical economic ideas. Malthus was a British philosopher and his work *An Essay on the Principle of Population*, published in 1798, pioneered the idea of demographic change and its economic impacts. He is still known for his Iron Law of Population,[13] which helped in developing early theories on demography. He was among those economists who supported Corn Laws in Britain during the early 19th century.[14]

During the same period, Malthus and Ricardo came into a long debate on political economy. Ricardo was an important proponent of the classical economic ideas. His work on *Principles of Political Economy and Taxation* (1817) laid down the foundation stone of the distribution of wealth of a nation. His main idea was related to the value theory based on the labour theory of value and the theory of rent. He also contributed to the idea of free trade system. One of

6. E. Roll, *History of Economic Thought*, London, 1948, p. 22.
7. See for example "Politics" by Aristotle, translated by Benjamin Jowett.
8. See for example Takeshi Amemiya (2004), The Economic Ideas of Classical Athens, *The Kyoto Economic Review*, Vol. 73, No. 2, p. 71.
9. *Ibid.*, p. 64.
10. *Division of labour* is an idea, which was developed by Adam Smith. This idea was not exclusively developed by Plato, but Plato identified different types of works by different individuals.
11. *Physiocracy* is considered as the first well-developed economic theory. The physiocrats believed that the wealth of nations is solely derived from agriculture. Their theories originated in France. They considered productive work as the source of national wealth, which was a significant contribution to the economic ideas.
12. *Scottish enlightenment* is a period of intellectual and scientific advancements in the 18th century Scotland. This period garnered active participation from academics, scholars, professionals, policy-makers and intellectuals of that time.
13. *Iron Law of Population* suggests that growing population rates would contribute to more labour supply and inevitably lower wages. It may also consequently lead to poverty.
14. For more information, see Geoffrey Gilbert, *Introduction to Malthus T.R. 1798: An Essay on the Principle of Population*, Oxford World's Classics reprint.

his most popular theoretical frameworks is the theory of comparative advantage,[15] which also explains the reasons why countries trade. The debate between Malthus and Ricardo emerged after Malthusian criticism on the Ricardian theory of rent. In his work, *Nature of Rent*, Malthus defined rent as the economic surplus. It was against the idea of Ricardo who thought of it as negative money.[16]

Also, J.S. Mill, an English philosopher, propagated the liberal political philosophy and emphasised on free markets, economic democracy and defended socialist ideas.[17] In his treatise, *Principle of Political Economy*, he also stressed on the importance of environment (see Box 4.1).

Box 4.1 Mill's Idea of Environment

If the earth must lose that great portion of its pleasantness, which it owes to things that the unlimited increase of wealth and population would extirpate from it, for the mere purpose of enabling it to support a larger, but not a better or a happier population, I sincerely hope, for the sake of posterity, that they will be content to be stationary, long before necessity compels them to it.

Source: *Principle of Political Economy*, Book 4, Chapter 6.

These major architects of classical economic ideas exclusively laid down the foundation of free market economy, which is an important and the main feature of classical economic idea. It was developed against the background of mercantilist system. In mercantilist system, government intervention was the main driving force in an economy. During industrial revolution, the system gradually outshined.

Against the backdrop of industrialisation and free market economy, a class struggle[18] within the economic system was evident during the 19th century. Emergence of heavy industries formed the same in different manner, which was between the industrial workers and the owners of industries.

Till the year 1824, labour union was illegal and not a well-structured representative body as it exists today.[19] In 1820, 60,000 workers went on strike in Scotland and gradually several trade unions like the London Trade Council came into existence.[20] This was the severity of a class struggle, and the contemporary philosophers as well as the economists of that time, including Karl Marx of Germany took up the concerns. He propagated the communist idea of political economy, which was gradually ingrained in the academic and policy discourses on capitalist and communist economic systems. He was a German philosopher, sociologist and economist. The road map of a communist economic system was laid down in his seminal works that include

15. Theory of comparative advantage maintains that a country should produce and export those goods in which it has a relative advantage in terms of labour productivity.
16. Leslie Stephen (1 March 2006). The English Utilitarians 1, Continuum International Publishing Group.
17. Ryan, Alann (Eds.) (2004), *Utilitarianism and Other Essays*, London: Penguin Books.
18. Class struggle is a conflict between the different classes with competing interests. In this case, it is generally referred to as a conflict between the proletariat (the wage-earners, generally the industrial workers) and the bourgeoisie (the middle class, generally skilled professionals).
19. John Foster (1974), *Class Struggle and Industrial Revolution Early Industrial Capitalism in three English Towns*, Methuen & Co Ltd: London.
20. Smout, T.C. (1985), *A History of the Scottish People 1560–1830*, London: Fontana.

Communist Manifesto and *Das Kapital*. His philosophical propositions later gave a boost to the labour movements, while he called for the proletarians of the world to unite together. Lenin and Mao were the main followers of Marxism. The October Revolution (also called the *Bolshevik Revolution*) took place in the erstwhile Soviet Union and overthrew the Czar. Also, in 1949, Mao Tse Tung (pronounced as *Mao Zedong*) founded the People's Republic of China. These countries followed the communist economic policies and later became socialist economies. We shall discuss these economic systems later in this chapter.

Until 1929, economic ideas were concentrated on the above classical ideas. The period of Great Depression, which started in 1929, brought new economic ideas and new economic systems. The Great Depression was followed by World War II, which asserted a new era in global political economy. As the war ended, the countries took several steps towards developing a new world order. Some of them were internationalism, multilateralism and regional economic integration. The economic ideas after the Great Depression can be broadly divided into Keynesianism, monetarism, neoclassical and institutionalism.

John Maynard Keynes in his book, *The General Theory of Employment, Interest and Employment* (published in 1936) investigated the causes of Great Depression. This book gave a shape to the philosophical outreach of modern macroeconomics by reflecting on the weaknesses of classical economic system. Keynes expressed the idea of reform in the international monetary systems to encourage investment and consumption by private sector.[21]

Monetarist idea is mainly associated with Milton Friedman, an American economist. He was described as the most influential economist during the 20th century.[22] He was a critique of Keynesian fiscal policy and conceptualised monetarist approach of macroeconomics through his theory of natural rate of unemployment. According to him, government can increase employment above the rate of natural employment only at the cost of rising inflation. He further argued that excessive supply of money leads to the increase in the rate of inflation. Also, Anna Schwartz in their book entitled *A Monetary History of the United States, 1867–1960* argued that the causes of Great Depression was massive contraction of money supply. Interestingly, this idea was also well-received during the oil shock of the 1970s. Therefore, monetary measures are actually significant determinants of a country's economic environment of business (see Box 4.2).

Moreover, neoclassical and institutionalism were other facets of new economic ideas after the Great Depression. The neoclassical economics gained momentum with the advent of marginalist revolution.[23]

The foremost ideas came from three books—William Stanley Jevon's *Theory of Political Economy* (1871); Carl Menger's *Principles of Economics* (1871) and Léon Walras' *Elements of Pure Economics* (1874–1877). These ideas still dominate economic thinking and analyses. Later, with Keynesian ideas, a neoclassical framework was developed by John Hicks and Paul Samuelson. This was the synthesis of classical idea of supply and demand model of markets into the Keynesian theory. It also synthesised the two distinct ideas of goods market and money markets.

21. Davidson, Paul (2002), *Financial Markets, Money and the Real World*, Cheltenham UK and Northampton US: Edward Elgar.
22. *The Economist*, 23 November 2006.
23. Marginalist revolution refers to a methodological development, which introduced marginal analysis such as marginal utility.

Box 4.2 Monetarist Policies

During 1970s, central banks of many industrial economies adopted monetary policies to regulate their economy. The adoption of growth targets for domestic money stock was evident in United States and Switzerland. In 1975, in the United States, Federal Reserve System introduced money stock growth target for the first time. In 1979, Federal Reserve Policy announced its policy for day-to-day operating procedures. The Open Market Committee published its report on targets for all the components of money supply, i.e., M_1, M_2 and M_3 for one year from March 1975 to March 1976. Similarly, in Switzerland, target for money stock growth was fixed in 1974. The shift towards monetary policies was an indication to strengthen central banking systems. The policy also aimed at reducing inflation. Later in 1978, Full Employment and Balanced Growth Act in the US compelled the Federal Reserve to set one year target ranges for money supply growth, which was supposed to be reported to the Congress.

Interest rates were low during 1990s. But the role of monetary policy in the modern world is, however, an important measure. Also, in the developing countries, the monetary policy is an important example of strong presence of monetarist ideas. In case of India, the Reserve Bank of India regulates the monetary policies through its instruments such as interest rates, repo rates, reverse repo rates, cash reserve ratios, etc. The monetary policy in India aims at controlled expansion of bank credit and money supply, which plays a vital role in achieving the growth targets and reducing the inflationary pressures.

Source: Based on the article by Benjamin M Freidman, NBER Working Paper 5465 and FRB.

Institutionalists proposed another important economic idea, which had a significant impact on the economic systems and the business environment as well. The institutionalists, whose ideas originated in the early 20th century in the writings of Thorstein Veblen (1857–1929) and Walton H. Hamilton (1881–1958), focused on the role of institutions, on economic behaviour.[24] But their ideas gained popularity when another group of economists, called the *institutional economists* proposed to include social and legal aspects to regulate the economic systems. Nevertheless, it has a significant impact on business environment. Due to regulatory measures and socio-economic aspects, the policy frameworks like those pertaining to environment clearance, land acquisition bill, safeguards measures, among others, are in place to regulate business transactions and facilitate trade.

Given this backdrop of the evolution of economic ideas, we shall now discuss the economic systems in detail.

4.4 MERCANTILISM

Mercantilism is an economic doctrine, which was prevalent in Europe during the 16th and 18th centuries. Under this system, the government controlled foreign trade through the state sponsored stakeholders. This system was the outcome of growing merchants in Europe during the 16th century. The main characteristic of mercantilism was the practice of keeping positive balance of trade.[25]

24. Veblen published, his book *The Theory of Leisure Class* (1899).
25. Balance of trade simply implies the difference between the value of exports and the value of imports. If this difference is positive, we call it positive balance of trade or the value of exports is higher than the value of imports and vice versa.

Both economic doctrines and commercial policies are the essence of mercantilist system.[26] Mercantilists mainly adopted import tariffs to maintain the positive balance of trade. In some cases, mercantilist countries such as France and Britain also issued Royal Decree to reduce imports and increase exports (see Box 4.3). Some of the important features of mercantilism included the following:

Box 4.3 A Note on Mercantilist Policy

France and Britain were the main countries that devised commercial regulations on mercantilist policies. Here, we have only highlighted the policy steps taken by France. Mercantilism started from France soon after legitimacy of monarchy during the early 16th century. Later, this idea spanned all across the Europe, even in Scandinavian countries like the Hubsburg, the Netherlands (Dutch). In 1539, a Royal Decree was issued in France. This Royal Decree banned the imports of woolen products from Spain and parts of Flanders (modern day Belgium and Netherlands). In addition, France also followed policies, which restrained exports of bullions (gold and silvers). Later, these policies were also introduced by Jean Baptist Colbert, the Finance Minister of France for almost 22 years during the early mercantilist period under King Louis XIV. His main work was the foundation of Royal Mirror Glass Factory. This was established in pursuits of increasing exports. In addition, Colber also raised tariffs to develop domestic economy.

Source: Based on John Maynard Keynes (1936), 'Notes on Mercantilism, the Usury Laws, Stamped Money and the Theories of Under-Consumption', The General Theory of Employment, Interest, and Money, London: Palgrave Macmillan.

1. Mercantilism put utmost attention on money. It was, therefore, also regarded as *bullionism.* Money was the source of power. Therefore, gold and silver were the main determinants of wealth of a country.
2. Interest was also charged under this idea on money. Nevertheless, the rate of interest was usually low in a mercantilist system. It was because high rate of interest was considered as the source scarcity of money.
3. Under the mercantilist system, land and labour were the only factors of production.
4. Commercial regulations were also prevalent in mercantilist system. These regulations were devised to restrain trade, particularly imports. This was also called *protectionism,* which was a policy generally adopted in national interest.

4.5 CAPITALISM

Capitalism is another important form of economic system, which still has its relevance. The main feature of capitalistic economy is the private ownership of resources. In other words, resources are owned by private individuals not by the state. In a capitalist economic system, individuals/ firms engaged themselves in the accumulation of capital and property. In other words, in a

26. Brezis, Elise S. (2003), 'Mercantilism', *The Oxford Encyclopedia of Economic History*, Oxford University Press.

capitalist economy, the consumers and producers are free to behave as per the demand and supply, which are primary market forces.[27] Classical economists like Adam Smith,[28] David Ricardo and John Stuart Mill criticised state restrictions under the mercantilist economic system (see Box 4.4 on the idea of capitalism and Box 4.5 on a recent instance to renew state capitalism).[29]

The main features of capitalism are as follows:

1. It involves private ownership of factors of production.
2. It includes the presence of competition among the capitalists.
3. Price mechanisms are free to be determined by market forces.
4. Labour market is also competitive and people are free to chose employment as per their existing skills and competencies.
5. There exists free market allocation of lands.
6. It abolishes all restrictions on interactions of market forces.
7. It advocates trade between the countries to help in enhancing their international trading position.
8. Specialised production systems based on the comparative or cost advantages are also included in the features of capitalism.

Box 4.4 Idea of Capitalism

During the 18th century, when economists like Adam Smith and others strongly advocated laissez-faire system, capitalist economic system gradually started taking shape in Britain. Adam Smith challenged the fundamental doctrine of mercantilist system and advocated free interactions of market forces. Not only this, the value of products was also examined and division of labour became an instrument for better productivity. Later, industrial revolution further strengthened the idea of capitalist economic system proposed in classical economic thoughts. The early essence of classical capitalist economic system in Britain was seen during the latter half of the 18th century. During the 19th century, British manufacturing companies dominated the world markets. This led to the adoption of free trade policy. In 1846, Sir Robert Peel's government abolished the famous Corn Law of 1815. This law was enacted to protect cereal producers in Britain. This law allowed the import of grains, but to sell them domestically only after a certain price cap (i.e., above 80 shillings). Moreover, by 1860, Britain abolished import duties on 400 items and income tax threshold was also reduced.

Source: Based on the article 'British Trade Policy in the 19th Century' published in *European Journal of Political Economy*, Vol. 16, pp. 829–842, 2000.

27. Fulcher, James (2004), *Capitalism A Very Short Introduction*, Oxford: Oxford University.
28. Adam Smith defined capitalism as the obvious and simple system of natural liberty in his treatise 'The Wealth of Nations' published in 1776.
29. For more information, see *History of Economic Thought: A Critical Perspective* by E.K. Hunt.

Box 4.5 State Capitalism in Europe

During the recent years, the governments have revived state interventions to renew state capitalism. They have started buying industrial stakes. A story of such incidence came into light that a planned merger of European Aeronautic Defence and Space Company (EADS), Airbus and BAE systems collapsed when the German government planned to take 15% stake in EADS. This policy was on anvil after losing share in Airbus to France. In view of French government stake in listed companies like Air France KLM, Aeroports de Paris, Areva, Renault and Dexia, etc., the German move was compared with Barack Obama's rescue of General Motors through bailing it out of crisis. This is considered to be the advent of state capitalism.

Source: Based on the article 'State Capitalism: Big Brother is Back', *The Economist*, November 3rd, 2012.

4.6 COMMUNIST SYSTEM

The communist economic system emerged as an alternate to the capitalist system. The main feature of this system was collective ownership of resources by the workers and the capitalists both.[30] The system was mainly advocated by Karl Marx and his friend Fredrick Angels. Owing to that, many a times, communism is also referred to as *Marxism*. In his magnum opus Das Capital, Marx laid the foundation of a communist economic system. The prime distinction between the capitalist and communist system is the concentration of capital among the capitalists, which is the outcome of surplus labour. Therefore, we need to understand what surplus labour means. Marx developed surplus labour theory, which advocates that profit from production is the outcome of extra works by labourers. They are not paid for the same. Therefore, the cost of production for a capitalist remains the same, whereas the profit increases. This further adds to the capitalists' profits, which need to be distributed among the labourers.

4.7 SOCIALIST SYSTEM

Socialist economic system is a further refinement of communist ideologies. Generally, socialist economic system belongs to Marxist school of thought. Besides, the system also belongs to the other school of thoughts such as intuitionalists, evolutionary economics and planned economies etc. The main idea of socialist economic system, though derived from Marxism, is that the production of goods and services do not aim at profits.[31] This is in contrast with the ideation of capitalist economic system. In this system, the state and public sector own the factors of production.

In most cases, economies which follow socialist structure are also planned economies. Some of the main characteristics of this system are as follows:

1. The state owns the factors of production.
2. Production does not have the motive of profit.
3. Economy is centrally planned.

30. Holmes, Leslie (2009), *Communism: A Very Short Introduction*, Oxford and New York: Oxford University Press.
31. Ludwig von Mises, *Socialism: An Economic and Sociological Analysis*.

4. Resources are nationalised.
5. The goal of economic activities is social welfare.
6. The prices of goods and services are not determined by market forces, but by states.
7. Competition is non-existent and there is a presence of state monopoly.
8. The state adopts protectionist measures in national interests.

The economic systems have gradually shaped the contemporary world economies. However, there has been a significant change in the applicability of the economic systems. Even most capitalist economies today have also resorted to government interventions. Particularly, after the 2008 global financial turmoil and Eurozone crisis, countries like US and those in Europe have re-formulated their economic policies. Similarly, economies like India, China, Myanmar, Vietnam and countries of Africa are now further liberalising their economies by removing restrictions on investments and trade. A scenario of the same is depicted in the opening case pertaining to reforms in Nigeria and Kenya. Most African countries are now encouraging foreign investment in their core economic sectors. These economies are socialist economies or have mixed economic system. Therefore, we study the current economic systems in terms of market economies, planned economies and mixed economies due to the policies adopted by various countries that amalgamate the features of these three economic systems.

4.8 MARKET ECONOMY

Market economy is the basis of capitalist economic system. It derives its basic features from the classical economic ideas. This system mainly refers to as where decisions regarding the regulating factors of production and the process of consumption are determined by market forces, i.e., demand and supply.[32] This system has free price mechanism, which automatically moves as per its determinants[33] in the market. As per the idea of laissez faire, in a free market economy, the government does not intervene in the economic activities. The private sector flourishes. Today, almost all the economies around the world are embracing free market mechanism through liberalisation policies. In fact, private entrepreneurship is an important determinant of economic growth. Due to market-friendly economic policies and economic environment conducive to private businesses, the market economy is now considered as the backbone of the evolving global economic order (see Box 4.6).

Box 4.6 Free Market Economy and the Private Sector

The development of free market economy in the world can be seen through increasing private sector participation. We can see the set of data pertaining to foreign direct investment (FDI) and banking credit to private sectors across the set of countries. The data on investment indicates that the foreign investment in almost all the regions across the globe has been increasing. This trend provides a suitable business environment for the foreign investors. Over the span of 40 years, FDI

32. Paul R. Gregory and Robert C. Stuart. *Comparing Economic Systems in the Twenty-First Century*, 7th ed., 2004, South Western, Cengage Learning, USA.
33. *Determinant of prices* implies that the supply of and demand for a commodity determine the price of that commodity in that market.

has grown steadily and its direction has also changed to a large extent. For instance, the share of FDI inflows in developing countries as against the global FDI inflows has increased from 28% in 1970 to more than 47% in 2010. The same has decreased for developed countries from 71% in 1970 to 47% in 2010. The share of least developed countries (LDCs) is still less than 2% during the same period.

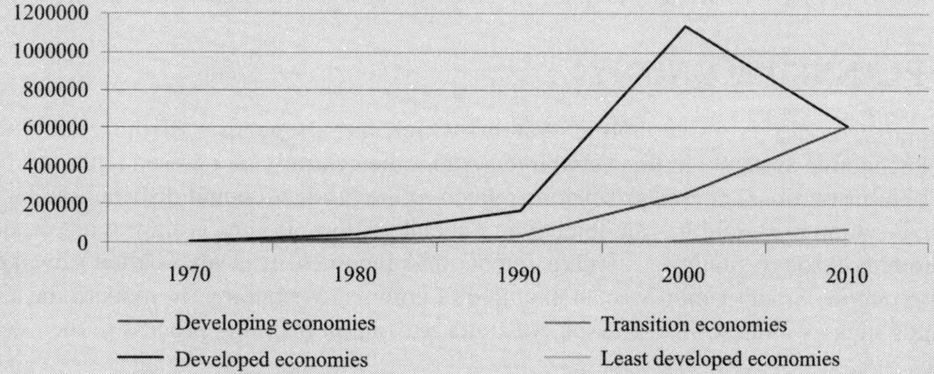

Exhibit 1 Global FDI flows (US$ million).
Source: Based on UNCTAD statistics.

In case of FDI stock, UNCTAD statistics reveals that the developed countries have accumulated the highest FDI in the world, with a share of more than 64% in 2010. The same has grown at the rate of 12% annually during 1980–2010. In case of developing countries, FDI has grown at the rate of 11% per year. These economies have a share of 31% in the world. The share is relatively much lower for the transition economies and LDCs. However, FDI stock in transition economies has grown at the rate of 23% annually during 1980–2010 and at 11% in LDCs during the same period. This indicates that most of the LDCs are still following restrain from the private sectors.

Another important indicator of the evolution of free market economy is the credit to private sectors globally. Every country gives credit to the private entrepreneurs to strengthen the private sector. In fact, the domestic credit to the private sectors refers to the financial resources provided to the private sector.

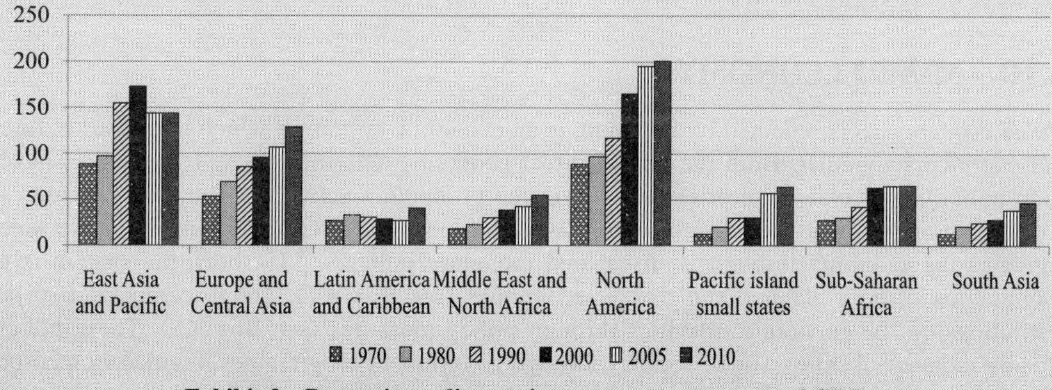

Exhibit 2 Domestic credit to private sector (percentage of GDP).
Source: Based on the data from World Development Indicator, World Bank.

A regional analysis of the indicators shows that the domestic credit to private sector as percentage of GDP has increased over the period. However, the credit is high in regions like East Asia and the Pacific, Europe, North America, etc. Most of the countries in South Asia, Southeast Asia and Latin America still have less domestic credit to the private sector.

Source: Based on UNCTAD World Investment Report 2013 and World Development Indicator, World Bank.

4.9 PLANNED ECONOMY

A *planned economy* is an economic system, which has its genesis in the communist and socialist economic systems. In this economic system, the centrally recognised authority (usually, government institutions) controls decisions related to the production and distribution. Generally, a planned economic system has an objective of social welfare. It aims at improving productivity of economies through planning of investments and incomes. It is also called *command and control economy*. Soviet Union was an example of command economy. In modern days, several economies such as India, China, Russia, Australia, etc. adopt planning process in their economic process.

Some of the main characteristics of a planned economy are as follows:

1. The government owns and manages all resources.
2. As against the free market forces, in a planned economy, price mechanism in the market is regulated by the government or its related institutions.
3. Consumers and producers do not have freedom of choices.
4. Production activities in such economies do not have profit motive.
5. It focuses on the creation of public enterprises.
6. There is an increase in public goods.

The proponents of this system also argue that free market or market economy cannot eradicate the social and economic ills prevalent in an economy. Market forces have a limited role. In view of this, the government has a responsibility to act on these fronts. Therefore, planning process is being followed by several countries, including some of the fast liberalising and developing economies like India.

4.10 MIXED ECONOMY

Mixed economy, as is reflected by its name, is an economic system in which both market forces and state work together. Both the agents direct economic activities. Mixed economies have a large public and private enterprise engaged in the production activities. The basic feature of a mixed economy is that the private sector owns the means of production and the government regulates the economy through its fiscal and monetary policies.[34] In short, the system is the combination of both planned and market economies (see Box 4.7). The government also puts restrictions on the economic activities through policy measures (see Box 4.8). These policies broadly include subsidies, social security through government programmes, regulatory measures like environmental protections, among others.

34. Frank Stilwell (2006), *Political Economy: The Contest of Economic Ideas*, 2nd ed., Oxford University Press.

Box 4.7 Recent Move Towards Mixed Economies

South Africa is a politically stable country in the African continent. It has well-developed regulatory regime and is endowed with the natural resources. In addition, South Africa provides a competitive market to the private sector players. Post the financial crisis of 2008, trust in South Africa's financial market is gaining momentum. Under this positive scenario, the government also came with a New Growth Plan in 2010. This plan is envisaged to restructure the economy to ensure inclusive and sustainable growth. It is in this context that the South African government is following a mixed economic system and has formulated policies relevant to this.

During the annual meeting of African National Congress (ANC) in January 2013, President Zuma clearly mentioned that his government would continue to pursue mixed economic policies. According to him, there is a need for decisive action to transform the economic patterns in the country, with a view to accomplish goals in future. In his view, the current policy of mixed economic system urges public, private, cooperative, and other forms of ownership to complement each other in the process of economic development of Africa. He also reaffirmed that the role of investment in building South Africa's growth prospects would be continued. There are several programmes in the country, which run under the idea of national development plan (NDP). These programmes include the introduction of central and national coordination of the building of dams, roads, bridges and other infrastructure development. His government pledged to continue implementing projects in 23 poorest districts of the country, which will ensure the provision of water, electricity and sanitation, and change the lives of approximately 19 million people. In his views, the private sector could also gain out of this and play a pivotal role in materialising infrastructure development programmes.

Source: Based on the article entitled 'Zuma Calls for Mixed Economy for Development Plans' in Mail and Guardian, 12 January 2013.

Box 4.8 Eurozone Crisis: The Case of Greece

Greece followed market economy after World War II. A crisis knocked at the doors of Greek economy in 2009. The Government of Greece had followed expansionary fiscal policies, which led the country into fiscal deficits. Moreover, shortage of financial liquidity to the banking system became a major reason. Public debt in the country became out of control as a result of rising public expenditure. In 2010, the Greek government revised its deficit at 13.6% of GDP. Total public debt was estimated to be at 120% of GDP in 2010, while as per OECD, it was over 140%. The trend of government debt rose up to 140% in the country in comparison to the other economies.

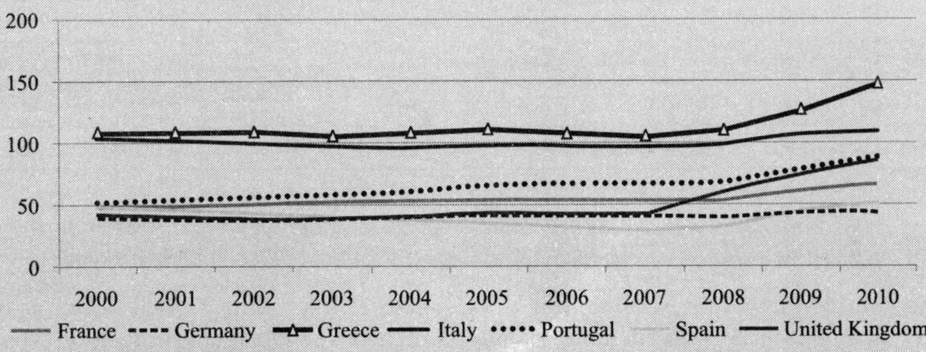

Exhibit 1 Central government debt in Europe (percentage of GDP).

Source: OECD.

This compelled the Greek government to follow economic reforms. The government initially targeted bailout plans. However, this programme was not successfully implemented. In November 2011, Greece passed the conditional reforms measures for Labour Market and Midterm Fiscal Plan 2015–2016. European Union (EU) also provided the rescue packages to Greece. The government started to adopt policies to keep public expenditure under control. It improved its monitoring and budget control system. Tax evasion was also kept under the scanner of the government. The country also started fiscal adjustment programmes. Thus, a free market economy resorted to government interventions under the circumstances of a crisis. Therefore, today's economy has multiple characteristics, which business executives and professionals ought to understand through the lens of economic systems.

Source: Based on OECD and Reuters, http://www.reuters.com/article/2009/11/05/greece-budget-debt-idUSATH00496420091105.

The main features of mixed economies are as follows:

1. Both public and private sectors exist in the system and work in coordination with each other.
2. Economic planning is an important instrument of government's economic policies.
3. There is a co-existence of both social welfare and private sector profits.
4. Government also acts to create economic environment conducive to business.
5. Consumers have freedom and choices and their rights are also protected by the government.
6. Government aims at reducing socio-economic problems such as poverty, inequality etc.

Having discussed the various economic systems, a comparative overview of the three major economic systems, namely, capitalist, socialist and mixed economies can be seen in Table 4.1.

Table 4.1 Comparative Overview of Economic Systems

Idea	*Capitalist Economy*	*Socialist/Communist Economy*	*Mixed Economy*
Resources	Own by private sector	Own by state	Owned by both
Market	Competitive and free	Regulated	Partially regulated
Motives	Profits	Social welfare	Both profits and welfare
Government	No intervention	Total intervention	Partial intervention
Labour market	Competitive wages	Regulated wages	Regulated wages

Closing Case: Think Twice Before You Google in China!

With the aim to start its operations in a vibrant market like China, Google which is a search engine company entered into the country and launched google.cn, an indigenous version. As per the requirements of the communist regime in China, Google registered itself as an internet service provider (ISP). It was also required to follow the local censorship rules, which prohibited searches and readings on issues such as democracy, Tibet, and many others. Google agreed to abide by these requirements.

Understanding the economic structure of China is very contextual in this case. It is a major world economy and has followed a socialist economic system since long. After the World War II, China emerged as a major communist power. During 1950s, China nationalised the banking systems and also brought the credit system under centralised leadership. The Chinese Communist Party also nationalised almost all the manufacturing units. It adopted a new land reform policy, which eliminated landlords from China. During the period of Mao, China became a unified socialist economy. From 1950 to the late 1970s, China was a closed economy and had state-owned enterprises (SOEs), which still exist. These enterprises are large industrial firms. In 1978, China adopted a new economic policy and went for reforms. It gradually started introducing aspects of capitalist measures in the socialist structure. FDI was allowed to the small economic zones. The government also agreed to reform SOEs and a large number of industries, which were not profit-making and brought out under non-public ownerships.

China also follows an economic planning model like India and Russia. Its first and the second five-year plans aimed at constructing around 700 large and medium size industrial projects, expanding heavy industry and strengthening the socialist structure of the economy. The objective to pursue reform was envisaged in the sixth plan. The planning has been evolutionary in China and has placed it as the second largest economy in the world, with an increasing share of industry and services in its GDP.

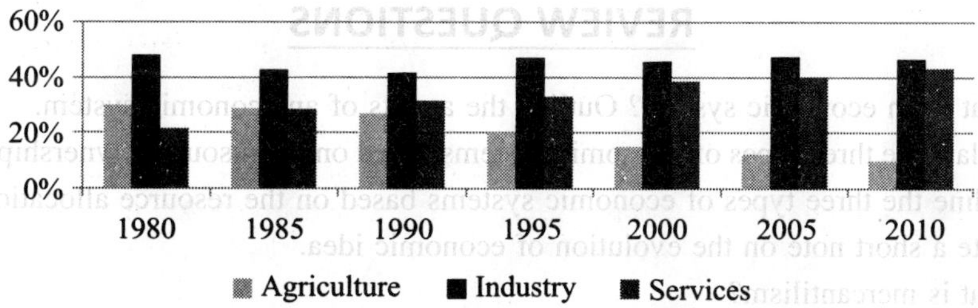

Exhibit 1 Sectoral share in Chinese GDP (%).
Source: World Bank.

With the evolving business climate, many multinational strived to enter into the Chinese market and build their businesses. Google was also one of them.

However, in 2010, Google was not in favour of abiding local censorship rules in China. It actually stopped censoring search results in China and started redirecting Chinese searches through google.com.hk (its server in Hong Kong). The Chinese government declared that Google's automatic redirection to Hong Kong-based website for accessibility of Chinese-based web pages is not acceptable. Owing to this, the company had to face the consequences of the state control over Chinese internet markets. However, Google maintained its sales team and research and development operation in Mainland China. This is essentially an issue which solicits managerial understanding of the economic systems. It was a unique departure and Google had nothing to gain, but only to lose. At the time when China was growing into an investment hub, it was really a hard luck for Google!

In 2007, Google China had a market share of 24%, which reduced to 5% in 2012 (BGR, 7 June 2013). In 2012, Deniel Alegere (president of Google Inc.) in an interview to Bloomberg TV told that Google never left Chinese market and Google is focusing on products that are non-sensitive to Chinese markets (Bloomberg, 24 June 2012). However, its share has been continuously declining. According to the latest data from Chinese Internet analytics company CNZZ, Google's share is merely 3% and ranks fifth of all the search engines in China, and held just 3% of the search market share in June 2013 (Jennifer Slegg, Search Engine Watch, 9 July 2013).

Source: This case is written by the authors based on inputs from the following sources:

1. Daily Finance, 9 July 2010.
2. Bloomberg, 24 June 2012.
3. BGR, 7 June 2013.
4. http://searchenginewatch.com/article/2280420/Googles-Search-Market-Share-in-China-Falls-to-Just-3, 9 July 2013.

CASE QUESTIONS

1. What strategies should Google formulate to re-enter the Chinese market?
2. Do you think it is advisable for Google to stay out of the Chinese market for too long? Give reasons to justify your opinion.
3. Economic systems shape the business environment. Argue with pertinent examples of Google's entry and stay in other markets like India.

REVIEW QUESTIONS

1. What is an economic system? Outline the agents of an economic system.
2. Explain the three types of economic systems based on the resource ownership classification.
3. Outline the three types of economic systems based on the resource allocation.
4. Write a short note on the evolution of economic idea.
5. What is mercantilism?
6. What is capitalism? State its main features.
7. Outline some of the main characteristics of a socialist system.
8. What is a free market economy? How does it help the private sector?
9. What is a planned economy? What are its characteristics?
10. Write a note on the features of a mixed economy with some examples.

SUGGESTED READINGS

Amemiya, Takeshi, 2004, 'The Economic Ideas of Classical Athens', *The Kyoto Economic Review*, Vol. 73, No. 2, p. 71.

Brezis, Elise S., 2003, 'Mercantilism', *The Oxford Encyclopedia of Economic History*, Oxford University Press.

Fulcher, James, 2004, *Capitalism: A Very Short Introduction*, Oxford University Press, Oxford, UK.

Hunt, E.K. and Lautzenheiser, M., 2011, *History of Economic Thought: A Critical Perspective*, 3rd ed., PHI Learning, Delhi.

Stilwell, Frank, 2006, *Political Economy: The Contest of Economic Ideas*, 2nd ed., Oxford University Press.

5

PLANNING AND REFORM

Learning Outcomes

After reading this chapter, you will

- Understand the features and objectives of planning in India, with a focus on five year plans
- Appreciate the various reforms in the country including the land reforms and the Green Revolution
- Comprehend the development of public sector enterprises in India

Opening Case: Direct Benefit (Cash) Transfer

The Government of India launched a Direct Benefit Transfer (DBT) scheme on 1 January 2013, with the aim to transfer subsidies directly into the bank account of the beneficiaries. The main purpose of the DBT programme is to ensure transparency in the distribution of funds through government schemes.

DBT is routed through the Central Plan Scheme Monitoring System (CPSMS). CPSMS manages 139 Centrally Sponsored Schemes (CSS) and more than 800 Central Sector Schemes (CS), along with state plans and Additional Central Assistance (ACA). It, thus, manages a fund to the tune of ₹3,00,000 crore annually.[1]

The Objectives of CPSMS include[2]

1. Establishment of an efficient fund management system by disbursing funds to states, NGOs, etc.
2. Establishment of an effective expenditure information network like maintaining databases of all implementing agencies at various levels including block and panchayat
3. Reforms in the area of Public Financial Management for better cash management
4. Public disclosure of all relevant information

1. http://cpsms.nic.in/Users/LoginDetails/Login.aspx?ReturnUrl=%2f
2. *Ibid.*

CPSMS is being implemented through a web-based application, *viz.* COMPACT and e-Lekha and has over 9,50,000 implementing agencies registered on its portal. Several agencies are being registered every day. The main users of CPSMS include Planning Commission, Ministry of Finance, all central ministries, state governments, programme managers, banks and NGOs which receive funds from the central government.

CPSMS has, thus, been a great support for the implementation of DBT. In fact, in April 2013, the government decided to extend DBT in 78 more districts across the country. There are several schemes, which have been attached to the DBT.[3] These include[4] the following:

A total of 12 schemes under the Ministry of Social Justice and Empowerment are as follows:

1. Post-matric Scholarship for SC Students
2. Pre-matric Scholarship for SC Students
3. Pre-matric Scholarship for Children of those engaged in Unclean Occupations
4. Upgradation of merit of SC Students
5. National Overseas Scholarship Schemes for SC students
6. Post-matric Scholarship for OBCs
7. National Overseas Scholarship for OBCs
8. Post-matric Scholarship for Economically Backward Class Students
9. Post-matric Scholarship for Students with Disabilities
10. National Overseas Scholarship for Persons with Disabilities
11. Scholarship for Top Class Education for Students with Disabilities
12. Top Class Education Scheme

A total of 4 schemes under the Ministry of Human Resources Development, Department of Higher Education are given below:

1. Scholarship to University/College Students
2. Fellowship Schemes of UGC
3. Fellowship Schemes of AICTE
4. Subsidy on Fee to Students

A total of 2 schemes under the Department of School Education and Literacy, Ministry of Human Resources Development are as follows:

1. National Means cum Merit Scholarship
2. National Scheme for Incentive for the girl child for secondary education

5 schemes under the Ministry of Tribal Affairs are as under:

1. National Overseas Scholarship for ST students
2. Post-matric Scholarship Scheme
3. Upgradation of Merit Scheme
4. Top Class Education System
5. Rajiv Gandhi National Fellowship

3 schemes under the Ministry of Minority Affairs are listed below:

1. Matric Scholarship Scheme

3. http://mhrd.gov.in/dbt
4. http://www.techeduhry.nic.in/SC-Welfare/3-List-of-Schemes-under-DBT.pdf

2. Maulana Azad National Fellowship
3. Merit cum Means Scholarship Scheme

2 schemes under the Ministry of Women and Child Development are as follows:

1. Indira Gandhi Matritva Sahyog Yojana (IGMSY)
2. Dhanalakshmi Scheme

1 scheme under the Ministry of Health and Family Welfare is given below:

1. Janani Suraksha Yojana

5 schemes under the Ministry of Labour and Employment are listed as under:

1. Scholarship to the Children of beedi workers
2. Housing subsidy to beedi workers
3. Stipend to children in the special schools under the Child Labour Project
4. Stipend to trainees under the Scheme of Welfare of SC/ST job seekers through Coaching, Guidance and Vocational Training
5. Payment of stipend to trainees under the Scheme of Skill Development in 34 Districts affected by Left Wing Extremism

2 schemes under the Ministry of Petroleum and Natural Gas are given below:

1. Domestic LPG Subsidy Scheme
2. Public Distribution System (PDS) Kerosene

1 scheme under the Department of Food and Public Distribution is as follows:

1. Targeted Public Distribution System (in union territories)

Source: This case is written by the authors based on inputs from the following sources:

1. http://cpsms.nic.in/Users/LoginDetails/Login.aspx?ReturnUrl=%2f
2. http://mhrd.gov.in/dbt
3. http://www.techeduhry.nic.in/SC-Welfare/3-List-of-Schemes-under-DBT.pdf

5.1 INTRODUCTION

Soon after independence, India adopted economic planning. The rationale behind economic planning was to progress towards sustainable development and equitable growth. Accordingly, an economic policy was devised as per the mandate.

Economic environment largely depends on the nature of economic policies and India's economic policy is primarily based on the economic planning. Development plans were accordingly formulated based on the idea of a mixed economy, in which co-existence of both private and public sector is still apparent. Economic planning started soon after independence. In 1950, Planning Commission of India came into existence, with the objective of carrying out policy formulations and development plans, aiming at enhancing living standard of the people of the country (see Box 5.1 for further details).

In 1951, the First Five Year Plan was implemented. The focus of development plans under the aegis of Planning Commission has always been to review and allocate state resources.

The rationale behind economic planning is to address the limitation of market forces for facilitating equitable resource allocation to all sections of the society. It has been pointed that market economy suffers from market failures. It is also believed that allocation of resources under economic planning is more rational and leads to social justice.

Box 5.1 Main Functions of Planning Commission

1. Make an assessment of the material, capital and human resources of the country, including technical personnel, and investigate the possibilities of augmenting such of these resources as are found to be deficient in relation to the nation's requirement.
2. Formulate a plan for the most effective and balanced utilisation of country's resources.
3. On determination of priorities, define the stages in which the plan should be carried out and propose the allocation of resources for the due completion of each stage.
4. Indicate the factors which are tending to retard economic development, and determine the conditions which, in view of the current social and political situation, should be established for the successful execution of the plan.
5. Determine the nature of the machinery which will be necessary for securing the successful implementation of each stage of the plan in all its aspects.
6. Appraise from time to time the progress achieved in the execution of each stage of the plan and recommend the adjustments of policy and measures that such appraisal may show to be necessary.
7. Make such interim or ancillary recommendations as it appear to be appropriate either for facilitating the discharge of the duties assigned to it, or on a consideration of prevailing economic conditions, current policies, measures and development programmes or on an examination of such specific problems as may be referred to it for advice by central or state governments.

Source: Planning Commission, Government of India.

With the above rationale, the First Five Year Plan set objectives to increase employment opportunities and argued for fuller utilisation of manpower in addition to the aim of reducing economic inequalities. It also advocated relative share of public and private sector in the ownership of productive capital in the country.[5] The First Five Year Plan period targeted 2.1% per annum increase in the national income. The performance of the plan was considered to be better than the targeted one.[6]

The Second Five Year Plan endorsed the performance of the First Five Year Plan and set target of 4.5% per annum increase in the national income. The national income during 1951–1956 increased from ₹9,110 crore in 1951 to ₹10,800 crore in 1956. This was estimated to be a growth of 18% over five years and 4.2% annually.[7]

The Second Five Year Plan period had seen some changes in the perspective and focus of economic planning in India. This was mainly influenced by P.C. Mahalanobis model of economic planning or development planning. The key priority was given to heavy industries. The model basically emphasised capital goods and consumer goods with priority.[8] This resulted

5. Planning Commission, Government of India, First Five Year Plan, 1951–1956.
6. Misra and Puri (2012), Indian Economy, Himalaya Publication House, New Delhi.
7. Planning Commission, Government of India, Second Five Year Plan, 1956–1961.
8. P. Mahalanobis (1953), Some observations on the Process of Growth of National Income, Sankhya, pp. 307–312.

in the increase in heavy industries under public sector.[9] The policies of economic planning continued to dominate with Mahalanobis idea. Industrialisation continued under state monitoring with Industrial Policy of 1956 in place (see Chapter 7 for more details).

Up to 1980s, economic growth in India had been modest and was close to 3.5% per annum. Economic planning was again renovated during 1980s. An attempt of economic reformation was made in 1987. Licensing was criticised and an attempt to attract the private sector in telecommunication was partially made. However, the policy for economic liberalisation was still away for Indian economy.

Prior to 1991, the Government of India attempted to close its economy for outsiders. High tariffs and import duty were imposed on imports. Licensing was also imposed on imports, which prevented foreign goods from entering into Indian market. It clearly indicates that Indian economy was not having economic environment conducive to business. Doing business was a lengthy process, which needed to satisfy a number of agencies, amounting to around 80 agencies.

By the mid of 1991, India was not having enough dollars to pay for imports and the government ran under huge deficit. This resulted in a new era of reformation with liberalised economic policy. Economic reform started on 24 July 1991. The key focus area of economic reform was liberalisation. Then, the Prime Minister, P.V. Narasimha Rao and Finance Minister, Manmohan Singh opened India's economy to the world through measures like deregulation, privatisation, tax reforms and delicensing. As a result of economic reforms, business environment gradually became conducive for private players as well for foreign investors.

This chapter discusses the economic planning and their features under various five year plans.

5.2 PRE-INDEPENDENCE PERIOD

Indian economy was considered to be the world's richest economy before 1000 AD.[10] Interestingly, India accounted for up to 25% of the world's GDP in 1500 AD. During 1820, the share went down to 16%. By the beginning of the 20th century, it further went down to 7.6%. In 1950, after India's independence, the share in the world GDP was estimated to be merely 4%.

India had the first urban settlement in the world during Indus Valley Civilisation (3000–1500 BC). During that period, people used to domesticate animals, practice agriculture and trade with the other cities. India's ancient economic history narrates a very progressive story. During the 5th century BC, silver ingots were in circulation. During Mauryan era (321–185 BC), infrastructure and trade routes attracted due consideration. Measures were taken to enhance trade and commerce. Later, during early Mughal period, India's economy was at its peak.

In 1500 AD, India accounted for 24% of the world's GDP, which was more than that of Europe which accounted for 20% of the world's GDP.[11] For details, please see Table 5.1. In 1757 AD, British won the Battle of Plassey and in 1764, the Battle of Buxar. Subsequently, in 1765, British got the right to collect revenue. The British East India Company became the colonial master of India up to 1857. From 1858 to 1947, India was under the direct rule of the British Crown.

9. P.T. Bauer (2011), *Indian Economic Policy and Development*, Routledge.
10. Maddison, Angus (2006), *The World Economy*, Vol. 1: *A Millennial Perspective* and Vol. 2: *Historical Statistics*, OECD Publishing, ISBN 9789264022621.
11. *Ibid.*

Table 5.1 Share of Countries and Region in World's GDP (0–1950 AD)

Region	0	1000	1500	1600	1700	1820	1950
Europe	13%	11%	20%	23%	25%	27%	30%
Western Offshoots (USA)	0%	1%	0%	0%	0%	2%	31%
Latin America	2%	4%	3%	1%	2%	2%	8%
Japan	1%	3%	3%	3%	4%	3%	3%
China	26%	23%	25%	29%	22%	33%	4%
India	33%	29%	24%	23%	24%	16%	4%
Rest of the world	24%	30%	24%	21%	22%	17%	20%

Source: Maddison (2006).

We have seen that during the 18th century, industrial revolution took place in Europe. Technological change occurred in India as well. Railway is an example of that. However, British policy towards India was not only to embrace new technology but also to influence every sphere of economic activities. India became a predominant supplier of raw material and ceased to be a major exporter of the finished goods. Some of the features of Indian economy during this period included major changes in taxation system, free trade and single currency with a fixed exchange rate. Taxes were imposed on property and land, and accordingly, Zamindari system was also rearranged.

On the eve of independence, India's economy was characterised as underdeveloped, with low per capita income, poor infrastructure, illiteracy, low industrialisation and an agrarian-based economy. The per capita income in 1947–1948 was merely ₹230. In 1950, almost half of the population was below poverty. Power generation was limited to 2100 MW on annual basis, whereas the transport infrastructure was also limited. With 82% population illiterate and most of them engaged in agriculture, India's GDP received the largest contribution from agriculture sector, i.e., more than 50%. However, due to backward production system, Indian agriculture was low in the level of productivity as compared to those of Japan and other countries.

5.3 NATIONAL DEVELOPMENT COUNCIL

The planning and development process of India was instituted by Planning Commission. This process had been supported by institutions like National Development Council, which was a forum of Union Ministers and Chief Ministers of States. Every five year plan was used to be discussed on this forum at different stages of plan formulations. Finally, these plans needed approval from National Development Council. The National Development Council was set up on 6 August 1952 and its first meeting was held in November 1952.

The objectives of National Development Council are as follows:

1. To strengthen and mobilise the effort and resources of the nation in support of the national development plans.
2. To promote common economic policies in all vital spheres.
3. To ensure the balanced and rapid development of all parts of the country.

The functions of the National Development Council are given below:

1. To review the working of the National Plan from time to time.
2. To consider important questions of social and economic policy affecting national development.
3. To recommend measures for the achievement of the aims and targets set out in the National Plan.

At the time of initiation, the National Development Council was constituted comprising the Prime Minister of India, the Chief Ministers of States and Members of the Planning Commission. The institution had been one of the vital linkages between State and Centre. It coordinated the two vital structures of Indian federalism concerning various tasks related to economic development of the country. In 1967, the Council was reconstituted, with all its functions redefined. Now, the Council comprised the Prime Minister of India, all Union Cabinet Ministers, the Chief Ministers of all States and Union Territories and the Members of the erstwhile Planning Commission. Delhi Administration was represented in the Council by the Lt. Governor and the Chief Executive Councillor, and the remaining Union Territories by their respective Administrators. So far, 56 meetings of the Council had been held. The last meeting of the National Development Council was held on 22 October 2011 to consider the Approach to the Twelfth Plan. The National Development Council was also dismantled by the new government along with the Planning Commission.

The functions of the Council that were redefined are as follows:

1. To prescribe guidelines for the formulation of the National Plan, including the assessment of resources for the plan.
2. To consider the National Plan as formulated by the Planning Commission.
3. To consider important questions of social and economic policy affecting national development.
4. To review the working of the Plan from time to time and to recommend such measures as are necessary for achieving the aims and targets set out in the National Plan, including measures to secure the active participation and co-operation of the people, improve the efficiency of the administrative services, ensure the development of the less advanced regions and sections of the community and through sacrifice borne equally by all citizens, build up resources for national development.

5.4 FIVE YEAR PLANS

As discussed earlier, post-independence India adopted economic planning on the pattern of socialist structure and mixed economy. The history of planning essentially becomes important to understand the business environment in the country. We will now discuss the important features, objectives and outcomes of each planning period in the country. It helps in understanding the evolution of India's economy and also, why economic planning continues to be relevant today.

Features of Indian planning

Planning in India has distinctive features as compared to that of socialistic economic planning.

It not only sets targets for the sectors which are under government control but also for those sectors which are under private sector. Moreover, the principal planning feature is the physical planning and also a combination of both social and economic planning. Economic planning has both physical and financial natures. At the nascent stage of Indian planning, Indian planners articulated that 'whatever is physically possible is financially possible too'.[12] The model of planning shaped the physical targets for the first and second plans.

Objectives of planning

Planning in India has both long- and short-term objectives. Every five year plan has its own objectives, targets and features. The objectives set in the First Five Year Plan are still relevant for the Indian economy.

The First Five Year Plan document states that in defining the objectives, priorities and techniques of planning in India, it is necessary to bear in mind the scale and dimensions of the problem as well as the basic values, which must find expression in the economic and social pattern to be evolved.

Also, for planning, it is vital to understand the development process and its implications for larger objectives like increasing production, creating employment, poverty alleviation, reducing economic inequalities, social justice, etc. A good planning process must give a balanced emphasis on all these interrelated factors. In fact, development is a process, which calls for effort and sacrifice on the part of the entire body of citizens. For such effort and sacrifice to come forth, psychological conditions have to be created, which provide an incentive for all to give their best.[13]

The long-term objectives of planning can be summarised as follows:

1. Achieving high economic growth
2. Increasing production
3. Attaining self-reliance
4. Alleviation of poverty
5. Generating employment opportunities
6. Reducing income inequalities
7. Ensuring social equity and social justice
8. Technological transformation and industrialisation
9. Promoting inclusive growth and economic development

Also, some of the objectives of planning, as emphasised in the Second Five Year Plan document, are as follows:

1. A sizeable increase in the national income so as to raise the level of living in the country
2. Rapid industrialisation, with particular emphasis on the development of basic and heavy industries

12. *A Critique of the Fourth Plan* in C.D. Wadhwa (Ed.) 'Some Problem of India's Economic Policy', Delhi, 1973.
13. First Five Year Plan Document.

3. A large expansion of employment opportunities
4. Reduction of inequalities in income and wealth and a more even distribution of economic power

The 12th Five Year Plan has also been advocating a faster inclusive and sustainable development. The document of the plan puts utmost attention on realising the vision to become a global leader as well as on achieving development needs such as food security. It also focuses on encouraging a sustainable process of economic development. Such objectives, thus, play a pivotal role in shaping the economic and the overall business environment in India.

We now discuss the economic policies during the planning periods. We have divided the planning periods in two phases, *viz.* early phase and later phase.

Early phase of economic planning

The First Five Year Plan (1951–1956) had a target to achieve 2.1% increase in the national income per annum during the planning period. The performance of the plan was better than the set target. Indian economy achieved a 4.2% increase per annum in its national income.

The Second Five Year Plan (1956–1961) was designed to carry out the same pace of economic growth that was achieved during First Five Year Plan. The plan was envisaged to provide a landscape and vision for large increase in production, investment and employment. At the same time, the plan also advocated for acceleration in the institutional changes, which was needed for the economic progress.[14] Overall, investments increased from ₹9,110 crore to ₹10,800 crore during the period. The economy was in surplus on current account balance at the outset of Second Five Year Plan. The investment further increased to ₹13,480 crore during 1956–1961. Accordingly, the Second Five Year Plan targeted for 4.5% growth per annum in the national income. The objective of the plan was set out to be distinct from the previous plan. A surge in the role of public sector undertakings was the prime objective. Heavy industries were planned as government undertaking. At the end of the plan, the national income grew at 4.2% per annum, which was slightly short of the actual target.

The Third Five Year Plan (1961–1966) aimed at little higher than those of the previous plans. The target was to achieve 5.6% per annum increase in the national income during the period. During the plan period, priority was given to the agriculture sector.

Similarly, the Fourth Five Year Plan (1969–1974) also put its utmost attention on strengthening the agricultural production. The production in organised industry during these two plan period increased by 8%; however, industrial sector experienced a decline during the same period. As stated in the document of the Fourth Five Year Plan, in the first four years, conditions were relatively favourable for industrial investments and growth, and the progress achieved was significant. Thereafter, for nearly three years, the economy was subjected to considerable stress and strain, and the growth rate in the industrial production declined, first slowly and then steeply till it reached virtual stagnation. To overcome the economic problems, the growth rate was targeted to be 5.7% per annum during the Fourth Five Year Plan. However, the actual achievement was merely 3.2%.

During the first phase of planning, Indian economy experienced fluctuating performance of agriculture, industries as well as inflation. Moreover, the economic growth that was achieved

14. Second Five Year Plan Document.

during this phase was averaged to 4.5%. Moreover, industrial growth slowed down considerably during the early 1960s. The industrial production index grew at the rate of 4% per year and value added in industry grew at 3.5% per year. The policy that was designed for Indian industrial sector affected its competitiveness at international level. Licensing was the major shortcoming of the industrial policy during this phase.

The draft document of Fifth Five Year Plan (1974–1979) was little more ambitious than that of the final document. In the draft document, the growth rate of 5.5% per annum national income was envisaged to be achieved, which was shortened down to 4.4%. At the outset of Fifth Five Year Plan, the Indian economy was suffering from inflationary pressure. During September 1974, the index increased up to 31.8%. It was noted in the final document of the plan, the food items and the industrial raw materials accounted for about two-third of the price increase. The oil prices increased four-fold.

Also, the trade gap took a downward turn from a surplus of ₹103.4 crore in 1972–1973 to a deficit of ₹432 crore in 1973–1974 and ₹1,190 crore in 1974–1975. Against this backdrop, economic policies were envisaged in the Fifth Five Year Plan to attract more investments. In addition, emphasis was also given to increase productivity of industries. The rate of increase in the GDP was about 4.9% per annum during 1974–1979. At the end of the plan, the economy went in negative growth. Table 5.2 gives an account of the targeted and actual growth rates till the Fifth Five Year Plan.

Table 5.2 Growth Rate (Targeted and Actual) During 30 Years of Plan Era

Plans	*Target (%)*	*Actual (%)*
First	2.1	3.6
Second	4.5	4.0
Third	5.6	2.2
Fourth	5.7	3.3
Fifth	4.4	5.2

Source: Sixth Five Year Plan Document, Planning Commission, Government of India.

Later phase of economic planning

Before the Sixth Five Year Plan (1980–1985), Indian economy experienced almost 30 years of planning with modest rate of economic growth. The level of economic growth was 3.5% during the first three decades of planning. Agricultural growth was merely 2.7%. Under such circumstances, the Sixth Five Year Plan set a target of 5.2% per annum. Against this target, the economy was able to achieve 5.4% of economic growth. The plan put special attention on the utilisation of the existing stock, increasing rate of investment and restraining the deficit in the balance of payments. This performance was the result of strong agricultural performance during the period. At the end of the plan, Indian economy was in a strong position coupled with some pertinent weaknesses. For instance, industrial performance was lower than the targeted performance. During this plan, technology policy statement was formulated. The application of technologies in industrial sector was initiated during the period.

The beginning of the Seventh Five Year Plan (1985–1990) remained modest and the economy grew at the rate of 3.8% per annum against the target of 5%. However, due to increased performance of agricultural sector, growth of the economy reached up to 5.5%, which resulted in the overall growth exceeding the actual target. Until the Seventh Five Year Plan period, Indian economy was concentrated to mixed economic policies, wherein heavy industries were still under government control. This was, in fact, the period of a major crisis for the economy owing to high inflation, increasing import bills, rising oil price in international market, and the resultant severe balance of the payments problem. The changing scenario of the economy and composition of the economy also resulted in the discourse of private sector participation.

The Eighth Five Year Plan (1992–1997) came just after the economy followed a comprehensive reforms and liberalisation programme. In the beginning, with liberalised business and economic environment as compared to the first phase of economic planning, the economy grew at 5.8%, which further accelerated to 7.4% for the last three years. The per annum growth rate was more than 6% during the Eighth Five Year Plan.

The Ninth Five Year Plan (1997–2002) was initiated after the positive experience of a new economic policy. With more than 6% economic growth per annum during the previous plan, the Ninth Five Year Plan set out the following objectives:[15]

1. Priority to agriculture and rural development, with a view to generate an adequate productive employment and eradication of poverty
2. Accelerating the growth rate of the economy with stable prices
3. Ensuring food and nutritional security for all, particularly the vulnerable sections of society
4. Providing the basic minimum services of safe drinking water, primary health care facilities, universal primary education, shelter, and connectivity to all in a time-bound manner
5. Containing the growth rate of population
6. Ensuring environmental sustainability of the development process through social mobilisation and participation of people at all levels
7. Empowerment of women and socially disadvantaged groups such as scheduled castes, scheduled tribes and other backward classes and minorities as the agents of socio-economic change and development
8. Promoting and developing people's participatory institutions like Panchayati Raj institutions, cooperatives and self-help groups
9. Strengthening efforts to build self-reliance
10. The process of reform was strongly advocated. In view of this, the target for the plan period was 6.5% growth in GDP per annum. This target was not achieved during this plan period, which also raised questions on the process of ongoing liberalisation. Again, owing to worst agricultural performance, the growth was claimed to be short of the actual targets.[16] The growth achieved during the period was 5.5% per annum.

However, the Tenth Five Year Plan (2002–2007) continued the higher economic growth target and set it at 8% per annum. The actual GDP growth was 7.8% in this plan period.

15. Ninth Five Year Plan Document, Planning Commission, Government of India.
16. Planning Commission, Government of India.

Similarly, the target of double digit growth was set during the Eleventh Five Year Plan (2007–2012). In fact, the first year of the plan was optimistic and achieved 9.3% growth. However, owing to the external environment, the desired growth could not be achieved. At the end of the Eleventh Five Year Plan, growth rate rather declined to 6.5%.

The Twelfth Five Year Plan (2012–2017) is already underway and has a targeted growth rate of 8%.

5.5 BEGINNING OF NEW PHASE OF PLANNING

Yojna Aayog to NITI Aayog

In May 2014, new government was formed under National Democratic Alliance ousting erstwhile United Progressive Alliance Government. The Prime Minister of India, Mr. Narendra Modi during his first speech at Lal Qila on 15 August 2014 announced dismantling the Planning Commission instituted in 1950s by the First Prime Minister of India. The dismantling of the old commission was accompanied by the constitution of new commission, i.e., NITI Aayog. Interestingly, NITI stands for National Institution for Transforming India.

The constitution of new commission has been justified with the ambitions of reforms and new market-led economic structure, which eventually does not need a planned economic development. The genesis of NITI Aayog (Commission) has been traced into the changing economic dynamism. The Cabinet Resolution for the constitution of NITI Aayog clearly states that

> The Planning Commission was set up on the 15th of March, 1950 through a Cabinet Resolution. Nearly 65 years later, the country has metamorphosed from an under-developed economy to an emergent global nation with one of the world's largest economies. ...From being preoccupied with survival, our aspirations have soared, and today, we seek elimination, rather than alleviation, of poverty. The people of India have great expectations for progress and improvement in governance, through their participation. They require institutional reforms in governance and dynamic policy shifts that can seed and nurture large-scale change. Indeed, the 'destiny' of our country, from the time we achieved Independence, is now on a higher trajectory.

Thus, the reforming and transforming Indian economy needs a transformation from planned economic development to market-led economic development process, including elimination of poverty. The document also lays down the objective of NITI Aayog.

The objectives of NITI Aayog are as follows:

1. To evolve a shared vision of national development priorities, sectors and strategies with the active involvement of states in the light of national objectives. The vision of the NITI Aayog will then provide a framework 'national agenda' for the Prime Minister and the Chief Ministers to provide impetus to.
2. To foster cooperative federalism through structured support initiatives and mechanisms with the states on a continuous basis, recognising that strong states make a strong nation.
3. To develop mechanisms to formulate credible plans at the village level and aggregate these progressively at higher levels of government.

4. To ensure, on areas that are specifically referred to it, that the interests of national security are incorporated in economic strategy and policy.
5. To pay special attention to the sections of our society that may be at risk of not benefitting adequately from economic progress.
6. To design strategic and long-term policy and programme frameworks and initiatives, and monitor their progress and their efficacy. The lessons learnt through monitoring and feedback will be used for making innovative improvements, including necessary mid-course corrections.
7. To provide advice and encourage partnerships between key stakeholders and national and international like minded think tanks, as well as educational and policy research institutions.
8. To create a knowledge, innovation and entrepreneurial support system through a collaborative community of national and international experts, practitioners and other partners.
9. To offer a platform for resolution of inter-sectoral and inter-departmental issues in order to accelerate the implementation of the development agenda.
10. To maintain a state-of-the-art Resource Centre, be a repository of research on good governance and best practices in sustainable and equitable development as well as help their dissemination to stakeholders.
11. To actively monitor and evaluate the implementation of programmes and initiatives, including the identification of the needed resources so as to strengthen the probability of success and scope of delivery.
12. To focus on technology upgradation and capacity building for implementation of programmes and initiatives.
13. To undertake other activities as may be necessary in order to further the execution of the national development agenda, and the objectives mentioned above.

The Aayog comprises the following:

1. Prime Minister of India as the Chairperson.
2. Governing Council comprising the Chief Ministers of all the states and Lt. Governors of union territories.
3. Regional Councils (These councils will be formed to address specific issues and contingencies impacting more than one state or a region. These will be formed for a specified tenure. The Regional Councils will be convened by the Prime Minister and will comprise the Chief Ministers of States and Lt. Governors of union territories in the region. These will be chaired by the Chairperson of the NITI Aayog or his nominee.)
4. Experts, specialists and practitioners with relevant domain knowledge as special invitees nominated by the Prime Minister.
5. The full-time organisational framework will comprise of the following:
   (i) Vice Chairman
   (ii) Full Time Members
   (iii) Part Time Members (maximum 2 from institutions)

(iv) Ex officio members (maximum 4 from Council of Ministers)
(v) Chief Executive Officer
(vi) Secretariat as deemed necessary

With the above objectives and structure, NITI Aayog has started its functioning as the high profile think tank of the Government of India. Renowned economist, Prof. Anil Panagariya is the Vice Chairperson of the Aayog supported by full-time members, which include Bibek Debroy, V.K. Saraswat and Ramesh Chand. The composition of Governing Council is similar to the composition of erstwhile National Development Council. With the objective of cooperative federalism, NITI Aayog has been promoting the new Government's development agenda. Now, planning is in the hand of Ministry of Finance. Disbursement of planned expenditure is being executed by the Ministry.

5.6 LAND REFORMS

In the post-independence India, land reform was directed towards the redistribution of lands. It aimed at removing the Zamindari system. There were three types of land tenure system, *viz.* Zamindari system, Mahalwari system and Ryotwari System. These systems were inherited from British land tenure systems and had inherent flaws such as inability to prevent exploitation of landless labourers.

Land tenure system refers to laws and regulations, which confer ownership rights upon an individual or actual tiller of the soil. It determines the status of the actual tiller of the land and his relations with the state. If the actual tiller is not the owner of the land, it determines the relation between the owner and the actual tiller of the land. It mentions the circumstances related to ownership rights, rent, sale or transfer his holding, etc.

Moreover, since after independence the focus had been on agricultural sector development, it was crucial to reform the agrarian structure and the prevailing institutional framework. Thus, in context of the optimal utilisation of resources, agrarian reform was accorded high priority. Therefore, the issue of land reforms became a significant national issue. As per the documents of the First Five Year Plan, land reform was a fundamental issue of national importance. Also, former Prime Minister, Indira Gandhi emphasised that land reform is the most crucial test, which our political system must pass in order to survive.

There were a large number of land tenure systems prevalent in India in the pre-independence period. Among them, three of them have been significant. These are as follows:

1. ***Zamindari system:*** This system provides for separation of ownership of land from its cultivators. The Zamindar owns a large area of land and is responsible for the payment of land revenues to the government. This system has been abolished in India.
2. ***Mahalwari system:*** In Mahalwari system, land is owned by a collective body belonging to the respective village, which plays a role of collecting land revenues from the owners and is responsible for any governmental activity.
3. ***Ryotwari (or Raiyatwari) system:*** In Ryotwari system, there is no intermediary between the government and the owner (i.e., registered holder of the land) and is responsible to the government for the payment of land revenues.

Land reform has several objectives, as enlisted in Figure 5.1.

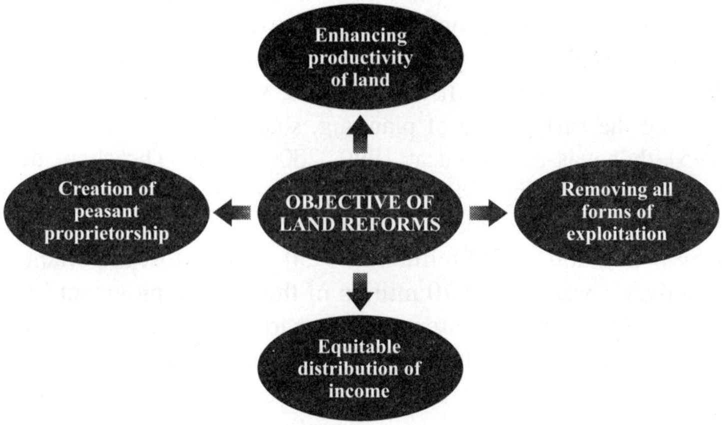

Figure 5.1 Objectives of land reforms.

In order to meet the objectives of land reforms, laws had been passed in the states to abolish Zamindari, Mahalwari and Ryotwari systems. The laws were enacted with two common principles, *viz.* abolition of intermediaries and the payment of compensation to the owners. Under the new act, nearly 57.7 lakh hectares were distributed to the landless agriculturists after the successful completion of the Zamindari Abolition Act, which had a favourable impact on the economy as well.

Impact of land reform

Reforms of any form have a large impact on the economic and business environment of an economy. Land reforms too had a meaningful impact. Some of the pertinent impacts of the land reforms can be summarised as follows:

1. It encouraged market-oriented farming practices.
2. It abolished the feudal system, which earlier dominated the agrarian economy.
3. It helped in shifting the focus from subsistence farming to commercial farming.
4. It also reduced the disparities prevalent in agricultural holdings.
5. It helped the cultivators in getting financial assistance to the boost productivity of land.
6. It also helped in increasing the income of small farmers and was instrumental in reducing poverty to some extent.

5.7 GREEN REVOLUTION

Post-independence, the agricultural output in India was a major concern. The country relied largely on food aid and food imports in order to meet domestic requirements. In 1965 and 1966, severe drought took place, which changed the course of policy-making in the field of agriculture. Ensuring food security, thus, became an increasingly important expected outcome. The country took to reforms in ensuring self-sufficiency in food grains through adoption of high yielding varieties of crops and advanced irrigation techniques to boost the agricultural productivity. This led to the Green Revolution. The states of Punjab, Haryana and western Uttar Pradesh were the ones which benefitted from this initiative and saw a rapid increase in farm productivity.

The share of agriculture in national income was more than 55% during 1950–1951. It was the main source of employment, with nearly 70% of the working population employed in the sector. As the process of industrialisation started, share of agriculture decreased over the period of time. During the early phase of planning, share of agriculture in GDP was 56.5% in the year 1950–1951 that was estimated at 1999–2000 prices. The share decreased to 45.9% during 1970–1971 and 34% during 1990–1991. The estimate was revised owing to the change in the base year. Moreover, employment in agriculture sector was estimated at 98 million out of the total working population of 140 million in 1950–1951. Most important aspect of this was that the share of cultivator was around 70 million of the total employment in agriculture, out of which 28 million were labourers. At present, this scenario has changed, but the fact remains that agriculture provides employment to almost 55% of the total working population in the country (see Figure 5.2).

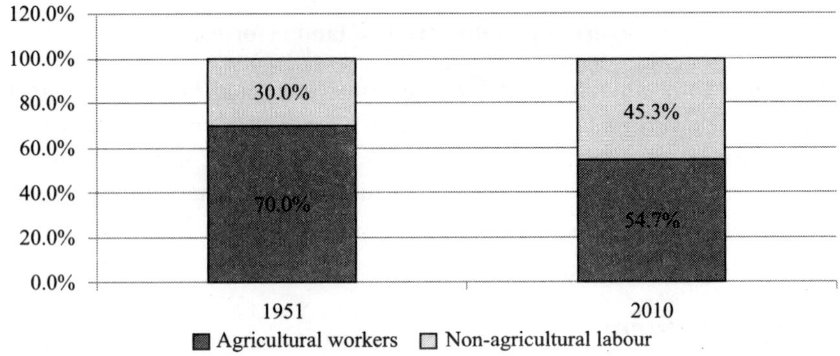

Figure 5.2 Changing share of employment in agriculture sector.
Source: Planning Commission of India, Plan Documents.

Need for a new policy

During the Second Five Year Plan, the use of technology in agriculture gradually started with an urge to modernise the sector. The Second Five Year Plan also pointed out the various ways and means of increasing agricultural productivity. As a pilot project, new technology was tried in seven districts during 1960–1961. This project was called *Intensive Agricultural District Programme* (*IADP*). The seven districts were selected on the basis of availability of drainage and irrigation facilities. The districts selected for the experiment included the following:

1. **For rice:** West Godavari (Andhra Pradesh), Shahabad (Bihar), Raipur (Madhya Pradesh) and Tanjavur (Tamil Nadu)
2. **For wheat:** Ludhiana (Punjab) and Aligarh (Uttar Pradesh)
3. **For millets:** Pali (Rajasthan)

Later in this experiment, *High Yielding Varieties Programme (HYVP)* was also added to this pilot project. This pilot project was extended in the remaining states and this was called *new agricultural strategy*. With the success of the projects, the Government of India further extended this programme in 114 districts in the country in 1965.

With the use of New Mexican varieties of seeds, multiple cropping was made possible. These varieties are known as *Lerma Rojo, Sonara-64, Kalyan and P.V.18*. These HYV of seeds were developed by Professor Norman Borlaug, which increased the level of per hectare yields to 5,000–6,000 kg in Mexico.

In addition, the new agricultural strategies also led to deviation from the traditional style of farming in India. It advocated the usage of fertilisers, pesticides and machinery for farming and hybrid seeds. Initially, the programme was implemented in a total area of 1.89 million hectares, which was extended up to 9.2 million hectares at the end of Third Five Year Plan. Table 5.3 shows the output of foodgrains during early phase of the Green Revolution.

Table 5.3 Output of Foodgrains During Early Phase of Green Revolution (in million tonnes)

Items	*1959–1960*	*1960–1961*	*1964–1965*	*1970–1971*	*1980–1981*
Wheat	29.3	30.3	12.3	23.8	36.3
Rice	9.7	9.8	39.3	42.2	53.6
Other cereals	21.5	22.5	25.4	30.5	29.0
Pulses	11.3	12.9	12.4	11.8	10.6
All foodgrains	71.8	71.8	89.4	108.4	129.6

Source: Economic Survey of India and RBI.

Also, Figure 5.3 depicts the average production of major foodgrains during the planning periods up to the Eleventh Five Year Plan. The data revealed that average productivity of rice and wheat increased over the period of time owing to the concentration of HYV of seeds used for these two commodities. However, the production of pulses remained constant or stagnant over the planning periods. This also highlighted the changing pattern of cropping in India after the Green Revolution.

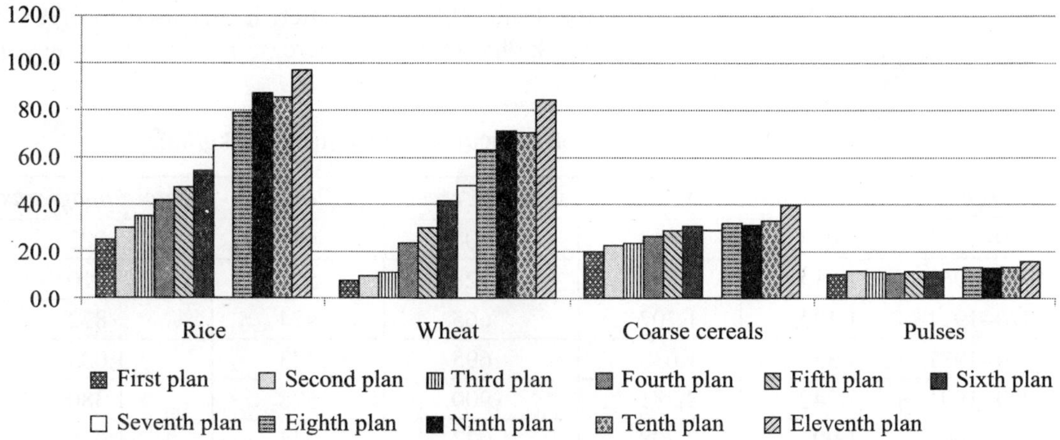

Figure 5.3 Average production during planning period (in million tonnes).

Source: Handbook of Statistics on Indian Economy, RBI.

As a result of this, agricultural production increased from an average of 81 million tonnes during the Third Five Year Plan to the average of 202 million tonnes during the Tenth Five Year Plan.

Some of the major impacts of the Green Revolution can be summarised as follows:

1. ***Agricultural production:*** The agricultural produce increased significantly. Yield of principle foodgrains such as wheat and rice was the main item in that category. On an average, wheat production grew from 11.1 million tonnes during the Third Five Plan to 70.2 million tonnes in the Tenth Five Year Plan. The overall contribution of wheat to the total foodgrains has increased from 13% in 1950–1951 to 35.7% in 2011–2012. On the other hand, the average annual production of rice increased from 35.1 million tonnes in the Third Five Year Plan to 85.6 million tonnes during the Tenth Five Year Plan.
2. ***Commercial crops:*** Green revolution led to significant increase in the productivity and production of commercial crops or cash crops. The output of sugarcane increased significantly during 1970s. A similar trend was also noted in case of oilseeds, potatoes, cotton, jute, etc. However, the output of pulses was low, which led to their import.
3. ***Greater interface between agriculture and industry:*** The modernisation of agriculture sector also strengthened its linkages with the industry. The production of commercial products provided industrial inputs to the industries. Both backward and forward linkages were strengthened due to green revolution.
4. ***Sectoral employment:*** It also led to the increase in the area under cultivation, and thus, created more employment opportunities in the agricultural sector. Adoption of new technologies, though displaced agricultural labour, also created newer avenues of employment because of its contribution to multiple cropping.

The overall impact of Green Revolution was the increase in productivity of agricultural sector. Per hectare yield increased from 522 kg/ha in 1951–1952 to 872 kg/ha during 1970–1971. This further increased to 1,023 kg/ha during 1980–1981. Thereafter, it increased to 1,798 kg in 2009–2010. At present, this crossed 2,000 kg/ha. In case of increase in specific foodgrains, Table 5.4 depicts a clear picture.

Table 5.4 Decadal Picture of Agricultural Productivity (kg/ha)

Year	*Rice*	*Wheat*	*Coarse Cereals*	*Pulses*	*Total Foodgrains*
1950–1951	668	663	408	441	522
1960–1961	1,013	851	528	539	710
1970–1971	1,123	1,307	665	524	872
1980–1981	1,336	1,630	695	473	1,023
1990–1991	1,740	2,281	900	578	1,380
2000–2001	1,901	2,708	1,027	544	1,626
2010–2011	2,240	2,938	1,528	689	1,921

Source: Handbook of Statistics on Indian Economy, RBI.

5.8 EVOLUTION OF PUBLIC SECTOR IN INDIA

Public sector implies those economic sectors, which are under the control of the governments at both centre and the states. In other words, the government-owned corporations constitute the public sectors. The majority of public held shares of these public sector undertakings (PSUs) are shared by central or state government. This share should not be less than 51%.

Before 1947, there were limited sectors, which were controlled by the government. These sectors were railways, postal services, telegraphs, ports, etc. After independence, industrial policy was designed, which strongly advocated the idea of large PSUs. As a part of 1956 industrial policy, a road map for the industrial sector in India was developed, envisaging the idea of a self-reliant economic growth. In order to boost public sector undertakings, the Industrial Policy Resolution 1956 classified the Indian industries into three broad categories, *viz.* schedule A category (which included industries that would be developed by the state), schedule B category (which included enterprises owned by state but private participation would be allowed) and schedule C category (which included industries left for private sectors) (see Chapter 7 for further details).

This was planned under the background of long gestation period of the industrial sector in India. The industry was weak after independence and not able to absorb large part of the working population. The country totally relied upon imports of industrial products. In order to increase export and industrial productivity, the government carried out planned programmes for the development of heavy industries under the state control. In 1969, government nationalised 14 major banks in India.

The Second Five Year Plan envisaged to establish three steel plants and a provision of ₹1.2 crore was made for Government Electric Factory. In addition, the plan also advocated the development of heavy industrial machinery through National Industrial Development Corporation (NIDC). The road map setup under the Second Five Year Plan and the Industrial Policy of 1956 led to the growth of state-owned enterprises (SOEs). Government entered in almost all the sectors. Later during 1960s and 1970s, a strong hold of public sector enterprises was evident in the economy. This is also being revealed by Table 5.5.

Table 5.5 Expansion of Public Sector and Investment in the Sector

Period	*Number of PSUs*	*Total Investment (in ₹ Crore)*
1950–1951	5	29
1960–1961	47	950
1970–1971	179	18,150
1980–1981	233	99,330

Source: Public Sector Enterprise Survey.

The statistics in Table 5.5 clearly indicates that during the various phases of planning, the number of PSUs increased from 5 in 1950–1951 to 233 in 1980–1981. During this period, the number of PSUs increased by 13% and their corresponding investment increased by 31%. The largest growth rate in their numbers was seen during the first phase of planning, i.e., 1950–1951 to 1960–1961. Growth rate was more than 25% during this decade and the case of investment was also the same with more than 40% increase in investment during the period.

At present, the public sector enterprises are divided into Maharatna, Navratna and Miniratnas. Seven heavy industries are under Maharatnas. These industries are Bharat Heavy Electricals Limited (BHEL), Coal India Limited, Gas Authority of India Limited (GAIL), Indian Oil Corporation Limited (IOCL), National Thermal Power Corporation (NTPC) Limited, Oil and Natural Gas Corporation (ONGC) Limited and Steel Authority of India Limited (SAIL). In addition to these Maharatnas, 14 Navratnas and 70 Miniratnas are under the public sector enterprises in India. In 2009, Maharatna status was established. The investment ceiling of public sector enterprises for Maharatna status was increased from ₹1,000 crore to ₹5,000 crore.

Over the years, PSUs have contributed in many developmental aspects, including employment generation, export promotion, reducing regional disparities, development of infrastructure, and industrial bases and capacity building for small scale industries. However, some PSUs have also faced the problems of inefficiency and have been subjected to disinvestment as well during the post-liberalisation period.

Box 5.2 Performance of Central Public Sector Enterprises

The story of India's public sector undertakings will always be accompanied by the success stories of the Central Public Sector Enterprises (CPSEs), which are under control of various ministries/ departments of the Central Government. These enterprises have been playing vital role in economic progress of the country. Up to 2015 298 CPSEs were under the administrative control of various ministries/departments, of which 235 were in operation and 63 under construction up to December 2015. As on 31 March 2015, financial investment in all the CPSEs was ₹10,96,057 crore, which registered a growth of 10.48% over the previous financial year. 157 CPSEs were profit-making and their net profit was ₹1,30,363 crore in 2014–2015. 77 CPSEs were loss-making and their combined net loss was ₹27,360 crore. The top five profit-making CPSEs were ONGC Ltd., Coal India Ltd., NTPC Ltd., the National Mineral Development Corporation (NMDC) Ltd. and Power Finance Corporation Ltd. in 2014–2015. During the same financial year, Bharat Sanchar Nigam Ltd., Air India Ltd., Mahanagar Telephone Nigam Ltd., Hindustan Photo Films Manufacturing Company Ltd. and Mangalore Refinery and Petrochemicals Ltd. stood as top five loss-making CPSEs. Generally, the profit-making CPSEs contribute to the central exchequer by paying dividends, interest on government loans and payments, etc. Total contribution of CPSEs, despite of increase in capital investment, decreased in 2014–2015 compared to 2013–2014. The decrease registered to be 9.2% in 2014–2015 over the previous financial year. This decrease was attributed to decrease in their contribution to dividend, corporate tax and custom duty in 2014–2015. On the other hand, their contribution to excise duty, dividend tax, sales tax and service tax was higher than that of the previous financial year. The major highlights of the performance of CPSEs during 2014–2015 are mentioned below.

Table 1 Highlights of Performance of CPSEs during 2014–2015 (₹ in crore)

Performance indicator	*2013–2014*	*2014–2015*
Net profit	1,28,295	1,03,003
Number of profit-making units	164	157
Net profit by profit-making units only	1,49,636	1,30,363
Net loss	21,341	27,360
Number of loss-making units	70	77
Total investment	9,92,096	10,96,057
Dividends paid	65,115	56,527

Source: Economic Survey of India and http://pib.nic.in/newsite/PrintRelease.aspx?relid=136895

5.9 ECONOMIC REFORMS

India is an emerging economy, with a GDP of US$1.84 trillion.[17] A series of reforms was initiated by the government in the external sector. These reforms aimed at integration of Indian economy with the world market, thereby promoting the tenets of globalisation and multilateral rule-making. Major reforms include devaluation of Indian currency in 1991 by 18–19%, which was subsequently appreciated against the currencies of industrialised nations. The government later adopted convertibility of Indian Rupee on both current account and capital account.

The year 1991 set forth the era of economic reforms in India, which accelerated the overall growth of the economy. In fact, in 1991, India saw one of the most comprehensive economic reforms in Asia. The reforms encompassed various aspects of the economy, including liberal trade policies, privatisation, deregulation, investment regime, etc.

Liberalisation of import regime and reduction of tariffs and quotas were among the external sector reforms. Import procedures were simplified and concurrently, a number of commodities were brought out of the purview of licensing system. Peak rate of import duty was reduced from 300% to 150% in 1991–1992. This was further reduced to 50% in 1995–1996.

In the first phase of liberalisation till 1997, the economy grew at more than 7% per annum and this was attributed to the growth in industry and services sectors. It even reached close to 9% in the few years just preceding the global financial crisis of 2007. The Indian economy, however, has remained resilient to this crisis because of its strong macroeconomic fundamentals.

Another vital step was industrial deregulation. Prior to liberalisation, India had been following several measures in order to control domestic activities. These activities included licensing, stringent process of starting a business and government control over distribution of industrial produce. The strictly regulated regime was criticised by various economist including Jagdish Bhagwati. In 1991, the Government of India abolished the licensing system and opened the sector for private players. Similarly, the number of sectors reserved for PSUs was reduced significantly from 17 to 3. Equity amounting to ₹1,13,650 crore in public sector enterprises was disinvested to public sector financial institutions and private companies, etc. in 2011–2012.

India has been striving to make the investment regime more investor-friendly. In the Doing Business Report 2014, published by the World Bank, India is ranked 134 out of 189 economies in the ease of doing business.[18] Though over the years, it has been seen that the country has eased business startups by establishing an online VAT registration system and replaced the physical stamp previously required with an online version.[19]

More reforms and schemes like Direct Benefit Transfer, MGNREGA, Right to Food, etc. have come up in the recent years. (A discussion on such reforms is presented in Chapter 8.)

Closing Case: Housing Sector Reforms in India

As per the preamble of the National Urban Housing and Habitat Policy 2007, at the end of

17. World Development Indicators (WDI), World Bank. The values are in current price as of 2012.
18. In preparing this report, a set of regulations affecting 9 stages of a business's life have been measured—starting a business, dealing with construction permits, registering property, getting credit, protecting investors, paying taxes, trading across borders, enforcing contracts and closing a business. The indicators are used to analyse economic outcomes and identify what reforms have worked, where, and why.
19. Doing Business Report 2011, World Bank and IFC. This study considered 183 countries.

the Tenth Five Year Plan, the housing shortage was estimated to be 24.7 million for 67.4 million households.[20] However, as per more recent estimates by Confederation of Real Estate Developers Association of India (CREDAI), India has a shortage of 18.1 million houses.[21]

CREDAI, which constitutes 9000 members, is the apex body for private real estate developers in India. It acts as a linkage between the developers and the government and customers. It spreads across the country with 22 state chapters and 143 city chapters.[22]

CREDAI advocates the reforms in housing policy so that the real estate sector can be developed in a better way. In fact, there is a growing need for affordable housing by the middle class as well as the poor. With such prospects ahead, the market size of the real estate sector is expected to touch US$180 billion by 2020.[23]

On the other hand, there are two schemes, namely, Indira Awas Yojana (IAY) and Rajiv Awas Yojana (RAY) run by the Government of India for providing housing facilities. The purpose of IAY scheme is to provide financial assistance to the weaker sections of society to own a house with basic amenities, whereas RAY looks forward to a slum-free India.

Some of the objectives of Rajiv Awas Yojana (2013–2022) are as follows:[24]

1. Providing housing, basic civic infrastructure and social amenities in slums
2. Reforms to identify and address the causes leading to creation of slums
3. Helping expand credit linkages for urban poor
4. Capacity building to strength institutional frameworks and human resource capacities
5. Community empowerment by enhancing their formal participation in decision-making

Housing development has received allocations since the First Five Year Plan. Table 1 provides the outlay in housing and urban development over the years as per the provisions of the five years plans.

Table 1 Plan Outlay in Housing and Urban Development Sector (₹ Million)

Plan	*Total Outlay*	*Housing and Urban Development*	*Percentage Share in the Total*
First plan	20,688	488	2.1
Second plan	48,000	1,200	2.5
Third plan	85,765	1,276	1.5
Annual plan (1966–1969)	66,254	733	1.1
Fourth plan	1,57,788	2,702	1.7

20. Policy document, Ministry of Housing and Urban Poverty Alleviation, http://nhb.org.in/Urban_Housing/HousingPolicy2007.pdf
21. Housing policy reform needed in India: CREDAI, Article by Vimukt Dave, Business Standard 18 January 2013.
22. http://www.credai.org/
23. *Ibid.*
24. Ministry of Housing and Urban Poverty Alleviation, Government of India, http://mhupa.gov.in/ray/Ray_index.htm

Plan	*Total Outlay*	*Housing and Urban Development*	*Percentage Share in the Total*
Fifth plan	3,94,262	11,500	2.9
Annual plan (1977–1980)	1,21,765	3,688	3
Sixth plan	9,75,000	24,884	2.6
Seventh plan	18,00,000	42,295	2.3
Annual plan (1990–1992)	13,38,350	3,001	2.2
Eighth plan	43,41,000	1,05,000	2.4
Ninth plan	–	1,58,800	–
Tenth plan	–	4,05,000	–
Eleventh plan	–	3,68,700	–

Source: Ministry of Housing and Urban Poverty Alleviation, Government of India.

Source: This case is written by the authors based on inputs from the following sources:

1. Policy document, Ministry of Housing and Urban Poverty Alleviation.
2. http://nhb.org.in/Urban_Housing/HousingPolicy2007.pdf
3. Housing policy reform needed in India: CREDAI, Article by Vimukt Dave, Business Standard, 18 January 2013.
4. http://www.credai.org/
5. Website of the Ministry of Housing and Urban Poverty Alleviation, Government of India.
6. Ministry of Housing and Urban Poverty Alleviation, Government of India, http://mhupa.gov.in/ray/Ray_index.htm

CASE QUESTIONS

1. What role should CREDAI play in the formulation of National Housing Policy?
2. Examine the current status of Rajiv Awas Yojana. What are the achievements and the implementation bottlenecks?

REVIEW QUESTIONS

1. Outline the main functions of the Planning Commission of India.
2. Examine the planning and resource allocation during pre-independence period.
3. What are five year plans?
4. Discuss the features and objectives of planning in India.
5. What were the major achievements during the early phase of economic planning in India?
6. What do you understand by land reforms? What are its objectives?
7. Outline the impact of land reform on business environment.
8. Describe Green Revolution. What were its major impacts on the economy?

9. Discuss the evolution of public sector in India.

10. Write a short note on economic reform and liberalisation in India.

SUGGESTED READINGS

Bauer, P.T., 2011, *Indian Economic Policy and Development*, Routledge, New York.

Economic Survey of India, 1992, 1993, 1994, Ministry of Finance, Government of India, New Delhi.

Five Year Plan Documents, Planning Commission of India.

Maddison, Angus, 2006, *The World Economy*, Vol. 1: *A Millennial Perspective* and Vol. 2: *Historical Statistics*, OECD Publishing.

Mahalanobis, P.C., 1953, 'Some Observations on the Process of Growth of National Income', *Sankhya*, Vol. 12, Part 4, pp. 307–312.

Misra, S.K. and Puri, V.K., 2012, *Indian Economy*, Himalaya Publication House, New Delhi.

6

MACROECONOMIC INDICATORS

Learning Outcomes

After reading this chapter, you will

- Understand the key macroeconomic indicators of the economy
- Be familiar with the concepts of inflation and business cycle
- Assess the concepts of socio-economic indicators like poverty, inequality and unemployment

Opening Case: Onion Price Rise in Delhi

Delhi witnessed increase in onion prices in the latter half of the year 2013. The price went as high as ₹100/kg in some places. It was argued that the cause of this price rise was the limited supply from the onion producing states, especially Maharashtra, Gujarat, Karnataka and Andhra Pradesh due to unfavourable climatic conditions at the time of harvesting.

The government took certain measures like reducing export of onions and also allowed its import, but still the price rise could not be controlled.[1] The Delhi government also ran subsidised Onion retail through *Safal* counters across the city, which was beneficial for the people.

The price rise took its toll politically on the ruling Congress party when it lost the Delhi assembly election in December 2013. The Union Agriculture Secretary, Ashish Bahuguna argued that the price rise in key vegetables like onion in the national capital was self-created, as there was no logic for the rate hike when the production was good.[2]

But after the polling, the onion price was stabilised and Congress saw it as a political conspiracy, wondering how it came down the very next day of poll.[3]

1. Onion prices back at ₹80/kg in Delhi, 21 October 2013, http://m.businesstoday.in//story/onion-prices-back-at-rs-80-a-kg-in-delhi/1/199873.html
2. Price spike of onion, tomato in Delhi self-created, The Financial Express, 7 November 2013.
3. Congress wonders how onion prices came down the day after polling, http://timesofindia.indiatimes.com/india/Congress-wonders-how-onion-prices-came-down-the-day-after-polling/articleshow/27191174.cms, 10 December 2013.

Onion is an important crop not only for domestic consumption but also as the highest foreign exchange earner among the fruits and vegetables. India is the second largest producer of onion in the world, next to China.

However, the productivity of onion in India is very low, i.e., 14.21 ton/ha as compared to China and other countries like Egypt, Netherlands, Iran, etc. It occupies an area of 1064 thousand/hectares, with a production of 15118 thousand tons. The export of onion during the year 2011–2012 was 13,09,863.26 thousand tons, with a value of ₹1,722.85 crore.[4]

Table 1 below depicts the major onion producers in the world:

Table 1 Major Onion Producing Countries of the World

Countries	*Area* (000 ha)	*Production* (000 mt)	*Productivity* (mt/ha)	*Share in world total* (%)
China	930.21	20507.76	22.00	26.99
India	1064.00	15118.00	14.20	19.90
Pakistan	124.70	1701.10	13.60	2.24
Bangladesh	117.56	872.08	7.40	1.15
Indonesia	109.47	1048.23	9.60	1.38
Vietnam	101.70	355.30	3.50	0.47
Russia	88.00	1536.30	17.50	2.02
Myanmar	78.90	1137.90	14.40	1.50
Brazil	67.25	1556.00	23.10	2.05
Turkey	62.69	1900.00	30.30	2.50
Others	1227.02	30244.54	24.60	39.81
World	3971.51	75977.21	19.10	100.00

Source: Indian Horticulture Database, 2011; APEDA Agrixchange.

The onion price rise reflected poorly on one of the most important macroeconomic indicators, i.e., inflation. Its spillover effect was felt in the realms of social-economic, business and political environment.

Source: This case is written by the authors based on inputs from the following sources:

1. Onion prices back at ₹80/kg in Delhi, 21 October 2013, http://m.businesstoday.in//story/onion-prices-back-at-rs-80-a-kg-in-delhi/1/199873.html
2. Price spike of onion, tomato in Delhi self-created, *The Financial Express*, 7 November 2013.
3. Congress wonders how onion prices came down the day after polling, http://timesofindia.indiatimes.com/india/Congress-wonders-how-onion-prices-came-down-the-day-after-polling/articleshow/27191174.cms, 10 December 2013.
4. APEDA Agrixchange, http://agriexchange.apeda.gov.in/Market%20Profile/one/ONION.aspx

6.1 INTRODUCTION

Macroeconomic indicators play a vital role in understanding a country's economic environment.

4. http://agriexchange.apeda.gov.in/Market%20Profile/one/ONION.aspx

It is a statistics about economic activity within a given economy. It helps in understanding the economic performance and predicting the future accordingly.

The total economic activity in an economy may be measured in three ways—gross domestic product (GDP), gross national income (GNI) and net national income (NNI).

In addition, several other indicators measure the economic health of a country, which directly or indirectly affects people, business and politics. These indicators are inflation, interest rate, exchange rate, poverty, employment, inequality and so on. If the inflation rises, purchasing power of disposable income decreases, thereby reducing consumption in the economy. Therefore, it is important to understand the macroeconomic indicators and their interpretation. This chapter brings out the discussion on major macroeconomic indicators, which are imperative to business and overall economic environment.

6.2 NATIONAL INCOME

It is important to understand the concept of national income accounting. GDP is a part of national income accounting system. Before understanding the national income accounting, we need to understand the structure of economy, and the generation of income through various economic activities. As we know, an economy comprises of consumers, producers and various other agents which links the economic activities. There also exist interlinkages between these activities. In a nutshell, generation of income can be understood through a circular flow of economic agents and their respective activities. (We have also highlighted this in Chapter 4 dealing with Economic Systems.) A modified version of circular flow of income generation in a realistic economy is presented in Figure 6.1.

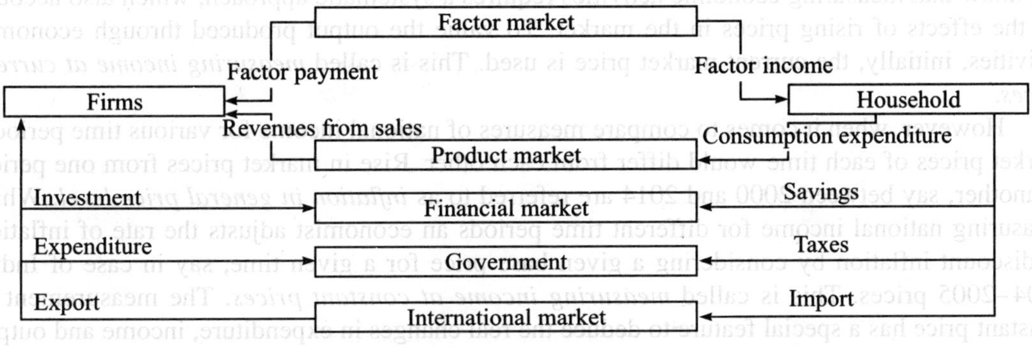

Figure 6.1 Circular flow of income generation in a realistic economy.

The national income accounting considers various agents to estimate the national income. It is a system of accounting akin to book keeping. The next section outlines the system of national income accounting and various measurements for national income.

6.2.1 National Income Accounting

National income accounting is a system which measures the aggregate outcome of economic activities in an economy at a given time period. The system is also referred to as the *book keeping system*. An important aspect is that the system estimates the total expenditure of an economy including the government expenditure, total revenues earned by the factors of production, *viz.* wages, interest, taxes, etc. It also shows how the economy is behaving in its broad and aggregate economic activities. It, thus, becomes an important system to analyse the health of an economy. Gross domestic product (GDP), gross national product (GNP) and gross national income (GNI) are some of the important measures that the system provides. Thus, national income is generally regarded as the income of a country. In other words, the total value of the final output of a country is the national income of that country. The value of the final output is estimated for a given year. In macroeconomics, there are three broad approaches to measure the national income which are as follows:

1. Expenditure approach
2. Production approach
3. Income approach

To assign the value of total production, income and expenditure, we need defined ways of valuating the economic activities. One important system of valuating economic activities is market prices.

At international level, there exists two broad categories of market pricing or valuing of economic activities, which include both goods and services. These two categories are valuing at constant price and current price.

Constant and current price

We know that measuring economic activities requires a systematic approach, which also account for the effects of rising prices in the market. To value the output produced through economic activities, initially, the current market price is used. This is called *measuring income at current prices*.

However, when it comes to compare measures of national income for various time periods, market prices of each time would differ from each other. Rise in market prices from one period to another, say between 2000 and 2014 are referred to as *inflation in general price level*. While measuring national income for different time periods an economist adjusts the rate of inflation or discount inflation by considering a given base price for a given time, say in case of India, 2004–2005 prices. This is called *measuring income at constant prices*. The measurement at constant price has a special feature to deduce the real changes in expenditure, income and output over different time periods, say over ten years.

The usage of constant price index has some limitations, the most important being the variation in portfolio of goods and services produced in a free market economy from year to year as new offerings comes to the market. Therefore, even if a constant price index is considered, at least every five years, a change in the base year (referred to as *rebasing*) is very much required.

Expenditure approach

The expenditure approach basically involves valuing of all the consumption expenditure. As outlined in the circular flow, the total national expenditure is equivalent to the expenditures incurred by the various agents in the economic activities such as households, firms, governments, etc. In this process, it is important to take into consideration that the national expenditure would only be the national income when the aggregation of only spending on the final consumption would take place.

Indicators and process of income estimation are as follows:

1. ***Final consumption expenditure:*** The final consumption expenditure accounts for the expenditure incurred by both households and government. Expenditure on final goods and services such as mobile phones, TV sets, food items and non-food items, which include both durable and non-durable goods are being taken into consideration. We refer C as private consumption in our discussion in this chapter.

Government also spends money as consumption expenditures on such goods and services. These goods and services include expenditure on education, health, defense and on maintaining law and orders, etc. We refer to G as government expenditure in our discussion in this chapter.

Thus, our total consumption expenditure is private expenditure plus private consumption.

Total consumption expenditure, $C_t = C + G$

2. ***Investment expenditure:*** Investment expenditure is also called *gross capital formation*. Expenditure made for investment has multiple aspects. It creates further assets. This type of expenditure includes spending on capital equipment, investment in real estate, spending on engineering goods and heavy machineries etc. Investment expenditure is also made by all the agents in economic activities such as private firms, government through public sectors, households, etc. It is also found that there are broadly three components of capital formations, which include gross fixed capital formation, change or investment in inventories and acquisition and disposal of values.

Total investment expenditure, I = Private investment expenditure, I_p + Total government investment expenditure, I_g

Gross fixed capital formation is the investment expenditure on acquiring new assets such as plants, equipment, buildings, etc.

Considering both consumption and investment expenditure in an economy as domestic expenditure, we can get the total domestic expenditure.

Thus, total domestic expenditure = $C_t + I$

Disaggregating this,

Total domestic expenditure = $C + G + I_p + I_g$

This can be referred to as the *total domestic income*, Y_d.

or $$Y_d = C_t + I$$

3. ***Export spending:*** In the circular flow model, export spending X on goods and services is also considered for calculating the national expenditure. However, while calculating the national income, we include net export expenditure which discounts expenditure on imports, M from the expenditure on export, X.

Total national income, $Y = C_t + G + I + (X - M)$

The calculation of national expenditure can be presented through Figure 6.2.

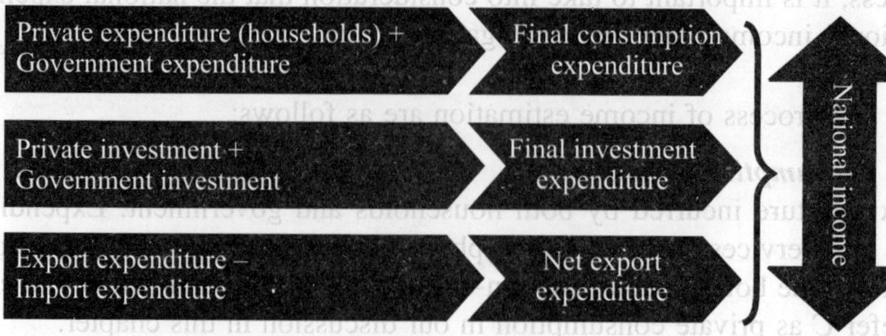

Figure 6.2 Calculation of national expenditure.

Production approach

The production approach is also known as *output approach* and *value-added approach.* To estimate the gross output in an economy, the approach identifies the process of production, which is related to both intermediate goods as well as final products. To avoid the issues related to double counting, the intermediate goods are not considered while estimating the national income used in the final production such as production of chips and usage of vegetables for the same. Thus, the approach estimates the total value of all final goods and services produced in an economy during a given time period. In this approach, the value added by firms and governments and other agents in producing goods and services are considered for national income accounting.

Income approach

Another approach to measure the national income is the estimation of total payments made to the factors of production of goods and services such as wage, interest, rent and profit. In an economy, factors of production are land, labour, capital and entrepreneurship. Today's economy is not only based on the production of goods but also has some activities such as services at domestic as well as international level. We also include remittances of these services when we calculate the total income of an economy. Thus, the total factor payments are the addition of wages, rents, interests and profits to entrepreneur. Therefore, the total income is the total factor payments.

Some of the measures undertaken while estimating the national income are as follows:

1. Final factor payments
2. Exclude subsidies from government or transfer receipts
3. Interest received on the net interest paid
4. Exclude remittances given to the foreign nationals
5. Exclude income from the sale of intermediate goods and services as well as income from more than one time sale of the final products
6. Exclude income from illegal activities such as illegal trade
7. Income from capital gains or addition of values in the asset owing to increase in its prices

With the above concepts, in India, measures of national income accounting broadly include the following:

1. ***Gross domestic product (GDP):*** GDP is the total value of all final goods and services produced in an economy in a year. GDP is estimated at both current and constant market prices.
2. ***Net domestic product (NDP):*** NDP is the total income generated within the country minus depreciation.
3. ***Gross national product (GNP):*** GNP is the value of total final product produced within an economy plus the income generated by its citizens outside its geographical boundary. For instance, in case of India, this would mean GDP plus remittances by Indians in abroad minus remittances by foreigners in India.
4. ***Net national product (NNP):*** NNP is a measure of GNP minus depreciation allowances of the existing capital.

6.2.2 National Income and the Economic Environment

Economic environment is always judged through indicators. Based on the performance of various sectors in India, performance of the economy is envisaged and the environment for economic activities is considered as good and bad. Growth in indicators such as GDP indicates the growth in overall economic activities such as production of goods and services, investments and exports of goods and services.

According to the performance of the economy and policies to catalyse the overall economic growth, the investors at both domestic and international level make their investment decisions. It also indicates the growing business opportunities, as the growth in income indicates the growing quantum of the economy.

At international level, the indicators of national income like GDP and GNP further facilitate international comparison and the analysts also highlight how economies are doing in terms of their economic activities. Growing income also delineates the increasing social standards of a country and its population. For better understanding of national income and its linkages with the business environment, let us take Indian economy as an example.

In September 2013, Economic Advisory Council (EAC) to the Prime Minister of India presented the economic outlook of India during 2013–2014 financial year. The report analysed the previous economic performance of India, which clearly indicates that the economic performance of the country over the last two years has not been upto the satisfactory level. The growth of the economy was almost touching the double digit figure earlier, which went down during the financial crisis of 2007–2008. The GDP grew at 8.6% in 2009–2010 and 9.3% in 2010–2011 after the economic crisis.

However, during the subsequent years, the economic growth unprecedentedly declined to 6.2% and 5.0%. Under this background, the report from EAC highlighted various factors responsible for the weaker economic performance in terms of GDP growth. These factors are mainly weak business confidence and disappointing corporate performance—simply, the overall business performance.

A growing GDP would attract a better faith in business, which further results in strengthening the overall economy. The report expected that the performance of the economy would be better in the forthcoming quarters of the economy. The overall projected economic growth was estimated to be 5.3% during 2013–2014 (see Table 6.1).

Table 6.1 GDP Growth—Actual and Projected (At constant 2004–2005 prices)

S. No.	*Annual Rates*	*2005–06*	*Average of 2005–06 in 2003–09*	*2009–10*	*2010–11*	*2011–12*	*2012–13*	*2013–14*
					P	*Quick Estimates*	*Revised Advance Estimates*	*Projected*
1	Agriculture and allied activities	5.1	3.8	0.8	–7.9	–3.6	–1.9	4.8
2	Mining and quarrying	1.3	3.7	5.9	4.9	–0.6	–0.6	0.1
3	Manufacturing	10.1	9.8	11.3	9.7	2.7	1.0	1.5
4	Electricity, gas and water supply	7.1	7.3	6.2	5.2	6.5	4.2	5.2
5	Construction	12.8	9.8	6.7	10.2	5.6	4.3	5.0
6	Trade, hotels, transport, storage and communication	12.0	10.5	10.4	12.3	7.0	6.4	5.1
7	Finance, insurance, real estate and business services	12.6	12.6	9.7	10.1	11.7	8.6	8.4
8	Community and personal services	7.1	7.3	11.7	4.3	6.0	6.8	7.3
9	Gross domestic product (factor cost)	9.5	8.8	8.6	9.3	6.2	5.0	5.3
10	Industry (2+3+4+5)	9.7	3.8	9.2	9.2	3.5	2.1	2.7
11	Services (6+7+8)	10.9	9.0	10.5	9.8	8.2	7.1	6.6
12	Non-agriculture (9–1)	10.5	10.3	10.1	9.6	6.6	5.5	5.4
13	GDP (factor cost) per capita	7.8	9.9	7.1	7.8	4.8	3.7	4.0
14	GDP at factor cost—2004–2005 prices in rupees lakh, crore (or trillion)	32.5	37.2	45.2	49.4	52.4	55.1	58.0
15	GDP market and current prices, in rupees lakh, crore (or trillion)	36.9	46.5	64.8	78.0	89.7	100.2	112.2
16	GDP at market and current prices in US$ billion	834.0	1,064.0	1,370.0	1,715.0	1,865.0	1,841.0	1,826.0
17	Population in million	1,106.0	1,130.0	1,170.0	1,186.0	1,202.0	1,217.0	1,232.0
18	GDP at market prices per capita at current prices	33,394.0	41,070.0	55,366.0	65,728.0	74,667.0	82,339.0	91,083.0
19	GDP at market prices per capita in US$	754.0	940.0	1,171.0	1,446.0	1,551.0	1,513.0	1,482.0

Source: Economic Advisory Council, Government of India.
Key Economic Indicators latest from Economic Advisor Report.

Recent economic performance

Indicators of national income along with their relation with economic environment are better understood with the current state of the economy. As per the Monetary Policy Review of Reserve Bank of India, the Indian economy is recovering steadily. The bank has assessed the macroeconomic environment in India and accordingly defined the monetary policy for the next quarter in April 2016. The policy review for the first quarter (Q1) of 2016 states that *gross value added* (*GVA*) in agriculture and allied activities moderated in second half of 2015–2016, pulled down by the contraction in the third quarter (Q3) due to the year-on-year decline in agricultural production. Whereas, during the same period, value added in industry has increased at high rate led by increase in value added in manufacturing sector. Services sector activity expanded steadily in 2014–2015, with trade, hotels, transport, communication and public administration, defence and related services turning out to be the main drivers.

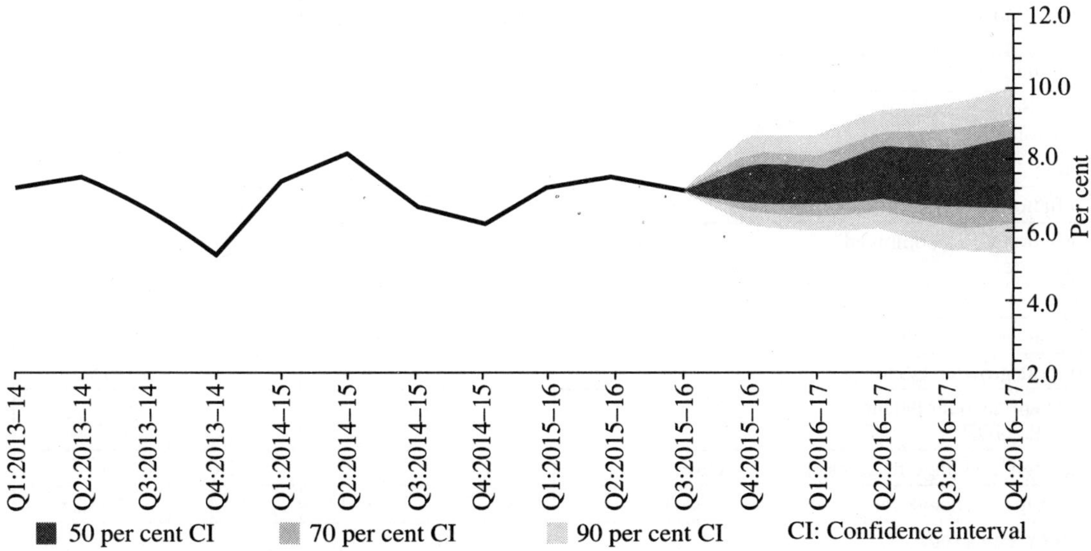

Figure 6.3 Quarterly projection of growth in GVA at basic prices (year-on-year).
Source: RBI, Monetary Policy Review, April 2016.

Figure 6.3 indicates the recovery path of Indian economy since the fourth quarter (Q4) of 2013–2014. The growth in gross value added is also expected to be more than 7% in the coming years. The prospects of good economic progress is reflecting. As per the Economic Survey of India, the state of the economy is rosy despite the fact that the global economy is in turmoil. Indian economy has registered a robust growth of 7.2% in 2014–2015 and 7.6% in 2015–2016. This led to the fact that India is now one of the fastest growing economies in the world. This is also dramatically improving perception regarding economic environment in India at global level. The key indicators of national income account suggest the same trend as outlined in Table 6.2.

Table 6.2 Key Indicators

Data Categories	*Unit*	*2012–2013*	*2013–2014*	*2014–2015*	*2015–2016*
GDP and related indicators					
GDP (2011–2012 prices)	₹ in crore	92,26,879*	98,39,434*	1,05,52,151	1,33,50,962**
Growth rate	%	5.6	6.6	7.2	7.6
GVA at basic prices (2011–2012 prices)	₹ in crore	85,46,552*	90,84,369*	97,27,490*	1,04,37,579**
Growth rate	%	5.4	6.3	7.1	7.3
Savings rate	Percentage of GDP	33.8	33.0	33.0	NA
Capital formation rate	Percentage of GDP	38.6	34.7	34.2	NA
Per capita net national income (At current market prices)	₹	71,050	79,412	86,879	93,231
Production					
Foodgrains	Million tonnes	257.1	265.0	252.0	253.2*
Index of industrial production (Growth)	%	1.1	–0.1	2.8	3.1*
Electricity generation (Growth)	%	4.0	6.0	8.4	4.4*
Prices					
Inflation (WPI) (average)	%	7.4	6.0	2.0	–2.8
Inflation CPI (Combined) (average)	%	10.2	9.5	5.9	4.9*
External sector					
Export growth (US $)	%	–1.8	4.7	–1.3	–17.6*
Import growth (US $)	%	0.3	–8.3	–0.5	–15.5*
Current account balance (CAB) GDP	%	–4.8	–1.7	–1.3	–1.4*
Foreign exchange reserves	US $ billion	292.0	304.2	341.6	349.6*
Average exchange rate	₹/US $	54.40	60.51	61.14	65.03*
Money and credit					
Broad money (M3) (annual)	Percentage of change	13.6	13.4	10.8	11.0*
Scheduled commercial bank credit	Percentage of change	14.1	13.9	9.0	11.3*
Fiscal indicators (centre)					
Gross fiscal deficit	Percentage of GDP	4.9	4.5	4.0	3.9*
Revenue deficit	Percentage of GDP	3.7	3.2	2.9	2.8*
Primary deficit	Percentage of GDP	1.8	1.1	0.8	0.7*

Notes

NA:	Not available	IR:	First revised estimates
2R:	Second revised estimates	AE:	Advance estimates
a:	Second advance estimates	b:	Base (2004–2005–100)
c:	As at end-January 2016	d:	April–December 2015–2016
e:	April–January 2015–2016	f:	April–September 2015–2016
g:	Year-on-year growth rate as on 8 January 2016	h:	Budget estimates
i:	Provisional actuals		

Source: Economic Survey of India, 2016.

6.2.3 National Income Accounting in India

At the international level, measurement of national income is based on the United Nations System of National Accounts (see Box 6.1). The system provides an integrated approach for national income accounting, which also synchronises the estimates across countries. The system covers the produced output, income generated by production, transfer payments, government expenditure, household consumption, balance sheets for assets and liabilities, balance of payments both at current and capital accounts, government expenditure, and so on.

As per the handbook of System of National Accounts (2008), the system is consistent in terms of its concepts as well as its accounting structure. The system is designed to undertake exercises such as economic analysis and understanding the process of the overall economic growth and development. The framework of the system provides a comprehensive account of all designated economic activities and for all the agents participating in the performance of these activities. The system uses identical values to establish scientific causal relations between the agents. Some of the important features of the system are given in Box 6.1.

Box 6.1 Illustration Based on United Nations System of National Accounts

Account	*Balancing Item*	*Main Aggregates*
Current accounts		
Production account		
Production account	Value added	Domestic product
Distribution of income accounts		
Primary distribution of income accounts		
Generation of income account	Operating surplus/mixed income	
Allocation of primary income account	Balance of primary income	National income (GNI, NNI)
Entrepreneurial income account	Entrepreneurial income	
Allocation of other primary income account	Balance of primary income	
Secondary distribution of income account	Disposable income	National disposable income
Redistribution of income in kind account	Adjusted disposable income	
Use of Income accounts		
Use of disposable income account	Saving	
Use of adjusted disposable income account	Saving	National saving
Accumulation account		
Capital account	Net borrowing (+√ net lending (–)	
Financial account	Net borrowing (+√ net lending (–)	
Other changes in assets account		
Other changes in the volume of assets account		
Revaluation account		
Balance sheets		
Opening balance sheet	Net worth	National wealth
Changes in assets and liabilities	Changes in net worth	
Closing balance sheet	Net worth	National wealth
Contributions to change in net worth		
Capital account	Change in net worth due to saving and capital transfers	
Other changes in the volume of assets account	Changes in net worth due to other changes in the volume of assets	
Revaluation account	Changes in the value of net worth due to nominal holding gains and losses	

Source: UNSN, 2008.

In India, the national income accounting system follows the basic guidelines of measuring the national income. The national accounting system is considered to be an important approach to estimate the national income. In order to account for the characteristics of the federal system, national accounting system follows a methodology, which is compatible for estimating the state level gross income. Central Statistical Organisation (CSO) is responsible for estimating the national income. It has some important features, which include revision of the base year from time to time as per the recommendation of the committee on national income accounting.

At present, the base year is revised from 2004–2005 to 2011–2012. CSO also publishes the basic document, describing methodologies for the national income accounting. The methodology to calculate the national income in terms of GDP is to divide the whole economy into broad economic sectors. These sectors include agriculture, forestry and logging, fishing, mining and quarrying, registered manufacturing, services, transport and trade, etc.

Recognising the importance of national income accounting, the Government of India constituted a committee under the chairmanship of P.C. Mahalanobis in 1949. The High Powered Expert Committee established the guiding principles for estimating the national income in India. Consequently, for the first time, the national income was estimated and the guiding principles were established by the Committee reports in 1951 and 1952.

Gross value added approach of Government of India

Based on the methodology, CSO estimated the national income indicators such as GDP and GNP at the constant prices of the year 1948–1949. These estimates were published in 1956 along with the estimation at current prices. Later, there has been gradual improvement in the methodologies as well as changes in the base years. Moreover, per capita income is also a measurement of the national income. This is also known as *income per person in a country.* This is used to measure the prosperity in an economy. As per the World Bank, GDP per capita is GDP divided by mid-year population.

6.2.4 National Income Accounting: Gross Value Added Approach of Government of India

As discussed above, System of National Accounts, 2008 (or SNA 2008) is internationally recognised and consistent system of national income accounting. The recommendations by SNA 2008 include the following:

1. Valuation of various gross value added, national value added and related aggregates at basic prices and estimation of GDP at market prices instead of factor cost (basic prices are prices before taxes on products).
2. Estimates of the institutional sectors—non-financial and financial corporations, general government and households are shown separately, in view of their intrinsic difference in their economic objectives, functions and behaviour.
3. Distinction between general government and public corporations has been made and units have been allocated to institutional sectors so that general government and other public units can be identified separately.

4. Unincorporated enterprises belonging to households, which have complete sets of accounts, tend to behave in the same way as corporations. Therefore, as recommended by SNA 2008, such enterprises have been treated as quasi-corporations. Some examples of quasi-corporations in the Indian context are proprietorship and partnership enterprises, maintaining accounts.
5. The head office has been allocated to the non-financial corporations sector unless all or most of its subsidiaries are financial corporations, in which case it is treated as a financial auxiliary in the financial corporations sector. In the 2004–2005 series, the recommendation had been adopted for service sector, wherein GVA estimates were compiled from enterprises in this sector. In the new series, this approach has been adopted for the mining and organised manufacturing sectors also.
6. Sub-sectoring of non-profit institutions (NPIs) in the corporate and government sectors has been done in respect of autonomous bodies and Section 25 companies.
7. Expenditure on research and development (R&D) has been capitalised in Government, public corporations and private corporations, and hence, has become part of capital formation.
8. Output of financial intermediation services indirectly measured (FISIM) has been calculated using a reference rate for the financial sector, except in the case of central bank (the Reserve Bank of India).
9. Output of the Reserve Bank of India (RBI) is measured at cost.
10. Non-financial assets in the earlier series were classified as 'construction' and 'machinery'. In the new series, as recommended by SNA 2008, non-financial assets have been classified as 'dwellings, other buildings and structures', 'machinery and equipment', 'cultivated biological resources' and 'intellectual property products'.
11. Consumption of fixed capital has been measured at the average prices of the period with respect to a constant-quality price index of the asset concerned.
12. Harmonisation between SNA and BPM (Balance of Payments and International Investment Position Manual) in respect of the external sector transactions has been achieved since the RBI has adopted BPM6 in its compilation.

The above recommendations are considered and a new series along with a new methodology for national income accounting is developed. CSO, with the above areas of interventions, introduced a new base year 2011–2012, in place of the previous series with base year 2004–2005 and released new series estimates of national income, consumption expenditure, saving and capital formation for the years 2011–2012 to 2013–2014.

One of the important reasons for changing the base year and methodology for national accounts is taking into account the structural changes influencing the economy. These structural changes are taking place in the economy, which has substantial impact on macreconomic aggregates. Macroeconomic aggregates, therefore, require to be updated periodically to take into account the current picture. In this new method, the estimates at the prevailing prices of the current year are also termed as *at current prices* as being done in all other methodologies for estimating macroeconomic indicators. However, the base year prices which are also 'constant prices' are changed in the new estimates. The new base year is 2011–2012, which is revised from the earlier base year 2004–2005. The revised indicators are given in Table 6.3.

Table 6.3 Advance Estimates of National Income and Expenditures of GDP, 2015–2016 at Constant Price (2011–2012) (₹ in crore)

Items	*2011–12 [2nd RE (NS)]*	*2012–13 [2nd RE (NS)]*	*2013–14 [2nd RE (NS)]*	*2014–15 (1st RE)*	*2015–16 (AE)*	*Percentage change over previous year*			
						2012–13	*2013–14*	*2014–15*	*2015–16*
Domestic product									
GVA at basic prices	81,06,656	85,46,552	90,84,369	97,27,490	1,04,37,579	5.4	6.3	7.1	7.3
Taxes on products including import duties	8,90,060	9,74,172	10,25,799	11,08,339	11,93,486	9.5	5.3	8.0	7.7
Less subsidies on products	2,60,677	2,93,845	2,70,734	2,83,679	2,80,102	12.7	–7.9	4.8	–1.3
GDP (1+2–3)	87,36,039	92,26,879	98,39,434	1,05,52,151	1,13,50,962	5.6	6.6	7.2	7.6
NDP	78,18,808	82,17,675	87,37,681	93,59,476	1,00,71,224	5.1	6.3	7.1	7.6
Final expenditures									
PFCE (Private Final Consumption Expenditure)	49,10,447	51,70,252	55,20,068	58,64,283	63,10,565	5.3	6.8	6.2	7.6
GFCE (Government Final Consumption Expenditure)	9,68,375	9,73,498	9,77,521	11,02,607	11,38,558	0.5	0.4	12.8	3.3
CIS (Change in Stocks)	29,97,619	31,43,531	32,50,539	34,05,251	35,87,515	4.9	3.4	4.9	5.3
Valuables	2,53,033	2,59,719	1,50,123	1,73,275	1,96,245	–3.8	–18.6	20.3	5.5
Exports of goods and services	21,43,931	22,88,581	24,66,632	25,08,402	23,49,643	6.0	–8.2	0.8	–6.3
Discrepancies	–28,667	70,586	–44,117	–35,284	58,745	–	–	–	–
GDP	87,36,339	92,26,879	98,39,434	1,05,52,151	1,13,50,962	5.6	6.6	7.2	7.6
Rates to GDP									
PFCE	56.2	56.0	56.1	55.6	55.6	–	–	–	–
GFCE	11.1	10.6	9.9	10.4	10.0	–	–	–	–
GFCF	34.3	34.1	33.0	32.3	31.6	–	–	–	–
CIS	2.4	2.2	1.6	1.8	1.8	–	–	–	–
Valuables	2.9	2.8	1.5	1.6	1.7	–	–	–	–
Exports of goods and services	24.5	24.8	25.1	23.8	20.7	–	–	–	–
Less imports of goods and services	31.1	31.2	26.9	25.2	22.0	–	–	–	–
Discrepancies	–0.3	0.8	–0.4	–0.3	0.5	–	–	–	–
GDP (Gross Domestic Product)	100.0	100.0	100.0	100.0	100.0	–	–	–	–
GNI (Gross National Income)	86,59,215	91,18,209	97,17,062	1,04,27,701	1,12,14,077	5.3	6.6	7.3	7.5
NNI (Net National Income)	77,42,074	81,09,505	86,15,309	92,35,026	99,34,339	4.7	6.2	7.2	7.6
Per capita income product and final consumption									
Production* (in million)	1,220	1,235	1,251	1,267	1,283	1.2	1.3	1.3	1.3
Per capita GDP	71,607	74,712	78,653	83,285	88,472	4.3	5.3	5.9	6.2
Per capital GNI	70,977	73,836	77,674	82,302	87,405	4.0	5.2	6.0	6.2
Per capita NNI	63,460	65,664	68,867	72,889	77,431	3.5	4.9	5.8	6.2
Per capita PFCE	40,250	41,864	44,125	46,285	49,186	4.0	5.4	4.9	6.3

Source: *Relates to mid-financial year. CSO, Government of India.

6.3 CONSUMPTION AND INVESTMENT

Consumption and investment are the two important economic activities, which broadly highlight the strength of an economy and the business environment therein. The business potential mainly depends on the market strength. The growing market has both consumption and investment opportunities. The increasing disposable income of individuals depicts the ability to increase their consumption. An increase in the consumption also reflects a scenario of increase in demand for goods and services. In other words, increase in the demand for goods and services would need supply of the same. Thus, the supply side of economy creates opportunities for the investments. It is in this context, the indicators, which that determine the consumption and investment level in an economy, become important. These two aspects have been discussed separately.

6.3.1 Consumption

Consumption in economics refers to the use of goods and services by households in an economy. It is important to note that the consumption differs from the consumption expenditure due to the consumption expenditure on intermediate goods and services. In this context, the consumption only includes the expenditure on consumption of final goods and services. In an economy, at macroeconomic level, determination of aggregate consumption is important for two important reasons, *viz.* to estimate the gross savings, and determine the business cycles.

In a simple Keynesian economics, aggregate consumption is the function of disposable income. In other words, disposable income level determines the consumption level.

This can be better understood by depicting a consumption function as follows:

$$C = a_0 + bY^d$$

where,

C = Total consumption
a_0 = Autonomous consumption
b = Slope of disposable income or marginal propensity to consume
Y^d = Disposable income (Total income – Taxes)

The calculation of the total consumption based on the above function is depicted in the Table 6.4.

Table 6.4 Calculation of Total Consumption

C	a_0	b	Y^d	*Aggregate Saving (S)*	*Marginal Propensity to Save (MPS)*
100	100		0	–100	–
200	100	0.5	200	0	0.5
300	100	0.5	400	100	0.5
350	100	0.5	500	150	0.5
400	100	0.5	600	200	0.5
450	100	0.5	700	250	0.5
500	100	0.5	800	300	0.5
550	100	0.5	900	350	0.5
600	100	0.5	1000	400	0.5

As per the theory of consumption function, the total consumption is directly related to the disposable income. This can further be understood by depicting a graph. A hypothetical graphical representation shows the linear consumption function (see Figure 6.4). Let us understand the figure through an example. When a household spends a minimum amount of U$100 at the time when it does not earn, it simply means the household is in debt. As the generation of disposable income takes place and increases over the period of time, the total consumption increases. The increase in consumption depends on the marginal propensity to consume (MPC). MPC defines that how much share of the increase in disposable income goes into for consumption.

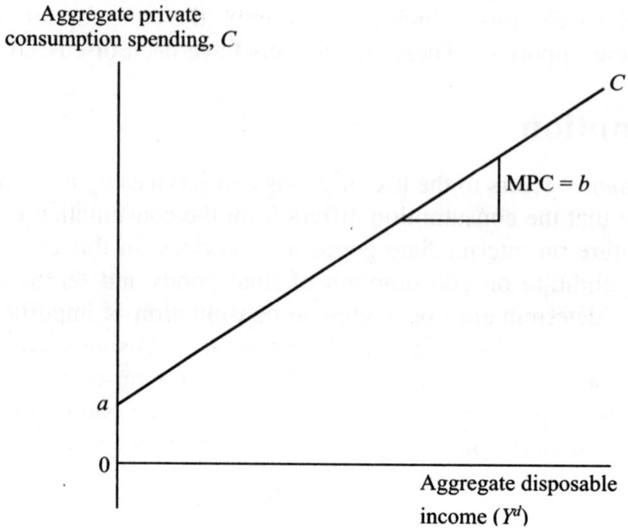

Figure 6.4 A linear consumption function.

Mathematically, it is expressed as follows:

MPC = $\Delta C/\Delta Y^d$ (ratio of the change in consumption due to change in income)

In the above example, 50% of the income is considered as MPC. Moreover, there is a concept of autonomous investment also. The term *autonomous* refers to the value of consumption, which is determined by the forces outside the income level.

The disposable income is considered as the determinant of consumption level. However, if there is no taxation and compulsory payments by government on the income, then the total income would determine the consumption level. Such a scenario is represented by Eq. (1) as follows:

$$C = a + bY \quad (1)$$

where,

Y = National income

a = Autonomous consumption

b = MPC

Illustration: Value for autonomous consumption spending, a is set at $10 million and that for marginal propensity to consume, c is set at 0.5. For every extra US$100 of aggregate disposable income (or national income), a household spends \$50. This can be written in terms of Eq. (2).

$$C = \$10 \text{ million} + 0.5Y^d \tag{2}$$

In a scenario of absence of taxation, this can be written as Eq. (3).

$$C = \$10 \text{ million} + 0.5Y \tag{3}$$

The marginal propensity to consume has a value, which is positive, stable and less than unity.

From the Eq. (2), we can also derive the average propensity to consume, which can be expressed by Eq. (4).

$$\text{Average propensity to consume} = C/Y^d \tag{4}$$

Savings

Savings also depend on the disposable income. If income increases, the MPC determines the level of consumption. If a consumer or household wants to spend 50% of its income, the savings would be another 50% of the income. In other words, we can derive saving functions from the consumption function, as expressed in Eq. (5) below:

$$S = -a_0 + (1 - b)Y^d \tag{5}$$

where,

S = Total savings

a_0 = Autonomous consumption

b = Slope of disposable income or marginal propensity to consume

Y^d = Disposable income (Total income – Taxes)

Marginal propensity to save (MPS) = 1 – MPC

Table 6.4 also highlights the calculation of the total savings as well as marginal propensity to save (MPS). Using a numerical example, the savings function can also be derived. Graphically, this is shown in Figure 6.5.

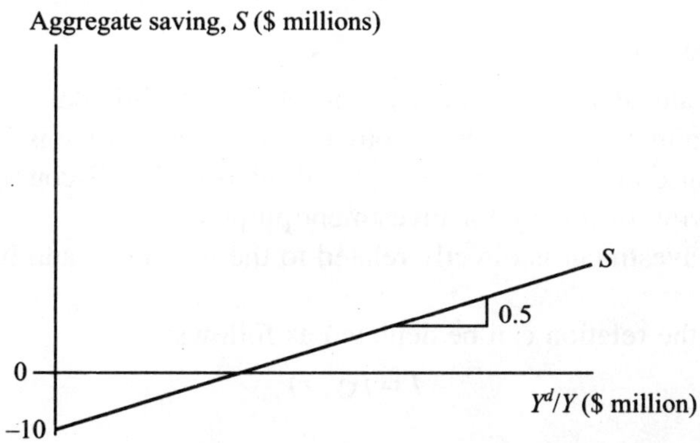

Figure 6.5 Savings function: Graphical representation.

6.3.2 Investment

Investment is an important economic factor and indicator. It not only highlights the bases of generation of income but also acts as a suggestive of the business environment. The indicators associated with the investment climate also reflect upon the overall economic policy of the country. We need to understand the concept of investment and indictors that are associated with it.

The total income accounts for the investment expenditure as well. We have already presented investment as I in the formula for national income, *viz.*

$$\text{National income} = C + I + G + (X - M)$$

This indicates that investment, I is the expenditure made apart from the expenditure of households and governments. There are two major types of investments, i.e., fixed investment and variable investment (stock). These are also of the nature of planned and unplanned. However, traditionally, the types of investment are considered to be of various categories, both in terms of stock and flows.

Investment may be of the following nature:

1. ***Autonomous investment:*** The investment, which is not influenced by the income is considered as autonomous investment.
2. ***Induced investment:*** This type of investment is influenced by the income level. Thus, the induced investment changes with the change in income level.
3. ***Real investment:*** Keynes always referred to the investment as real investment. Real investment is the investment made in the new area such as purchasing new plants, equipment, etc.
4. ***Gross investment:*** It represents the total investment made on value creation of the existing asset as well as of new assets.
5. ***Net investment:*** Net investment is the total investment in an economy minus capital consumption in maintaining the asset for a given time period (depreciation).

Investment level in an economy also depends on the following two main factors:

1. Income, y
2. Rate of interest, r

Notably, if the rate of interest is high, households would like to save their income in financial system to earn more returns. On the other hand, if the income is high, it is expected that the investment would also be high. A higher level of interest also discourages the investment, as it causes costly borrowing of money for investment purposes.

In other words, investment is directly related to the income, y and inversely related to the rate of interest, r.

Mathematically, the relation can be depicted as follows:

$$I = f(y, r)$$

where,

I = Investment
y = Income
r = Rate of interest

$$I = i + a_0 y - a_1 r$$

where,

i = autonomous investment

a_0 and a_1 are coefficients

Thus, it is noteworthy that for business purposes, rate of interest level is an important determinant, as it may discourage and encourage investments. Figure 6.6 graphically represents the investment function.

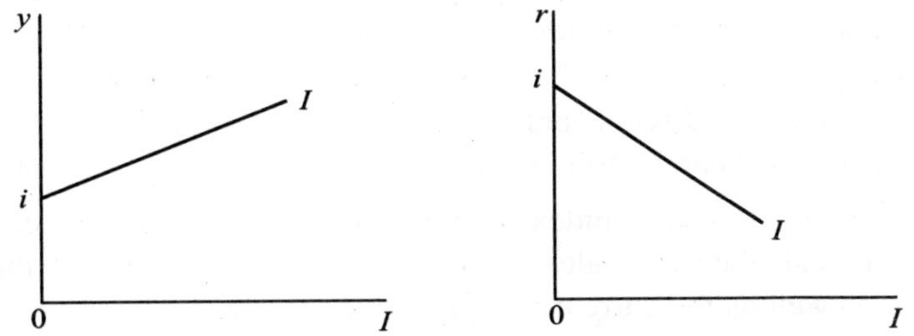

Figure 6.6 Investment function: Graphical representation.

6.4 INFLATION

Generally, *inflation* is defined as the increase in prices of commodities, which resultantly decreases the purchasing power of money. Thus, it occurs when there is a rise in the prices in general in an economy. Inflation is generally considered as a macroeconomic indicator, which can also destabilise the economic progress. It directly affects the household expenditure and well-being of the people.

An increase in the general prices of commodities can also affect the investment scenario, given the rise in prices of raw materials such as construction materials. In this context, governments give a particular attention towards controlling the inflation.

In India, inflation is regulated through both fiscal and monetary measures. *Fiscal measures* include reducing deficit financing by contracting expenditure. *Monetary measures* include reducing money supply through various indicators such as rate of interest, CRR and liquidity reserves.

The start of financial year 2013–2014 saw high inflation rates in India. Since 2011–2012, inflation for both primary goods and manufactured goods had moved almost together. High incidence of increasing oil prices on the movement of goods led to an increase in the prices of primary commodities.

In recent times, the price of primary items such as vegetables and fuel increased by multiple times. For instance, prices of onion increased by 27.8% in October 2013 over the prices in October 2012. The overall price of vegetables increased by 78.4% during this period. In addition, the wholesale price index increased to an eight-month high and was estimated to be 7% on year-on-year basis in October 2013. Such an increase in the inflation has resulted in monetary adjustments by the Reserve Bank of India (RBI).

In September 2013, RBI estimated that the retail inflation measured by the consumer price index (CPI) would continue to be higher. However, RBI hiked the lending rates by 0.25% to curb the inflationary pressure in the economy. The most important factor that caused high inflationary pressure was strengthening of US Dollar in comparison to Indian Rupee. This resulted in the increase in prices of oil imports thereby, increasing the price of commodities.

6.4.1 Measurement of Inflation

Generally, inflation is measured by the price index. The *price index* is a system through which we estimate the percentage change during a given time period. In some cases, rise in the prices are measured in terms of retail price index or consumer price index.

In India, inflation is measured by the wholesale price index and the consumer price index. To measure through indices of retail and consumer prices as well as wholesale prices, the following important methods can be followed:

1. ***Paasche index:*** Paasche index was developed by an eminent economist, Herman Paasche. To calculate the index, we consider the prices of both the current and the base year as well as the current year quantities. Thus,

$$\text{Paasche price index} = \left(\frac{\sum_{i=1}^{n} P_{it} \times Q_{it}}{\sum_{i=1}^{n} P_{i0} \times Q_{it}}\right) \times 100$$

where,

P_{it} = Current price
Q_{it} = Current quantity
P_{i0} = Constant price of the previous year

2. ***Laspeyres index:*** Laspeyres index is another important method to measure the price change over time. In this index, the base year quantities are used, rather than the base year prices (as in the case of Paasche index). This method can be expressed mathematically as follows:

$$\text{Laspeyres index} = \frac{\sum_{i=1}^{n} P_{it} \times Q_{i0}}{\sum_{i=1}^{n} P_{i0} \times Q_{i0}} \times 100$$

where,

P_{it} = Current price
P_{i0} = Base price
Q_{i0} = Base quantity

These two measures separately consider the base year quantity and the current year quantity to measure the price index. However, the two methods do not concurrently account for the base year quantity and the current year quantity to measure the price index. These two limitations are dealt with in the later indices like those developed by Marshall–Edgeworth and Fisher.

3. ***Marshall–Edgeworth index:*** It is the arithmetic mean of quantities and prices.

$$\text{Marshall–Edgeworth index} = \frac{\sum [P_{ct1} \times (Q_{ct0} + Q_{ct1})]}{\sum [P_{ct0} \times (Q_{ct0} + Q_{ct1})]}$$

where,

P_{ct1} = Prices in time 1, i.e., current year
P_{ct0} = Prices in the base year or previous year
Q_{ct1} = Quantity in time 1, i.e., current year
Q_{ct0} = Quantity for the base year

4. ***Fisher index:*** It is calculated as the geometric mean of both Laspeyres index and Paasche index.

$$\text{Fisher index} = \sqrt{L \times P}$$

where,

L = Laspeyres index
P = Paasche index

6.4.2 Types of Inflation

In today's economic environment, there are multiple factors affecting the prices of commodities. We have seen in the past, due to regional instability in West Asia and Gulf, the supply of crude oil was affected during 1990s. In the international market, crude oil was short of demand. Countries like India and China need more crude oil. In the case of excess demand and presence of short supply, the prices of crude oil dynamically rose. This resulted in the rise in the prices of commodities. On the other hand, there also exists an economic policy, which leads to price rise in an economy. Some of the policies are easing money supply in the economy and decreasing the interest rates.

Another important factor that affects inflation is the factor market. Rise in the cost of capital, wage rates to labourer, cost of technologies, and the cost of fixed capital lead to an increase in the cost of production. This also results in the rise in inflation.

This entails that there are two important types of inflation, which are described below:

1. ***Demand pull inflation:*** Demand pull inflation refers to the rise in prices of commodities owing to the presence of excess demand in the economy. It occurs when the aggregate demand in an economy outpace the aggregate supply. In the Keynesian economics, demand pull inflation occurs when the aggregate employment increases in the economy. As the aggregate demand increases, the aggregate demand shifts. This also has cyclical impacts, i.e., as the demand increases, firms also increase their employees to produce more in order to meet the increasing demand by capturing more market. But the immediate impact is an increase in the aggregate employment and output, leading to an increase in the aggregate demand. However, there exist capacity constraints for firms. This finally results in the increase in prices of commodities. This can be better understood through Figure 6.7.

According to Figure 6.7, the aggregate demand is AD_0, aggregate supply is AS_0 and the aggregate price level is r_0, with the aggregate output level Y_0. In case, there is an increase in the employment, it leads to an increase in the demand from AD_0 to AD_1. The movement of aggregate demand curve along the aggregate supply curve indicates an increase in the total output from

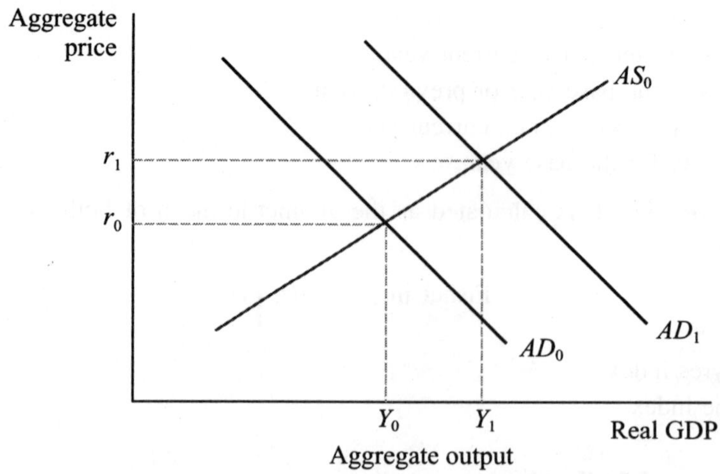

Figure 6.7 Demand pull inflation.

Y_0 to Y_1. This increase in the output is the result of more workers employed. However, owing to capacity constraints, the output produced is less than the increase in demand. This factor leads to an increase in the price level, creating inflationary pressures in the economy.

2. ***Cost push inflation:*** Cost push inflation occurs when the cost of production rises. This may occur due to an increase in the factor payments or due to some other reason. It is caused by an increase in the cost of factor of production, leading to an increase in the cost of production of the aggregate output. The condition for increase in the prices of commodities in this case is that there is no linkage between the cost of production and the factors affecting demand. The cost of production increases for a number of reasons such as increase in the cost of raw materials, increase in the wage rates, or there may be increase in the cost of supplying the products such as increase in the transport fuels. In this case, the supply of commodities and the aggregate demand also decrease. Accordingly, price rise can be seen in the economy.

This can be better understood through the graph, as depicted in Figure 6.8.

Figure 6.8 indicates that the aggregate demand in an economy moves along the curve *AD*. $SRAS_1$ is a short run aggregate supply curve, which shows that the economy has a supply of commodities along this curve. By intersecting *AD*, the aggregate supply curve forms the aggregate output level in the economy at Y_1. In case, if there is an increase in the cost of raw materials such as crude oil, the firms producing output related to petroleum, vehicles will start producing less owing to a decrease in the consumption level of oil by the households. The aggregate demand decreases from Y_1 to Y_2. This further led to a shift in the aggregate supply curve from $SRAS_1$ to $SRAS_2$, leading to an increase in the prices of commodities from P_1 to P_2. $SRAS_1$ and $SRAS_2$ intersect at LRAS (long term aggregate supply).

In addition to the above types of inflation, there are also some characteristics of inflation which form its basic nature. On the basis of the difference in magnitude as well as length of time or period, inflation can be classified into hyperinflation, stagflation, agflation and deflation.

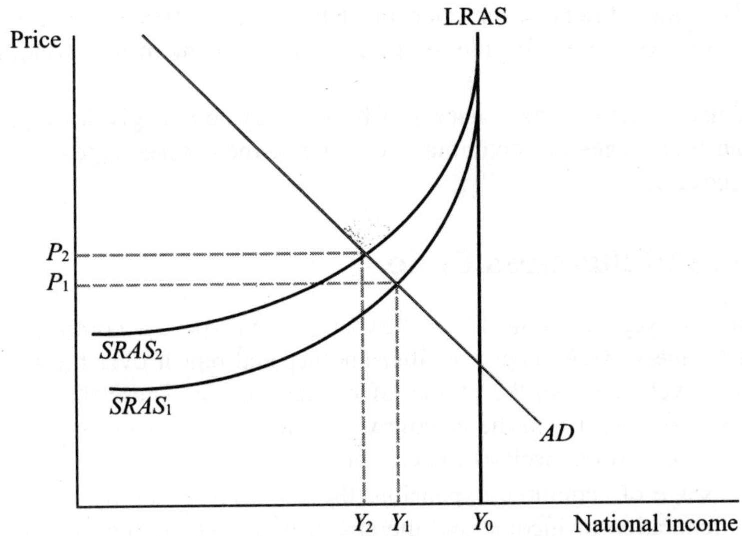

Figure 6.8 Cost push inflation.

1. ***Hyperinflation:*** When a country experiences unprecedentedly high inflation, which significantly affects the holdings of money of the people of the country, it is called *hyperinflation*.
2. ***Stagflation:*** *Stagflation* occurs when the inflation rate is high, growth rate is low and the unemployment is increasing. The situation of stagflation is dangerous for an economy, as the policies designed to curb inflation would further lead to decrease in the economic growth and employment.
3. ***Agflation:*** *Agflation* refers to the increase in the general price levels of agricultural goods.
4. ***Deflation:*** *Deflation* stands for the decrease in prices of commodities in terms of negative inflation rate. The negative inflation increases the real value of money or increases the purchasing power of the households' given income in a given time period. It also occurs when the money supply is reduced in an economy.

6.5 BUSINESS CYCLE

Business cycle is a concept, which shows the periodic movements of economic indicators. In fact, it also shows the periodic fluctuation of macroeconomic variables in an economy, which broadly represent the situation of economic activities. It also measures fluctuations in the macroeconomic variables such as real GDP, employment, trade, investment, etc.

The evolution of the concept of business cycle dates back to the publication of the 'Report to the Committee of the Association for the Relief of the Manufacturing Poor by Sismondi and Owen' in 1817, wherein they pointed out the issues of economic cycle and also identified the causes of the same. However, the concept of business cycle was not exclusively outlined as a systematic tool to understand the economic environment in an economy as well as in the world.

The broad and systematic explanation of business cycle was given by Joseph Shumpeter. He identified the four stages of economic cycle and termed these stages as expansion, crisis, recession and recovery.[5]

6.5.1 Stages of Business Cycle

In general, business cycle has four stages—expansion, prosperity, contraction and recession. These stages of business cycle occur one after another and repeat over the period of time. The stages of business cycle are also the phases of business cycle. These phases are characterised by the macroeconomic scenario in the economy, which broadly covers the employment, output growth, investment scenario as well as the consumer demand.

In a higher stage of economic expansion, the economy generally experiences high level of employment, generation of income and thereby, a higher economic growth, increasing level of investments as well as a higher consumer spending, leading to an increase in the consumer demands. This phase is called *boom* in the economy.

As the consumer spending decreases owing to the decreasing level of income or due to rise in the prices or increase in the unemployment, the consumer demand decreases, leading to decrease in the economic growth. A sharp decrease in these phenomenon is called *recession.*

If this recession continues for a long period, then it leads to many economic failures such as sharp decrease in the prices leading to deflation, rise in unemployment, no capital formation, and thus, the hope for economic expansion dooms for a long time period. This is also called *recession.*

Further, economic policies are designed to counter such problems. These policies may attract more investment, leading to the creation of employment, generation of income and gradually spending power. This stage is called *recovery stage*. The cycle is presented through the following illustration (shown in Figure 6.9) (see Figure 6.10 also):

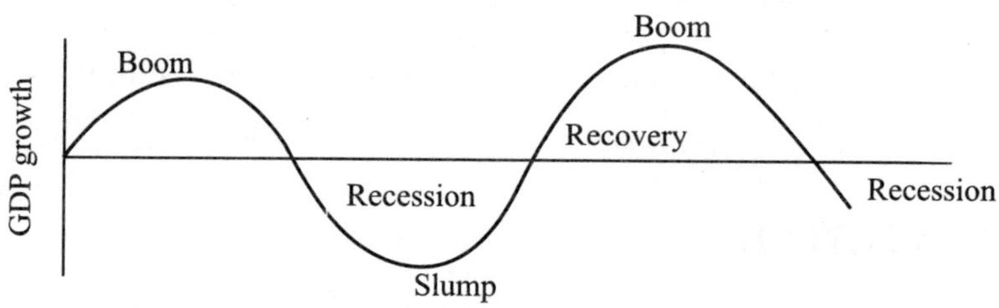

Figure 6.9 Stages of business cycle.

5. J.A. Schumpeter (1954), *History of Economic Analysis*, London: George Allen and Unwin. Also, see A.F. Burns and W.C. Mitchell, *Measuring Business Cycles*, New York, National Bureau of Economic Research, 1946.

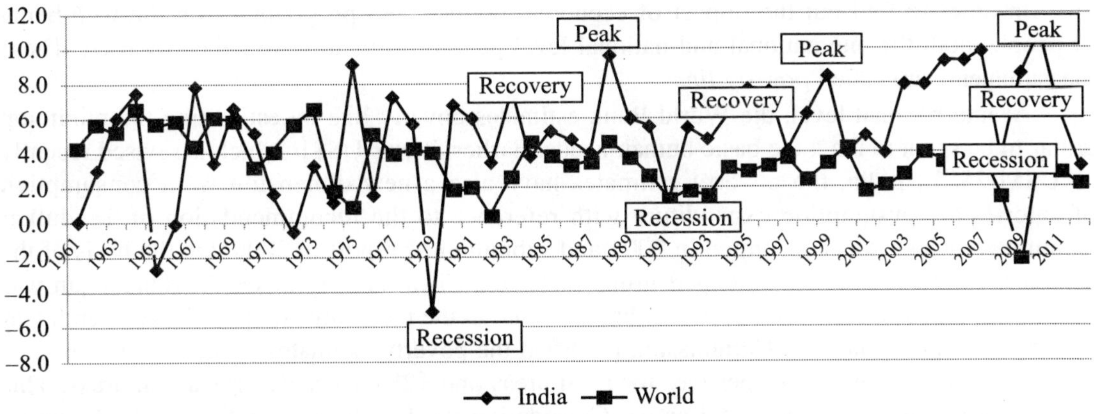

Figure 6.10 GDP growth of India and the world: Depicting stages of business cycle.
Source: World Development Indicator, World Bank.

6.6 SOCIO-ECONOMIC INDICATORS: POVERTY, INEQUALITY AND UNEMPLOYMENT

Social indicators are the indicators, which broadly define the success of economic policies and economic progress. There are several indicators at macrolevel, which generally present social and economic positioning of the people of a country. In view of understanding the performance of the people of an economy in general at various social indicators, human development indices are constructed at international level by United Nations. However, we are generally concentrated to three major social indicators, which have a lot to do with the economic and business environment of a country. These indicators are poverty, inequality and unemployment, which suggest the improvement of an economy at various aspects.

6.6.1 Poverty

Poverty is the scarcity of resources to supplement the rudimentary human needs. There are broadly two categories of poverty, *viz.* relative poverty and absolute poverty.

1. ***Relative poverty:*** It is defined in terms of availability of resources for individuals in relation to other individuals, who are relatively better off. Therefore, the measurement of relative poverty varies from society to society and from country to country.
2. ***Absolute poverty:*** It is the dearth of basic needs such as availability of food, shelter and other resources like water, sanitation facilities, health, education and so on.

The World Bank also defines poverty as follows:

Absolute poverty is anchored in some absolute standard of what households should be able to count on, in order to meet their basic needs. For monetary measures, these absolute poverty lines are often based on the estimates of the cost of basic food needs (i.e., the cost a nutritional basket considered minimal for the healthy survival of a typical family), to which a provision is added for non-food needs.

In order to find out the impact of economic policies and programmes on the well-being of people, both the international and national level poverty estimates are generally used. These measurements are called *poverty lines*.

At international level, the World Bank estimates poverty line by estimating the minimum dollar to be spent to meet the basic human needs. Earlier, it was US$1, which is revised recently as US$1.25. In India, the poverty estimates have also a new dimension from consumption of calories to consumption expenditure with reference to the recommendation of Tendulkar Committee, which was constituted in 2005 and submitted its report in 2009. On the basis of the estimates of the committee, an expert group under the Chairmanship of Dr. C. Rangarajan was constituted for the estimation of poverty line in India. In the meantime, on the basis of Tendulkar Committee report, Planning Commission modified the poverty estimates. Tendulkar Committee fixed the threshold at ₹22.42 per day for rural areas and ₹28.65 per day for urban areas. This estimate was criticised in political arena. Considering the low level of estimate, the Planning Commission revised this estimate as per the same methodology for the 68th round survey of household expenditure. As per the revised estimate, the line is increased to ₹27.2 per day for rural areas and ₹33.3 per day for urban areas.

As per the new estimates, it is said that there is a decrease in the poverty in India. The decline of poverty also entails that there is an increase in the per capita income, which is a result of increase in the overall economic growth. This depicts a close relationship between the economic environment and the poverty reduction.

The global poverty level has been a major problem faced by humanity. In order to eradicate extreme poverty and hunger, the United Nations in its millennium development goals put a target to halve the total population living under the poverty line in the world (i.e., living on less than $ 1.25 a day) by 2015. Though it is likely to be attained in some countries, in most of them, it is very unlikely to be achieved by 2015. Recently, the international standard for poverty is raised from $ 1.25 to $ 1.90 per day. The scenario across the region in 2010 is given in Table 6.5. The table still presents scenario at $ 1.25 per day.

Table 6.5 Share of Population Living below Poverty Line (%)

Region	**US $ 1 Per Day**			**US $ 1.25 Per Day**		
	1990	*1999*	*2011*	*1990*	*2000*	*2010*
Asia and the Pacific	15.4	12.3	9.1	77.2	14.3	12.8
Europe and Central Asia	3.6	1.3	1.0	1.9	0.5	0.66
Latin America and Caribbean	9.6	9.1	8.6	11.9	6.5	5.53
Middle East and North Africa	2.1	1.7	1.5	9.6	2.7	2.41
South Asia	35.0	33.4	30.8	61.1	36.0	31.03
Sub-Saharan Africa	46.1	42.6	41.1	51.5	47.5	48.47
World	–	–	–	52.2	22.4	20.63

Source: World Bank.

The latest estimate at regional level also highlights the progress of reduction in poverty in the world. However, the two regions like South Asia and Africa as well as some countries of Asia (except China) are not doing well (see Figure 6.11).

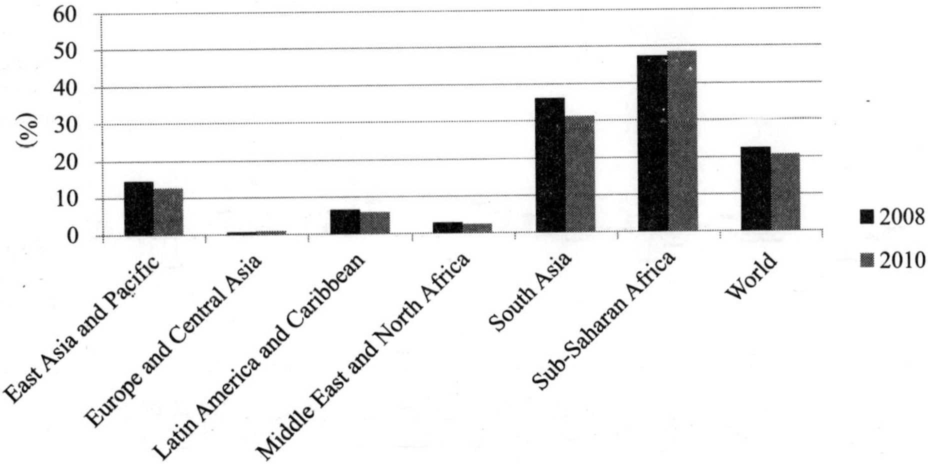

Figure 6.11 Poverty headcount ratio (%) in 2008 and 2010.
Source: World Bank.

Poverty and economic environment

Business environment has a lot to do with poverty, both directly and indirectly. A country having large population and suffering from absolute poverty means less business opportunities. It simply implies that per capita consumption of the country suffering from poverty is very low. In other words, demand for goods and services would be decreasing. It is important for a country to strengthen domestic consumption by eliminating the absolute poverty to attract more business and make business-friendly policies.

6.6.2 Inequality

Economic inequality is considered as an important socio-economic problem of global magnitude. It is referred to as a gap between rich and poor during a given time period. This may occur due to flawed distribution process of income. In setting up post-2015 global agenda, inequality is considered to be as one of the major problems.

In a report, the United Nations University—World Institute for Development Economics Research (UNU–WIDER) indicates that 1% of world's adult were holding 40% of the world's asset in the year 2000. It was also estimated that the US had higher income inequality than Europe. The widening gap between rich and poor across the world as well as across the region is evident.

Moreover, the market income inequality rose considerably. Percentage point change in the Gini coefficient of household market and disposable incomes between 2007 and 2010 are depicted in Figure 6.12.

Measurement of inequality

Economists and statisticians measure the economic inequality through various estimates. Most

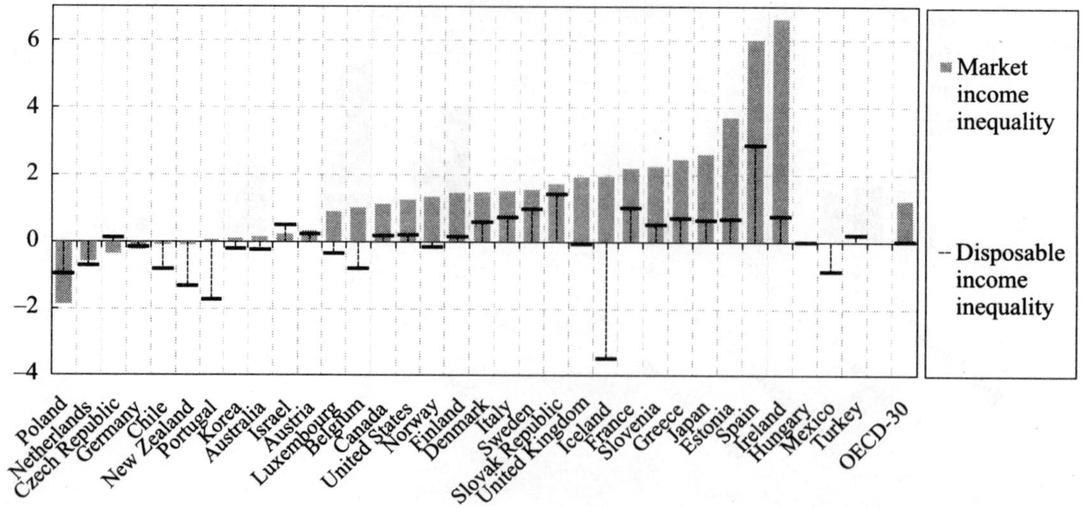

Figure 6.12 Percentage point change in the Gini coefficient of household market and disposable incomes.
Source: OECD.

prominent among the method is Lorenz curve. The other method of measurement is Gini coefficient. We will broadly discuss these two methods of measurement of income inequality. However, we will also mention some important methods such as Robin Hood index and quantile ratio.

1. ***Lorenz curve:*** Lorenz curve was developed by Lorenz in 1905 for representing the inequality through graphical presentation of cumulative distribution of wealth among population. The graph plots cumulative distribution of wealth as a percentage of income at vertical axis and cumulative distribution of population as percentage of total population at horizontal axis. As indicated in Figure 6.13, the straight line is 45° line, which shows the presence of absolute equality. Any deviation from this line downwards indicates the higher percentage of population living at lower income. This line is presented as *Lorenz curve*. As more bending occurs in the Lorenz curve, the income inequality increases.

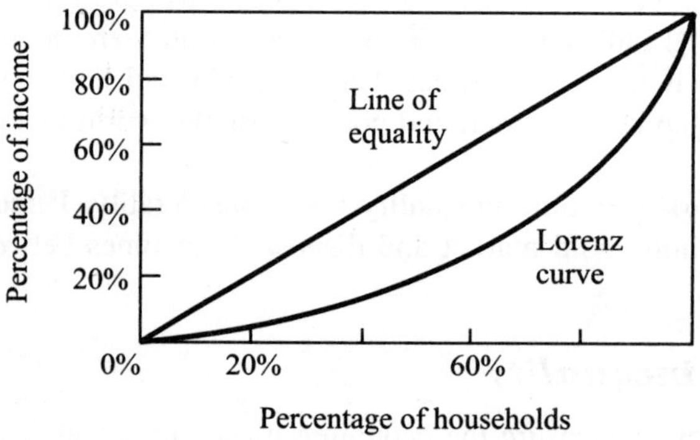

Figure 6.13 Lorenz curve.

2. ***Gini coefficient:*** The coefficient, developed by Carrodo Gini, measures inequality in the income distribution. This is a mathematical explanation of Lorenz curve. It is expressed in terms of ratio of the area divided by Lorenz curve into two regions, say *A* and *B*. Figure 6.14 presents this division clearly.

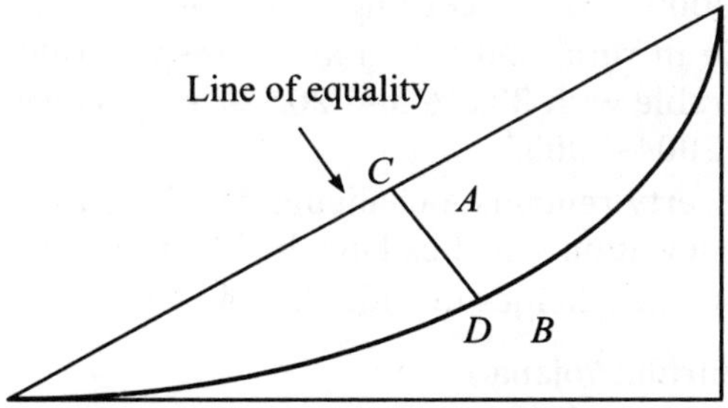

Figure 6.14 Gini coefficient.

As per the area defined in the graph shown in Figure 6.14, Gini coefficient is the ratio of area *A* to the areas *A* and *B*. Thus,

$$\text{Gini coefficient, } G = \frac{A}{A+B}$$

The ratio can be shown in terms of percentage or in terms of value ranging from 0 to 1. If the coefficient equals to 1 or 100%, it simply implies that there is no equality of income in the economy. As the ratio decreases, the equality in the income distribution increases.

In addition to these two measures of inequality, Robin Hood index, which is also known as *Schutz index*, measures the income inequality by estimating the value of longest possible distance between the line of equality and the Lorenz curve, say distance between *C* and *D*, as indicated in Figure 6.14. Similarly, quantile ratio is another method which measures the income inequality by ranking the population as per the income level from lower strata to higher.

6.6.3 Unemployment

Unemployment is another major macroeconomic indicator, which not only defines the strengths and weaknesses of an economy but also shows the demographic pattern of working people and their respective engagement. The term *unemployment* is defined as unavailability of works for the working population.

As per the International Labour Organisation (ILO), more than 197 million people are unemployed in the world, as of 2012. In other words, the estimate suggests that about 6% of the workforce in the world is unemployed. The unemployment rate (percentage) is calculated by dividing the total number of unemployed workers by the total workforce.

Mathematically,

$$\text{Unemployment rate} = \frac{\text{Total number of unemployed workers}}{\text{Total workforce}} \times 100$$

Closing Case: Poverty Alleviation—A Continuing Challenge

In 2013, Planning Commission revealed that poverty in India has declined to a record of 22% in 2011–2012. This trend is seen over the last decade and poverty levels have declined from 37.2% in 2004–2005 to 29.8% in 2009–2010. According to the release from the Planning Commission, 25.7% and 13.7% of people in rural and urban areas, respectively, were below the so-called poverty line. This is comparable with 33.8% and 20.9%, respectively, in 2009–2010, and 42% and 25.5%, respectively, in 2004–2005.[6]

However, the rural poverty remains a challenge for the government, despite the various development and poverty alleviation schemes launched by the government.

Some of such development schemes include the following:

1. Jawahar Gram Samridhi Yojana
2. National Old Age Pension Scheme
3. National Family Benefit Scheme
4. National Maternity Benefit Scheme
5. ANNAPURNA (providing food to senior citizens)
6. Integrated Rural Development Programme
7. Rural Housing: Indira Awaas Yojana
8. National Rural Employment Guarantee Act (NREGA)

Such schemes have been helpful in contributing to the alleviation of poverty to a large extent. In India, poverty is officially linked to a nutritional baseline, measured in calories (food-energy method).[7]

The constitution of various committees formed by the government since independence reveals that there has been concerted effort for the alleviation of poverty over the years. Some of the committees set up for the purpose include Planning Commission working group (1962), Alagh Committee (1979) and Lakdawala Committee (1993).

The Tendulkar Committee constituted in 2009 made four major recommendations—a shift away from calorie consumption-based poverty estimation, a uniform poverty line basket (PLB) across the rural and urban India, a change in the price adjustment procedure to correct the spatial and temporal issues with price adjustment, and incorporation of private expenditure on health and education while estimating poverty.[8]

Further, in 2012, the Planning Commission constituted another committee, called *Rangarajan Committee*, as an expert panel on poverty estimation.

Using the Tendulkar methodology, the Planning Commission has calculated the national poverty line at ₹816 per capita per month in villages and ₹1,000 per capita per month in cities.

6. India's poverty level falls to record 22%: Planning Commission, 23 July 2013, http://www.livemint.com/Politics/1QvbdGnGySHo7WRq1NBFNL/Poverty-rate-down-to-22-Plan-panel.html
7. India: Achievements and Challenges in Reducing Poverty, The World Bank, http://web.worldbank.org/WBSITE/EXTERNAL/TOPICS/EXTPOVERTY/EXTPA/0,contentMDK:20208959~menuPK:435735~pagePK:148956~piPK:216618~theSitePK:430367~isCURL:Y~isCURL:Y,00.html
8. Report of the Expert Group to Review the Methodology for Estimation of Poverty, 2009, Planning Commission; PRS.

The methodology employed by the Planning Commission to calculate the poverty has created a lot of debate among the political parties as well as among the civil society in the country.

Source: This case is written by the authors based on inputs from the following sources:

1. India's poverty level falls to record 22%: Planning Commission, 23 July 2013, http://www.livemint.com/Politics/1QvbdGnGySHo7WRq1NBFNL/Poverty-rate-down-to-22-Plan-panel.html
2. India: Achievements and Challenges in Reducing Poverty, The World Bank, http://web.worldbank.org/WBSITE/EXTERNAL/TOPICS/EXTPOVERTY/EXTPA/0,contentMDK:20208959~menuPK:435735~pagePK:148956~piPK:216618~theSitePK:430367~isCURL:Y~isCURL:Y,00.html
3. Report of the Expert Group to Review the Methodology for Estimation of Poverty, 2009, Planning Commission.
4. PRS, http://www.prsindia.org/theprsblog/?p=2848.

CASE QUESTIONS

1. Compare and contrast the recommendations of the Lakdawala Committee and Tendulkar Committee.
2. What were the methodologies applied by the two committees for calculating the poverty line?

REVIEW QUESTIONS

1. What do you understand by macroeconomic indicators?
2. What is national income? How is it measured?
3. Define GDP and GNP.
4. What is the role of Central Statistical Organisation (CSO)?
5. What is a linear consumption function?
6. Graphically represent the investment function.
7. What is inflation? How is it measured?
8. What are the various types of inflation?
9. Outline the stages of a business cycle.
10. What is Lorenz curve?

SUGGESTED READINGS

Basu, Kaushik, 2011, 'Understanding Inflation and Controlling It', Ministry of Finance, Government of India.

Samuelson, Paul and Nordhaus, William, 2009, *Macroeconomics*, McGraw-Hill Education, New Delhi.

Sarkar, S. and Pal, N., 2005, *Statistics: Concepts and Applications*, PHI Learning, Delhi.

Schumpeter, J.A., 1954, *History of Economic Analysis*, George Allen & Unwin, London.

Shapiro, Edward, 2003, *Macroeconomic Analysis*, Galgotia Publication, New Delhi.

System of National Accounts, 2008, The United Nations, 2009, New York, USA.

World Investment Report, 2014, UNCTAD, Geneva.

7

INDUSTRIAL POLICIES

Learning Outcomes

After reading this chapter, you will

- Be familiar with the evolution of the industrial policy frameworks of India since independence
- Understand the economic environment of the country within the framework of the industrial policy
- Appreciate the significance of the industrial policy framework for assessing the contemporary and future challenges and opportunities in industrial and manufacturing sector

Opening Case: The 'Made in India' tag?

The manufacturing sector plays a vital role in the economic growth of a country. For a fast developing country like India, the sector becomes even more significant in terms of ensuring export competitiveness as well as for job creation in the domestic market. The government has been taking several measures to give a boost to this sector. The industry, which constitutes approximately 19% of the labour force in India, contributes 17.6% to the GDP.

India's manufacturing sector has a tremendous potential and the industry players are now deeply engaged in research and development also. As a result of this, manufacturing activities recovered a 10-month high in January 2014 owing to a rise in the new orders. HSBC's purchasing managers' index (PMI) for manufacturing rose to 51.4 in January 2014—the highest reading on the survey-based index since March 2013. Earlier a McKinsey study estimated that India's manufacturing sector would grow six-fold by 2025, to US$1 trillion, and has a potential to create upto 90 million domestic jobs because of the rising domestic demand, coupled with the MNCs desire to diversify their production by including low-cost plants in the countries other than China. Also, Deloitte's global index for 38 nations ranked India as the fourth most competitive manufacturing nation in the year 2013. Indian economy saw a massive expansion during 2006–2011, attaining a five-year CAGR of 7.8%.

The manufacturing exports are also on a rise in the sectors like auto components, plastics and articles thereof, metals and minerals, engineering goods, pharmaceuticals, and fertilisers, among others. As per Indian Brand Equity Foundation (IBEF), the sector has been attracting foreign investments also. For instance, Saudi Arabia-based Sabic, a manufacturer of fertilisers, polymers and raw materials used in polyester fibres, has started a technology centre in Bangalore. The company has invested US$100 million and it intends to double the number of its employees in a few years. Also, Cadbury India has signed MoU with Andhra Pradesh government to develop a plant worth ₹1,000 crore in Chittoor, which is deemed to be operational by mid-2015. There are several instances like these, which suggest the potential and prospects of the growth in the manufacturing sector.

Moreover, India's automobile sector has witnessed a high growth in the recent years. The automobile and auto components sector is likely to generate an output of US$145 billion by the end of 2016. As per Automotive Component Manufacturers Association (ACMA), the auto component industry has grown at a CAGR of 12% from 2008–2012 and is expected to grow at 14% CAGR during 2013 –2021. The turnover of the auto component industry in India stands at US$40.6 billion as of 2012–2013, and is estimated to be US$66 billion in 2015–2016 and US$115 billion in 2020–2021.

Such a huge potential in the manufacturing sector is already well-assessed by the National Manufacturing Policy 2011, announced by the Government of India, which aims to enhance the share of manufacturing in GDP to 25% within a decade and also create 100 million jobs. As per the policy document, some of the key features of the policy include its focus on some issues, *viz.* empower rural youth by imparting necessary skill sets to make them employable, sustainable development, technological value addition in manufacturing, principle of industrial growth in partnership with the states. According to the document, the central government will create the enabling policy framework, provide incentives for infrastructure development on a PPP basis through appropriate financing instruments, while the state governments will identify the suitable land and become the equity holders in the National Investment and Manufacturing Zones (NIMZs).

As per the policy document (Press Information Bureau, Government of India, 16 December 2011), the following are the key policy instruments for achieving the objectives:

1. Establishment of National Investment and Manufacturing Zones (NIMZs)—green field integrated Industrial Townships with state-of-the-art infrastructure and land use on the basis of zoning; clean and energy efficient technology and requisite social infrastructure. NIMZ proposed with land area of at least 5000 ha.
2. Industrial townships are proposed to be self-governing and autonomous bodies under Article 243(Q-c) of the Constitution.
3. The trunk infrastructure will be financed appropriately by the central government including through viability gap funding, while SPV will develop the zone infrastructure in public-private partnership (PPP) mode.
4. NIMZ will be managed by special purpose vehicle, headed by government officials and experts, including those of environment.

The policy wili also help in improving access to finance for SMEs in the manufacturing sector. Thus, understanding policy frameworks and their evolving role is crucial for defining the future road map of industrial development in the country.

Let us hope for more 'Made in India' tags in days to come.

Source: This case is written by the authors based on inputs from the following sources:

1. Article by ET Bureau, http://articles.economictimes.indiatimes.com/2014-02-04/news/46964118_1_new-orders-manufacturing-activity-leif-eskesen
2. CIA World Fact Book.
3. Automotive Components Manufacturer Association of India (ACMA), Auto Industry Profile, http://acma.in/pdf/Status_Indian_Auto_Industry.pdf; Fulfilling the promise of India's manufacturing sector, March 2012, Rajat Dhawan, Gautam Swaroop and Adil Zainulbhai http://www.mckinsey.com/insights/operations/fulfilling_the_promise_of_indias_manufacturing_sector
4. Manufacturing Sector in India, December 2008, http://www.ibef.org/industry/manufacturing-sector-india.aspx

7.1 INTRODUCTION

Industrial policies are designed to promote the development of industrial sector in an economy. This sector encompasses both heavy industries as well as small-scale industries. Generally, the industrial policies cover heavy manufacturing sector in an economy. Through a policy framework designed for the purpose, the government tries to strengthen the productivity and competitiveness of domestic firms.

Industrial policies are also integral to the economic environment of a country. They provide an overall framework to ascertain whether the policy is conducive to private sector participation or not. In an era of liberalisation and globalisation, industrial sectors act as an important area, which attracts investment from private sectors both at domestic as well as international level.

In accordance with the Indian economic policies that characterise a mixed economy, the government initially supported state-owned enterprises in the heavy industries sector. But gradually, the need for privatisation was felt. In 1991, Indian industrial policies abolished state control over some of the pertinent industrial sectors. These initiatives helped solicit inflow of foreign investments in the country. In this context, we discuss India's industrial policies in this section and also reflect on the business environment of the country, as per the policies followed during various time periods.

7.1.1 Manufacturing in Defence Sector

The manufacturing in India's defence sector has been an important base for India's bid to become an economic power. India has been pursuing indigenous defence manufacturing for decade. However, the defence procurements still depend on foreign-manufactured arms and machineries. India has the third largest army, the fourth largest air force and the seventh largest navy in the world and 31.5% of the budget in defence is spent on capital acquisitions. 60% of the total requirements of India's defence sector is still being fulfilled by imports, making India as one of the largest importers of defence-related equipment. India's defence-related budget is more than 4% of India's GDP. In other terms, India has US $ 362 per capita expenditure on defence sector. In terms of share of GDP, India is the fifth largest economy in the world spending major portion of GDP on defence sector.

During the post-independent era, industrial policies were designed to promote public sector undertaking. Defence sector production units were reserved for public sector units only. Private investment in this sector was not open. 100% Indian private investment was allowed only in 2001. Thus, Indian defence sector is dominated by defence public sector undertakings (DPSUs) and ordnance factories (OFs), which contribute about 90% of the total domestic defence manufacturing output.

With new government in 2014, the sector has been experiencing radical changes and major economic reforms are taking place. On one hand, for the first time, foreign investment is allowed in the defence manufacturing, and on the other hand, the government has placed this sector under its ambitious 'make in India' project. Up to 49% investment is allowed under the government route and investment by foreign portfolio investors is open up to 24% under automatic route. The current FDI policy in defence sector has removed the clause that mandated 51% ownership by single largest Indian equity holder. However, investment in defence sector is subject to other security conditions.

Box 7.1 From Delicensing to Make in India

India's quest of market economy started with the advent of policy framework for liberalisation in the country's economic structure covering all the core sectors such as industrial sector, monetary policies, external sector, public sector, etc. on the eve of 20th century. Economic reforms were initiated in 1991 to promote private sector. Liberalisation policies of 1991 are, thus, considered as a milestone in Indian economy.

Despite the fact that the country followed market-friendly approach in economic policies, the country remained a planned economy and the importance of planning was, at the outset of 12th Five Year Plan, reignited. The fact remains that delicensing was started in 1991 yet, during the post-reform period, restrictions were still imposed on several sectors for both private and foreign investment. The prominent among the reserve sectors for public sector investments were railways and defence manufacturing. These were further accompanied by major business-related impediments in terms of paper works and red tapism. As a result, the manufacturing sector has been facing many problems and has not been able to attract foreign investment in major sectors. The story of delicensing needed another flip to uplift India's manufacturing sector, which was in turmoil after the economic crisis in 2008, and subsequently, slowdown in European economies.

The new government, therefore, took a radical step for reform and announced Make in India campaign. The government called for major policy reforms to attract foreign investment and announced new FDI policies. Make in India campaign has promising future. It has been supported by government's initiatives in the area of digitisation of business-related approvals and also by the programmes started for production of skill labourers in specific sectors. In addition, several incentives-related schemes are being announced for attracting private investment in sectors like defence and others. Some of the policies that the government has started recently as the effort to support Make in India campaign are listed below:

1. Doing business in India just got easier—new delicensing and deregulation measures are reducing complexity, and significantly increasing speed and transparency.
2. States asked to introduce self-certification and third party certification under Boilers Act.
3. Major components of defence products' list excluded from industrial licensing.
4. Services of all Central Government Departments and Ministries will be integrated with the eBiz—a single window IT platform for services by 31 December 2014.
5. No inspection should be undertaken without the approval of the Head of the Department.
6. For all non-risk, non-hazardous businesses, a system of self-certification to be introduced.
7. A new 'National Industrial Corridor Development Authority' is being created to coordinate, integrate, monitor and supervise development of all industrial corridors.
8. Work on 5 smart cities in progress as a part of the Delhi–Mumbai Industrial Corridor: Dholera, Shendra-Bidkin, Greater Noida, Ujjain and Gurgaon.
9. Policy in defence sector liberalised and FDI cap raised from 26% to 49%.
10. 100% FDI allowed in defence sector for modern and state-of-the-art technology on case-to-case basis.
11. 100% FDI under automatic route permitted in construction, operation and maintenance in specified rail infrastructure projects like suburban railways, high-speed rail projects, DFCs manufacturing of rolling stocks, electrification of railway lines, etc.

Source: Department of Industrial Policy Promotion, Ministry of Commerce.

With the above changes in defence manufacturing, the Government of India has approved 36 proposals of foreign investment in defence sector up to March 2016. The Indian defence industry's import-export ratio is inferior to countries which have smaller base in manufacturing in the defence sector. Even in case of India, import has much larger base than the export from India. With the objective to reverse the current imbalances in defence sector between imports and exports of defence-related equipment and machinaries, "Make in India" programme aims at promoting indigenous manufacturing in the sector without affecting the current requirements and preparedness of India's defence sector.

The notable point here is India's Make in India initiative in defence sector not only aims at fulfilling domestic requirements but also acts as a firm step taken to boost India's defence exports. The government accordingly has devised strategies for export promotion in this sector. The government, in its strategies, proposed to form a body, which specifically promotes and facilitates exports of defence-related equipment. It is expected that the proposed body will identify the suitable export markets in consultation with the Ministry of External Affairs and Department of Commerce. More importantly, considering the foreign policy dimensions and international export control and arms control regimes, it may play important role in promoting exports of defence-related articles/equipment.

In addition, regulatory regime for private players (both foreign and domestic) is needed to comply with India's defence procurement policy (DDP), industrial licensing policy, foreign trade policy and fiscal regimes for the sector. The government has revisited and decided to revise it every year. The defence procurement policy, 2016 is a revised policy. However, industrial licensing policy, 1951 is an important component in India's defence sector. As far as fiscal regime is concerned, the Government of India has suggested the following provisions in its annual budget as fiscal incentives in the sector:

1. The important provisions of the Union Budget 2015–2016 are as under:
   - (i) During the financial year 2015–2016, a provision of ₹2,46,727 crore has been made for defence services.
   - (ii) Total capital outlay for Defence in the year 2015–2016 is ₹94,588 crore.
   - (iii) Out of the provision of capital outlay of ₹94,588 crore, maximum has been allocated for defence-related capital acquisition amounting to ₹77,704 crore.
   - (iv) Other capital acquisition in defence sector is also important and an allocation of ₹17,181 crore was provided for the purpose during 2015–2016. The provision is under 'Other than Capital Acquisition' segment for capital expenditure of Defence R&D Organisation (DRDO), Ordnance Factory Board, Inspection Organisation and other agencies and capital works projects of the services.
   - (v) Either of the following two deductions can be availed:
     - (a) Investment allowance (additional depreciation) at the rate of 15% to manufacturing companies that invest more than ₹1 billion in plants and machinery acquired and installed between 1 April 2013 to 31 March 2015, provided the aggregate amount of investment in the new plants and machinery during the same period exceeds ₹1 Billion.
     - (b) To support the companies engaged in the sector in manufacturing, in addition to the benefit of investment allowance at the rate of 15% as above, additional

deduction at 15% of the cost of new plants will be provided, exceeding ₹250 million, acquired and installed during any previous year until 31 March 2017.

2. Tax incentives are given below:
   (i) Tax incentives are to be given for research and development (R&D) in the sector as R&D incentives for R&D programmes supported by private sector.
   (ii) A weighted tax deduction is given under Section 35 (2AA) of the Income Tax Act.
   (iii) A weighted deduction of 200% is granted to assesses for any sums paid to a national laboratory, university or institute of technology, or specified persons with a specific direction that the said sum would be used for scientific research within a programme approved by the prescribed authority.
   (iv) For companies engaged in the manufacture of an in-house R&D centre, a weighted tax deduction of 200% is granted under Section 35 (2AB) of the Income Tax Act for both capital and revenue expenditure incurred on scientific research and development. Expenditure on land and buildings are not eligible for deduction.
3. State incentives include the following:
   (i) Apart from the above, each state in India offers additional incentives for industrial projects. Incentives are in areas like subsidised land cost, relaxation in stamp duty exemption on sale/lease of land, power tariff incentives, concessional rates of interest on loans, investment subsidies/tax incentives, backward areas subsidies, special incentive packages for mega projects.
4. Export incentives are given below:
   (i) Export promotion capital goods scheme.
   (ii) Duty remission scheme.
   (iii) Focus product scheme, special focus product scheme, focus market scheme.
   (iv) Incentives as per 'Merchandise Exports from India Scheme (MEIS)' under new Foreign Trade Policy.
5. Area-based incentives include the following:
   (i) Incentives for units in Special Economic Zone (SEZ)/National Investment Manufacturing Zone (NIMZ) as specified in respective Acts or for the setting up of projects in special areas such as the North-east, Jammu and Kashmir, Himachal Pradesh and Uttarakhand.

7.2 INDUSTRIAL POLICY RESOLUTION, 1948

On 6 April 1948, Government of India came out with an industrial policy resolution. An understanding of the Directive Principles of State Policy, as provided in the Constitution of India, clearly indicates that India in its early stage of framing policies embraced a socialist structure aimed at bringing social equity and welfare in the society. In view of this, the industrial policy resolution was also a reflection of the same objective. The policy, thus, laid down the foundation stone of the mixed economy (discussed in Chapter 4) in India's industrial structure.

The Industrial Policy Resolution, 1948 emphasised that the economy should have a secure process of increasing production and the framework should be based on an equitable distribution.

Accordingly, industries were divided into four broad categories, *viz.*

1. Government controlled sectors such as arms and ammunition, atomic energy, and production and maintenance of railways equipment and ownership of railways
2. Development of new industries by states undertaking such as coal, iron and steel, aircrafts, etc.
3. Sectors of basic importance under the plan of central government
4. The remainder sectors, where private sector was supposed to participate

Thus, the main objective of the policy was to lay down the foundation of a mixed economy. It emphasised that the state must play a vital role in the process of development of industrial base in the country. In fact, it clearly divided industries (as indicated above), where state can only dominate the sector. It highlighted the roles of the central and state governments in this process, wherein the centre was supposed to have a monopoly in the first category of industries, while the state governments were supposed to work on the subsequent two categories of industries. Moreover, owing to the socialist pattern, it was deemed crucial that the industries of basic and strategic necessities remained in the hand of the public sector. Moreover, since the private sector at that time was not strong enough in terms of finances, several other essential industries that required investments were also placed in the hand of the government.

7.3 INDUSTRIAL POLICY RESOLUTION, 1956

At the outset of First Five Year Plan, India, which was a newly independent economy, had a backward industrial structure. In 1948–1949, India's industrial establishment accounted for only 6.6% of the national income. Also, only a small chunk of the working population was engaged in this sector. After the World War I, cotton and textiles were the only major industries, though steel and paper industries were also prevalent even before independence. However, the period during and after the World War II saw some more industries coming up like those based on metals and minerals, chemicals, diesel engines, pumps, bicycles, sewing machines, and certain types of machine tools.

Since after the independence, the major industrial produce was concentrated to consumer produce, there is little evidence of production of capital goods. This set the way for India to rely on the imports of capital goods for its manufacturing units. At the outset of First Five Year Plan (see Box 7.2 for strategies suggested during the first plan), it was found that iron and steel,

Box 7.2 Strategies of the First Five Year Plan

1. Fuller utilisation of the existing capacity in producer goods industries like jute and plywood and consumer goods industries like cotton textiles, sugar, soap, vanaspati, paints and varnishes
2. Expansion of capacity in capital and producer goods industries like iron and steel, aluminium, cement, fertilisers, heavy chemicals, machine tools, etc.
3. Completion of industrial units on which a part of the capital expenditure has already been incurred
4. Establishment of new plants, which would lend strength to the industrial structure by rectifying, as far as resources permit the existing lacunae and drawbacks, e.g., manufacture of sulphur from gypsum, chemical pulp for rayon, etc.

Source: **As outlined in the document of First Five Year Plan.**

which was domestically produced, accounted for only 50% of its total demand in the country. Similarly, India had to depend on the imports of equipment for power sector industries. During 1951–1956, the First Five Year Plan put special attention on defining the industrial priorities. However, due to the highest priority accorded to agricultural sector, the plan focused on the completion of projects which were underway during the period.

The Second Five Year Plan document highlighted that the expansion process of industrial establishments in the country was satisfactory. The economy was able to establish some of the important industrial units such as Sindri Fertiliser Factory, Chittaranjan Locomotive Factory, Indian Telephone Industries, the Integral Coach Factory, the Cable Factory and the Penicillin Factory.

The performance of some of the industrial sectors was also good during the First Five Year Plan. For instance, locomotives were produced more than the targeted one and similarly, the production of Penicillin was supposed to be more than the target of the First Five Year Plan.

However, the Second Five Year Plan also highlighted the need for regulatory reforms, considering the need for industrial development in the country. Before, the Industrial Policy, 1956, the sector was regulated by the Development and Regulation Act, 1951, which was further amended in 1953, in addition to the Industrial Policy, 1948. The amendment covered more industries in the schedule. These policies were brought out under the idea that puts more emphasis on the promotion of agricultural sector. A new policy was indeed required to supplement the earlier one looking at the need for bases for industrialisation in the country. Therefore, the Second Five Year Plan also focused on the establishment of large-scale industries.

In order to restructure the industrial sector, Government of India brought out the Industrial Resolution on 30 April 1956. This was a timely and accorded priority to the necessities of the Second Five Year Plan. The policy was envisaged to expedite industrialisation process, leading to the development of industries and machine-making industries to garner a better industrial and transport sector output. The policy was also considered as a landmark step to strengthen public sector undertaking in India.

The new Industrial Policy, 1956 divided the Indian industries into two schedules, popularly known as

1. ***Schedule A:*** The industries under schedule A were kept as the state-based industrial units.
2. ***Schedule B:*** The industries under schedule B were open for private sector but state was encouraged to develop these as well and the private sector was supposed to supplement the state (also see Box 7.3 for more details).

However, for those industries not listed in any of the two schedules, private sector was encouraged to develop them.

7.3.1 Objectives of Industrial Policy Resolution, 1956

In the Industrial Policy Resolution, 1956, it was clearly stated that the policy had a broad objective to achieve the goals that were outlined in the Directive Principles of State Policy in the Constitution of India. These objectives were mainly associated with the economic well-being of the people of the country and also highlighted that the state would not lead to the concentration

Box 7.3 Industries under Schedule A and Schedule B

Schedule A	*Schedule B*
1. Arms and ammunition and allied items of defence equipment	1. All other minerals, except minor minerals, as defined in Section 3 of the Minerals Concession Rules, 1949
2. Atomic energy	2. Aluminium and other non-ferrous metals not included in Schedule A
3. Iron and steel	3. Machine tools
4. Heavy castings and forgings of iron and steel	4. Ferro-alloys and tool steels
5. Heavy plant and machinery required for iron and steel production, mining, machine tool manufacture and such other basic industries, as specified by the central government	5. Basic and intermediate products required by chemical industries such as the manufacture of drugs, dyestuffs and plastics
6. Heavy electrical plant including large hydraulic and steam turbines	6. Antibiotics and other essential drugs
7. Coal and lignite	7. Fertilisers
8. Mineral oils	8. Synthetic rubber
9. Mining of iron ore, manganese ore, chrome ore, gypsum, sulphur, gold and diamond	9. Carbonisation of coal
10. Mining and processing of copper, lead, zinc, tin, molybdenum and wolfram	10. Chemical pulp
11. Minerals specified in the Schedule to the Atomic Energy (Control of Production and Use) Order, 1953	11. Road transport
12. Aircraft	12. Sea transport
13. Air transport	
14. Railway transport	
15. Shipbuilding	
16. Telephones and telephone cables, telegraph and wireless apparatus (excluding radio receiving sets)	
17. Generation and distribution of electricity	

of capital. Clearly, a socialist structure of the economic system was again envisaged. Thus, in order to achieve the goals identified in the directive principles, the Industrial Policy Resolution, 1956 intended to produce outcomes on the following parameters:

1. Accelerate economic growth.
2. Expedite industrial progress.
3. Develop heavy industries.
4. Expand public sector undertakings.
5. Strengthen the growing cooperative sector.
6. Ensure progress towards socialist pattern of society and mixed economic system.

7.3.2 Characteristics of Industrial Policy, 1956

The main characteristic of the policy was a clear division of the industrial sectors into two schedules. This envisaged that there would be a limited participation of the private sector, as only industries listed in schedule B were open to the private investors. Moreover, the policy also emphasised that the state should progressively participate in the development of industries listed in schedule B as well. The industrial policy resolution supported the process of industrialisation in the country. In the first category, i.e., Schedule A, the policy put those industrial sectors or units which were supposed to be the future industries. Thus, the state was solely responsible for the development of future industrial base as per the Industrial Policy, 1956. The second category, i.e., Schedule B consisted of those industries which were to be state-owned but the private sector was expected to support the state in developing these industries. Another important feature of the policy was the third category. This category did not include industries which were included in Schedules A and B. These industries were supposed to be developed by the private sector.

Under the framework of Industrial Policy, 1956, the Second Five Year Plan set priorities for the industrial sector during 1956–1961. These priorities mainly concentrated on the development and expansion of industrial capacity of the country. Thus, as per the Second Five Year Plan, the following areas were prioritised for the expansion of industrial capacity:

1. Strengthening iron and steel, and heavy chemical industries including fertiliser industries, and development of engineering and machine building industries
2. Expansion of capacity of other developmental commodities such as capital goods
3. Undertake modernisation as well as mechanisation of national industries such as cotton and sugar industries
4. Achieving full capacity utilisation of the existing industries during the plan period
5. Expedite the expansion of capacity for producing consumer goods, considering the need for industries at state levels

In order to fulfill these priorities, the government also made a provision of ₹60 to ₹65 crore aimed at the establishment of National Industrial Development Corporation (NIDC) to provide assistance to the industrial sector.

7.3.3 Outcome of the Policy

The outcome of the policy was evident from the industrial progress of the country during the first two decades of economic planning. It was recognised by the Third Five Year Plan document that the growth and diversification of industries were remarkable during the Second Five Year Plan. Notably, three new steel works with one million tonnes capacity were completed as public sector undertaking and also capacity of two existing steel works in the private hands was doubled. In addition, a landmark achievement was to expedite the process of development of heavy electrical and heavy machine tools industry.

Similarly for the first time, paper and cement industries were started. The production of basic chemical industries increased with the addition of a number of new products such as urea, ammonium phosphate, penicillin, synthetic fibres, industrial explosives, polyethylene, newsprint and dyestuffs. As a result of the rapid development of industries, output increased substantially and broadly included the production of commodities like bicycles, sewing machines, telephones, electrical goods, textiles and sugar machinery. As a result of these developments, the index of industrial production increased from 100 in 1950–1951 to 194 in 1960–1961.[1]

As per the plan document, during the Second Five Year Plan, the index number of industrial production increased from 139 to 194—an increase of about 7% per annum. Similarly, an increase in the industrial production index of iron and steel was recorded as 14%. The highest growth was seen in case of production of machineries, which accounted for an increase of 21%

1. Document of the Third Five Year Plan, Chapter 26: Industries, Review of progress under the two plans, Planning Commission, Government of India.

per annum, whereas increase in the production of chemicals was recorded as 10% per annum from 1955–1956 to 1960–1961. However, the production of textiles was relatively weaker during the same period of time, recorded only about 1% (see Figure 7.1).

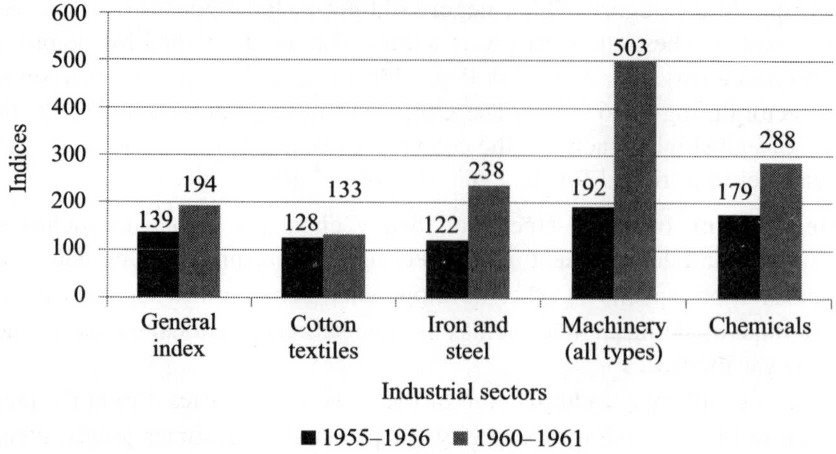

Figure 7.1 Index number of industrial production (1950–1951 = 100).
Source: Plan Document of Third Five Year Plan, Planning Commission.

In addition to the general rise in production of industrial sector, it is important to understand the role of specific industries during the first two periods of economic planning in the country. From the Figure 7.1, we can see the rise in production of steel ingots from 1.4 million tonnes in 1950–1951 to 1.7 million tonnes in 1955–1956, which further increased during 1955 to 1961. Production of steel ingots increased from 1.7 million tonnes to 3.5 million tonnes—an increase of 16% per annum as compared to the annual increase of only 4% in the First Five Year Plan (also see Boxes 7.4 and 7.5 for more information). Similarly, revenue from the production of

Box 7.4 Impact of Industrial Policy, 1956

To augment the industrial base of the country, during the period of Second Five Year Plan, three new steel plants were established as public sector undertakings. This was a major step taken forward by the government. The new projects started producing output of steel ingots during the Second Five Year Plan only. In 1960–1961, the total output of steel ingots has increased to 3.5 million tonnes and the output of pig iron reached 9 lakh tonnes.

Moreover, the rapid growth of production units of machinery items was another big achievement of the industries in India after the new industrial policies. This enabled India to produce indigenous machinery items and equipment to feed the demand for such products. The value of graded machine tools in the country increased by more than sixteen-fold during 1950–1961.

Some of the heavy machine building plant at Ranchi and coal mining machinery plant at Durgapur were established during this period. The extraction of mineral and production also received attention after the new industrial policy. The main mineral products were coal, iron ore and bauxite. In fact, the production of coal increased by more than 5% per annum from 32.3 million tonnes in 1950–1951 to 54.6 million tonnes in 1960–1961. Similarly, the output of bauxite increased from 64,000 in 1950 to 3,77,000 tonnes in 1960.

Source: Third Five Year Plan, Planning Commission.

Box 7.5 Bhilai Steel Plant

The Bhilai Steel Plant, located in Bhilai, Chhattisgarh is India's first and the main producer of steel rails as well as a major producer of wide steel plates and the other steel products. The plant also produces and markets various chemical by-products from its coke ovens and coal chemical plant. It was set up with the help of former USSR in 1955.

A ten-times winner of Prime Minister's Trophy for the best integrated steel plant in the country, this plant is India's sole producer of rails and heavy steel plates as well as the sole supplier of the country's longest rail tracks of 260 m. With an annual production capacity of 3.153 million tonnes of saleable steel, the plant also specialises in other products such as wire rods and merchant products.

machines tools was only 18% per annum during 1950–1956, but rose to an annual increase of 48% during the subsequent five years of economic planning.

In addition to the above performance, Table 7.1 also indicates the same trend due to the Industrial Policy, 1956. The policy expedited the process of industrialisation through government participation.

Table 7.1 Performance of Some Major Industrial Units

Items	*Unit*	*1950–1951*	*1955–1956*	*1960–1961*
Index of industrial production	1950–1951 = 100	100.00	139.00	194.00
Production of steel ingots	Million tonnes	1.40	1.70	3.50
Aluminium	1000 tonnes	3.70	7.30	18.50
Machine tools (graded)	Value in rupees crore	0.34	0.78	5.50
Sulphuric acid	1000 tonnes	99.00	164.00	363.00
Mill made cloth	Million yards	3,720.00	5,102.00	5,127.00
Minerals (iron ore and coal)	Million tonnes	35.50	42.70	65.30

Source: Documents of Third Five Year Plan, Planning Commission.

7.4 MONOPOLIES INQUIRY COMMISSION, 1964

Further, in 1964, the central government appointed a commission under the chairmanship of K.C. Dasgupta, to evaluate the position of concentration of economic power. The commission submitted its report and recommended for restrictive trade practices. This commission was known as *Monopolies Inquiry Commission* (*MIC*). It also highlighted the issues pertaining to the operations of industrial licensing system under the Industrial Development and Regulation Act, 1951.

On the basis of the report submitted by the commission, the Government of India brought out Monopolies and Restrictive Trade Practices (MRTP) Act in 1969. The main objective of the Act was to rectify the process of distribution of wealth in the economy, in view of MIC's conclusion that industrial licensing was responsible for the development of biased and disproportionate capital distribution. The MIC also recommended that the larger industrial houses should get a license for heavy industries. This further brought the need for restructuring the existing licensing policies. Thus, the Act categorised the business houses in India, and accordingly, the large industries were allowed in the areas of investment, which were not allocated for government or the small-scale sector.

In accordance with the MRTP Act, the new Industrial Licensing Policy, 1970 categorised the industries into four categories:

1. Core sector (included industrial units of strategic importance)
2. Heavy investment sector (included projects having more than ₹5 crore of value)
3. Middle sector (included projects with investment ranging between ₹1 crore to ₹5 crore)
4. Delicensed sector (broadly included investment in the industries, which amounted for less than ₹1 crore).

Thus, the policy exempted such projects from the requirement of license.

7.5 INDUSTRIAL POLICY STATEMENT, 1973

The Industrial Policy Statement, 1973 gave preference to the small and medium entrepreneurs. It was aimed to prevent excessive concentration of industrial activity in the large industrial houses. It encouraged entrepreneurs in setting up of new capacity, particularly in the production of mass consumption goods. With this view, new undertakings of up to rupees one crore by way of fixed assets were exempted from the requirements of licensing, unlike the foreign companies or those with fixed assets of ₹5 crore or more.

7.6 INDUSTRIAL POLICY STATEMENT, 1977

In the year 1977, a new government was formed in India, popularly known as *Janata Party Government*, led by Morarji Desai. The Janata Party government had a distinct approach towards the economic planning in India. Most importantly, though it also advocated the idea of socialism, yet its policies were different. It proactively advocated the idea of decentralisation and thereby, the idea of strengthening small and medium-scale industries. With these objectives, the government put the new industrial policy statement on the floor in 1977.

The new policy was inclined towards seeking self-reliance. The statement highlighted the fact that some elements of the Industry Policy Resolution, 1956 remained valid, but there existed many areas of reform too. After a long period of Industrial Policy that the country followed, the economy faced problems of certain structural distortions in addition to the continuous presence of poverty. The country suffered from the economic ills such as unemployment, regional disparities, rural-urban disparities, and stagnated real investment. In order to avoid these distortions in the economy, the Policy Statement, 1977 adopted decentralisation as well as promotion of small industries.

Some of the main characteristics of this statement are listed below:

1. This statement aimed to focus on small-scale industries and cottage industries, especially in rural areas and small towns.
2. It called for the protection of sick industrial units in order to prevent unemployment.
3. It redefined the role of large-scale industries to complement the requirements of small-scale industries.

4. It called for strengthening the public sector enterprises to meet the basic consumer needs in the country.

7.7 INDUSTRIAL POLICY STATEMENT, 1980

The Industrial Policy Statement, 1980 came during the rule of new government, after the fall of Janta Party Government in early 1980. The policy was spelled out to be based on the Policy Resolution, 1956. The objectives included optimal utilisation of the existing industrial capacity, higher productivity, employment generation, tackling regional disparities, export promotion, strengthening agricultural base of the country, consumer protection, etc. In a sense, the policy statement also emphasised on strengthening the domestic market.

Policy measures were announced to rejuvenate the public sector undertakings. However, it also increased the investment limits of small-scale industries, proving beneficial for the opening of private sector as well. Some of the measures of this policy statement are as follows:

1. The main focus was on the human resource development in public sector.
2. Automatic capacity expansion of public sector units was allowed.
3. Focus was given to industrially backward districts to correct the regional imbalances.
4. Investment limits of small-scale industries were reviewed and enhanced to ₹2 lakh for small units, ₹20 lakh for medium or ancillary units and ₹25 lakh for large units.
5. Fully export-oriented industries were given special priorities.

7.8 REVIEW OF INDUSTRIAL POLICY MEASURES BEFORE 1991

Prior to 1991, licensing was the main instrument to tackle the problem of capital concentration. The era is generally referred to as *Licence Raj*. Some general features characterising the industrial policies prior to 1991 are as follows:

1. Licensing was the main instrument to augment the existing capacity.
2. The economy followed a combination of policies culminating in the development of mixed economy that gave special priorities to the public sector units.
3. The private sector participation was low. The policies could not ensure a considerable role for private sector in achieving broader economic objectives of the country.
4. Industries were promoted, but generally suffered from underutilisation of capacities.
5. Regional disparities emerged as one of the major challenges that the economy faced. It was noted by Dutt Committee that the industrialised states, *viz.* Maharashtra, Gujarat and Tamil Nadu benefitted the most from the existing policies. States such as Bihar, Madhya Pradesh, Uttar Pradesh and Rajasthan remained industrially backward, and were often referred to as *BIMARU states*.
6. However, most significantly, it cannot be denied that a good mix of consistent evolution in policy measures and the continuous reform agenda coupled with the need for removing the deterrents to industrialisation paved the way for a smooth transition to economic openness, duly witnessed in 1991.
7. It is also noteworthy that the industrial policies also led to the development of export-oriented industries.

7.9 INDUSTRIAL POLICY STATEMENT, 1991

In view of the constraints of the existing industrial policies and in order to extend the process of industrial liberalisation, the Industrial Policy Statement, 1991 was announced by the Government of India on 24 July 1991. The objective of the policy was stated as follows:

> The government will continue to pursue a sound policy framework encompassing encouragement of entrepreneurship, development of indigenous technology through investment in research and development, bringing in new technology, dismantling of the regulatory system, development of the capital markets and increased competitiveness for the benefit of common man.[2]

Moreover, in order to remove industrial backwardness, the policy advocated a need for investment in the country. It was further put on the table due to India's economic crisis in 1991. The policy was brought out to supplement a sustained economic growth. Thus, the policy highlighted its major objective to build on the gains already made, correct distortions or weaknesses that might have crept in and maintain a sustained growth in productivity. It highlighted the need for foreign investment and technological penetration in the country for achieving the economic self-reliance. To achieve the objectives, the government announced a series of policy measures, which broadly included abolition of Licence Raj, allowing foreign investments in select areas, disinvestment of public sector units and review of MRTP Act, among others.

The industrial performance decelerated during 1989–1990. Compared with the astonishing performance of the industrial sector in the previous year, i.e., 8.7% growth in the index of industrial production, the industrial growth declined to 8.6% and further decelerated by 0.1% in 1990–1991. The industrial performance was not conducive to economic growth. The overall economic growth also substantially declined to 2.5% in 1991–1992, which was caused by both the slowdown in agricultural production as well as by the sharp decline in industrial production. The industrial production declined to negative.

In addition, India suffered from payment crisis during 1991–1992. This occurred due to increase in the oil prices during the Gulf War of 1990s. The foreign exchange reserves of India declined from US$3.11 billion during August 1990 to US$896 million in January 1991. To overcome the payment crisis, the government approached the International Monetary Fund (IMF) and had to drew US$660 million from the reserve tranche during the third quarter of 1990. In January 1991, the government again drew more than US$1 billion under Compensatory and Contingency Financing Facility (CCFF) and US$789 million under first credit tranche (FCT) arrangement. However, India's economic problem continued to be persistent.

It was felt that the payment crisis was not an outcome of the trade deficit alone. In fact, the industrial structure also suffered from Licence Raj, which was a deterrent to doing business in the country. Thus, a new policy reform was imminent and the 1991 reforms of liberalisation, privatisation and globalisation were the much sought steps in this direction.

2. Statement on Industrial Policy, 1991 Document, DIPP, Ministry of Commerce and Industry, Government of India.

7.9.1 Objectives of the 1991 Policy

The Industrial Policy Statement, 1991 stated that

> A broad-based infrastructure had been built up. The basic industries had been established. A high degree of self-reliance in a large number of items—raw materials, intermediates, finished goods—had been achieved. New growth centres of industrial activity had emerged, as had a new generation of entrepreneurs. A large number of engineers, technicians and skilled workers had also been trained.

It further stated that

> The seventh plan recognised the need to consolidate on these strengths and take initiatives to prepare Indian industry to respond effectively to the emerging challenges. A number of policies and procedural changes were introduced in 1985 and 1986 under the leadership of Shri Rajiv Gandhi, aimed at increasing productivity, reducing costs and improving quality. The accent was on opening the domestic market to increased competition and readying our industry to stand on its own in the face of international competition. The public sector was freed from a number of constraints and given a larger measure of autonomy. The technological and managerial modernisation of industry was pursued as the key instrument for increasing productivity and improving our competitiveness in the world. The net result of all these changes was that Indian industry grew by an impressive average annual growth rate of 8.5% in the seventh plan period.

With the above background, the policy statement reassured that the government would continue to follow the policy of self-reliance. It also called for strengthening the domestic economy to enable payment for India's imports through its own foreign exchange earnings. This implied that the government aimed to strengthen India's industrial base and follow new policy regimes for the foreign exchange management. Thus, the main objectives of the Industrial Policy, 1991 can be summarised as under:

1. Enable the country to achieve sustained growth in its industrial productivity.
2. Achieve a higher employment.
3. Develop the human resources and their optimum capacity utilisation.
4. Strengthen the domestic industries on account of their competitiveness.
5. Carry out the promotion of exports.
6. Deregulate the industrial sector.

7.9.2 Features of Industrial Policy Statement, 1991

The basic thrust of this resolution was on simplifying the regulations and procedures by delicensing deregulating and decontrolling. Some of its salient features are given below:

1. The industrial landscape of private sector was enhanced through dereservation of public sectors in some of the industrial areas. In fact, after 1956, 17 sectors were reserved for public sector only. But the 1991 Policy reduced the reserved category from 17 to 8. This helped in increasing the private sector participation in the core industrial sectors.
2. Restructuring of sick industrial units was called for, as the policy statement stated that sick units accounted for more than 30% of the total losses incurred by the central public sector enterprises.

3. Delicensing was another important feature of the Industrial Policy Statement, 1991. Licensing, in fact, was a strong deterrent to doing business in the country. Since the industrial base of the country was diversified and needed a new approach of competitive market, licensing was abolished.
4. Small-scale industries were also exempted from licensing for all articles of manufacture.
5. The government also announced trade policy reforms along with the devaluation of Indian currency. India removed the import licenses, which were required for the import of raw materials.
6. Industrial policy statement also allowed foreign investment through automatic route and in some cases with prior approval of the government. However, the major reform was the automatic entry of foreign investors for technological agreements.

7.9.3 Micro, Small and Medium Industries and Policies

Micro, Small and Medium Enterprises (MSMEs) are an important part of the industrial base of Indian economy. The new industrial policy of 1991 has dramatically removed restrictions on industrial sector in India for private players. While the new industrial policy focused on large-scale industrial base, the small- and medium-scale industries were also thriving. These industries became intermediary and support base for large industries. One of the important examples of this is small industries in automotive parts supporting manufacturing of automobiles by large enterprises.

During post-1991 reform period, the performance of small- and medium-scale industries sector has grown at higher rate. Fixed investment has also been increasing in this sector. In order to give impetus to MSME sector, a separate policy statement was announced in 1991 related to the sector. The statement was the first and foremost step in terms of policy for small and decentralised economic activities in the guise of small industries. Some important policy measures were highlighted to mitigate risks faced by the sector. Important features of the small industrial policy of 1991 are as follows:

1. MSME sector were opened for private investment with equity participation of 24%.
2. Introduced factoring services by banks.
3. Adequate credit to the small entrepreneurs.
4. Sub-contracting exchanges were allowed to be set up.
5. Government committed to have technology development cell dedicated to the sector.
6. Programmes and schemes aimed at new technology upgradation.
7. The small and tiny sector was to be accorded priority in allocation of indigenous raw materials.
8. The policy envisaged marked promotion of small and tiny sectors' products to be undertaken by cooperatives, public sector institutions and other professional agencies.

In the context of growing importance of small- and medium-scale industries, the government announced Micro, Small and Medium Enterprises Development Act, 2006. The Act aims at facilitating the small- and medium-scale industries and promoting it as an essential component of Indian economy. The Act came into force in October 2006. The main feature and importance of the Act is the provision of legal instruments for the promotion of the sector. For the first time, small- and medium-scale industries were subjected to government's recognition. Accordingly, benefits were planned to uplift the sector.

The Act categorises enterprises in terms of (i) manufacturing and (ii) providing/rendering of services and further classifies into micro, small and medium enterprises, based on their investment in plant and machinery. In manufacturing category, micro enterprises are firms with investment up to ₹25 lakh, small enterprises are firms with investment between ₹25 lakh to ₹5 crore and medium enterprises are those with investment between ₹5 crore and ₹10 crore. In case of services enterprises, the classification between micro, small and medium enterprises is also based on investment. Enterprises with investment up to ₹10 lakh are micro enterprises in service category, enterprises with investment between ₹10 lakh to ₹2 crore are classified as small-scale enterprises, whereas medium-scale enterprises in service category need investment up to ₹5 crore and above ₹2 crore.

With the above classification, the Act also provides provisions related to establishment of specific funds for the promotion of the sector, notifying schemes and programmes, policies related to credit to the sector and simplification of the opening and closure of the business under the specified categories of the sector, and so on. In 2005, the government had announced policy for credit to small- and medium-scale industries. The policy is known as *Policy Package for Stepping up Credit to Small and Medium Enterprises*. The policy included measures to increase quantum of credit to the sector. Some of the important measures are as follows:

1. Fixing targets for funding SMEs by public sector banks to achieve a minimum 20% year-on year growth in credit to the sector.
2. Follow a transparent rating system with cost of credit linked to the credit rating of the enterprises by public sector banks.
3. Concerted efforts to be made by commercial banks to provide credit cover on an average to at least 5 new enterprises in the sector at each of their semi-urban/urban branches per year.
4. Issuing detailed guidelines relating to debt restructuring mechanism for all eligible enterprises of the sector by the RBI.
5. Introduction of one-time settlement scheme to apply to MSE non-performing asset (NPA) accounts in the books of the banks as on 31 March 2004.
6. Taking the exiting RBI guidelines as indicative minimum, banks to formulate a comprehensive and more liberal policy relating to advances to the sector.
7. Banks to adopt cluster-based approach for financing enterprises in the sector.

In addition, the government periodically announced several promotional schemes for the improvement of small- and medium-scale industries in the country. Considering the growing importance of this sector and its contribution to GDP, the new government undertook a number of schemes and programmes for the promotion of the sector after 2014. These schemes include the Prime Minister's Employment Generation Programme (PMEGP), Credit Guarantee Trust Fund for Micro and Small Enterprises (CGTMSE), Credit Linked Capital Subsidy Scheme (CLCSS) for Technology Upgradation, Scheme of Fund for Regeneration of Traditional Industries (SFURTI), and Micro and Small Enterprises-Cluster Development Programme (MSECDP) for the establishment of new enterprises and development of the existing ones.

Udyog Aadhar Memorandum (UAM) scheme was notified in September 2015 under Section 8 of the MSME Development Act 2006. Under this scheme, doing business in the sector has become easier, as the scheme promotes online registration. Small- and medium-scale entrepreneurs are now required to file an online entrepreneurs' memorandum to get a unique identification number named as *Udyog Adhaar Number* (*UAN*). No supporting documents are required for this purpose. Similarly, Employment Exchange for Industries was launched in June 2015 in line with Digital India to facilitate easy employability in the sector. It matches job seekers with the requirement of entrepreneurs of small- and medium-scale industries. Another important initiative was the announcement of Framework for Revival and Rehabilitation of Micro, Small and Medium Enterprises (MSMEs) in May 2015 under which banks have to constitute a Committee for Distressed MSMEs at zonal or district level to prepare a corrective action plan (CAP) for these units. A scheme for promoting innovation and rural entrepreneurs (ASPIRE) was also launched in March 2015.

Make in India is an important initiative of the Government of India. The initiative aims at providing ease of doing business in the country in manufacturing sector. MSME falls under all the vibrant sectors included in the Make in India campaign. Ease of doing business in sectors identified in Make in India include automotive parts, pharmaceuticals, textiles, food processing, leather, IT, construction sectors, and so on. These sectors have potential to invite MSME players to support large industries in these sectors. Therefore, the incentives for MSME to uplift India's manufacturing base would be an important initiative.

7.10 INDIA'S INDUSTRIAL PROGRESS AFTER 1991

The new reforms incorporated in the industrial sector strengthened the industrial base of the country. The economic performance of the country during post-reform period has been sound. In fact, the country experienced close to double-digit economic growth during this period despite the fact that many financial turbulences affected the economy severely.

The economic performance during the first decade of economic reform continued to be robust and achieved almost over 6% growth on an average. The performance of industrial sector was also remarkable. As compared to the previous decade, the industrial sector achieved more than 6% growth on an average for the first decade of economic reforms. The macroeconomic indicators given in Table 7.2 depict the overall performance of the economy during the period.

Table 7.2 Selected Macroeconomic Indicators 1989–2003

	Indicators	*1989–1990*	*1994–1995*	*1999–2000*	*2000–2001*	*2001–2002*	*2002–2003*
1.	Growth of GDP (%)	5.60	6.30	6.10	4.40	5.60	4.40
2.	GDP growth by sectors (%)						
	(i) Agriculture and allied	2.70	4.90	0.30	–0.40	5.70	–3.10
	(ii) Industry of which manufacturing	6.70	8.30	4.00	7.30	3.40	6.10
	(iii) Services	6.70	6.00	10.10	5.60	6.80	7.10
3.	Inflation rate [WPI index (%)]	9.10	10.40	4.80	2.50	5.20	3.20
4.	Current account balance as percentage of GDP	–	–3.10	–1.10	–0.50	–0.50	–

	Indicators	1989–1990	1994–1995	1999–2000	2000–2001	2001–2002	2002–2003
5.	Foreign exchange reserves (US$ billion)	3.37	19.65	35.06	39.55	51.05	69.89
6.	Exchange rates (₹/US$)	16.60	31.40	43.33	45.51	47.69	48.44
7.	Rate of growth of						
	(i) Exports (%)	18.90	18.40	10.80	21.00	–1.60	20.40
	(ii) Imports (%)	8.80	22.90	17.20	1.70	1.70	14.50
	(iii) Exports as percentage of GDP	6.40	9.60	9.10	10.40	9.90	–
	(iv) Imports as percentage of GDP	9.30	10.50	12.40	11.80	11.60	–
8.	Fiscal deficit as percentage of GDP	7.90	4.70	5.40	5.60	5.90	5.50
9.	Revenue deficit as percentage of GDP	2.60	3.10	3.50	4.10	4.20	3.90
10.	Saving ratio as percentage of GDP	22.30	24.90	24.10	23.40	24.00	–
11.	Investment as percentage of GDP	24.90	25.40	25.20	24.00	23.70	–

Source: Ministry of Finance, Government of India, Economic Survey (various years), as compiled by Wadhva, 1991.[3]

Further, Table 7.3 indicates the performance of industrial sector.

Table 7.3 Performance of Industrial Sector

Annual Growth Rates of Industrial Production in Major Sector (%) (Base Year: 1993–1994 = 100)				
Year	***Mining***	***Manufacturing***	***Electricity***	***General***
1992–1993	0.5	2.2	5.0	2.3
1993–1994	3.5	6.1	7.4	6.0
1994–1995	9.8	9.1	8.5	9.1
1995–1996	9.7	14.1	8.1	13.0
1996–1997	–1.9	7.3	4.0	6.1
1997–1998	6.9	6.7	6.6	6.7
1998–1999	–0.8	4.4	6.5	4.1
1999–2000	1.0	7.1	7.3	6.7
2000–2001	3.7	5.3	4.0	5.0

Note: Base: 1993–1994 = 100 and those for the year 1992–1993 Index of Industrial Production (IIP) Base: 1980–1981 = 100.

Source: Economic Survey of India, 2001–2002.

3. Wadhva, C.D. (1991), "India trying to liberalise: Economic reforms since 1991", Chapter 16, APCSS, http://www.apcss.org/Publications/Edited%20Volumes/RegionalFinal%20chapters/Chapter16Wadhva.pdf

As per the growth in the, industrial productivity index (IPI), average growth of industrial output was 6.6% during 1992–2001. During the period from 1981 to 1990, the average performance of the sector was good (7.8%) and the average IPI growth was higher than that of the first decade after reform. With respect to the different industrial types, the production of consumer goods such as beverages, food products, chemical products, machinery equipment, etc. was going on efficiently.

Details of some of the industrial reforms post-1991 are given in Box 7.6. Also, a selected industry-wise industrial performance for the period of 2007 and 2015 can be seen in Table 7.4.

Box 7.6 Reforms in Industrial Sector Post-1991

Some of the key reforms in industrial sector post-1991 include the following:

1. 13 minerals, which were reserved for public sector, were opened for private sector with effect from 26 March 1993. This resulted in a reduction in the number of industries reserved for the public sector, decreasing to 6. These industries were defence products, atomic energy, coal and lignite, mineral oils, railways and minerals, as specified in the Schedule to the Atomic Energy Order 1953.
2. Motor car and white goods industries were delicensed in 1993. Some other sectors were also delicensed in the same year, which included raw hides and skins, and, leather and patent leather (excluding chamois leather).
3. The manufacturing of readymade garments was opened for large-scale undertakings. It was reserved for exclusive manufacture by the ancillary/small-scale undertakings. The notification for the same was made on 29 July 1993. However, this was made subject to an export obligation of 50% and investment in fixed asset of the plants exceeding ₹3 crore.
4. Further, in June 1993, the Development Commissioners for Export Promoting Zones (EPZs) were delegated some specific powers for 100% Export Oriented Units (EOUs) and EPZs. These powers earlier rested with the zonal authority under Ministry of Commerce.
5. Excise duty on capital goods was rationalised and import duty was reduced, which lowered the capital costs and led to the increase in investment.
6. Concessional tax rate of 30% on the short-term capital gains for foreign institutional investors was introduced to increase foreign investment in Indian stock market.
7. Five-year tax holiday for new industries in industrially backward states and union territories and for power generation anywhere in India was introduced.
8. Export credit finance limit was increased.
9. Compulsory consortium lending was having limit of ₹5 crore, which was raised up to ₹50 crore.
10. CRR and SLR were reduced, thereby enabling money market to make more credit.
11. Minimum lending rate for the highest slab decreased to 15%.
12. Sick Industrial Companies (Special Provision) Act 1985 (SICA) was amended in December 1993 to facilitate early detection of the sickness of the industry and accordingly, to take remedial measures.

Source: Economic Survey of India, 1993–1994.

Table 7.4 Growth in Productivity of Selected Industries During 2007–2015 (%)

Industry Group	*Weight*	*2007–08*	*2008–09*	*2009–10*	*2010–11*	*2011–12*	*2012–13*	*2013–14*	*2014–15*
Food products and beverages	7.28	147.5	135.4	133.5	142.9	164.8	169.5	167.7	175.5
Tobacco products	1.57	98.4	102.7	102	104.1	109.7	109.2	110.2	111.2
Textiles	6.16	124.6	120.1	127.4	135.9	134	142	148.3	152.4
Wearing apparel, dressing and dyeing of fur	2.78	149.9	134.6	137.1	142.2	130.1	143.6	171.6	180.5
Luggage, handbags, saddlery, harness and footwear, tanning and dressing of leather products	0.58	110	104.4	105.8	114.3	118.5	127.1	133.7	147.2
Wood and products of wood and cork except furniture, articles of straw and plating materials	1.05	148	155.3	160.1	156.5	159.2	147.9	144.6	150.8
Paper and its products	1	112.6	118	121.1	131.4	138	138.7	138.6	143.1
Publishing, printing and reproduction of recorded media	1.08	140.2	142.4	133.8	148.8	192.8	183	183.4	175.9
Coke, refined petroleum products and nuclear fuel	6.71	119.6	123.4	121.8	121.5	125.8	136.4	143.5	144.7
Chemicals and their products	10.06	118.4	115	120.7	123.1	122.7	127.3	138.6	138.2
Rubber and plastics products	2.02	135.7	142.6	167.4	185.2	184.6	185	181.1	189.4
Other non-metallic mineral products	4.31	130.6	134.9	145.4	151.4	158.6	161.6	163.3	167.4
Basic metals	11.33	156.3	159	162.4	176.7	192.1	195.8	196.4	219.4
Fabricated metal products, except machinery and equipment	3.08	143.8	144	158.6	182.8	203.3	193.8	180.2	179
Machinery and equipment n.e.c.	3.76	185	171	198	256.3	241.3	230	219.2	227.7
Office, accounting and computing machinery	0.3	164.8	148.8	154.4	146.3	148.7	128.1	108	67
Electrical machinery and apparatus n.e.c.	1.98	373	530.8	459.2	472.1	367.1	369.2	422.6	511.6
Radio, TV and communication equipment and apparatus	0.99	604.2	726.7	809.1	911.5	950.5	1003.7	730.1	332.7
Medical, precision and optical instruments, watches and clocks	0.57	111.4	119.8	100.9	107.8	119.5	117.1	111.1	108.6
Motor vehicles, trailers and semi-trailers	4.06	151.2	138	179.1	233.3	258.6	244.8	221.3	226.8
Other transport equipment	1.82	129	134	171.1	210.7	235.8	235.7	249.5	265.5
Furniture, manufacturing n.e.c.	2.99	132.7	142.5	152.7	141.2	138.6	131.5	113.3	121.4
Manufacturing index	75.53	150.1	153.8	161.3	175.7	181	183.3	181.9	186.1

Source: Handbook of Statistics on Indian Economy, RBI.

With a base of 1980–1981, during 1982–1990, the growth of consumer non-durable goods was 4.3%, which rose to 5% during 1991–2001. However, the average growth of consumer durables during 1981–1990 was higher than that during 1991–2001. Similarly, the growth in the production of basic goods also reduced during this period. The case of capital goods was also similar. This indicated that there exists space for more reforms in this sector (see Table 7.5 for index number of industrial production use-based classification). An analysis of the growth in industrial production vis-à-vis GDP growth is given in Figure 7.2.

Table 7.5 Index Numbers of Industrial Production: Use-based Classification

Base Year: 1980–1981 = 100						
Year	*Basic Goods*	*Capital Goods*	*Intermediate Goods*	*Consumer Goods*	*Consumer Durables*	*Consumer Non-durables*
1981–1982	110.9	106.7	103.7	113.8	110.9	114.1
1982–1983	118.7	110.6	104.7	112.0	121.0	110.9
1983–1984	125.8	123.5	115.0	113.8	140.5	110.5
1984–1985	139.8	127.2	126.2	122.0	178.8	116.1
1985–1986	149.3	140.7	135.7	137.3	212.2	129.5
1986–1987	163.2	166.3	141.2	145.7	241.3	134.1
1987–1988	172.2	192.8	145.0	160.0	259.6	147.9
1988–1989	189.2	206.4	161.9	166.2	317.5	148.0
1989–1990	199.4	251.5	168.9	177.0	325.0	159.0
1990–1991	213.0	291.8	177.1	188.0	359.0	167.3
1991–1992	226.9	266.8	173.2	190.8	320.5	175.1
1992–1993	232.9	266.4	182.6	194.2	318.1	179.3
1993–1994	254.9	255.4	203.9	202.0	369.4	181.7
Base Year: 1993–1994 = 100						
1994–1995	109.6	109.2	105.3	112.1	116.2	111.2
1995–1996	121.4	115.0	125.7	126.5	146.2	122.1
1996–1997	125.0	128.2	135.9	134.3	152.9	130.2
1997–1998	133.6	135.6	146.8	141.7	164.9	136.5
1998–1999	135.8	152.7	155.8	144.8	174.1	138.1
1999–2000	143.3	163.3	169.5	153.0	198.7	142.5
2000–2001	148.5	166.2	177.4	165.2	227.6	150.8

Source: Handbook of Statistics on Indian Economy, RBI.

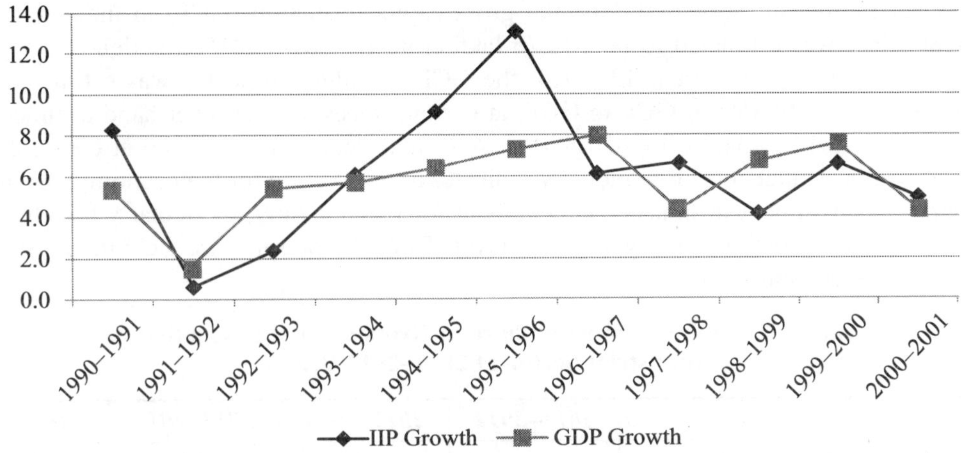

Figure 7.2 Growth in industrial production and growth in GDP.
Source: Handbook of Statistics on Indian Economy, RBI.

Post-reforms, there was a general change in not only the pattern of industrialisation in the country but also in terms of ownership of Indian Industries. In addition, the composition of output has also emerged as a symbol of change after the new Industrial Policy, 1991, i.e., the post-liberalisation. The role of public and private sector was reviewed. New ways of public-private partnerships (PPP) were evolved, with the aim of enhancing industrial progress in the country. Later in the Ninth Five Year Plan, the sector further slowed down and growth rate during the period was recorded as 5% in contrast with 7.3% during the Eighth Five Year Plan. But later in the Tenth Five Year Plan, the industrial performance was better than those of previous two plans. Disinvestment of major public sector was followed during the Tenth Five Year Plan. The performance of industrial sector during the recent years is given in Table 7.6.

Table 7.6 Performance of Industrial Sector

GCF in Industry (₹ Crore at 2004–2005 Prices)								
	2004–05	***2005–06***	***2006–07***	***2007–08***	***2008–09***	***2009–10***	***2010–11***	***CAGR (Eleventh Five Year Plan)***
Mining	37,322	52,259	60,456	68,372	57,045	65,984	70,389	3.9%
Manufacturing	3,44,517	4,04,928	4,74,405	6,11,928	4,20,506	5,98,445	6,40,982	7.8%
Construction	54,445	57,531	95,799	1,15,157	88,523	86,290	98,426	0.68%
Total industry	4,89,584	5,79,391	7,07,029	8,81,464	6,65,067	8,52,999	9,13,051	6.6%
Share of GCF in industry as percentage to total GCF	48.4	49	51.8	54.9	42.5	49.6	48.3	
CAGR has been calculated for a period of four years.								

Source: Economic Survey of India, 2011–2012.

As per the recently released data, the gross capita formation (GCF) in industrial sector at current prices was estimated to be ₹42.76 lakh crore for 2014–2015 experiencing a growth of 9.3% over the last year. In 2013–2014, the GCF in industrial sector was estimated to be ₹39.12 lakh crore. The rate of GCF to GDP, at current prices, on the other hand declined from 34.7% in 2013–2014 to 34.2% in 2014–2015. A similar decline is also seen at constant price. However, rise in estimated GCF in industry indicates a rosy picture for the economy. An upward momentum in investment in industry is beneficial for the economy, particularly to achieve the place of the fastest growing country at global level. Table 7.7 presents the GCF in industry with its share in selected sub-sector.

Table 7.7 Sub-sector-wise Share in Gross Capital Formation in Industrial Sector at 2011–2012 Prices

	2011–2012	*2012–2013*	*2013–2014*	*2014–2015*
Rate of growth of GCF in industry		2.8	–3.7	3.6
Mining	2.1	2.3	4	3.3
Manufacturing	19.2	18.4	17.4	16.9
Electricity	9.6	9.1	8.6	9.2
Construction	7.2	7.7	5.5	5.4

7.11 PERFORMANCE OF SMALL AND MEDIUM SCALE INDUSTRY (SME) SECTOR

Micro, Small and Medium Enterprises (MSMEs) sector contributes significantly to the manufacturing output, employment and exports of the country. Overall, the sector contributes a significant portion of GDP, with share of 37.5% to the country's GDP. A total of 3.6 crore units of such enterprises have been spread across the country providing employment more than 8 crore people constituting more than 6% of India's total population (Economic Survey of India, 2016). Moreover, the sector accounts for more than 45% of the manufacturing output and 40% of the total exports of the country (Ministry of MSME).

As per the revised methodology suggested by the Central Statistics Office (CSO), Ministry of Statistics and Programme Implementation (MoSPI), on the basis of the data on gross domestic product (GDP) published by CSO, MoSPI and final results of the latest Census (Fourth Census), the estimated contribution of MSME sector to GDP and output during 2006–2007 to 2012–2013 are as noted in Table 7.8.

Recent trend of MSME sector in terms of its contribution to GDP and also sectoral output suggests that share of manufacturing MSME in GDP is hovering between 7.73% in 2006–2007 and 7.045% in 2012–2013. On the other hand, the share in case of MSME in services to GDP has been increasing over time. It was estimated to be 27.40% in 2006–2007, which increased to 30.70% in 2011–2012. In the year 2012–2013, the share of MSME sector in service sector output was 30.505%. The share of MSME in manufacturing output of the country decreased from 42.02% in 2006–2007 to 37.33% in 2012–2013 (annual reports, Ministry of MSME).

Table 7.8 Contribution of MSME Sector in GDP and Output (at 2004–2005 Prices)

Year	*Gross value of output of MSME manufacturing sector (₹ in crore)*	*Share of MSME sector in total GDP (%)*			*Share of MSME manufacturing output in total manufacturing output (%)*
		Manufacturing sector MSME	*Services sector MSME*	*Total*	
2006–2007	11,98,818	7.73	27.40	35.13	42.02
2007–2008	13,22,777	7.81	27.60	35.41	41.98
2008–2009	13,75,589	7.52	28.60	36.12	40.79
2009–2010	14,88,352	7.45	28.60	36.05	39.63
2010–2011	16,53,622	7.39	29.30	36.69	38.50
2011–2012	17,88,584	7.27	30.70	37.97	37.47
2012–2013	18,09,976	7.04	30.50	37.54	37.33

Source: **1.** Fourth All India Census of MSME 2006–2007, **2.** National Account Statistics (2014), CSO, MoSPI and **3.** Annual Survey of Industries, CSO, MoSPL.

7.12 REVIEW OF ECONOMIC ENVIRONMENT IN INDUSTRIAL SECTOR

As per the erstwhile Planning Commission Working Group on Manufacturing Industries, the country's economic growth is not derived by manufacturing industry, rather it is sourced by an increase in the service industries. However, it remains a matter of concern as to why the manufacturing sector is not able to attract such progress as in the case of services sector. The percentage of working group shows that the main reasons are poor planning and inadequate consensus. In fact, the absence of competitive regime in the manufacturing sector has led to a decrease in the performance of manufacturing sector. This is also caused by inadequacy in policy implementation. Therefore, to strengthen the industrial sector of the country, a clear vision with set target would be required along with the competitive regulatory regime.

Some of the concerns are as follows:

1. Even after a long period of economic reforms, the manufacturing industry is yet to give the desired outcome.
2. The issue of land acquisition to set up manufacturing units has always been a political issue. A new bill on land acquisition, namely, Right to Fair Compensation and Transparency in Land Acquisition, Rehabilitation and Resettlement Bill, 2013 has already been implemented on 1 January 2014. This act replaces the century-old Land Acquisition Act, 1894, enacted during the British times.
3. Ensuring environmental sustainability also remains a challenge to the manufacturing and mineral industries. In some areas of the country, large projects have failed to materialise. An important example is the project of POSCO. The state government of Odisha allowed constructing a steel plant with a value of US $ 12 billion to POSCO, an Indian subsidiary of Korean company. The MoU expired in 2011 and the project was not even materialised due to various delays and interventions. Due to delays, however, the construction of Phase I is expected to be completed by 2017–2018.

4. Settlement of industrial disputes is another area of concern, wherein a clear policy framework is needed. For instance, industrial dispute in Maruti Plant in India resulted in the decrease in production of vehicles due to the continuous protest of labourers. This unrest happened in Manesar in Haryana (see Box 7.7).

Box 7.7 Industrial Dispute: Maruti at Manesar

- **91** workers arrested • **1** official dead • **100** managers and executives in hospital
- **2** Japanese executives injured • **1,200** policemen deployed
- **THE PLANT**—5.5 lakh is the number of cars rolled out every year
- **DAMAGE**—Office facilities burnt beyond repairs
- **STRIKES AT PLANT IN 2011—October 7–October 21**
- **August 29–October 1:** Company locked out workers asking them to sign a good conduct agreement
- **July 27–28** • **June 4–16**
- **60,000** less vehicles were manufactured because of the strikes last year
- **₹2,300 cr** loss suffered by carmaker last year • **29%** drop in carmaker's profits last year
- **8.74%** drop in Maruti-Suzuki's India Ltd. shares on Thursday

Source: *India Today*, 20 July 2012.

Moreover, the document of the Twelfth Five Year Plan (2012–2017) highlights the following issues:

1. Industry has not given sufficient importance to the documentation of knowledge and creation of intellectual property (IP). As a result, not only the opportunities were lost to create IP but also we lost IPs to the other countries, such as in traditional agricultural products (IPs filed by western countries on neem, turmeric and basmati rice, which India has contested). We need a robust regulatory framework for speeding up award of IPs and also for enforcement of IP regulations. A holistic and better management of IP is required.
2. Considerable focus should be given to improve industry-academia collaborations and interface in creating patents/technologies.
3. It is also important to ascertain that the free trade agreements (FTAs) signed by India do not have trade distorting effects.
4. Micro, small and medium enterprises (MSMEs) have limited information and access to risk capital for sourcing/developing and internalising new technologies. This requires the utmost importance.
5. There is a need to strengthen the standards so that the industry gets benefitted from the mutual learning and improves its technology depth (see Box 7.8).

Box 7.8 Examples of Weak Domestic Standards

1. Absence of standards

The import of poor quality products becomes easy when there is an absence of technical standards. This process is one of the important causes of the weakness of domestic industries and it hurts the industries. Owing to the competitive prices of the imported products which the domestic industries may not be able to match, these poor-quality products gradually capture markets. In India, this seems to be happening in product markets. For example, we see the mobile telephones market, batteries for the mobile telephones, digital blood pressure measuring equipment, decorative lights (imported from China during Diwali festival), and medical equipment, which are all imported products. More importantly, from the consumer point of view, these also expose harmful effects of spurious products. It is important to curb such influx of products into market through adequate technical standards. In the absence of such standards, it would not be possible to make such technical regulations, which would curb the import of poor-quality products.

In case of mobile telephones, lack of manufacturing standards and testing/sampling laboratories is continuously prompting dumping by foreign manufacturers. For example, till 2009, there was no standard mandating all imported mobile phones to have an International Mobile Station Equipment Identity (IMEI) number. This resulted in an increase in the Chinese handsets without IMEI numbers in the Indian market, which had a share of around 13% in 2009.

2. Lack of a clear framework for voluntary and mandatory compliances

In some situations, where Indian standards exist for products or processes, the central government has not notified them for mandatory compliance.

In case of toys, standards have been laid out for safety of toys, which theoretically take care of the safety through standardisation of quality of plastics and paints, electrical and mechanical hazards, migration of heavy elements (lead, cadmium), etc. But it is also true that these standards are not mandatory to comply with, leading to an increase in the imports of toys from other countries in India through dumping strategies.

Structural steel is used for building dams, bridges, etc. Standards for the manufacturing of structural steel are voluntary and lack the need to specify end user. Due to the lack of compliance to such voluntary guidelines and the absence of the need for requisite certification, dumping of poor-grade structural steel is being done in the Indian market.

Source: Twelfth Five Year Plan Document, Planning Commission, Government of India, 2013.

7.13 POLICIES ON FOREIGN DIRECT INVESTMENT IN INDIA

Foreign direct investment is a way to accumulate foreign capital. An economy, which is a backward in its industrial base, technological advancements and employment generation, need to look for foreign collaboration to meet the basic objectives of industrial progress and technological advancement to generate employment. This is persuaded due to lack of domestic funds. In addition, foreign capital also enables to import more to meet the rising domestic demands. Therefore, most of the countries, particularly the developing countries which are being embarked on the process of economic progress, tend to attract the foreign investment through policy measures. India as a developing nation has also formulated policies to drive the economic progress by attracting more foreign investments.

The requirement of foreign capital can be analysed with the following illustration shown in Figure 7.3.

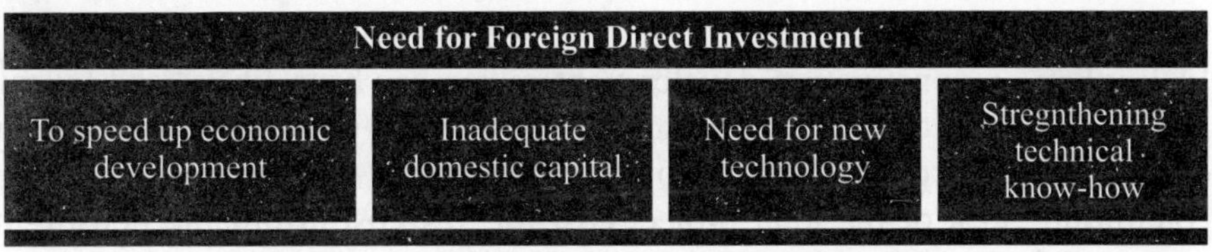

Figure 7.3 Need for foreign direct investment.

There are various forms of foreign investment. These broadly include foreign direct investment, intergovernmental loans, and loans from international institutions and commercial borrowings from external sources. The need and development of policies regulating foreign exchange have been criticised for various reasons. However, the development of policies needs to be understood through the various policy guidelines. These guidelines reflect the need for FDI as well as for reformation over the period of time in India.

Opening of new sectors for FDI after 2014

India is one of the important economies transforming towards market-based economic policies. Radical changes in economic policies are taking place. The reform agenda, which started in 1991, is further strengthened by the new government formed in 2014. The government has opened up 15 major sectors for foreign investment. Striving for better positioning in doing business at global level, the new sectors are also getting other policy supports such as online permit, single window system for registering firm and other initiatives under Make in India campaign. Following are the new sectors where government has eased FDI norms:

1. Townships, shopping complexes and business centres—all allow up to 100% FDI under the automatic route. Conditions on minimum capitalisation and floor area restrictions have now been removed for the construction development sector.
2. India's defence sector now allows consolidated FDI up to 49% under the automatic route. FDI beyond 49% will now be considered by the Foreign Investment Promotion Board. Government approval route will be required only when FDI results in a change of ownership pattern.
3. Private sector banks now allow consolidated FDI up to 74%.
4. Up to 100% FDI is now allowed in coffee/rubber/cardamom/palm oil and olive oil plantations via the automatic route.
5. 100% FDI is now allowed via the automatic route in duty-free shops located and operated in the customs bonded areas.
6. Manufacturers can now sell their products through wholesale and/or retail, including through e-commerce without government approval.
7. Foreign equity caps have now been increased for establishment and operation of satellites, credit information companies, non-scheduled air transport and ground handling services from 74% to 100%.
8. 100% FDI is allowed in medical devices.
9. FDI cap has increased in insurance and sub-activities from 26% to 49%.
10. FDI up to 49% has been permitted in the pension sector.
11. Construction, operation and maintenance of specified activities of railway sector has opened to 100% foreign direct investment under automatic route.
12. FDI policy on construction development sector has been liberalised by relaxing the norms pertaining to minimum area, minimum capitalisation and repatriation of funds or exit from the project. To encourage investment in affordable housing, projects committing 30% of the total project cost for low-cost affordable housing have been exempted from minimum area and capitalisation norms.

13. Investment by NRIs under Schedule 4 of Foreign Exchange Management Act (FEMA) (Transfer or Issue of Security by Persons Resident Outside India) Regulations will be deemed to be domestic investment at par with the investment made by residents.
14. Composite caps on foreign investments introduced to bring uniformity and simplicity is brought across the sectors in FDI policy.
15. 100% FDI allowed in white label ATM operations.

7.14 FOREIGN EXCHANGE REGULATION ACT

The Foreign Exchange Regulation Act (FERA) was a legislation passed by the Parliament of India in 1973 during the Indira Gandhi government. It came into effect on 1 January 1974. The Act imposed stringent regulations on dealings and transactions related to foreign exchange. This Act continued for a long period of time in the country. It also led to the departure of some major companies such as Coca-Cola and Pepsi Co. The main features of the Act were restricted exchange control regime. The Act also advocated the process of Indianisation and did not allow foreign equity of more than 49%.

7.15 INDUSTRIAL POLICY RESOLUTION, 1991

Industrial policy, 1991 freed the industries of the country from the restrictions imposed on them. The policy, 1991 is still considered as the catalyst for foreign investment in the country. The need for foreign reserves was the result of balance of payment crisis in India in 1991. This need was envisaged to be fulfilled by the new structure of foreign investment and exchange control policy. The 1991 reforms was one of the most comprehensive economic reforms.

Closing Case: Industrial Policy Post-2015—The Global Concern

Year 2015 is the deadline for the millennium development goals (MDGs) set by the United Nations to be achieved by the countries of the world. However, a major concern is that many countries may not be able to meet the targets specified within the goals. Therefore, keeping this context in mind and understanding the pivotal role of industrial policies in helping the countries to attain MDGs, the United Nations Industrial Development Organisation (UNIDO) has asserted that the industrial policy in the years beyond 2015 should be rooted in the three dimensions of sustainable development—economic, social and environmental.

Before moving ahead, it is imperative to understand the MDGs as well as the role of UNIDO.

Millennium development goals

There are eight universally agreed upon goals to be achieved by 2015. These goals are known as *MDGs.* Each target is further divided into indicators, which vary from country to country depending on their level of development. The fulfillment of MDGs by a country is to be measured on the basis of their attainment of the respective indicators. The goals and their related targets are given as follows:

1. Eradicate extreme poverty and hunger.
   (i) **Target 1A:** Halve, between 1990 and 2015, the proportion of people living on less than $1.25 per day.
   (ii) **Target 1B:** Achieve decent employment for women, men and young people.
   (iii) **Target 1C:** Halve, between 1990 and 2015, the proportion of people who suffer from hunger.
2. Achieve universal primary education.
   (i) **Target 2A:** By 2015, all children (both girls and boys) can complete a full course of primary schooling.
3. Promote gender equality and empower women.
   (i) **Target 3A:** Eliminate gender disparity in primary and secondary education preferably by 2005, and at all levels by 2015.
4. Reduce child mortality rates.
   (i) **Target 4A:** Reduce by two-thirds, between 1990 and 2015, the under-five mortality rate.
5. Improve maternal health.
   (i) **Target 5A:** Reduce by three quarters, between 1990 and 2015, the maternal mortality ratio.
   (ii) **Target 5B:** Achieve, by 2015, universal access to reproductive health.
6. Combat HIV/AIDS, malaria, and other diseases.
   (i) **Target 6A:** Have halted by 2015 and begun to reverse the spread of HIV/AIDS.
   (ii) **Target 6B:** Achieve, by 2010, universal access to treatment for HIV/AIDS for all those who need it.
   (iii) **Target 6C:** Have halted by 2015 and begun to reverse the incidence of malaria and other major diseases.
7. Ensure environmental sustainability.
   (i) **Target 7A:** Integrate the principles of sustainable development into the country's policies and programmes; reverse the loss of environmental resources.
   (ii) **Target 7B:** Reduce biodiversity loss, achieving, by 2010, a significant reduction in the rate of loss.
   (iii) **Target 7C:** Halve, by 2015, the proportion of the population without sustainable access to safe drinking water and basic sanitation.
   (iv) **Target 7D:** By 2020, achieve a significant improvement in the lives of at least 100 million slum-dwellers.
8. Develop a global partnership for development.
   (i) **Target 8A:** Develop further an open, rule-based, predictable, non-discriminatory trading and financial system.
   (ii) **Target 8B:** Address the special needs of the least developed countries (LDCs).
   (iii) **Target 8C:** Address the special needs of landlocked developing countries and small island developing states.
   (iv) **Target 8D:** Deal comprehensively with the debt problems of developing countries through national and international measures in order to make debt sustainable in the long term.

(v) **Target 8E:** In cooperation with pharmaceutical companies, provide access to the affordable, essential drugs in developing countries.

(vi) **Target 8F:** In cooperation with the private sector, make available the benefits of new technologies, especially information and communications.

United Nations Industrial Development Organisation (UNIDO)

UNIDO is the specialised agency of the United Nations that promotes industrial development, with the aims of ensuring poverty reduction, inclusive globalisation and environmental sustainability, thereby achieving an equitable development. Its mandate is to promote its aims and objectives to meet the requirements of the developing countries and economies in transition. UNIDO provides the following mutually reinforcing services:

1. Technical cooperation
2. Analytical and policy advisory services
3. Standard setting and compliance
4. A convening function for knowledge transfer and networking.

It focuses on the following four main thematic areas:

1. Poverty reduction through productive activities
2. Trade capacity building
3. Energy and environment
4. Cross-cutting issues like South-South Cooperation, LDCs, etc.

UNIDO is efficient in meeting the interlinked challenges of reducing poverty through productive activities, integrating developing countries in global trade through trade capacity building, fostering environmental sustainability in industry, and improving access to clean energy.

Given this backdrop, it is now imperative to know that UNIDO is already working on post-2015 strategic planning to ascertain the future challenges and necessities.

In fact, Ulla Heher, the post-2015 Strategic Planning Coordinator at UNIDO also remarked that for many developing countries, accelerating the transformation of their productive structures is increasingly an integral part of their strategies for achieving inclusive and sustainable development. As per his views, this is supported by the fact that almost one-third of the manufacturing value added is now created in developing countries, up from under 20% about 15 years ago. In fact, the real question about industrial policy in the years beyond 2015 is not whether but how it should be practiced to best strengthen the global approach to development.

Therefore, it becomes evident that a concerted effort is required by the stakeholders including international organisations, private sectors and industry to work towards an industrial policy framework that is capable of ensuring sustainable industrial development and consequently, inclusive growth.

Source: This case is written by the authors based on inputs from the following sources:

1. UNIDO proposes post-2015 industrial policy, Franklin Alli, http://www.vanguardngr.com/2014/01/unido-proposes-post-2015-industrial-policy/, 30 January 2014.
2. http://www.unido.org/
3. http://www.un.org/millenniumgoals/

CASE QUESTIONS

1. Find out the indicators of MDGs for India and their current status of attainment.
2. What role should the private sector play in helping India to fulfill the MDGs?
3. Is there any interface between India and UNIDO and what are the issues of common concerns?

REVIEW QUESTIONS

1. Outline the provision of Industrial Policy, 1948.
2. What are Schedule A and Schedule B?
3. Examine the features of the Industrial Policy, 1956.
4. Outline the characteristics of the industrial policies prior to liberalisation.
5. What were the objectives and features of the 1991 industrial policy?
6. Examine the performance of industrial sector post-1991.
7. What is FDI?
8. What are MDGs? Outline the concerns related to the global industrial policy post-2015.

SUGGESTED READINGS

Ahluwalia, I.J., 1991, *Productivity and Growth in Indian Manufacturing*, Oxford University Press, Delhi.

Ahluwalia, I.J. and Little, I.M.D. (Eds.), 2012, *India's Economic Reforms and Development: Essays for Manmohan Singh*, 2nd ed., Oxford University Press, Delhi.

Bauer, P.T., 2011, *Indian Economic Policy and Development*, Routledge, New York.

Economic Survey of India, 1992, 1993, 1994, Ministry of Finance, Government of India, New Delhi.

Economic Survey of India, 2013–2014, Ministry of Finance, Government of India, New Delhi.

Mahalanobis, P.C., 1953, 'Some Observations on the Process of Growth of National Income', *Sankhya*, Vol. 12, Part 4, pp. 307–312.

Misra, S.K. and Puri, V.K., 2012, *Indian Economy*, Himalaya Publication House, New Delhi.

Samuelson, Paul and Nordhaus, William, 2009, *Macroeconomics*, McGraw-Hill Education, New Delhi.

Twelfth Five Year Plan Document, Planning Commission of India, New Delhi.

8

FISCAL POLICY

Learning Outcomes

After reading this chapter, you will

- Comprehend the concepts and applications of public revenue, public expenditure and public debt
- Appreciate how development activities are financed by public expenditure and how fiscal policy plays a pivotal role in the development initiatives
- Know the current budgetary allocations

Opening Case: Right to Food

The Government of India implemented National Food Security Act in 2013, with the aim to provide subsidised food grains to almost two-third of the country's population. The Act entitles the beneficiaries to purchase 5 kg of cereals per person per month at a subsidised price, which includes: rice at ₹3/kg, wheat at ₹2/kg and coarse grains (millet) at ₹1/kg. Moreover, certain section of the society including pregnant women, lactating mothers, and some categories of children are eligible for daily free meals.

The National Advisory Council (NAC) of the Government of India proposed the salient features of the National Food Security Bill. NAC, in fact, is mandated with the role to provide inputs to the formulation of policy by the government and to provide support to the government in its legislative businesses.

As per the Report of the Expert Committee on National Food Security Bill, the salient features of the Food Security Bill are as follows:

1. 75% of the rural and 50% of the urban population are entitled for three years from enactment to 5 kg food grains per month at ₹3 (4.8¢US), ₹2 (3.2¢US), ₹1 (1.6¢US) per kilogram for rice, wheat and coarse grains (millet), respectively.
2. The states are responsible for determining eligibility.
3. Pregnant women and lactating mothers are entitled to a nutritious take home ration of 600 cal and a maternity benefit of at least ₹6,000 for six months.

4. Children from 6 months to 14 years of age are to receive free hot meals or take home rations.
5. The central government will provide funds to the states in case of short supplies of food grains.
6. The current food grain allocation of the states will be protected by the central government at least for six months.
7. The state government will provide a food security allowance to the beneficiaries in case of non-supply of food grains.
8. The public distribution system is to be reformed.
9. The eldest woman in the household, 18 years or above, is the head of the household for the issuance of the ration card.
10. There will be state and district-level redress mechanisms.
11. State Food Commissions will be formed for the implementation and monitoring of the provisions of the act.
12. The cost of implementation is estimated to be US$22 billion (1.25 lakh crore), approximately 1.5% of GDP.
13. The poorest, who are covered under the Antodaya Anna Yojna, will remain entitled to the 35 kg of grains allotted to them under the mentioned scheme.

Given the features of this bill, it is important to note that we are already spending ₹67,310 crore on food subsidies. With this Act being implemented, there will be an increase of another ₹30,000 crore only, and it will help in feeding 77 crore people sleeping hungry in the country. In other words, the Government of India will only be giving a subsidy of ₹1,188 per person per year or ₹3.25 per day.[1]

There has been considerable criticism of the bill because of political reasons. It carries a mandate to contribute to the sustainable livelihood and inclusive growth.

The resource allocation is huge and it serves a major development purpose.

Source: This case is written by the authors based on inputs from the following sources:

1. National, Advisory Council, Government of India, http://nac.nic.in/
2. Report of the Expert Committee on National Food Security Bill, http://eac.gov.in/reports/rep_NFSB.pdf
3. Food Security Bill—Making sense of the numbers, Article by Sachin Kumar Jain, http://infochangeindia.org/agriculture/analysis/food-security-bill-making-sense-of-the-numbers.html

8.1 INTRODUCTION

Fiscal policy primarily deals with the state's policy measures to regulate taxation and public expenditure. In India, as a planned economy, fiscal policy remains an important instrument for both revenue collections as well as financing various programmes. Thus, the government decisions on account of fiscal measures influence the business environment as well. In day-to-day life, our activities are influenced by the government decisions. For instance, at the end of the fiscal year, households look at the changes in the tax slabs, etc. Any rebate on personal income increases the household's consumption capability as well as investment potential. In other words,

1. 'Food Security Bill — Making sense of the numbers', Article by Sachin Kumar Jain, http://infochangeindia.org/agriculture/analysis/food-security-bill-making-sense-of-the-numbers.html

fiscal policies also determine the business environment from micro to macro level. It is in this context that it becomes important for us to examine the policies related to government's earnings (revenues) and government's expenditure. For instance, projects like the one discussed in the opening case requires a dedicated government expenditure.

The measures under fiscal policy deal mainly with the approaches to revenue collection and decisions related to expenditure. These policies are announced by the Finance Minister of the Government of India in the budget speech. Fiscal policies are now important macro-economic instruments, particularly as an instrument for the government intervention. This policy was mainly advocated by Keynesian economics. In a pure capitalist economy, the government intervention was not considered healthy for market economy. However, these days, the market alone cannot fulfill the socio-economic needs of the population. In order to strike a balance in a free market economy, fiscal instruments are used by the government.

Government not only imposes measures to collect revenues but also follows policies to finance the various programmes. Therefore, it also incurs expenditures. These expenditures are incurred in various developmental programmes such as building infrastructure, maintaining infrastructure, supporting social development programmes like health and education. In recent years, the government has adopted a food security programme through the National Food Security Act, 2013. These expenditures are being financed by both the central and state governments.

The sources of financing these expenditures differ depending on the magnitude of expenditure. The sources also determine the kind of impacts on the economy. For instance,

1. Expenditure through deficit financing increases the inflationary pressure on the economy.
2. On the other hand, increased expenditure on social welfare of the households increases the consumption capability, leading to an increase in the overall demand in the economy.

In both cases, fiscal policy has a major role to play in determining the economic and business environment.

Following are the two important heads under which fiscal policies are divided:

1. ***Policies of revenue collection:*** Taxation is an important instrument for revenue. Thus, government imposes direct taxes on income and indirect taxes on economic activities.
2. ***Policies of government expenditures:*** The collected revenues from taxes and charges are spent on the development of various infrastructure such as building roads, rails, ports, airports, hospitals, educational institutions, etc. These projects incur heavy expenditure. Thus, financing of these projects is also an important part of fiscal policies. One such scheme has been discussed in the opening case of this chapter.

As we know, government expenditure on social sector, infrastructure sector as well as education sector leads to an increase in the consumption expenditure. It increases market demand among the population as the expenditure in social sector strengthens the human capital, creates employment and reduces poverty. The wider impacts of such policies are always recognised in the economic arena.

The financing instruments of the government also influence the monetary policies (Chapter 9 discusses monetary policy). For instance, if the government expenditure exceeds its revenue, then the financing depends on the market borrowing and deficit financing. In this situation, money supply in the economy increases. This further leads to an increase in the inflation in the economy. In this context, a careful selection of fiscal policy is indeed important to tackle the economic situation. This chapter deals with it and also highlights the fiscal policies of the Government of India.

8.2 PUBLIC REVENUE

To understand the basic concepts of fiscal policy, we need to look upon the budget sheet of the government. See 2013–2014 budget at a glance[2] in Box 8.1.

Box 8.1 Union Budget of India, 2013–2014 (₹ Crore)

S. No.	Items	Sub-items	*2014–2015* Actuals @	*2015–2016* Budget Estimate	*2015–2016* Revised Estimate	*2016–2017* Budget Estimate
1.	Revenue receipts		11,01,472	11,41,575	12,06,084	13,77,022
	(a)	Tax revenue (net to centre)	9,03,615	9,19,842	9,47,508	10,54,101
	(b)	Non-tax revenue	1,97,857	2,21,733	2,58,576	3,22,921
2.	Capital receipts (c+d+e)$		5,62,201	6,35,902	5,79,307	6,01,038
	(c)	Recoveries of loans	13,738	10,753	18,905	10,634
	(d)	Other receipts	37,737	69,500	25,312	56,500
	(e)	Borrowings and other liabilities*	5,10,725	5,55,649	5,35,090	5,33,904
3.	**Total receipts (1+2)$**		**16,63,673**	**17,77,477**	**17,85,391**	**19,78,060**
4.	Non-plan expenditure (f+g)		12,01,029	13,12,200	13,08,194	14,28,080
	(f)	On revenue account	11,09,394	12,06,027	12,12,669	13,27,408
	(f')	Of which, interest payments	4,02,444	45,61,145	4,42,620	4,92,670
	(g)	On capital account	91,635	10,61,73	95,525	1,00,642
5.	Plan expenditure		4,62,644	4,65,277	4,77,197	5,50,010
	(h)	On revenue account	3,57,597	3,30,020	3,35,004	4,03,628
	(i)	On capital account	1,05,047	1,35,257	1,42,193	1,46,382
6.	**Total Expenditure (4+5)**		**16,63,673**	**17,77,477**	**17,85,391**	**19,78,060**
	(j)	Revenue expenditure (f+h)	14,66,992	15,36,047	15,47,673	17,31,037
	(k)	Of which, grants for creation of capital assets	1,30,760	1,32,472	1,32,004	1,66,840
	(l)	Capital expenditure (g+i)	1,96,681	2,41,430	2,37,718	2,47,023

2. *Revenue deficit* refers to the excess of revenue expenditure over revenue receipts. *Effective revenue deficit* is the difference between the revenue deficit and grants for the creation of capital assets. *Fiscal deficit* is the difference between the revenue receipts plus non-debt capital receipts and the total expenditure including loans, net of repayments. This indicates the total borrowing requirements of government from all sources. Primary deficit is measured by fiscal deficit less interest payments.

7.	Revenue deficit (j – 1)	3,65,519	3,94,472	3,41,589	3,54,015
		(2.9)	(2.8)	(2.5)	(2.3)
8.	Effective revenue deficit (7 – k)	2,34,759	2,68,000	2,09,585	1,87,175
		(1.9)	(2.0)	(1.5)	(1.2)
9.	Fiscal deficit [6 – (1 + c + d)]	5,10,725	5,55,649	5,35,090	5,33,904
		(4.1)	(3.9)	(3.9)	(3.5)
10.	Primary deficit (9 – f')	1,08,281	99,504	92,469	41,234
		(0.9)	(0.7)	(0.7)	(0.3)
US $ Excluding receipts under Market Stabilisation Scheme. * Includes draw-down of cash balance.					

Note: Actuals for 2011–2012 in this document are provisional. In parentheses, deficits are expressed as percentage of GDP.

Source: Ministry of Finance, Government of India.

The budget at a glance indicates some important variables to be understood. These variables are the contents of revenues, expenditures and their respective estimates. It is, therefore, imperative to understand the basic difference between the revenue and the capital flows.

By definition, the *capital flows* or *capital expenditure* is an expenditure, which creates asset in short as well as long term.

On the other hand, *capital receipts* are the receipt from the process of liquidation of an asset. In other words, the capital receipts are the part of government revenue. Revenues, as a whole, come out from the various sources, which include regular earnings, taxation, etc. Similarly, *revenue expenditure* is a regular phenomenon in which the revenue incurs on maintaining the law and order, defense expenditure, social expenditure, etc. Thus, capital expenditure is also a part of the government expenditure.

Broadly, there are three types of revenues, *viz.* tax revenues, non-tax revenues and capital receipts. These are described in the subsequent sections.

8.3 TAX REVENUES

Tax revenues are the receipts collected on account of collection of tax and duties. This is further divided into direct and indirect taxes. Direct taxes include income tax levied upon earnings of households, business earnings or capital gains. On the other hand, indirect taxes which include service tax, excise duty, etc., are levied upon economic activities and services availed. Thus, taxes collected through these means are known as *tax revenues*.

Taxation in India has been an important instrument of government's revenues. The significance of the taxation can be understood by the fact that today tax-GDP ratio is more than 16% as against the 6.3% in 1950–1951. Total tax revenue of the central government was estimated at ₹9198.42 billion in 2015–2016. The same was ₹2,451 billion in 1970–1971. It is important to see the share of other revenues. In 1970–1971, the share of tax revenues was about 46%, which rose to 52.1% in 2015–2016. Similarly, the share of non-tax revenue has decreased from 15.8% in 1970–1971 to 12.5% in 2015–2016. However, the share of capital receipts remains fluctuating, around 38% in 1970–1971, 41% in 2010–2011 and about 35% in 2015–2016. The changing dynamics of these revenues are presented in Figure 8.1.

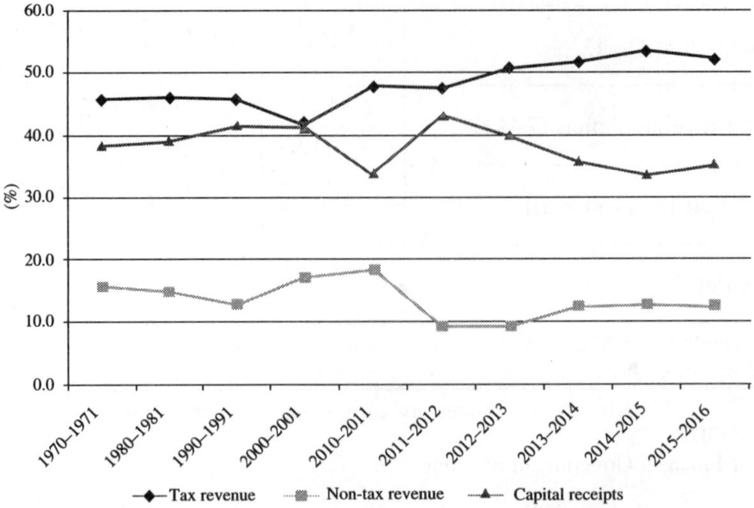

Figure 8.1 Share of components of revenues of central government.
Source: Handbook of Statistics on Indian Economy, RBI.

8.3.1 Direct and Indirect Tax Revenue

Table 8.1 indicates the various components of direct and indirect tax revenues. The trend indicates that the share of personal income tax in the total direct tax revenue was 22.3% in 1970–1971, with ₹1.14 billion out of ₹5.11 billion total direct tax revenue. The same (in percentage) total tax revenue was 4.7% in 1970–1971. The share of personal income in direct tax increased to about 40.1% in 2015–2016 from 22.3% in 1970–1971, which also led to an increase in its share in the total tax revenues up to about 22% in the same year. The interesting phenomenon recorded after the economic reform was revenue collection through indirect taxes. In 1970–1971, direct tax in the total tax revenue accounted for 21%, which went up to 54.1% in 2015–2016. Similarly, the share of indirect tax in the total tax revenue went down to 46% in 2015–2016 from 78.7% in 1970–1971. Table 8.1 indicates the revenue from taxation and Figure 8.2 represents the changing share of direct and indirect tax revenue in the total revenue collected from the various taxes.

Table 8.1 Direct and Indirect Tax Revenue (₹ in billion)

Year	*Direct Tax*	*Indirect Tax*	*Total*
1970–1971	5.11	18.9	24.04
1980–1981	18.93	71.3	90.25
1990–1991	69.03	347.4	416.47
2000–2001	496.51	839.2	1335.72
2010–2011	3135.01	2078.2	5213.21
2011–2012	3433.10	2218.4	5651.50
2012–2013	3973.45	2532.7	6506.15
2013–2014	4728.61	2883.2	7611.81
2014–2015	4992.53	4092.10	9084.63
2015–2016	4951.96	4246.46	9198.42

Source: Handbook of Statistics on Indian Economy, RBI.

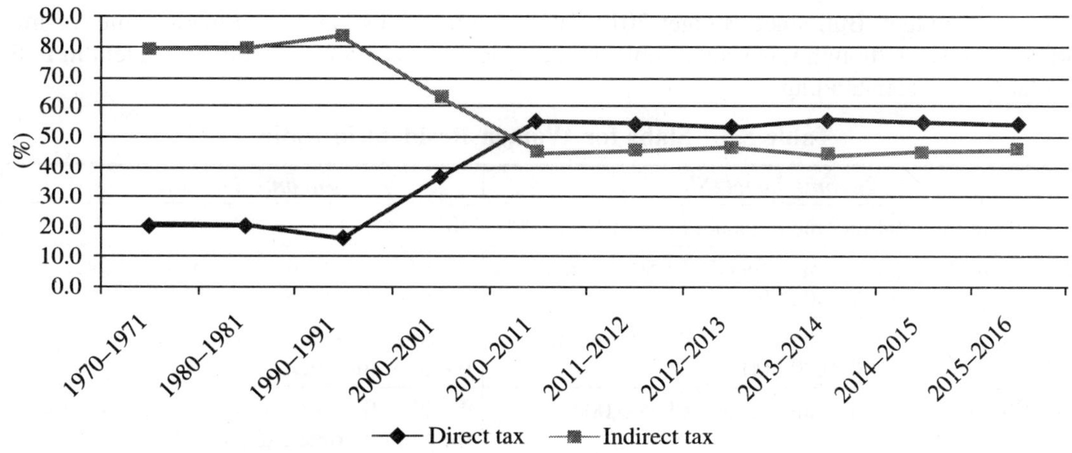

Figure 8.2 Share of direct and indirect tax in total tax revenue.

Source: Handbook of Statistics on Indian Economy, RBI.

Direct taxes

The taxes on income are considered as the *direct taxes*. Government of India imposes mainly income tax and corporation tax on the income of individuals and firms respectively. Income tax is known as the *personal income tax*. The Government of India has tried to lay down a progressive tax structure when it comes to imposition of personal income tax. It is not levied on all the people of the country. It is slab-based. In fact, this taxation is being followed by the government on the basis of ability to pay principle.[3] Thus, the households with lower income are exempted from the personal income tax. The exemption parameter has been changing. In fact, the minimum income which was exempted from tax was ₹40,000 in 1995–1996 while it is ₹2,50,000 in 2014–2015. In the recent budget, there is no change in tax slabs. However, some more exemptions are given to senior citizens. It is found that there has been a continuous decrease in tax rates on personal income. The tax rates are illustrated in Table 8.2.

Table 8.2 Tax Rates

	Income Level/Slab	*Income Tax Rate*
1	Where the total income does not exceed ₹2,50,000	Nil
2	Where the total income exceeds ₹2,50,000 but does not exceed ₹5,00,000.	10% of amount by which the total income exceeds ₹2,50,000
3	Where the total income exceeds ₹5,00,000 but does not exceed ₹10,00,000.	₹30,000 + 20% of the amount by which the total income exceeds ₹5,00,000
4	Where the total income exceeds ₹10,00,000.	₹1,30,000 + 30% of the amount by which the total income exceeds ₹10,00,000

Source: Union Budget 2014–2015, Ministry of Finance, Government of India.

In case of individual being a woman resident in India and below the age of 60 years at any time during the previous year, there used to be a separate provision in budgets before the

3. Ruddar Datt and K.P.M. Sundharam, *Indian Economy*, S. Chand & Company, 40th ed., 1999.

2013–2014 budget. But, since Budget 2013–2014, the tax slabs have been made same for men and women. Even though it is same, Table 8.3 provides the tax slabs for women resident in India for clarity of understanding.

Table 8.3 Slabs for Women Resident in India

	Income Level/Slab	*Income Tax Rate*
1	Where the total income does not exceed ₹2,50,000	Nil
2	Where the total income exceeds ₹2,50,000 but does not exceed ₹5,00,000	10% of the amount by which the total income exceeds ₹2,50,000
3	Where the total income exceeds ₹5,00,000 but does not exceed ₹10,00,000	₹30,000 + 20% of the amount by which the total income exceeds ₹5,00,000
4	Where the total income exceeds ₹10,00,000	₹1,30,000 + 30% of the amount by which the total income exceeds ₹10,00,000

Source: Union Budget 2014–2015, Ministry of Finance, Government of India.

In case of an individual resident who is of the age of 60 years or more at any time during the previous year, the slabs are illustrated as follows (Table 8.4):

Table 8.4 Slabs for an Individual of Age 60 Years or More

	Income Level/Slab	*Income Tax Rate*
1	Where the total income does not exceed ₹3,00,000	Nil
2	Where the total income exceeds ₹3,00,000 but does not exceed ₹5,00,000	10% of the amount by which the total income exceeds ₹2,00,000
3	Where the total income exceeds ₹5,00,000 but does not exceed ₹10,00,000	₹20,000 + 20% of the amount by which the total income exceeds ₹5,00,000
4	Where the total income exceeds ₹10,00,000	₹1,20,000 + 30% of the amount by which the total income exceeds ₹10,00,000

Source: Union Budget 2014–2015, Ministry of Finance, Government of India.

In case of an individual resident who is of the age of 80 years or more at any time during the previous year, the slabs are illustrated as follows (Table 8.5):

Table 8.5 Slabs for an Individual of Age 80 Years or More

	Income Level/Slab	*Income Tax Rate*
1	Where the total income does not exceed ₹5,00,000	Nil
2	Where the total income exceeds ₹5,00,000, but does not exceed ₹10,00,000	20% of the amount by which the total income exceeds ₹5,00,000
3	Where the total income exceeds ₹10,00,000	₹1,00,000 + 30% of the amount by which the total income exceeds ₹10,00,000

Source: Union Budget 2014–2015, Ministry of Finance, Government of India.

Corporation tax

Corporation tax is another direct tax levied on the net income of the companies/firms. The rates are kept different for domestic firms and foreign firms in India. The tax was very high, which gradually decreased over the period of time, particularly since 1990–1991 (or after the liberalisation process). The reduction was aimed at assisting the private sector in driving the economic growth. At present, the corporate tax rate for domestic companies is 30%, while the same for foreign companies is 50%. In fact, the 2005–2006 budgets aligned the income of firms for domestic firms to the highest marginal personal income tax, which was 30%. The budget also included depreciation rate by 15% in case of firms producing general machinery, which was increased to 20%. In addition to corporation taxes, there were some surcharges levied by the government, which were later removed in a phased manner. As per the budget of 2015–2016, the surcharges are applicable for income level exceeding ₹1 crore on individual income excluding firms which is 15%. New manufacturing companies incorporated on or after 1 March 2016 are to be given an option to be taxed at 25% + surcharge and cess, provided they do not claim profit linked or investment-linked deductions and do not avail of investment allowance and accelerated depreciation. It is also proposed to reduce corporate tax for small business enterprises to 29% plus surcharges.

Due to tax evasion, the Finance Minister in 1996–1997 levied a Minimum Alternate Tax (MAT). The tax was supposed to be levied on the firms which have the total corporation tax less than 30% of the total book profit after availing exemptions. This was initially 12% of the book profit, which later increased to 15% in 2009–2010. Some of the firms engaged in power and infrastructure sector were exempted from this tax. Revenue collection from corporation tax was very high and more than 70% of the revenue collected through direct tax measures. Revenue collected through personal income tax was as low as 22.3% in 1970–1971. In 1990–1991, the direct tax revenue was collected mainly through corporation tax. However, the share of personal income in the total direct tax revenue increased to over 47% in 2000–2001, which is now 60%. Figure 8.3 indicates the trend of share of these two tax revenue in the direct tax collections.

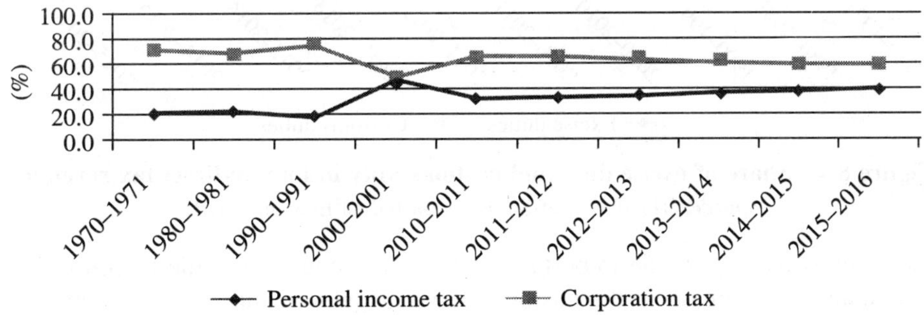

Figure 8.3 Share of income tax and corporation tax in total direct tax revenues.
Source: Handbook of Statistics on Indian Economy, RBI.

Indirect taxes

Indirect taxes are the duties levied on commodities and services purchased and availed. There are various forms of indirect taxes. However, in India these indirect taxes are broadly divided into excise duties and customs duties.

Excise duties are found to be an important source of revenues, when it comes to indirect tax revenue sources. These duties are levied by the centre for goods, which are produced domestically and administered by the centre under the authority of entry 84 of the Union List I under Article 246 of the Constitution. In addition, on some products such as liquor, the state governments are also imposing excise taxes, which are exempted from the central excise taxes. The excise duty is levied as per the Central Excise Act, 1944 and under the Schedules I and II of the Central Excise Tariff Act, 1985. Some products yield the maximum revenue through excise duties, which include production of commodities like sugar, cotton, cloth, tobacco, motor spirit, etc. In 1950–1951 the tax revenue collected through excise duties was ₹70 crore, which rose to ₹1,369 crore in 1970–1971 and ₹1,77,223 crore in 2015–2016.

Customs duties are imposed on the commodities which are imported from abroad as well as exported from India. There are two major components of customs duties, *viz.* import and export duties. These two duties are important, when it comes to competitiveness of the products produced in India and abroad. Increasing export duty would reduce the competitiveness of Indian products in the global market. Increasing import duties would deter globalisation. In the multilateral rule-making, WTO members adhere to a minimum commitment and mainly towards a gradual reduction in the import tariff. Figure 8.4 depicts the share of excise and customs duty in the total indirect tax revenue of India.

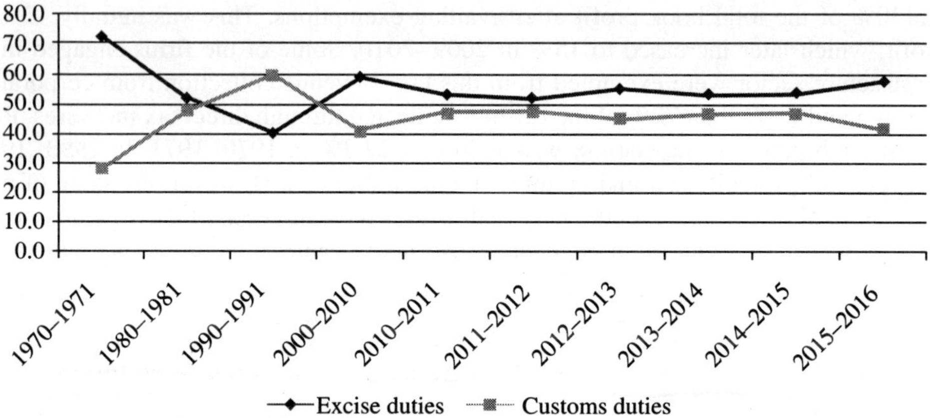

Figure 8.4 Share of excise duty and customs duty in total indirect tax revenues.
Source: Handbook of Statistics on Indian Economy, RBI.

Import duties have been the important source of revenue. Over the period of time, there has been a significant increase in the customs duties. However, the share of customs duties in the total revenues collected through indirect taxation remains almost constant during the recent decades, with registering a slight increase from about 41% in 2000–2001 to 45% in 2013–2014 and 42% in 2015–2016. It clearly indicates the reduction on duties on imports. The central government has collected over ₹1,27,482 crore.

Other taxes are the taxes imposed by the government along with direct taxes. These other taxes are imposed in the form of indirect tax collection on expenditure and services rendered, etc. These taxes are service tax, wealth tax, gift tax, interest tax, advertisement tax, expenditure tax, etc. Some of the taxes are levied by the centre and some of these are levied by the state. The clear distinction has been made by the Constitution by taking some of the taxation in union list and some of these in concurrent list and state list.

The clear distinction has been made by the Constitution by taking some of the taxations in union list and some of these in state and concurrent lists. A new proposal is to introduce Goods and Service Tax (GST) (see Box 8.2), which will streamline indirect tax system in India, and is likely to be rolled out on 1 July 2017. This is also discussed in detail in Chapter 12 of this book.

Box 8.2 Goods and Service Tax (GST) and Its Benefits

In the backdrop of India's complex taxation system which has multiple layers and several agencies involved, the Government of India embarked upon to streamline the indirect tax system in India by adopting new tax structure called goods and services tax (GST). This initiative was taken up in 2000 during the tenure of the then Prime Minister, A.B. Vajpayee, and was later evolved during the tenure of the former Prime Minister, Manmohan Singh. Later, in a budget speech, the then Finance Minister, P. Chidambaram announced the target date for the implementation as 1st April 2010. The new tax regime required constitutional amendments, which was later cleared by the Prime Minister, Narendra Modi's government on 3rd August 2016 by both the houses of the Parliament after having political consensus on the amendments and tax structure. It is, however, expected that the GST regime will be effective from 1st July 2017.

Policy-makers, including economists and technocrats, have long backed the GST, which, as per their assessment, could boost economic output by 1–2% points a year. However, the bill which is now passed requires to be passed by at least 15 state legislatures for which negotiations are held between the Central and the State Governments. Efforts have been taken to finalise rates under the GST, for which a GST Council has been formed. The GST Council has decided a four-tier GST rates of 5%, 12% 18% and 28% with lowest for essential goods and highest for luxury goods.

The following are the benefits of the new GST regime:

- A simple tax regime, GST, will replace a complex tax regime in which 17 indirect taxes were included.
- A simple tax regime will strengthen the system and has potential to save costs to the economy.
- Tax evasion will set to decrease and exemptions will decrease.
- Encourage seamless movement of goods vehicle across states leading to increase in the output of vehicles (In India, goods vehicles travel 280 km a day less than the 50% of the productivity in the US where it travels with 800 km a day).
- The GST will provide input tax credit to many capital goods leading to a 12–14% drop in the costs, and is expected to lift up investment in capital goods by 6%.
- Manufacturing will get more competitive as GST addresses cascading of tax, inter-state tax, high logistics costs and fragmented market.
- The current 2% inter-state levy means production is kept within a state which can be removed under GST creating a national level market.
- The GDP is expected to increase by more than 1% due to cost saving. National Council of Applied Economic Research (NCAER) estimates rise in the GDP from 0.9% to 1.7% due to the elimination of tax cascading and state restrictions and levies have complicated e-commerce.

Source: Based on 'The advantages of GST: Take a look at benefits', August 4, 2016, *The Economic Times*; http://economictimes.indiatimes.com/news/economy/policy/the-advantages-of-gst-take-a-look-at-benefits/articleshow/53514291.cms

8.4 NON-TAX REVENUES

Non-tax revenues are those which are collected through dividends, profits from public undertakings, fees, fines, etc. There also include revenue from sale of telecom spectrum in the country.

8.5 CAPITAL RECEIPTS

Capital receipts are another important instrument of government revenues. These include revenues from liquidation of government asset such as disinvestment, fresh borrowings and interest receipts, etc.

The three of these have been depicted through the following illustration shown in Figure 8.5.

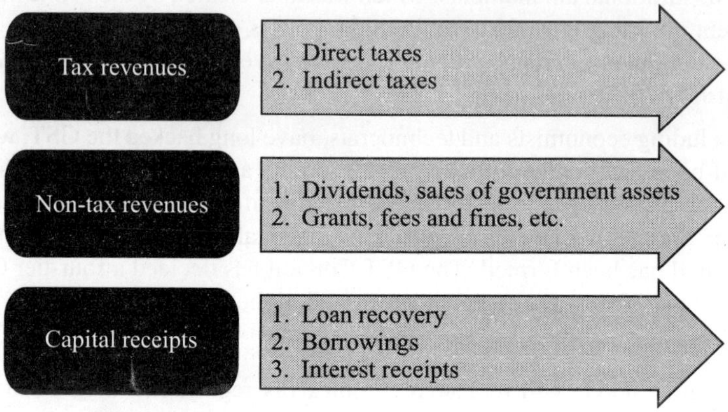

Figure 8.5 Instruments of government revenue.

8.6 PUBLIC EXPENDITURES

In addition to the concept of revenues receipt, the government also incurs expenditures. The basic concepts of expenditures are given as follows:

1. ***Planned expenditure:*** Planned expenditure incurs under the central and state plans. In India, the centre and states are running various schemes and programmes. To finance these programmes and schemes, an agreed sum of expenditure by the Planning Commission is categorised under planned expenditure.
2. ***Non-planned expenditure:*** Non-planned expenditure are those which incur upon interest payments, expenditure on completing the schemes and programmes of the previous plans and those expenditure which are not included in the five year or yearly plans of both the centre and state governments.

In India, there has been continuous increase in the expenditure of the central government. The increase is significant in case of revenue expenditure, which is financed by the tax and non-tax revenues. Table 8.6 shows the statistics on revenue and capital expenditures of the central government.

Table 8.6 Expenditure of Central Government (₹ in Crore)

Year	Revenue Expenditure	Capital Expenditure	Total Expenditure
1970–1971	3,130.00	2,494.00	5,624.00
1980–1981	14,410.00	8,358.00	22,768.00
1990–1991	73,516.00	31,782.00	1,05,298.00
2000–2001	2,77,839.00	47,753.00	3,25,592.00
2010–2011	10,40,723.00	1,56,605.00	11,97,328.00
2011–2012	11,45,785.00	1,58,580.00	13,04,365.00
2012–2013	12,43,514.00	1,66,858.00	14,10,372.00
2013–2014	13,71,772.00	1,87,675.00	15,59,447.00
2014–2015	14,88,780.00	1,92,378.00	16,81,158.00
2015–2016	15,36,047.00	2,41,430.00	17,77,477.00

Source: Handbook on Indian Economy, Reserve Bank of India.

As per the guidelines for the classification of public expenditure for the Twelfth Five Year Plan, planned and non-planned expenditures are redefined. The guidelines say that the plan expenditure is under the central and state plans, and non-planned expenditure are those which do not come under the plan expenditure of the centre and state governments.

The non-planned expenditure is further categorised under the revenue and capital expenditure. Revenue expenditure is financed out of the collected revenue from taxes and non-taxes sources. It includes interest payments, subsidies, defence, social services, economic services, grants to states and UTs, etc. On account of capital expenditure loans, equipment for defence, loans to states and UTs and foreign governments are included. Table 8.7 shows the details of expenditure of central government under non-planned expenditure.

Table 8.7 Details of Expenditure of Central Government under Non-planned Expenditure

		2014–2015	2015–2016	2015–2016	2016–2017
		Actuals	Budget Estimate	Revised Estimate	Budget Estimate
1.	Revenue expenditure				
(i)	Interest payments and prepayment premium	4,02,444	4,56,145	4,42,620	4,92,670
(ii)	Defence services	1,36,807	1,52,139	1,43,236	1,62,759
(iii)	Subsidies	2,58,258	2,43,811	2,57,801	2,50,433
(iv)	Grants to state and UT governments	77,125	1,08,552	1,08,233	1,18,356
(v)	Pensions	93,611	88,521	95,731	1,23,368
(vi)	Police	47,767	51,791	52,681	59,796

(vii)	Assistance to states from National Calamity Contingency Fund/National Disaster Response Fund (NDRF)	3,461	5,690	5,910	6,450
(viii)	Other general services (organs of state, tax collection, external affairs, etc.)	26,147	30,936	30,345	35,003
(ix)	Social services (education, health, broadcasting etc.)	25,829	29,143	32,149	32,134
(x)	Economic services (agriculture, industry, power, transport, communications, science and technology, etc.)	26,632	28,984	33,722	34,266
(xi)	Postal deficit	6,121	6,665	6,749	8,416
(xii)	Expenditure of union territories without legislature	4,833	4,998	5,109	5,677
(xiii)	Amount met from National Calamity Contingency Fund/ Contribution to National Disaster Response Fund (NDRF)	–3,461	–5,690	–5,910	–6,450
(xiv)	Grants to foreign governments	3,820	4,432	4,293	4,530
	Total revenue non-plan expenditure	**11,09,394**	**12,06,027**	**12,12,669**	**13,27,408**
2.	Capital expenditure				
(i)	Defence services	81,887	94,588	81,400	86,340
(ii)	Other non-plan capital outlay	8,180	10,582	13,187	13,348
(iii)	Loans to public enterprises	650	954	668	898
(iv)	Loans to state and UT governments	73	79	79	81
(v)	Loans to foreign governments	...	158	158	...
(vi)	Others	845	–188	33	–45
	Total capital non-plan expenditure	**91,635**	**1,06,173**	**95,525**	**1,00,622**
	Total non-plan expenditure	**12,01,029**	**13,12,200**	**13,08,194**	**14,28,030**

Source: Ministry of Finance, Government of India.

8.7 FISCAL DEFICIT

Budgetary deficit has close relations with the policies which govern the economic environment. As we know, budgetary deficits are higher expenditure of the government budget over its budgetary revenues. Significant increase in the budgetary deficit implies that the government runs under heavy debt. It can also deter the economic growth in the long-run. In its World Economic Outlook 2013, International Monetary Fund (IMF) warns that countries with large fiscal deficits must consolidate.

As per the projection of IMF, the government debt in developed countries has been increasing from 60% of GDP in 1992 to 107% in 2012, which will continue to increase up to 104% in 2018. The projection has accounted for fiscal adjustment in these countries, which would eventually lead to decrease in debt as a percentage of GDP. In case of developing countries like Asia, the government debt was around 34% in 2012, which is estimated to reduce to 24% by 2018. The same shows a rise in case of European Union, reaching from 69% in 1996 to about 87% in 2012.[4] As per the data of the World Bank, the governments of most of the countries are suffering from cash deficit. Figure 8.6 indicates the same. Fiscal deficits build a pressure on the government. Thus, a decline in public debt and fiscal deficit would reveal the strong financial position of the government. Through sound fiscal position, governments also act against some of the global setbacks. For instance, government through fiscal stimulation tried to avert the impacts of crises of 2008 on various industrial sectors.

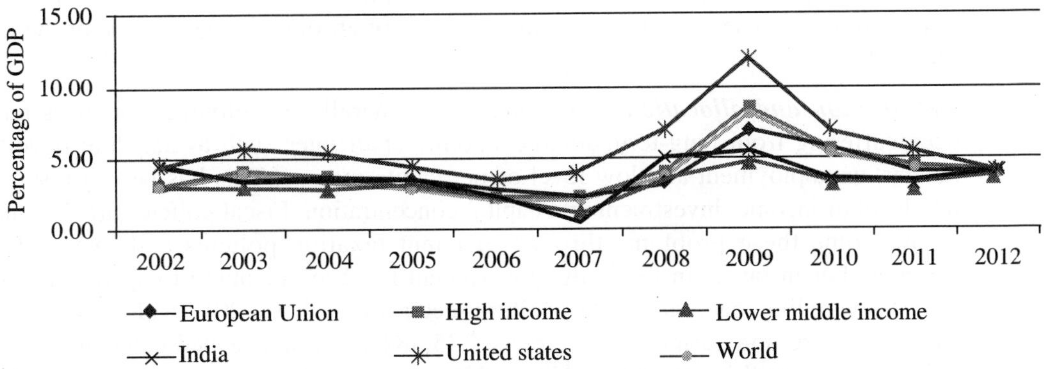

Figure 8.6 Trend of cash deficit of central government.
Source: World Bank.

8.7.1 Types of Deficits

The role of expenditure and revenue is also important in understanding the government deficits. These occur when the expenditure exceeds revenue. However, there exist some differences. These are various ways to represent the deficit experienced by the government.

There are broadly three types of deficit, which are discussed below:

1. ***Revenue deficit:*** The most significant is the revenue deficit, which is just the difference between the revenue receipts and the revenue expenditures.

   Revenue deficit = Revenue expenditure – Revenue receipts
   (that is, Tax + Non-tax Revenue)

2. ***Fiscal deficit:*** This deficit occurs when the total expenditure including capital expenditure exceeds the total revenues including capital receipts.

   Fiscal deficit = Total expenditure (that is, Revenue expenditure + Capital expenditure) – (Revenue receipts + Recoveries of loans + Other capital receipts, i.e., all revenue and capital receipts other than loans taken)

4. World Economic Outlook, IMF.

3. ***Primary deficit:*** Primary deficit appears when we deduct interest payments from the total deficit or fiscal deficit.

   Primary deficit = Fiscal deficit – Interest payments

8.8 OBJECTIVES OF FISCAL POLICY

The objectives of fiscal policies are both macro and micro in nature. In an economy, there exist various socio-economic problems such as unemployment, poverty, hunger, inequality, etc. In order to remove these problems, fiscal instruments remain practical. Recently, the Government of India has passed the food security bill to tackle the issue of absolute hunger. Some of the key objectives are as follows:

1. ***Mobilisation and allocation of resources:*** Generally, developing countries have been suffering from long-term socio-economic challenges such as absolute poverty, hunger, unemployment and low level of per capita income. This has been a result of low level of income, investment and capital concentration. Fiscal policies are designed to overcome these problems through efficient taxation policies and expenditure methods. For instance, in India, the government has been planning to spend more on infrastructure like road, rail and agriculture sector. In the 2016–2017 budget, allocation for agriculture and farmers' welfare is ₹35,984 crore and a dedicated long-term irrigation fund will be created in NABARD, with an initial corpus of about ₹20,000 crore. Total investment in the road sector, including PMGSY allocation, would be ₹97,000 crore during 2016–2017.
2. ***Equitable distribution of wealth:*** By increasing the planned and non-planned expenditure on various programmes and schemes, the government tries to reduce income inequality prevalent in the economy. For instance, the 2016–2017 budget indicates that there is an allocation of ₹87,765 crore for the rural sector and 2.87 lakh crore will be given as grant in aid to gram panchayats and municipalities as per the recommendations of the 14th Finance Commission. A sum of ₹38,500 crore is allocated for MGNREGS. Allocation for social sector, including education and health care is ₹1,51,581 crore and ₹2,000 crore are allocated for initial cost of providing LPG connections to BPL families, etc.
3. ***Creating employment opportunities:*** Aggregate demand in an economy is related to the aggregate output and employment. This means, an increase in the aggregate demand would lead to an increase in the employment. An increase in the government expenditure, therefore, creates opportunities for employment.
4. ***Economic stability:*** Economic stability relates to fiscal stability and price stability. The short-term and long-term objectives of fiscal policy are to strengthen economic stability in an economy. For instance, in case of price instability, government uses its fiscal instruments such as market borrowings to neutralise the prices in the economy. On the other hand, government expenditure and fiscal deficits are important for business cycle, which indicates the fiscal stability. In the long-term, fiscal instruments are used to stabilise these variables.

5. ***Inflation control:*** Fiscal policy is an important instrument for controlling the rate of inflation as well.
6. ***Maximise welfare in the economy:*** It also aims to create maximum welfare for the people of the country.

8.9 FISCAL INSTRUMENTS

We have already discussed that the fiscal policy uses two main instruments, i.e., public revenue and public expenditure. These instruments are outlined in the annual financial statement of any government. In this section, we elaborate some of the concepts related to public revenue, public expenditure and taxation.

Public revenue and public expenditure

We know that revenues are mainly of two types, *viz.* tax revenue and non-tax revenue. Similarly, expenditures are classified into revenue expenditure and capital expenditure. The revenue receipts and quantum as well as the type of expenditure define the public debt situation in an economy.

Taxation

We know taxation is an important instrument or source of revenue for a government. Total tax revenue is the outcome of the tax rate in a country. In other words, the level of tax revenue depends on the tax base or tax rate. This is expressed as the percentage of the total income. Sometimes, it is also expressed as marginal and average tax rate.

1. ***Marginal tax rate:*** It is defined as the changes in tax liability as a result of the change in income. For instance, if the income is increasing, tax liability will increase and thereby, tax rate will increase. This can be expressed as follows:

   Marginal tax rate = Change in tax liability/Change in the total taxable income
2. ***Average tax rate:*** Average tax rate is the total tax liability as a share of the total taxable income. This can be expressed as follows:

   Average tax rate = Total tax liability/Total taxable income

8.10 GUIDING PRINCIPLE OF TAX POLICIES

Generally, taxation is levied to finance government programmes, which are mostly developmental in nature. In view of the developmental process of the country, a government also needs to have a progressive framework as the guiding principles of taxation. The following are the principles that guide a progressive tax structure in an economy:

1. ***Equity and fair taxation:*** *Equity* refers to equitability in terms of distribution of burden of taxation. Fair taxation refers to levying taxes on consumption and higher levels of income. This also refers to as the simplification of taxes with an objective to promote equity.
2. ***Certainty:*** A good taxation system should define the situations in which the tax is levied, and should devise appropriate methods to determine the ability to pay tax.

3. ***Easy payment and efficient tax collection mechanism:*** A good taxation system should have a user-friendly tax payment mechanism.
4. ***Simplicity:*** A taxation system should be simple so as to make taxpayers convenient to understand the tax rules, law and regulations. The simplicity would make tax payment efficient for the taxpayers, which would enable them to comply with the rules of taxation.
5. ***Generate economic growth:*** The taxation should assist economic growth in order to maximise the developmental process.
6. ***Transparent and visible:*** The taxation system should enable taxpayers to easily understand the transparency of the system.
7. ***Minimum tax gap:*** A tax system should minimise the tax compliance of taxpayers so as to maximise the welfare.

In addition to the above guiding principle of taxation, we need to understand the nature of taxation. As we have discussed the type of taxation earlier, it is important to find out the welfare aspect of taxation policies too. As we know, different taxation policies have impacts on the different sections of society. The policies that are being followed define the nature of taxation. There are three broad nature of taxation, *viz.* progressive, regressive and proportional. These are discussed below:

1. ***Progressive taxation:*** A tax is called progressive tax when the rate of taxation increases as a result of increase in taxable income. The tax liability on taxpayers, therefore, increases in absolute terms. Progressive taxation shows the distributional effects of increase in income. In a progressive tax, the average tax rate is less than the marginal tax rate.[5] The progressive taxation is measured by the various methods, which include Gini coefficient, marginal and effective tax rate, etc.
2. ***Regressive taxation:*** A tax policy is regressive in nature when the tax imposed on taxpayers targets low income segment. The peculiarity of this tax system is that the rate of tax does not increase as per the increase in income level of tax payers. Such tax is applied uniformly to all the income groups. This creates a situation where tax rates declines as income increases. This creates more difficulty for lower income group as compared to higher income groups.
3. ***Proportional taxation:*** A tax rate is said to be proportional when the tax imposed not only increases with the increase in income but also increases as a proportional to the increase in income. This is a fixed tax rate, which does not change with the change in income.[6]

8.11 BURDEN OF TAXATION AND INCIDENCE OF TAXATION

The two concepts of burden and incidence of taxation are also important to understand the economic environment affected by fiscal policies. These are as follows:

5. Hyman, David M. (1990), *Public Finance: A Contemporary Application of Theory to Policy*, 3rd ed., Dryden Press: Chicago, IL.
6. *Ibid.*

1. *Burden of taxation* is the total tax liability as the percentage of the total income on taxpayers. Thus, the burden of tax is directly related to the liability of taxpayers.
2. But in several cases, burden of taxation is shifted from those who are legally liable to pay tax to those who are not legally liable to pay. This is called *incidence of taxation.*

8.12 EFFECT OF TAXATION

Effect of taxation can be seen on consumption, production, economic growth, investment and welfare of the population. It is closely related to the changes in tax rates as well. The government's policies towards the taxation have multiple effects. Some of the important areas, wherein taxation plays an important role and impacts directly or indirectly are as follows:

1. ***Economic growth and production:*** A higher tax rate reduces the consumption expenditure, as it also lead to the reduction in the total disposable income. As a result of this, the total consumption expenditure decreases, leading to a short fall in demand. It also reduces savings and investment, and consequently, negatively impacts the production and economic growth in the country.
2. ***Distribution of resources:*** Taxation has a direct impact on the distribution of resources in the economy. Again, this depends on the type of taxation followed by the government. A regressive tax structure has a little impact on the distribution of resources, whereas a progressive taxation has beneficial impacts on the equitable distribution of resources. It reduces inequality and attracts more revenue for the government, enabling to spend more for the poor.
3. ***Effects on social welfare:*** An increase in the tax rates in terms of progressive tax structure increases the ability of the government to spend more for the welfare of the government. Some populist measures are taken from revenue collected. This results in the increase in social welfare of the economy. For instance, India is now following some programmes such as those pertaining to food security, *sarva sikhsa abhiyan* and mid-day-meal scheme, etc. These programmes need financing. Taxation is an important method to finance these programmes.
4. ***Inflation and taxation:*** Increase in tax rates decreases the disposable income. In turn, it also reduces the ability to spend. However, this has a little impact on inflation. Affects on inflation depend on the type and structure of taxation. For example, imposition of direct taxes does not increase inflation, whereas imposition of indirect taxes such as import duty, customs duty, service tax, sales tax, transportation-related tax, etc. increases the cost of production and the prices of commodities consequently.

8.13 PUBLIC DEBT

The Constitution of India, as per the provisions of Article 292, allows the central government to borrow against the security of the consolidated fund of the country. This is called *public debt.* However, certain conditions are laid down for borrowing for both the centre and state governments in the country. The tradition of borrowing from various sources dates back to British period when British borrowed to meet the capital expenditure for constructing Indian

Railways. In 1939, the total Indian public debt was estimated at ₹1,200 crore, out of which nearly ₹925 crore was debt under the various interest yielding assets.[7] Internal debt accounted for about 61% of the total debt and the rest was represented by India's external debt, i.e., 39% of the total debt or ₹470 crore.

In the post-independence era, the government has used various instruments for public borrowings such as borrowing from market and mobilisation of small savings from people. The Planning Commission advocated these methods to raise funds for financing development projects in the country. However, one of the main reasons for raising the public debt borrowings has been the rapid economic growth. Table 8.8 indicates the summary of public debt and other liabilities of the government.

Table 8.8 Public Debt and Other Liabilities of the Central Government (₹ in crore)

Particulars	*1950–1951*	*2002–2003*	*2013–2014*	*2014–2015*	*2015–2016*
Public debt	2,054	10,80,300	44,86,172	62,78,554	68,94,691
Internal	2,022	10,20,690	43,03,310	47,75,900	52,98,217
External	32	59,610	1,82,862	1,94,286	2,05,459
Other liabilities	511	4,78,600	11,65,612	13,08,367	13,91,014
Total	**2,565**	**1,55,89,600**	**56,51,734**	**62,78,553**	**68,94,690**

Source: Budget at Glance, Various Issues, Government of India.

The public debt of the Government of India consists of internal and external debts, which are discussed as follows:

1. Internal debt is basically sourced from market loans, compensation bonds and 15-year annual certificates. The internal public debt also includes debt treasury bills of the RBI, borrowings from commercial banks and also non-negotiable, non-interest bearing and securities from the international financial institutions such as IMF.
2. External debt refers to the borrowings of the central government from the external sources such as borrowings from the international community, international financial institutions such as IMF, World Bank, Multilateral lending and bilateral lending, etc.

The aggregate liabilities or debt of the central government and state government was ₹3,059 crore in 1950–1951, which rose to ₹4,03,613 crore in 1990–1991. This further increased to ₹83,77,981 crore in 2015–2016. Out of the total liabilities, in 2015–2016, the central liabilities accounted for the maximum (about 84% of the total liabilities). In terms of percentage of GNP, the total liabilities of both the central and state governments accounted for 62.5% of the GNP at current prices in 2015–2016. Table 8.9 shows the liabilities of the central and state governments, while Table 8.10 shows the select debt indicators of the central and state governments.

The broad classification of the government debt is shown in terms of external and internal debt. The total external debt as a percentage of total liabilities has been decreasing over the period of time. It was 19% of the total liabilities in 1980–1981, which decreased to 5%

7. *Op. cit.*, 3.

in 2012–2013. The external debt was also 5% of the total liabilities in 2010–2011. The domestic liabilities were 81% in 1980–1981, which rose to 95% in 2012–2013. The internal debt came from the various sources. Other liabilities of the central and state governments also accounted for these estimates. However, in Table 8.9 below, these liabilities are not shown separately. Table 8.10 shows the trend of debt indicators of the Central and State Governments for the period of 1980–2016.

Table 8.9 Liabilities of the Central and State Governments (₹ in crore)

Year	*Centre*			*States' Liabilities*	*Grand Total*
	Domestic	*External*	*Total*		
1980–1981	48,451	13,479	61,930	26,783	88,713
1990–1991	2,83,033	66,314	3,49,347	1,28,155	4,77,502
1995–1996	5,54,983	1,48,398	7,03,381	2,49,535	9,52,916
2000–2001	11,02,596	1,89,990	12,92,586	5,94,147	18,86,733
2005–2006	21,65,902	1,94,070	23,59,972	11,47,717	35,07,689
2010–2011	37,81,135	2,78,877	40,60,012	18,28,976	58,88,988
2011–2012	43,47,164	3,22,897	46,70,061	19,93,916	66,63,977
2012–2013	48,93,303	3,32,005	52,25,308	22,05,988	74,31,296
2013–2014	54,85,600	3,74,494	58,60,094	24,52,664	83,12,758
2014–2015	60,84,568	4,00,734	64,85,302	27,50,934	92,36,236
2015–2016	66,89,532	4,11,907	71,01,439	–	–

Source: Handbook of Statistics on Indian Economy, RBI.

Table 8.10 Select Debt Indicators of the Central and State Governments (Percentage of GDP)

Year (End-March)	*Domestic Liabilities of Centre*	*External Liabilities of Centre*	*Total Liabilities of Centre (2+3)*	*Total Liabilities of States*	*Combined Domestic Liabilities of Centre and States*	*Combined Total Liabilities of Centre and States (3+6)*
(1)	(2)	(3)	(4)	(5)	(6)	(7)
1980–1981	32.38	9.01	41.39	17.90	38.93	47.94
1990–1991	48.28	11.31	59.59	21.86	57.54	68.85
1995–1996	45.24	12.10	57.34	20.34	55.18	67.28
2000–2001	50.64	8.73	59.36	27.29	64.94	73.67
2005–2006	58.64	5.25	63.90	31.08	73.82	79.07
2010–2011	48.51	3.58	52.08	23.46	61.95	65.53
2011–2012	48.28	3.60	51.88	22.33	61.92	65.52
2012–2013	48.57	3.31	51.88	22.23	62.72	66.03
2013–2014	48.7	1.6	50.3	–	–	–
2014–2015	48.1	1.5	49.6	–	–	–
2015–2016	47.4	1.5	48.9	–	–	–

Source: Handbook of Statistics on Indian Economy, RBI.

8.14 DEVELOPMENT ACTIVITIES FINANCED BY PUBLIC EXPENDITURE

The Government of India has been financing several development activities through public expenditure. The planning policy has laid down the importance of public expenditure in meeting developmental programmes. Some of the recent developmental programmes include financing of food security, MNREGA, Direct Cash Transfer Benefits, etc. In addition, the government also undertakes financing of infrastructure development such as road connectivity and railway line construction in the rural areas.

Some of such programmes, among others, are discussed as follows:

1. ***Bharat Nirman:*** It is a business plan for creating and augmenting the basic rural infrastructure. It includes projects related to
   (i) Irrigation
   (ii) Roads (Pradhan Mantri Gram Sadak Yojana)
   (iii) Housing (Indira Awaas Yojana and Rajiv Awas Yojana)
   (iv) Water supply (National Rural Drinking Water Programme)
   (v) Electrification (Rajiv Gandhi Grameen Vidyutikaran Yojana)
   (vi) Telecommunication
2. ***National Rural Livelihood Mission (NRLM):*** NRLM is a poverty alleviation project of the Ministry of Rural Development with a US$5.1 billion budget. The World Bank also supports this project. It aims at promoting self-employment and organisation of self-help groups (SHG) for rural poor.
3. ***National Rural Health Mission (NRHM):*** NRHM aims to provide accessible, affordable and quality health care to the rural population, especially the vulnerable groups.
4. ***Integrated Childhood Development Scheme:*** This scheme aims at tackling the menace of malnutrition and other health-related problems in children less than 6 years of age and their mothers. The programme focuses on girl child also.
5. ***Sarv Siksha Abhiyan (SSA):*** SSA aims for Universalisation of Elementary Education (UEE), as mandated by 86th amendment to the Constitution of India. This amendment has made free and compulsory education to children between 6 to 14 years age group a fundamental right. SSA addresses the needs of 192 million children and seeks to open new schools and strengthen school infrastructure.
6. ***Mid-day Meal Scheme:*** This programme run by the government is the world's largest school feeding programme reaching out to over 12 crore children in over 12.65 lakh schools and centres across the country.
7. ***Mahatma Gandhi National Rural Employment Guarantee Act (MNREGA):*** MNREGA guarantees the right to work by ensuring at least 100 days of guaranteed wage-based employment in a financial year to every household. This has helped in sustaining livelihoods across the country.
8. ***Food Security Programme:*** The Government of India is already running a Food Security Programme enacted through the National Food Security Act, 2013. This is

a Food Subsidy Programme, which entitles almost two-third of the population of the country to the subsidised food grains.

9. ***Direct Cash Transfer Scheme:*** This scheme is aimed at ensuring that subsidy amount goes directly into the bank accounts of the beneficiaries. It implies that instead of giving a subsidy, the subsidy amount is transferred to the beneficiary's account directly. It applies to LPG gas cylinders, kerosene subsidies, pension payments, scholarships, employment guarantee scheme payments, and for other benefits under the various welfare programmes run by the government. The direct transfer is linked to the unique Aadhar number provided to the citizens through the Unique Identification Authority of India (UIDAI).

8.15 THE UNION BUDGET 2017–2018

The government, discontinuing the previous norms, chose to present general budget for the financial year 2017–2018 on the 1st February 2017. The budget speech of the Finance Minister indicates that the auspicious season of spring is symbol of "optimism". Moreover, this was the first budget after the government's demonetisation initiative.

This budget focuses on ten important sectors, as mentioned by the Finance Minister in his budget speech in the Parliament on 1st February 2017:[8]

1. **Farmers:** Commitment to double the income in 5 years
2. **Rural population:** Providing employment and basic infrastructure
3. **Youth:** Energising them through education, skills and jobs
4. **Poor and the underprivileged:** Strengthening the systems of social security, health care and affordable housing
5. **Infrastructure:** For efficiency, productivity and quality of life
6. **Financial sector:** Providing growth and stability through stronger institutions
7. **Digital economy:** For speed, accountability and transparency
8. **Public service:** Effective governance and efficient service delivery through people's participation
9. **Prudent fiscal management:** To ensure optimal deployment of resources and preserve fiscal stability
10. **Tax administration:** Honouring the honest

It has been declared that the priority of the government is to "transform, energise and clean India" (TEC India) as the future roadmap. Therefore, TEC India aims at:[9]

11. Transforming quality of both governance and life of people of India
12. Energising people, especially the youth and the vulnerable, to enable them to utilise their potential, and

---

8 Finance Minister's Budget Speech in Parliament on 1st February 2017, Union Budget 2017–2018,: http://pib.nic.in/eventsite/budget2017/pdf/bs.pdf and "Union Budget 2017: Full speech of Finance Minister Arun Jaitley", http://timesofindia.indiatimes.com/business/india-business/union-budget-2017-full-speech-of-finance-minister-arun-jaitley/articleshow/56913593.cms

9 *Ibid.*

13. Cleaning the economy from the evils like corruption, black money and non-transparent political funding

The key highlights of this budget include the following:[10]

Allocation for farmers and rural population

1. Total budgetary allocation for rural, agriculture and allied sectors is ₹1,87,223 crore for the year 2017–2018.
2. Target for agricultural credit is ₹10 lakh crore in 2017–2018.
3. Benefits to farmers from 60 days' interest waiver was announced on 31 December 2016.
4. There will be a support NABARD for modernisation through computerisation and integration of all 63,000 functional Primary Agriculture Credit Societies with the Core Banking System of District Central Cooperative Banks at an estimated expenditure of ₹1,900 crore in 3 years.
5. Coverage under Fasal Bima Yojana increased from 30% of cropped area in 2016–17 to 40% in 2017–2018 and 50% in 2018–2019, with a budget provision of ₹9,000 crore for the year 2017–2018.
6. Long term Irrigation Fund, which was already set up in NABARD, increased by 100% and the total corpus of this fund will increase to ₹40,000 crore.
7. A dedicated Micro Irrigation Fund in NABARD is to be set up with corpus of ₹5,000 crore for the year 2017–2018 to achieve the objective of 'per drop more crop'.
8. A model law on contract farming is on the anvil.
9. Dairy Processing and Infrastructure Development Fund is to be set up in NABARD with a corpus of ₹2,000 crore in 2017–2018 and is likely to increase to ₹8,000 crore over 3 years.
10. Budgetary allocation for MGNREGA is ₹48,000 crore in 2017–2018.
11. Pace of construction of PMGSY roads accelerated to 133 km roads per day in 2016–2017, against an average of 73 km during 2011–2014.
12. Allocation for Pradhan Mantri Awaas Yojana–Gramin is ₹23,000 crore in 2017–2018.

Allocation for youth and poor

1. The government intends to launch Skill Acquisition and Knowledge Awareness for Livelihood Promotion (SANKALP) programme with estimated expenditure of ₹4,000 crore, with the aim to provide market relevant training to 3.5 crore youth.
2. The government intends to launch next phase of Skill Training for Industrial Value Enhancement (STRIVE) in 2017–2018 at a cost of ₹2,200 crore.
3. There will be an extension of Pradhan Mantri Kaushal Kendras to more than 600 districts across the country and establishment of 100 India International Skills Centres.

---

10 *Ibid.*

4. In health sector, the government has prepared an action plan to eliminate Kala-Azar and Filariasis by 2017, Leprosy by 2018, Measles by 2020 and Tuberculosis by 2025.
5. The allocation for scheduled tribes is ₹31,920 crore and for minority affairs is ₹4,195 crore for the year 2017–2018.

Allocation for infrastructure

1. Allocation for transportation sector including rail, road shipping and aviation is ₹2,41,387 crore in 2017–2018.
2. In Railways, the total capital and development expenditure would be ₹1,31,000 crore, including ₹55,000 crore provided by the government in 2017–2018.
3. For Railways passenger safety, a Rashtriya Rail Sanraksha Kosh is to be set up with a corpus of ₹1 lakh crore over a period of 5 years.
4. A new Metro Rail Policy is on the anvil, and also, a new Metro Rail Act will be enacted by rationalising the existing laws.
5. For road transport, budgetary allocation is ₹64,900 crore in 2017–2018.
6. 2,000 km of coastal connectivity roads have been identified for construction and development.
7. Select airports in Tier 2 cities will be taken up for operation and maintenance in the PPP mode.

Targets for financial sector and fiscal management

1. Government, to liberalise the economy, intends to abolish Foreign Investment Promotion Board in 2017–2018.
2. A Computer Emergency Response Team for our Financial Sector (CERT-Fin) will be established.
3. ₹10,000 crore will be invested for recapitalisation of banks in 2017–2018 as part of 'Indradhanush' roadmap'.
4. Lending target under Pradhan Mantri Mudra Yojana is to be set at ₹2.44 lakh crore.
5. Allocation for capital expenditure increased by 25.4% over the previous year in 2017–2018.
6. Target for fiscal deficit is at 3.2% of GDP in 2017–2018 and 3% in 2018–2019.
7. Net market borrowing of the government is restricted to ₹3.48 lakh crore after buyback in 2017–18, lower than ₹4.25 lakh crore in 2016–2017.
8. In the current financial year, revenue deficit stands reduced to 2.1% lower, and therefore, the government targets for revenue deficit at 1.9% of GDP in 2017–2018.

Others including taxation reforms

1. Maximum amount of cash donation, a political party can receive, will be ₹2,000 from one person.

2. To augment domestic consumption particularly after demonetisation, the existing rate of taxation for individual assesses between income of ₹2.5 lakh to 5 lakh reduced from 10% to 5%.

Table 8.11 Budget at Glance: 2017–2018 (₹ in crore)

S.No.	*Particulars*	*2016–2017 Revised estimate*	*2017–2018 Budget estimate*
1	**Revenue receipts**	**14,23,562**	**15,15,771**
2	Tax revenue (net to centre)	10,88,792	12,27,014
3	Non-tax revenue	3,34,770	2,88,757
4	**Capital receipts**	**5,90,845**	**6,30,964**
5	Recoveries of loans	11,071	11,932
6	Other receipts	45,500	72,500
7	Borrowing and other liabilities	5,34,274	5,46,532
8	**Total receipts (1 + 4)**	**20,14,407**	**21,46,735**
9	**Scheme expenditure**	**8,69,847**	**9,45,078**
10	On revenue account	6,31,511	6,74,057
11	On capital account	2,38,336	2,71,021
12	**Expenditure on other than schemes (13 + 15)**	**11,44,560**	**12,01,657**
13	On revenue account	11,03,049	11,62,877
14	Of which, interest payments	4,83,069	5,23,078
15	On capital account	41,511	38,780
16	**Total expenditure (9 + 12)**	**20,14,407**	**21,46,735**
17	On revenue account (10 + 13)	17,34,560	18,36,934
18	Of which, grants in aid for creation of capital assets	1,71,472	1,95,350
19	On capital account (11 + 15)	2,79,847	3,09,801
20	Revenue deficit (17 – 1)	3,10,998 (2.1)	3,21,163 (1.9)
21	Effective revenue deficit (20 – 18)	1,39,526 (0.9)	1,25,813 (0.7)
22	Fiscal deficit [16 – (1 + 5 + 6)]	5,34,274 (3.2)	5,46,532 (3.2)
23	Primary deficit (22 – 14)	51,205 (0.3)	23,454 (0.1)

Source: Government of India, Ministry of Finance, Budget Documents

Note: Figures in parenthesis are as a percentage of GDP.

3. There will be a surcharge of 10% of tax payable on categories of individuals whose annual taxable income is between ₹50 lakh and ₹1 crore.
4. The government to carry out extensive consultation for implementing GST from 1st April, 2017.
5. For MSME companies, income tax for companies with annual turnover upto ₹50 crore is reduced to 25% in 20017–2018.
6. Basic customs duty on LNG is reduced from 5% to 2.5% in 2017–2018.
7. No transaction above ₹3 lakh would be permitted in cash.

The summary of the budget is presented in Table 8.12.

8.16 THE UNION BUDGETS OF 2014–2015 AND 2016–2017

8.16.1 The Union Budget 2014–2015

The then Finance Minister of India, P. Chidambaram presented the interim budget on 17 February 2014. In his budget speech, he stated that "whether it is a regular budget for the full year or an interim budget, some things remain the same". Thus, the things which remain same are broad goals of the government.

Interim budget by UPA government: 17 February 2014

Considering the goals of the government which were focused on curtailing fiscal deficits, the interim budget proposed some changes in indirect taxes. The government also aimed at reviving economic growth, and therefore, it eased the manufacturing sector from the burden of excise duty.

As per the Minister, the growth in the Indian economy is expected to be 4.9% during the financial year (2014–2015). The major targets of the government, as highlighted in the budget, are as follows:

1. The budget projected the fiscal deficit for the country for the year 2014–2015 as 4.1% of the GDP.
2. The government would need to bring down fiscal deficit to 3% of the GDP by 2016–2017.
3. The current account deficit is likely to be reduced from US$88 billion in 2012–2013 to US $45 billion in 2013–2014, almost half of the previous year.
4. The government is expected to spend ₹2.5 trillion on subsidies, out of which 46% is likely to be spent on food subsidy.

In order to achieve the targeted economic growth and goal to curtail the fiscal deficit, the government decided to keep the plan expenditure at the same level as in case of the financial year 2013–2014. The total plan expenditure provided by the government was ₹5,55,322 crore. In this budget, the defence saw a major hike in its budget allocation. The budget allocation to defence rose by 10% from ₹2,03,672 crore in 2013–2014 to ₹2,24,000 crore in 2014–2015.

As per the interim Union Budget 2014–2015, the major initiatives proposed by the government to achieve the targets and goals are as follows:

1. Merchandise export is likely to be at US$ 326 billion in 2013–2014, and is expected to grow at 6.3% during 2013–2014 as compared to the previous year.

2. Factory gate tax would be reduced to 10% from 12% on some capital goods and consumer durables.
3. Cut in excise duty on small cars, two wheelers, commercial vehicles to 8% from 12% is the main highlight of this budget to achieve a higher manufacturing growth.
4. Excise duty reductions are recommended on larger vehicles.
5. The excise duty on sport utility vehicles (SUVs) is likely to be reduced to 24% from 30%.
6. It is also proposed to make appropriate reductions in the excise duties on chassis and trailers—the rates can be reviewed at the time of regular budget.
7. The minister also appealed to build consensus on goods and services tax (GST).
8. In addition, the government proposed to take measures to encourage domestic production. These measures include
   (i) Restructure the excise duty on all categories of mobile.
   (ii) Custom duty on soaps and chemicals, etc. is fixed to 7%.
   (iii) A concessional custom duty of 5% is fixed on capital goods imported by the Bank Note Paper Mill India Private Limited for the production of papers used for printing currency.

Union budget by NDA government: 10 July 2014

The outgoing Congress-led United Progressive Alliance (UPA) government presented the interim budget in February 2014 for the financial year 2014–2015. Later, in the 2014 general elections, the Bharatiya Janata Party (BJP) led by Narendra Modi won full majority in Lok Sabha elections and formed the National Democratic Alliance (NDA) government in May 2014. The Finance Minister of the new government, Arun Jaitley presented the Union Budget on 10 July 2014. The key goal of the present budget is to recover economic growth in the country. In order to attain this, the Finance Minister in his speech highlighted the need for reducing fiscal and current account deficits.

The government has an aim to increase tax-GDP ratio in the economy. This budget has also highlighted that the reduction in fiscal deficit from 5.7% in 2011–2012 to 4.5% in 2013–2014 was due to the reduction in expenditure, rather than through higher revenues. It has also mentioned that the reduction in current account deficit has been achieved by imposing restrictions on some imports, including gold.

The key highlights of the Union Budget of 2014–2015 presented by the new government in July 2014 are as follows:

1. It aims at reducing fiscal deficit to 3.6% for 2015–2016 and 3% for 2016–2017.
2. Special priority is on reducing inflation in the wholesale prices.
3. Attracting FDI to the infrastructure is also one of the aims.
4. Composite cap of FDI is to be 49% in the insurance sector and the defence sector.
5. The government allocates ₹7,060 crore for developing 100 smart cities across the country.
6. The budget also puts special attention on the rural development and agricultural sector, particularly for supply chain management of agricultural products.
7. Tax slabs on personal income remain unchanged. The income tax exemption limit has been raised by ₹50,000 (i.e. from ₹2,00,000 to ₹2,50,000). For senior citizens, the limit is now raised to ₹3 lakh.

8. It provides for reintroducing *Kisan Vikas Patra* and launching National Savings Certificate (NSC) with insurance cover.
9. Colour picture tubes have been exempted from basic customs duty; so, LED and LCD TVs have now become cheaper.

The summary of the budget is presented in Table 8.12.

Table 8.12 Budget at Glance: 2014–2015 (₹ in crore)

		2012–2013	*2013–2014*	*2013–2014*	*2014–2015*
		Actuals	*BE*	*RE*	*BE*
1	**Revenue receipts**	**8,79,232**	**10,56,331**	**10,29,252**	**11,89,763**
	2 Tax revenue (net to centre)	7,41,877	8,84,078	8,36,026	9,77,258
	3 Non-tax revenue	1,37,355	1,72,252	1,93,226	2,12,505
4	**Capital receipts (5+6+7)$**	**5,31,140**	**6,08,967**	**5,61,182**	**6,05,129**
	5 Recoveries of loans	15,060	10,654	10,802	10,527
	6 Other receipts	25,890	55,814	25,841	63,425
	7 Borrowings and other liabilities*	4,90,190	5,42,499	5,24,539	5,31,177
8	**Total receipts (1+4)$**	**14,10,372**	**16,65,297**	**15,90,434**	**17,94,892**
9	**Non-plan expenditure**	**9,96,747**	**11,09,975**	**11,14,902**	**12,19,892**
	10 On revenue account of which	9,14,306	9,92,908	10,27,689	11,14,609
	11 Interest payments	3,13,170	3,70,684	3,80,066	4,27,011
	12 On capital account	82,441	1,17,067	87,214	1,05,283
13	**Plan expenditure**	**4,13,625**	**5,55,322**	**4,75,532**	**5,75,000**
	14 On revenue account	3,29,208	4,43,260	3,71,851	4,53,503
	15 On capital account	84,417	1,12,062	1,03,681	1,21,497
16	**Total expenditure (9+13)**	**14,10,372**	**16,65,297**	**15,90,434**	**17,94,892**
	17 Revenue expenditure (10+14)	12,43,514	14,36,169	13,99,540	15,68,111
	18 Of which, grants for creation of capital assets	1,15,710	1,74,633	1,38,228	1,68,104
	19 Capital expenditure (12+15)	1,66,858	2,29,129	1,90,894	2,26,781
20	**Revenue deficit (17–1)**	**3,64,282**	**3,79,838**	**3,70,288**	**3,78,348**
		(3.6)	**(3.3)**	**(3.3)**	**(2.9)**
21	**Effective revenue deficit (20–18)**	**2,48,572**	**2,05,205**	**2,32,060**	**2,10,244**
		(2.5)	**(1.8)**	**(2.0)**	**(1.6)**
22	**Fiscal deficit {16–(1+5+6)}**	**4,90,190**	**5,42,499**	**5,24,539**	**5,31,177**
		(4.8)	**(4.8)**	**(4.6)**	**(4.1)**
23	**Primary deficit (22–11)**	**1,77,020**	**1,71,814**	**1,44,473**	**1,04,166**
		(1.8)	**(1.5)**	**(1.3)**	**(0.8)**

BE = Budget estimates, RE = Revised estimates $ excludes receipts under Market Stabilisation Scheme.
* includes draw-down of cash balance.

Source: http://www.indiabudget.nic.in/, Ministry of Finance.
Note: Actuals for 2012–2013 in this document are provisional.

8.16.2 The Union Budget 2016–2017

Budget 2016–2017 reflects government's firm commitment to substantially boost investment in agriculture, social sector, infrastructure and employment generation on one hand and simultaneously sticking to the fiscal consolidation path on the other hand. This is substantiated by a huge 15.3% jump in plan outlay and 9% increase in non-plan outlay in 2016–2017 Over Revised Estimate for the year 2015–2016 while simultaneously conforming to the fiscal deficit target of 3.5%. Besides additional allocation to meet the obligations of 7th pay commission, recommendation and implementation of one rank one pension (OROP) in Defence have also been provided.

In RE (2015–2016), the plan outlay at ₹4,77,197 crore is more than the BE (2015–2016) by ₹11,920 crore. With minor reduction in non-plan, the total expenditure outlay in RE (2015–2016) at ₹13,08,194 crore is ₹7,914 crore more than BE (2015–2016). Accordingly, the fiscal deficit target of 3.9% has been achieved without reduction in expenditure outlay at RE stage. The total plan outlay for 2016–2017 is ₹5,50,010 crore and non-plan outlay is ₹14,28,050.45 crore.

Since 2015–2016, the devolution of states' share in taxes has witnessed a major jump in total resources being transferred to states. Continuing with this trend, the total resources going to states, including the devolution of state's share in taxes, plan and non-plan grants/loans, and releases under centrally sponsored scheme in BE (2016–2017), is ₹9,11,330 crore, with a jump of ₹99,846 crore over RE (2015–2016) and ₹2,43,093 crore more than the actual (2014–2015). These facts reflect the government's firm commitment to co-operative federalism and strong belief in the principle that 'the Nation grows when states grow'.

The funding pattern of 'core' schemes, which also form part of the national development agenda, will be shared 60:40 between the centre and the states (90:10 for the 8 north-eastern states and 3 Himalayan states). A list of these schemes is given in Annexure B. In case a scheme/sub-scheme in this list has a central funding pattern of less than 60:40, the existing funding pattern will continue.

For effective outcome-based monitoring of implementation of the programmes and schemes and to ensure optimum utilisation of resources, an exercise to rationalise plan and non-plan schemes of all ministries and departments has been undertaken. The existing programmes and schemes have been re-organised into outcome-based umbrella programmes and schemes to avoid thin spread of resources. The rationalised set of schemes will further pave way for merging of schemes/sub-schemes reflected in the respective detailed demands for grants of the ministries/departments, for a more compact framework. This will help the ministries/departments gain more flexibility in budget management and ensure effective monitoring of the implementation of the schemes.

Key highlights of the budget are as follows:

1. Growth of economy accelerated to 7.6% in 2015–2016.
2. Fiscal deficit in RE 2015–2016 and BE 2016–2017 retained at 3.9% and 3.5%.
3. Revenue deficit target decreased from 2.8% to 2.5% in RE 2015–2016.
4. Total expenditure projected at ₹19.78 lakh crore.
5. Plan expenditure pegged at ₹5.50 lakh crore under plan, increase of 15.3%.
6. Non-plan expenditure kept at ₹14.28 lakh crore.
7. Special emphasis to sectors such as agriculture, irrigation, social sector, including health, women and child development, welfare of scheduled castes and scheduled tribes, minorities, infrastructure.

8. *Ek Bharat Shreshtha Bharat* programme will be launched to link states and districts in an annual programme that connects people through exchanges in areas of language, trade, culture, travel and tourism.
9. Raise the ceiling of tax rebate under Section 87A from ₹2,000 to ₹5,000 to lessen tax burden on individuals with income up to ₹5 lakh.
10. Increase the limit of deduction of rent paid under Section 80GG from ₹24,000 per annum to ₹60,000, to provide relief to those who live in rented houses.
11. Total investment in the road sector, including PMGSY allocation, would be ₹97,000 crore during 2016–2017.
12. To approve nearly 10,000 km of national highways in 2016–2017.

The summary of the budget is shown in Table 8.13.

Table 8.13 Budget at Glance: 2016–2017 (₹ in crore)

		2014–2015	*2015–2016*	*2015–2016*	*2016–2017*
		Actuals @	*Budget estimates*	*Revised estimates*	*Budget estimates*
1	**Revenue receipts**	**11,01,472**	**11,41,575**	**12,06,084**	**13,77,022**
	2 Tax revenue (net to centre)	9,03,615	9,19,842	9,47,508	10,54,101
	3 Non-tax revenue	1,97,857	2,21,733	2,58,576	3,22,921
4	**Capital receipts (5+6+7)$**	**5,62,201**	**6,35,902**	**5,79,307**	**6,01,038**
	5 Recoveries of loans	13,738	10,753	18,905	10,634
	6 Other receipts	37,737	69,500	25,312	56,500
	7 Borrowings and other liabilities*	5,10,725	5,55,649	5,35,090	5,33,904
8	**Total receipts (1+4)$**	**16,63,673**	**17,77,477**	**17,85,391**	**19,78,060**
9	**Non-plan expenditure**	**12,01,029**	**13,12,200**	**13,08,194**	**14,28,050**
	10 On revenue account of which	11,09,394	12,06,027	12,12,669	13,27,408
	11 Interest payments	4,02,444	4,56,145	4,42,620	4,92,670
	12 On capital account	91,635	1,06,173	95,525	1,00,642
13	**Plan expenditure**	**4,62,644**	**4,65,277**	**4,77,197**	**5,50,010**
	14 On revenue account	3,57,597	3,30,020	3,35,004	4,03,628
	15 On capital account	1,05,047	1,35,257	1,42,193	1,46,382
16	**Total expenditure (9+13)**	**16,63,673**	**17,77,477**	**17,85,391**	**19,78.060**
	17 Revenue expenditure (10+14)	14,66,992	15,36,047	15,47,673	17,31,037
	18 Of which, grants for creation of capital assets	1,30,760	1,32,472	1,32,004	1,66,840
	19 Capital expenditure (12+15)	1,96,681	2,41,430	2,37,718	2,47,023
20	**Revenue deficit (17–1)**	**3,65,519**	**3,94,472**	**3,41,589**	**3,54,015**
		(2.9)	**(2.8)**	**(2.5)**	**(2.3)**
21	**Effective revenue deficit (20–18)**	**2,34,759**	**2,68,000**	**2,09,585**	**1,87,175**
		(1.9)	**(2.0)**	**(1.5)**	**(1.2)**
22	**Fiscal deficit {16–(1+5+6)}**	**5,10,725**	**5,55,649**	**5,35,090**	**5,33,904**
		(4.1)	**(3.9)**	**(3.9)**	**(3.5)**
23	**Primary deficit (22–11)**	**1,08,281**	**99,504**	**92,469**	**41,234**
		(0.9)	**(0.7)**	**(0.7)**	**(0.3)**

Source: Government of India, Ministry of Finance

Note: $ = under market stabilisation, *= includes draw dawn of cash balance, 1. GDP for BE 2016–2017 has been projected at ₹1,50,65,010 crore assuming 11% growth over the advance estimates, of 2015–2016 (₹1,35,67,192 crore) released by CSO.

8.17 FINANCE COMMISSION

Finance Commission of India was established by the Finance Commission (Miscellaneous Provisions) Act, 1951 in pursuant to the provisions of Article 280 of the Constitution of India. The commission aims at ensuring smooth functioning of the centre-state fiscal relations.

The Constitution mandates the following three responsibilities for the Finance Commission:

1. Distributing the net proceeds of shareable central taxes between the union and the states (also see Box 8.3)
2. Determining the grants to states which are in need of assistance
3. Recommending measures to augment the consolidated fund of a state to supplement the resources of local bodies

Box 8.3 Constitutional Provisions on Distribution of Revenues between the Union and the States

Article 268: Duties levied by the union but collected and appropriated by the states.
Article 269: Taxes levied and collected by the union but assigned to the states.
Article 270: Taxes levied and collected by the union and distributed between the union and the states.
Article 271: Surcharge on certain duties and taxes for purposes of the union.
Article 274: Prior recommendation of President required to bills affecting taxation in which States are interested.
Article 275: Grants from the union to certain states.
Article 280: Finance Commission.
Article 281: Recommendations of the Finance Commission.

Source: Finance Commission of India.

The Thirteenth Finance Commission recommended the following sharing basis in revenues for different states (see Box 8.4).

Box 8.4 Revenue Share of Different States as per the Thirteenth Finance Commission

States	*Share*	*States*	*Share*
Andhra Pradesh	6.937	Maharashtra	5.199
Arunachal Pradesh	0.328	Manipur	0.451
Assam	3.628	Meghalaya	0.408
Bihar	10.917	Mizoram	0.269
Chhattisgarh	2.470	Nagaland	0.314
Goa	0.266	Odisha	4.779
Gujarat	3.041	Punjab	1.389
Haryana	1.048	Rajasthan	5.853
Himachal Pradesh	0.781	Sikkim	0.239
Jammu and Kashmir	1.551	Tamil Nadu	4.969
Jharkhand	2.802	Tripura	0.511
Karnataka	4.328	Uttar Pradesh	19.677
Kerala	2.341	Uttarakhand	1.120
Madhya Pradesh	7.120	West Bengal	7.264

Source: Thirteenth Finance Commission.

Closing Case: MGNREGA—What is it doing?

The *Mahatma Gandhi National Rural Employment Guarantee Act (MGNREGA)* is one of the most crucial nation-wide development initiatives, requiring financial expenditure from the government. As per the MGNREGA, 2005, it aims at enhancing the livelihood security of the people in rural areas by guaranteeing 100 days of wage employment in a financial year to a rural household, who volunteer to do unskilled manual work.

Some of the key features and highlights of MGNREGA include the following:

1. MGNREGA is in line with the provisions of Directive Principles of State Policy enlisted in the Constitution of India.
2. This law guarantees the right to work in line with the provisions of Article 41 of the Constitution of India and also relates to Article 23 of the Universal Declaration of Human Rights that defines the right to work as a basic human right.
3. It aims to create durable assets that would augment the basic resources available to the poor.
4. It is an obligation on the government to provide employment under this act at minimum wage rate and within 5 km radius of the village.
5. It includes community participation and is implemented by the *Gram Panchayats.*
6. Payment of wages is done through bank's or post office's accounts directly.
7. It includes mostly labour-intensive works aimed towards the local infrastructure development.
8. The whole mechanism works through a comprehensive Management Information System (MIS), which includes job card details and muster rolls.
9. As per the Ministry of Rural Development, since 2010–2011, all details with regard to the expenditure of the MGNREGA are available on the MIS and are present in the public domain.

Though MGNREGA has also been criticised owing to some limitations in its implementation mechanism, yet it has been able to create opportunities for a sustainable livelihood for millions of people in the country. Table 1 gives an account of the achievements of MGNREGA from 2011 to 2014 on the basis of financial years.

Table 1 Mahatma Gandhi NREGA at a Glance

		Financial Year 2013–2014	*Financial Year 2012–2013*	*Financial Year 2011–2012*
Total number of districts		644.000	636.000	635.000
Total number of blocks		6,576.000	6,568.000	6,378.000
Total number of Gram Panchayats (GPs)		2,47,643.000	2,47,643.000	2,47,643.000
Total number of villages		7,78,134.000	7,78,134.000	7,78,133.000
Total number of households (HHs) registered (₹ crore)		13.000	13.000	12.600
Total number of workers in job card (in ₹ crore)		28.700	28.700	27.800

		Financial Year 2013–2014	Financial Year 2012–2013	Financial Year 2011–2012
Number of GPs with nil expenditure		29,944.000	25,749.000	25,065.000
Number of ongoing works (in ₹ lakh)		115.200	79.600	53.200
Total number of works taken up (new + spill over) (in ₹ lakh)		131.300	105.000	80.800
Total expenditure (₹ crore)	Wages (₹ crore)	22,032.700	27,168.700	24,306.200
	Material and skilled wages (₹ crore)	7,504.900	10,417.700	10,650.500
	Administrative expenditure			
	GP level	171.900	307.600	301.800
	Block level	958.700	1,328.300	1,191.700
	District level	423.400	482.000	514.400
	State level	148.346	32.936	108.055
	Total administrative expenditure	1,702.300	2,150.900	2,116.000
	Total expenditure (₹ crore)	31,240.000	39,737.300	37,072.700
	Labour versus material (%)	74.600	72.300	69.500
	Administrative expenditure (%)	5.400	5.400	5.700
Wage employment provided (₹ lakh)	Households	432.100	498.800	506.400
	Individuals	649.700	797.300	820.000
	Men	335.500	422.000	446.600
	Women	314.300	375.200	373.300
	SCs	150.100	181.700	185.000
	STs	113.500	142.900	147.400
	Persons with disability	4.200	4.200	4.000
Person days (₹ crore)	Total as per Labour Budget (LB)	259.500	278.700	199.600
	Person-days generated so far	173.300	230.400	218.800
	Percentage of total Labour Budget (LB)	66.800	82.700	109.600
	Percentage as per proportionate Labour Budget (LB)	74.800	94.300	155.800
	SC person-days	40.000	51.200	48.500
	ST person-days	28.500	41.00	40.900
Average wage rate per day per person		131.300	121.400	114.500

	Financial Year 2013–2014	*Financial Year 2012–2013*	*Financial Year 2011–2012*
Average days of employment provided per household	40.100	46.200	43.200
Total number of households completed 100 days of wage employment (₹ lakh)	24.500	51.700	41.700
Percentage of payments generated within 15 days	64.500	63.200	57.800
Percentage of payments disbursed through Electronic Fund Management System (EFMS)	20.200	0.900	0.000
Performance since inception		Person-days generated (₹ crore): 1,613.59	Total expenditure (₹ crore): 2,37,262.76

Source: This case is written by the authors based on inputs from the following sources:

1. http://nrega.nic.in/netnrega/home.aspx 2. MNREGA website.

CASE QUESTIONS

1. Discuss the relations between fiscal policy and MGNREGA.
2. Examine the problems in proper implementation of MGNREGA at grass roots.

REVIEW QUESTIONS

1. What do you understand by fiscal policy?
2. What are the three types of public revenue?
3. What is corporation tax?
4. Define customs and excise duties.
5. What is non-tax revenue?
6. What do you understand by planned and non-planned revenues?
7. Explain fiscal deficit.
8. Examine the key objectives of fiscal policy.
9. What are fiscal instruments?
10. Outline the effects of taxation.
11. What is public debt? Outline its characteristics.
12. Examine some development activities financed by public expenditure.

SUGGESTED READINGS

Approach to the Twelfth Five Year Plan, 2011, Planning Commission of India, New Delhi.

Dasgupta, Dipak and Supriyo De, 2011, 'Fiscal Deficit', in *New Oxford Companion to Economics in India*, Kaushik Basu and Annemie Maertens (Eds.), Oxford University Press, New Delhi.

De, Supriyo, 2012, *Fiscal Policy in India: Trends and Trajectory*, Available at the website of Ministry of Finance, Government of India, New Delhi.

Economic Survey of India, 2013–2014, Ministry of Finance, Government of India, New Delhi.

Misra, S.K. and Puri, V.K., 2012, *Indian Economy*, Himalaya Publication House, New Delhi.

9

MONETARY POLICY

Learning Outcomes

After reading this chapter, you will

- Understand the objectives and instruments of the monetary policy
- Learn the mechanism of demand and supply of money
- Appreciate importance of central banking and the role of the Reserve Bank of India in the contemporary and evolving business environment

Opening Case: Rupee versus Dollar and the RBI

The rapid movements of rupee to dollar exchange rate made headlines in the media during the latter half of the year 2013. The Indian Rupee hit a record low and posted its biggest percentage fall in 18 years in August 2013. It even breached the 68 rupee per dollar mark. This had its own impact on both the socio-economic as well as the political fabric of India.

The change in the exchange rate is not a new phenomenon. Exhibit 1 gives an account of the same. In 2011–2012, on a month-to-month basis, rupee depreciated by 12.4% and exchange rate rose to ₹51.34 per US$ in January 2012 as compared to ₹44.97 per US$. In 2013–2014, rupee depreciated sharply. But a cause of the recent depreciation has been the current account deficit, which led the depreciation of rupee from ₹51.34 in January 2012 to ₹68 per US$ in 2013. Moreover, the global oil prices too played a role and had a spillover effect in India.

During the recent times, the WPI inflation remained persistently high, particularly during 2011–2012. The inflations were started with 9.7% in 2011–2012, which came down to 6.6% in the last quarter of the same financial year. Similarly, there was a decrease in the consumer price index (CPI) during 2011–2012, which declined below 7%. Despite the significant decline in CPI, inflation remained high near 10%, except food inflation. On the other hand, fuel prices remained high at 8.0% during the last quarter of the year 2013 –2014.

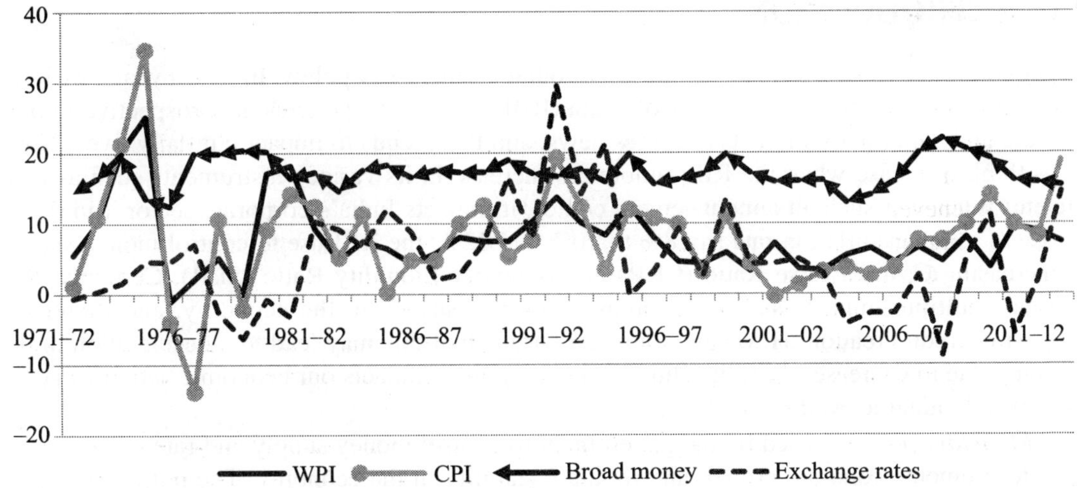

Exhibit 1 Business cycle of monetary indicators (average annual growth).
Source: RBI, Exchange rates are in terms of US$ and average of calendar year.

On 15 July 2013, the Reserve Bank of India issued a press release and argued that the market perception of likely tapering of US Quantitative Easing has triggered outflows of portfolio investment, particularly from the debt segment. This led to the depreciation of the rupee. However, it is also true that India was not the only country affected by this crisis.

The RBI through its press release 2013–2014/100, dated 15 July 2013 announced several measures to restore stability in the forex market, which are enlisted as follows:

1. The Marginal Standing Facility (MSF) rate is recalibrated with immediate effect to be 300 basis points above the policy repo rate under the Liquidity Adjustment Facility (LAF). Consequently, the MSF rate will now be 10.25%.
2. Accordingly, the bank rate also stands adjusted to 10.25% with immediate effect.
3. The overall allocation of funds under the LAF will be limited to 1.0% of the Net Demand and Time Liabilities (NDTL) of the banking system, reckoned as ₹75,000 crore for this purpose. The allocation to individual banks will be made in proportion to their bids, subject to the overall ceiling. This change in LAF will come into effect from 17 July 2013.
4. The Reserve Bank conducted open market sales of government securities of ₹12,000 crore on 18 July 2013.

However, in August 2013, rupee was able to breach the 68 dollar mark and many thought that it would touch 70! However, the exchange rate improved later.

Source: **This case is written by the authors based on inputs from the following sources:**

1. Reserve Bank of India, Press Release 2013–2014/100, dated 15 July 2013.
2. Reuters, 27 August 2013.
3. http://www.reuters.com/article/2013/08/27/us-india-economy-rupee-idUSBRE97Q0KT20130827

9.1 INTRODUCTION

All economic activities are closely related to a country's monetary policy. In recent years, we have seen that whenever the Reserve Bank of India (RBI) reviews its policies, its prospective impact on share and commodity markets becomes news, and thus, tends to impact our daily lives. Now, let us think of a case when the RBI announces increase in its various instruments such as repo rate etc. Whenever such an announcement comes, it impacts India's corporate sector. Similarly, in case of a higher inflation rate say 8% to 10% and 12%, the RBI use to control money supply by increasing Cash Reverse Ratio (CRR) and Statutory Liquidity Ratio (SLR). Certainly, this also has multiple impacts such as decreasing money supply in the economy, and therefore, decreasing credit creation. However, some may argue that this may lead to a deceleration in the economy due to decrease in credit. Thus, monetary policy impacts our economic activities at the level of individual as well as the firm.

Monetary policy is used by the government to control money supply and rate of interest in order to promote economic growth and to attain stability in the economy. The policy also aims at stabilising the prices and increasing the employment opportunities.

The countries use monetary policies to stabilise their economic growth and development. Generally, the central banking system plays a vital role for effective monetary policies. In India, the RBI is the central bank controlling monetary policies, whereas in other countries like the United States, the Federal Reserve System looks after the US monetary policy. Some of the central bank institutions are Bank of England (UK), People's Bank of China (China), Reserve Bank of New Zealand (New Zealand), Bank of Japan (Japan), Nepal Rashtra Bank (Nepal), etc.

9.2 OBJECTIVES OF MONETARY POLICIES

Monetary policy relates to the functioning of central bank in the economy. It also presents the policy reaction as per the prevailing economic environment and contributes to achieving the sustainable growth.

Thus, generally, the objective of monetary policy in an economy is to support and supplement the stable growth process of the country by controlling three basic instruments of monetary policy, *viz.* money supply, interest rate and inflationary pressure. By using monetary policy instruments, the central bank of a country also tries to control various illegal economic activities such as black marketing.

The major objectives of the monetary policies can be summarised as follows:

1. ***Growth stabilisation:*** Achieving a higher economic growth in a developing country like India remains a major target for the economy. In order to achieve it, expansion in both industrial supply and domestic consumption will be pre-requisite. This would require an increase in the investment as well as in the consumption expenditure. Therefore, through monetary policies, governments are able to regulate the supply of money in the economy so that the price remains stabilised. As a result, the real purchasing power of consumers does not decrease. This causes an increase in the consumption as per the increase in income. On the other hand, it also aims at attracting more investment through interest rate-related policies. This strengthens supply side

of the economy. Thus, the monetary policy promotes stable growth process in the country.

2. ***Price stability:*** Another objective of monetary policy is price stability. Price stability is an important factor to strengthen the process of savings and capital formation, as it deters the decrease in real purchasing power of money or income of household as well as firm. Thus, it promotes investment, savings and consumption owing to the increase in income. Therefore, for achieving a higher economic growth, we need stabilised price. Highly fluctuating price would lead to destablisation in the economy by increasing inflationary pressure, which in turn would lead to decrease in investments, expenditures as well as in savings.
3. ***Stability in exchange rates:*** Exchange rate stability is a major concern for any market economy. If an economy practises a rigid and fixed exchange rate system, then it is decided by the central bank of the country. However, in an open economy, exchange rate is determined by all other policies including monetary policy. *Exchange rate* simply means value of domestic currency in the exchange of foreign currency. It also depends on the balance of trade of the country as well as on capital flows. To regulate the exchange rates, monetary policy uses instruments like interest rates. For favourable exchange rates, monetary policies are designed in such a way so that more foreign capital inflows can take place, which would reduce the capital account deficits.
4. ***Stability in financial markets:*** *Financial stability* refers to the performance of the financial markets, which depends on the investor's confidence. Thus, to attract more confidence in the financial markets, monetary policies are designed so as to attract more investments. It is also designed to safeguard the financial system from any unprecedented crisis.

Moreover, the 2007–2008 financial crisis created the need for a more inclusive monetary policy. Some of such developments are enlisted in Box 9.1.

Box 9.1 Select Monetary Policy Objectives Post-2007–2008 Crisis

Central Banks	*Objectives*
Federal Reserve Bank (USA)	Promote employment, price stability, moderate interest rate.
People's Bank of China (China)	Maintain stability of the currency, promote economic growth.
Reserve Bank of Australia (Australia)	Price stability, full employment, and the economic prosperity and welfare of the Australian people.
Bank of England (England)	Monetary stability and financial stability
Bank of Japan (Japan)	Price stability

Source: Based on the inputs from websites of the central banks of respective countries.

9.3 TYPES OF MONETARY POLICIES

There are various types of monetary policies. The types and framework of the monetary policies change as per the economic environment and economic goals to be achieved through the policies. Monetary policies, thus, can be expansionary, contractionary, discretionary and countercyclical as per their design.

1. ***Expansionary monetary policy:*** It aims at increasing money supply in the economy and allows more credit creation. It has a goal of increasing economic activities.
2. ***Contractionary monetary policy:*** This kind of monetary policy is imposed on the reduction in the level of supply of money to contract economic activities. It has a goal to stabilise the economy and is practised when the prices are rising.
3. ***Discretionary monetary policy:*** This type of monetary policy is used by the central bank at its discretion when the government gives autonomy to the bank to regulate monetary policies.
4. ***Countercyclical monetary policy:*** It is used to counteract the business cycle of the economy. It tries to control the economy during rapid expansion and speed it up during contraction.

9.4 DEMAND AND SUPPLY OF MONEY

Before coming to the topic of instruments of monetary policies, we need to understand the constituents of demand and supply of money. We will first understand the concept of demand for money.

Demand for money

Demand for money refers to the instinct to keep financial assets in the form of money. In other words, it is the desire to have money as financial assets in the form of cash, bank deposits, etc. In our day-to-day life, we carry out several transactions. Money plays a vital role in carrying out these transactions. In fact, demand for money arises as a result of trade-off between holding money and the interest of holding assets in place of money. In short, the demand for money arises out from motives to keep money.

Traditionally, various motives for keeping money are as follows:

1. ***Transaction motive:*** Transactions are an important economic activity. Before the invention of money, transactions happened through barter. The classical quantity theory of money outlines that monetary transactions carried out in the economy further determine the level of income in the economy. According to this theory, level of prices and income determines the demand for money in the economy.
2. ***Asset motive:*** Asset motive is another important factor that creates demand for money. To keep financial assets, money is needed to carry out transactions of even these assets. Thus, the value of financial assets is assumed in terms of money.
3. ***Speculative motive:*** Besides, in the analysis of Keynes, the demand for money also arises out of speculations. For instance, the holding of money or demand for money

also depends on the level of interest rates on money or other financial instruments such as bonds.

Supply of money

Supply of money implies the available money stock in an economy at a specific point of time. The *total stock of money* is defined as the total currency in circulation and demand deposits in financial institutions. This is a basic definition of supply of money. However, today, there are several other forms of money existing in an economy (like India) such as time deposits, saving deposits and bonds, etc. Broadly, the usage of money as a medium of exchange, a unit of account and as a store of value is the function of money that constitutes the total supply of money as well.

Therefore, money supply is divided into broad money and narrow money. *Broad money* relates to the definition of money that accounts for currency in circulation, deposits with financial institutions and currency with banks, etc. On the other hand, *narrow money* is the total currency in circulation only. Thus, the definition of money supply depends on the primary conceptualisation of money supply.

We now discuss a broad classification of money supply under the various heads in some specific countries. Generally, monetary aggregates are defined as M_0, M_1, M_2, M_3 and M_4 or different types of money are classified as M, which ranges from M_0 to M_4 depending on the country-specific frameworks (see Box 9.2). These types of money aggregates constitute the total supply of money in an economy, which starts from narrow definitions to broad and the broadest definitions.

Thus, M_0 is currency in circulation (narrow money), M_1 is currency in circulation plus deposits (broad money), M_2 is M_1 plus demand deposits, saving deposits and time deposits, M_3 is M_1 plus all the deposits with all the financial institutions.

The Reserve Bank of India defines the monetary aggregates as given in Box 9.2.

Box 9.2 Money Aggregates in India

Money Aggregates in India	M_0	M_1	M_2	M_3	M_4
Currency with the public	×	√	√	√	√
Post office savings deposits	×		√		√
Bankers' deposits with the RBI	×			√	√
Demand deposits	×	√	√	√	√
Time deposits with the banking system	×			√	√

Source: RBI, http://rbidocs.rbi.org.in/rdocs/Publications/PDFs/78902.pdf

In India, M_0 is not used as the classification of money. M_1 is narrow money, whereas M_3 is broad money. The measurement of money stock in India is presented by the RBI according to the above classification. (A detailed analysis of money supply in the country is presented in Chapter 11). However, we present here an overview of the trend of money supply in the country, as depicted in Table 9.1.

Table 9.1 Trend of Types of Money stock in India: 1950–1951 to 2015–2016 (₹ in Billion)

Year	Currency in Circulation	Cash with Banks	Currency with the Public	'Other' Deposits with the RBI	Bankers' Deposits with the RBI	Demand Deposits	Time Deposits	Reserve Money	Narrow Money	Broad Money
1950–1951	–	–	14.1	0.2	0.6	5.9	3.3	14.9	20.2	23.5
1951–1952	12.9	0.4	12.5	0.2	0.5	5.5	3.3	13.6	18.1	21.4
1952–1953	12.7	0.5	12.3	0.1	0.5	5.2	3.6	13.3	17.6	21.2
1953–1954	13.3	0.4	12.9	0.1	0.4	5.3	3.7	13.9	18.3	22.0
1954–1955	14.2	0.4	13.8	0.1	0.5	5.7	4.2	14.7	19.6	23.8
1955–1956	16.1	0.4	15.7	0.1	0.5	6.4	4.7	16.8	22.2	26.8
1956–1957	16.7	0.5	16.2	0.1	0.6	7.1	5.3	17.3	23.4	28.7
1957–1958	17.2	0.5	16.7	0.2	0.7	7.2	7.5	18.0	24.1	31.6
1958–1959	18.5	0.5	17.9	0.2	0.7	7.2	9.5	19.3	25.3	34.8
1959–1960	20.0	0.7	19.3	0.2	0.9	7.7	11.6	21.1	27.2	38.8
1960–1961	21.5	0.6	21.0	0.1	0.7	7.6	11.0	22.4	28.7	39.6
1961–1962	22.6	0.5	22.0	0.2	0.7	8.2	12.0	23.5	30.5	42.5
1962–1963	24.4	0.6	23.8	0.3	0.8	9.1	12.4	25.5	33.2	45.6
1963–1964	26.7	0.6	26.1	0.3	0.8	11.2	12.9	27.8	37.5	50.4
1964–1965	28.4	0.7	27.7	0.2	1.0	12.9	14.2	29.6	40.8	55.0
1965–1966	31.1	0.8	30.3	0.2	1.0	14.8	16.1	32.3	45.3	61.3
1966–1967	32.9	0.9	32.0	0.4	1.3	17.1	18.7	34.6	49.5	68.2
1967–1968	34.7	0.9	33.8	0.6	1.4	19.2	21.1	36.6	53.5	74.6
1968–1969	37.9	1.1	36.8	0.8	1.9	20.2	25.3	40.7	57.8	83.1
1969–1970	41.6	1.7	40.0	0.6	1.7	24.8	31.0	43.9	65.4	96.4
1970–1971	45.6	1.9	43.7	0.6	2.1	29.4	36.5	48.2	73.7	110.2
1971–1972	50.1	2.1	48.0	0.8	3.0	34.4	43.7	53.8	83.2	126.9
1972–1973	56.8	2.4	54.4	0.6	3.0	42.0	53.1	60.3	97.0	150.1
1973–1974	66.0	2.7	63.2	0.5	6.3	48.3	64.2	72.7	112.0	176.2
1974–1975	67.0	3.5	63.5	0.8	8.3	55.5	75.7	76.0	119.8	195.5
1975–1976	70.5	3.5	67.1	0.8	6.8	65.4	91.6	78.1	133.3	224.8
1976–1977	82.9	4.2	78.7	1.2	13.9	80.3	117.6	98.0	160.2	277.8
1977–1978	91.5	5.2	86.3	0.7	17.2	56.9	185.2	109.4	143.9	329.1
1978–1979	108.4	6.0	102.3	1.7	30.8	69.0	228.2	140.8	172.9	401.1
1979–1980	123.8	7.3	116.5	3.9	38.0	79.6	272.3	165.7	200.0	472.3
1980–1981	143.1	8.8	134.3	4.1	47.3	95.9	323.5	194.5	234.2	557.7
1981–1982	154.1	9.4	144.7	1.7	54.2	103.0	378.2	210.0	249.4	627.5
1982–1983	176.4	9.8	166.6	1.9	52.9	116.9	446.5	231.1	285.4	731.8
1983–1984	206.4	10.4	196.0	2.9	80.6	135.0	531.3	289.9	334.0	865.3
1984–1985	238.8	12.0	226.7	6.0	107.5	166.5	630.2	352.2	399.2	1,029.3

Year	*Currency in Circulation*	*Cash with Banks*	*Currency with the Public*	*'Other' Deposits with the RBI*	*Bankers' Deposits with the RBI*	*Demand Deposits*	*Time Deposits*	*Reserve Money*	*Narrow Money*	*Broad Money*
1985–1986	265.2	14.7	250.6	2.9	113.5	187.5	753.0	381.7	441.0	1,193.9
1986–1987	299.1	15.3	283.8	3.1	145.9	228.3	901.2	448.1	515.2	1,416.3
1987–1988	351.2	15.6	335.6	4.0	179.7	246.0	1,057.2	534.9	585.6	1,642.8
1988–1989	401.2	17.9	383.3	6.9	221.5	277.6	1,267.1	629.6	667.9	1,934.9
1989–1990	482.9	19.9	463.0	6.0	287.1	341.6	1,498.9	775.9	810.6	2,309.5
1990–1991	552.8	22.3	530.5	6.7	318.2	391.7	1,729.4	877.8	928.9	2,658.3
1991–1992	637.4	26.4	611.0	8.9	348.8	524.2	2,026.4	995.1	1,144.1	3,170.5
1992–1993	713.3	30.5	682.7	13.1	381.4	544.8	2,399.5	1,107.8	1,240.7	3,640.2
1993–1994	854.0	31.0	823.0	25.3	507.5	659.5	2,803.1	1,386.7	1,507.8	4,310.8
1994–1995	1,046.8	40.0	1,006.8	33.8	612.2	881.9	3,353.4	1,692.8	1,922.6	5,276.0
1995–1996	1,225.7	43.1	1,182.6	33.4	685.4	932.3	3,843.6	1,944.6	2,148.3	5,991.9
1996–1997	1,372.2	51.3	1,320.9	31.9	595.7	1,053.3	4,554.0	1,999.9	2,406.1	6,960.1
1997–1998	1,510.6	54.8	1,455.8	35.4	718.1	1,187.3	5,534.9	2,264.0	2,678.4	8,213.3
1998–1999	1,758.5	69.0	1,689.4	37.4	797.0	1,363.9	6,718.9	2,592.9	3,090.7	9,809.6
1999–2000	1,970.6	79.8	1,890.8	30.3	804.6	1,496.8	7,823.8	2,805.6	3,418.0	11,241.7
2000–2001	2,182.0	86.5	2,095.5	36.1	814.8	1,662.7	9,337.7	3,033.0	3,794.3	13,132.0
2001–2002	2,509.7	101.8	2,407.9	28.3	841.5	1,792.0	10,755.1	3,379.5	4,228.2	14,983.4
2002–2003	2,824.7	108.9	2,715.8	32.2	833.5	1,987.6	12,443.8	3,690.4	4,735.6	17,179.4
2003–2004	3,270.3	120.6	3,149.7	51.0	1,043.6	2,586.3	14,269.6	4,364.9	5,786.9	20,056.5
2004–2005	4,295.8	174.5	4,121.2	68.4	1,355.1	4,074.2	18,931.0	5,719.3	8,263.9	27,194.9
2005–2006	4,295.8	174.5	4,121.2	68.4	1,355.1	4,074.2	18,931.0	5,719.3	8,263.9	27,194.9
2006–2007	5,041.0	212.4	4,828.5	74.7	1,973.0	4,776.0	23,421.1	7,088.6	9,679.3	33,100.4
2007–2008	5,908.0	223.9	5,684.1	90.3	3,284.5	5,783.7	28,620.5	9,282.7	11,558.1	40,178.6
2008–2009	6,911.5	257.0	6,654.5	55.3	2,912.7	5,886.9	35,351.0	9,879.6	12,596.7	47,947.8
2009–2010	7,995.5	320.6	7,674.9	38.1	3,523.0	7,179.7	41,134.3	11,556.5	14,892.7	56,027.0
2010–2011	9,496.6	378.2	9,118.4	36.5	4,235.1	7,228.6	48,657.7	13,768.2	16,383.5	65,041.2
2011–2012	10,672.3	435.6	10,236.7	28.2	3,562.9	7,109.0	56,474.4	14,263.4	17,373.9	73,848.3
2012–2013	11,909.8	499.1	11,410.6	32.4	3,206.7	7,532.3	64,922.9	15,148.9	18,975.3	83,898.2
2013–2014	13,010.7	552.5	12,458.2	19.7	4,297.0	8,119.8	74,576.2	17,327.4	20,597.6	95,173.9
2014–2015	14,483.1	621.3	13,861.8	145.9	4,655.6	8,916.3	82,577.6	19,284.6	22,924.0	1,05,501.7
2015–2016	16,634.6	653.7	15,981.0	154.5	5,018.3	9,970.2	90,437.7	21,807.4	26,105.7	1,16,543.4

Source: Handbook of Statistics on Indian Economy, RBI.

9.5 INSTRUMENTS OF MONETARY POLICY

There are direct and indirect instruments of monetary policies. Direct instruments include Cash Reserve Ratio (CRR) and Statutory Liquidity Ratio (SLR), whereas, indirect measures include bank rate, repo rate, reverse repo rate, open market operations, etc. We present here the concept of these measures and how it operates in an economy.

Cash reserve ratio (CRR)

CRR is the amount that comes as a ratio of funds of banks required to be deposited with the central bank. It is levied at the available amount of the bank, which is required to be maintained with the central bank. For example, suppose CRR in a country is 3%. It implies that every bank needs to maintain 3% of the available funds with the central bank. It is one of the most important instruments for controlling money supply in the economy. The central bank has the power to increase the rate, which means larger share of funds of banks would be maintained by the central bank, leading to a decrease in the credit by banks. The required reserves in some countries are: 4% (Russia), 6% (Bangladesh), 8.5% (Turkey), while in UK it has been removed. In India, CRR is 4%.

The range of CRR in India is defined as 3% to 15%. It means in no case, CRR would exceed 15% and also, it could not be less than 3% of NDTL of Banks. During pre-liberalisation period in India, CRR varied between 4% and 15%. During post-liberalisation period, it decreased from 15% in 1994 to 4% at present (see Table 9.2). Thus, CRR during the pre-reform period played a pivotal role as a monetary policy instrument.

Table 9.2 Pre-reform and Post-reform CRR in India

Pre-Reform Period CRR		*Post-Reform Period CRR*	
Effective Date	*Rate*	*Effective Date*	*Rate*
29-06-1973	5.00	17-04-1993	14.50
08-09-1973	6.00	15-05-1993	14.00
22-09-1973	7.00	11-06-1994	14.50
08-12-1973	7.00	06-08-1994	15.00
01-07-1974	5.00	11-11-1995	14.50
23-07-1974	5.00	09-12-1995	14.00
14-12-1974	4.50	18-01-1997	10.00
28-12-1974	4.00	25-10-1997	9.75
27-11-1981	7.25	29-08-1998	11.00
25-12-1981	7.50	13-03-1999	10.50
27-08-1983	8.50	20-11-1999	9.00
04-02-1984	9.00	10-03-2001	8.00
24-10-1987	10.00	15-06-2002	5.00
02-07-1988	10.50	14-06-2003	4.50
30-07-1988	11.00	03-03-2007	6.00
01-07-1989	15.00	09-02-2013	4.00

Source: RBI.

How CRR is being used as an instrument can be understood by the following illustration given in Figure 9.1.

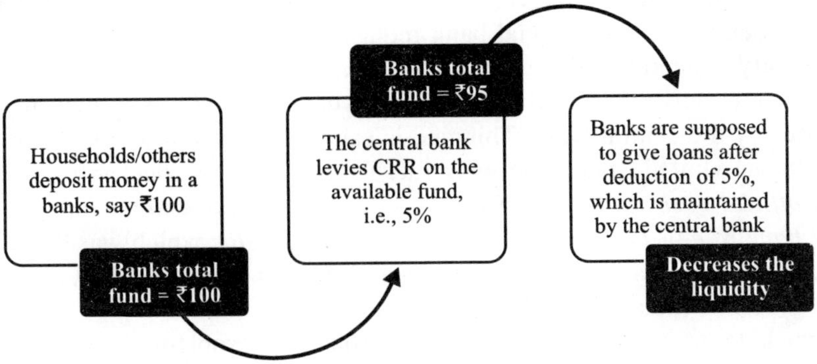

Figure 9.1 Use of CRR as an instrument.

Statutory Liquidity Ratio (SLR)

Statutory Liquidity Ratio is the amount that commercial banks are required to maintain or keep with themselves as a ratio of available funds. This approves security for the customers. The basic difference between CRR and SLR is related to the impact of these two instruments on liquidity and credit growth. On one hand, CRR aims to control liquidity in an economy, while on the other hand, SLR has a direct impact on the credit growth. In the United States, for instance, no CRR is required if the net transaction accounts for less than US$12.4 million. In case of transaction greater than US$12.4 million, banks are supposed to maintain 3% with the Federal Reserve Bank, subject to an amount less than US$79.5 million. In case, net transaction exceeds $79.5 million, banks are required to maintain reserves of 10% of the available funds. In USA, it is liquidity ratio. The SLR in India was 1.25% in June 2016.

Earlier, the SLR was usually very high in India, which can be seen in Table 9.3. In 1991, Narasimham Committee recommended that the RBI should reduce SLR. It was, therefore, reduced to 25% and now SLR is kept as 23%.

Table 9.3 SLR in India (1964–1981)

Effective date	*SLR*	*Effective date*	*SLR*
16-09-1964	25.00	28-07-1984	35.50
05-02-1970	26.00	06-07-1985	37.00
24-04-1970	27.00	02-01-1988	38.00
28-08-1970	28.00	22-09-1990	38.50
04-08-1972	29.00	06-03-1993	37.75
17-11-1972	30.00	20-08-1994	34.25
08-12-1973	32.00	25-10-1997	25.00
01-07-1974	33.00	08-11-2008	24.00
01-12-1978	34.00	07-11-2009	25.00
25-09-1981	34.50	18-12-2010	24.00
30-10-1981	35.00	11-08-2012	23.00

Source: RBI.

Bank rate

Bank rate is the interest rate that the central bank charges when it lends loan to the other banks in the market. Whenever, a commercial bank requires funds, they can borrow from the central bank of the country concern. In lieu of this, the central bank would levy interest. This is called *repo rate*, as the transaction is carried out by repos, wherein *repo* is an agreement of purchase or sale of securities by the central bank. This rate is called in different terms as per the definition by countries. In the United States, the bank rate is known as discount rate, in Australia, it is referred to as *official cash rate* and in Canada, it is known as *overnight rate*. In England, it is called *official bank rate* or *bank of England base rate (BOEBR)*, which was 0.5% in June 2016. In June 2016, the official cash rate in Australia was 1.25% and the overnight rate in Canada was 0.5%. The bank rate in India was 7.00% in June 2016.

During the latter part of 1990s, India passed through the problem of severe liquidity crunch, which resulted in the reduction in bank rates gradually from 12% in 1995 to 6% in 2003. The bank rates in India before 1991 are given in Table 9.4.

Table 9.4 Effective Dates of Bank Rates in India

Effective date	*Bank rate*	*Effective date*	*Bank rate*
5-07-1935	3.50	16-04-1997	11.00
28-11-1935	3.00	26-06-1997	10.00
15-11-1951	3.50	17-01-1998	11.00
03-01-1963	4.50	29-04-1998	9.00
26-09-1964	5.00	02-03-1999	8.00
09-01-1971	6.00	02-04-2000	7.00
31-05-1973	7.00	23-10-2001	6.50
23-07-1974	9.00	29-04-2003	6.00
12-07-1981	10.00	13-02-2012	9.50
04-07-1991	11.00	17-04-2012	9.00
09-10-1991	12.00	15-07-2013	10.25

Source: RBI.

Now, an important point to understand is how the changes in bank rate affect the credit demand in an economy. This can easily be understood by the following illustration given in Figure 9.2.

Open market operations

Open market operation is another indirect instrument of the central bank to regulate monetary system of the economy. It is an activity of the central bank through which the bank sells government bonds and securities and other financial instruments to the market. Similarly, it is also referred to as purchase of such assets by the central bank from the market. It is used to regulate the short-term interest rate and supply of monetary aggregates (see Box 9.3).

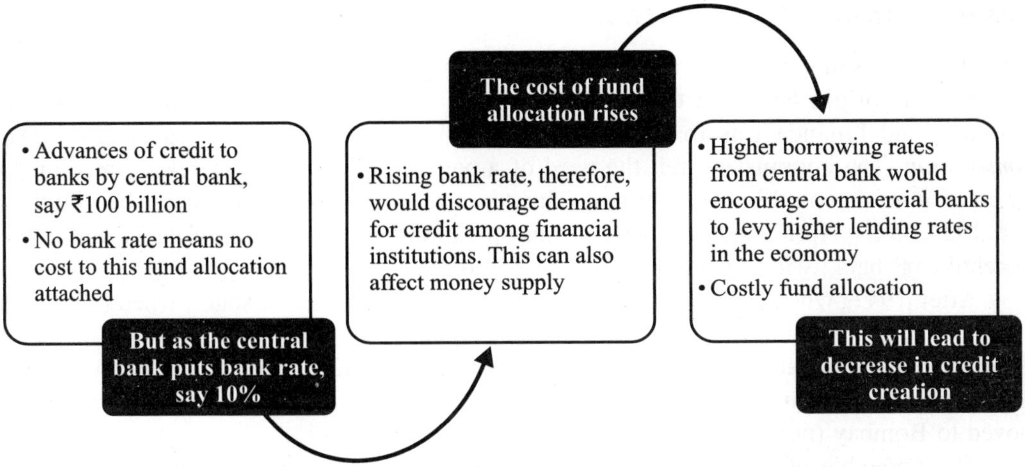

Figure 9.2 Impact of changes in bank rate on credit demand.

Box 9.3 China uses Open Market Operation to Avoid Liquidity Crunch

In January 2014, the People's Bank of China announced that it will inject a net 375 billion yuan ($62 billion) into the banking system through its regular open market operations. The step was aimed to avoid a liquidity crunch in the economy. Accordingly, the central bank has offered 120 billion yuan of 21-day reverse repurchase agreements, short-term lending for liquidity, in its one day open-market operations on 23 January 2014.

Source: Report by Nasdaq, 22 January 2014.

It operates with various goals as per the situation of the economy. In a situation of boom, the central bank uses to sell assets to the market. When the operation takes place, the bank's reserves reduce, leading to the decline in its credit creation capacity. This process continues. On the other hand, when the economy suffers from slowdown, the central bank purchases the government securities from public. This means the reserve of commercial bank increases, leading to increase in its reserves and the capacity of credit creation. This increases credit in the economy and money supply by creating more liquidity.

9.6 CENTRAL BANKING IN INDIA: RBI

India's central bank is named as the *Reserve Bank of India*. The system is akin to the other central banking across the globe. In fact, the concept of central banking suggests that it tries to influence the interest rates, money supply by adopting contractionary or expansionary monetary measures. The influence of monetarist approach began to influence economic systems in the second half of the 20th century. This approach also advocated an independent central banking system. Accordingly, the Federal Reserve Bank in the United States, Central Banks in England and France began to play pivotal roles. The central banking system of China also played a vital role in stabilising the Chinese economy. Thus, the role of the RBI is imperative in Indian context, particularly in establishing the business environment conducive to investors.

Reserve Bank of India (RBI)

The RBI was established as a bank in participation with various shareholders in April 1935. However, its origin has been traced to 1926–1927 when the Royal Commission on Indian Currency and Finance was formed. The commission is popularly known as *Hilton-Young Commission*. The commission felt the need of a banking system, and therefore, recommended for creation of a central banking system. Thus, as a result, the RBI was established by the RBI Act, 1934. On 1 April 1935, the RBI began operations as India's central bank and a private shareholders' bank, with a paid-up capital of ₹5 crore.

After 1947, when India got independence, the RBI became a state-owned central bank, which suited the planning policies of the Indian economy, i.e., planned economy. On 1 January 1949, the RBI was nationalised under the Reserve Bank (Transfer of Public Ownership) Act, 1948. Initially, the bank was located in Calcutta (now, Kolkata). In 1937, the RBI permanently moved to Bombay (now Mumbai).

The Preamble of the Reserve Bank of India describes the basic functions of the Reserve Bank as to regulate the issue of bank notes and keeping of reserves, with a view to secure monetary stability in India and generally, to operate the currency and credit system of the country to its advantage.

Functions of RBI

As per the RBI Act, the main functions of the RBI are as follows:

1. Monetary policy
2. Regulation and supervision of the banking and non-banking financial institutions, including credit information companies
3. Regulation of money, forex and government securities markets as also certain financial derivatives
4. Debt and cash management for the central and state governments
5. Management of foreign exchange reserves
6. Foreign exchange management-current and capital account management
7. Banker to banks
8. Banker to the central and state governments
9. Oversight of the payment and settlement systems
10. Currency management
11. Developmental role
12. Research and statistics

In fact, the RBI, like any other central bank in the world, performs the functions which are affiliated to a central bank. In addition to the traditional functions of central banking, RBI is also involved in promoting the development in India. Some of the main functions can be discussed in detail as follows:

1. ***Issue of currency notes:*** As per the RBI Act, under section 22, the RBI reserves the right of issuing the currency. In case of coins and one rupee notes, it works as a distributor across the country. It has a separate department, which takes care of

issuing the currency and is called *Issue Department*. The currency department of RBI looks after the currency management. This department forecasts the demand for new currency in the economy and keeps an account of the currency notes.

2. ***Banker to the government:*** In section 20 of the RBI Act, 1934, the provision is made that the RBI shall have obligation to undertake receipts and payments on behalf of the central government. Later, the state government came into agreement with section 21A of the Act, which makes the RBI as the main banker of the state governments as well. As a banker of the government, the RBI maintains the principal accounts of both the centre and state governments. It has well-established mechanism, which facilitates revenue collection and payments on behalf of the governments. It keeps cash balances, makes payments and carries out other banking-related operations. It also manages public debts and loans for the central as well as federal governments.
3. ***Bankers to the banks:*** According to the provision of Banking Companies Act, 1949, the RBI has been made as the bank of last resort. Provision was made in the Act that every scheduled bank in India has to maintain a cash balance with the RBI. The schedule bank was also given right to borrow from the RBI as per the conditions laid down by the central bank. As per the Banking Regulation Act, the scheduled banks were supposed to keep 5% of demand liabilities and 2% of time liabilities, which later became portion of the Net Demand and Time Liabilities (NDTL).
4. ***Custodian of foreign exchange and exchange rate management:*** The exchange rate in India is being managed by the RBI. It is also the custodian of foreign exchange reserves in the country. Initially, it was responsible for buying and selling foreign currency at a fixed exchange rate as per the RBI Act of 1934.
5. ***Credit control:*** The other main function of the RBI is to control liquidity or credit in the economy. Thus, as a controller of credit, the RBI has a right to influence the credit creation by banks through its various monetary instruments such as bank rates, open market operations, etc. the RBI has many arms to influence the Indian money market. It is a supreme banking authority and every bank has to obtain license from the RBI to start a banking business in India. Moreover, it also directs the banks in India for their operations such as the banks are required to get permission from the RBI to open new branches. It also directs banks across the country on account of customer-related issues. In such a scenario, if the RBI wants to control credit creation, then it will use its power to reduce the money supply by increasing its holdings of cash reserves of all the scheduled banks.
6. ***Monetary policy framework:*** The monetary policy framework of the RBI has been roaming around the basic objectives of the central bank, which advocates price stability and accordingly, adequate flow of credit and liquidity. In view of its broad objectives, the RBI monetary policy framework has a goal to ensure financial stability and assist the economy in achieving a higher rate of economic growth. Since the functions and tasks of the RBI have been complex, the policies, therefore, have a broad framework for not only stabilising the prices and credit creation but also for fulfilling the development needs of the people of the country.

As per the rules and regulations of the RBI under the RBI Act, every year in the month of April, it announces the monetary policy. Previously, on quarterly basis, and now, on bimonthly basis, it reviews its monetary policy for the year. Thus, there is one announcement of yearly monetary policy starting from April 1 and ending on March 31; it was followed by three announcements of quarterly review in July, October and January. Now, bimonthly monetary policy statements are followed starting from the month of April for a financial year. The monetary policy for a financial year consists of part A and part B. Part A deals with the monetary policy, whereas part B provides a synopsis of the actions and the status of policies of the RBI followed in the past and the proposed policies. In other words, part A deals with the current state of the economy, domestic macroeconomic aggregates, outlook of the economic policies, monetary measures undertaken and the proposed monetary measures. On the other hand, part B deals with the current financial stability in the economy, situation in financial markets, financial inclusion and policy guidelines for these. This part also proposes regulatory measures to regulate the financial markets and banking institutions. Bimonthly monetary policy statements also consist of two parts.

The body of the released document on the first quarter monetary policy review of the year 2013–2014 is illustrated in Box 9.4.

Box 9.4 First Bimonthly Monetary Policy of RBI, 2016–2017

Part A: Monetary Policy	
Monetary and liquidity measures	The section outlines details of measures taken by the RBI.
Assessment	It presents the economic scenario and situation in financial markets outlining the context of the new policy measures.
Policy stance and rationale	It outlines the situation of macroeconomic indicators and reasons for measures taken by the RBI.
Part B: Developmental and Regulatory Policies	
Liquidity framework for monetary policy operations	It sets out the objective of liquidity adjustments.
Banking structure	It provides measures and suggestion related to banking structuring.
Financial markets	It brings out discussion on the components of financial markets.
Non-banking financial sector, financial inclusion and payment and settlement	It outlines measures in non-banking financial sector.

Source: RBI, First Bimonthly Monetary Policy of RBI, 2016–2017.

9.7 INSTITUTIONAL FRAMEWORKS

The monetary policy framework of the RBI has a defined institutional mechanism also. These institutions are listed below:

1. ***Financial Markets Committee (FMC):*** The Financial Markets Committee was formed in 1997. The committee was interdepartmental and chaired by the Deputy

Governor incharge of monetary policy formulation of the RBI. The core function of FMC is to review developments in money, foreign exchange and government securities markets and assess the possible liquidity and credit condition in the economy. The committee assesses this on day-to-day basis.

2. ***Monetary Policy Strategy Group:*** Another important institution is the Monetary Policy Strategy Group, which is headed by the Deputy Governor. The group is an integral part of the policy formulation process. Its core function is to review the monetary and credit conditions in the country on quarterly basis and also suggest the strategies for the quarter. It has an important role while formulating the monetary policy for a quarter.
3. ***Technical Advisory Committee (TAC) on Monetary Policy:*** In the year 2005, the RBI constituted a Technical Advisory Committee (TAC) on Monetary Policy. The committee consists of five external experts and two directors of the RBI. The external experts are eminent scholars and experts who deal with the field of central banking and monetary policies. The committee is chaired by the Governor of the RBI. The aim of the committee is to assist the RBI in strengthening the process of consultations during formulating the monetary policy. The main function of the committee is to review the macroeconomic and monetary developments in the country.
4. ***Pre-Policy Consultation Meetings:*** Since October 2005, the RBI has made the policy-making process consultative, and in the process has reached out to multiple stakeholders ahead of each monetary policy and quarterly review. These stakeholders include Indian Banks' Association, market participants, representatives of trade and industry, credit rating agencies and other institutions such as urban co-operative banks, micro-finance institutions, small and medium enterprises, non-banking finance companies, rural cooperatives and regional rural banks.
5. ***Liquidity Adjustment Facility (LAF):*** In June 2000, the RBI introduced the Liquidity Adjustment Facility in order to manage the market liquidity on a daily basis. This measure was actually recommended by Narsimhan Committee on Banking Sector Reforms. LAF has now become an important instrument for regulating the interest rates in the economy. Under LAF measures, the RBI has introduced repo rate and reverse repo rate to regulate the sale and purchase of government securities. *Repo rate* is the price at which the RBI injects liquidity in the market. Contrary to that, *reverse repo rate* is the price at which the RBI tightens liquidity in the market. In other words, repo rate is the rate at which the RBI sells government securities to public and reverse repo rate is the rate at which it purchases government securities from public. Reverse repo rate is pegged at 100 basis points below the rupee rate, which means the reverse repo rate would automatically be adjusted, whereas the repo rate is fixed.

9.8 RECENT TRENDS IN MONETARY POLICY

Monetary policies are important when it comes to understand the business environment of an economy. With the objectives to follow a contractionary or an expansionary monetary policy, the RBI defines its approach towards the currency stabilisation as well as towards the economic progress. The indicators that are being used by the RBI play a vital role in defining the economic environment conducive to business. In June 2016, the rates of the RBI indicators are given in Table 9.5.

Table 9.5 Current Rates of the RBI Indicators

Indicators	*Rate (%)*	*Indicators*	*Rate (%)*
Bank rate	7.00	Cash reserve ratio	4
Repo rate	6.50	Statutory liquidity ratio	21.25
Reserve repo rate	6.00	Base rate	9.3–9.70
Marginal standing facility rate	7.00	Term deposit rate	7.0–7.5

Source: RBI, 7 June 2016.

Some of the recent features and trends are as follows:

1. The monetary policy for the year 2016–2017 is designed in view of the lower inflationary pressure on the economy. An ease in policy rates was followed during first bimonthly monetary policy statement, which was continued during the second bimonthly statement by the RBI.
2. The second bimonthly policy statement outlines that domestic conditions for growth are improving gradually, mainly driven by consumption demand, which is expected to strengthen with a normal monsoon and the implementation of the Seventh Pay Commission award. On a reassessment of balance of risks, therefore, the GVA growth projection for 2016–2017 has been retained at 7.6% with risks evenly balanced.
3. Global financial markets have recorded gains through Q2 of 2016, spurred by risk-on investor sentiment. Portfolio flows are returning, albeit hesitantly, to EME debt and equity markets. The firmness in crude prices that set in around mid-March has been supported in subsequent weeks by some temporary reductions in the global supply. Gold prices remain elevated on safe haven demand. Other non-energy commodity prices remain stable with a hint of upside, while steel prices have firmed appreciably.
4. On the domestic front, the recently released provisional estimate of gross value added (GVA) for 2015–2016 marginally scaled down the annual growth rate to 7.2%, on a deceleration of services sector activity in relation to the advance estimates.
5. Given weak private investment in the face of low capacity utilisation, a reduction in the policy rate by 25 basis points will help strengthen activity and aid the government's initiatives.
6. The Reserve Bank's liquidity framework was changed significantly in September 2014 in order to implement key recommendations of the Expert Committee to revise and strengthen the monetary policy framework (Chairman: Dr. Urjit R. Patel). With over six quarters of implementation history, it is appropriate to review the experience, with a view to making necessary adjustments as well as to more fully implementing the report of the Expert Committee.
7. Smooth the supply of durable liquidity over the year using asset purchases and sales as needed.
8. Narrow the policy rate corridor from +/– 100 bps to +/– 50 bps, with a view to ensuring finer alignment of the Weighted Average Call-money Rate (WACR) with the repo rate.

9. Ease liquidity management for banks without abandoning liquidity discipline by reducing the minimum daily maintenance of CRR from 95% of the requirement to 90% with effect from the fortnight beginning 16 April 2016;
10. Allow substitution of securities in market repo transactions in order to facilitate development of the term money market.
11. Consult with the government on how to moderate the build-up of cash balances with the Reserve Bank.
12. The RBI shall focus on the areas like strengthening of financial market infrastructure; improving credit flow to the productive sectors, including agriculture; implementation of a dynamic provisioning regime for banks; designing of a framework for monitoring liquidity risk; finalisation of guidelines for licensing of new banks in the private sector; reviewing the banking structure in India; regulation of wealth management activities; customer service initiatives; expansion of payment system infrastructure and mitigation of concentration risk in the system; streamlining the system of distribution of banknotes and coins; and improving the mechanism for detection and reporting of counterfeit banknotes.[1]
13. The government of India on the recommendation of Central Board of Directors of the Reserve Bank of India (RBI) ceased the legality of bank notes of ₹500 and ₹1000 on 8th November 2016 through its Gazette Notification REGD. No. D.L.-33004/99 published on 8th November, 2016 (see Box on Demonetisation in India)

Box 9.5 Demonetisation in India

The demonetisation decision was taken owing to the presence of fake currency notes as legal tender in large amount in circulation in public. In fact, it was very difficult to identify the fake notes of ₹500 and ₹1000, which were causing adverse effects on Indian economy. In addition, the government also realised that the unaccounted banknotes of the high denomination currency in public were the main source of black money in the economy. This was largely due to the share of these notes in the total currency in circulation. It is believed that high denomination currency of ₹500 and ₹1000 accounted for more than 85% of the total currency in circulation. Thus, with the objective to erase black money as well as fake currency from the economy, the government in exercise of the powers conferred under sub-section (2) of Section 26 of the Reserve Bank of India Act, 1934 (2 of 1934) declared that the specified bank notes would cease to be the legal tender with effect from 9th November 2016. However, the government allowed that the old notes may be deposited in banks and can also be changed with new notes from any banks in the country till 31st December 2016. From 1st January 2017, the old notes of ₹500 and ₹1000 were allowed to be deposited in the RBI till 31st March 2017. In place of these notes, the RBI announced new notes of ₹500 and ₹2000 denominations to be printed and circulated in the economy.

The decision of the government has direct impact on not only the ills prevailing in the economy but also on the supply of money which can be contracted drastically in the short-term leading to lower economic growth and unemployment in the economy. The withdrawal of almost 86% of the currency from the economy may lead to less credit as well. As per fresh estimates, decline in economic growth is estimated to be 0.3% to 1% due to demonetisation. This step is considered as a landmark decision of the government in its fight against black money. The government is also gradually making the country move towards becoming a cashless economy.

Source: Based on 'Inputs from the Gazzette Notification on Demonetisation', http://finmin.nic.in/172521.pdf, and 'The High Economic Cost of India's Demonetisation', *The Economist.*

1. See https://www.rbi.org.in/scripts/NotificationUser.aspx?Id=7956&Mode=0

Closing Case: RBI's Crucial Role!

There has been a problem of rising both the capital and current account deficits. The inflation and exchange rate problem was also persistent. In order to take corrective measures, the RBI took some stances. The background of this policy was the global and domestic economic environment, wherein GDP growth was 4.5% in the third quarter of 2012–2013.

The industrial activities also slowed down to 0.6% in the month of February 2013. As we know the objective of monetary policy of the RBI is to stabilise the prices and promote the economic expansion, the RBI called for a controlled expansion. To do this, the RBI has been using both quantitative and qualitative measures. Table 1 presents the statistics, showing the average annual growth of the major indicators.

Table 1 Average Annual Growth of Major Indicators

Year	*Wholesale Price Index (WPI)*	*Consumer Price Index (CPI)*	*Broad Money*	*Exchange Rates*	*Year*	*Wholesale Price Index (WPI)*	*Consumer Price Index (CPI)*	*Broad Money*	*Exchange Rates*
1971–1972	5.6	1.0	14.4	–0.6	1992–1993	10.1	12.3	17.7	14.2
1972–1973	10	10.7	16.4	0.4	1993–1994	8.4	3.5	15.9	21.3
1973–1974	20.2	21.2	19.8	1.6	1994–1995	12.6	11.9	19.8	–0.2
1974–1975	25.2	34.6	13.6	4.7	1995–1996	8	10.7	15.6	3.3
1975–1976	–1.1	–4.0	12.5	4.6	1996–1997	4.6	9.9	16.2	9.3
1976–1977	2.1	–13.8	19.9	7.1	1997–1998	4.4	3.1	17	2.5
1977–1978	5.2	10.6	19.9	–2.7	1998–1999	5.9	11.0	19.8	13.6
1978–1979	0	–2.2	20.4	–6.3	1999–2000	3.3	4.4	17.2	4.3
1979–1980	17.1	9.1	20.2	–0.8	2000–2001	7.2	–0.3	15.9	4.4
1980–1981	18.2	14.2	16.4	–3.3	2001–2002	3.6	1.3	16	5
1981–1982	9.3	12.4	17.3	10.3	2002–2003	3.4	3.2	16.1	3
1982–1983	4.9	5.2	14.6	9.2	2003–2004	5.5	3.8	13	–4.2
1983–1984	7.5	11.3	17.6	6.8	2004–2005	6.5	2.7	14	–2.7
1984–1985	6.5	0.2	18.3	12.1	2005–2006	4.5	3.8	15.9	–2.7
1985–1986	4.4	4.8	16.6	8.8	2006–2007	6.6	7.6	20	2.7
1986–1987	5.8	4.8	17.6	2	2007–2008	4.7	7.6	22.1	–8.7
1987–1988	8.1	10.0	17.3	2.8	2008–2009	8.1	10.0	20.5	5.2
1988–1989	7.5	12.6	17.3	7.4	2009–2010	3.8	14.0	19.2	11.3
1989–1990	7.5	5.4	19	16.6	2010–2011	9.6	9.9	16.1	–5.5
1990–1991	10.3	7.6	17.1	7.9	2011–2012	8.9	8.3	15.8	2.1
1991–1992	13.7	19.3	16.7	29.7	2012–2013	7.4	18.9	15.4	14.5

Source: RBI rates are in terms of US$ and average of calendar year.

The RBI has undertaken some measures to make Indian Rupee competent enough to be resilient against the global volatility, which is partially successful. The RBI raised the Marginal Standing Facility (MSF) rate by 200 bps in July 2013, as in the opening case. There have been measures undertaken by the RBI to ease the liquidity condition. But later, the liquidity condition was tightened by raising the repo rate. Thus, during the course of 2013–2014, the RBI monetary policies have been changing as per the global and domestic environment. Liquidity condition can easily be seen in the following exhibit.

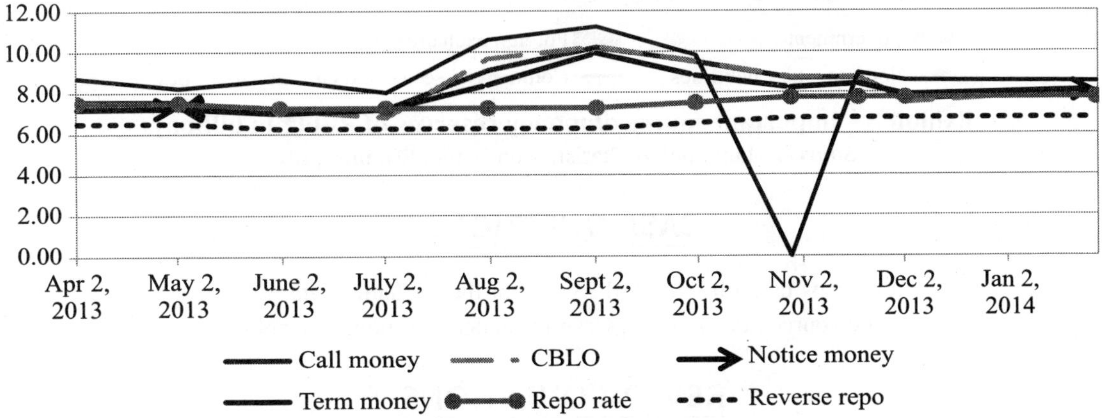

Exhibit 1 Monetary rates (%).
Source: Handbook of Statistics on Indian Economy, RBI.

The reserve money in India and their sources have been depicted in the exhibit which are as follow:

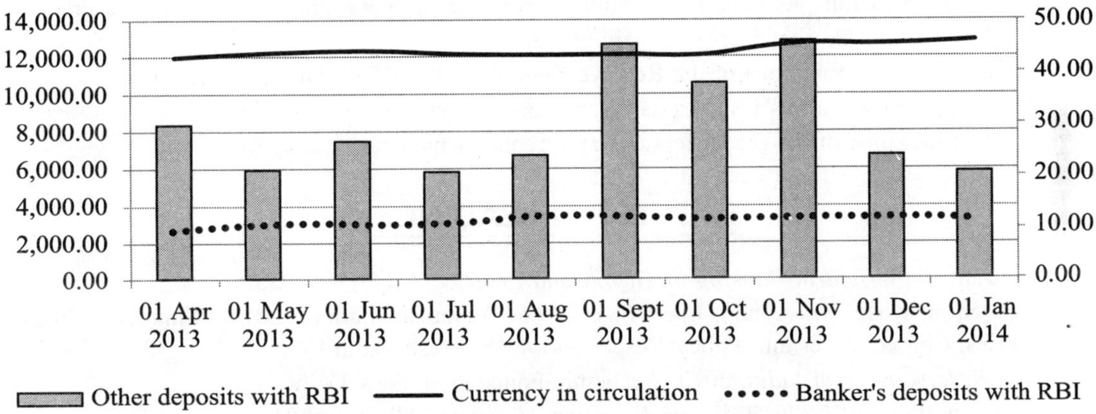

Exhibit 2 Reserve money in India (₹ in billion).
Source: Handbook of Statistics on Indian Economy, RBI.

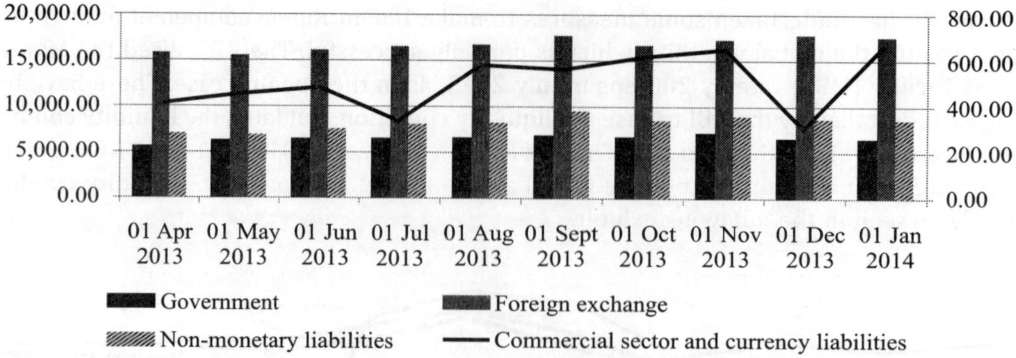

Exhibit 3 Important source of money reserves of RBI (₹ in billion).
Source: Handbook of Statistics on Indian Economy, RBI.

CASE QUESTIONS

1. Evaluate the steps taken by the RBI to control the exchange rate.
2. How does the sources of money reserve influence the monetary policy.

REVIEW QUESTIONS

1. What is monetary policy? What are its objectives?
2. Discuss the types of monetary policies.
3. What do you understand by demand and supply of money?
4. Examine the various instruments of monetary policy.
5. Explain how changes in the bank rate affect the credit demand.
6. How does China get benefitted from the open market operations to avoid liquidity crunch?
7. What is a bank rate? Explain its significance.
8. What are the functions of the Reserve Bank of India (RBI)? Discuss in detail.
9. Describe the various institutional frameworks governing monetary policy.
10. Outline some of the recent features and trends of monetary policy.

SUGGESTED READINGS

Blinder, Alan, 1998, *Central Banking in Theory and Practice*, MIT Press, USA.

Claessens, Stijn, Kose, M. Ayhan, Laeven, Luc, and Valencia, Fabian, 2014, 'Financial Crises: Causes, Consequences and Policy Responses', IMF, Washington DC.

History of Reserve Bank of India, 2013, Academic Foundation, New Delhi.

Misra, S.K. and Puri, V.K., 2012, *Indian Economy*, Himalaya Publication House, New Delhi.

Rangarajan, C., 2009, *India: Monetary Policy, Financial Stability and Other Essays*, Academic Foundation, New Delhi.

Ray, Partha, 2013, *Monetary Policy*, Oxford University Press, New Delhi.

Vasudevan, A., 2012, *Monetary Governance in Search of New Space*, Academic Foundation, New Delhi.

10

BALANCE OF PAYMENTS

Learning Outcomes

After reading this chapter, you will

- Understand the concept and components of balance of payments (BoP) and its accounting
- Learn the key indicators of balance of payments
- Appreciate the linkages between balance of payments and contemporary business environment

Opening Case: India's BoP Challenges and the Business Environment

The business environment in a country depends on various factors. India's economic growth in recent years has been slow owing to the slow growth in India's manufacturing sector. Moreover, this is an era of economic interdependence, and consequently, Indian economy is also affected by the global economic environment. The eurozone crisis and the depleting global demand scenario have led to a decrease in the investment inflows.

Concurrently, India's export has been performing slowly as compared to its imports due to lower demand size in European countries. Now, the question arises as to how these issues can be taken together to understand the relation between the economic and business environment and the balance of payments situation.

Often we come across several news related to the Indian economy in both print and electronic media. One of the important news is related to India's external sector problems. In 2013, Indian Rupee weakened to 68 per dollar as compared to 45 per dollar in 2011. This weakening of rupee created multiple effects on the Indian economy. It led to the rise in the fuel prices, which further had an impact on the prices of essential commodities. As a result, inflation was on peak. This reduction was caused by India's current account deficit.

The current account deficit increased to US$189.8 billion in 2011–2012, which was 10.2% of the GDP. It is also believed that India's balance of payments trouble increases owing to the global trading environment and the outgoing capital from the country. The following exhibit depicts the widening trade deficit and takes a stock of the other important indicators of Indian economy:

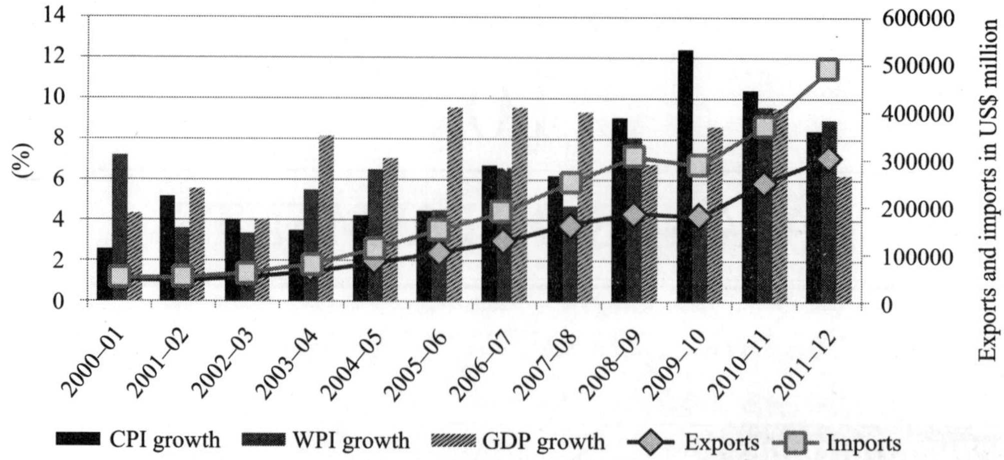

Exhibit 1 Widening trade deficit and other indicators.

Note: Indicators like CPI growth, WPI growth and GDP growth are measured at primary Y-axis (%) and exports and imports are shown at secondary Y-axis (US$ million).

Source: Economic Survey of India.

In August 2013, India was left with only enough cash in the RBI to pay for seven months of imports. This created a challenge for India's balance of payments position. Also, because of this, it was difficult for the economy to defend the falling rupee.[1] The government took some measures including imposition of further restrictions on gold imports. The rupee is now stable but the challenges of stabilising the balance of payments position continue to exist.

Source: This case is written by the authors based on inputs from the following sources:

1. Economic Survey of India.
2. RBI.
3. India's balance of payment problems hamper rupee rescue, *Reuters, Live Mint* and *Wall Street Journal*, 12 August 2013, http://m.livemint.com/Money/zi7NqefFHpujFPxndYnatK/Indias-balance-of-payment-problems-hamper-rupee-rescue.html

10.1 INTRODUCTION

Current account deficit is a major concern for Indian economy. In recent times, lot of restrictions have been imposed on the import of gold, because it is believed that it adds to the current account deficit. The question then arises as to why the widening of current account deficit is a matter of concern for the government. We know that the current account deficit means adverse trade payment situation. In this case, India's values of imports are higher than India's value of exports. Certainly, for higher import value, India needs to pay more in terms of US$. This has adverse impacts on both the foreign exchange reserves and the exchange rate mechanism. The Government of India has already imposed restrictions on the imports of gold in the country to reduce the current account deficit.

1. India's balance of payment problems hamper rupee rescue, Reuters, Live Mint and Wall Street Journal, 12 August 2013, http://m.livemint.com/Money/zi7NqefFHpujFPxndYnatK/Indias-balance-of-payment-problems-hamper-rupee-rescue.html

An increase in the current or capital account deficit has a potential to impede the economic progress by putting more pressure on the economy's overall balance of payments situation. It is, therefore, required to understand the concept of balance of payments. In this chapter, we discuss the concept balance of payments and its overall impact on the business environment of an economy.

10.2 BALANCE OF PAYMENTS

Every country maintains its accounts of transactions with the world. The method of this transaction is double-entry book keeping of countries' international transactions. This account detail is called *balance of payments* of a country. In this account, details of debit are entered on one side, and credits are maintained on the other side. In other words, the total outflow and inflow in terms of currency of the country or international currency such as US$ are maintained in this account details.

In this balance of payments account details, a systematic summary of economic transaction is presented as per the guidelines of IMF for specific time periods. In India, RBI is responsible for the management of balance of payments data that is broadly based on the guidelines of RBI, and are compatible with the manual of IMF. The recent manual of RBI was published in the year 2010.

Now, consider the fact that Indian exporters and importers are involved in trade with the rest of the world. The trade is carried out in both goods and services. For exports and imports, payment mechanism is regulated by RBI in collaboration with the other international banking systems for transfer payments. Now, once Indian exporters earn revenues from their businesses, RBI keeps them in the form of receipts or credits. Similarly, for the payments related to imports, RBI manages them on debits. In case, the total credit is equal to the total debit, then the balance of payments in terms of trade in goods and services is neither favourable and nor unfavourable for a country.

However, consider a scenario, wherein India's imports are more than its exports. In this case, the country's foreign exchange earned by exports is limited to India's total imports. Such a scenario reflects that India's current account is in deficit. It has to manage the payments from other sources such as by borrowings and so on. Then, the country needs to look into its capital accounts. In case, if the capital account is in deficit, then this is going to impact the business environment in the country. We shall now discuss the components of balance of payments, which would give us an idea about its structure.

10.3 COMPONENTS OF BALANCE OF PAYMENTS AND ITS ACCOUNTING

Balance of payments account for trade in goods and services as well as other payments and receipts such as borrowings, aid and loan, etc. The trade in goods and services is the part of current account and the rest is the part of capital account. Thus, the balance of payments comprises the current account, capital account, errors and omissions, and changes in the foreign exchange reserves. Transaction, on account of trade, is classified into merchandise exports and imports, and exports and imports of services. Thus, the current account is classified into merchandise (exports and imports) and invisibles. The classification of invisible transaction consists of services, which include commercial, government, financial and other services like travel and transportation, income and transfers like grants, gifts, remittances, etc.

On the other hand, capital account is classified into foreign investment, which comprises FDI, portfolio investment, institutional investment, non-debt liabilities, loans like external assistance, external commercial borrowings and trade credit, and banking capital such as non-resident Indian (NRI) deposits. Components of balance of payments are presented in Figure 10.1.

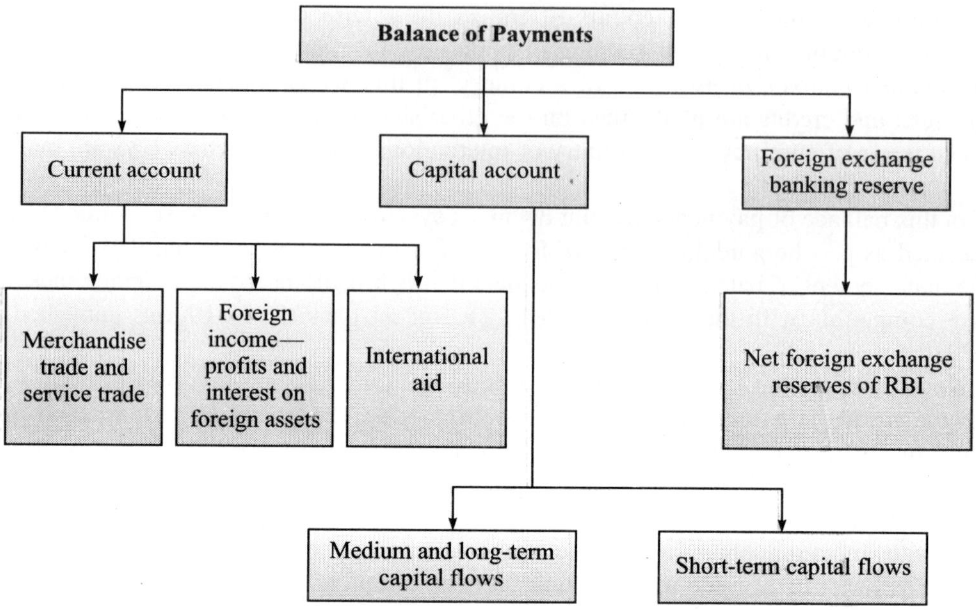

Figure 10.1 Components of balance of payments.

Balance in merchandise trade account

This account in the balance of payments is the part of current account balance. It primarily represents the difference between the exports and the imports, which includes trade in goods only. Trade account balance indicates whether the country is enjoying a surplus on goods trade with the rest of the world or it is suffering from trade deficit. Generally, the countries which dominate in producing manufacturing items enjoy the trade surplus. In addition, the countries which produce high-value commodities or endowed with natural resources (such as oil and gas) have also trade surplus while trading with the major trade partners. Countries like the United States, Germany, China, Iran, Russia and Saudi Arabia fall in this category.

Invisible transactions

Invisible transactions are the accounts of trade in services. Generally, trade between the countries on account of providing services such as financial services, transportation services, education services, tourism services, etc. are the main areas of trade in services. The current account of a country includes both the trade in merchandise as well as in services.

Balance in current account

This represents the overall current account balance, including the trade in goods and services. In today's dynamic and globalised world, developing countries like China, India, Brazil, etc. have comparative advantages in providing services to the developed nations, as these countries also own human capital necessary to do so. For instance, providing information and outsourcing-related services to the countries like USA has become one of the leading sectors which drive India's growth story. In this scenario, trade services emerge as an important part of the current account of BoP. The current account also includes primary income and secondary income. The difference between these components in terms of credits and debits represents the overall balance of the current account.

Capital account balance

Capital account balance is primarily the difference between the receipts and the payments through capital transfers such as borrowings and lending of capital. The capital account of a country maintains the details on account of its total capital inflow and outflow, including the long-term and short-term borrowings. Capital inflows are categorised into various instruments such as debt, equity, loans, etc. Thus, the main components of capital account are loans from banking system, bilateral grants and loans, foreign investments, foreign institutional investments, portfolio investment, etc. A country may experience surplus or deficit on account of the capital inflows and outflows, which describes that the country is having balance of payments surplus/deficit on capital account. This indicator has its own implications for the economy.

Foreign exchange reserves

The foreign currency held in a country is also taken into account while maintaining the balance of payments' accounts. The reserve may be held in the form of Special Drawing Rights (SDR) as per IMF rule, gold, US Dollar, Euro, etc. Technically, when a country exports, it receives more foreign exchange. It implies that if the current balance of payments account is in surplus, the country has a potential to increase its foreign exchange reserves. The same is also true for capital account. On the other hand, if a country imports more, it has to pay from its foreign exchange reserves.

Errors and omission

Errors and omissions can be either due to statistical discrepancies or due to certain unrecorded transactions.

As discussed, the components of balance of payments form the structure of its accounting system. The balance of payments statement is based on the double entry accounting system. The standard balance of payments statement is presented in Table 10.1.

Table 10.1 indicates that the basic principle that is involved in accounting of balance of payments of a country is the method of double entry recording system.

Table 10.1 A Standard BoP Statement

Items	*Receipts (Credits)* +	*Payments (Debits)* −	*Balance (Surplus)* +	*Balance (Deficit)* −
1. Current account				
(i) Merchandise (goods)	Exports	Imports	Exports > Imports	Exports < Imports
(ii) Invisible (services)	Exports	Imports	Exports > Imports	Exports < Imports
2. Capital account				
(i) Foreign investment	Inflows	Outflows	Inflows > Outflows	Inflows < Outflows
(ii) Loans	Received	Supplied	Received > Supplied	Received < Supplied
3. Banking capital	Deposits in India	Deposited from India	If deposits in India, is higher	Deposits from India is higher
4. Rupee debt services	Inflows	Outflows	Inflows > Outflows	Inflows < Outflows
5. Other capital	Inflows	Outflows	Inflows > Outflows	Inflows < Outflows

Source: Based on Balance of Payment Manuals, IMF.

10.4 STRUCTURE OF BOP IN INDIA

Based on parameters and guidelines by IMF (discussed in the previous section), RBI publishes data on the balance of payments. The latest data on balance of payments is published as two statements. Statement I bring out data on BoP based on the guidelines of IMF and statement II presents data on BoP based on the old framework of RBI. RBI publishes these statements both in US Dollar and Indian Rupee. We use the statement published for the year 2014–2015 as an illustration.

There are four broad components in the new statement, *viz.* current account, capital account, financial account, and the net errors and emissions. The current account is broadly sub-divided into goods and services, primary and secondary income categories. There are sub-categories of this categorisation, which can also be seen in the statement I (see Table 10.2). The capital account is divided into gross acquisition/disposal of non-financial assets and capital transfers. Similarly, the financial account is divided into direct investment in India and direct investment by India, portfolio investment, and other investment such as loans, credit lines etc.

In case of statement II (see Table 10.3), the old version of RBI's BoP statement has five broad categories. The first category includes detailed accounting of current account and capital account, second category is loans and advances, third is banking capital, fourth is rupee debt services and fifth category is other capital. The details of sub-categories under each category are presented in statement II.

Table 10.2 Statement I: Standard Presentation of BoP in India as per the Sixth Edition of IMF's Balance of Payments and International Investment Position Manual (BPM6) (US$ in million)

Items	*2014–2015*		
	Credit	*Debit*	*Net*
1 Current account (1.A + 1.B + 1.C)	5,54,717	5,82,108	–27,392
1.A Goods and services (1.A.a + 1.A.b)	4,71,482	5,40,709	–69,227
1.A.a Goods (1.A.a.1 to 1.A.a.3)	3,15,495	4,60,598	–1,45,105
1.A.a.1 General merchandise on a BoP basis	3,15,495	4,26,162	–1,10,667
1.A.a.2 Net exports of goods under merchanting	–	–	–
1.A.a.3 Non-monetary gold	–	34,437	–34,437
1.A.b Services (1.A.b.1 to 1.A.b.13)	1,55,987	80,111	75,878
1.A.b.1 Manufacturing services on physical inputs owned by others	109	30	80
1.A.b.2 Maintenance and repair services n.i.e.	174	227	–53
1.A.b.3 Transport	17,446	16,176	1,270
1.A.b.4 Travel	20,333	15,306	5,028
1.A.b.5 Construction	1,613	1,153	460
1.A.b.6 Insurance and pension services	2,197	1,118	1,079
1.A.b.7 Financial services	5,661	3,580	2,081
1.A.b.8 Charges for the use of intellectual property n.i.e.	529	4,820	–4,290
1.A.b.9 Telecommunications, computer, and information services	75,333	4,094	71,240
1.A.b.10 Other business services	28,422	27,644	778
1.A.b.11 Personal, cultural, and recreational services	1,191	1,440	–249
1.A.b.12 Government goods and services n.i.e.	543	961	–418
1.A.b.13 Others n.i.e.	2,435	3,563	–1,129
1.B Primary income (1.B.a to 1.B.c)	13,116	37,229	–24,114
1.B.a Compensation of employees	3,558	2,737	821
1.B.b Investment income	8,073	33,875	–25,801
1.B.b.1 Direct investment	4,207	13,531	–9,323
1.B.b.2 Portfolio investment	120	7,367	–7,247
1.B.b.3 Other investment	496	12,971	–12,475
1.B.b.4 Reserve assets	3,250	5	3,245
1.B.c Other primary income	1,484	618	867
1.C Secondary Income (1.C.a + 1.C.b)	70,118	4,169	65,950
1.C.a General government	291	614	–324

Items	2014–2015		
	Credit	Debit	Net
1.C.b Financial corporations, non-financial corporations, households, and Non-Profit Institutions Serving Households (NPISHs)	69,828	3,555	66,273
1.C.a.1 Personal transfers (current transfers between resident and/non-resident households)	67,331	3,218	64,113
1.C.b.2 Other current transfers	2,496	337	2,160
2 Capital account (2.A + 2.B)	469	603	–134
2.A Gross acquisitions (DR.)/disposals (CR.) of non-produced non-financial assets	244	134	110
2.B Capital transfers	225	470	–244
3 Financial account (3.A to 3.B)	5,50,265	5,21,852	28,413
3.A Direct investment (3.A.a + 3.A.b)	51,644	20,047	31,596
3.A.a Direct investment in India	44,996	9,865	35,131
3.A.a.1 Equity and investment fund shares	41,620	9,612	32,008
3.A.a.1.A Equity other than reinvestment of earnings	31,910	9,612	22,298
3.A.a.1.B Reinvestment of earnings	9,710	–	9,710
3.A.a.2 Debt instruments	3,376	253	3,123
3.A.a.2.A Direct investor in direct investment enterprises	3,376	253	3,123
3.A.b Direct investment by India	6,648	10,184	–3,535
3.A.b.1 Equity and investment fund shares	6,648	6,702	–53
3.A.b.1.A Equity other than reinvestment of earnings	6,648	3,941	2,708
3.A.b.1.B Reinvestment of earnings	–	2,762	–2,762
3.A.b.2 Debt instruments	–	3,481	–3,481
3.A.b.2.A Direct investor in direct investment enterprises	–	3,481	–3,481
3.B Portfolio investment	2,55,490	2,14,556	40,934
3.B.a Portfolio investment in India	2,54,777	2,13,855	40,923
3.B.a.1 Equity and investment fund shares	1,92,213	1,77,459	14,753
3.B.b.2 Debt securities	62,565	36,395	26,170
3.B.b Portfolio investment by India	713	701	11
3.C Financial derivatives (other than reserves) and employee stock options	14,463	16,747	–2,284
3.D Other investment	2,28,668	2,09,094	19,573
3.D.1 Other equity American Depository Scheme/Global Depository Scheme (ADRs/GDRs)	–	–	–
3.D.2 Currency and deposits	64,994	49,205	15,789

Items	2014–2015		
	Credit	Debit	Net
3.D.b.1 Central bank (rupee debt movements; NRG)	1,733	–	1,733
3.D.b.2 Deposit-taking corporations, except the central bank (NRI deposits)	63,262	49,205	14,056
3.D.b.3 General government	–	–	–
3.D.b.4 Other sectors	–	–	–
3.D.c Loans (external assistance, ECBs and banking capital)	59,073	59,102	–31
3.4.c.1 Loans to India	57,403	58,443	–1,042
3.4.c.2 Loans by India	1,670	661	1,011
3.D.d Insurance, pension, and standardised guarantee schemes	365	288	76
3.D.e Trade credit and advances	89,729	90,653	–924
3.D.f Other accounts receivable/payable—other	14,508	9,846	4,663
3.D.g Special drawing rights	–	–	–
3.E Reserve assets	–	61,407	–61,407
3.E.a Monetary gold	–	–	–
3.E.b Special drawing rights n.a.	–	–	–
3.E.c Reserve position in the IMF n.a.	–	–	–
3.E.d Other reserve assets (foreign currency assets)	–	61,407	–61,407
4 Total assets/liabilities	5,50,265	5,21,852	28,413
4.A Equity and investment fund shares	2,56,019	2,11,512	44,509
4.B Debt instruments	2,79,737	2,39,089	40,648
4.C Other financial assets and liabilities	14,508	71,251	–56,745
5 Net errors and omissions	–	616	–887

Source: Handbook of Statistics on Indian Economy, RBI.

Table 10.3 Statement II: India's Overall Balance of Payments (US$ in Million)

Item	2014–2015		
	Credit	Debit	Net
A.1 Merchandise	3,16,545	4,61,484	–1,44,940
A.2 Invisibles	2,41,238	1,23,098	1,18,139
A.2.a Services	1,57,700	81,113	76,588
A.2.a.1 Travel	20,334	15,306	5,028
A.2.a.2 Transportation	17,485	16,177	1,308
A.2.a.3 Insurance	2,202	1,119	1,084
A.2.a.4 G.n.i.e.	543	961	–418
A.2.a.5 Miscellaneous	1,17,135	47,550	69,585

Item	2014–2015		
	Credit	**Debit**	**Net**
A.2.a.5.a Miscellaneous—of which software services	73,108	2,708	70,400
A.2.a.5.b Business services	28,422	27,644	778
A.2.a.5.c Financial services	5,661	3,580	2,081
A.2.a.5.d Communication services	1,997	1,023	975
A.2.b Transfers	70,141	4,449	65,692
A.2.b.1 Official transfers	322	893	–572
A.2.b.2 Private transfers	69,819	3,555	66,264
A.2.c Income	13,397	37,537	–24,140
A.2.c.1 Investment income	9,839	34,801	–24,962
A.2.c.2 Compensation of employees	3,558	2,737	821
A Current account	5,57,783	5,84,583	–26,800
B.1 Foreign investment	3,08,556	2,35,100	73,456
B.1.a Foreign direct investment	51,796	20,544	31,251
B.1.a.1 Foreign direct investment in India	45,147	9,864	35,283
B.1.a.1.a Foreign direct investment in India—Equity	31,910	9,612	22,298
B.1.a.1.b Foreign direct investment in India—Reinvested earnings	9,988	–	9,988
B.1.a.1.c Foreign direct investment in India—Other capital	3,249	252	2,997
B.1.a.2 Foreign direct investment abroad	6,649	10,680	–4,031
B.1.a.2.a Foreign direct investment abroad—Equity	6,649	3,867	2,782
B.1.a.2.b Foreign direct investment abroad—Reinvested earnings	0	3,337	–3,337
B.1.a.2.c Foreign direct investment abroad—Other capital	0	3,476	–3,476
B.1.b.1 Foreign portfolio investment	2,56,761	2,14,556	42,205
B.1.b.1.a Foreign portfolio investment in India	2,56,048	2,13,854	42,193
B.1.b.1.a.1 Portfolio investment in India of which FIIs	2,54,777	2,13,854	40,923
B.1.b.1.a.2 Portfolio investment in India of which GDRs/ADRs	1,271	0	1,271
B.1.b.2 Foreign portfolio investment abroad	713	702	11
B.2 Loans	1,23,355	1,20,170	3,184
B.2.a External assistance	5,780	4,054	1,725
B.2.a.1 External assistance by India	60	388	–327
B.2.a.2 External assistance to India	5,719	3,667	2,053

Item	2014–2015		
	Credit	Debit	Net
B.2.b Commercial borrowings	27,847	26,276	1,570
B.2.b.1 Commercial borrowings by India	1,611	273	1,338
B.2.b.2 Commercial borrowings to India	26,236	26,004	232
B.2.c Short-term credit to India	89,729	89,840	–111
B.2.c.1 Suppliers' credit >180 days and buyers' credit	87,643	89,230	–1,587
B.2.c.2 Suppliers' credit up to 180 days	2,086	610	1,476
B.3 Banking capital	90,094	78,476	11,618
B.3.a Commercial banks	88,361	78,476	9,885
B.3.a.1 Assets of commercial banks	17,031	18,546	–1,515
B.3.a.2 Liabilities of commercial banks	71,329	59,930	11,399
B.3.a.2.a Of which: Non-resident deposits of commercial banks	63,262	49,205	14,057
B.3.b Others	1,733	0	1,733
B.4 Rupee debt service	0	81	–81
B.5 Other capital	28,898	27,789	1,109
B Capital account	5,50,903	4,61,617	89,286
C Errors and omissions	1,025	2,104	–1,080
D Overall balance	11,09,710	10,48,304	61,406
E Monetary movements	0	61,406	–61,406
E.1 IMF	0	0	0
E.2 Foreign exchange reserves (Increase –/Decrease +)	0	61,406	–61,406
E.3 SDR Allocation	–	–	–

G.n.i.e.: Government not included elsewhere.
Notes: 1. Data for 2014–2015 are preliminary estimates and for 2013–2014 are partially revised.
2. Total may not tally due to rounding off.

Source: Handbook of Statistics on Indian Economy, RBI.

10.5 KEY INDICATORS OF BALANCE OF PAYMENTS

As per the manual of IMF, the key indicators of BoP are current account balance, capital account balance and financial account balance. When we deal with the current account balance, the value of exports and imports of goods and services are the main indicators which play a vital role in the national income accounting.

Similarly, in case of capital account, the net capital received and transfers are the indicators of a partial representation of economic environment. For financial accounts, FDI and institutional investments are the main indicators of the BoP structure. These indicators are closely related to the macroeconomic situations. We can now discuss the scenario of these indicators in case of India.

Trade scenario

The Ministry of Finance's Mid-year Economic Analysis for the year 2015–2016 indicates that the external sector of India appears to be robust. Trade deficit has declined considerably and is at comfortable level. Trade deficit is estimated to be 1.2% of the GDP. International trade has been affected in recent years by the global economic slowdown and since the second half of 2014–2015, it has also been affected in value terms by the decline in global commodity prices. India's exports (on customs basis) reached a peak level of US$314.4 billion in 2013–2014 and decelerated marginally to US$310.3 billion in 2014–2015, mainly on account of subdued global demand. During 2015–2016 (April–November), exports declined by 18.5% on account of subdued global demand coupled with falling commodity prices, particularly crude oil prices (see Figure 10.2).

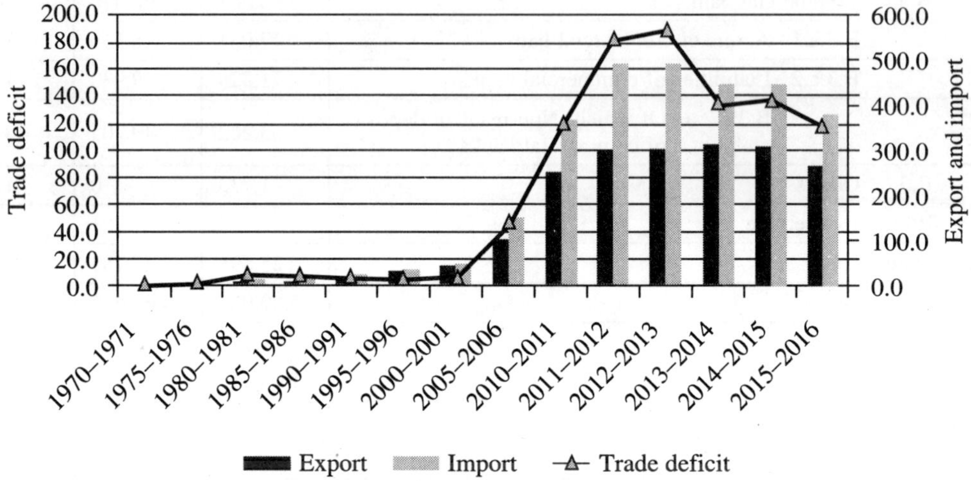

Figure 10.2 India's total trade deficit (US$ in billion).

Note: Trade deficit is measured at primary *Y*-axis (in US$ billion; and expressed through line graph) and exports and imports are shown at secondary *Y*-axis (in US$ billion; and expressed through bar graph).

Source: Handbook of Statistics on Indian Economy, RBI.

The historical performance of exports and imports in India suggests that India's merchandise trade increased from US$4.2 billion in 1970–1971 to US$791.1 billion in the year 2012–2013 and US$642.4 billion in 2015–2016. During this period, India's merchandise exports and imports have grown at compound annual growth rate (CAGR) of more than 11% and 12%, respectively. The CAGR of merchandise export was above 9.8% between 2005–2006 and 2015–2016, increasing from US$103 billion in 2005–2006 to US$262 billion in 2015–2016.

On the other hand, India's merchandise imports increased further to US$380.4 billion, registering a negative growth over the last year. The merchandise imports were US$448 billion in 2014–2015. At present, the total imports stand at US$380.4 billion as against the exports standing at US$262.0 billion in 2015–2016. Clearly, there exists a trade deficit on account of merchandise trade. At present, the total trade deficit in merchandise trade is US$18.4 billion. While, on account of the services trade, India has a positive balance of trade, with surplus of US$83.4 billion.

Foreign investments

Foreign investment is categorised under two components, *viz.* foreign direct investment (FDI) and foreign institutional investment (FII). The net FDI to India has increased during the recent years, whereas the net FII has decreased in 2015–2016. Overseas investments done by India have also shown a declining graph during 2011–2012, 2012–2013 and thereafter. FDI in India increased from US$4,031 million in 2000–2001 to US$29,029 million in 2010–2011 and US$34,426 million in 2014–2015. The increase during the period of 2000–2001 to 2010–2011 was at an average annual rate of more than 30% and CAGR of 22%. In the year 2014–2015, the increase was recorded to be 12% over 2013–2014.

As per Economic Survey of India, 2016, net FDI inflows in India grew to US$27.7 billion in April–December, 2015–2016 compared to US$21.9 billion in April–December, 2014–2015. This indicates the continuous increase in trend of net capital inflow in the country since the new policy was opted by the Government of India to attract foreign investment in several areas such as Railways.

The case of overseas investments (FDI outflow or OFDI) has also been significant, which increased at an average annual growth of more than 45% during 2000–2001 to 2010–2011. During 2013–2014, FDI outflow increased to US$9,199 million compared to US$7,134 million in 2012–2013, but in 2014–2015, this decreased to US$1,799 million. The overseas investment by India has decreased by 80% in 2014–2015 over 2013–2014. The net portfolio investment increased by more than 80% on an average during the period of 2000–2001 to 2010–2011. It has also increased in 2014–2015. Table 10.4 shows the trend in India's FDI inflow and outflow.

Table 10.4 Foreign Investment in India (US$ Million)

Year	*FDI inflow*	*FDI outflow*	*Net FDI*	*Net portfolio investment*
2000–2001	4,031	759	3,272	5,862
2001–2002	6,125	1,391	4,734	6,686
2002–2003	5,036	1,819	3,217	4,161
2003–2004	4,322	1,934	2,388	13,744
2004–2005	5,987	2,274	3,713	13,000
2005–2006	8,901	5,867	3,034	15,528
2006–2007	22,739	15,046	7,693	14,753
2007–2008	34,729	18,835	15,893	43,326
2008–2009	41,737	19,365	22,372	8,341
2009–2010	33,107	15,144	17,966	50,362
2010–2011	29,029	17,195	11,834	42,127
2011–2012	32,957	11,097	21,860	39,031
2012–2013	26,953	7,134	19,819	46,710
2013–2014	30,763	9,199	21,564	4,822
2014–2015	34,426	1,799	32,627	40,934

Source: Handbook of Statistics on Indian Economy, RBI.

The government has initiated various reform measures for simplification and rationalisation of procedures and processes to attract more FDI. The impact of them has started becoming visible. After the launch of the initiatives in September 2014, there was nearly 40% increase in FDI inflows during October 2014 to June 2015 over the corresponding period of the previous year. During April–November 2015–2016, the total FDI inflows were US $ 34.8 billion as compared to US $ 27.7 billion during April–November 2014–2015, showing a 26% surge. The FDI equity inflows also increased from US $ 18.9 billion during April–November 2014–2015 to US $ 24.8 billion during April–November 2015–2016, showing a 31% growth.

Considering the direction of investment inflows in India, statistics indicates that Mauritius has the largest share in India's total FDI inflows. Singapore has the second largest share followed by UK.

The huge increase in foreign investment was due to increase in both FDI and portfolio investment. In gross terms, inflows under FDI were at US$35.2 billion in 2014–2015. Net FDI (Net FDI into India and net outward FDI) reached an all-time high of US $ 31.3 billion in 2014–2015 (US $ 22.4 billion in 2008–2009). Similarly, net portfolio investment also reached their highest level so far of US $ 42.2 billion in 2014–2015 (US $ 32.4 billion in 2009–2010). During the first half of 2015–2016, net foreign investment fell to US $ 7.9 billion as against US $ 37.3 billion in the first half of 2014–2015, mainly due to outflows of portfolio investment.

Net portfolio investment logged an outflow of US $ 8.7 billion in H1 of 2015-16 as against net inflow of US $ 22.2 billion in first half (H1) of 2014–2015. Foreign institutional investor (FII) investment is the major component of portfolio investment and net FII was US $ 40.9 billion in 2014–2015, which was negative in 2015–2016.[2] Net FDI reached US $ 16.7 billion in H1 of 2015–2016 as against US $ 15.1 billion in H1 of 2014–2015.

NRI deposits

Capital account also consists of deposits by non-resident Indians (NRIs). The capital inflows from these NRIs stood at US $ 58.6 billion in 2011–2012 as compared to US $ 51.7 billion in 2010–2011. The NRI deposit in the year 2012–2013 was recorded to be US $ 70.8 billion, showing an increase of US $ 12.2 billion over the previous year. In the year 2015–2016, NRI deposit was recorded to be US $ 126.9 billion, which is an increase of US $ 11.8 billion over 2014–2015.

Official development assistance (ODA)

External assistance is another important part of balance of payments, which also constitutes the components of external debt. Generally, the official assistance by multilateral and bilateral institutions or countries constitute loans or grants. India's official assistance on account of loans was recorded to be US $ 7.5 billion in 2014–2015, which was less than that of 2013–2014. In 2013–2014, the total authorisation of assistance on account of loan was US $ 9.0 billion. Considering grants, the total assistance received by India was US $ 19 million in 2014–2015, which is less than that what it was in the previous year. In 2012–2013, the total grant was US $ 350 million, and in 2013–2014, it was US $ 23 million. India's total official external assistance was estimated to be US $ 7.6 billion in 2014–2015. Table 10.5 outlines the external assistance received by India during the recent times.

---

2. As per FDI statistics from Department Industrial Policy and Promotion.

Table 10.5 External Assistance Received by India (US$ Million)

Year	*Authorisation*			*Net Inflow of Aid*
	Loans	*Grants*	*Total*	
2000–2001	3,769	206	3,975	–537
2001–2002	4,439	711	5,150	332
2002–2003	4,115	254	4,369	–3,912
2003–2004	3,223	571	3,794	–3,225
2004–2005	3,961	663	4,624	952
2005–2006	2,542	356	2,898	1,545
2006–2007	6,557	801	7,358	1,290
2007–2008	7,145	1,070	8,215	1,655
2008–2009	6,268	322	6,590	2,179
2009–2010	10,321	204	10,525	3,129
2010–2011	7,795	331	8,126	4,721
2011–2012	12,343	232	12,575	2,612
2012–2013	12,301	350	1,265	891
2013–2014	9,004	23	9,027	1,475
2014–2015	7,582	19	7,601	1,171

Source: Handbook of Statistics on Indian Economy, RBI.

External debt

External debt plays an important role in setting out favourable balance of payments situation. As of 2014–2015, India's external debt stock is US$475.3 billion, which was an increase of US$29.13 billion as compared to the external debt of 2013–2014. This rise in external debt was primarily due to an increase in external commercial borrowings. As per the RBI statistics presented in Table 10.6, the overall external debt of India was recorded to be US$475.5 billion in 2014–2015.

Table 10.6 External Debt of India: By Component (US$ Million)

S. No.	*Item*	*1990–91*	*2000–01*	*2010–11*	*2011–12*	*2012–13*	*2013–14*	*2014–15*
1	Multilateral	20,900	31,105	48,475	50,453	51,590	53,418	52,392
2	Bilateral	14,168	15,975	25,712	26,884	25,158	24,727	21,752
3	IMF	2,623	0	6,308	6,163	5,964	6,149	5,488
4	Trade credit	4,301	5,923	18,647	18,990	17,760	15,518	12,650
5	ECBs	10,209	24,408	1,00,476	1,20,136	1,40,125	1,49,375	1,80,854
6	Rupee debt	12,847	3,719	1,601	1,354	1,258	1,468	1,506
7	Long-term debt	75,257	97,698	2,52,901	2,82,587	3,12,677	3,54,500	3,89,805
8	Short-term debt	8,544	3,628	64,990	78,179	96,697	–	–
9	Gross total debt	83,801	1,01,326	3,17,891	3,60,766	4,09,374	4,46,178	4,75,303

Source: Handbook of Statistics on Indian Economy, RBI.

Some of the key features of this statistics, as outlined by the Reserve Bank of India, are as follows[3]:

1. External debt on account of commercial borrowings increased by US$31.5 billion during 2014–2015 as compared to the increase of US$9.2 billion in 2013–2014.
2. Trade credit components of external debt (both long term and short term) showed a decrease of US$2.9 billion in 2014–2015 over the year 2013–2014.
3. The long-term debt increased by US$35.3 billion in 2014-15. It was US$354.5 billion in 2013–2014, which increased to US$389.8 billion in 2014–2015 mainly on account of the rise in external commercial borrowings.
4. The loans under external assistance (multilateral and bilateral debt) declined by around US$4.0 billion during 2014–2015 as compared with an increase of US$1.4 billion in the preceding year.

10.6 TRENDS OF BALANCE OF PAYMENTS IN INDIA

The overall trend of balance of payments in India was estimated to be positive during 2014–2015 as compared to 2013–2014. However, in India's balance of payments situation, the current account deficit is the notable factor to be handled carefully. This was increasing in recent years prior to 2013–2014. Several measures taken by the Government led to the situation where decreasing trend in the current account deficit has been seen in the previous few years. The current account was recorded to be US$27 billion in 2014–2015, which was the decreasing trend in trade deficit (see Figure 10.3). The net capital account was positive for India (see Table 10.7).

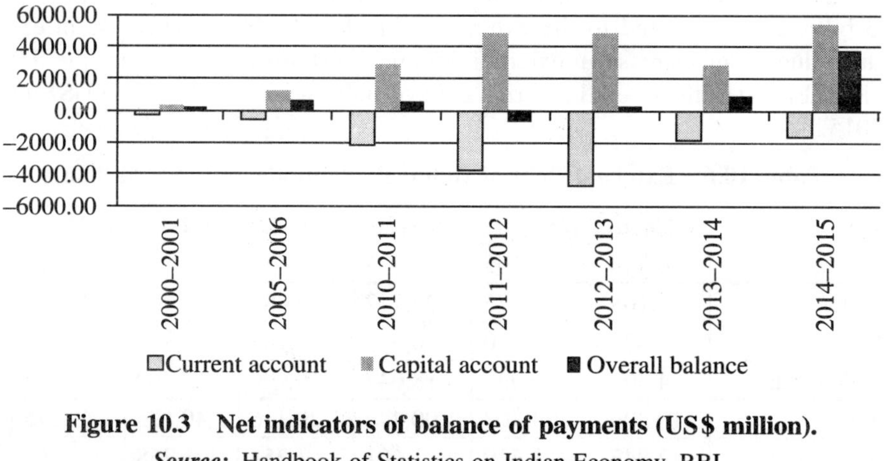

Figure 10.3 Net indicators of balance of payments (US$ million).

Source: Handbook of Statistics on Indian Economy, RBI.

3. RBI Press Release, 27 June 2013, http://rbi.org.in/scripts/BS_PressReleaseDisplay.aspx?prid=28957.

Table 10.7 Net Indicators of Balance of Payments (₹ in billion)

Items	*2000–01*	*2005–06*	*2010–11*	*2011–12*	*2012–13*	*2013–14*	*2014–15*
Merchandise	–567.37	–2,296.6	–5,805	–9,121	–10,645	–8,848.4	–8,858.6
Services	79.1	1,026.1	2,006.0	3,079.0	3,532.0	4,422.6	4,686.8
Transfers	599.7	1,094.3	2,421.0	3,051.0	3,484.0	3,947.2	4,016.6
Income	–227.33	–261.16	–818	–768	–1,168	–1,398.9	–1,474.3
FDI	149.2	134.3	541.0	1,032.0	1,082.0	1,299.7	1,912.2
Foreign portfolio	118.2	553.6	1,394.0	856.0	1,465.0	296.8	2,578.5
External assistance	20.0	75.9	225.0	113.0	53.0	62.0	106.2
Commercial borrowings	201.7	105.1	554.0	479.0	461.0	724.2	95.6
Banking capital	–91.44	58.0	220.0	710.0	903.0	1,516.6	720.8
Rupee debt	–27.6	–25.57	–3	–4.0	–3.1	–3.0	–4.9
Other capital	13.1	55.5	–567	–301	–279.5	–671.0	71.4
Errors and omissions	–13.69	–23.32	–121	–116	146.0	–60.0	–66.7
Overall balance	276.4	659.0	595.0	–685	207.0	960.5	3,779.2

Source: Handbook of Statistics on Indian Economy, RBI.

Closing Case: India's Strategies to Reduce Trade Deficit

As per the World Economic Outlook 2013, the currencies of emerging market are experiencing depreciation. In fact, they have depreciated significantly. The scenario of currency depreciation is presented in the Exhibit 1.

It indicates that currencies of Brazil, India and South Africa have depreciated by 8%–16% against the US Dollar. This has its own impact on many emerging economies including India.

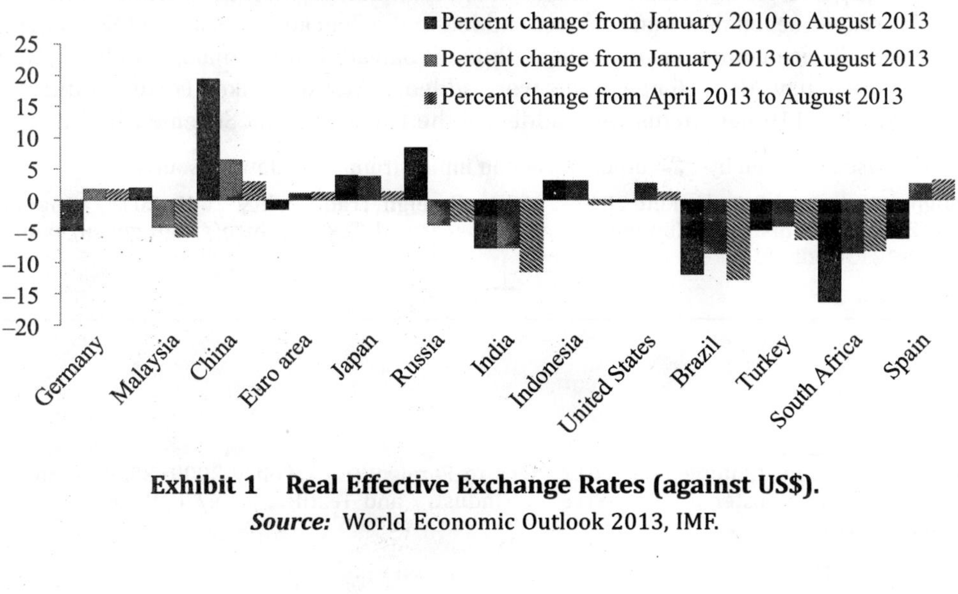

Exhibit 1 Real Effective Exchange Rates (against US$).

Source: World Economic Outlook 2013, IMF.

Given this fact, it is important to focus on foreign trade policy and its measures to manage the trade deficit better. In 2009, India announced foreign trade policy for the period of 2009–2014. The objective of the policy was to increase India's share in global trade, increase employment, market diversification, technological upgradation, etc. The trade policy exclusively came out with the policies to promote exports from India to the various markets.

To increase exports from India, it also announced several incentives for the manufacturing sector as well as the small and medium-scale industries. In May 2011, the Department of Commerce, Government of India unleashed its strategies to double India's goods export during the next three years from US$246 billion in 2010–2011 to US$500 billion in 2013–2014.

The strategy highlighted various measures to enhance India's total exports and achieve reduction in the level of current account deficit. The strategy paper advocated multipronged approach to do so. Its policy instruments include fiscal incentives, institutional changes, enhanced market access across the world, diversification of export markets, improvements in infrastructure and reduction in transaction cost.[4]

Some of the features of the strategy, among others, are as follows:

1. 2% Interest Subvention Scheme earlier available only to handlooms, handicrafts, carpets and SMEs till 31 March 2012 was continued till 31 March 2013 and also extended to labour-intensive sectors like toys, sports goods, processed agricultural products and ready-made garments, etc.
2. Zero Duty Export Promotion Capital Goods (EPCG) Scheme was extended up to 31 March 2013.
3. The scope of Zero Duty EPCG Scheme was enlarged.
4. A new Post-Export EPCG Scheme was introduced.
5. EPCG scheme for North Eastern region was promoted.
6. It was focused on promoting exports of 16 identified green technology products under the EPCG Scheme.
7. Seven new markets were added to Focus Market Scheme (FMS). These countries are Algeria, Aruba, Austria, Cambodia, Myanmar, Netherland Antilles, and Ukraine. Moreover, seven new markets were added to the Special Focus Market Scheme (Special FMS). These countries are Belize, Chile, El Salvador, Guatemala, Honduras, Morocco, and Uruguay. Also, 46 new items were added to Market Linked Focus Product Scheme (MLFPS). 110 new items were added to the Focus Product Scheme (FPS) list.

Source: This case is written by the authors based on inputs from the following sources:

1. Highlights of Annual Supplement 2012–2013 to Foreign Trade Policy 2009–2014, announced on 5 June 2012 by Minister of Commerce and Industry and Textiles, http://dgft.gov.in/exim/2000/highlights1213e.pdf
2. WEO 2013.

4. Highlights of Annual Supplement 2012–2013 to Foreign Trade Policy 2009–2014, announced on 5 June 2012 by Minister of Commerce and Industry and Textiles, http://dgft.gov.in/exim/2000/highlights1213e.pdf

CASE QUESTIONS

1. Examine the role of Focus Market Scheme in export promotion.
2. What is Zero Duty EPCG Scheme? Discuss the new policies related to it.

REVIEW QUESTIONS

1. What is Balance of Payments (BoP)? Name its components.
2. What is the difference between current account and capital account?
3. Examine the structure of BoP in India.
4. Discuss the key indicators of BoP.
5. What is external debt?

SUGGESTED READINGS

Balance of Payments Manual for India, 2010, Reserve Bank of India, Mumbai.

Economic Survey of India, 2013–2014, Ministry of Finance, Government of India, New Delhi.

'Global Financial Stability Report: A Report by the Monetary and Capital Markets Department on Market Developments and Issues', 2014, IMF, Washington DC.

World Development Report, 2014, World Bank.

'World Trade Report: Factors Shaping the Future of World Trade', 2013, WTO, Geneva.

11

MONEY AND CAPITAL MARKETS

Learning Outcomes

After reading this chapter, you will

- Understand the structure of the Indian financial system
- Appreciate the role and importance of money market and capital market in the economy
- Know about the developments in stock market and the role of Securities and Exchange Board of India (SEBI)

Opening Case: Repo Rate kept Unchanged

In the first bi-monthly monetary policy announcement on 1 April 2014, the Reserve Bank of India (RBI) kept the repo rate unchanged at 8%. In fact, owing to inflation, the repo rate kept changing many a times in the last one year. The CRR was also remained unchanged at 4%.

It was argued by RBI Governor, Rahuram Rajan that policy rates may not be further tightened if the retail inflation remains in control, i.e., 8% by January 2015 and 6% by January 2016. However, food and fuel are the major drivers of inflation in recent times.

Earlier, RBI had announced its monetary policy in which it kept its lending rates unchanged and raised the repo rates to address the concern of the economy related to high inflation. Contrary to this, the industrial sector of the country has expected a rate cut in the major policy rates.

In December 2013, growth in India's industrial output reduced by 0.6%. Considering this, industrial houses asked RBI to cut the key rates. It is believed that the cut in key rate would help in reviving the manufacturing sector, as industrial growth in the country remained negative. It is also believed that the reduction in industrial growth is the result of contracting demand in the country due to high level of interest rates. In case of cut in policy rates, the high interest rates are reduced, which increases the demand in the economy. It further leads to increase in the manufacturing sector.[1]

1. See news, Worried industry asks RBI to cut rates after December IIP contracts, *Economic Times*, 12 February, 2014.

The 2014–2015 interim budget speech of the Finance Minister shows that as per the estimates, India would have attained a growth of 4.9% during 2013–2014. For this, the government has taken fiscal measures and reduced the excise taxes on capital goods. However, the concern that was raised by the industry, given the slower industrial growth, attracted more attention. It was deemed that the fiscal measures would reduce the prices of these commodities, whereas the reduction in policy rates in the money market would lead to increase the credit in the economy.

If the rates are lower, its lending rates will also decrease, which means loans and advances for the manufacturing products will increase. These two measures have important role to play in the economy, and therefore, have a close association with the economic growth. Such an interlinkage reflects on the evolving business environment in the country.

Source: This case is written by the authors based on inputs from the following sources:

1. Rajan sticks to the script, holds key rates, *The Hindu Business Line*, 1 April 2014, http://www.thehindubusinessline.com/economy/policy/rbi-monetary-policy-review-rajan-delivers-no-surprises-holds-interest-rates/article5857861.ece
2. Worried industry asks RBI to cut rates after December IIP contracts, *The Economic Times*, 12 February 2014, http://articles.economictimes.indiatimes.com/2014-02-12/news/47270095_1_manufacturing-sector-negative-growth-december-iip

11.1 STRUCTURE OF INDIAN FINANCIAL SYSTEM

Money market and capital market are the integral parts of the financial system. Financial system emerges out of the financial needs and transactions of households, firms and the governments.

Individuals, firms or the government require finances to meet long-term plans, short-term plans and contingencies. Financial system regulates these financial transactions, and therefore, constitutes an important part of business process as well as the economic environment of a country. A stable financial structure, which includes both money market and capital market, provides sustained support to booming business in the economy.

There is also a strong linkage between the financial systems and the economic progress which makes an important aspect to be understood. In fact, the financial system is linked with several real economic activities and facilitates economic transactions. It reduces the financial cost of commercial and economic activities by smoothening financial or commercial transactions. Thus, in many ways, it serves as a vehicle for boosting business. For instance, boosting business through trade in both goods and services needs smooth financial transaction which has seamless characteristics. An efficient financial system plays an imperative role in this direction, as it reduces transaction costs. The financial system also encourages savings and leads to capital formation in the economy.

During early stages of human civilisations, economic and financial assets were kept in terms of commodities, land, cattle, etc. This mechanism was prevalent during the barter system. As the economic system evolved, financial mobilisations and savings started to take shape in different forms. The old mechanism was restrictive for financial transactions. As a result, the new systems evolved. These systems are known as *money market* and *capital market*. In addition, changes in money market also influence the changes in capital market and *vice versa*.

At the global level, financial markets are closely integrated. It is in this context that financial globalisation becomes imperative for the stable condition of financial markets. The experience of 2008 liquidity crunch suggests that there is also a negative impact of financial globalisation. Therefore, regulation of financial markets becomes an important aspect for the emerging economies like India. As per the global financial stability report released by IMF in May 2013, the global financial market is still in transition phase and moving towards greater stability.

In the Euro area, monetary policies were revisited at national levels to stabilise the financial situation. In emerging economies like India, Brazil, South Africa and Indonesia, slower economic growth and devaluation of currencies have resulted in focused policy towards reducing current trade deficit, wherein monetary policies are not getting large space to move on. However, some countries in Latin America are performing well owing to their robust financial performance.[2] With a view to understand the financial system and its functions, its impact as well as its relations with the economic activities, this chapter deals with the concept and structure of Indian financial system.

India's financial system comprises money market and capital market. *Money market* refers to the market for short-term lending, whereas for medium-term and long-term financial transactions, *capital market* plays a vital role.

The *money market* describes a market, where borrowers and lenders exchange short-term funds to address their liquidity needs. It pertains to very short-term debt securities, especially those debts that mature within one year. The money market investments are also called *cash investments*. Thus, some of the money market instruments include financial claims that have low default risk, maturities under one year and high marketability.

The capital market, on the other hand, is a market for buying and selling equity and debt instruments. It comprises institutions and mechanisms through which medium-term and long-term funds are made available to the business, government and individuals. Figure 11.1 presents the structure of the financial market in India.

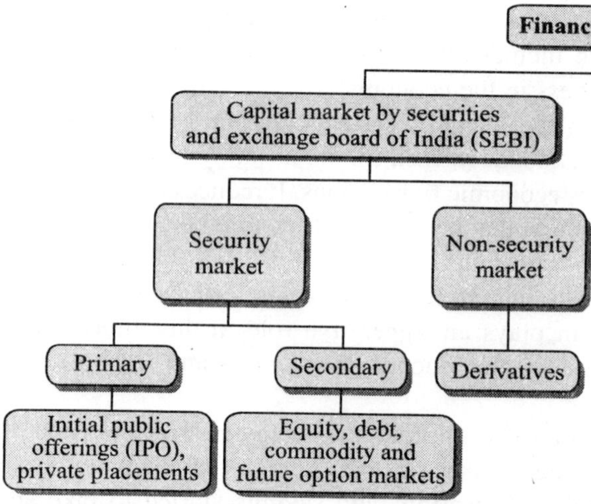

Figure 11.1 Structure of financial market in India.

Source: SEBI and RBI.

2. IMF, Global Financial Stability Report, May, 2013, http://www.imf.org/External/Pubs/FT/GFSR/2013/02/pdf/text.pdf

Further, security market is a part of capital market. It has two segments—primary market and secondary market, which are interdependent. *Primary market* provides the channel for sale of new securities. The issuer of securities can sell securities in the primary market to raise funds for the purpose of investment. On the other hand, *secondary market* helps the holder of the securities in adjusting their holdings by making a re-assessment of their risk and return.

11.2 MONEY MARKET

Money market, which regulates money supply, credit and advances, is an integral pillar of the economic and business environment of a country. The money market, which broadly consists of operations of banking system, has a lot of linkages with the economic progress. This can easily be seen at the time of announcement of monetary policy measures by RBI. Notably, India's capital market has strong linkages with RBI's monetary policies, particularly the policies related to lending rates both for the government and commercial banks. The close relations can be seen in terms of the fluctuations in capital market as a result of policy announcements in the money market. Not only this, industrial productivity, too, is linked with these policy measures.

Generally, Indian money market is classified into organised and unorganised money market. The *organised sector of the market* is regulated by RBI and consists of banking systems including commercial banks. On the other hand, the *unorganised money market* is the financial system that is traditionally present in India. It is basically based on the non-banking lending system such as indigenous bankers, money lenders, non-banking financial companies like Life Insurance Corporation of India, etc. The broad structure of the market is presented in Figure 11.2.

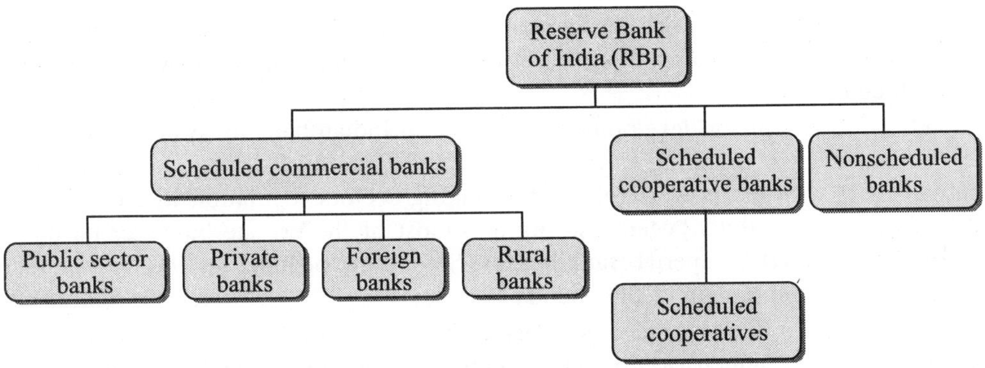

Figure 11.2 Structure of organised banking system in the country.
Source: RBI.

The organised banking in India is classified into three categories—central bank, commercial banks and cooperative banks. The banking system is also classified into scheduled and non-scheduled banking systems. RBI is the central bank of the country about which we have discussed in detail in Chapter 9. However, in this section, we will discuss the organised banking system in the country.

In fact, the total number of scheduled banks at the end of financial year 2011–2012 was 169 as compared to 73 in 1969. The number of non-scheduled commercial banks reduced to 4 in 2011–2012 as compared to 16 in the year 1969. Also, the total number of public sector banks stood at 27 as on 31 March 2007. The development of private sector banks and foreign banks has been a milestone in the Indian banking system. The number of private sector bank as on 31 March 2007 was recorded to be 25; and 39 foreign banks were also operating. Moreover, the total number of regional rural banks was 357 in the year 2006–2007.

The progress of these numbers indicates the progress of organised money market in the country. At present, the banking sector of the country is valued at ₹81 trillion (US$1.31 trillion). It is believed that the sector has a potential to become one of the largest banking systems globally. The Indian banking system already has an outreach across the length and breadth of the country through a network of nationalised and private banks.[3]

Moreover, the unorganised money market is dominated by the presence of indigenous bankers. Such a process of money lending has existed in India long before the evolution of commercial money lending systems. The old system evolved with the evolution of feudal social structure in India agrarian society.

The various types of indigenous bankers include the following:

1. Professional money lenders
2. Those who do both banking business and trading business
3. Commission agents
4. Money changers, etc.

These sources of credit mostly dominate in the rural areas. Generally, the indigenous bankers put their own capital and grant loans and advances to such needy people who are known to them directly or through their friends or relatives.

In fact, Indian banking system has a short history. The pre-independence banking system was characterised as the agglomeration of various private sector banks, which were organised as joint stock companies.[4]

After 1947, some major developments occurred in Indian banking system, which broadly include the enactment of Banking Companies Act and Banking Regulation Act, 1949. These Acts entitled RBI with the powers related to banking sectors regulation in the country. The central banking system, thus, became strong and most of the private banks came under the purview of RBI. Similarly, Imperial Bank became State Bank of India in 1951, with a mandate to support the economic growth of the country.

But, the banking system lacked grass roots reach owing to the various market-related issues, such as information asymmetries, dominated agrarian structure and lack of fund. In order to bring reforms, the Government of India followed the programme that advocated nationalisation of banks. In this process, the money market became part of the government business. Most of the banks existing in the country were nationalised. As a result of this programme, 14 banks which possessed deposits more than ₹50 crore were nationalised by a banking companies ordinance in 1969. These banks were the Central Bank of India, Bank of Maharashtra, Dena Bank, Punjab National Bank, Syndicate Bank, Canara Bank, Indian Overseas Bank, Indian Bank, Bank of Baroda, Union Bank, Allahabad Bank, United Bank of India, UCO Bank and Bank of India.

---

3. http://www.ibef.org/industry/banking-india.aspx
4. http://rbi.org.in/scripts/PublicationsView.aspx?id=10487

Later, in the 1990s, reforms were started in the Indian financial sectors as well, and private banking systems were encouraged to operate in the economy. As per the objectives of banking sector nationalisation programme, the goals of these nationalised banks were

1. Mobilisation of resources through branch expansion
2. Lending funds for productive purposes
3. Lending funds to weaker section of the society
4. Increase agricultural credits
5. Spreading branches in semi-urban and rural areas
6. Ensure adequate credit to priority sectors

Some specific programmes were carried out to address the issue of expansion of branches in the semi-urban and rural areas. These schemes were related to specific branch license policy and some bank schemes such as Lead Bank Scheme (LBS). Today, 25% of branches, which are planned to be expanded in a financial year by a domestic commercial bank, need to be opened in the rural areas. These policies led to change in the banking structure of the country.

Another important step was allotting branches of public sector banks in all districts of the country. Initially, 22 public sector banks (SBI and its 7 associate banks and 14 nationalised banks) and 3 private sector banks (Andhra Bank Limited, Bank of Rajasthan Limited and Punjab and Sind Bank Limited) were allotted to open branch in all districts of the country. Each bank was allotted districts in more than one state. The next section highlights the branch expansion of banking sector in the country.

Branch expansion

As per the new monetary policy, all the domestic commercial banks need to allocate at least 25% of their total number of branches in unbanked rural areas, i.e., tier 5 and tier 6 centres. It implies that these commercial banks have to open their branches in rural areas, and therefore, have to keep this rule into consideration when the banking sector is planning its annual expansion plans. Figure 11.3 suggests that the overall branches of commercial banks increased from 8,262 in 1969 to 1,05,753 in the year 2013. In 1969, the total number of branches in rural areas was only 22% of the total commercial banks branches in the country, which increased to 37% in 2013, which further increased to 39% in 2015. This implies that there has been a massive expansion of bank branches in the rural areas. An overall picture of the same is presented in Figure 11.3.

Credit by commercial banks

We know that banks play an important role of financial intermediaries and collect deposits as well as lend it to the investors and others. Total deposits in a bank is the ability that a bank possesses to lend to the others including industries. But this depends on various monetary measures undertaken by the central banking system in India, i.e., RBI. The detail of sector deployment of bank credit is maintained by RBI for 47 scheduled banks and nearly 97% of the total credit flow.

Table 11.1 presents the total credit provided by these scheduled banks to the various sectors. As per the latest statistics, credit provided by these scheduled banks in the country goes to industries. The share of industrial sector remains highest in the total credit from banking sector.

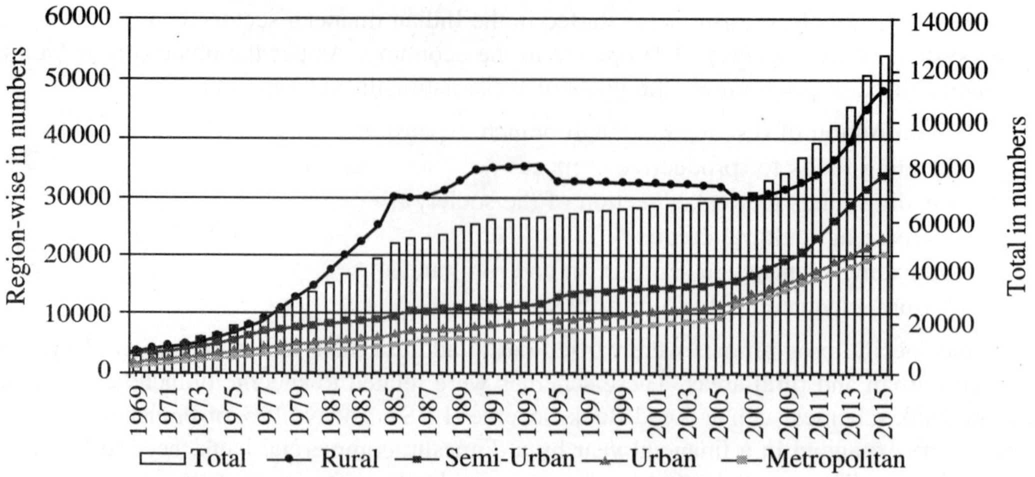

Figure 11.3 Population (group-wise) number of branches of scheduled commercial banks (in numbers).

Note: The line graphs are measured on primary Y-axis and the bar graph is measured on secondary *Y*-axis.

Source: Handbook of Statistics on Indian Economy, RBI.

Table 11.1 Sectoral Deployment of Non-food Gross Bank Credit–Outstanding, 2007–2016 (₹ in billion)

Sectors	*2007–08*	*2008–09*	*2009–10*	*2010–11*	*2011–12*	*2012–13*	*2013–14*	*2014–15*
Agriculture and allied activities	2,753	3,387	4,161	4,835	5,484	5,899	6,660	7,659
Industry (micro and small, medium and large)	8,583	10,544	13,115	16,132	19,374	22,302	25,165	26,576
Services	5,493	6,463	7,268	8,908	10,166	11,486	13,375	14,131
Personal loans	5,218	5,625	5,856	6,997	7,873	9,009	13,375	14,131
Priority sector	7,481	9,325	10,922	12,694	14,203	15,398	18,297	20,103
Total non-food credit	22,048	26,018	30,400	36,871	42,897	48,696	55,296	60,030
Food credit	438	455	490	624	816	946	912	994
Total credit	22,486	26,474	30,890	37,495	43,714	49,642	56,208	61,023

Source: Handbook of Statistics on Indian Economy, RBI.

Note: Data are provisional and relate to select 47 banks, which account for 95% of the total non-food credit extended by all scheduled commercial banks. For 2013–2014 and 2014–2015, data are related to 46 banks.

It accounted for about 43.5% of the total credit in 2014–2015. Banking credit to the agricultural sector remains low hovering around 12.5% during recent years. The overall credit to the other sectors except industrial sector went down in terms of share during 2007–2015. In 2014–2015, a slight decrease in banking credit was witnessed from 44.7% in 2013–2014 to 43.55% in 2014–2015.

We see in Table 11.1 that sectoral allocation of credit is classified into food credit and non-food credit. In fact, non-food credit constitutes banking credit to the industrial sectors. The share of priority sector in non-food category also decreased from 34% in 2006–2007 to 32% in 2012–2013 and 33% in 2014–2015.

Table 11.2 shows that maximum bank credit went to infrastructure sector in 2014–2015 so far as bank credit to industry is concerned. The share of infrastructure sector in banking credit to industry was 24% in 2006–2007, which rose to 33% in 2012–2013 and 35% in 2014–2015.

Table 11.2 Industry-wise Industrial Bank Credit During 2007–2013 (₹ in billion)

Industry	*Outstanding as on*				
	28 March 2008	*26 March 2010*	*23 March 2012*	*21 March 2014*	*20 March 2015*
Mining and quarrying (including coal)	**122.77**	**180.84**	**324.46**	**358.45**	**359.51**
Food processing	**493.97**	**656.77**	**941.45**	**1,462.54**	**1,714.95**
Sugar	160.80	192.55	315.79	344.66	414.11
Edible oils and vanaspati	72.43	103.80	132.37	212.93	210.64
Tea	24.83	19.95	19.91	32.41	31.95
Others	235.91	340.46	473.38	872.53	1,058.24
Beverage and tobacco	**62.94**	**109.69**	**150.55**	**182.86**	**186.48**
Textiles	**963.98**	**1,213.75**	**1,594.14**	**2,022.13**	**2,019.19**
Cotton textiles	477.46	612.28	838.96	1,007.07	1,000.45
Jute textiles	10.80	13.80	13.95	19.98	22.36
Man-made textiles	52.85	116.72	159.16	215.60	203.57
Other textiles	422.88	470.96	582.06	779.47	792.81
Leather and leather products	**57.42**	**62.32**	**76.33**	**102.08**	**102.47**
Wood and wood products	**31.63**	**43.71**	**61.45**	**94.23**	**98.31**
Paper and paper products	**134.69**	**190.74**	**249.80**	**328.20**	**340.66**
Petroleum, coal products and nuclear fuels	**420.67**	**785.79**	**611.75**	**648.40**	**561.45**
Chemicals and chemical products	**625.62**	**857.13**	**1,269.93**	**1,663.36**	**1,544.87**
Fertiliser	91.86	138.47	157.62	305.90	253.96
Drugs and pharmaceuticals	235.02	359.80	460.46	486.55	492.95
Petrochemicals	87.79	100.46	332.82	421.88	330.74
Others	210.96	258.40	319.02	449.03	467.22

Industry	*Outstanding as on*				
	28 March 2008	*26 March 2010*	*23 March 2012*	*21 March 2014*	*20 March 2015*
Rubber, plastic and their products	**112.13**	**156.17**	**299.04**	**370.71**	**377.73**
Glass and glassware	**27.83**	**48.31**	**62.69**	**87.04**	**88.39**
Cement and cement products	**125.44**	**247.22**	**369.10**	**539.33**	**560.38**
Basic metal and metal product	**1,075.93**	**1,629.29**	**2,618.09**	**3,607.80**	**3,853.89**
Iron and steel	826.96	1,274.64	1,959.00	2,673.98	2,834.29
Other metal and metal product	248.99	354.65	659.09	933.82	1,019.61
All engineering	**544.39**	**738.21**	**1,130.10**	**1,463.62**	**1,540.05**
Electronics	158.43	221.00	287.20	346.76	367.90
Others	385.96	517.22	842.90	1,116.86	1,172.15
Vehicles, vehicle parts and transport equipment	**293.23**	**387.80**	**517.81**	**665.33**	**682.09**
Gems and jewellery	**251.01**	**317.51**	**513.26**	**698.89**	**718.19**
Construction	**279.45**	**442.19**	**486.16**	**625.71**	**743.03**
Infrastructure	**2,053.36**	**3,798.87**	**6,299.91**	**8,363.56**	**9,245.31**
Power	950.75	1,878.40	3,309.26	4,869.02	5,575.67
Telecommunications	382.82	593.62	939.95	882.04	918.90
Roads	344.76	735.69	1,109.41	1,578.60	1,686.91
Other infrastructure	375.01	591.15	941.29	1,033.90	1,063.83
Other industries	**906.98**	**1,248.21**	**1,797.24**	**1,880.60**	**1,839.34**
Industries	**8,583.44**	**13,114.52**	**19,373.26**	**25,164.84**	**26,576.29**

Source: Handbook of Statistics on Indian Economy, RBI.

Note: Data are provisional and relate to select 47 banks, which account for 95% of the total non-food credit extended by all scheduled commercial banks.

Instruments of money market

Money market promotes investment. This is carried out through its defined instruments, which meet short-term requirements of the borrowers. The following are the main instruments through which money market operates in India:

1. ***Call market:*** *Call money* refers to the market which deals with the short-term credit. The maturity period for such transactions varies from 1 day to 14 days. It generally facilitates lending and borrowings between the banks and the other entities.
2. ***Treasury bill:*** Another instrument for short-term borrowings is treasury bills. The government issues this bill with a promise note. The type of treasury bills include *ad hoc bills*, which are the instruments issued by the state governments and government

departments for investment purposes; whereas *regular bills* are sold to the general public and banks. The bills are also classified as per their maturity periods, which include 14-days, 91-days, 182-days and 364-days treasury bills.

3. ***Ready forward contract:*** It is called *repo or repurchase agreement*. By using this agreement, at the repo rate, banks borrow funds from RBI to meet their requirements if they have shortage of funds. This is a short-term agreement.

11.3 CAPITAL MARKET

Capital market is the other important segment of financial system. It is considered as the backbone of India's industrial sector. It stimulates growth and injects resources in the economy. It helps business units in generating financial resources for investments. We know that the business houses in the country need financial resources. To raise their capital requirements, business communities go for both short-term and long-term options. The long-term options belong to capital market operations. In other words, business units raise capital by borrowings of funds by selling their stock in the capital market. Both capital and money markets are interdependent, and therefore, their policies affect each other.

Structure of Indian capital market

India's capital market consists of the financial institutions and securities market. The financial institutions provide long-term loans and advances to the business units. These financial institutions include Industrial Finance Corporation of India (IFCI), EXIM Bank, etc. The securities market in India, on the other hand, consists of national stock exchange markets and other stock exchanges.

The securities market is divided into

1. Primary market
2. Stock or secondary market

Primary market deals with new securities, while the secondary market deals with the securities already sold in the market. Security and Exchange Board of India (SEBI) is responsible for the regulation of the market. SEBI was created by SEBI Act enacted in 1992.

The capital market is also classified into the following:

1. ***Gilt edged market:*** This includes government securities and bonds which have a consistent earnings record and are backed by RBI.
2. ***Corporate securities market:*** It includes securities issued by joint stock companies and consists of shares and debentures.

Thus, capital market consists of borrowers and lenders. The lenders in this market sell share and securities and get funds out of it. On the other hand, borrowers also look forward to a good return on investment.

Role of capital market in India

Capital market plays an important role in promoting and sustaining the economic growth. It also provides a sustained support to the various sectors of the economy through advancing credits and meeting sectoral requirements. Broadly, the role of the capital markets can be summarised as follows:

1. It meets the requirement of capital and plays a role of intermediary for capital formation by selling and purchasing securities and acting as a lender to market for a long period of time.
2. It provides liquidity in stock exchange and also return on stock purchases and sales.
3. It raises long-term capital for business units through the sales of its securities to the public.
4. It helps in improving the efficiency of capital allocation through competitive pricing mechanism.
5. It provides technical assistance and advisory services to the entrepreneurs.
6. It acts as an important source for resource transfer to industrial sector through attracting investments from public.
7. It also attracts foreign capital through foreign institutional investments (FIIs).
8. It provides an institutional support for public to make investment in the productive sectors of the economy. In other words, capital market helps in promoting the industrial growth.
9. It can help in promoting public–private partnerships (PPP).

Progress of India's capital market

India's capital market has been meeting the long-term financial needs of the country's industrial sector and continues to play a significant role. During the early phase of the economic planning, capital market had a limited role to play. The initial development of the capital market in India took place under the aegis of legal frameworks, *viz.* Capital Issues (Control) Act, 1947, Securities Contracts (Regulation) Act, 1956 and Companies Act, 1956. These legislations provided a legal framework for the development of capital market in the country. Initially, the stock exchanges were dominated by Bombay Stock Exchange (BSE). BSE's dominant role in Indian capital market continued up to 1992.

After the liberalisation process in India, capital market witnessed remarkable structural changes during 1990s. The broad financial sector reforms led to the reforms in capital market as well. The reforms were aimed at enhancing the efficiency of capital market in the country as well as strengthening competition therein. Reforms were advocated to adopt international standards. The previous legislation, the Capital Issues Act was replaced by another act, which established the National Stock Exchange (NSE) in 1992. The office of the Controller of Capital Issues was repealed. In 1993, NSE started functioning as a recognised stock exchange. Furthermore, SEBI was also established to regulate the securities market in the country.

After the reforms started in the financial sector, capital market emerged as the major source of finance for both manufacturing as well as services sectors. New companies are now having direct access to the capital markets. The functioning of capital markets are now made easy for the companies to raise their funds by issuing securities through public issues. Thus, the mobilisation that took place during post- and pre-reform periods by issuing new capital by private companies can be seen in Table 11.3 and Table 11.4.

Table 11.3 New Capital Issues by Non-Government Public Limited Companies (₹ in crore)

Financial year	Equity shares		Preference shares		Debentures/Bonds		Total	
	Number of issues	Amount	Number of issues	Amount	Number of issues	Amount	Number of issues	Amount
1970	64	38	41	13	8	15	113	66
1980	0	89	0	2	0	73	237	164
1990	269	1,220	4	8	134	5,282	407	6,510
2000	69	2,753	0	0	10	2,401	79	5,153
2010	67	25,299	0	0	4	2,680	71	27,979
2011	70	24,830	0	0	6	2,626	76	27,456
2012	49	8,152	0	0	14	7,528	63	15,680
2013	48	13,884	0	0	6	2,217	54	16,101
2014	53	5,812	–	0	17	5,869	70	11,681
2015	63	9,315	–	0	23	7,741	86	17,056

Source: Handbook of Statistics on Indian Economy, RBI.

Table 11.4 Resource Mobilisation in the Private Placement Market (₹ in crore)

Year	Private Sector						Public Sector						Grand total	
	Financial institutions		Non-financial institutions		Total		Financial institutions		Non-financial institutions		Total			
	No. of issues	Amount	No. of issues	Amount	No. of issues	Amount	No. of issues	Amount	No. of issues	Amount	No. of issues	Amount	No. of issues	Amount
2001–02	363	16,019	309	12,601	672	28,620	167	17,358	119	18,898	286	36,256	958	64,876
2002–03	327	9,454	550	15,623	877	25,077	157	20,407	110	21,464	267	41,871	1,144	66,948
2003–04	344	12,551	296	6,209	640	18,760	132	26,461	102	18,679	234	45,141	874	63,901
2004–05	255	20,974	462	14,820	717	35,794	124	25,531	69	22,080	193	47,611	910	83,406
2005–06	375	26,463	571	14,727	946	41,190	137	39,165	32	16,119	169	55,284	1,115	96,473
2006–07	632	48,414	892	33,426	1,524	81,841	127	52,117	30	11,908	157	64,025	1,681	1,45,866
2007–08	905	88,291	711	41,386	1,616	1,29,677	132	56,186	67	26,863	199	83,048	1,815	2,12,725
2008–09	687	60,586	383	35,103	1,070	95,689	123	65,615	91	42,753	214	1,08,369	1,284	2,04,057
2009–10	1,630	1,42,441	640	90,853	2,270	2,33,294	151	74,290	67	35,696	218	1,09,985	2,488	3,43,280
2010–11	878	71,977	460	49,476	1,338	1,21,453	212	98,983	38	17,960	250	1,16,943	1,588	2,38,396
2011–12	530	38,937	62	24,001	592	62,938	231	1,23,507	35	31,804	266	1,55,311	858	2,18,249
2012–13	640	86,973	141	54,708	781	1,41,680	246	1,37,254	58	51,269	304	1,88,523	1,085	3,30,204
2013–14	862	87,529	150	33,797	1,012	1,21,327	256	1,80,267	104	97,587	360	2,77,852	1,372	3,99,179
2014–15	1,901	1,83,842	535	93,176	2,436	2,77,018	135	1,34,984	85	34,482	220	1,69,466	2,656	4,46,484

Note: Data for 2014–2015 are Provisional.
Sources: Handbook of Statistics on Indian Economy, RBI.

During the reform period, SEBI issued the guidelines for companies issuing securities for comprehensive disclosure to protect investors' interests. Thus, it was mandated for the companies to comply with the disclosure norms, which were internationally recognised. In addition, market became deregulated and therefore, prices of securities, bonds, debentures, etc. were determined by the market. This was applicable to the government undertakings as well. The reformation in economic system also changed the resource mobilisation method for the public sector undertakings. Therefore, government undertakings also started utilising capital market. In addition, several undertakings were disinvested. Their shares and securities are also placed into the market for resource mobilisation. The bonds issued by government undertakings are summarised in Table 11.5.

Table 11.5 Bonds Issued by Public Sector Undertakings (₹ in crore)

Year	*Tax-free bonds*	*Taxable bonds*	*Total bonds*
1985–1986	0	353.7	353.7
1989–1990	3,317.0	912.0	4,229.0
1994–1995	1,198.3	1,871.8	3,070.1
1999–2000	400.0	8,296.8	8,696.8
2004–2005	–	7,590.6	7,590.6
2009–2010	1,926.4	46,482.7	48,409.1
2010–2011	1,642.0	58,791.0	60,433.0
2011–2012	28,082.0	59,983.0	88,065.0
2012–2013	14,860.0	37,857.0	52,717.0
2013–2014	34,244.0	16,621.0	50,865.0
2014–2015	–	37,283.0	37,283.0

Source: Handbook of Statistics on Indian Economy, RBI.

11.4 RECENT DEVELOPMENTS IN STOCK EXCHANGES

In a modern economy, a large amount of capital is required for strengthening its manufacturing base. In view of this requirement, corporations and companies form joint stocks which could raise such funds. In India, these funds are raised through stock exchanges. The Government of India has so far recognised 23 stock exchanges in the country under the Securities Contract (Regulation) Act, 1956.

Businesses in stock exchanges function through various stages. A client of a broker or intermediary gives order to its broker. The order is set to be appeared in stock exchange. This stage indicates the daily stock prices of the order. In the next stage, a client of a broker places its order to purchase the stock at the given price on the day. In the final stage, the investors buy stock of company and also settle the transaction.

The stock market works on the basis of speculations. In fact, investment in stock is related to the long-term return on it. Therefore, speculation for stock is important while making such long-term investments. In India, the investors generally invest in a stock which has a speculation of good return in the long-term, and therefore, speculation plays a vital role in doing business in the stock market. The developments in terms of reform in recent years are important to understand the stock market. We know that the functioning of stock exchanges has several issues associated with it. Therefore, it is imperative to examine the developments in primary and secondary markets in the recent years.

Developments in primary market

We have already discussed that primary market includes sales and purchase of securities. It plays a vital role in mobilising resources from both government and non-government securities. In fact, it is believed that an efficient primary market also leads to stabilise the economy. In recent years, primary markets, therefore, have been significant in raising funds. In fact, ₹15,474 crore of equity capital has been raised in 2012–2013 through 49 issues as compared to ₹12,857 crore in 2011–2012.[5] In 2014–2015, primary market mobilised ₹19,202 crore through 89 issues, which was less than ₹55,652 crore mobilised in 2013–2014 through 90 issues. The resource mobilisation through primary market during recent years is presented in Table 11.6.

Table 11.6 Resource Mobilisation through the Primary Market (₹ in crore)

Year/ Month	*Total*		*Categorywise*				*Issuer Type*				*Equities*			
			Public		*Rights*		*Listed*		*IPOs*		*At Par*		*At Premium*	
	No.	*Amount*	*No.*	*Amount*	*No.*	*Amount*	*No.*	*Amount*	*No.*	*Amount*	*No.*	*Amount*	*No.*	*Amount*
2010–11	91	67,609	68	58,105	23	9,503	38	32,049	53	35,559	2	50	78	57,617
2011–12	71	48,468	55	46,093	16	2,375	17	6,953	54	41,515	4	104	47	12,753
2012–13	69	32,455	53	23,510	16	8,945	36	25,926	33	6,528	4	571	45	14,902
2013–14	90	55,652	75	51,075	15	4,576	52	54,416	38	1,236	19	824	36	12,445
2014–15	88	19,202	70	12,452	18	6,750	42	15,891	44	3,311	8	49	55	8,740

Source: Securities and Exchange Board of India.

Trends in resource mobilisation during recent years indicate that resource mobilisation through primary market has been experiencing a downward movement, while the total mobilisation has reached ₹19,202 crore through primary equity market in 2014–2015. The new companies have issued a total of 44 IPOs and allocated ₹3,311 crore in 2014–2015. Sizewise classification of resource mobilisation indicates that in 2014–2015, primary market has accumulated ₹18,702 crore with size more than 100 crore. In 2014–2015, there were total 41 issues having size of more than ₹100 crore. However, the number is less than that of 2010–2011 when 55 issues were having size of more than ₹100 crore. The case of mutual funds has been positive. Figure 11.4 shows resource mobilisation by mutual funds. The total mutual fund mobilisation stood at ₹1,09,377 crore in 2014–2015. The mutual funds of Unit Trust of India (UTI) also mobilised ₹4,629 crore in 2012–2013 as against the debt of ₹3,179 crore in 2011–2012. In 2014–2015, net mobilisation by UTI is negative and the debt is estimated to at ₹1,278 crore.

Some of the important developments in primary securities market took place in the recent years. As per the annual report of SEBI, a total of ₹8,740 crore of equity capital has been raised in 2014–2015 through 55 issues as compared to 36 issues in 2013–2014 in which mobilisation

5. Annual Report 2012–2013 and 2014–2015.

was of ₹12,445 crore. This indicates that the value of securities issued has decreased. The trend of the other components of net resource mobilisation through mutual fund is also presented in Table 11.7.

Table 11.7 Trend of Net Mobilisation of Funds through Mutual Funds (₹ in crore)

Year	*UTI*	*Bank*	*Financial institution*	*Private sector*	*Total*
1993–1994	9,297	148	238	1,560	11,243
1994–1995	8,611	766	576	1,322	11,275
1995–1996	-6,314	113	235	133	–5,833
1996–1997	-3,043	7	137	864	–2,035
1997–1998	2,875	237	204	749	4,065
1998–1999	170	–89	547	2,067	2,695
1999–2000	4,548	336	296	16,938	22,118
2000–2001	322	249	1,273	9,292	11,136
2001–2002	-7,284	863	406	16,134	10,119
2002–2003	-9,434	1,033	861	12,122	4,582
2003–2004	1,049.9	4,526	787	41,510	47,873
2004–2005	–2467	706	–3,384	7,933	2,788
2005–2006	3,423.8	5,365	2,112	41,581	52,482
2006–2007	7,326	3,033	4,226	79,477	94,062
2007–2008	10,678	7,597	2,178	1,38,224	1,58,677
2008–2009	–4,112	4,489	5,954	–30,538	–24,208
2009–2010	15,653	9,855	4,871	47,968	78,347
2010–2011	–16,636	1,304	–16,988	–16,281	–48,600
2011–2012	–3,179	389	–3,098	–39,525	–45,413
2012–2013	4,629	6,708	2,241	65,284	78,862
2013–2014	401	4,845	2,572	46,761	54,579
2014–2015	–1,278	–700	–1,035	1,12,390	1,09,377

Source: Handbook of Statistics on Indian Economy, RBI.

During last few years, there have been several uncertainties in the primary capital market. In order to boost the investors' confidence, some measures have been undertaken by SEBI. A mechanism has been designed and put in place to see the irregularities of book of account of companies listed with the stock exchanges. Thus, now companies are required to file audits with the listed stock exchange. SEBI has also made mandatory for the companies to include business responsibility report in their annual report. In addition to these, other measures have been also undertaken, which include revised timeline for disclosing financial information prior to issue opening, revision of requirement stock exchanges and companies in respect of scheme of arrangements, manner of achieving minimum shareholding requirements, etc.

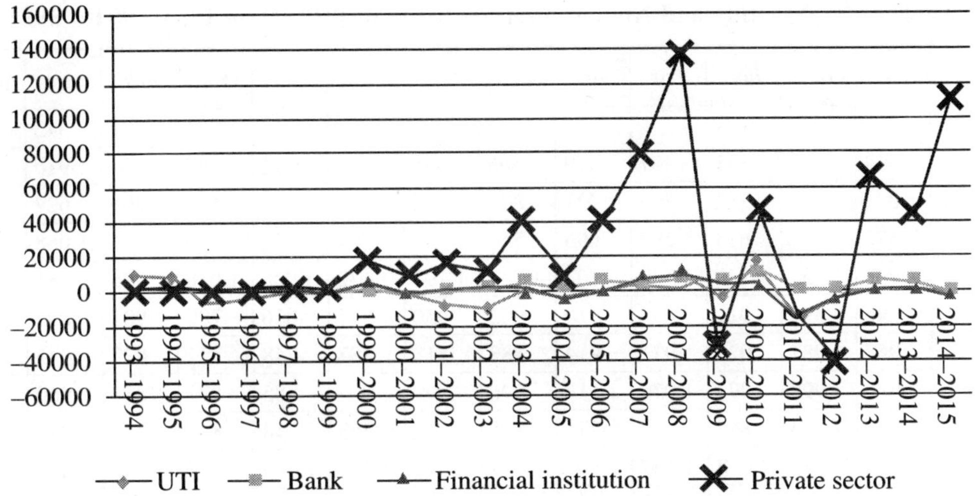

Figure 11.4 Trend of mobilisation of funds through mutual funds (₹ in crore).
Source: Handbook of Statistics on Indian Economy, RBI.

Developments in secondary market

The secondary market in India operates through stock exchanges, and benchmark indices are the indices of NSE and BSE. It is considered as the barometer to a nation's economic health.[6] The ups and downs in the indices of these two stock exchanges indicate the increase and decrease in the stock prices. Market capitalisation by BSE has increased from ₹74,15,296 crore in 2013–2014 to ₹10,149,290 crore in 2014–2015, which was estimated on last working day of the respective years. This shows an annual increase of 37% over the last year. Similarly, the market capitalisation of NSE increased from ₹72,77,720 crore in 2013–2014 to ₹99,30,122 crore in 2014–2015 recorded on the last working day of the trading years, showing an increase of 36%.

In addition, the indices of NSE and BSE in recent years have also been fluctuating. The capital market has seen the recovering impacts of the Indian economy. The annual average of BSE index increased from 3,621 in 2006–2007 to 5,041 in 2007–2008, but decreased to 3,731 in 2008–2009 due to global slowdown (see Figure 11.5). In recent years, the index was recorded to be 8,111 in 2015–2016 and 8,049 in 2014–2015. The annual average of the index was 5,540 in 2012–2013 and 5,999 in 2013–2014 (Table 11.8).

To strengthen the barometer of the health of the economy, SEBI has undertaken several steps. The 2013–2014 year saw the indices of secondary market touching new heights. Some of the important policies which are undertaken by SEBI include the following:

1. Establishment of centralised know your client (KYC) for new clients
2. Rationalisation of KYC requirements such as flexibility in PAN card verification
3. Preventing money laundering by making mandatory for intermediaries to identify beneficial owner, reducing timeline for transfers of equity share, etc.

6. Annual Report, SEBI, 2012–2013, p. 18.

Table 11.8 Monthly and Annual Average Index of BSE (Base 1983–1984 = 58)

Year/ Month	*April*	*May*	*June*	*July*	*Aug*	*Sept.*	*Oct.*	*Nov.*	*Dec.*	*Jan.*	*Feb.*	*Mar.*	*Annual*
1990–91	–	–	–	–	–	–	–	–	–	294	321	342	322
1991–92	364	372	371	407	479	506	495	544	511	557	654	916	508
1992–93	1,072	861	784	735	731	838	798	693	674	673	709	627	755
1993–94	576	597	613	597	696	744	750	794	922	1,060	1,126	1,068	796
1994–95	1,076	1,057	1,141	1,130	1,207	1,237	1,192	1,142	1,088	1,018	976	961	1,102
1995–96	946	893	911	899	910	902	930	837	816	795	903	893	885
1996–97	957	987	1,028	971	914	883	818	787	748	872	873	945	901
1997–98	983	998	996	1,070	1,117	996	999	907	885	877	851	960	971
1998–99	1,047	1,004	846	834	774	795	743	753	758	843	841	940	845
1999–00	874	976	1,018	1,137	1,204	1,251	1,318	1,254	1,409	1,637	1,969	1,803	1,321
2000–01	1,545	1,230	1,354	1,360	1,265	1,305	1,120	1,170	1,226	1,236	1,278	1,061	1,259
2001–02	952	1,017	964	912	905	797	787	862	921	929	993	1,013	921
2002–03	995	964	962	941	891	883	851	876	947	952	941	905	927
2003–04	873	892	1,003	1,069	1,192	1,301	1,406	1,475	1,632	1,822	1,742	1,715	1,343
2004–05	1,799	1,608	1,487	1,539	1,594	1,687	1,769	1,850	2,004	1,976	2,064	2,085	1,785
2005–06	1,990	2,020	2,144	2,274	2,401	2,556	2,525	2,615	2,805	2,928	3,076	3,298	2,548
2006–07	3,544	3,484	2,938	3,093	3,325	3,549	3,731	3,951	3,993	4,113	4,132	3,750	3,621
2007–08	3,944	4,202	4,288	4,580	4,405	4,810	5,561	5,923	6,261	6,105	5,473	4,851	5,041
2008–09	5,004	5,210	4587	4,143	4,469	4,220	3,151	2,798	2,821	2,785	2,708	2,650	3,731
2009–10	3,233	3,894	4,477	4,441	4,671	4,957	5,123	5,094	5,252	5,332	5,008	5,326	4,749
2010–11	5,447	5,213	5,345	5,526	5,637	5,983	6,255	6,190	6,043	5,836	5,442	5,572	5,707
2011–12	5,886	5,554	5,541	5,658	5,145	5,080	5,088	5,016	4,767	4,908	5,422	5,319	5,278
2012–13	5,287	4,984	5,075	5,235	5,318	5,464	5,698	5,700	5,944	6,091	5,933	5,789	5,540
2013–14	5,710	6,077	5,780	5,888	5,486	5,768	6,063	6,127	6,251	6,221	6,075	6,482	5,999
2014–15	6,777	7,152	7,668	7,773	7,866	8,133	8,014	8,485	8,377	8,604	8,842	8,782	8,049
2015–16	8,660	8,431	8,291	8,595	8,509	7,948	8,298	8,032	7,947	7,673	7,283	7,631	8,111

Note: The averages are based on daily closing index.
Source: Handbook of Statistics on Indian Economy, RBI.

In addition to the steps taken by SEBI in 2013–2014, recent years have also modernised its operations and also put in place modern surveillance to ensure smooth functioning of investor friendly redressal mechanism. Exchanges have to ensure that the 'ISIN' details of the securities are included in the bills/contract notes/statements issued by stock brokers to their clients. In addition, many other steps were undertaken by SEBI to circumvent investors benefits from risks and uncertainty, which cover inclusion of inspections on account of AML/CFT issues, risk assessment of securities markets and international cooperation with global bodies in its attempt to keep regulatory framework for AML robust in Indian markets.

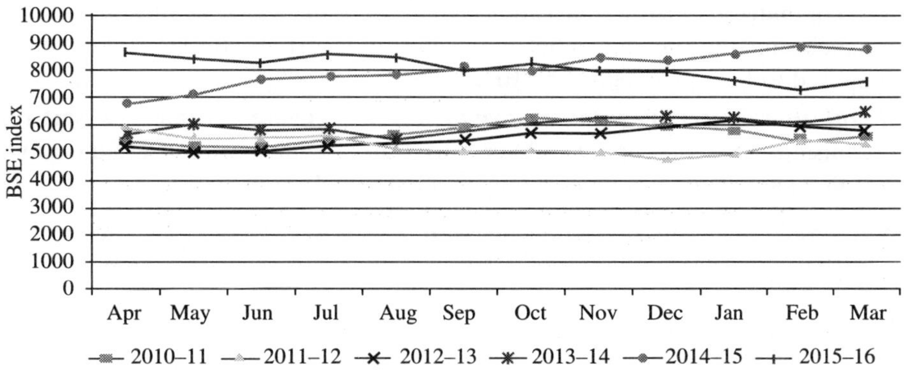

Figure 11.5 Monthly BSE 100 index (base year 1983–1984 = 58).
Source: Handbook of Statistics on Indian Economy, RBI.

11.5 SECURITIES AND EXCHANGE BOARD OF INDIA (SEBI)

In accordance with the provisions of the Securities and Exchange Board of India (SEBI) Act, 1992, SEBI was established on 12 April 1992. The Board was established to safeguard the interest of investors. The preamble of the Act clearly spelt out that it is

> An Act to provide for the establishment of a Board to protect the interests of investors in securities and to promote the development of, and to regulate, the securities market and for matters connected therewith or incidental thereto.[7]

The head office of SEBI is located in Mumbai, while it has regional and local offices at other places in the country as well. The Act also provides the powers and functions of SEBI. SEBI, thus, regulates the activities of the issuers of securities, investors and the market intermediaries. Its functions are divided into quasi-legislative, quasi-judicial and quasi-executive. The major functions of SEBI are as follows:[8]

1. ***Inspection of stock exchanges:*** SEBI has an important regulatory tool through which it does on-site inspection of stock exchanges such as NSE, BSE, Calcutta Stock Exchange (CSE), Ahmedabad Stock Exchange (ASE), etc. The main objective of on-site inspection is to make market fair and growing so that the investors are attracted and feel safe.
2. ***Inspection of intermediaries:*** It also does on-site inspection of intermediaries in the capital market. The number of inspections carried out during 2011–2012 was 111, which rose to 300 in 2012–2013.
3. ***Curbing of illegal trading in securities:*** SEBI keeps a supervisory eye upon the capital market to curb the illegal trading incidence. For this, it does not allow trading in securities which is outside the purview of stock exchanges.
4. ***Registration of intermediaries:*** SEBI has continuously been streamlining the process of registration of intermediaries in the capital market. In context to this, SEBI has

7. Website of SEBI, http://www.sebi.gov.in/
8. Section 11 of SEBI Act 1992, http://www.sebi.gov.in/cms/sebi_data/commondocs/0203c_p.pdf

also continued to ensure transparency by responding to the applicants within 30 days. Financial institutions and other custodian of securities, mutual funds, etc. are also supposed to be registered with SEBI.

5. ***Regulation of self-regulatory organisation:*** There are various self-regulatory organisations in the capital market. SEBI also regulates these organisations. These self-regulatory organisations can also include stock exchanges.

The SEBI Act, 1992 is mandated to safeguard the interest of investors. Section 11(1) of the Act highlights those powers that rest with SEBI to enable SEBI to protect the investors. The Act clearly says that SEBI has a duty to protect the interest of investors in securities. The Act calls for promoting investors' education and training of intermediaries of securities markets.

Closing Case: Banking Sector Reforms

Nationalisation of banking sector in India led to a massive expansion of banks' branches across the country. However, the banking sector was operating under low profitability and weak capital base. The aggregate bank deposits increased from 11% of GDP at the time of nationalisation to 67.2% of GDP in the year 2010–2011.

Moreover, rural expansion and also credit to rural areas expanded due to the nationalisation policy. It is also considered that the performance of 14 nationalised banks have also been commendable since there nationalisation.

However, the banking sector was not very profit-oriented, which led to the weak capital base. Thus, to ensure the financial viability of banking sector in an economic environment, which proposed liberalised economic systems after 1991, the Government of India started banking sector reforms. The main objective of these reforms was to improve the health of banking sector and accept the globally recognised norms and practices in the sector. These are started under the ambit of massive financial sector reforms in the country.

Banking sector reforms were also the result of the deep economic crisis in the country during 1990s. The government was already on the verge of introducing comprehensive economic reforms in the country. Therefore, the reform packages also included banking sector reforms.

To carry out the task, the Government of India appointed a committee under the chairmanship of M. Narasimhan in August 1991. The committee is known as *Narasimhan Committee* on banking sector reforms. The committee submitted its report in April 1998. Before adopting the recommendations of the committee, the government planned to introduce reforms in the sector in a phased manner. The banks were directed not to charge any interest on non-performing assets in April 1992. Thus, the banking sector recognised international standards of asset classification in the country.

Banks were required to classify loans advances in terms of standard assets, sub-standard assets, doubtful assets and loss assets. The government also introduced various measures to strengthen the capital base of the banking system such as capital to risk-weighted assets ratio (CRAR) system. In addition, the government started a recapitalisation programme of nationalised banks during the period of 1993–1994. It strengthened the financial health of the banking sector.

Some of the major reforms in the banking sector at that time included the following:

1. Introduction of prudential norms related to income recognition, asset classification, etc.

2. Rehabilitation programme of public sector banks
3. Setting up of the Board for Financial Supervision under RBI
4. Introduction of guidelines for private sector banks and promoting competition
5. Reduction in ratios such as SLR and CRR
6. Liberalisation programme in banking sector to attract foreign investment
7. Increase in the FDI limit in banking sector

Source: This case is written by the authors based on inputs from the following source:

1. RBI website.

CASE QUESTIONS

1. Discuss the reforms made in the banking sector after 1991.
2. Examine the evolution of rural banking sector after 1991.

REVIEW QUESTIONS

1. Describe the structure of the financial system in India.
2. What is money market? Discuss its characteristics.
3. What do you understand by capital market? Examine its structure.
4. Discuss the role of capital market.
5. Outline some of the recent developments in the secondary markets in India.
6. What is SEBI? What are its major functions?

SUGGESTED READINGS

Economic Survey of India, 1992, 1995, 2012 and 2013, Ministry of Finance, Government of India.

Misra, S.K. and Puri, V.K., 2012, *Indian Economy*, Himalaya Publication House, New Delhi.

Rangarajan, C., 2009, India: Monetary Policy, *Financial Stability and Other Essays*, Academic Foundation, New Delhi.

Rangarajan, C. and Kannan, R., 2004, *Selected Essays on Indian Economy*, Academic Foundation, New Delhi.

Sarma, V.N., 2013, *Banking and Financial Systems*, Cambridge University Press, India.

12

LEGAL FRAMEWORK

Learning Outcomes

After reading this chapter, you will

- Understand the basic regulations governing the legal environment for business in India
- Comprehend the impact of Consumer Protection Act, 1986, Companies Act, 1956 and 2013 and Foreign Exchange Regulation Act (FERA)/Foreign Exchange Management Act (FEMA) on business environment
- Appreciate the importance of Competition Law and Competition Commission of India in the evolving business environment

Opening Case: Dial 1800-11-4000!

An advertisement on television may be misleading! A matchbox may not contain 50 sticks as promised by its label! The air conditioner you bought may be of lesser capacity than what is communicated to you! Therefore, the Government of India has already come up with an awareness campaign called *Jaago Grahak Jaago* (wake up consumers). Also, there is a National Consumer Helpline (NCH) toll-free number 1800-11-4000 and the NCH Mobile Application called *NCHMobiApp* (see http://www.nationalconsumerhelpline.in/NCH-MobileApp.aspx) to address consumers concerns and advice them. The sole aim of NCH is to provide information, advice and guidance to empower Indian consumers and persuade businesses to reorient their policy and management systems to address consumer concerns and grievances and adopting world class standards.[1]

Moreover, in order to protect the consumers, the Department of Consumer Affairs, Government of India has enlisted the following rights that the consumers can, and indeed must, exercise:[2]

1. http://www.nationalconsumerhelpline.in/NCH-MobileApp.aspx
2. Department of Consumer Affairs, Ministry of Consumer Affairs, Food and Public Distribution, Government of India http://consumeraffairs.nic.in/consumer/?q=node/6

1. ***Right to safety:*** This right entails that consumers should be protected against the marketing of such goods and services, which are hazardous to life and property. The consumers should be aware in the sense that they should insist on purchasing quality marked products such as ISI, AGMARK, etc.
2. ***Right to be informed:*** It implies that the consumers have the right to be informed about the quality, quantity, potency, purity, standard and price of goods so as to protect the consumers against unfair trade practices. They should insist on seeking such information from the seller so that they make an informed choice and do not fall prey to high pressure selling techniques of the companies.
3. ***Right to choose:*** The consumers have the right to get access to a variety of goods and services at a competitive price. Therefore, a competitive market is also necessary.
4. ***Right to be heard:*** Consumers have the right to represent themselves in various non-consumer and non-political committees/forums formed to consider the consumer's welfare.
5. ***Right to seek redressal:*** It implies that consumers have the right to seek redressal against unfair trade practices and exploitation. They also have the right to get their genuine demands settled through a fair hearing.
6. ***Right to consumer education:*** The ignorance of consumers, especially in rural areas, leads to their exploitation. Therefore, this right gives the consumers a right to acquire the knowledge to be an informed consumer throughout life.

The Consumer Protection Act was passed in 1986. There is also a Consumer Protection Unit, which deals with many aspects pertinent to consumer welfare. As per the provisions, these include the following:[3]

1. Administration of Consumer Protection Act, 1986 and its rules and regulations
2. Matters related to National Consumer Disputes Redressal Commission and also those concerning the Central Consumer Protection Council
3. Formulating Plan Schemes for consumer protection and monitoring of such schemes
4. Pertaining to international cooperation in the area of protecting consumer rights
5. Questions on Consumer Protection Act, rules, regulations, etc. raised and discussed in the Parliament
6. Coordination with states/UTs for reviewing the same
7. Conducting meetings, seminars and capacity-building programmes on relevant theme

Source: This case is written by the authors based on inputs from the following sources:

1. http://www.nationalconsumerhelpline.in/NCH-MobileApp.aspx
2. http://www.nationalconsumerhelpline.in/NCH-MobileApp.aspx
3. Department of Consumer Affairs, Ministry of Consumer Affairs, Food and Public Distribution, Government of India.
4. http://consumeraffairs.nic.in/consumer/?q=node/6
5. Consumer Protection Unit, http://consumeraffairs.nic.in/consumer/?q=hi/node/396

3. Consumer Protection Unit, http://consumeraffairs.nic.in/consumer/?q=hi/node/396

12.1 LEGAL PROCEDURE

Legal framework in a country primarily describes the laws and regulations, which have a vital impact on the business environment. These regulations and the acts are important in terms of their nature and characteristics. In India, legal framework, which deals with business and macro-economic environment of a country, covers a wide range of areas. These areas include industrial structure, environmental protection, competition policy, regulatory frameworks, etc.

Broadly the legal framework for economic activities in India is governed under the aegis of the Constitution of India and executed by relevant ministries. The Constitution has maintained a federal framework of the economy, and therefore, created Finance Commission and Planning Commission. For law-making pertaining to economic laws, the Constitution has defined the procedure for both the state and union governments. The legal procedure for the union government to make a law requires approval from both houses—*Lok Sabha* (the lower house) and *Rajya Sabha* (the upper house)—of the Parliament. In case of bills proposed to be passed by states, it is required to get the approval from both Legislative Assembly (the lower house; also known as *Vidhan Sabha*) and Legislative Council (the upper house; also known as *Vidhan Parishad*). However, only approval from the lower house legally makes it a law in case of states.

Any bill which is prepared by the government is presented before the Parliament. Prior to doing so, government also seeks suggestion from the Ministry of Law and Justice and various stakeholders which are being affected by the proposed bill through a stakeholder consultation. The Parliament either passes it or suggests amendments. The government incorporates amendments suggested by the parliamentarians and again presents it to the Parliament. Ultimately, it is the Parliament which passes the bill and finally the bill passed by both the houses of the Parliament is sent to the President of India for his consent. After the approval from the President of India, the bill is published in the Gazette of India and becomes an act from the date of consent by the President.

Having discussed the process of an act, we are now in a position to examine some of the acts which can help in improving our understanding of the business environment of the country.

12.2 SICK INDUSTRIAL COMPANIES ACT (SPECIAL PROVISIONS), 1985

India was suffering from industrial sickness during 1970s and 1980s. *Sick industrial units* are defined as those units which continuously incur losses or are not making profits over the years. There were some units as large public sector undertakings (PSUs) experiencing the same. In view of this, the Government of India set up a committee under the Chairmanship of T.T. Tiwari to look into the problems and suggest remedial measures. Based on the recommendations of the Tiwari Committee, the government enacted the Sick Industrial Companies Act (SICA) (Special Provisions) in 1985.

This act was the most important regulation pertaining to industrial sickness. The act was made applicable to both public and private industrial undertakings. However, specifically, SICA was enacted in relation with those industries which were specified in the First Schedule to the Industries (Development and Regulation) Act, 1951.

Purpose of the act

The main purpose of the act was to determine the sickness of an industry and help in expediting the process of recovery of these units. Concurrently, the act aimed to ensure closure of unviable units. The broad objectives of the act as defined are as follows:

1. Timely detection of sick and potentially sick companies
2. Speedy determination by a body of experts of the preventive, ameliorative, remedial and other measures which need to be taken with respect to such companies
3. The expeditious enforcement of the measures so determined and for all matters connected therewith or incidental thereto

Main provisions

SICA was enacted in public interest and also revised twice, *viz.* in 1991 and 2003. But the provision made in the act passed in 1985 was an important pillar of India's industrial structure. Some of the key provisions of this act are as follows:

1. The act provided for the establishment of two quasi-judicial bodies—Board for Industrial and Financial Reconstruction (BIFR) and Appellate Authority for Industrial and Financial Reconstruction (AAIFR). Section 4 of the act provides that BIFR shall consist of a Chairman and minimum of two and a maximum of fourteen other members. These people shall be the persons qualified to be High Court Judges or those with eminent professional expertise drawn from the various disciplines like science, economics, industrial finance, and technology, among others. They shall be appointed by the central government. Moreover, Section 5 of the act calls for constituting an appellate body known as *AAIFR* to hear appeals against the orders of the Board (i.e., BIFR) under this act.
2. The act also defined the criteria of sickness of an industry. It provided for references and criteria of sickness under its Chapter III and section 15. Also, Section 16 of the act provides for inquiry into the working of sick industrial companies.
3. The act also highlighted the preparation of sanctioned scheme under various sub-sections of Sections 17 and 18.
4. The act also had provisions pertaining to directions to dispose the asset of sick industry, dealing with losses of industrial companies, penalty on offenses and offenses by companies, etc.

However, SICA was a failure, and repealed and replaced by Sick Industrial Companies (Special Provisions) Repeal Act, 2003. This act aimed not only to combat industrial sickness but also to reduce the same by ensuring that companies do not exploit the loopholes in the act by using declaration of sickness as an escapist route.

12.3 BOARD FOR INDUSTRIAL AND FINANCIAL RECONSTRUCTION (BIFR)

We have seen the philosophy behind the formation of BIFR while discussing SICA. BIFR was set up in January 1987 and became functional with effect from May in the same year. It is an agency of the Government of India and works under the aegis of the Department of Financial Services of the Ministry of Finance. The objective of BIFR is to determine the sickness of industrial companies. It also assists in reviving those companies that may be viable and in shutting down those which are not worthy of revival. Thus, primarily BIFR deals with and manages the companies and PSUs which are in poor financial and commercial conditions.

BIFR collects official complaints from industries and tries to resolve it. There are two main categories in which filings were collected from industries. The first category is the filing of references reporting sickness of the industry and also requesting for adequate measures. The second category is miscellaneous filing through applications and request letters. As per the procedure outlined in 2009, the references are to be listed within 60 days and then taken up for hearing by the bench. In case of the listing of miscellaneous applications in pending references, a monthly list is published in the beginning of the month and it includes daily cause list.

At the close of the financial year 1991–1992, BIFR registered 1,020 cases related to industrial sickness and 954 cases were heard. In the year 2013, the total references registered by BIFR were 92, which were higher than those in the year 2012. There is a gradual increase in the total number of cases registered by BIFR during post-liberalised era.

It is worth mentioning that BIFR has a story of successful recoveries like the recovery of Bharat Heavy Electricals Limited (BHEL) in the 1980s, and it also played a turnaround in cases of Arvind Mills, Scooters India, etc.

12.4 CONSUMER PROTECTION ACT, 1986

Consumer Protection Act was enacted by the Government of India in 1986. The act aims at protecting the interests of the consumers. It has enabled consumers in the country to seek speedy redressal of their grievances. In fact, rapid growth of consumerism and the expanding business domains created the need for consumer protection regulations in the country. Though various acts like the Indian Penal Code (1860), Indian Contract Act (1872) etc. provided for the consumer rights, but they were only partially developed to do so.

Considering the importance of protecting consumer's rights, the act was enacted. The objectives of the act as mentioned are as follows:

> An act to provide for the better protection of the interest of consumers and for that purpose to make provision for the establishment of consumer councils and other authorities for the settlement of consumers' disputes and for matters connected therewith.[4]

Provisions of the act

As per the provisions of the act, several institutions were established which included Consumer Protection Council, State Consumer Protection Council and District Consumer Protection Council. The act has extensively elaborated the concepts pertaining to consumers and consumer activities. Some of the broad provisions of the act are as follows:

1. The act has defined the consumption activities for which protection is required. It says the one who buys goods for which he partly pays or fully pays is considered to be the

4. Provisions of the Consumer Protection Act, 1986, Government of India.

consumer. A person who hires goods or a service for which he makes a payment is also a *consumer*. However, if the purchase and hiring of goods and services is for a commercial purpose, as per the act, it will not come under the definition of a consumer as per Section 2(d) of the act.

2. Beneficiaries of services for which payment has been made or is promised to be made will also be termed as *consumers*. A complainant can seek relief under the act which may include removing defect, replacing the product with a new product of similar description, receiving payment in lieu of the defect in product or services and asking for the provision for adequate cost, etc., as envisaged under Article 2.11 of the act.
3. The act also provides for the consumers in case of unfair and restrictive trade practices. For instance, in case of provision of warranty or guarantee when there are no prospects of such promises, a consumer can seek compensation on such false promises. Any kind of false promises during marketing and sales maneuvering are considered as unfair trade practices. The act also defines restrictive trade practices in its Section 2(r), as given in Box 12.1.
4. The act also provides for the consumer protection in case of goods and services being made available on the basis of services and goods supplied by others. In this case, the provider of services and goods is liable to protect consumer's interests in the event of non-availability of goods or services on account of the other party.
5. The act also mentions about the rights to consumers like right to choose a good or service, right to education, right to redressal. Thus, companies selling the product need to furnish complete and adequate information needed by the consumer related to the product to make a purchase decision.

Box 12.1 Restrictive Trade Practices as per Consumer Protection Act, 1986

Section 2(r) of Consumer Protection Act, 1986 defines *restrictive trade practices* as the practice of making any statement, whether orally or in writing or by visible representation which

1. Falsely represents that the goods are of a particular standard, quality, quantity, grade, composition, style or model
2. Falsely represents that the services are of a particular standard, quality or grade
3. Falsely represents any re-built, second hand, renovated, reconditioned or old goods as new goods
4. Represents that the goods or services have sponsorship, approval, performance, characteristics, accessories, uses or benefits which such goods or services do not have
5. Represents that the seller or the supplier has a sponsorship or approval or affiliation which such seller or supplier does not have
6. Makes a false or misleading representation concerning the need for, or the usefulness of, any goods or services
7. Gives to the public any warranty or guarantee of the performance, efficacy or length of life of a product or of any goods that is not based on an adequate or proper test thereof
8. Makes to the public a representation in a form that purports to be
   (i) A warranty or guarantee of a product or of any goods or services
   (ii) A promise to replace, maintain or repair an article or any part thereof or to repeat or continue a service until it has achieved a specified result, if such purported warranty

or guarantee or promise is materially misleading or if there is no reasonable prospect that such warranty, guarantee or promise will be carried out

9. Materially misleads the public concerning the price at which a product or like products or goods or services, have been or are, ordinarily sold or provided, and, for this purpose, a representation as to price shall be deemed to refer to the price at which the product or goods or services has or have been sold by sellers or provided by suppliers generally in the relevant market unless it is clearly specified to be the price at which the product has been sold or services have been provided by the person by whom or on whose behalf the representation is made
10. Gives false or misleading facts disparaging the goods, services or trade of another person

Source: Consumer Protection Act, 1986, Government of India.

In recent times, the protection of consumer rights has taken the form a global movement. The World Consumer Rights Day is celebrated on March 15. It was on this day that the US President John F. Kennedy raised the issue of consumer rights in a formal forum during his address to the Congress in 1962.

Moreover, there are a lot of consumer rights organisations in the country which work as non-government organisations and engage in research, advocacy and networking with the aim to protect the rights of the consumers from corporate abuses like false advertising, unsafe products, etc. Some of such organisations include Consumers International, Consumer Unity and Trust Society, Consumer Protection Council, Citizen Consumer and Civic Action Group, and Consumer Education and Research Centre, among others.

12.5 COMPANIES ACT, 1956 AND 2013

To register a new company in India, it is mandatory to obtain director identification number (DIN). After getting digital certificate, the company name needs to be approved. This whole process is being conducted by Ministry of Corporate Affairs in India. Previously, the Companies Act, 1956 was the sole legal framework for new companies to be registered and for registered companies to be functioning in the country. The act was enacted by the Parliament in 1956 and aimed at providing legal framework of the registration process of corporate sector and setting out the responsibilities of directors of a company.

The act was administered by the Government of India through Ministry of Corporate Affairs as well as through the offices of Registrar of Companies, etc. It was amended several times and has been replaced by the Companies Act, 2013.

The Companies Act, 2013, which consists of 29 chapters, 470 sections and 7 schedules as against 658 sections and 14 schedules in the Companies Act, 1956, has been lauded by the corporate sector and other stakeholders.

Some of the main features and provisions of the Companies Act, 2013 are as follows:

1. This act applies to companies incorporated under this act or under the previous act.
2. It provides business-friendly corporate regulations.
3. It provides for enhanced disclosure norms and better corporate governance practices.
4. It calls for limiting the term of auditors of the company.

5. It gives adequate impetus to investor protection.
6. It provides for reserving board seats for women.
7. It incorporates new definitions such as those pertaining to financial statement (to include details of unlisted subsidiaries), key managerial personnel, small company other than public company and annual return, etc.
8. It permits the incorporation of one person company as private limited. Section 3 of Chapter II of the act deals with the procedure of incorporation of a company. It says that a company may be formed for any lawful purpose by
   (i) Seven or more persons, where the company to be formed is to be a public company
   (ii) Two or more persons, where the company to be formed is to be a private company
   (iii) One person, where the company to be formed is to be one person company that is to say, a private company
9. The numbers of permissible members in private company has been raised to 200 as against the existing limit of 50 members. The limit of members in association or partnership without incorporation has also been increased to 100.
10. The act allows that a company can issue securities to the public. Chapter III and Section 23 of the act deals with the provisions related to public offers by a company.
11. The act focuses on improving management and administration and advocates the use of new technologies such as e-governance.
12. The act has also made a provision for the constitution of national company law tribunal.

12.6 MONOPOLIES AND RESTRICTIVE TRADE PRACTICES (MRTP) ACT, 1969 AND COMPETITION ACT, 2002

In India, the competition regime has been evolving over the years. Article 39 (clauses b and c) of the Constitution of India has already mentioned the importance of competition regime.[5] The first law related to competition in India was the Monopolies and Restrictive Trade Practices (MRTP) Act, 1969. This act aimed at prevention of concentration of economic power to the common detriment, control of monopolies, prohibition of monopolistic trade practices, prohibition of restrictive trade practices, and the prohibition of unfair trade practices.

Based on the provisions of this act, MRTP Commission was constituted in 1984. The MRTP Act was amended in 1991. In October 1999, the government appointed a High Level Committee on Competition Policy and Law to suggest a legislative framework, which could either propose a new law or make appropriate amendments to the MRTP Act.

The recommendations of this Committee led to the Competition Act, 2002. The act has four major provisions mentioned as follows:

1. ***Anti-competitive agreements:*** It restricts competitors entering into agreements, which in from restricts the competition.

---

5. Article 39 of the Constitution of India states that the State shall, in particular, direct its policy towards securing—(clause b) that the ownership and control of material resources of the community are so distributed as best to subserve the common good; and, (clause c) that the operation of the economic system does not result in the concentration of wealth and means of production to the common detriment.

2. ***Abuse of dominance:*** It restricts large players from dominating the market, both product market and geographical market, and also restricts predatory pricing.[6]
3. ***Combinations regulation:*** It restricts any such mergers or acquisitions that reduce or harm competition and adversely affect welfare.
4. ***Competition advocacy:*** It is aimed to promote competition advocacy and create awareness about competition issues, and also capacity building of all stakeholders.

The Competition Act, 2002 was amended by the Competition (Amendment) Act, 2007. It provided for the establishment of the Competition Commission of India (CCI) and Competition Appellate Tribunal (CAT). In further developments, the Ministry of Corporate Affairs through its notification on 28 August 2009 repealed the MRTP Act, 1969, and replaced it by the Competition Act, 2002 with effect from 1 September 2009.

The CCI is also mandated to give opinion on competition issues on a reference received from a statutory authority established under any law. It also undertakes advocacy, training and public awareness programmes on competition policy and related issues. The CCI functions as a law enforcement agency as well as an agency mandated to initiate proceedings against those who interfere with the fair, open and free functioning of markets.

12.7 FOREIGN EXCHANGE REGULATION ACT (FERA) AND FOREIGN EXCHANGE MANAGEMENT ACT (FEMA)

Another important legal framework regulating the business environment is the one related to foreign exchange. The Government of India passed a legislation to regulate foreign exchange in 1973, with a view to impose stringent regulatory measures on its inflows and outflows. The legislation is known as the *Foreign Exchange Regulation Act (FERA)*, which came into effect on 1 January 1974. The act imposed regulatory measures on international payments dealing with foreign exchange and securities.

In fact, this act was enacted when India experienced the impact of global oil crisis in 1973. The Indian economy was losing its foreign exchange reserves and prices were high. In order to save India's foreign exchange, the government introduced this act, which was also aimed at regulating foreign exchange.[7]

Article 8 also restricted the conversion of Indian currency into foreign currency until and unless it was approved by RBI. Article 9 prevented payments of foreign exchange by Indians to anyone outside India without prior permission from RBI. FERA also took its toll on the business environment of the country owing to its stringent nature. For instance, see a case in point in Box 12.2 about the Coca Cola's departure from the Indian market in 1977.

---

6. As per the provisions of the act, *predatory pricing* means the sale of goods or provision of services, at a price which is below the cost, as may be determined by regulations, of production of the goods or provision of services, with a view to reduce competition or eliminate the competitors.
7. Article 8(a) of the act deals with the restrictions on dealing with foreign exchange. According to this, except with the previous general or special permission of the Reserve Bank, no person other than an authorised dealer shall in India, and no person resident in India other than an authorised dealer shall outside India, purchase or otherwise acquire or borrow from, or sell, or otherwise transfer or lend to or exchange with, any person not being an authorised dealer, any foreign exchange, provided that nothing in this sub-section shall apply to any purchase or sale of foreign currency effected in India between any person and a money-changer.

Box 12.2 Coca Cola's Departure from India in 1977

A classic case in point is the departure of Coca Cola in 1977 from the Indian market because of non-compliance to FERA guidelines. In 1977, when the Prime Minister Morarji Desai's government came to power in India, the company was asked to have an Indian partner. It was supposed to hand over the controlling stake of its Indian operations to the Indian investors, as per the provisions of FERA. This implied that the company might have to share its secret formula with its Indian partners. The company refused to do so and had to stop its operations in India, thereby quitting the Indian market. It was only in 1993, during the post-liberalisation era, that changes in government policy allowed foreign brands to operate without Indian partnerships, and thus, the company re-entered the Indian market.

Therefore, in order to cope with the evolving nature of foreign exchange mechanism in the wake of liberalisation, which called for a complete management and not merely regulation of foreign exchange, FERA was repealed in 1999.

A new legislation called *Foreign Exchange Management Act (FEMA)* was enacted in the year 1999. Thus, FERA was replaced by FEMA. The new act came into effect on 1 July 1999. Some of the key objectives and features of this act are as follows:

1. The objective of this act was to make India's regulatory framework relating to foreign exchange management comply with the new economic regime.
2. This could facilitate India's external trade and payments, leading to promoting the orderly development and maintenance of foreign exchange market in the country.
3. The act envisioned a consistent foreign exchange management system in the country, which could fulfill the obligations envisaged under the WTO regime.
4. It gave authority to the central government to impose restrictions.

FEMA was definitely an improvement over FERA. Box 12.3 reflects on some of the differences between the two acts.

Box 12.3 Difference between the Provisions of FERA and FEMA

S. No.	*FERA*	*FEMA*
1	It constitutes 81 sections and is complex.	It constitutes 49 sections and is simplified.
2	It is meant for regulation of foreign exchange.	It is meant for complete management of foreign exchange.
3	A major objective was to conserve foreign exchange and prevent its misuse.	A major objective was to facilitate foreign trade and payments in the wake of the demands of liberalisation.
4	Definition of 'Authorised Person' in FERA is a narrow one.	'Authorised Person' has been defined to include banks and off-shore banking units.
5	There existed presumption of negative intention (*Mens Rea* which means *guilty mind*) and joining hands in offence (i.e., abatement) in case of an offence.	Such presumptions have been excluded in FEMA.
6	Violation of FERA regulations was a criminal offence.	Violation is a civil offence.
7	It does not define the current account and capital account transactions.	It clearly distinguishes between the current account and capital account transactions.
8	Residential status of a person was determined by citizenship.	Residential status is determined based on stay of more than 182 days in India.

12.8 GOVERNMENT'S REFORM AGENDA AND REGULATORY BILLS

To boost India's economic performance, the Government of India embarked upon reform agenda during early 1990s. This reform agenda has since been continued in different areas. The most important endeavours in the quest of economic reforms have been in the areas of industrial policy and also in the areas of foreign investment. Measures of liberalisation have continuously been taken in various economic spectra such as reforms in fiscal policies, reforms in industrial policies, reforms in monetary policies and also reforms in foreign exchange and trade policies, etc. During recent years, the Government of India has continuously been trying to carry out reforms in regulatory frameworks for the faster implementation of liberalised economic policies and to attain higher economic growth. Two important bills are pending, which aim at reforms in the area of implementation. These include Goods and Service Tax bill and Land Bill.

12.8.1 The Right to Fair Compensation and Transparency in Land Acquisition, Rehabilitation and Resettlement Act, 2013

In 2013, the Government of India introduced the Right to Fair Compensation and Transparency in Land Acquisition, Rehabilitation and Resettlement Act, 2013 in Parliament which was passed by both the houses of the Parliament. The act was a major reform undertaken by the government since independence in the area of land acquisition. It may be noted that due to lack of reforms in these areas, several projects related to infrastructure development were stuck. The major features of the act are outlined as under:

1. For private projects, the consent of 80% land owners is required, and in case of public-private partnership projects, the requirement is 70%. For the government projects, no consent is required.
2. A social impact assessment is mandatory for all projects with few exceptions.
3. The act exempted 13 laws (such as the National Highways Act, 1956 and the Railways Act, 1989) from its ambit. It also provides that any unutilised land for 5 years duration acquired under the provisions of the act must be returned to the original owners.
4. It also provides for the establishment of a Land Acquisition, Rehabilitation and Resettlement (LARR) Authority, which shall look into grievances.
5. For any government department, the head of that department would be held guilty in case of any offence and the person concerned has to prove that they exercised due diligence to prevent the commission of that offence.
6. Private hospitals and private educational institutions are excluded.

In 2014, the Government of India proposed further amendment in the LARR Act. With new proposed amendments, the bill was introduced in the Parliament and passed by Lok Sabha (the lower house). The bill came into force in 2014 with special ordinances. Later in 2015, the amendments were introduced in the Parliament. New amendments aim at amending the principle act passed in 2013.

The bill enables the government to exempt five categories of projects from the following requirements:[8]

1. Social impact assessment
2. Restrictions on acquisition of multi-cropped land
3. Consent for private projects and public–private partnerships (PPPs) projects.

These five categories of projects include the following:

1. Defence
2. Rural infrastructure
3. Affordable housing
4. Industrial corridors
5. Infrastructure, including PPPs where government owns the land.

12.8.2 Goods and Services Tax (GST) Bill

One of the major steps in the area of fiscal reform was value added tax (VAT) at the central and the state levels. This has simplified the indirect tax regime in the country. However, major bottlenecks towards simplification remain in the distribution of power between different layers of the Indian federal structure, which varies across industries and services types. Therefore, a comprehensive indirect tax reform was needed. The Goods and Services Tax (GST) regime was announced by the Government of India during 2007–2008 budget. However, the regime required constitutional amendment from Parliament. With the objective to introduce GST, a constitution amendment bill was introduced in Parliament in 2014 and the bill was passed by the lower house of the Parliament.

It is important to note that an ideal GST regime aims at harmonising the taxation regimes in the country by putting all indirect taxes levied in one category. Therefore, it deals with the process of simplifying the current tax regime, broadening of the tax bases and reducing distortions due to several stakeholders involvement such as centre, states and municipalities. Considering the complexity of the existing tax regimes, fiscal reform is an important endeavour of the Government of India. Therefore, the GST bill has been introduced to achieve the objective of simplified tax regime (see Box 12.4).

The features of the bill are as follows:

1. It enables Parliament and state legislatures to frame laws on GST. The GST is applicable on the supply of goods or services.
2. Initially, GST will not apply to (i) petroleum crude, (ii) high speed diesel, (iii) motor spirit (petrol), (iv) natural gas, and (v) aviation turbine fuel. A law made in Parliament in context of GST will not override a state law.
3. The government at the centre will have the exclusive rights to levy and collect GST during interstate trade or imports. This will be known as *Integrated GST* (*IGST*). The IGST will be shared between the centre and states.

8. http://www.prsindia.org/uploads/media/Land%20and%20R%20and%20R/Brief%20-%20LARR%20 Bill_2015.pdf

Box 12.4 Justification of GST

Taxation in India has been defined in accordance with the provision of the Constitution of India vide its three lists, i.e., union list, state list and concurrent list as per Article 246 of the Seventh Schedule. This provision exclusively divides the power of imposition and implementation of taxation in the country between the centre and the state. However, there exist several shortcomings in the fiscal regime of the country. Even today, the regime of value added tax (VAT) does not include all the indirect taxes levied by Central Government in the domain of CENVAT additional customs duty, surcharges, etc. An example is given below for transport sector, wherein several types of taxes are levied by the centre and state governments.

Table 1 Important Taxes in Transport Sector

Name of Tax	*Levying Authority*	*Important Component*	*Mode*
Taxes on vehicles	State governments	Regulatory Framework Indian Motor Vehicles Act, State Motor Vehicles Taxation Act, state toll tax, etc.	Road
Taxes on goods and passengers	State governments	Passenger tax, goods tax, tax on entry of goods into local areas, tolls on roads, etc.	Roads and IWT
Other taxes and duties on commodities and services	State governments	Foreign travel tax	Air and IWT
Taxes on sales, trade, etc.	State governments	Regulatory Framework State Sales Tax Act, Central Sales Tax Act, etc.	All modes
Service tax on transport services	Central government	All services in transport sector	All modes
Excise	Central government	Excise duty and cess on transport goods	All modes, fuel
Customs	Central government	Excise duty and cess on transport goods	All modes, fuel

Source: National Transport Development Policy Committee Report, 2014.

Closing Case: Can DCHL be Declared Sick under BIFR Provisions?

Deccan Chronicle Holdings Limited (DCHL), the publisher of Deccan Chronicle newspaper, filed a reference on 26 August 2013, seeking registration as a sick industrial company under Section 15(1) of the Sick Industrial Companies (Special Provisions) Act, 1985 (SICA). The company was in debt of ₹3,777 crore. It had posted a loss of ₹3.65 crore for the quarter ended 31 December 2013.

However, the Board for Industrial and Financial Reconstruction (BIFR) rejected its application to be declared a sick company. BIFR held it responsible for withholding some crucial information and argued that the company misrepresented itself as an industrial entity, as it was primarily engaged in publishing business. Therefore, it was not considered as being engaged in manufacturing activity under the Industries (Development and Regulation) Act. DCHL is registered under Press and Registration Books Act, 1867.

This decision implies that the company may have to consider selling parts of the business. If it was declared as a sick company, it would have given it protection from the creditors. As per BIFR, a large number of secured creditors and asset reconstruction companies—India Bulls Financial Services Limited, Canara Bank, Kotak Mahindra Bank Limited, State Bank of India, JM Financial Asset Reconstruction Company Private Limited, Pegasus Assets Reconstruction Private Limited and IDFC Limited—had initiated steps to recover their dues under the Sarfaesi Act, contrary to DCHL's claim that action had been taken only on 9.78% of its securities.

The matter reached the Delhi High Court, which directed BIFR to constitute a special bench to decide the maintainability of a plea by the company. Now, BIFR, which already passed three administrative orders against DCHL, has to pass a judicial order after hearing both DCHL and its lenders. It is now interesting to see whether a company registered as a newspaper can claim the status of an industry or not.

The summary records of the proceedings of the hearing held on 18 February 2014 before the special bench revealed the following:[9]

1. Company to provide a copy of Form-'A' to all concerned by 22 February 2014.
2. All concerned to file their objection on the validity of Registration to Board's office, with a copy to the company by 27 February 2014. Those who will not file their objection by 27 February 2014 forfeit their right to file objection.
3. Company to file reply on the objections received from the creditors to Board's office, with a copy to all concerned by 14 March 2014.
4. The Bench fixed the next date of hearing on 19 March 2014 at 11.00 hours for final arguments on the validity of registration.

Further, the order dated 19 March 2014 gave another date of 7 April 2014 for the final argument on the Validity of Registration which took place.[10]

Source: This case is written by the authors based on inputs from the following sources:

1. DCHL running out of options after BIFR rejects application, *Live Mint* and *Wall Street Journal*, 26 December 2013.
2. DCHL posts ₹3.6-cr loss in quarter ended Dec, The Hindu Business Line, 13 February 2014.
3. BIFR Special Bench, http://www.bifr.nic.in/18_02_2014_Decan_Order.pdf
4. Board for Industrial and Financial Reconstruction bench to decide Deccan Chronicle Holdings Ltd's plea, *The Times of India*, Hyderabad, 6 February 2014.
5. http://www.bifr.nic.in/19_03_2014_Decan_Order.pdf

CASE QUESTIONS

1. Cite two learnings about the role of BIFR that you have understood from this case.
2. What should be the way ahead for DCHL in the context discussed in this case?

9. http://www.bifr.nic.in/18_02_2014_Decan_Order.pdf
10. http://www.bifr.nic.in/19_03_2014_Decan_Order.pdf

REVIEW QUESTIONS

1. Examine the importance of legal frameworks in influencing the business environment.
2. What were the provisions of Sick Industrial Companies Act (Special Provisions), 1985?
3. What is BIFR? Describe.
4. Outline the major provisions of the Consumer Protection Act, 1986.
5. What are the main features of the Companies Act, 2013?
6. Outline the provisions of the Competition Act, 2002.
7. What is the role of Competition Commission of India?
8. Distinguish between FERA and FEMA.

SUGGESTED READINGS

Companies Act, 2013 with Rules, 2014, Taxman.

Mehta, Pradeep S. (Ed.), 2012, *Evolution of Competition Laws and Their Enforcement: A Political Economy Perspective*, Routledge Publications in association with Consumer Unity and Trust Society (CUTS International), Jaipur.

13

PRINCIPLES OF INTERNATIONAL LAW FOR BUSINESS

Learning Outcomes

After reading this chapter, you will

- Be familiar with the sources of international law
- Understand the various principles of international law
- Comprehend and appreciate the scope of international trade law

Opening Case: GIPC Index and India-US Legal Dispute

The Global Intellectual Property Center (GIPC) is a part of the United States Chamber of Commerce. It looks after intellectual property rights (IPRs). GIPC periodically carries out study on the environment of IPRs in various countries. With a specified methodology, it also prepares index to compare intercountry intellectual property environment. As per the latest index, which is called the *GIPC International IP Index 2014*, India has scored the lowest. The highest score on this index has been estimated for the United States (US) among 25 countries.

Considering the worst performance by India on this index, GIPC urged US Trade Representative Office that India should be on a priority list for engagement to address the issue of deteriorating IPR environment in the country. Both the US and India should engage for cooperation on IPR issues.

The Indian pharmaceutical industry took this index surprisingly and has been sceptical on the methodologies used for construction of the index. The industry experts expressed further apprehensions that this may be the goal or motive that they can target the Indian market. Consequently, IPR experts, generic drug-makers and the Indian industry questioned the methodology. They considered the index as a tool to push the interests of American industry by pressurising India. The industry chamber, Confederation of Indian Industry (CII) also argued that the GIPC index is not truly representative of the IPR environment in India.

Taking note of the deteriorating IPRs in India, the US International Trade Commission (USITC), a quasi-judicial body was asked by the US to investigate the violation and discrimination of IPRs due to industrial policies. Earlier in 2012, India made provision of compulsory licence to a pharmaceutical company named *Natco Pharma* to manufacture and sell cancer-treatment drug *Nexavar*. It was priced at ₹30, which was comparatively very low compared to what was charged by the patent holder companies. Consequently, the pharmaceutical companies in the US opposed this move. The USITC raised the issue sighting that the law was not in compliance with the WTO provisions.

On this issue, the USITC is to investigate into this matter. The stakeholders are supposed to be part of the hearing process, which includes Ron Somers, the President of the US-India Business Council, Pallavi Shroff, Confederation of Indian Industry (CII), and Jerry Rao, former Chairman National Association of Software and Service Companies (NASSCOM). They are supposed to present their testimonials to the USITC on this issue.

Earlier, the Senators' letter to USITC specifically pointed out that India has been able to enforce and protect the copyrights. The discrimination is enforcing, in particular, against the innovative US pharmaceutical companies, providing a competitive advantage to the domestic industries and protecting it. The traders and the chambers of commerce are urging for listing India in the list of Priority Foreign Country for IPRs.

In case, the US brings out India into the priority list, it is believed that India would bring this issue before WTO. This should be noted that listing India into priority list means, as per the US Trade Act, it is the country which does not provide adequate protection to IPRs.

This is not a new case between India and the US. Both the countries are fighting several cases in WTO's dispute settlement body.

Source: This case is written by the authors based on inputs from the following sources:

1. US International Trade Commission to hear cases of bias against American companies in India, *The Economic Times*, http://www.thehindu.com/business/Industry/india-likely-to-drag-us-to-wto-if-classified-priority-country/article5726702.ece
2. GIPC, http://dev.theglobalipcenter.com/wp-content/themes/gipc/map-index/assets/pdf/Index_Map_Index_2ndEdition.pdf

13.1 SOURCES OF INTERNATIONAL LAW

The business environment in a cross-country context is directly affected by the principles of international law. The international law acts as a regulatory framework besides the country's own legal environment. It is, therefore, imperative that while doing business internationally, managers need to comprehend the principles of international law, as it applies to their business interests.

Before we discuss the principles of international law, it is important to understand the sources of international law. The sources of international law are not confined to the national legal systems alone, but encompass provisions relating to bilateral and multilateral agreements as well.

As per Article 38 of the Statute of the International Court of Justice (ICJ), the sources of international law are as follows:

1. International conventions, whether general or particular, establishing rules expressly recognised by the contesting states

2. International custom, as evidence of a general practice accepted as law
3. The general principles of law recognised by civilised nations
4. Judicial decisions and the teachings of the highly qualified publicists of various countries, subject to the provisions of Article 59.[1]

13.2 PRINCIPLES OF INTERNATIONAL LAW

The international legal framework is guided by certain principles which have to be followed by the countries. The principles of international law are as follows:

1. ***Principle of sovereignty and sovereign immunity:*** The principles of sovereignty and sovereign immunity are an essential part of all the international laws. These principles are judicially created to safeguard the interest of national sovereignty. The existence of legal equality and comity is a priority of international law. The international laws under these principles legally recognise the rights of property, territorial integrity and its associated jurisdiction, and also make mention of interstate relationships. The doctrine of sovereign immunity gives the states immunity from prosecution assuming that the state cannot commit anything wrong in legal terms.
2. ***Principle of international jurisdiction:*** International jurisdiction is another important principle of international law derived from the doctrine of universal jurisdiction. It allows a state to bring criminal proceedings against a crime, irrespective of its location. This doctrine of universal jurisdiction principally allows that one state or international organisation should have a right for claiming justice in case of violation of code of conduct or incidence of crime, regardless of their origin. If there is an international dispute between two parties from different states, then disputes settlements in the national courts will vary country to country due to different jurisdictions and procedures of dispute settlement in different countries. This principle also allows national courts to carry out procedures on international crimes even if the crime has not been committed in its national territory. However, in order to carry out international criminal procedure for international crimes, an International Criminal Court was created in 2001.
3. ***Principle of comity:*** In international law, the principle of comity is another important pillar. It is based on the doctrine of comity. This doctrine refers to the legal principle through which jurisdiction of one court is expected not to violate the jurisdiction of other courts. It implies mutual respects for each other's country's laws and regulations.
4. ***Principle of the act of state doctrine:*** The act of the state doctrine is another principle of international law. This doctrine is closely related to the principles of sovereignty and sovereign immunity. It highlights that the state is sovereign and it has a right to safeguard its domestic interests. Therefore, according to the principle, the state actions related to domestic activities are set to be free and need not be internationally questioned.

---

1. Article 59 of the Statute of ICJ states that the decision of the court has no binding force except between the parties and in respect of that particular case.

13.3 SCOPE OF INTERNATIONAL TRADE LAW

Understanding the framework of international trade law is important for us in the context of understanding the business environment. International trade law has been defined by the United Nations General Assembly resolution 2102 (XX) as the body of rules governing commercial relationships among countries.

Some of the areas which lie within the scope of the international trade law include provisions pertaining to the following:

1. ***International sale of goods:*** The United Nations Convention on the International Sale of Goods was held in Vienna in 1980. It was an essential part of international business law. This is known as *Convention on Contracts for the International Sale of Goods (CISG)*. As described in the contract, the main objective of this arrangement is to provide a modern, uniform and fair regime for contracts for the international sale of goods.[2] This framework governs contracts for the international sales of goods between the private companies.

   The main aspects of CISG includes formation of contracts, agency arrangements, and exclusive sales arrangements. These arrangements deal with the detailed process of business between the parties. The model contract arrangements generally contain rules and regulations for the international sales contracts. It highlights the rights and obligations of parties, which are involved in trade or sale and purchase. They have to comply with the rules under the multilateral trading system (for more details on multilateralism, read Chapters 18 and 19).

2. ***Instrument of payments:*** While entering into a sales contract, the instruments for payments need to be identified. The UN convention on international bill of exchange and international permissible notes indicated the uniformity in bilateral exchange. The most prominent methods for payment are negotiable instruments and banker's commercial credits. Negotiable instruments are the documents, which guarantee the payment of a specified amount of money during a specified time period. The payment mechanisms for international sale of good are, thus, envisaged to lower the risk of non-payment. In terms of negotiable instruments, letter of credit (L/C) is widely used in international trade.

3. ***International business laws:*** There are several laws that govern international trade. These laws may be bilateral trade agreements, regional trade agreements or multilateral trade arrangements (see Chapters 18, 19 and 20 for detailed information). Moreover, there are laws pertaining to customs examination and customs clearing process as well. The multilateral rules under WTO have been one of the key arrangements through which international sale of goods and trade are being governed. These laws include General Agreements on Tariffs and Trade (GATT) and other agreements under the aegis of WTO such as agreements of trade facilitation, intellectual property rights (IPRs) and Sanitary and Phytosanitary agreement (SPS measures), etc. Besides, there

2. http://www.uncitral.org/uncitral/en/uncitral_texts/sale_goods/1980CISG.html

is a UN organisation called *United Nations Commission on International Trade Law (UNCITRAL),* which also has provisions for smooth conduct of international trade (for details on UNCITRAL, see Chapter 14).

4. ***Industrial property and copyright:*** Industrial property and copyright has been advocated in international business law to protect and encourage innovations from scientists and other creators of new ideas or products. The laws relating to intellectual property and copyrights confer exclusive rights to the owners. Under the ambit of WTO, Trade-Related Intellectual Property Rights (TRIPS) agreement governs the copyrights for sales of goods in international market (for more information on TRIPS, see Chapter 19). Also, World Intellectual Property Organisation (WIPO), consisting of 187 members and headquartered in Geneva, is a UN agency specialised for intellectual property rights' issues.
5. ***Transportation:*** Transportation is another part of international business law. We broadly divide transportation into land or surface transport, sea transport and air transport. Trade in goods largely depends on sea transportation. Transportation also has a significant impact on the cost of trade of particular goods. The cost-effective transportation is sea transport, which makes goods competitive in international market as compared to those transported through other transports such as road and air. Rail is also an efficient mode of transportation. However, due to intercontinental connectivity, sea transportation plays a pivotal role in the international transportation of goods. Apart from the provisions made in WTO agreements, the UN conventions on Contracts for the International Carriage of Goods Wholly or Partly by Sea is also governing international transportation for goods.

   These laws provide rights to the landlocked countries to use sea ports of the neighbouring countries. For example, Nepal and Bhutan are landlocked countries, which are using Kolkata port as the port for their transit trade with the other countries. Similarly, Afghanistan, another landlocked country in South Asia, uses the Chahbahar port situated in Iran and Karachi port situated in Pakistan for its transit trade. These provisions are made under the ambit of both international and bilateral arrangements. For instance, the bilateral arrangement between Indian and Nepal also allows Nepal to use Indian Railways as the alternate mode of transport from Kolkata port to Nepal, and also from Bangladesh to Nepal.
6. ***Insurance:*** Insurance is one of the key pillars of modern business laws. The rise of international trade and the involvement of various stakeholders have created new opportunities for insurance industry for goods in transit for the international trade. This has become an integral part of the international commercial law. In the event of loss and damage during transit, the insurance mechanism provides opportunities for the insured party to recover the loss. The international Cost, Insurance and Freight (CIF) sale contract includes the cost of insurance and makes it mandatory to have insurance of goods for international sale. Marine insurance mechanisms are also used for insuring goods in transit through sea routes.

13.4 SOME OTHER INTERNATIONAL CONVENTIONS PROMOTING TRADE AND COMMERCE

The ensuing chapters will discuss international conventions or regulatory regimes which are important for trade and businesses. Some chapters are also dedicated to international organisations such as World Trade Organisation (WTO). However, this section deals with an introduction to some of the pertinent international conventions, which are promoting international trade and commerce and facilitating transnational businesses. We know that the world has numerous legal regimes that have direct and indirect impact on the international trade and commerce. There exist national laws regulating business in countries and also international laws which try to safeguard and facilitate international business. Therefore, a company or a firm or an individual, who is involved in international trade, has to face regulation both at local and international levels. In addition, regulation in host and home countries are also in practice for international business. Thus, the composition of business laws may be categorised as international conventions, home country laws and host country laws (see Figure 13.1).

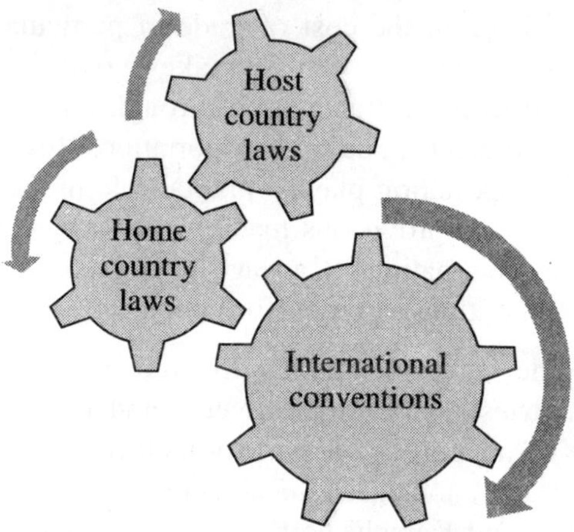

Figure 13.1 Composition of business laws.

In modern times, international trade and business laws relate to trade in goods and services between countries, trade and international property rights, cross border trade facilitation and customs harmonisation, dispute resolution, risk management, investment, etc. International agreements related to trade in goods and services, etc. are discussed in Chapter 19. This section deals with the principles of conventions on customs, transport (road and rail) and also convention on climate change. These are important conventions, and the principles and objectives of these conventions highlight the guiding framework of international laws.

13.4.1 Revised Kyoto Convention

The international convention on the simplification and harmonisation of customs procedures (Kyoto Convention) first came into force in 1974. Considering the evolving demands from stakeholders, the convention was revised. The revised Kyoto Convention outlines several guiding principles aiming at seamless trade between countries. This convention promotes trade facilitation through the use of technology for effective customs controls and procedure. Some of the important principles are as follows:[3]

1. Transparency and predictability of customs actions
2. Standardisation and simplification of the goods declaration and supporting documents
3. Simplified procedures for authorised persons
4. Maximum use of information technology
5. Minimum necessary customs control to ensure compliance with regulations
6. Use of risk management and audit-based controls
7. Coordinated interventions with other border agencies
8. Partnership with the trade

The revised Kyoto Convention was adopted by the World Customs Organisation in June 1999 and entered into force on 3 February 2006. The convention has 101 contracting parties.

13.4.2 TIR Convention

TIR is a multilateral treaty popularly known as TIR Convention concluded in November 1975. The convention aims at harmonising and simplifying the administrative formalities of international road transport. TIR stands for transport internationaux routiers in French, which means international road transports in English.

Initial coverage of TIR Convention, 1975 was limited to Europe. The expansion of membership gradually started in regions like Central Asia and South West Asia. Now, 69 countries have acceded to the convention, including those from Europe, North Africa and the Middle East. The TIR system is promoted under the aegis of the United Nations to make it accessible for all countries desirous of using it. In 1984, the Economic and Social Council (ECOSOC) of the United Nations adopted a resolution (1984/79), which recommends that countries world-wide examine the possibility of acceding to the convention and introducing the TIR system.

The five pillars of TIR convention

In order to ensure that goods may travel with a minimum interference "en route" and yet offer maximum safeguards to customs administrations, the TIR regime contains five basic requirements—the five pillars of the TIR customs transit system:[4]

1. Goods should travel in customs secure vehicles or containers.
2. Throughout the journey, duties and taxes at risk should be covered by an internationally valid guarantee.

3. World customs Organisation, http://www.wcoomd.org/en/topics/facilitation/instrument-and-tools/conventions/pf_revised_kyoto_conv.aspx
4. TIR Handbook, The United Nations.

3. Goods should be accompanied by an internationally accepted customs document (TIR Carnet), opened in the country of departure and serving as a customs control document in the countries of departure, transit and destination.
4. Customs control measures taken in the country of departure should be accepted by all countries of transit and destination.
5. Access to the TIR procedure for national associations to act as guarantor, international organization for the effective and smooth functioning of international guarantee system and natural and legal persons to utilize TIR Carnet for international movement of vehicles.

13.4.3 Convention Concerning International Carriage by Rail (COTIF)

The Convention Concerning International Carriage by Rail (COTIF) is an international convention regulating traffic and passenger movement by rail transport. The convention provides international rule and regulatory framework for international carriage of goods and passenger by railways, uniform rules for the use of vehicles and uniform rules for contract of rail infrastructure, etc. An inter-governmental organisation was set up in 1985 for operationalisation of the COTIF among member countries as per the provision of the convention. The organisation is called the Intergovernmental Organisation for International Carriage by Rail [In French, it is Organisation Intergouvernementale Pour Les Transports Internationaux Ferroviaires (OTIF)]. The convention was further amended in 1999 and came into force in 2006 with its protocols in place.

The UN General Assembly is the highest decision-making body of the OTIF. It comprises the representatives from all member states. The Secretary General convenes the General Assembly once every three years. Contracting parties to the convention include 48 countries spread across Europe, Central Asia and the Middle East. As per the COTIF, the principle aims of the OTIF are as under:[5]

1. To establish a uniform system of law applicable to the carriage of passengers, luggage and goods in international trade through traffic by rail between member states, and to facilitate the application and development of this system.
2. To apply the system of law provided to international transit traffic using in addition to services on railway lines, land and sea services and inland waterways.

Other internal carriage performed under the responsibility of the railway, complementary to carriage by rail, shall be treated as carriage performed over a line.

13.4.4 The United Nations Framework Convention on Climate Change (UNFCCC)

The United Nations Framework Convention on Climate Change (UNFCCC) is an international environmental treaty having the objective to tackle climate change globally. The Convention was negotiated during Earth Summit in Rio, Brazil in 1992, which came into force in 1994.

5. See CIT documents, Available: http://www.cit-rail.org/en/rail-transport-law/cotif/

The UNFCCC has 197 parties. The parties to the convention meet annually since 1995, and the meeting is called the conferences of the parties (COP). The purpose of the COP is to assess the progress in dealing with the climate change mitigation and adaptation. Initially, the convention did not set any binding commitment for reducing global emissions to contracting parties.

The main principles of the Convention are listed below:

1. To protect the climate system for the benefit of present and future generations taking into account the specific needs and special circumstances of developing country parties, and particularly their vulnerability to climate change.
2. To take precautionary measures to anticipate, prevent or minimise the causes of climate change and mitigate its adverse effects. The parties should promote sustainable development, and the policies and measures to protect the climate system against human-induced change should be integrated with national development programmes of the parties. The parties should cooperate to promote a supportive and open international economic system and their moves should not lead to unjustifiable discriminations and restrictions on international trade.

Further, in the year 1997, Kyoto Protocol to the UNFCCC was concluded and it established legally binding obligations for developed countries to reduce their greenhouse gas emissions in the period 2008–2012. The 2010 Cancún agreements state that the future global warming should be limited to below 2.0°C (3.6°F) relative to the pre-industrial level. The protocol was amended in 2012 to encompass the period 2013–2020 in the Doha Amendment, but not yet entered into force. In 2015, the Paris Agreement was adopted, governing emission reductions from 2020 through commitments of countries in ambitious nationally determined contributions.

Closing Case: Supreme Court of India Judgement on Sovereign Immunity

In case of Ethiopian Airlines (a state-owned company) which lost its appeal against a Consumer Commission ruling, it was clearly stated by the Supreme Court of India that in cases of trade and business, the principle of sovereign immunity is not absolute. The countries have to abide by the law of the country in which they are doing business. This case was related to a complaint filed by Ganesh Narain Saboo, who had booked a consignment with the airline. Owing to much delay in delivery at Dar es Salaam in Tanzania, the goods were spoiled.

The Court held the Ethiopian Airlines accountable for its commercial obligations made in India, and ruled that it exercised no sovereign immunity.

To abide by the doctrine of sovereign immunity is an international obligation for all countries. Section 86 of the Civil Procedure Code (CPC) of the Indian legal framework provides that *no foreign State may be sued in any Court otherwise competent to try the suit except with the consent of the Central Government certified in writing by a Secretary to that Government.*

However, the rise of globalisation and increase in trade relations created opportunities for judicial interventions beyond the traditional frameworks of sovereign immunity.

In earlier judgements, courts in India rejected the plea that a foreign company, which is state-owned, would get the benefit of sovereign immunity. In this direction, decision by a consumer court rejected that a foreign state could claim sovereign immunity.

In a similar case, the Mumbai High Court in 2013 had rejected the application of the Section 86 of CPC against Qatar Airways. The company argued that as it is a state-owned company, it, therefore, has privilege to attract the Section 86 of the CPC. But, the High Court sighting the reason that the company is an independent entity and also engaged in commercial business in India, ruled that this Section does not apply to the company.

Source: This case is written by the authors based on inputs from the following sources:

1. Sovereign immunity out of the question in commercial transactions: court, *The Hindu*, by J. Venkatesan, 16 August 2011, http://www.thehindu.com/news/national/article2359813.ece
2. Bombay High Court on Sovereign Immunity, 10 July 2013, http://indiacorplaw.blogspot.in/2013/07/bombay-high-court-on-sovereign-immunity_10.html
3. Sovereign Immunity Not Absolute: Supreme Court of India, by Shashank Kumar, 16 August 2011, http://ilcurry.wordpress.com/2011/08/16/sovereign-immunity-not-absolute-supreme-court-of-india/

CASE QUESTIONS

1. Explain Section 86 of the CPC.
2. Read further about the cases of Ethiopian Airlines and Qatar Airways on the issue of sovereign immunity raised in the case, and compare and contrast the two.

REVIEW QUESTIONS

1. What are the sources of international law?
2. Discuss the principle of sovereignty and sovereign immunity.
3. What do you understand by the principle of international jurisdiction?
4. Describe the meaning and concept of international sale of goods.
5. What are the provisions related to transportation in International Business Law?

SUGGESTED READINGS

Brierly, J.L., 1984, 'The Origins of International Law' in *The Law of Nations: An Introduction to the International Law of Peace*, 6th ed., Sir Humphrey Waldock (Ed.), Cambridge.

Herdegen, M., 2013, *Principles of International Economic Law*, Oxford University Press, Oxford, UK.

Subedi, S.P., 2006, *International Economic Law*, *Study Guide*, University of London, UK.

14

INTERNATIONAL ORGANISATIONS

Learning Outcomes

After reading this chapter, you will

- Understand the evolution of international organisations like the United Nations, World Trade Organisation and others
- Become familiar with the role played by such organisations in the emerging global order
- Appreciate their significance in the contemporary business environment

Opening Case: Business Partners with the UN

One may ponder that how a business or a corporate house and an international organisation like the United Nations (UN) can work closely with each other. But it is true that businesses continue to partner with the UN through a strategic model and help the UN and its specialised agencies in their efforts to address global development challenges.

Though these partnerships do have a philanthropic side, but they may not necessarily be a non-profit initiative. The businesses can realise their commercial needs as well, which are partnering with the UN.

Some of the ways in which businesses can partner with the UN include the following:

1. Leverage their core competencies to support the national development policies in developing countries and least developed countries. Companies can also adapt their business models to develop innovative technique to fulfill millennium development goals (MDGs), which also fulfill their commercial needs.
2. Create awareness about global issues like climate change and develop innovative products to meet the challenge, for instance, developing green products.
3. Partner in funding the various developmental projects of the UN across the world. This may include projects related to addressing the challenges of hunger in a poor country through collaboration with World Food Programme (WFP) or funding for girl child education through UNESCO in a developing country.

4. Send their key personnel to work closely with the UN in poor countries or conflict-ridden countries to build capacity. This will help the companies in becoming a part of the mainstream development initiative in such areas and also in providing the basic utility products therein.

This case, in fact, gives an account of some such select partnerships that would help in enhancing the understanding of the context.

Business Call to Action

There is an initiative called the *Business Call to Action*, which was launched as a coalition among a dozen of international companies, with an urge to apply business expertise to tackle the menace of poverty. This was launched at an event in London organised by United Nations Development Programme (UNDP) and the British Government in May 2008.

Besides the various international development agencies and foundations like AusAid and Clinton Global Initiative, companies like Vodaphone, Coca Cola, Microsoft, SABMiller, Thomson Reuters, Citi and Cisco have also come forward to contribute to the poverty alleviation through job creation in the global South. These companies also have some new business initiatives aimed towards helping the countries of the global South in meeting their respective MDGs. In fact, the objective of the 'Business Call to Action' is to build capacity of the poor people to access desired information flows, earn money and a sustainable livelihood and gain some professional competence.

Digital Opportunity Initiative

In another such initiative of business partnership, Accenture partnered with Markle Foundation and UNDP to design a framework known as *Digital Opportunity Initiative (DOI)*, that helps the global South in leveraging the benefits of information and communication technology (ICT) for better human development. This is, thus, supporting the countries in realising their MDGs, as ICT is being utilised by the countries to meet their development priorities in the sectors like health, primary education, infrastructure and governance.

Moreover, ICT has also been playing a significant role in better policy formulation for the development of small businesses, industries, trade and investments in the global South. Thus, the use of ICT has become complementary to the development, and thus, businesses have a larger role to partner with the UN System and enhance the scope of their business models.

Cisco Networking Academy Programme in LDCs

Cisco Networking Academy Programme is another such initiative in which the IT company Cisco Systems, Inc. partnered with UNDP in Africa, Arab, Asia and the Caribbean. This programme, launched in the year 2000, provides training to the students in least developed countries to bridge the digital divide and enhance their employability. For instance, in Asia and the Pacific region, Cisco Systems and UNDP have already flourished this partnership by establishing 18 academies in 9 countries and providing internet education to the students. This programme is striving to enhance the capacity of students in at least 40 LDCs of the world.

Ericsson in Haiti

To recall, a massive earthquake measuring 7.2 on Richter scale struck Haiti in early 2010, and brought untold miseries to the people living there. One of the devastating effects was on the telecom infrastructure of the country, which was actually becoming a hindrance to the relief operations being carried out by the UN.

At this juncture, Ericsson, a leading telecom company, partnered with the United Nations to establish a mobile network and also provided the required technical support to coordinate the relief operations successfully.

Ericsson Response deployed the Brage GSM system that provided coverage for approximately 200 km^2. It was connected to the centralised gateway of the UN telephony via satellite, which enabled better coordination through voice communication between UN staffs in Haiti and the UN offices worldwide. Importantly, since the year 2000, Ericsson Response has provided such systems and technical cooperation during humanitarian crisis in many countries including Afghanistan, Congo, India, Indonesia, and even the USA.

Allianz's Microinsurance Initiative

Allianz, a German insurance company, partnered with UNDP and Gesellschaft für Technische Zusammenarbeit (GTZ) to carry out market studies to analyse the demand for microinsurance products in India, Indonesia and Lao PDR.

This initiative asserted that microinsurance would help the poor, and also in financial inclusion of the consumers at the bottom of the pyramid. It will, thus, encourage private sector to contribute to addressing development challenges by their offerings.

Indian Solar Loan Programme

In order to develop clean and reliable sources of electric power, Canara Bank and Syndicate Bank agreed to give loans for photovoltaic solar home systems to the rural households in Karnataka. This was a first of its kind initiative and such loans were not available before. This initiative, which benefitted more than 19,000 households, was carried out by the two banks in partnership with the United Nations Environment Programme (UNEP).

Moreover, this initiative also helped the school children in devoting more time to their studies and enhancing the productivity of cottage workers in rural areas as well. This was an innovative UN led project, which also helped in creating new employment opportunities in factories that produced solar panels and related accessories.

Source: This case study is written by the author taking cues from the various evidences of such partnership as enlisted by UN Business on its website http://business.un.org/en.

14.1 INTRODUCTION

An *international organisation* is the one which has sovereign states as its member. Some of such organisations include the United Nations Organisation (UNO or simply UN), the World Bank, and the International Monetary Fund (IMF or simply the Fund). There are several other international organisations as well, but for the ease of understanding and in-depth discussion, only the above mentioned ones have been included in this chapter.

Some of the important characteristics of international organisations are that they

1. Operate globally to fulfill the developmental and economic needs of the members (as illustrated in the Opening Case of this chapter)
2. Have a defined agenda, objectives, policies and programme areas to operate in a multilateral setting, not necessarily confined to a region

3. Promote international understanding and cooperation on issues of global concerns
4. May be broad-based in scope (like the UN) or of specific concern like Asia-Africa Legal Consultative Organisation (AALCO) or Interpol (for international cooperation on police and policing)
5. Have an institutional mechanism to implement their programmes and projects worldwide
6. Work with a rigour across geographies and for humanity by providing equal opportunity to all
7. Are in themselves a well-defined institutional framework to support countries in fulfilling their development needs
8. Work independently and also in close cooperation among themselves and with the other economic congregations and international non-governmental organisations to fulfill its objectives
9. Support and actively participate in capacity building, human resource development, technical assistance to members and overall in ensuring sustainable livelihoods

The chapter starts the discussion on the United Nations and some of its specialised agencies like the United Nations Conference on Trade and Development (UNCTAD), United Nations Commission on International Trade Law (UNCITRAL), United Nations Development Programme (UNDP), World Food Programme (WFP) and International Labour Organisation (ILO). This is followed by the discussion on the Bretton Woods institutions (including the World Bank and IMF) and later on the World Trade Organisation (WTO) is discussed. This chapter also discusses some other intergovernmental organisations like G8 and G20.

14.2 THE UNITED NATIONS

The *United Nations (UN)* is an international organisation which was established on 24 October 1945. It was the result of the signing of the UN Charter on 26 June 1945 by 51 countries including India, which is also one of the founder members of the UN (see Box 14.1 for Preamble of the United Nations). In fact, it was established after the World War II, with the aim of promoting peace and international understanding (see Box 14.2 for more details).

UN has six official languages, namely, Arabic, Chinese, English, French, Russian and Spanish. It works across the globe on various areas including humanitarian assistance, peacebuilding, refugee protection, disaster relief, human rights, and a host of other developmental challenges facing mankind.

The UN replaced the League of Nations, which was similar, but a weak organisation established after the World War I as a result of the Treaty of Versailles in 1919. Every year 24 October is celebrated as the UN Day. India made a net contribution of US$ 16.97 million to the regular budget of UN for 2013, which stands at US$ 2.6 billion. Just for comparison, the contributions of China, Brazil and USA accounted for US$ 131.18 million, US$ 74.76 million and US$ 618.48 million, respectively.[1]

1. 'Assessment of Member States' contributions to the United Nations regular budget for the year 2013 and of new Member States' advances to the Working Capital Fund for the biennium 2010–2011 and contributions to the United Nations regular budget for 2011 and 2012', ST/ADM/SER.B/866, published by United Nations Secretariat, 24 December 2012. http://www.un.org/ga/search/view_doc.asp?symbol=ST/ADM/SER.B/866

Box 14.1 Preamble of the United Nations

We the Peoples of the United Nations Determined

- to save succeeding generations from the scourge of war, which twice in our lifetime has brought untold sorrow to mankind
- to reaffirm faith in fundamental human rights, in the dignity and worth of the human person, in the equal rights of men and women and of nations large and small, and
- to establish conditions under which justice and respect for the obligations arising from treaties and other sources of international law can be maintained, and
- to promote social progress and better standards of life in larger freedom,

And for These Ends

- to practice tolerance and live together in peace with one another as good neighbours, and
- to unite our strength to maintain international peace and security, and
- to ensure, by the acceptance of principles and the institution of methods, that armed force shall not be used, save in the common interest, and
- to employ international machinery for the promotion of the economic and social advancement of all peoples.

Have Resolved to Combine Our Efforts to Accomplish These Aims

Accordingly, our respective governments, through representatives assembled in the city of San Francisco, who have exhibited their full powers found to be in good and due form, have agreed to the present Charter of the United Nations and do hereby establish an international organisation to be known as the United Nations.

Source: www.un.org

Box 14.2 Purpose of the United Nations

The UN has the following four main purposes:

1. To keep peace throughout the world
2. To develop friendly relations among the nations
3. To help nations in working together to improve the lives of poor people, conquer hunger, disease and illiteracy, and encourage respect for each other's rights and freedoms
4. To be a centre for harmonising the actions of nations to achieve these goals

Source: www.un.org

Structure of the UN

UN has six main bodies, which includes the following:

1. ***General Assembly (also UN General Assembly or UNGA):*** UNGA comprises representatives from all its member states. The present UNGA membership (commonly referred to as *members of the UN*) stands at 193. UNGA is a key organ of the UN responsible for providing mandate to the UN to fulfill its various responsibilities and obligations. Within UNGA, there are various subsidiary organs like boards, commissions, committees and working groups, among others, that work on specific issues and submit their draft resolutions to UNGA for consideration.

2. ***Security Council (also UN Security Council or UNSC):*** UNSC is a key body responsible for maintaining international peace and security, a primary reason of the existence of the UN. It comprises 5 permanent members that include China, France, Russia, the United Kingdom, and the United States. Moreover, it also constitutes 10 non-permanent members, who are included for a period of 2 years on a rotating basis among the member states (excluding permanent members). In the contemporary scenario, there have been talks about reforming the UNSC and increasing the number of permanent members. India has also staked its claim for permanent membership and has gathered a lot of support from several countries.
3. ***Secretariat:*** The Secretariat is an integral body of the UN responsible for carrying out the day-to-day activities. Its work ranges from operational level decisions to a wide range of activities which may include those related to peacekeeping operations or even studying global economic trends.
4. ***Economic and Social Council (ECOSOC):*** As the name suggests, ECOSOC is responsible for coordinating the socio-economic and developmental work of the United Nations and its specialised agencies. It works towards helping the countries in achieving the MDGs (see Chapter 1 to know more about MDGs). It also provides policy guidance to enhance the impact of development cooperation like South-South Cooperation (see 'Trade and Development' section of Chapter 17 to know more about development cooperation). ECOSOC also has several subsidiary bodies, which can be categorised into Functional Commissions (like Statistical Commission), Regional Commissions (like Economic and Social Commission for Asia and the Pacific, i.e., UNESCAP), Standing Committees (like Committee on Non-Governmental Organisations), and Ad-hoc and Expert bodies.

   ECOSOC has 54 member countries, which are elected by UNGA for a term of 3 years. This election of members is done on a basis, which ensures a considerable geographical representation, that is, 14 countries from Africa, 11 from Asia, 6 from Eastern Europe, 10 from Latin America and the Caribbean and 13 from Western Europe and others. Presently, India is a member of ECOSOC and its term expires on 31 December 2014.
5. ***Trusteeship Council:*** After the World War II, there were 11 territories which were called *Trust Territories*. These Trust Territories gradually became independent states through a period of time. For instance, New Guinea, which was an Australian Trust Territory, united with another territory Papua to become independent as Papua New Guinea in 1975. Likewise, Somaliland, an Italian Trust Territory united with British Somaliland Protectorate in 1960 to become Somalia.[2] All these initiatives behind reorganisation, self-governance or independence of trust territories could be attributed to the Trusteeship Council, which was established in 1945 to provide international supervision to these Trust Territories. All Trust Territories attained self-government or independence by 1994, and thus, the mandate of this council was accomplished. Trusteeship Council, however, exists even today with the amended rules that will be applicable if such situations emerge in future.

2. See United Nations and Decolonisation. Available: http://www.un.org/en/decolonization/selfdet.shtml

6. ***International Court of Justice (ICJ):*** The International Court of Justice, headquartered at Hague in The Netherlands, is the main judicial body of the UN. It serves the purpose of dispute resolution between the member states. It is also mandated to give advice and opinion on issues of legal relevance to the UN and its specialised agencies. The ICJ has 15 judges elected by UNGA and the Security Council to hold office for a term of 9 years.

14.3 UNITED NATIONS CONFERENCE ON TRADE AND DEVELOPMENT (UNCTAD)

UNCTAD was established as a platform for deliberations on developmental issues and challenges facing the world. It is a principal organ of the UN. It also develops guidelines and frameworks for cooperation on all issues of development related to trade, finance, investment, development aid and technical assistance. UNCTAD works to maximise the trade, investment and development opportunities of developing countries and assist them in their efforts to integrate into the world economy on an equitable basis.

In fact, in the early decades of the post-1945 era, developing countries had significant concerns related to their global positioning in the world trading system. This led to a call for international attention to identify and address their challenges of trade and trade-led development. The first United Nations Conference on Trade and Development was, thus, organised in Geneva in 1964. However, since the issues were critical and not too small to be resolved within a few years or a decade, this conference was assigned a permanent secretariat. The institutionalisation of UNCTAD was a major step towards addressing the concerns of the developing world. UNCTAD meets every four years. The most recent conference was UNCTAD XIII, which was held in Doha, Qatar, in April 2012.

Since its inception, UNCTAD has gained prominence in contributing to research, related policy discourses and trade policy-making in the developing world. Some of its key initiatives and achievements include the following:[3]

1. Providing an intergovernmental platform for dialogue on development cooperation, especially North-South cooperation.
2. Developing the Generalised System of Preferences in the year 1968, seeking developed countries to grant better market access to exports from developing countries.
3. Facilitating several International Commodities Agreements, aimed at stabilising the prices of export products crucial for developing countries.
4. Developing a convention on a Code of Conduct for Liner Conferences that strengthened the ability of developing countries to maintain national merchant fleets.
5. Adoption of a Set of Multilaterally Agreed Equitable Principles and Rules for the Control of Restrictive Business Practices (This work later evolved into what is today known as *Trade and Competition Policies*).
6. Contributing to the definition of target of 0.7% of gross domestic product (GDP) to be given as official development aid by developed countries to the poorest countries, as adopted by the United Nations General Assembly in 1970.

3. UNCTAD, http://unctad.org/en/Pages/About%20UNCTAD/A-Brief-history-of-UNCTAD.aspx

7. It identified the least developed countries in 1971, which garnered attention of the international community. UNCTAD is also credited for organising the first LDC Conference in 1971.
8. It helped in bringing about a paradigm shift in economic discourses through its enriching practices of macroeconomic management.
9. It was instrumental in the Uruguay Round of negotiations and also contributed to the negotiations on General Agreement on Trade in Services (GATS).
10. It contributed to the promotion of South-South Cooperation and other forms of development cooperation for the benefits of the global South.
11. It was responsible for linking the global financial architecture to the development and stressed the need to make it more development-centric.
12. It provided technical assistance to the countries on a variety of issues including capacity building of trade negotiators, investment policy review, competition policy, debt management, and trade and environment.
13. UNCTAD has a well-defined structure, and its management and institutions are looked after by the Trade and Development Board, which meets in Geneva at regular intervals.

Work areas

Some of its key work areas/programmes include the following:

1. Africa, LDC and special programmes
2. Globalisation, interdependence and development (to contribute to global debates and discourses on globalisation for developing countries)
3. International trade and commodities (to build consensus, trade negotiations, strengthen capacity and promote global partnerships)
4. Investment and enterprise
5. Technology and trade logistics

UNCTAD secretariat is located in Geneva. In fact, one of its other major achievements has been the conceptualisation and implementation of the Generalised System of Preferences (GSP). It is well-argued by UNCTAD that developing countries need to promote their exports of manufacturing goods, and therefore, it is necessary that they should be given special tariff concessions. This has led to the formulation of GSP, wherein developed countries would allow the goods from developing countries to enter their territory either duty-free or at reduced rates. This has given a competitive edge and a better market access to such goods from developing countries.

UNCTAD XIII

The 13th session of UNCTAD (known as *UNCTAD XIII*) was held in Doha, Qatar in April 2012 (see Box 14.3). Its main theme was 'Development-centred globalisation: Towards inclusive and sustainable growth and development'. The conference successfully undertook all the three spheres of activities—general debate (in which ministers and heads of delegations made their statements), negotiations (in which diplomats engaged themselves to finalise an agreed outcome document), and the side events [which were organised by Civil Society Organisations (CSOs) and other organisations]. It had four sub-themes focusing on enabling economic environment; all forms of cooperation and partnership for trade and development including North-South, South-South and Triangular Cooperation; addressing persistent and emerging development challenges; and promoting investment, trade, entrepreneurship and related development policies.

Box 14.3 Major Outcome of Ministerial Meeting of UNCTAD in Doha, 2012 (UNCTAD XIII)

1. Adopted Doha Manar, 2012
2. Reiterated commitment to UNCTAD
3. Adhere the mandate of MDG as committed under UNMDGs
4. The Ministerial meeting recognised the economic significance of the revolutionary protests by arguing that global economic recovery has been slow after the 2008 economic crisis.
5. Development-centered globalisation was recognised as the factor for inclusive growth and development.

This conference affirmed the three pillars of UNCTAD's mandate of consensus building, policy-oriented analysis and technical cooperation. Amidst the evident North-South divide, the last day of UNCTAD XIII came out with two outcome documents—Doha Mandate (a 15-page, 64-paragraph document which gives guidelines for the organisation's activities for the next four years), and Doha Manar (an Arabic word meaning a strong light visible from a distance that serves to direct travellers, which is the closing declaration of UNCTAD XIII on behalf of 194 member states).

Whereas, The Doha Mandate calls for development strategies to be inclusive and be designed to meet human needs, and that the multilateral trading system must remain open, transparent, inclusive, non-discriminatory and rules-based, the Manar maintains that responsive policies that foster participatory and inclusive approaches to development in order to achieving prosperity for all is the need of the hour.[4]

UNCTAD XIV, 2016

From 17–22 July 2016, UNCTAD XIV was held in Nairobi, Kenya. The theme of the conference was 'From decisions to actions'. The conference ended with the adoption of the Nairobi 'Maafikiano', or the Nairobi consensus document. The title of the outcome was 'From decision to actions: Moving towards an inclusive and equitable global economic environment for trade and development'.[5] It was also agreed that UNCTAD would contribute to the implementation of the outcomes for boosting trade and development in the developing countries. It especially focused on the implementation of the 2030 Sustainable Development Goal (SDG) agenda for the LDCs.

14.4 UNITED NATIONS COMMISSION ON INTERNATIONAL TRADE LAW (UNCITRAL)

International trade law (as discussed in Chapter 13) is a significant factor affecting the global

4. Ahmed, Faisal (2012). "UNCTAD XIII and the Development-centred Globalisation", Diplomatist, May 2012.
5. See http://www.twn.my/title2/wto.info/2016/ti160723.htm

business environment. It has been evolutionary and has continued to influence multinationals and their international business decisions (see Box 14.4 for mandate of UNCITRAL).

Box 14.4 Mandate of United Nations Commission on International Trade Law

1. Coordinating the work of organisations active in this field and encouraging cooperation among them
2. Promoting wider participation in the existing international conventions and wider acceptance of the existing model and uniform laws
3. Preparing or promoting the adoption of new international conventions, model laws and uniform laws, and promoting the codification and wider acceptance of international trade terms, provisions, customs and practices in collaboration, where appropriate, with the organisations operating in this field
4. Promoting ways and means of ensuring a uniform interpretation and application of international conventions and uniform laws in the field of the law of international trade
5. Collecting and disseminating information on national legislation and modern legal developments, including case law, in the field of the law of international trade
6. Establishing and maintaining a close collaboration with the United Nations Conference on Trade and Development
7. Maintaining liaison with the other United Nations organs and specialised agencies concerned with the international trade
8. Taking any other action it may deem useful to fulfill its functions

Source: General Assembly Resolution 2205 (XXI), Section II, Paragraph 8, set forth in Annexure I.

Therefore, there was a need to harmonise the international trade law regulations so that each country follow some commonly established global norms on international trade. With this view, the UN General Assembly through one of its resolutions in December 1996 established UNCITRAL to promote the progressive harmonisation and unification of international trade law. UNCITRAL works through its annual session held alternately in Vienna and New York. Just like the ECOSOC membership composition, the membership of UNCITRAL is elected by UNGA and represents different geographical regions and more importantly, distinct legal traditions. Its membership includes 14 countries from Africa, 14 from Asia, 14 from Western Europe, 8 from Eastern Europe, and 10 from Latin America and the Caribbean.

UNCITRAL seeks to promote the participation of a large number of countries in the existing international conventions. Besides, it also promotes the adoption of new international conventions as well as works towards ensuring their uniform interpretation and wider acceptance of international trade terms and related provisions. Some of the conventions are as follows:

1. The Convention on the Limitation Period in the International Sale of Goods (1974)
2. The United Nations Convention on the Carriage of Goods by Sea (1978)
3. The United Nations Convention on Contracts for the International Sale of Goods (1980)
4. The United Nations Convention on International Bills of Exchange and International Promissory Notes (1988)
5. The United Nations Convention on the Liability of Operators of Transport Terminals in International Trade (1991)

6. The United Nations Convention on Independent Guarantees and Stand-by Letters of Credit (1995)
7. The United Nations Convention on the Assignment of Receivables in International Trade (2001)
8. The United Nations Convention on the Use of Electronic Communications in International Contracts (2005)
9. The United Nations Convention on Contracts for the International Carriage of Goods Wholly or Partly by Sea (2008)

14.5 UNITED NATIONS DEVELOPMENT PROGRAMME (UNDP)

UNDP is the largest development network in the world, operating in around 177 countries. It provides expert advice, capacity building, and grants to meet the local challenges and aims to develop local capacity. It was established in 1965 through the merger of the Expanded Programme of Technical Assistance (EPTA) and the United Nations Special Fund. An important feature of UNDP development assistance is that it works with the country systems and within the guidelines/provisions laid out by a country's national development policy.

Some of its key areas of work include the following:

1. ***Fulfillment of MDGs:*** UNDP promotes inclusive growth and sustainable development. Under its mandate, it also assists member countries in achieving MDGs and it works to improve living standard of the people across the globe. More than 6000 development projects are underway and being implemented in 117 countries worldwide.
2. ***Poverty alleviation:*** Poverty alleviation is one of the key targets under MDGs. In this context, poverty reduction is the core of the work undertaken by UNDP. UNDP provides nearly US$1 billion per year as an aid for poverty alleviation. It also assists member countries in enhancing employment opportunities that has a direct impact on poverty reduction.
3. ***Crisis prevention:*** Building peace and resilience in the areas affected from crisis and natural disaster is another core mandate of UNDP. It works to ensure immediate life-saving requirements in the areas, which are affected from civil crisis, natural disaster, etc. It works in more than 80 countries to strengthen the gains of development process in a post-crisis scenario. For instance, in Afghanistan, UNDP runs programme of US$53.79 million, aiming at reducing poverty and improving livelihoods during post-crisis period. Similarly, a programme to support police remunerations, police infrastructure, police capacity development of US$65.2 million is also underway.
4. ***Democratic governance:*** UNDP through its programme on democratic governance enhances linkages between the people and the democratic institutions. It fosters partnership between governmental institutions, civil society, and the people of a particular country. Through such partnership, its mandate is to strengthen accountability, effectiveness of democratic institutions and ensure participation of people. 27% of the total aid was planned for this focus area in 2013. Again, Afghanistan was the largest receiver of aid under this category amounting to US$880.02 million in 2013.

5. ***Women empowerment:*** Women empowerment is another goal of UNDP. It works for ensuring the voice of women reaching towards establishment of democratic institutions for their welfare as well. It advocates equality among genders and facilitates women to be self-motivated and economically as well as socially empowered through its programmes.
6. ***Sustainable development:*** Under this programme, UNDP aims at strengthening national capacity of member countries in managing environment and using natural resources in a sustainable manner. Around 16% of the total budget was devoted to such projects in 2013.

Some projects of UNDP in India

There are almost 39 projects undertaken by UNDP in India (see an example in Box 14.5). Out of the total budget of US$42.72 million, projects under poverty reduction and MDG achievement programmes accounts for 19%, whereas budget for democratic governance is allocated to be 43% of the total budget. Almost 38% of this is allocated to the projects under environment and

Box 14.5 Health Care Waste Management: A Case from India

King George Medical University (KGMU), Lucknow participated in the Global Health Care Waste Management project, an initiative to demonstrate and promote the best practices for reducing health and environmental risks and hazards generated by hospital wastes. This initiative was run in eight countries and implemented by the UNDP, with a support from World Health Organisation (WHO) and Health Care Without Harm. The project was funded by Global Environment Facility. In March 2013, the Bio-medical Waste Management Committee of the hospital received a Special Recognition Award from the global project team.

The 3000-bed hospital, with 500 resident doctors and more than 2000 outpatients every day, is spread across 1.5 km and constitutes 49 buildings. But owing to a low ratio of one nurse to every sixty patients and also because of the limited human and financial resources, it was a challenge for the hospital to implement sound bio-medical waste management practices.

Before the project began in 2010, an estimated 2,500 kg of waste generated at the hospital every day was disposed off in the open area. The health-related risk of such an approach has been summarised by Dr. Kirti Srivastava, Member Secretary, Bio-medical Waste Management Committee, KGMU, who said "Between 10–20% of waste generated by a hospital is infected waste but, if you do not segregate this infected waste from the general waste, similar to say household waste, then you will actually need to treat 100% of the waste generated in your hospital."

But now, the situation is completely transformed. Some of the major changes which have helped in the proper management of waste include the following:

1. Waste treatment infrastructure is in place now.
2. The hospital now uses specially designed waste segregation storage containers.
3. There are now special trolleys for collection and transportation of wastes.
4. The Bio-medical Waste Management Committee has appointed a doctor from each of forty nine departments to monitor the progress of each unit.
5. Moreover, the hospital staff now receives regular training in waste management practices.

Source: UNDP, India.

sustainable development programmes. In the health care area, UNDP is undertaking 'Improving Efficiency of Health Care Projects' in several states. Budget allocated for this programme was US$12.2 million in 2013 and the source of budget was Government of India. Similarly with multiple sources of budget, poverty reduction and livelihood promotion programmes are also underway. The programme aims at inclusion of poor in disadvantaged area, especially covering tribes, schedule castes and minorities.

14.6 WORLD FOOD PROGRAMME (WFP)

WFP is the largest humanitarian organisation in the world. Headquartered in Rome, it addresses the problems of hunger and malnutrition globally. This is, in fact, a multilateral programme on food aid established by the UN in 1963. Its ultimate goal, however, is to eliminate the need for food aid itself. The organisation is governed by the Executive Board, which broadly consists of representatives from 36 member states and meets four times every year.

The major function of the Executive Board is to

1. Help in evolving and coordinating the short-term and long-term food aid policies
2. Provide intergovernmental supervision and direction to the management of WFP
3. Review and approve programmes, projects and activities submitted to it
4. Approve budgets of programmes, projects and activities, and review the administration and execution of approved programmes, projects and activities

As per its mission statement, the core strategies of WFP are as follows:

1. To provide food aid to save life in refugee and emergency situation
2. To improve nutrition and quality of life
3. To build assets and promote self-reliance of the poor through labour intensive work programmes

To fulfill the broad objective, WFP has set its strategic plan in phased manner, which has five prominent objectives commensurate with its mission statement.[6]

1. Save lives and protect livelihoods in emergencies.
2. Prevent acute hunger and invest in disaster preparedness and mitigation measures.
3. Restore and rebuild lives and livelihoods in post-conflict, post-disaster or transition situations.
4. Reduce chronic hunger and under nutrition.
5. Strengthen the capacities of countries to reduce hunger through handover strategies and local purchase.

WFP in India

WFP has been engaging with the Government of India and works closely on hunger-related issues. With the objectives to ensure food security for vulnerable sections as well as to

6. World Food Programme.

combat malnutrition, WFP has administered Below Poverty Line (BPL) Scheme initiated by the Government of India. India and WFP have also signed a Country Programme Action Plan (CPAP) 2008–2012. The programme has envisaged the allocation of food grains to WFP for the utilisation of WFP projects and programmes. This programme also enables India to achieve targets set forth by MDGs.

The programme was envisaged to assist Eleventh Five Year Plan to ensure achieving its social goals during the period. WFP is now assisting India in capacity development for attaining its nutritional objectives under MDGs by 2015. The programme will continue its emphasis on the malnutrition of children. Main objectives of the programme is highlighted in Figure 14.1.

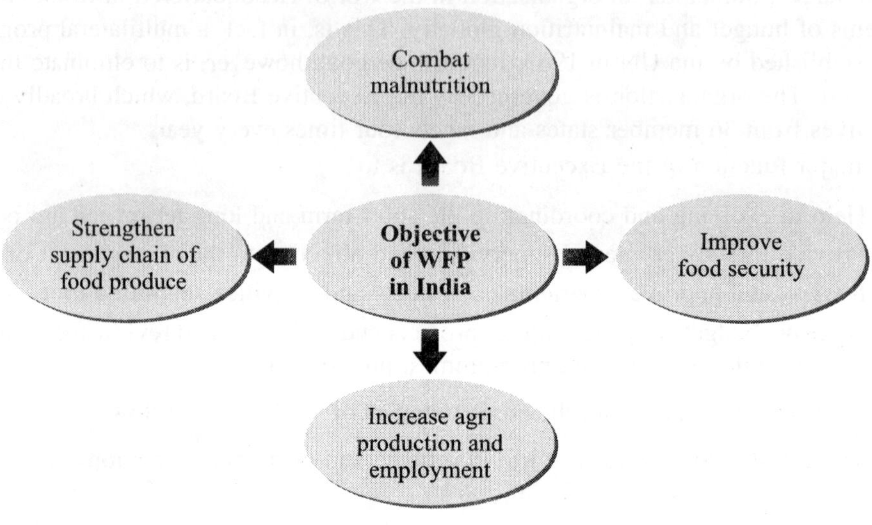

Figure 14.1 Objectives of World Food Programme.

14.7 INTERNATIONAL LABOUR ORGANISATION (ILO)

ILO was founded in 1919 after the World War I. The organisation was the part of Treaty of Versailles. After the World War II, the organisation became the integral part of the United Nations. It became a specialised agency of the United Nations in 1946. Almost all the member countries of the UN are the part of ILO. The programme under ILO continued during the post-war period. In 1969, ILO received Nobel Peace Prize for its contribution to attain justice for the workers. The prize also recognised its technical assistance to the developing nations. During pre-war period (World War II), the constitution of the organisation was amended in 1922, which came into force in 1934. After World War II, the instrument of amendment of 1945 came into force in 1946. ILO was created to promote social progress to overcome the economic and social backwardness through dialogue and cooperation. Its aim remains the same during the post-war era. ILO works for promoting social justice and pursues its basic idea of labour peace (see Figure 14.2). It has continuously been promoting the human and labour rights (see Figure 14.3).

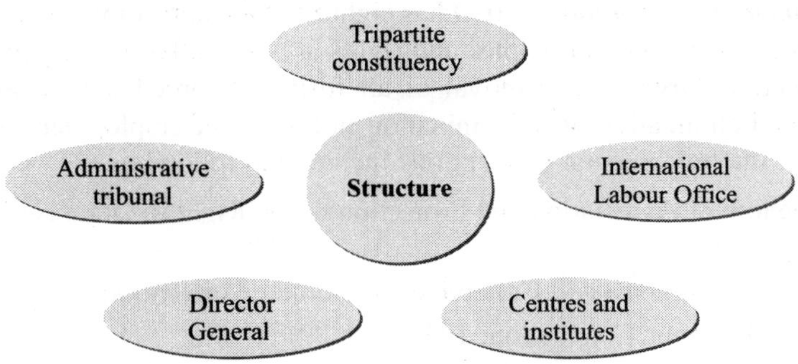

Figure 14.2 Structure of ILO.

ILO's four strategic objectives			
Promote fundamental principles, standard and rights	Create better opportunities for employment for both men and women	Enhance social protection of all	Strengthen tripartism and social dialogue

Figure 14.3 ILO's Strategic Objectives.

The constitution of ILO has set the structure and working principle of the organisation. The organisation has a tripartite structure unlike the other bodies of the United Nations. The agency has government, employer and workers as the representative. As per the constitution of ILO, there are four means of governance of the organisation, which broadly includes the following:

1. ***Tripartism:*** It implies equal representation of workers and employers, who enjoy equal status with that of the governments through democratic decision-making.
2. ***Ratification:*** The adopted conventions have to be ratified by the local authorities in the member countries.
3. ***Inspection:*** A system of inspection is there to ensure enforcement of the laws and regulations.
4. ***Global partnerships:*** It is to ensure social well-being through cooperation between the countries and the concerned stakeholders.

Governing body

Governing body is the executive body of ILO. It decides the agenda of the International Labour Conference. It consists of 28 governments, 14 employers and 14 workers (56 titular members) and 66 deputy members (comprising 28 governments, 19 employers and 19 workers). Ten of the titular government seats are permanently held by states of chief industrial importance (Brazil, China, France, Germany, India, Italy, Japan, the Russian Federation, the United Kingdom and the United States). The other government members are elected by the conference held in every three years.[7] The framework of ILO comprises the fundamental conventions, governance conventions and declarations.

7. ILO.

1. ***Fundamental conventions:*** ILO has eight fundamental conventions, which primarily cover the fundamental principles and rights at work, effective recognition of the right of collective bargaining, removal of all forms of forced labour, abolition of child labour and elimination of discrimination in respect of employment of occupation. As per ILO, the fundamental conventions include the following:
   (i) Freedom of Association and Protection of the Right to Organise Convention, 1948 (No. 87)
   (ii) Right to Organise and Collective Bargaining Convention, 1949 (No. 98)
   (iii) Forced Labour Convention, 1930 (No. 29)
   (iv) Abolition of Forced Labour Convention, 1957 (No. 105)
   (v) Minimum Age Convention, 1973 (No. 138)
   (vi) Worst Forms of Child Labour Convention, 1999 (No. 182)
   (vii) Equal Remuneration Convention, 1951 (No. 100)
   (viii) Discrimination (Employment and Occupation) Convention, 1958 (No. 111)
2. ***Governance conventions:*** Governance conventions are related to the subjects that monitor the international labour standards and set out the international labour standard systems. The member states are supposed to ratify governance conventions as a matter of priority. There are four governance conventions, which are listed below:
   (i) Labour Inspection Convention, 1947 (No. 81)
   (ii) Labour Inspection (Agriculture) Convention, 1969 (No. 129)
   (iii) Tripartite Consultation (International Labour Standards) Convention, 1976 (No. 144)
   (iv) Employment Policy Convention, 1964 (No. 122)
3. ***Declarations:*** Declarations are the resolutions of International Labour Conference. These are not subject to ratification, yet these are significant in terms of their applicability. The declarations were also set out by the governing body of ILO and used as guidelines for the application of international labour standards, particularly in multinational enterprises. The declarations are periodically updated by the ILO. Table 14.1 shows the declarations stated by International Labour Conference.

Table 14.1 Declarations Stated by International Labour Conference

Declarations stated by International Labour Conference	*Year*
Declaration on Social Justice for Fair Globalisation	2008
Declaration on Fundamental Principles and Rights at Work	1998
Declaration on Gender Equality	1981
Declaration concerning the Policy of “Apartheid” of the Republic of South Africa	1964
Declaration concerning the aims and purposes of the ILO (Declaration of Philadelphia)	1944

Source: ILO.

14.8 INTERNATIONAL MONETARY FUND (IMF)

International Monetary Fund (IMF) is a global organisation and a child of Bretton Woods Conference. It was formally created in 1945 and is one of the organisations of Bretton Woods Sisters. With a view to reconstruct the world economy after the World War II, a conference was held at Bretton Woods, New Hampshire during 1–22 July 1944. The conference was called *the United Nations Monetary and Financial Conference*. The conference was aimed at addressing the need for new world economic order through the creation of international institutions governing global economic policies. IMF was also conceived. IMF came into formal existence in December 1945 and the articles of agreement were initially signed by 29 member countries. It is headquartered in Washington D.C.

With the agenda to promote international monetary cooperation and exchange rate stability, IMF, with the cooperation of member states, provides opportunities for the balanced growth of trade (see Box 14.6). It also helps in creating favourable environment for the member states for their balance of payments difficulties. It has 188 member states.

Box 14.6 Purpose of IMF

The purpose of the IMF can be enlisted as follows:

1. To promote international monetary and provide machinery for consultation and collaboration on international monetary problems
2. To facilitate the expansion and balanced growth of international trade
3. To contribute to the promotion of employment, real income and the development of productive resources of the member countries
4. To promote exchange rate stability and maintain orderly exchange arrangements among member countries
5. To assist in the establishment of a multilateral system of payments in respect of current transactions to eliminate foreign exchange restrictions that hamper the world trade
6. To provide adequate safeguards to help member countries to correct maladjustments in their balance of payments
7. To shorten the duration and lessen the degree of disequilibrium in international balance of payments

Source: IMF.

The management of IMF is under the management team and its 17 departments. Through its organisational structure, it carries out country policies. The Managing Director is the Head of the staff and Chairman of the Executive Board. Four Deputy Managing Directors assist the Managing Director of IMF. The Executive Board is composed of 24 directors, who look after the day-to-day operations at IMF.

Finances of IMF

There are three main pools for resource allocation of IMF, which include quotas, Special Drawing Rights (SDRs) and gold. In addition, IMF also believes that it may experience shortage of funding, as in case of major financial crisis. In this case, IMF can supplement its main resources by borrowings. Therefore, borrowing arrangement is another important source of resource allocation. There are two important arrangements under this principle, *viz.* New Arrangements to Borrow and General Arrangements to Borrow. A number of member countries and institutions are ready to lend IMF in case of such requirements. For instance, in 2009, the Group of Twenty countries (G20) agreed to increase its lending to US$750 billion, which was intended to enable IMF to inject extra liquidity[8] into the world economy.

The three main pools for resource allocation of IMF are discussed below:

1. ***Quotas:*** Each member country has a quota, which is decided as per the size of the economy and the size of trade. The larger the economy, the larger is the quota. A country can pay 25% of its quota through Special Drawing Rights or in currencies such as US Dollar, euro, pound, or yen. The remaining 75% is paid through its own currency. This is the main resource of IMF.
2. ***Special Drawing Rights (SDRs):*** This is an international reserve asset. It was created in 1969. The basic purpose of the creation of IMF was to supplement or support the existing official reserve of the IMF. SDRs are not considered as the currency or as a claim on IMF, but these are the claims on the freely usable currencies of IMF for their respective SDRs (these currencies are US Dollar, euro, pound and yen). The value of SDRs in terms of US Dollar is posted daily at IMF website. The Executive Board reviews basket composition of countries in every five years.
3. ***Gold:*** A large amount of gold is maintained by IMF. The purpose of this is to maintain its financial soundness and also to meet the unexpected contingencies. IMF has about 2.8 thousand tonnes of gold and the total gold holding is valued as US$4.9 billion or SDR 3.2 billion. IMF has a restricted policy on the use of gold. However, IMF may sell gold or accept payment in terms of gold from the member countries (see Box 14.7 for more information).

Box 14.7 Sale of Gold by IMF

The Executive Board of IMF approved sale of 403.3 tonne gold, with an aim to stabilise the IMF finances for long-term implementation of the new income model. The IMF sold 212 tonne gold to the Reserve Bank of India, the Bank of Mauritius, and the Central Bank of Sri Lanka. Later, additional amount was sold to the Bangladesh Bank. In December 2010, the IMF concluded the gold sales programme with the total sales of 403.3 metric tonne of gold. The total proceeds amounted to about $15 billion (SDR 9.5 billion).

Source: IMF.

14.9 WORLD BANK

The *World Bank* or the *World Bank Group (WBG)* came into existence in December 1945 as a result of the Bretton Woods Conference and started functioning in June 1946. It is a group of five international organisations that gives loans to the poor and developing countries. These five organisations are listed as follows:

8. *Liquidity* implies the ability to convert or degree to convert an asset into cash. It is also known as *marketability.*

1. ***International Bank for Reconstruction and Development (IBRD):*** This is a major constituent of the World Bank Group and provides long-term loans (with sovereign guarantees) to the governments of middle-income and creditworthy low-income countries for reconstruction and development purposes. It provides capital investment and advisory services. For instance, there are several development projects running in India through World Bank funding like National Rural Livelihoods Project, 2011($1000 million), National Dairy Support Project, 2012 ($352 million), India: Secondary Education Project ($500 million), among others.[9] It was established in 1945 and has been raising its funds from the global financial markets.
2. ***International Development Association (IDA):*** The aim of IDA is to help the world's poorest countries. Established in September 1960, it provides long-term interest-free loans (called *credits*) and grants to the poorest countries. Usually, the repayment period of IDA loans is 35 to 40 years. Contrary to IBRD, IDA is funded largely by the contributions from rich member economies also while drawing from the IBRD income and repayment of IDA credits.
3. ***International Finance Corporation (IFC):*** IFC was established in 1956 and provides financing without sovereign guarantees, primarily to the private sector. Being the largest development institution globally that focuses on the private sector, IFC also contributes to the international financial markets and advises the businesses and governments on pertinent issues. IFC also works extensively in India and has been focusing on thrust areas like improving rural productivity, helping in strengthening supply chain linkages and facilitating access to finance in underserved rural and urban markets. It also promotes private investments in infrastructure and encourages the growth of microfinancing in rural areas.[10] For instance, through Lok Capital, a collective investment vehicle, it has supported the growth of microfinance institutions. IFC, along with its portfolio client, Usha Martin, has also provided capacity-building services for better income opportunities to more than 3,000 small farmers in Jharkhand. Moreover, it is also engaged in the Cairn-IFC Linkage Programme in Rajasthan, which focuses on local supplier development, child and maternal health care, and a dairy development project.[11]
4. ***Multilateral Investment Guarantee Agency (MIGA):*** The Multilateral Investment Guarantee Agency (MIGA), established in 1988, provides insurance against certain types of risk, including political risk, primarily to the private sector. The agency was created as a member of the World Bank Group to promote foreign direct investment into developing countries to support economic growth, reduce poverty, and improve people's lives. MIGA fulfills this mandate by offering political risk insurance (guarantees) to the investors and lenders.
5. ***International Centre for Settlement of Investment Disputes (ICSID):*** The International Centre for Settlement of Investment Disputes (ICSID), established in 1966, works with

9. See the web link: http://www.worldbank.org/en/country/india/projects/all
10. IFC in India: A Focus on Inclusive Growth, http://www.ifc.org/wps/wcm/connect/region__ext_content/regions/south+asia/news/ifc+in+india+a+focus+on+inclusive+growth
11. *Ibid.*

the governments to reduce investment risk. It also settles disputes between the states and the nationals of the other states. The Washington convention sets forth the mandate of ICSID and establishes the core functions of the organisation. The convention is a multilateral treaty.

Organisational structure of World Bank Group

Each of the parts of the World Bank Group works as per the guidelines and procedures established under the Articles of Agreement. In fact, Articles of Agreement of the WBG are the governing document of the group functioning. The Articles of Agreement are concluded for each of the constituents of WBG. These agreements were concluded at the Bretton Wood conference. Therefore, these organisations are also considered as the Bretton Wood sisters.

The IBRD Articles of Agreement were concluded in 1944, which came into effect in 1945. The first amendment was done in 1965. The executive directors of the bank have drawn the Articles of Agreement of IDA, which came into effect in 1960. The Articles of Agreement for IFC came into effect in 1956. The Washington Convention came into force in 1966.

14.10 WORLD TRADE ORGANISATION (WTO)

WTO was established on 1 January 1995 as a result of Uruguay Round of General Agreement on Tariffs and Trade (GATT). In the post-war era, a need was felt to regulate and institutionalise the frameworks of international trade and economic agreements. Owing to this, an international conference was organised in Geneva (Switzerland) in 1947 to consider a draft charter for the establishment of a proposed International Trade Organisation (ITO). However, there was no consensus on establishing such an organisation, but the conference gave shape to a formal agreement, known as *General Agreement on Tariffs and Trade (GATT)*.

GATT came into existence on 1 January 1948, signed by 23 contracting parties and was applicable to trade in goods. Several rounds of GATT negotiations were held successively in Geneva (1947), Annecy (1949), Torquay (1950), Geneva (1956), Dillon (1960), Kennedy (1964), Tokyo (1973) and finally, in Uruguay (1986). It was the result of Uruguay Round that lasted 7 years due to which the World Trade Organisation (WTO) came into existence. In fact, GATT faced some limitations like its failure to considerably liberalise trade in agricultural goods. Moreover, it also needed an organisational set-up to deal with the emerging issues in international trade at a time when many countries (including India) were going for structural economic reforms.

As of 29 July 2016, the WTO has 164 members. Some of the new members, who acceded to the WTO between 2012 and 2016 include: Afghanistan (29 July 2016), Liberia (14 July 2016), Kazakhstan (30 November 2015), Seychelles (26 April 2015), Yemen (26 June 2014), Lao People's Democratic Republic (2 February 2013), Tajikistan (2 March 2013), Vanuatu (24 August 2012), Russia (22 August 2012), Samoa (10 May 2012) and Montenegro (29 April 2012).

WTO provides a forum for trade negotiations and settling trade disputes as well as technical assistance to the developing countries, and also monitors the national trade policies of its member countries. Most importantly, the main objective of the WTO is to help trade flow smoothly, freely, fairly and predictably. It is headquartered in Geneva, Switzerland and headed by Roberto Carvalho de Azevedo, who assumed office in October 2013.

Some of the key activities of the WTO include the following:

1. Undertake multilateral negotiations for reducing and/or eliminating trade barriers (tariff and non-tariff barriers).
2. Make rules for international trade and try to develop consensus on crucial issues like subsidies and antidumping, among others.
3. Monitor the implementation of its agreed rules for trade in goods, trade in services, and trade-related intellectual property rights (TRIPS).
4. Review trade policies of its members including those related to regional or bilateral trade agreements signed by them.
5. Capacity building of government officials and official negotiators from developing country on international trade issues.
6. Disseminate trade-related data and conduct research on various facets of international trade and multilateral trading system. For instance, through its annual publication, The World Trade Report, WTO provides a deeper understanding about multilateralism and trade policy issues.
7. Settle disputes between the member countries on international trade issues.

Among the several points mentioned above, an important function of the WTO is building trade capacity. This is pertinent because there are several least developed countries (LDCs), where the contribution of trade to the country's economic development has been marginal. It provides technical assistance to build the capacity of government officials and negotiators in comprehending and implementing the WTO agreements. This also helps the countries in developing better negotiation practices, especially when entering into a trade agreement with their trading partners.

In fact, building trade capacity is not merely about capacity building of government officials. It includes human capacity, institutional capacity and infrastructure as well. It helps in providing assistance in various fields such as developing ports and road networks, enhancing support to the entrepreneurs and helping the small businesses in tapping the opportunities in the international markets.

The Aid for Trade (AfT) initiative is one such programme of the WTO, which builds trade capacity. AfT initiative was launched at the Hong Kong Ministerial in 2005 and later, in early 2006, a Task Force, established by WTO, was entrusted with the responsibility of executing it. It is an official development assistance (ODA) to help LDCs in building trade capacity and infrastructure to help in increasing their participation in the international trade. It is generally in the form of grants and concessional loans. It is usually provided in the form of technical assistance (as discussed earlier), infrastructure (as mentioned earlier), productive capacity (helps in diversifying the export portfolio to build comparative advantages), and adjustment assistance (supports the costs of tariff reductions etc. by LDCs).[12]

Structure of the WTO

The structure of the WTO consists of the following:

12. Aid-for-Trade Fact Sheet, WTO; http://www.wto.org/english/tratop_e/devel_e/a4t_e/a4t_factsheet_e.htm

1. ***Ministerial Conference:*** Ministerial Conference is the topmost decision-making body in the WTO. It constitutes the Trade/Commerce Ministers of the member countries and the conference meets at least once in every two years.
2. ***General Council:*** Next in the hierarchy is the General Council, which consists of member countries' ambassadors or permanent representatives or heads of delegation based in Geneva. Depending on the requirements, it meets several times in a year in Geneva. Trade Policy Review Mechanism and the Dispute Settlement System are the integral parts of the General Council.
3. ***Goods Council, Services Council and Intellectual Property (TRIPS) Council:*** The Goods Council, Services Council and Intellectual Property (TRIPS) Council come next in the hierarchy and report to the General Council.
4. ***Specialised Committees:*** There are several other specialised committees, working groups and working parties with specific interests and mandates like environment, regional integration, membership applications, etc., which are at the lower end of the hierarchy.

Decision-making

An important characteristic of the WTO is its decision-making process, which has always been by consensus of its entire membership, though a majority voting is also possible. This makes the WTO highly democratic in its governance. Each country has only one vote, and therefore, all members exercise equal powers.

Principles of WTO

The WTO and the multilateral trading system work on some underlying principles to ensure transparency, equity and opportunities for its member countries. The five core principles of WTO are listed below (see details in section 'WTO Principles' of Chapter 19):

1. Principle of non-discrimination (including most favoured nation and national treatment)
2. Principle of binding and enforceable commitments
3. Principle of transparency
4. Principle of single undertaking
5. Principle of safety valves

The main constituents of the WTO agreements include the following (see details in Chapter 19):

1. General Agreement on Tariffs and Trade (GATT)
2. General Agreement on Trade in Services (GATS)
3. Trade-related Intellectual Property Rights (TRIPS)
4. Trade-related Investment Measures (TRIMS)
5. Trade Policy Review Mechanism (TPRM)
6. Dispute Settlement Body (DSB)

Ministerial Conferences

The Ministerial Conference (also called *WTO Ministerial*) is the highest decision-making body in the WTO. As of now, ten Ministerial Conferences have been held, which are as follows:

1. First Ministerial Conference: Singapore, 9–13 December 1996
2. Second Ministerial Conference: Geneva, Switzerland, 18–20 May 1998
3. Third Ministerial Conference: Seattle, USA, 30 November 1999–3 December 1999
4. Fourth Ministerial Conference: Doha, Qatar, 9–13 November 2001
5. Fifth Ministerial Conference: Cancún, Mexico, 10–14 September 2003
6. Sixth Ministerial Conference: Hong Kong, 13–18 December 2005
7. Seventh Ministerial Conference: Geneva, Switzerland, 30 November 2009–2 December 2009
8. Eighth Ministerial Conference: Geneva, Switzerland, 15–17 December 2011
9. Ninth Ministerial Conference: Bali, Indonesia, 3–6 December 2013
10. Ninth Ministerial Conference: Nairobi, Kenya, 15–19 December 2015

World Customs Organisation

The World Customs Organisation (WCO) was established in the year 1952 as the Customs Co-operation Council (CCC). It is an independent inter-governmental organisation, which aims at enhancing the efficiency and effectiveness of customs administrations. Its mission statement is "The WCO provides leadership, guidance and support to customs administrations to secure and facilitate legitimate trade, realise revenues, protect society and build capacity".[13]

It represents 180 customs administrations across the globe that collectively process approximately 98% of the world trade. It is the voice of the international customs community.[14]

The strategic goals of WCO, whose Secretariat is based in Brussels, Belgium, are as follows:[15]

1. **Strategic goal 1: Economic competitiveness package**—To promote the security and facilitation of international trade, including simplification and harmonisation of customs procedures
2. **Strategic goal 2: Revenue package**—To promote fair, efficient, and effective revenue collection
3. **Strategic goal 3: Compliance and enforcement package**—To protect society, public health and safety
4. **Strategic goal 4: Organisational development package**—Strengthen capacity building
5. **Strategic goal 5:** Promote information exchange between all stakeholders
6. **Strategic goal 6:** Raise the performance and profile of customs
7. **Strategic goal 7:** Conduct research and analysis

13. http://www.wcoomd.org/en/about-us/what-is-the-wco/mission_statement.aspx
14. See WCO, Available: http://www.wcoomd.org/en/about-us/what-is-the-wco.aspx
15. See http://www.wcoomd.org/en/about-us/what-is-the-wco/goals.aspx

Closing Case: Dispute on China's Rare Earth Elements in WTO

China imposed export restrictions on various forms of rare earths elements (REE), tungsten and molybdenum. This raised an alarm, as the European Union (EU) believed that such restrictions would violate the WTO principles. Since China is a leading producer of these materials, its policies significantly affect the supply and prices of these materials, thereby creating competitive advantages for China's domestic manufacturing industry at the expense of manufactures abroad.

The EU, jointly with the United States and Japan, requested consultations with China on 13 March 2012. This came when the several efforts to resolve the issue over the past years were not successful. Consultations took place at the WTO in Geneva on 25 and 26 April 2012. The consultations did not lead to a solution, but confirmed the EU's claims. The EU, US and Japan then together requested the establishment of a WTO panel to look into this trade dispute.

Raw materials covered in this case are various forms of rare earth elements (REE), molybdenum and tungsten. REEs, in fact, serve as raw materials for the industries engaged in manufacturing car components, mobile phones, cameras, flat panel screens, computers, and various gadgets that work on renewable energy like wind turbines, hybrid vehicles, etc. There are 17 REEs, which include elements like Scandium (used in aerospace components) and Cerium (used as a catalyst in oil refineries), among others.

China has gradually tightened its export restrictions on REEs by raising export taxes and sharply reducing export quota. In June 2010, China implemented a considerable reduction of the quota by 32% for domestic exporters and 54% for foreign-invested exporters of rare earths. This led to a global decline in the supply of these materials as compared to the demand overseas. It is noteworthy that due to such supply shortages, industries in the EU either have to stop manufacturing of some products or relocate to China. In fact, such export restrictions create serious disadvantages for the foreign producers.

Source: This case is written by the authors based on inputs from the following source:

1. European Commission Press Release, 27 June 2012 vide MEMO/12/499, EUROPA., http://europa.eu/rapid/press-release_MEMO-12-499_en.htm

CASE QUESTIONS

1. Has China violated any WTO principle? If yes, identify which WTO principle(s) has/have been violated in this case.
2. Do you see the case going to the Appellate body?
3. What would be your suggestions for China to resolve this case?

REVIEW QUESTIONS

1. Outline some of the important characteristics of international organisations.
2. Describe the structure of the United Nations.
3. What is UNCTAD? Highlight some of its key initiatives and achievements.

4. What are the various work areas of UNCTAD?
5. What is UNCITRAL? What is its role?
6. Discuss the key work areas of UNDP.
7. What is World Food Programme? Examine its interventions in development sector in India.
8. What are the four key strategic objectives of ILO?
9. What is the role of IMF?
10. Outline the five organisations that make up the World Bank Group.
11. Highlight some of the key activities of the WTO.

SUGGESTED READINGS

Banerjee, A.M. and Sharma, M.R. (Eds.), 2007, *Reinventing the United Nations*, PHI Learning, Delhi.

Reinalda, B., 2013, *Handbook of International Organization*, Routledge.

Rittberger, Volker, 2002, *Global Governance and the United Nations System*, United Nations University Press, Tokyo, Japan.

VanGrasstek, Craig, 2013, *The History and Future of the World Trade Organization*, WTO, Geneva.

15

MODELS AND FRAMEWORKS OF INTERNATIONAL TRADE

Learning Outcomes

After reading this chapter, you will

- Understand the reasons why countries engage into international trade
- Comprehend the concept and significance of classical trade theories, including theory of absolute advantage, theory of comparative advantage and factor endowment theory
- Appreciate the application and utility of new trade models in the international trade

Opening Case: China—The World's Factory

China has been growing rapidly. The country has become a leading economy in the world. In fact, it is the largest exporter and the second largest importer of the world's merchandise. The growth story of China is not just a miracle, but also a result of economic efficiency. With the increasing efficiency in its production owing to cheap labour cost, China is now the world's largest manufacturing hub. It produces a range of products from textiles to electronics to heavy machinery. It is the largest exporter of textile products. Moreover, its products such as televisions, smart phones, steel pipes and other items such as toys are now moving all across the world. It accounts for more than a fifth of global manufacturing. In textiles, China's share in world's exports has increased to 33% as of 2012. But a major concern is its rising domestic demand for oil.

As per the United States Energy Information Administration (EIA), China's oil imports will reach 9.4 million barrels per day by 2025.[1] It is deemed that a major chunk of it would contain the Gulf Oil, thus establishing the possibilities of its closer geopolitical ties with the

1. 'China: Seeking Oil in Troubled Waters' by Antoaneta Bezlova, 8 September 2008, *IPS News*, http://www.ipsnews.net/2005/09/china-seeking-oil-in-troubled-waters/

Gulf region.[2] China's imports of oil and mining products have already surpassed that of the US. In case of non-fuel/mining products, China's imports fell by 8% in 2012 as compared to 2011.

China's oil industry contributes 45.3% of the Chinese GDP as of 2013 estimates, and the industrial production growth rate is 7.7%.[3] Its industrial output ranges in a variety of sectors including metals and mining, footwear, electronic appliances, coal, automobiles, machinery and Original Equipment Manufacturer (OEMs), textiles, fertilisers and consumer goods, among others.

Shanghai is the largest industrial and commercial city in China. Also, the Guangdong Province, with more than 500 companies, has emerged as a new hi-tech industrial region in the country. As per the National Bureau of Statistics (NBS), in March 2014, the country's industrial value added increased by 8.8% from an average growth of 8.6% in the January–February period, as reported by *Shanghai Daily* on 6 April 2014.[4]

However, a question related to the issue of sustainable of the Chinese growth story has been raised by many scholars. Though most people also argue that Chinese model is workable and sustainable because poverty is reducing there and domestic consumption is on the rise.

Source: This case is written by the authors based on inputs from the following sources:

1. Bloomberg, http://www.bloomberg.com/news/2014-02-11/china-s-exports-top-estimates.html
2. WTO Trade Profiles.
3. China's industrial production picks up in March, 16 April 2014, http://www.shanghaidaily.com/business/economy/Chinas-industrial-production-picks-up-in-March/shdaily.shtml

15.1 TRADE AND ITS RELEVANCE

Every country has its own culture and social fabric. In addition, countries also have different geographical and physical characteristics. Based on their geographical locations and features, countries are endowed with natural resources. They also strive to develop their competitiveness in other resources or economic activities like services, etc. Based on their characteristics, it is generally implied that an agri-based region would produce more of food grains, while labour-intensive products are produced by those countries which have low cost of labour. Similarly, some countries produce capital goods. In this era of multilateralism, some countries have also developed cost advantages in producing certain services. These differences in countries' production and consumption systems also create possibilities of trade.

A basic question is why trade happens. Some of the rudimentary reasons for the same could be because of the differences in endowment of natural resources across the geographies (or countries) or owing to the cost advantages and disadvantages in producing certain commodities. If a country is not able to produce certain commodity (to meet domestic demand) owing to the lack of resources or due to cost disadvantage, it would rather import it. For example, India and China have limited endowment and production of crude oil. This is a geographical limitation. Therefore, the two countries import crude oil from the Organisation of the Petroleum Exporting Countries (OPEC) like Saudi Arabia, Iran or Nigeria.

---

2. Faisal Ahmed (2014), 'Exploring an 'India-GCC-China' Geopolitical Equilibrium in the Emerging Global Order', A.K. Pasha (Ed.), *India's Political and Foreign Relations with the Gulf Region*, ISBN: 978-93-81505-69-4, Delhi, Wisdom Publications.
3. CIA World Fact Book.
4. China's industrial production picks up in March, 16 April 2014, http://www.shanghaidaily.com/business/economy/Chinas-industrial-production-picks-up-in-March/shdaily.shtml

To understand it better in case of India, we have to assess the demand for oil in India. Being a developing economy, India needs more industrial output to attain the desired economic growth. It is expected that the growth in India's oil consumption would be more than that of the China's oil consumption in future. In India, energy consumption is expected to grow at 39.5% in the long term as per the *BP Energy Outlook 2035*. It is also estimated that during 2005–2012, the total energy consumption by India grew at 53.63%. In the current scenario of production of oil in the country, India produced 38 million tonnes of crude oil in 2012–2013. On the other hand, in the same year, it consumed 219 million tonnes of crude oil. The data itself says that rest of the oil is sourced from other countries. As per the statistics of Ministry of Petroleum and Natural Gas, Government of India, the net crude oil import by India was 185 million tonnes in 2012–2013.

Most important reasons for trade, therefore, could be the differences in resource endowments of countries, transfer technological know-how and to earn from exports. The need for trade has been developed through various theoretical and empirical foundations by several economists. The classical economists advocated free market mechanism, and therefore, advocated free trade for profit optimisation. Later, the economists also came with other ideas such as welfare maximisation, trade as engine of economic growth, trade for reducing poverty and inequality, etc. The modern economic ideas also advocate trade for regional and international cooperation among the countries. There are several regional blocks which have free trade regime to strengthen the political economy of regionalism in global economic order (see Chapter 18).

Thus, following are the main reasons for international trade:

1. ***Varying factors of production:*** Countries are naturally endowed with various resources. Some countries are endowed with resources like crude oil, natural gas, minerals and other commodities such as iron ore. These countries have advantages in producing petroleum products and natural gas used for both households and industries. On the other hand, some countries are endowed with fertile land, which can be used to produce food grains and other agricultural produce such as vegetables, rice and other cereals. Similarly, geographical factors like climatic conditions also bring changes in the production patterns. For example, countries, like Brazil produce more sugarcane for ethanol, whereas India produces more sugarcane for sugar. In addition, countries, with cheap labour can produce labour-intensive products, for instances, Bangladesh has an advantage in producing textile products and ready-made garments (RMG), which have a competitive edge in the global market. Such differences in the factors of production across countries create new avenues for the international trade.
2. ***Gains from trade:*** To make gains from trade is another important reason for trade. Usually, the countries tend to specialise in the production of those products only which offer cost advantage to them. These products are also produced to meet the domestic requirements. However, due to cost-effective production and specialised production sector, several countries gain from trade. The gains from trade arise due to the differences in cost ratio, huge demand in global market, factor endowments and terms of trade, etc.
3. ***Welfare through trade:*** The production of specialised products has both comparative and cost advantages. This allows countries to attain more gains from trade with the countries, where demand for specialised products is rising. For instance, by exporting

oil, Iran and Saudi Arabia get more benefit, and on the other hand, India, by importing oil, also gets benefitted, as its industrialisation process gets energy resources. In this case, both the countries are able to generate revenue—one by exporting and the other through the impact of industrialisation—which can be used for the welfare of the people living in these countries.

4. ***Engine of economic growth:*** A noted economist, Nurks Ragner, coined the idea and correlated trade with the growth. Modern economists consider trade as the key factor for economic development. In fact, interlinkages among trade, growth, poverty reduction and finally, development are the recent developments in the discourses and practices, and many countries now plan for a trade-related process of economic development. WTO agreements have recognised these close links. It has special provisions for trade-related activities in the global market. For instance, LDCs get some benefits like duty-free quota-free (DFQF) market access (see provisions for LDCs in Chapter 20). In addition, the Bali Ministerial Conference of the WTO held at Bali, Indonesia in December 2013 also adopted a number of decisions for LDCs (see a Box in Chapter 20 on LDC Package of the Bali Round 2013).

With the above benefits from trade, models and frameworks have been developed to understand the need and reasons for trade between the countries. These models have also identified the gains from trade. In the subsequent section, we discuss the models of trade starting from the classical ideas to the modern international trade theories.

15.2 THEORY OF ABSOLUTE ADVANTAGE

The theory of absolute advantage was proposed by a noted economist, Adam Smith in 1776. In his book, 'An Inquiry into the Nature and Causes of the Wealth of Nations', Smith conceptualised the idea of this theory. The principle of absolute advantage, as discussed by Smith, refers to the specialisation in production and export of goods in which a country has absolute cost advantage.

In order to understand this theory, let us consider two countries A and B, and two commodities X and Y. Assume that both commodities X and Y are produced by both the countries A and B.

Now, see the following illustration given in Table 15.1:

Table 15.1 Units of Labour (Labour Hour) Required to Produce 1 Unit of Commodities

	Commodity X	*Commodity Y*
Country A	12	18
Country B	22	10

As per Table 15.1 given above,

1. Country A requires 12 units of labour (i.e., 12 labour hour) to produce 1 unit of X, and 18 units of labour to produce 1 unit of Y.
2. Country B requires 22 units of labour to produce 1 unit of X, and 10 units of labour to produce 1 unit of Y.

As evident from this illustration, the following conclusions may be derived:

1. Country A requires less labour cost to produce Commodity X vis-à-vis Commodity Y. Therefore, Country A has an absolute cost advantage in producing Commodity X.
2. Country B requires less labour cost to produce Commodity Y vis-à-vis Commodity X. Therefore, Country B has an absolute cost advantage in producing Commodity Y.

Based on this, the following may be implied:

1. Country A should specialise in producing and exporting Commodity X.
2. Country B should specialise in producing and exporting Commodity Y.

Thus, the theory of absolute advantage implies that a country should specialise in producing and exporting those commodities in which it has an absolute cost advantage.

The basic assumptions of this theory are as follows:

1. There are only two countries and two commodities.
2. There is a perfect competition.
3. There is a *laissez-faire* free trade system.
4. Labour is the only scarce factor of production.
5. The focus is on the division of labour.

Significance of the theory

1. This theory is based on the idea of division of labour. The division of labour leads to increase in the productivity of the labour force.
2. It advocates the idea of gains from trade. Departing from the mercantilist idea, Smith pointed out that in the international trade, both exports and imports are advantageous for the participating countries. International trade also decreases monopoly and increases competition.
3. Trade leads to the process of transfer of technological know-how between the participating countries.
4. Trade also improves the domestic performance of an economy. It can produce more of a specialised good.
5. This theory advocates the idea of free trade.

Criticism

1. The most significant criticism of absolute advantage theory is the absence of absolute advantage in many countries. In this scenario, trade for those countries seems to be a disadvantage. However, this is also a fact that trade happens between the countries which do not have absolute advantage.
2. The theory considers labour as the only factor of production. Proposition is based on the idea of division of labour. The roles of capital and technology in producing commodities have not been brought out into picture in the model.
3. Every country has its own geographical features. Thus, the size and population of a country vary. Countries' specialisation also varies.

4. The theory of absolute cost advantage neglects the cost of trade and other non-tariff barriers. It does not include transport cost. Even if a country has specialisation and absolute cost advantage, the cost of trade could be higher if the transportation cost is neglected. For example, landlocked countries face high transport cost.

15.3 THEORY OF COMPARATIVE ADVANTAGE

In order to understand this theory, first the concept of opportunity cost (i.e., the cost of an opportunity foregone) should be understood through the illustration given in Figure 15.1 and Table 15.2.

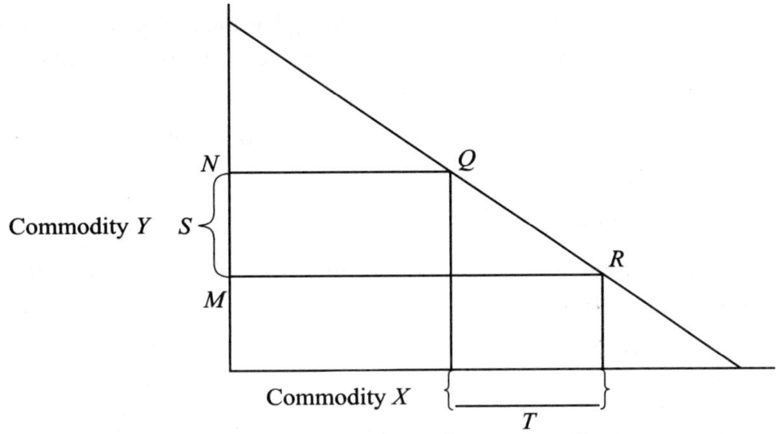

Figure 15.1 Understanding opportunity cost for Country A.

Say for example, a country (i.e., A) produces commodities X and Y. Let us assume that Country A wants to produce more of Commodity X. Also, let us consider that all the labour resources are attributed to produce both X and Y. To produce an extra unit of X, Country A needs to employ more labour in the area of production that produces X from the area of production that produces Y. In this process, if Country A may lose the production of Commodity Y, then this is called the *cost of an opportunity lost* or simply, the *opportunity cost*.

Consider that L is the labour available for Country A, which has employed it for producing both Commodities X and Y. As per Figure 15.1, if it increases the production of X by an amount represented by T, then it would shift the production of X to point R from point Q. It also leads to decrease in the production of commodity Y by an amount shown by S by shifting the production from point N to point M. This means that Country A has to sacrifice the production of Commodity Y on account of increase in production of Commodity X. This is called *opportunity cost* for producing Commodity X in terms of Commodity Y.

Let us understand about opportunity cost through another illustration given in Table 15.2.

Table 15.2 Units of Commodity Produced by 1 Unit of Labour

	Commodity X	*Commodity Y*
Country A	20	10
Country B	10	20

From Table 15.2, we can conclude the following:

1. With 1 unit of labour, Country A can produce 20 units of X and 10 units of Y.

   Therefore, 20X = 10Y

   or 2X = 1Y

   or for Country A, 1X = 1/2Y (15.1)

2. With 1 unit of labour, Country B can produce 10 units of X and 20 units of Y.

   Therefore, 10X = 20Y

   or for Country B, 1X = 2Y (15.2)

If we look at Eqs. (15.1) and (15.2), we understand that the opportunity cost for Country A is lower. Therefore, Country A has a comparative advantage in the production of Commodity X.

Now, let us know about the Commodity Y.

1. With 1 unit of labour, Country A can produce 20 units of X and 10 units of Y.

   Therefore, 10Y = 20X

   or for Country A, 1Y = 2X (15.3)

2. With 1 unit of labour, Country B can produce 10 units of X and 20 units of Y

   Therefore, 20Y = 10X

   or 2Y = 1X

   or for Country B, 1Y = 1/2X (15.4)

If we look at Eqs. (15.3) and (15.4), we understand that the opportunity cost for Country B is lower. Therefore, Country B has a comparative advantage in the production of Commodity X.

Thus, as per the theory of comparative advantage, a country should specialise in the production and export of those commodities in which it has a comparative advantage.

The theory was developed by David Ricardo. Ricardo carefully examined the existence of the idea of comparative advantage. In his book 'On the Principles of Political Economy and Taxation' published in 1817, he developed this theory.

The comparative advantage model says that trade occurs due to the differences in production technology and factors. It also explains that trade is beneficial for countries and establishes the conditions for trade in case of existence of comparative advantage of a country in producing certain commodities. The basis of trade between the countries is the presence of comparative advantage.

The comparative advantage expands the concept and applies it to formulate the trade model. It says that if a country has a comparative advantage in terms of lesser opportunity cost to produce another goods relative to other countries, then it can gain from trade by specialising the productions.

Assumptions of comparative advantage

1. The model clearly says that if there is a presence of comparative advantage in terms of factors of production in relation to other country, then there will be a case of specialisation of production, and thus, the trade will be advantageous.

2. The model is based on two countries and two commodities analysis.
3. There is a perfect competition and free trade, and the gains from trade can only be possible in the presence of these two essential characteristics of market.
4. Opportunity cost forms the critical criteria for trade.
5. There are no externalities and no transportation cost.

Criticism

1. The assumption of no externalities is flawed. The model does not take care of the externalities emerging out of the factors such as social cost, environmental cost, etc.
2. It does not account for the transport cost while providing the possibilities of advantage of trade.
3. The model does not incorporate the significant impact of international mobility of the factors of production.

15.4 FACTOR ENDOWMENT THEORY

The factor endowment theory has its genesis in the Ricardian model of comparative advantage. However, it has different aspects for determining the gains from trade. We know the fact that Ricardian model of comparative advantage considers only labour as the factor of production and technology as the factor influencing the labour productivity. The current model, however, assumes similar technology available to the countries for producing commodities. Thus, the current model does not consider variability in technology in different countries, although it assumes the other factors of production such as capital endowments as the factors which influence productivity and comparative advantage as well.

As per the Heckscher–Ohlin (HO) model, possibility of trade emerges when there is a difference between the prices of inputs of production. This creates difference in the cost of production between the countries. The model suggests that factor prices differ due to the availability of factors of production in a country. For example, if a country has abundant capital, then it is considered that the country has capital endowment. Similar is the case for labour. Thus, as per the model, countries which are rich in labour will have an advantage in exporting labour-intensive products, whereas the countries which are rich in capital will have an advantage in producing capital-intensive goods.

The factor endowment theory or HO theory, thus, implies that a country should specialise in producing and exporting those commodities in which it is endowed with the most of the factors of production for producing the commodity.

Assumptions of factor endowment (HO) theory

The basic assumptions of HO theory are as follows:

1. It assumes that there is no artificial barrier to trade and there is a free trade.
2. There is a perfect competition in the world market—both commodity and factor markets.

3. It is based on two countries, two factors and two products. There are two countries which produce two products using both capital and labour.
4. The two countries have varying factors of production.
5. Factors mobility between the countries is restricted.
6. The model considers identical production process and technologies across the countries.
7. Factor pricing in countries also varies.

Limitations of HO theory

1. Some of the assumptions of the model are unrealistic such as identical production technology in different countries.
2. Assumption of constant returns to scale is another limitation of HO theory.
3. It does not take into account the dynamic production function.
4. The model only considers the factor prices and ignores the demand of commodity.

15.5 LEONTIEF PARADOX

In context of HO theory, another key economist, Wassily Leontief in his research found that the capital-intensive country exported labour-intensive goods. This study was done in context of the United States' economy, which was capital-intensive, but exported labour-intensive goods. This finding was in contrast to the arguments build by HO theory that capital-intensive countries would export capital-intensive goods. This finding was a surprise for Leontief, and has gradually been brought into the trade literature as Leontief paradox.

15.6 NEW TRADE THEORY

The classical theories continue to be the most important frameworks of trade, as they explain the reasons for why trade happened between the countries. However, there are several new trade models, which are also serving as important tools for analysis. This collection of economic models pertaining to the analysis of international trade is together known as the *new trade theory*. These models were developed during the second half of 20th century.

The earlier trade theories highlighted that significant amount of trade can happen only between the countries, which have different factor endowments. However, the current trade indicators suggest that a significant trade can happen even between the similar economies. For instance, India and China are developing countries, yet the trade between these two countries reached about US$70 billion in 2012. Similarly, intraregional trade among ASEAN is over 25% of ASEAN's global trade. The regional export of EU (15) is more than 50% of its global export. This suggests that various other factors are also affecting trade between the countries apart from the factors identified by the classical economists.

The new trade theorists have also argued that a country may follow the approach of quantitative restrictions. This is not the environment, wherein free trade can happen. Thus, the quantitative restrictions are also taken into consideration while developing the new trade models. The new trade models are associated with the economists like Jagdish Bhagwati,

Paul Krugman, Avinash Dixit, Jan Timbergen and others. These economists not only laid down the ideas of increasing returns to scale and incorporated it in the trade models but also highlighted the existence of monopolistic competition and its relevance in the trade models. Some of the new trade models also consider geographical interactions. For instance, in early models of trade, geographical factors were neglected such as the presence of transport cost. Thus, the new economic geography has become an important tool to analyse the patterns of trade flow in the world. Krugman laid down the theoretical foundation of the new economic geography.[5]

In addition, economists also developed gravity model to show that the economies of similar characteristics and geographically located nearer to each other can engage in more mutual trade. Timbergen was the first economist who did the econometric studies for trade flows through the gravity model of trade. During 1960s and 70s, trade economists also used game theory to negotiate the terms of trade. Even today, game theory is being applied in various areas of trade. In this section, we discuss the main assumptions of new trade theories and present a critical analysis of the new trade models in general.

Features of the new trade theory

1. It takes into account various issues like revealed comparative advantages, intra-industry trade, etc.
2. Increasing returns to scale forms the basis of trade. Thus, economies of scale, at the firm level, tend to impact the trade between the countries.
3. Economic geography is a significant factor affecting the international trade, and thus, the new trade theory takes it into account.
4. The new trade theory also takes into account the importance of rising multinationals and their own production networks.

15.6.1 Revealed Comparative Advantage (RCA)

In 1965, Bela Balassa developed the revealed comparative advantage (RCA) index to understand the revealed comparative advantage of a country.[6] The basic idea behind the formulation of this index is to understand the specialisation of a country producing certain commodities.

RCA can be calculated using the following formula:

$$RCA_{ij} = (X_{ij}/X_{wj})/(X_i/X_w)$$

where, X_{ij} = i_{th} country's export of Commodity j

X_{wj} = World exports of Commodity j

X_i = Total exports of Country i

X_w = Total world exports

An RCA index value of more than one reveals that the country has a comparative advantage.

5. See Lecture Delivered by Paul Krugman, Prize Lecture, December 8, 2008, http://www.nobelprize.org/nobel_prizes/economic-sciences/laureates/2008/krugman_lecture.pdf
6. Balassa, B. (1965), *Trade Liberalisation and Revealed Comparative Advantage*, The Manchester School, 33, pp. 99–123.

15.6.2 Trade Complementarity Index (TCI)

The trade complementarity index (TCI) can show how well the structures of imports and exports of two countries match. It enables a comparison of export and import profiles of two countries by assessing how the export of one country complements the import of another country. TCI can be calculated using the following formula:

$$TCI = \left[1 - \left(\sum_i \left| \frac{\sum_w m_{iwd}}{\sum_w m_{wd}} - \frac{\sum_w m_{isw}}{\sum_w m_{sw}} \right| \right) \div 2 \right] \times 100$$

where, d = Importing country
s = Exporting country
w = Set of all countries in the world
i = Set of industries
x = Commodity export flow
X = Total export flow
m = Commodity import flow
M = Total import flow

The value of TCI ranges between 0% and 100%. A higher complementarity value indicates a better export/import match, while 0% indicates no complementarity at all.

15.6.3 Intra-Industry Trade (IIT) Model

Intra-industry trade (IIT) model is an important idea that the new trade theorists presented. It refers to the trade happening in the similar industries between the countries. In other words, it is the exchange of goods between two countries in a similar industry. For instance, if both India and Bangladesh produce cotton and garments, then it does not mean that they should not trade with each other in this sector. Of course, they can trade with each other in this sector (industry) by harnessing each others' value chains.

The intra-industry trade happens in commodities like automobiles, machinery, electronic goods, apparel, etc. As per the World Trade Report 2013 by the WTO, both industrialised and developing economies (where rapid industrialisation is in process) tend to engage more in the intra-industry trade.[7]

In the real world, though the products vary in their forms but they belong to the same industry. These products are not the perfect substitutes of each other, but compete with each other in the world market. Thus, creating a variety in the products of the same industry leads to the development of intra-industry trade between the countries. For example, Germany exports automobiles to the United States and also imports automobiles from the United States.

To analyse this pattern through intra-industry trade model, economists have also developed indices. Initially, Joseph Micheal Finger and later, Paul Krugman highlighted the occurrence of

7. See World Trade Report, 2013.

intra-industry trade, though Krugman did it more comprehensively.[8] A measure of IIT index was also proposed by Gurbel and Lloyd.

The IIT index is based on the premise that when the factor endowments and consumer preferences are identical between the two countries, then the economies of scale could provide an incentive for bilateral trade between them.

It can be calculated by using the following formula:

$$IIT_{jk} = 1 - [\text{sum}_i\ |X_{ijk} - M_{ijk}|/(X_{ijk} + M_{ijk})]$$

where, X_{ijk} = Exports of products from Industry i in Country j to Country k
M_{ijk} = Imports of products from Industry i in Country j from Country k

The value of IIT index ranges between 0 and 1; 1 indicates the perfect level of trade between the firms in the same industry and 0 represents no intra-industry trade. Higher the index towards 1, higher is the incidence of intra-industry trade.

15.6.4 Gravity Model of Trade

The gravity model of trade was first used by Jan Tinbergen in 1962. In order to explain the global trade flows, and to ascertain the export potential of countries, this model is widely used. It is actually based on the Newton's law of gravitation. Mathematically, the gravity model of trade can be expressed in the following form:

$$F_{ij} = G \times \frac{M_i \times M_j}{D_{ij}}$$

where, F_{ij} = Trade flow from Country i to Country j
M = Economic mass of each country (GDP or population is considered)
D = Geographical distance between the two countries
G = Proportionality constant

Using logarithm, it can be converted into a linear form for the purpose of econometric analysis, which can be expressed as follows:

$$\log (T_{ij}) = \alpha + \beta_1 \log (GDP_i) + \beta_2 \log (GDP_j) + \beta_3 \log (Distance) + \varepsilon$$

where, T_{ij} = Bilateral trade between Country i and Country j
GDP_i = Economic mass (gross domestic product) of Country i
GDP_j = Economic mass (gross domestic product) of Country j
$Distance$ = Geographical distance between the two countries i and j
β_1, β_2 and β_3 = Coefficients to be estimated
ε = Error term

To find the trade or export potential, the gravity model can be augmented by using several other variables, an instance of which is given as follows:

8. Krugman, P. (1979), 'Increasing Returns, Monopolistic Competition, and International Trade,' *Journal of International Economics,* 9, pp. 469–479.

$$\log(E_{ij}) = \alpha + \beta_1 \log(GDP) + \beta_2 \log(Distance) + \beta_3 (Contiguity) + \beta_4 (Common\ language) + \beta_5 (Common\ coloniser) + \varepsilon$$

where, E_{ij} = Exports from Country i to its trading partner (country j)

GDP = GDP of Country j

Distance = Distance between the two countries

Contiguity = Dummy variable to identify a pair of countries that are contiguous or share a border (we can assign a value of 1 if the other country is contiguous, else 0)

Common language = Dummy variable which includes both ethnic and official language (If two countries share a common ethnic or official language, we can assign 1, otherwise 0)

Common coloniser = Dummy variable (if the two countries have been colony of the same coloniser before 1945, we assign 1, otherwise 0)

β_1, β_2, β_3, β_4 and β_5 = Coefficients to be estimated

ε = Error term

15.7 EVOLVING WORLD TRADE

In 2014, as per the WTO, the world merchandise export has seen a slowdown and registered growth of 2.5% over 2013. World merchandise exports recorded annual growth of 3% in 2013 over 2012. World trade remained sluggish during the years. As per WTO's World Trade Report 2014, the slowdown in world trade in recent years was caused by the European economic slowdown, debt crisis and geopolitical tensions, which further aggravated in 2014. The growth in world trade during 2012–2013 was considered to be the lowest growth in world merchandise trade from the average growth rate of 5.3% during the last 20 years.[9] In value terms, world merchandise trade growth averaged just 1% per year from 2012 to 2014.

As per IMF's World Economic Outlook 2016, amid increasing financial turbulence, global recovery has been weakening. Economic activities in advance economies are curtailed and emerging economies like China are experiencing rebalancing in its economic progress. Economic slowdown in China has spillover effects on world trade, as China is trade partner of more than 100 countries.

The global export and import data suggests that the growth in the North American region has started to revive. Particularly in Mexico in the North America, trade has persistently grown higher than what it was in the previous years. The regions where world merchandise export and import have seen a little or negative growth are Europe, Canada, South and Central America, and the Commonwealth Independent States (CIS) region. Table 15.3 shows the growth in merchandise trade over the years.

As per the statistics of the WTO, world's leading exporters are China, the United States, Germany, Japan and The Netherlands, whereas the United States, China, Germany, Japan and the UK are the leading importers. At present, China's overall share in the world's exports is

9. World Trade Report 2015, WTO.

12.3%, whereas its share in the world's imports is 10.3%. The United States is the second largest exporter in the world with 8.5% share in world's exports, and the largest importer in the world with 12.6% share (see Table 15.4).

Table 15.3 Growth in the Volume of World Merchandise Trade by Select Region and Economy, 2010–2014

Exports			*Region*	*Imports*		
2010–14	*2013*	*2014*		*2010–14*	*2013*	*2014*
3.5	**3.0**	**2.5**	**World**	**3.0**	**2.0**	**2.5**
4.5	2.5	4.0	North America	3.5	1.0	4.5
4.0	2.0	5.5	Canada	2.5	1.5	2.0
6.0	4.5	7.0	Mexico	6.0	3.0	7.0
4.5	2.5	3.5	United States	3.0	1.0	4.5
2.0	2.0	–1.5	South and Central America	3.5	3.5	–2.5
2.5	2.5	1.5	Europe	1.0	0.0	2.5
2.5	2.0	2.0	European Union (28)	1.0	–0.5	3.0
–1.5	–5.0	1.5	Norway	1.5	1.5	1.0
4.5	16.0	–6.0	Switzerland	–2.5	2.0	–13.0
1.0	1.0	0.0	Commonwealth of Independent States (CIS)	2.5	–1.0	–10.0
4.5	5.0	4.5	Asia	4.5	5.0	3.5
3.5	6.0	6.0	Australia	2.5	–2.5	2.0
7.5	7.5	7.0	China	6.5	10.0	4.0
6.0	8.5	3.0	India	4.5	–0.5	3.0
–1.0	–2.0	0.5	Japan	3.0	0.5	2.5
3.5	3.0	4.0	Six East Asian traders*	3.0	3.5	3.0

*Hong Kong, China; Malaysia; Republic of Korea; Singapore; Separate Customs Territory of Taiwan, Penghu, Kinmen and Matsu (Chinese Taipei) and Thailand.

Source: International Trade Statistics, WTO.

Table 15.4 Leading Exporters and Importers in World Merchandise Trade, 2014 (Billion Dollars and Percentage)

Rank	*Exporters*	*Value*	*Share in World's Export*	*Rank*	*Importers*	*Value*	*Share in World's Export*
1	China	2,342	12.3	1	United States	2,413	12.6
2	United States	1,621	8.5	2	China	1,959	10.3
3	Germany	1,508	7.9	3	Germany	1,216	6.4
4	Japan	684	3.6	4	Japan	822	4.3
5	The Netherlands	672	3.5	5	United Kingdom	684	3.6
6	France	583	3.1	6	France	678	3.5
7	Korea, Republic of	573	3.0	7	Hong Kong, China	601	3.1

Rank	Exporters	Value	Share in World's Export	Rank	Importers	Value	Share in World's Export
8	Italy	529	2.8	8	The Netherlands	588	3.1
9	Hong Kong, China	524	2.8	9	Korea, Republic of	526	2.8
10	United Kingdom	506	2.7	10	Canada	475	2.5
11	Russian Federation	498	2.6	11	Italy	472	2.5
12	Canada	475	2.5	12	India	463	2.4
13	Belgium	471	2.5	13	Belgium	452	2.4
14	Singapore	410	2.2	14	Mexico	412	2.2
15	Mexico	398	2.1	15	Singapore	366	1.9
16	United Arab Emirates	360	1.9	16	Spain	358	1.9
17	Saudi Arabia, Kingdom of	354	1.9	17	Russian Federation	308	1.6
18	Spain	325	1.7	18	Switzerland	276	1.4
19	India	322	1.7	19	Chinese Taipei	274	1.4
20	Chinese Taipei	314	1.7	20	United Arab Emirates	262	1.4

Source: International Trade Statistics, WTO.

The trade in services has also evolved over the years. Some of the services which have benefitted from liberal trade practices across the globe include transportation, banking and financial services, information and communication technology, telecommunication and education. Importantly, services trade have not been affected by the slowdown, and have not been so volatile. Table 15.5 gives a list of leading commercial services trading countries.

Table 15.5 Leading Exporters and Importers in World Trade in Commercial Services, 2012 (Billion Dollars and Percentage)

Rank	Exporters	Value	Share in World's Export	Rank	Importers	Value	Share in World's Export
1	China	2,342	12.3	1	United States	2,413	12.6
2	United States	1,621	8.5	2	China	1,959	10.3
3	Germany	1,508	7.9	3	Germany	1,216	6.4
4	Japan	684	3.6	4	Japan	822	4.3
5	The Netherlands	672	3.5	5	United Kingdom	684	3.6
6	France	583	3.1	6	France	678	3.5
7	Korea, Republic of	573	3.0	7	Hong Kong, China	601	3.1
8	Italy	529	2.8	8	The Netherlands	588	3.1
9	Hong Kong, China	524	2.8	9	Korea, Republic of	526	2.8
10	United Kingdom	506	2.7	10	Canada	475	2.5

Rank	Exporters	Value	Share in World's Export	Rank	Importers	Value	Share in World's Export
11	Russian Federation	498	2.6	11	Italy	472	2.5
12	Canada	475	2.5	12	India	463	2.4
13	Belgium	471	2.5	13	Belgium	452	2.4
14	Singapore	410	2.2	14	Mexico	412	2.2
15	Mexico	398	2.1	15	Singapore	366	1.9
16	United Arab Emirates	360	1.9	16	Spain	358	1.9
17	Saudi Arabia, Kingdom of	354	1.9	17	Russian Federation	308	1.6
18	Spain	325	1.7	18	Switzerland	276	1.4
19	India	322	1.7	19	Chinese Taipei	274	1.4
20	Chinese Taipei	314	1.7	20	United Arab Emirates	262	1.4

Source: International Trade Statistics, WTO.

The United States is the leading exporter and importer of commercial services. India ranks at 19th place as an exporter and 12th as an importer of commercial services in the world.

Closing Case: Global Value Chains

The rise in international production, trade and investments across the globe is creating opportunities for an organised interaction of global production and distribution networks. These networks are now increasingly organised through global value chains. Various forces are working together.

As a part of the global production and distribution networks, global value chain has been contributing towards the global trade and development. In fact, globalisation of trade relations between companies compels them for innovations in their operations internationally. These innovations decrease the cost of trade and strengthen the global integration process.

In the global value chains, there is an evident fragmentation of the economic activities. Most of the global manufacturing imports are now happening in the intermediate goods. A summary of the growing process of world's production and trade networks suggests that the world's manufacturing exports are rising gradually.

Considering the growth in world's production and the overall GDP, the total exports in the world slowed down to 2.5% as against 5.5% in 2011 and 14.0% in 2010. The world's export in manufacturing items has reduced to 7.5% in 2011 from 18% in 2010. It further decreased to 2.5% in 2012. This is basically caused by the decrease in the production of manufacturing item in the world from 9.0% in 2010 to 2.0% in 2012 (Table 1). The decrease in the rest of the sectors is also evident in Table 1. This has resulted in decrease in GDP. The growth rate of world economy reduced to 2.0% in 2012 from 4.0% in 2010. Also see the figure given in Exhibit 1 for more information about growth of world exports, production and GDP.

Table 1 Growth in the Volume of World Merchandise Exports and Production, 2005–2012

	2005–2012	*2010*	*2011*	*2012*
World merchandise exports	3.5	14.0	5.5	2.5
Agricultural products	4.0	7.5	6.0	2.0
Fuels and mining products	2.0	5.5	2.5	2.5
Manufactures	4.0	18.0	7.0	2.5
World merchandise production	2.0	6.5	2.5	2.0
Agriculture	2.0	0.0	2.0	1.5
Mining	1.0	2.0	1.5	3.0
Manufacturing	2.5	9.0	3.0	2.0
World GDP	2.0	4.0	2.5	2.0

Source: International Trade Statistics, WTO.

It is, thus, imperative that the global value chains be embedded in the industrial development policies of the country. A strengthening global value chain would benefit the multilateral rule-making system as well.

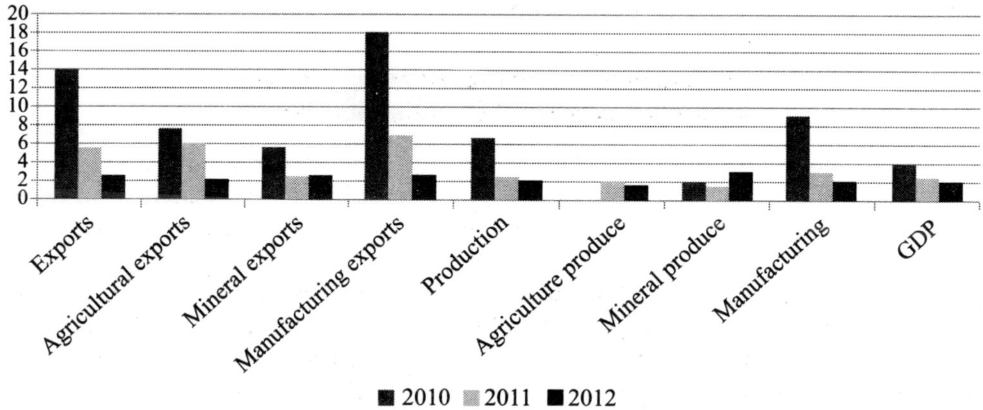

Exhibit 1 Growth in world exports, production and GDP.

Source: International Trade Statistics, WTO.

Source: This case is written by the authors based on inputs from the following sources:

1. OECD.
2. WTO.
3. UNCTAD, http://unctad.org/en/PublicationChapters/wir2013ch4_en.pdf

CASE QUESTIONS

1. What is global value chain?
2. How is the global value chain different from the regional value chains?

REVIEW QUESTIONS

1. What are the main reasons for countries to engage in the international trade?
2. Describe the theory of absolute advantage.
3. What is opportunity cost?
4. Explain the theory of comparative advantage.
5. What is factor endowment theory?
6. What do you understand by Leontief paradox?
7. What are the limitations of the classical models?
8. What is revealed comparative advantage (RCA) index?
9. What is the gravity model of trade?
10. Discuss the evolving trend in world trade.

SUGGESTED READINGS

Bhagwati, Jagdish N. (Ed.), 1987, *International Trade: Selected Readings*, 2nd ed., MIT Press, Cambridge, MA, UK.

Buckley, Peter J. and Casson, Mark C., 1976, *The Future of the Multinational Enterprise*, Macmillan, London.

Krugman, Paul, and Obstfeld, Maurice, 2008, *International Economics: Theory and Policy*, Addison-Wesley, Boston, MA, *A Practical Guide to Trade Policy Analysis*, 2012, WTO, Geneva.

Mattoo, Aaditya, Stern, Robert M., and Zanini, Gianni, 2008, *Handbook on International Trade in Services*, The World Bank, Oxford University Press, Washington DC.

World Investment Report, 2014, UNCTAD, Geneva.

16

INTERNATIONALISATION OF FIRMS

Learning Outcomes

After reading this chapter, you will

- Understand the reasons why firms internationalise
- Comprehend the various modes of entry into a foreign market
- Appreciate the importance of national competitive advantage

Opening Case: Domestic Airlines Industry—Moving beyond Indian Airspace!

India's domestic private sector carriers have started looking beyond the Indian airspace. They are now set to increase their market share in the international flights. The support from Ministry of Civil Aviation, which intends to provide approvals for Indian domestic private carriers for their overseas operation, is encouraging this scenario. In this connection, domestic airlines, such as IndiGo and SpiceJet had filed their applications for starting overseas operations. This shows the fact that Indian domestic airlines are keenly interested in choosing a new market. This move is specially directed towards the destinations like Dubai (an emirate of the UAE), Singapore, etc., where they are already operating their flights.

Previously, Indian domestic airlines were only allowed to operate when the national airlines refused to operate on a certain route. This is known as *right of first refusal*. This right was ended by the government, which mainly benefitted Air India. This opened new avenues for privately maintained carriers. For example, IndiGo has got approval from Ministry of Civil Aviation to operate in 63 new international routes every week. However, a large part of the flights is destined to Dubai. Similarly, SpiceJet has also got 49 new routes to operate in the Gulf region, including Dubai and Riyadh. On the other hand, Jet Airways got 56 new flights every week as to operate in the new routes, out of which 14 are destined to Kuwait. This decision from the government came with a view to reduce the dependency of India's overseas operations on Air India.

Also, the Indian civil aviation industry is thriving and experiencing higher growth. As per the statistics of Airports Authority of India (AAI), the international passenger traffic in India has increased by 14% in February 2014. This is also believed that the largest contributors of this growth are the passengers travelling to the Gulf countries, such as the UAE.

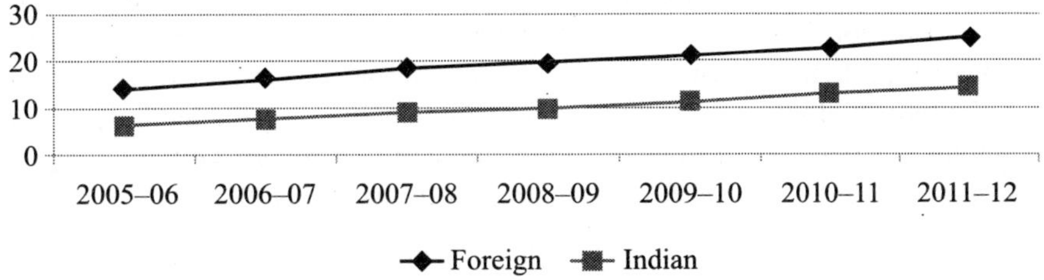

Exhibit 1 Trend of international passenger by Indian and foreign airlines in India (million).
Source: Directorate General of Civil Aviation (DGCA), Government of India.

The international aircraft movements have shown an increase of 1.5% during 2012–2013 over 2011–2012. The increase in international aircraft movements is attributed to the increase in frequencies of the existing international airlines and introduction of services by the new airlines, *viz.*, four airlines at Delhi airport (All Nippon Airways, Kalitta Airways, Kenya Airways and Mihin Lanka Airlines), three airlines at Chennai airport (Air Austral, IndiGo Airlines and Maldivian Airlines), three airlines at Ahmedabad airport (Etihad Airways, SpiceJet and Thai Airways International), and three airlines at Cochin airport (IndiGo Airlines, SpiceJet and Tiger Airways).

The international passenger traffic has registered a growth of 5.5% at all airports taken together. International passenger traffic around the world has continued to grow. The overall air traffic demand is increasing globally. As per the International Air Transport Association (IATA), the international passenger demand grew by 5.4% in 2013 compared to 2012, with all the regions reporting a steady growth. The capacity rose to 4.9%, boosting the load factor to 79.3%, which was up by 0.4% points over 2012. The growth is seen in the region of Asia and the Pacific. The region's traffic rose to 5.3% in 2013, the highest increase among the three major regions and slightly above the annual growth of 5.2% in 2012.

Similarly, Middle East carriers recorded the strongest increase in passenger traffic in 2013, which was a rise of 12.1% compared to 2012. However, the growth was not as much as was recorded in 2012, i.e., 15.4% from the year 2011. Carriers in the region have benefitted from the continued strength of the regional economies, particularly Saudi Arabia and the UAE, and from the solid growth in business-related premium travel, particularly to the developing markets such as Africa.

This provides an opportunity for Indian domestic airlines to grab the increasing trend of passenger travel demand across these regions.

Source: This case is written by the authors based on inputs from the following sources:

1. *The Economic Times*, http://articles.economictimes.indiatimes.com/2012-07-31/news/32961889_1_gulf-carriers-air-india-express-overseas-flights
2. Airports Authority of India, http://www.aai.aero/traffic_news/AnnualReviewTraffic2012-13.pdf
3. IATA, http://www.iata.org/pressroom/pr/Pages/2014-02-06-01.aspx

16.1 WHY COMPANIES CROSS BORDERS?

Internationalisation of firms occurs when a firm enters into a foreign market. The new era of economic liberalisation has resulted in an increase in the cross-border operations of firms. Globalisation has strengthened the incidences of internationalisation and is also strengthened by it. *Internationalisation* is defined as the process through which a firm tends to operate beyond its national boundary. There are various purposes for which firms go global.

Some of the important reasons for internationalisation are as follows:

1. ***Increasing revenues:*** One of the reasons why firms internationalise is their urge to expand to different markets and enter into profitable ventures. This helps in reducing cost by sourcing cheaper raw materials from different countries and increasing their revenues. This is a primary motive for most of the companies.
2. ***Market diversification:*** After having catered to a home market and realising the potential of its offerings in other countries, a firm may look forward to internationalise. For instance, Airtel (a telecommunication company), after defining the industry boundaries in India, has now moved to Sri Lanka and Africa. Also, India's leading domestic airline company, IndiGo moved international and started flying to the other destinations like Dubai, Singapore and London.
3. ***Increasing life cycle of its products:*** A company can internationalise its operations to increase the life cycle of its products, i.e., increasing the duration for which its product stays in the market. If it has only domestic operations, its product follows the normal product life cycle (PLC). But if it internationalises, it gives its products an opportunity to be used by different markets abroad. For instance, a new Sony camcorder launched in Japan (an industrialised country) may take a few months or a year to be launched in a developing country market (say Brazil) and may further take another couple of years or even more to be launched in the market of a least developed country (LDC), say Botswana in Africa.
4. ***Investment opportunities:*** An investment opportunity abroad also creates avenues for internationalisation. For instance, the Bangalore-based GMR Group, a lead member of the joint venture Delhi International Airport (P) Ltd. (DIAL; that constructed Terminal-3 in Delhi), has also invested in the Maldives.
5. ***Investment in natural resources:*** Different countries are endowed with different natural resources. Depending on expertise, a company can internationalise its operations to explore and extract the natural resources in and from other countries. For instance, ONGC carries out exploration in oil and gas basins in many countries like Vietnam and others through ONGC Videsh Limited (OVL).

16.2 MODES OF ENTRY INTO A FOREIGN MARKET

Firms cross borders for business purposes. However, the process of cross-border operations of a firm depends on its mode of entry into the foreign market. In fact, the central idea behind the entry into market and choice of a mode of entry into a market is the relation between the risks associated with the market and the type of economic system that controls the market. The firms intend to choose that mode of entry which has the potential to lower their risks in that particular market.

There are two different types of entry into a foreign market, *viz.* entry through equity modes and entry through non-equity modes. The equity modes of entry include joint ventures, wholly-owned subsidiaries, partially-owned subsidiaries, mergers and acquisitions. On the other hand, non-equity entry includes exports and contracts.

Some of the modes of entry into a foreign market are as follows:

Exporting

An initial way of entering into a foreign market is through exporting. This requires lower level of investments, and thus, has low risk associated with it. The concept of exports and imports is primarily based on the idea of supply and demand. A product, which is produced by a firm in China and has demand in India, has an opportunity to enter into the Indian market. This occurs when firms engage themselves in the international trade.

Exports can happen in the following two ways:

1. ***Indirect exporting:*** The firm exports goods to a foreign country through engaging with intermediaries, export and import management companies and export merchants.
2. ***Direct exporting:*** The firm sells its goods in a foreign market through its own branches or subsidiaries.

Licensing

Licensing is another important form of entry into a foreign market. The *licensing agreement* refers to an agreement through which a firm grants the right to a foreign firm to use its expertise, technology and industrial property for manufacturing. The firm which grants the license is known as the *licensor*, while the foreign firm which receives it is known as the *licensee*. It involves less risk and helps the licensor in getting benefits by entering into a foreign market and using innovative technology.

Franchising

Franchising is another mode of entry into a foreign market in which a firm (the *franchisor*) grants the right to use its brand name and trademark to a foreign firm (the *franchisee*). This mode has successfully been used for the industries like fast food chains, consumer services and hotel business, etc. The franchisee has to follow the same standards of operation and guidelines as directed and followed by the franchisor. Firms like McDonald's and KFC are some important examples of such kind.

The franchise obligation is defined in countries with various legal frameworks to protect the respective interests of both franchisor and the franchisee. The evolving trend of consumerism and globalisation in India has helped in increasing the potential of franchising in the country. There are international laws like those under TRIPS, which help in securing the cross-border trademarks of firms while entering into a franchising agreement.

Turnkey projects

Turnkey projects are also a mode of entry into a foreign market. They are generally long-term investment-based projects and may be related to the development of airports, dams, power plants, roads, etc. in a foreign country. They work on a build-operate-transfer (BOT) basis, and are expertise-based assignments granted to a firm to carry out the project in a foreign country. They are time-bound in nature.

Foreign Direct Investment (FDI)

Foreign direct investment (FDI) is also an important mode of entry into a foreign market. Foreign firms enter into a market by investing in business through equity or non-equity modes of entry. A firm can incorporate its own subsidiary in a foreign country and make investments. In order to increase investment potential in their country, governments also promote policies for attracting such investments.

MNCs also operate through subsidiaries. They set up their own subsidiaries in a foreign market. Audi India is a subsidiary of Volkswagen group in India, selling its products in the Indian market. ONGC is an Indian firm engaged in doing business in the gas and oil sector. ONGC Videsh Limited (OVL) is a subsidiary formed by ONGC for participating in the foreign countries. It is now doing business in 30 countries. (Chapter 17 discusses about FDI in detail.)

Joint ventures

Joint venture is a business arrangement through which firms make investment in foreign countries by collaborating with the foreign firms. The firms involved in the joint ventures usually employ their resources to attain a specific business goal. For example, a joint venture can have an equity participation of 50:50. This may happen when the foreign investment is restricted to a certain level in some industries. For example, Indian Oil has joint ventures with the MNCs like PETRONAS—a Malaysian oil company. Maruti Udyog and Suzuki of Japan also show an example of joint ventures.

Mergers and acquisitions

Merger refers to the merging of two different firms into one so as to form a new firm. *Acquisition* implies acquiring of a firm by another firm. These are also important modes of entry into a foreign market.

16.3 PORTER'S DIAMOND

Michael Porter in his book, 'The Competitive Advantage of Nations' presented the Diamond model. This model deals with ascertaining the national competitive advantage of a country and its way of impacting the competitiveness of a firm engaged in the international business. There are four factors of national competitive advantage which make up the Porter's diamond. These factors include factor conditions, demand conditions, firm's structure, strategy and rivalry, and related and supporting industries.

This model tries to address a basic question that why firms belonging to certain countries are capable of consistent innovation. Porter called it a system which constitutes the diamond of national advantage. This system is based on the national attributes.

Accordingly, the four attributes or conditions are mentioned as follows:

1. ***Factor conditions:*** This attribute reflects the availability of resources and factors of production in a nation, which helps in strengthening the competitiveness of an industry in that particular country. These factors include natural resources, capital, labour, physical resources, technological advancements and infrastructure support.
2. ***Demand conditions:*** The demand condition reflects the scenario of consumption in a country. As per the model, it is an essential element to determine the competitiveness of a country's home market. The condition of demand for a product determines the prospects for the firms' business.
3. ***Firm's, structure, strategy and rivalry:*** The structure of a firm and its strategy is also significant. The conditions that are related to legal and institutional framework to govern starting a business and also its operations in a country help in understanding the prospects of that business in the country. The simpler the procedure, the competitive is the environment for the business.
4. ***Related and supporting industries:*** The national competitiveness is also determined by the related and supporting industry in the country. For example, the availability of raw materials and its supply in a country for certain industry provides a competitive advantage.

16.4 MULTINATIONAL CORPORATIONS (MNCs)

A *multinational corporation (MNC)* is a company, which is headquartered in one country and has business operations in two or more countries. Their number has increased to a large extent owing to globalisation triggered by liberal trade policies across the world.

Some of the key characteristics of MNCs are as follows:

1. They can operate through subsidiaries and branches in two or more countries.
2. They have the potential to cater to a larger market and are capable of market diversification.
3. They spend a considerable amount of capital on research and development for bringing about innovation to create value for their customers.
4. They provide quality products and services to their customers in different markets both through standardisation or customisation.
5. They undertake large projects in the home country and international markets, as they have good market capitalisation.
6. They tend to manage a cost-effective supply and value chain both at regional and global levels.
7. They are engaged in foreign direct investment.
8. They are engaged in technology sharing to be continuously involved in innovation at all levels of their value chain.
9. They manage a large set of individuals (human resources) and train them to work in a multicultural setting.
10. They also create large employment opportunities.

16.4.1 Classification of MNCs

Multinational Corporations (MNCs) have been defined in various ways. The attributes of MNCs characterise their organisational framework and structure. Thus, they have been viewed in terms of their geographical coverage, management styles and organisational structures.

1. ***Geographical coverage:*** Based on the geographical coverage, there are two types of multinationals, i.e., global and multidomestic multinationals. The MNCs which are having high coordination in their value chains are called *global*, whereas the MNCs having relatively lesser coordinated industry value chains are called *multidomestic*.
2. ***Management style:*** In terms of management style, firms are categorised as ethno-centric, polycentic and geocentric. *Ethnocentric* organisations have their headquarters in home country and follow home country standards in organisational decision-making and communications wherever they operate. The *polycentric* multinationals focus on doing business in the host country through a host country-oriented approach. The *geocentric* organisations have a global orientation and are not particular to focus on a home or host-country orientation.
3. ***Organisational structure:*** In terms of its organisational structure, MNCs are categorised as centralised and decentralised multinationals. *Centralised* multinationals are typically controlled by the headquarter, with a centralised controlling system, just like the ethnocentric organisations. On the other hand, *decentralised* structure of MNCs gives freedom to the locally-based executives operating in different countries to make decisions on their operations.

Closing Case: Unilever in the Indian Subcontinent—Hindustan Unilever Limited (HUL), Unilever Nepal, Unilever Sri Lanka

Unilever Limited has a presence across the Indian subcontinent. The business of Unilever is expanding both in India and overseas, particularly in countries like Nepal. The kind of performance that Unilever is showing in India as one of the major players in fast moving consumer goods (FMCG) is commendable. In India, this company is known as Hindustan Unilever Limited (HUL), which has a market capitalisation of ₹1,19,899.88 crore.

During the period of undivided India in the year 1888, Lever Brothers of England sent consignments of soaps to India. After this event, they sent the consignment of Lifebuoy in 1895. It launched other famous brands such as Pears, Lux and Vim. Considering the market in India, in the year 1931, Unilever Limited set up the first Indian subsidiary named as Hindustan Vanaspati Manufacturing Company and then Lever Brothers India Limited. United Traders Limited was also formed subsequently.

Later in 1956, these subsidiaries were merged to Hindustan Lever Limited (HLL). A 10% of its equity was offered to the public and Unilever accounted for 67.25% of the equity. In 1991, liberalisation of economic policies started. A new dimension for business was opened. HLL started to expand its wings beyond India. Its business plan advocated taking up all the opportunities provided to it.

HLL planned to enter into foreign market by following different modes of entry. It formed joint venture with the US-based Kimberly Clark Corporation in 1994 and also set up a subsidiary in Nepal named as Unilever Nepal Limited. Unilever Nepal represents the largest manufacturing investment in the Himalayan kingdom. Its factory manufactures HUL's products like soaps, detergents and personal products both for the domestic market and also for exports to India.

In Nepal, around 4 April 2014, the production at Unilever Nepal and exports from there came to a standstill owing to disruption caused by 29 outsourced workers, who wanted a proper appointment letter. They were not issued appointment letter by the outsourced company, which had hired them to work with the Unilever Nepal. The company has 140 permanent and temporary workers and produces products like Lux, Lifebuoy, Liril (soaps), Pepsodent, Close Up (toothpastes) and Fair & Lovely (fairness cream).

In Sri Lanka, the Unilever Sri Lanka was incorporated in 1938 and produces 29 brands, including Pears, Sunlight, Lux, Bru and Vim. It deals in several product categories, including household care, skin care, oral care, tea and personal grooming, among others.

Source: This case is written by the authors based on inputs from the following sources:

1. HUL, http://www.hul.co.in/aboutus/ourhistory/, Outsourced workers grind Unilever factory to a halt, 6 April 2014.
2. Unilever Sri Lanka, http://www.unilever.com.lk/
3. http://www.nepalsharemarket.com/NepalShareMarket/NEPSE/Analysis/news/company_news.aspx?news_id=NEW-007052

CASE QUESTIONS

1. Describe the expansion of Unilever in South Asia.
2. What are the various products offered by HUL in India? Are they all manufactured by HUL?

REVIEW QUESTIONS

1. What are the important reasons of internationalisation of companies?
2. Discuss the modes of entry into a foreign market.
3. What do you understand by licensing and franchising?
4. Describe Porter's diamond.
5. What are the key features of an MNC?

SUGGESTED READINGS

Daniels, J.D., Radebaugh, Lee H., Sullivan, Daniel P., and Salwan, Prashant, 2009, *International Business: Environments and Operation*, 12th ed., Dorling Kindersley (India).

Hill, C.W.L. and Jain, A.K., 2009, *International Business: Competing in the Global Marketplace*, Tata McGraw-Hill Education, New Delhi.

Rugman, A.M. and Hodgetts, R.M., 2004, *International Business*, Pearson Education, Delhi.

Sundaram, A.K. and Black, J.S., 1995, *The International Business Environment: Text and Cases*, PHI Learning, Delhi.

17

FOREIGN DIRECT INVESTMENT (FDI)

Learning Outcomes

After reading this chapter, you will

- Understand the concept and types of FDI
- Learn the various theories of FDI and their relevance
- Analyse the trend of FDI inflows in India and globally

Opening Case: FDI in Multi-brand Retail

The Government of India took various decisions to attract foreign investments to the country. Allowing 51% FDI in multi-brand retail is one of them. Single-brand retail sector was already opened for the foreign investors. Retail sector is an important pillar of India's economy and also has a huge market, as it serves the growing consumers in the country. It is estimated that retail market has a share of 14%–15% in the GDP of the country, and has marketability potential of US$500 billion. The growing income of 1.2 billion people of the country has opened an arena for more consumption-based supply chain and retailing market. As per the study by a consulting firm Technopak, Indian retail market is further expected to grow at 6% per annum and will reach US$865 billion by 2023.[1]

Considering the changing dynamics of world retail market and India's consumer's capability, multi-brand retail is considered to be one of the important areas, where FDI can be attracted. Up to 2011, the Government of India does not allow FDI in multi-brand retail. Several rounds of debate took place among the policy-makers. Even government restricted foreign ownership in single-brand retail up to 51%.

After taking new measures of reforms, FDI has been allowed in this sector. However, the decision to implement it lies with the respective states. The new market has been opened for

1. http://www.ibef.org/research/reports/indian-retail-market-set-to-touch-865-billion-dollar-by-2023; Modern retail to help sector clip at 6% CAGR till 2023: Report, 22 August 2013, http://articles.economictimes.indiatimes.com/2013-08-22/news/41437210_1_organised-retail-retail-sector-alternate-channels.

the foreign investors. Some of the multi-brand retail companies became keenly interested to invest in India. These included Walmart, Carrefour, etc. Moreover, the Government of India also approved 100% ownership in single-brand retail for the foreign investors.

However, these reforms got mixed opinion from retailers, political parties, farmers and state governments. Most of the states did not agree to adopt this new reform. The industry was, however, happy.

The FDI in multi-brand retail had a lot of arguments both in favour and against it. Some of the benefits include the following:

1. Farmers are likely to get a fair price, as the role of middlemen would be eliminated.
2. It would create many job opportunities.
3. It would offer more choice to the consumers at competitive rates.
4. This may lead to a reduction in the wastage of perishable goods like fruits and vegetables.
5. It is likely to provide benefit to the SMEs.
6. It would help in strengthening the supply chain.

Some of the arguments which were given against it by political parties and other stakeholders included the following:

1. It would create problems for small traders (*kirana* stores).
2. Farmers may be exploited by big firms.
3. It would become difficult for domestic players to compete.
4. Foreign companies would focus on the repatriation of money.

The outcome of the opening up of this sector is yet to be seen in the days to come. Foreign companies like Walmart are there in the Indian market, but are yet to open up into multi-brand retailing.

Source: This case is written by the authors based on inputs from the following sources:

1. http://www.ibef.org/research/reports/indian-retail-market-set-to-touch-865-billion-dollar-by-2023
2. Modern retail to help sector clip at 6% CAGR till 2023: Report, 22 August 2013, http://articles.economictimes.indiatimes.com/2013-08-22/news/41437210_1_organised-retail-retail-sector-alternate-channels

17.1 MEANING OF FDI

Foreign direct investment (FDI) is defined as the direct investment by any entity of one country into the industry engaged in the production of goods and services in another country. FDI, therefore, differs from the indirect investments such as portfolio investments. FDI is considered as one of the key elements of global economic integration process.

As per the Organisation for Economic Cooperation and Development (OECD).

> *FDI is defined as* a cross-border investment made by a resident entity in one economy (the direct investor), with the objective of establishing a lasting interest in an enterprise (the direct investment enterprise) that is resident in an economy other than of the direct investor. The lasting interest implies the existence of a long-term relationship between the direct investor and the enterprise, and a significant degree of influence by the direct

investor on the management of the enterprise. Ownership of at least 10% of the voting power, representing the influence by the investor, is the basic criterion used.[2]

As per the fifth edition of the International Monetary Fund's (IMF) Balance of Payments Manual, the *direct investors* are those who are the owner of 10% or more of the capital of a corporation, organisation or a company.

It is important to mention here that this percentage is recommended as the base to demarcate investment as direct investment and portfolio investment in terms of shareholdings of a company. The IMF defines the owner of 10% or more of a company's capital as a direct investor. Accordingly, *direct investment* is the investment made in shares of a company or in equity of a company, which constitutes or equals to more than 10% of the company's capital. If the investment is less than that, the investment is considered as *portfolio investment.*

An individual, private or public enterprise, government, multilateral donor agency, etc. may use direct investment as an instrument of FDI. Direct investment can be made in both assets and liabilities using various instruments like equity, shares, loans, debentures, etc. Therefore, FDI has been classified on the basis of the structure of investor, instruments and the type of industry in which investment has been made. FDI has also two directions—outward and inward.

Equity and debt are the main FDI instruments. Equity broadly includes shares, reserves, capital, etc. Direct investment in equity through these vehicles by one country into another country is considered as a cross-border investment and is included in FDI. On the other hand, investments in debt instruments are securities, loans, deposits and others (see Box 17.1 for details on financial instruments related to FDI).

Box 17.1 Financial Instruments Related to FDI

1. ***Equity:*** It comprises equity in branches; all shares in subsidiaries and associates (except non-participating, preferred shares that are treated as debt securities and included under direct investment, debt instruments); and other contributions of an equity nature. Ownership of equity is usually evidenced by shares, stocks, participations, depositary receipts or similar documents. Shares and stocks have the same meaning while depositary receipts are securities that represent ownership of securities by a depositary.
2. ***Deposits:*** Typical forms of deposits include savings deposits, term deposits, transferable and non-transferable deposits in local or foreign currencies [see the System of National Accounts (SNA) guidelines for a more specific definition of deposits].
3. ***Debt securities:*** These include non-participating preferred shares, bonds, debentures, commercial paper, promissory notes and other non-equity securities.
4. ***Loans:*** Loans are financial assets that are created when a creditor lends funds directly to a debtor through an instrument that is not intended to be traded. This category includes all loans and advances (except accounts receivable/payable, which are treated as a separate category of financial assets). It also covers the treatment of financial leases and repurchase agreements.
5. ***Trade credit (receivables and payables) between FDI-related enterprises:*** It represents short-term credit in the ordinary course of business by suppliers/buyers of goods and services. These credits are registered from the time the goods or services are provided until payment is received (or *vice versa*).

Source: OECD, http://www.oecd.org/daf/inv/investmentstatisticsandanalysis/40193734.pdf

2. Organisation for Economic Co-operation and Development (OECD), Benchmark Definition of Foreign Direct Investment, 4th ed., 2008.

FDI is also classified based on the control by the government on investment in various sectors. Suppose the government allows investment in retail but if it is subject to approval from government, it is called *FDI through government route*. While, if the government allows FDI in infrastructure, and it can happen without prior approval of the government, it is called *FDI through automatic route*.

As per the United Nations Conference on Trade and Development (UNCTAD), the components of FDI are defined as follows:

> The components of FDI are equity capital, reinvested earnings and other capital (mainly intra-company loans). As countries do not always collect data for each of those components, reported data on FDI are not fully comparable across countries. In particular, data on reinvested earnings, the collection of which depends on company surveys, are often unreported by many countries.

As the world becomes more and more interconnected, increased globalisation and liberal trade practices are now creating further opportunities for the entrepreneurs at global level. This also contributes to a higher degree of economic and financial integration. This results in cross-country capital flows in the form of investments. Of course, markets are quickly moving towards internationalisation of firms, which not only are helping business in meeting the demand side of consumption but are also making investments in the supply side of the economy, for instance, investment in infrastructure. Thus, by attracting FDI, countries are flourishing and meeting their objectives of higher economic growth. Global competition is increasing in various sectors and processes such as transport, real estate, mining, telecommunication, and supply chain, among others.

Developing countries are also becoming investor-friendly these days through their FDI policies and regulations, which can protect investor rights. Besides investment inflows, a new trend has also emerged in the recent years in which the developing countries are also looking forward to the outward foreign direct investment (OFDI) opportunities for participating in economic as well as business opportunities in other countries. For instance, China's investment in African mining sector and infrastructure sector in Asia such as ports are notable.

In this chapter, we discuss about the concept of FDI, in general, and trends of FDI in India, in particular. We also examine the current status of FDI in the world and its linkages with the economic development.

17.2 TYPES OF FDI

FDI is classified as per its direction, its process through government or automatic route and also through merger types. As per these characteristics, the FDI is classified as follows:

1. ***Inward and outward (FDI):*** As per the direction of FDI, inward FDI is directed as capital inflow in a country, whereas outward FDI is the capital outflow from the country (home country) directed towards another country (host country). Thus, outward FDI is the local capital invested in the other countries, whereas inward FDI is the foreign capital invested in the home country.
2. ***Greenfield investment:*** Greenfield investments are the investments made in new projects, particularly in infrastructure projects. This type of investment is being

attracted by the various sectors, which are usually the result of government's policies for attracting the foreign investment. For instance, in India, foreign investments are attracted to the airports infrastructure-related Greenfield projects, which aim at transforming the existing infrastructure of Delhi airports and Mumbai airports, etc. through public private partnerships (PPP). New terminals at these airports are important projects.

3. ***Horizontal and vertical investment:*** Horizontal investment is the investment made to produce same or similar kind of goods or commodities in the host country as in the home country. In this kind of investment, product differentiation is the key element in market structure. On the other hand, vertical investment is also the investment abroad in the same industry of operation as in home country, but as a supplier or forwarder. Moreover, vertical investment is categorised as *backward vertical FDI* (when it integrates the sources of supply) and *forward vertical FDI* (when it acts as a forwarded or becomes closer to the consumers in terms of supply chain).
4. ***Automatic route and government route:*** FDI in a country is controlled by the government through its FDI policies. If a government lifts its control from foreign investment in a particular sector, it is called *automatic route*, whereas if the government puts obligations on the foreign investors to acquire permission from the government for investment in some sectors, then it is called *investment through government route*.

In India, these are the main routes of investment, wherein the government has a control either fully or partially over the various sectors, except those sectors where investment is through fully (100%) automatic route. Moreover, from the perspective of a host country, and depending on the utilisation of FDI, it can also be classified into *import-substituting FDI* and *export-increasing FDI*.

17.3 THEORIES OF FDI

We have already discussed trade theories in Chapter 15. Some economists have argued that there are limitations in the trade theories. Of course, every trade theory has limitations when it comes to link cross-border economic relations and the country's own economic development. Therefore, some economists also argued that there is an important instrument for broader economic engagement, which is called *cross-border investment*. Notably, these days, countries are not only looking for free trade agreements (FTA) in goods and services but also for comprehensive agreements, which include host of other factors like competition policy, intellectual property rights (IPRs), government procurement, and more significantly in this context, investments.

Generally, there are three major dimensions of looking at FDI. These dimensions are market imperfections theory, international production theory and internalisation theory.[3] Let us first start with the classical trade theories. We know that classical trade theory points out that countries gain when they specialise in production. These theories have never highlighted the gains from investment. In contemporary economic order, investment flows from one country to another have become a general phenomenon.

---

3. http://www.st-andrews.ac.uk/business/distance/Economics/Reading/Critique_trade_theories.pdf

Thus, the theories like market imperfection theory, international production theory and eclectic theory intend to address this global concern. Thus, up to 1950s, international investment flows were looked upon under the assumptions of traditional theory of international capital movements.[4] Moreover, FDI was mainly considered as the movement of capital emerging out due to the differences in rate of interests in two countries. This approach was redefined by Stephen Hymer.

Some of the important theoretical frameworks for FDI are discussed as follows:

1. ***Theory of market imperfection:*** Stephen Hymer, a Canadian economist, propounded the theory of market imperfection. Hymer's research focused on multinational corporations. In his theory of market imperfection, Hymer pointed out that the firms use foreign investment as their strategy to capitalise on certain capabilities, which are not present in its competitors investing in the other countries. These differences in the production capabilities of firms in home countries and in firms from abroad who tend to invest are viewed as market imperfections. In other words, differences in production capabilities between the firms across countries are the result of varying factors of production. Thus, the investment is attracted from more capable firms operating abroad to the home countries.
2. ***International production theory:*** This approach was developed by Peter Buckley and Mark Casson. Their theory of internationalisation of multinational enterprises explains that multinational enterprises integrate with the other firms both horizontally and vertically. The type of integration depends on the relationship among knowledge, market imperfections and the internalisation of markets for intermediate goods.[5] Thus, capital movement in terms of FDI uses the process of vertical and horizontal integration. As per the theory, the cross-border movement of investments between vertically integrated firms is the result of internalisation of market for intermediated products, whereas investment for horizontally integrated firm is the result of internalisation of market for assets. Also, the resource differentials and the government intervention play a significant role in determining the overseas investment activities.
3. ***Eclectic theory or OLI model:*** The eclectic theory, also known as the *OLI Model*, was proposed by Dunning. This is said to be an extension of the internalisation theory, which argues that the firms aspire to develop their own internal markets wherever they get an opportunity to carry out transactions at a lower cost within the firm.

The OLI Model relies on the following factors:

(i) *Ownership:* Ownership-specific advantages like trademarks, etc. can create competitive advantages for the firm if it intends to engage in production through FDI.

(ii) *Location:* Advantages pertaining to location like availability of raw materials, tariff regimes, wage rate, etc. can make a country attractive to foreign investors.

(iii) *Internalisation:* Advantages pertaining to internalisation like advantages of having own production process also endows the firm to engage in the foreign production on its own.

---

4. http://www.fep.up.pt/docentes/fcastro/chapter%202.pdf
5. Buckley, Peter J. and Casson, Mark C. (1976), *The Future of the Multinational Enterprise*, Macmillan, London.

In fact, eclectic theory takes into account the country-specific and company-specific variables as well. *Country-specific variables* include those pertaining to the macroeconomic environment like political environment, regulatory environment, cultural environment, foreign trade and fiscal policies, and other economic environment factors. Company-specific variables include human resources, strategy, organisational structure, technical prowess, knowledge management, etc.

17.4 GLOBAL TRENDS IN FDI FLOWS

The World Investment Report by UNCTAD presents a comprehensive analysis of the current trend in global investment flows. As per the 2013 report, globally, investment inflows in terms of FDI fell by 18% in 2012 from a revised US$1.65 trillion in 2011 to US$1.35 trillion.[6]

As per the World Investment Report 2016, the recovery process in FDI inflows was strong in 2015 resulting in 38% increase over 2014. Global FDI was estimated to be US$1.76 trillion in 2015, achieving highest level since the financial crisis in 2008–2009.

Despite the fact that there has been a positive growth in GDP, employment, trade and production, investment inflows have seen a negative growth in recent years. However, some recovery in investment is taking place, which would in turn increase employment in the world. Figure 17.1 indicates these developments. Trade and GDP growth are now attracting FDI across the world, particularly in emerging countries, and FDI has increased in 2015.

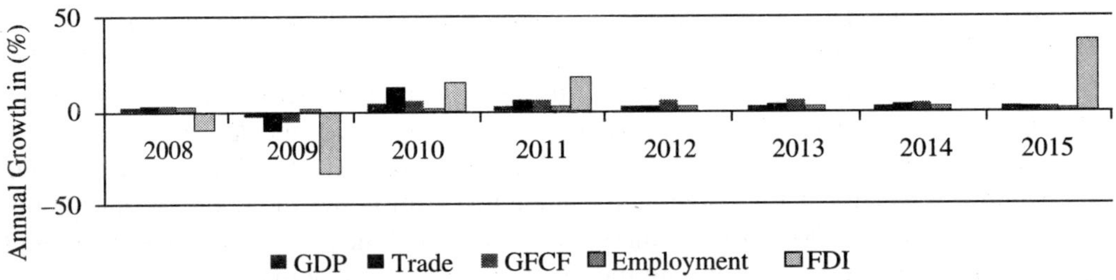

Figure 17.1 Growth rates of global GDP, gross fixed capital formation (GFCF), trade, employment and FDI, 2008–2015.

Source: UNCTAD, World Investment Report, 2013, IMF and ILO.

17.5 GEOGRAPHICAL DISTRIBUTION OF WORLD FDI

The geographical distribution of FDI needs to be understood in two ways, viz. country-wise and region-wise, and also on the basis of level of development (i.e., developed, developing and least developed categories). Statistics reveal that for the first time, the developing world is able to attract FDI more than the developed countries. In fact, FDI inflows in developing countries have been resilient, as FDI reached more than US$1,762 billion in 2015 in the world and US$765 billion in developing countries.

On the other hand, FDI inflows in the developed nations increased to US$962 billion in 2015 with 55% share in global FDI. Now, the developing countries account for about 45% of

6. World Investment Report 2013, UNCTAD.

FDI inflows in the world. Figure 17.2 represents the changing direction of global FDI flows. The developing countries are gradually getting more FDI inflows.

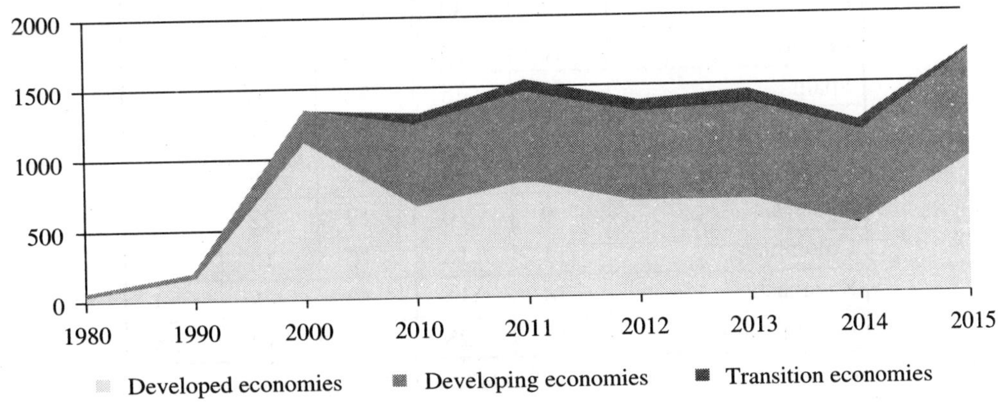

Figure 17.2 Trend of global FDI inflow (US$billion at current prices).
Source: UNCTAD Statistics.

However, it is important to note that among the developing countries, China has been dominating the statistics. The total share of developing Asian countries in FDI is now approximately 30.7%.

A country-wise analysis indicates that the United States (US) remains the most favourable destination for the investors. After the US, China is the most favourable destination for FDI. The global ranking of the largest recipient of FDI indicates that there is an increase in FDI inflows in most of the top developing countries over 2014, which attracted more FDI, after experiencing decrease during the recent past. Similarly, top FDI in the developed nations like US also experienced increase after experiencing decline in 2012. The FDI inflows in top 20 countries are presented in Table 17.1. Among the developed countries, the US had 21% share in the world FDI inflows in 2015, whereas the UK and Australia had a share of 2.2% and 1.2%, respectively, in 2015 experiencing decrease in share compared to 2014.

Table 17.1 FDI Inflows in Top 20 Countries (US$ Billion at Current Prices)

Countries	*2008*	*2012*	*2013*	*2014*	*2015*
United States	306	168	212	107	380
China	108	121	124	129	136
Hong Kong	67	75	75	114	175
Brazil	45	65	53	73	65
British Virgin Islands	52	65	112	50	52
United Kingdom	89	62	48	52	40
Australia	47	57	57	40	22
Singapore	12	57	66	68	65
Russian Federation	75	51	53	29	10

Countries	2008	2012	2013	2014	2015
Canada	62	45	72	59	49
Chile	16	30	18	21	20
Ireland	–16	29	45	31	101
Spain	77	28	33	23	9
India	47	26	28	35	44
France	64	25	43	15	43
Indonesia	9	20	19	22	16
Colombia	11	16	16	16	12
Kazakhstan	14	14	10	8	4
Luxembourg	17	28	15	12	25

Source: UNCTAD Statistics and World Investment Report, 2016.

In case of developing countries, China alone has 7.7% share in World's FDI inflows, whereas China together with Hong Kong has 17.7% share in the world FDI inflows in 2015. The share of India is about 2.5%. The global share of major countries in 2008 as compared to 2012 is presented in Figure 17.3. The recent trend depicts that the developing countries like China, Hong Kong and Brazil have witnessed an increase in FDI. On the other hand, countries like US,

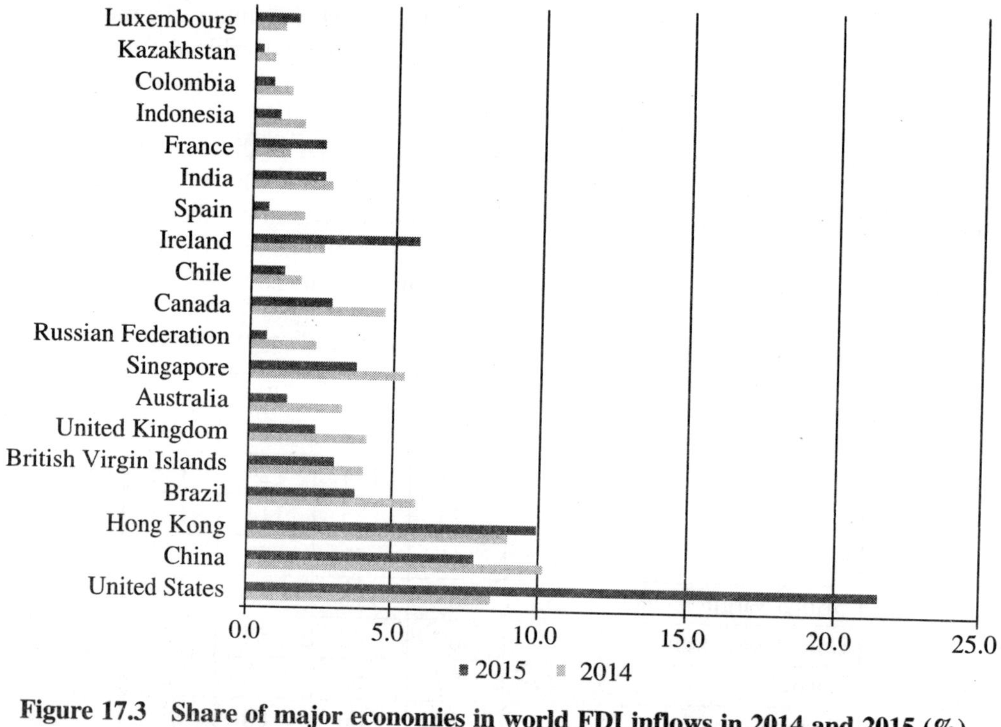

Figure 17.3 Share of major economies in world FDI inflows in 2014 and 2015 (%).

Source: UNCTAD.

UK, Canada and Spain had witnessed contraction in the FDI inflows between 2008 and 2015. However, the developed countries like Australia and Singapore witnessed an increase in their respective FDI inflows. India has also been experiencing a decrease during the two time periods.

Africa

As far as the regional distribution is concerned, Africa emerged as one of the important destinations for investment from abroad. Africa remains one of the few regions, which experienced year on year growth of 15.4% in 2012, but in 2015, experienced a decrease of 7.2% in FDI inflow over 2014. An important development in Africa is that the transnational companies from the developing world are increasingly making their presence by expanding their operations. In addition, countries like Egypt and Tunisia are experiencing increase in FDI inflows. As per the World Investment Report, 2016, after experiencing years of political instability, North Africa regained momentum and FDI inflow increased by 9% in the region in 2015 led by investment inflow in Egypt which rose by 49% in 2015 over 2014. However, FDI inflows to West Africa declined by 18% in 2015 over 2014 due to decrease in investment in Nigeria. FDI inflow to Nigeria was US \$4.7 billion in 2014, which declined to US \$3.1 billion in 2015. Similarly, FDI inflows to Central Africa also recorded a decline of 36% in 2015 over the last year. This decrease in Central Africa was led by sharp decrease in FDI inflows to Congo, which recorded FDI inflows of US \$1.5 billion after record US \$5.5 billion in 2014.

East Africa received US \$7.8 billion in FDI in 2015—a 2% decrease from 2014. In an effort to attract more foreign investors, both Tanzania and Kenya now allow 100% foreign ownership of companies listed on their stock exchanges. In southern part of Africa, large inflows were seen in Angola. It attracted a record of \$8.7 billion of FDI in 2015, becoming the largest recipient in Africa. However, in South Africa, FDI inflows decreased by 69% and were recorded as \$1.8 billion, the lowest in 10 years lackluster. This was because of low economic performance, lower commodity prices and higher electricity costs.[7]

Developing Asia

Developing Asia is the largest recipient region of FDI inflows in the world accounting for more than 30% of the total FDI inflows in the world. In 2015, developing Asia has experienced a growth of 15.6% over the last year in FDI inflows amounting to US\$540.7 billion. However, it is important to mention here that the major recipient countries of FDI inflows are large countries of the region. These countries include China, Hong Kong-China, India, Singapore, Turkey, etc. The distribution of FDI is uneven in developing Asia when it comes to the counting of small countries. The total FDI inflows to East Asia increased by 25% to become US\$322 billion in the year 2015 over the last year. It was mainly driven by Hong Kong-China, which experienced the increase of 53% in FDI inflows in 2015 over 2014. The FDI inflows to Southeast Asia experienced a steady increase of 1% in 2015 amounting to US\$126 billion. Singapore is the leading recipient of FDI in Southeast Asian countries, which also experienced decrease of 5% in FDI inflow in 2015 over 2014. However, low income countries in Southeast Asia performed well. The FDI inflows in Myanmar increased by 200% in 2015 and accounted for about US\$3 billion.

7. See http://www.oecd-ilibrary.org/docserver/download/5k4376zqcpf1.pdf?expires=1394018260&id=id&accname=guest&checksum=B7290A9B56856D55006DD9ACA69CCC11

Considering the performance of India, the FDI inflows in South Asia also soared by 22% in 2015. The FDI inflows to South Asia were US$50 billion, of which US$44 billion were received by India only. The FDI inflows to Bangladesh also increased by 44% in 2015 due to labour intensive manufacturing units, which were opened for FDI. However, the FDI inflows in other countries of South Asia have witnessed a decline. In case of West Asia, the FDI inflows were US$42 billion in 2015, which was a decrease of 2% over the preceding year, i.e., 2014. The largest recipient of FDI in developing Asia was Turkey. The FDI inflows to Turkey was US$17 billion in 2015, experiencing a growth of 36% when compared with the FDI inflows to Turkey in 2014.

Latin America and the Caribbean

In 2015, the FDI inflows in Latin America and the Caribbean accounted for US$167.6 billion, which were less than the FDI inflows of US$244 billion in 2012 and US$249 billion in 2011. The share of developing countries in the region in the World's FDI inflows was recorded to be 9.5% in 2015. Major countries in developing Latin America experienced decrease in FDI inflows. These countries are Brazil, Columbia and Chile, with decline of 11.5%, 25.85% and 5%, respectively, in 2015 over the year 2014. On the other hand, FDI inflows to Mexico and Argentina increased by 18% and 130%, respectively, in 2015 over the last year.

Transition Economies

The FDI inflows to transition economies have also been declining. They fell by 38% in 2015 over 2014. The FDI inflows to transition economies were US$35 billion in 2015 compared to US$56.5 billion in 2014. The FDI performance of transition subgroups differed. In South-East Europe, FDI inflows increased by 6% to $4.8 billion, as better macroeconomic situations and the EU accession process continued to improve investors' risk perception. In contrast, FDI inflows to the CIS and Georgia declined by 42% to $30 billion.

The Russian Federation and Kazakhstan saw their FDI inflows more than halve from their 2014 level, while inflows to Belarus declined slightly. The FDI inflows to Ukraine, by contrast, increased more than seven times to $3 billion. The Russian Federation recorded FDI inflows of $9.8 billion, a 66% decline from the previous year.

The region-wise trend is given in Table 17.2 and Figure 17.4.

Table 17.2 Region-wise FDI Trend (US$ Billion at Current Prices)

Region	*1970*	*1980*	*1990*	*2000*	*2010*	*2011*	*2012*	*2013*	*2014*	*2015*
Africa (developing)	1.3	0.4	2.8	9.6	43.6	47.6	50.0	52.2	58.3	54.1
Americas (developing)	1.6	6.4	8.9	98.0	189.9	249.4	243.9	176.0	170.3	167.6
Asia (developing)	0.9	0.5	22.7	156.6	400.7	436.2	406.8	431.4	467.9	540.7
Oceania (developing)	0.0	0.0	0.3	0.3	2.9	2.0	2.2	2.8	1.9	2.3
America (developed)	0.0	0.0	0.0	380.9	227.2	268.2	213.1	283.3	165.1	428.5
Asia (developed)	0.1	0.3	1.9	15.3	4.3	9.3	12.1	14.1	8.5	–
Europe	5.2	21.4	104.4	728.5	429.2	472.9	275.6	323.4	306.0	503.6
Oceania (developed)	1.0	2.2	10.2	17.0	35.7	69.6	59.9	55.8	55.3	–

Source: UNCTAD and World Investment Report, 2016.

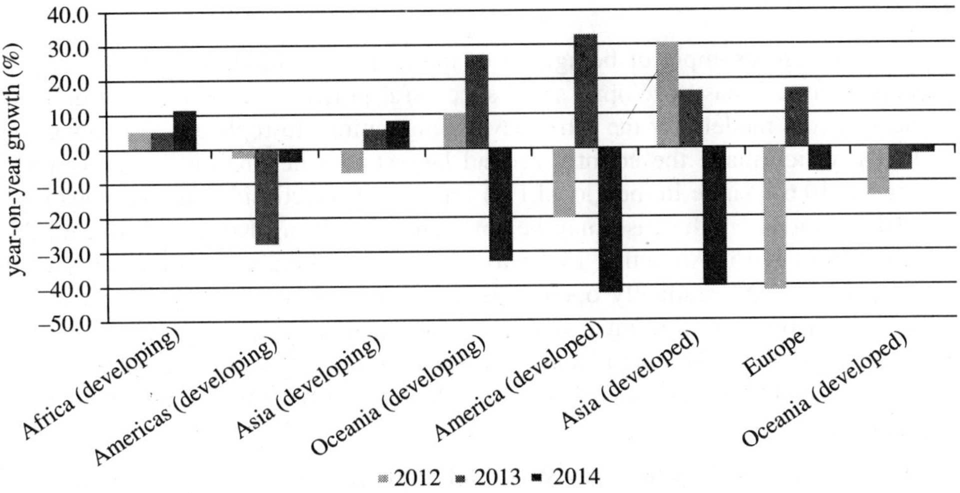

Figure 17.4 Growth of FDI inflows in developing and developed region (%).
Source: UNCTAD.

17.6 IMPORTANCE OF FDI IN WORLD ECONOMY

We have discussed the trend of cross-country investment inflows. The world has witnessed an increasing pace of globalisation. This has contributed to an increase in the investment inflows also, and has even contributed to the process of national development in many countries. During 1970 to 1980, the FDI inflows in the world grew at an average rate of about 16%, which in the subsequent decade, grew at an average rate of 17%, and during 1990 and year 2000, the growth rate reached to 23%. The rate of growth after 2000 has also been increasing, but the world experienced a fluctuating trend with high negative growth rates. Thus, the average growth rate of FDI inflows in the world during the decade of 2000–2010 was merely 5%. However, the trend suggests that during 1970 to 1990, total FDI inflows in the world reached to US$207 billion from US$13 billion. The global FDI inflows in 2012 were US$ 1350 billion, which were less than that of the year 2011. In 2015, FDI inflows in the world are estimated to be US$1.76 trillion, 38% higher than that of the preceding year, i.e., 2014.

In addition, share of developing countries in both outflow and inflow of capital is also increasing. This trend suggests that the world has seen a tremendous cross-country capital flow, which in turn, has the potential to enhance the global growth.

FDI is an important tool for cross-country capital mobility, an important factor of economic growth. These days FDI in various sectors has also become a mechanism for technology transfer from one country to another, thereby contributing to cost-effective production technologies. Such benefits can be witnessed both virtually and physically in the developing countries. The presence of transnational corporations provides a platform for the local firms to acquire technological know-how and use it in the production of goods and services. Countries like China and Brazil have been very successful in attracting the FDIs.

Now, we will review some of policies and practices adopted by few countries aimed at attracting investment in the form of FDI.

China

China is an important example of being one of the largest countries attracting foreign capital to its various sectors. It has developed some successful practices, which can be defined as the best practices or role models for the other developing nations to replicate. China's government promoted FDI, which made the country second largest FDI destination in the world. Today, China alone has 10.6% share in the global FDI inflows. If we consider autonomous regions (or administered territories, as the case may be) of China like Hong Kong and Macau, this share increases to 25% in 2015. Attracting FDI was the core of China's economic reforms process. China systematically and gradually opened its economic sectors for the foreign investments. During the reform process, foreign investment was opened by China's Vice Premier, Deng Xiaoping, who called for reforming China's economy for the first time. Special economic zones (SEZ) were set up and FDI was allowed. The main features of the policies and practices in China regarding FDI are as follows:

1. In 1992, FDI policy was revisited and strategies were made for nation-wide FDI inflow.
2. Special incentive policies for FDI in first four SEZs in coastal region were put on place.
3. Incentives to foreign investors were provided for encouraging foreign joint ventures.
4. An important feature was that priority was given to the export-oriented sectors for FDI.
5. In 2006, China announced new policy to regulate FDI.
6. In 2007, China withdrew preferential tax rates and introduced uniform tax rates.
7. Now, the country attracts FDI to the newer areas like recycling, clean production and renewable energy sectors.
8. Chinese FDI is now concentrated to services sector which accounts for 61% of the FDI inflow, and which expanded by 17% in the services sector.
9. FDI in manufacturing sector is dropping in China and recorded a share of 31% in 2015. This is the result of rising wages and increase in production costs in Chinese coastal regions.

Brazil

Brazil is another important developing country, which successfully attracted FDI over the period of time. Brazil is the largest recipient of FDI in Latin America. In 2012, it had a share of 5% in the world FDI inflows, which is now 3.7%. FDI inflows touched to US$96.2 billion in 2011, which became US$64.7 billion in Brazil in 2015. The country had a liberal regime for FDI and opened almost all the sectors, except a few. It also managed to get FDI without following any incentive-related policy. The investment regime is liberalised and there is no discrimination between the local and foreign investors. Some of the important features of FDI policy of Brazil are as follows:

1. There are incentives for making investment in the areas of export of technological information services, and also in new technology.
2. Import tariff for importing capital goods was reduced.

3. In 2005, the government in Brazil provided special tax breaks for investment in information technology, and research and development.
4. Focus on infrastructure increased by the introduction of sector investment regime.
5. Manaus free trade zone (FTZ) was established on the Amazon River.
6. A national privatisation programme was initiated to boost further liberalisation efforts.

In recent years, Brazil has carried out sizeable disinvestment in telecommunications. The overall investment activity in Brazil—measured by gross fixed capital formation—registered a cumulative decline of 14% in real terms by the end of 2015.

Republic of Korea (South Korea)

Republic of Korea integrated the FDI policies with its economic policies. FDI became an integral part of the South Korean economy and resulted in a significant increase in the number of foreign companies operating there. There was a sharp increase in FDI inflows in Korea due to the change in economic policy of the country. During 1997, FDI in South Korea was US$2.8 billion, which increased to US$9.3 billion in 2000. During 2001–2007, most of the investment attracted. South Korea was in new Greenfield projects.[8] In 2015, FDI inflows in South Korea were recorded at US$5 billion compared to US$9.3 billion in 2014. Following are the main features of FDI policy in South Korea:

1. Foreign Investment Promotion Act (FIPA) was passed in 1998.
2. FIPA focused on strengthening technological capacity by indigenising the foreign technology.
3. National investment promotion agency was established, with the aim to develop an investor-friendly climate for attracting FDI to its various sectors.
4. There was a reduction in the corporate taxes.

17.7 FDI REGIME IN INDIA: TRENDS AND PATTERN

India has been pursuing policies to support the liberalisation process. In this process, India has been gradually allowing foreign investment in various sectors. India has been ranked 7th by the Organisation for Economic Cooperation and Development (OECD) in FDI restrictiveness index in the year 2013.[9] However, the government has allowed automatic foreign investment, that too up to 100% in many sectors. Prior to the reform period, India has restrictive policy for the foreign investment. Public sector undertakings were promoted by the government and a few sectors were opened for private investment within the country.

During the reform period, special attention was put forth on attracting investment to India. This process is still continuing. The government has set up a Foreign Investment Implementation Authority (FIIA) to facilitate quick assessment of foreign direct investment (FDI) approvals and to implement them by providing services to the foreign investors in terms of getting approvals

8. OECD.
9. Consolidated FDI Policy, DIPP, Ministry of Commerce and Industries, Government of India, March 2011.

and for managing other challenges they might face. FIIA is assisted by Fast Track Committee (FTC), which has been established in 30 ministries/departments for monitoring and resolution of difficulties for sector-specific projects.

Major areas for foreign investments were opened in the country. The consolidated FDI policy of India was launched in March 2011, with the intent of promoting foreign direct investment through a policy framework which is transparent, predictable, simple and clear and reduces regulatory burden. The system of periodic consolidation and updation was also introduced as an investor-friendly measure'.[10]

Features of FDI in India before the announcement by the new government in 2014 and in 2016 are listed below:

1. ***Agriculture and animal husbandry:*** 100% FDI is allowed through automatic route in the activities including floriculture, horticulture, cultivation of vegetables and mushrooms under controlled conditions; development and production of seeds and planting material; animal husbandry (including breeding of dogs), pisciculture, aquaculture under controlled conditions; and services related to agro and allied sector.[11]
2. ***Development of townships, housing, built-up infrastructure and construction-development projects:*** 100% FDI is allowed through automatic route in the areas of developing townships, housing, built-up infrastructure and construction development projects (which would include, but not be restricted to, housing, commercial premises, hotels, resorts, hospitals, educational institutions, recreational facilities, city and regional level infrastructure).
3. ***Development of industrial parks:*** 100% FDI is allowed through automatic route in the areas of both developing new and the existing industrial parks.
4. ***Electricity generation, transmission and distribution:*** 100% FDI is allowed through automatic route in the activities including generation and transmission of electric energy produced in hydroelectric, coal/lignite-based thermal; oil-based and gas-based thermal power plants; non-conventional energy generation and distribution; distribution of electric energy to households, industrial, commercial and other users; and power trading.[12]
5. ***E-commerce:*** FDI up to 100% is permitted for e-commerce activities subject to the condition that such companies would divest 26% of their equity in favour of the Indian public in five years, if these companies are listed in the other parts of the world.[13]
6. ***Food processing:*** 100% FDI is allowed in the sector through automatic route.

10. It also mentions that in case, any company is dealing with transgenic/genetically modified seeds, relevant clearance from the Genetic Engineering Approval Committee (GEAC) and Review Committee on Genetic Manipulation (RCGM) has been made mandatory. Further, the policy also mandates compliance to the Environment Protection Act.
11. FDI in the atomic energy sector is prohibited and is reserved for the public sector.
12. Such companies would engage only in business-to-business (B2B) e-commerce and not in retail trading, inter alia, implying that the existing restrictions on FDI in domestic trading would be applicable to e-commerce as well.
13. Excludes titanium bearing minerals and its ores and is subject to the Mines and Minerals (Development and Regulation) Act, 1957.

7. ***Mining:*** 100% FDI is allowed through automatic route in the activities which involve mining and exploration of metal and non-metal ores including diamond, gold, silver and precious ores;[14] coal and lignite mining for captive consumption by power projects, iron and steel and cement units;[15] setting up coal processing plants like washeries;[16] and mining and mineral separation of titanium bearing minerals and ores, its value addition and integrated activities.[17]
8. ***Petroleum and natural gas sector:*** 100% FDI is allowed through automatic route in the activities like exploration activities of oil and natural gas fields, infrastructure related to marketing of petroleum products and natural gas, petroleum product pipelines, natural gas pipelines, LNG regasification infrastructure, market study and formulation, and petroleum refining in the private sector.[18]
9. ***Telecommunication:*** 74% FDI is allowed in the sector out of which 49% is allowed through automatic route. Any investment above 49% but up to 74% is allowed only through the government route.[19]
10. ***Trading-related activities:*** 100% FDI through automatic route is allowed in trading activities pertaining to cash and carry trading, e-commerce marketing and test marketing.

Besides, FDI is prohibited in some sectors also. Some of the key areas in which FDI is prohibited in India include lottery business including government/private lottery, online lotteries; gambling and betting including casinos; business of chit fund; trading in transferable development rights; real estate business or construction of farm houses; manufacturing of cigars, cheroots, cigarillos and cigarettes, tobacco or substitutes; activities/sectors not opened to private sector investment including atomic energy and railway transport.

Consolidated FDI Policy effective from 7 June 2016

Through its consolidated FDI policy in June 2016, the Government of India announced further opening of the economy through liberalising the investment regime. Some of the important sectors like manufacturing in defence, railways, and energy were further liberalised by the

14. Includes other eligible activities permitted under and subject to the provisions of Coal Mines (Nationalisation) Act, 1973.
15. This is subject to the condition that the company shall not do coal mining and shall not sell washed coal or sized coal from its coal processing plants in the open market and shall supply the washed or sized coal to those parties who are supplying raw coal to coal processing plants for washing or sizing.
16. This is subject to sectoral regulations and the Mines and Minerals (Development and Regulation Act, 1957).
17. This is subject to the existing sectoral policy and regulatory framework in the oil marketing sector and the policy of the government on private participation in exploration of oil and the discovered fields of national oil companies. However, an FDI cap of 49% has been put on the activities pertaining to petroleum refining by the public sector undertakings (PSUs), without any disinvestment or dilution of domestic equity in the existing PSUs.
18. Similar FDI route and FDI cap also apply to ISP with gateways, ISP's not providing gateways, i.e., without gateways (both for satellite and marine cables), radio paging, and end-to-end bandwidth.
19. 100% FDI is allowed in telecom services with automatic route upto 49% and Government route beyond 49% as per new FDI policy.

government. The government also announced liberalisation in single-brand retail sector. Some of the important features of the present FDI regime in India are mentioned as follows:[20]

1. 100% FDI under automatic route is permitted in floriculture, horticulture, apiculture and cultivation of vegetables and mushroom under controlled conditions (artificially).
2. 100% FDI under automatic route is permitted in development and production of seeds and planting material.
3. 100% FDI under automatic route is allowed in services related to agro and allied sector.
4. 100% FDI under automatic route is permitted in plantation sector limited to tea, coffee, rubber, cardamom, palm oil tree, olive oil tree plantation.
5. 100% FDI under automatic route is permissible in mining and exploration on metal and non-metal ores, coal and ignite and in setting up coal processing plants like washeries. These permissions are subject to the provisions of acts related to the respective sectors of mining ores and coal.
6. 100% FDI through government approval is permissible in mining and mineral separation of titanium bearing minerals and ores, its value addition and integrated activities.
7. 100% FDI through automatic route is permissible in exploration activities of oil and natural gas fields, infrastructure related to marketing of petroleum products and natural gas, marketing of natural gas and petroleum products, petroleum product pipelines, natural gas/pipelines, LNG regasification infrastructure, market study and formulation and petroleum refining in the private sector, subject to the existing sectoral policy and regulatory framework in the oil marketing sector and the policy of the government on private participation in exploration of oil and the discovered fields of national oil companies.
8. 49% FDI through automatic route is permissible in petroleum refining by the public sector undertakings (PSUs), without any disinvestment or dilution of domestic equity in the existing PSUs.
9. In manufacturing sector, FDI is permissible through automatic route and a manufacturer is permitted to sell its products manufactured in India through wholesale and/or retail, including through e-commerce, without government approval.
10 Up to 49% FDI is permissible in defence industry subject to Industrial licence under the Industries (Development and Regulation) Act, 1951 without prior approval from Government or through automatic route. Above 49% FDI under government route on case-to-case basis is allowed, wherever it is likely to result in access to modern and state-of-the-art technology in the country. However, the cap through automatic route is 49% FDI in equity in this sector.
11. 100% FDI is allowed in broadcasting carriage services with automatic route up to 49% and with government approval above 49% FDI in equity. These services are teleports (setting up of up-linking HUBs/teleports), direct to home (DTH), cable networks, mobile TV, headend-in-the sky broadcasting service (HITS).

20. Consolidated FDI Policy, DIPP, Ministry of Commerce and Industry, Government of India, See http://dipp.gov.in/English/policies/FDI_Circular_2016.pdf

12. 49% FDI in equity with government approval is allowed in terrestrial broadcasting FM (FM radio), subject to such terms and conditions, as specified from time to time, by Ministry of Information and Broadcasting, for grant of permission for setting up of FM radio stations and up-linking of 'news and current affairs' TV channels.
13. 100% automatic route FDI is allowed in up-linking of non-news and current affairs TV channels/down-linking of TV channels.
14. In case of print media, the new FDI policy permits 26% FDI through government approval in publishing of newspapers and periodicals dealing with news and current affairs and publication of Indian editions of foreign magazines dealing with news and current affairs.
15. In civil aviation, 100% FDI through automatic route is allowed in greenfield projects and 100% FDI is permissible in the existing projects with 74% through automatic route and beyond 74% through government approval.
16. 100% FDI is permissible in non-scheduled air transport service, helicopter service through automatic route with Directorate General of Civil Aviation (DGCA) approval and 49% FDI is permissible in scheduled air transport services. 100% FDI is also permitted in maintenance and repair, training institutes, etc. and also in ground handling services subject to sectoral clearance.
17. 100% FDI is permitted in satellites—establishment and operation, subject to the sectoral guidelines of Department of Space/ISRO through government approval.
18. 100% FDI is permitted in e-commerce through automatic route.
19. 51% FDI through government approval is permitted in multibrand retail.
20. 100% FDI through automatic route is permitted in rail infrastructure, including (i) suburban corridor projects through PPP, (ii) high speed train projects, (iii) dedicated freight lines, (iv) rolling stock including train sets, and locomotives/coaches manufacturing and maintenance facilities, (v) railway electrification, (vi) signalling systems, (vii) freight terminals, (viii) passenger terminals, (ix) infrastructure in industrial park pertaining to railway line/sidings including electrified railway lines and connectivities to main railway line and (x) mass rapid transport systems.

In addition to the above steps, the new policy on FDI also permitted foreign investment in banking sector both private and public with limited permissible FDI through government approval, infrastructure company in the security market and financial and insurance sector.[21] The latest announcement of the year 2016 envisages opening of the major sectors in India, which was earlier closed for foreign investment. This regime will have a long-term beneficial impact.

The data collected on foreign investments before and after the year 2000 are not comparable due to the change in the concept and definition of FDI in the country. Therefore, the trend analysis is concentrated to the data after 2000. The coverage of FDI as per its recent definition has made it compatible to international conceptualisation by IMF. Thus, now FDI covers investment as equity, reinvested earnings, and other direct capital in the form debt transaction, etc. The earlier definition included investment under designated heads such as under RBI's automatic approval, approval in larger projects as equity, and other investment under FERA, etc. This resulted in

21. *Ibid.*

difference in the statistics of foreign investment based on the two measures. The new definition came under FEMA enactment. Considering this, we discuss the trend of FDI in India using data by UNCTAD. As per the statistics of UNCTAD, there has been a significant increase in the FDI inflows in India since 1970. The decadal growth in FDI inflows in India is presented in Figure 17.5.

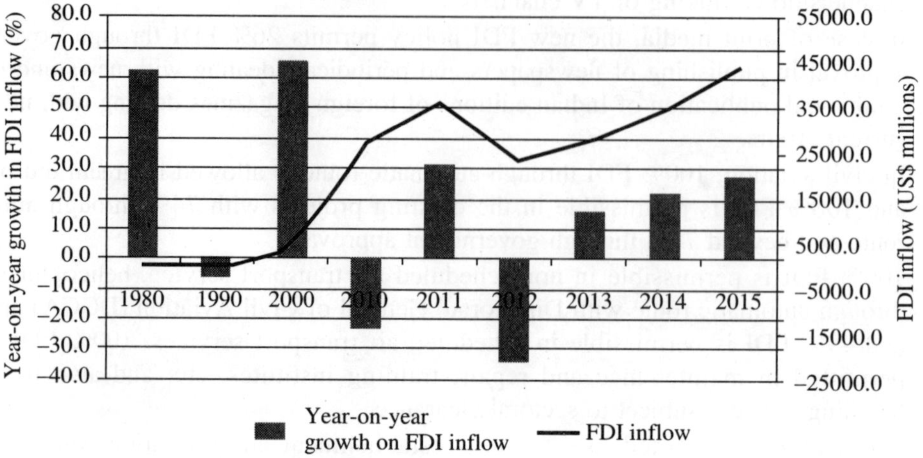

Figure 17.5 Growth of FDI inflows in India (US$ million).

Note: FDI growth rate (%) is measured by bar graph along primary Y-axis, while FDI inflow is measured by line graph along secondary Y-axis.

Source: UNCTAD.

As per the FDI statistics in India, the total number of FDI inflows has increased from US$4,031 million in 2000–2001 to US$34,298 million in 2012–2013 and US$55,457 million in 2015–2016. A higher level of increase in FDI was witnessed after 2000. The annual average increase in FDI inflows has been more than 25% during 2000 and 2016. In the year 2006–2007, India received massive increase in FDI. The FDI inflow in the year was US$22,826 million, registering more than 150% growth as compared to the previous year. On the other hand, if we consider portfolio investments by foreign institutional investment (FII), the growth in the total foreign investment was highest in the year 2003–2004. Foreign investment was US$15,699 million in the year 2003–2004, registering a growth of more than 160% over the previous year.

Table 17.3 presents the trend of investment in the country after 2000.

Table 17.3 Foreign Investment Inflows in India (Direct and Portfolio) (US$ Million)

Year	*Direct Investment*				*Portfolio Investment*		
	Investment in Equity	*Investment Reinvested Earnings*	*Investment Other Capital*	*Total*	*Portfolio Investment in India of which FIIs*	*Portfolio Investment in India of which GDRs/ADRs*	*Total*
2000–2001	2,399	1,352	280	4,031	–	–	13,619
2001–2002	4,096	1,644	390	6,130	–	–	9,259
2002–2003	2,825	1,832	438	5,095	–	–	8,833

Year	Direct Investment				Portfolio Investment		
	Investment in Equity	Investment Reinvested Earnings	Investment Other Capital	Total	Portfolio Investment in India of which FIIs	Portfolio Investment in India of which GDRs/ADRs	Total
2003–2004	2,229	1,460	633	4,322	–	–	28,218
2004–2005	3,779	1,904	369	6,052	0	0	40,847
2005–2006	5,976	2,760	226	8,962	0	0	68,120
2006–2007	16,481	5,828	517	22,826	1,05,756	3,776	1,09,534
2007–2008	26,866	7,680	300	34,844	2,26,621	6,645	2,33,564
2008–2009	32,094	9,032	776	41,902	1,27,349	1,162	1,28,511
2009–2010	27,146	8,668	1,931	37,745	1,56,570	3,328	1,59,897
2010–2011	22,250	13,102	695	36,047	2,51,125	2,049	2,53,175
2011–2012	35,852	8,205	2,494	46,552	1,84,150	597	1,84,747
2012–2013	22,885	9,880	1,534	34,298	1,73,575	187	1,73,762
2013–2014	25,274	8,978	1,794	36,046	–	–	–
2014–2015	31,911	9,988	3,249	45,148	–	–	–
2015–2016	41,043	10,049	4,365	55,457	–	–	–

Source: Department of Industrial Policy and Promotion.

The category of share of foreign investment in the country indicates that direct investment in the total foreign investment was 23% in 2000, which increased to 37% in 2001–2002 and recorded 25% share in 2008–2009. The current share of direct investment in the total foreign investment is 16%, which decreased from the previous years. Portfolio investment has been dominating the total foreign investment in the country. As far as the category of direct investment is concerned, investment in equity has been very high. The share of equity in the total direct foreign investment increased over 75% in 2008–2009. At present, it is 74%, which increased from 2013–2014. In the year 2013–2014, the share of direct foreign investment in equity was 70.7%. However, in 2011–2012, the same was 77%. The new format of portfolio investment provides data on net portfolio investment. Therefore, the data from 2014 onward is not given in the table above.

17.8 SOURCES OF FDI IN INDIA

The direction of FDI in India suggests that the main sources of FDI are Mauritius, the UK, Singapore and the USA. In the year 2015–2016, Singapore contributed highest FDI inflows in equity in India with a share of 34% and Mauritius accounted for 21%. The UK had a share of 2%, a sharp decrease from the previous years. In 2011–2012, the UK accounted for 25% of India's total FDI in equity. The United States was the third largest source of FDI in equity in India accounting for 10% in 2015–2016. Table 17.4 shows the FDI inflow in India from country of sources. When we consider cumulative FDI from 2000 to 2016, Mauritius is the highest contributor in FDI in equity with share of 33%. Similarly, Singapore accounts for 16% of FDI in equity.

Table 17.4 FDI Inflows in India: Major Sources (US$ Million)

Country	*2010–11*	*2011–12*	*2012–13*	*2013–14*	*2014–15*	*2015–16*	*2000–16*
Mauritius	6,987	9,942	–	4,859	9,030	8,355	95,910
Singapore	1,705	5,257	–	5,985	6,742	13,692	45,880
UK	755	9,257	–	3,215	1,447	898	23,108
Japan	1,562	2,972	–	1,718	2,084	2,614	20,966
USA	1,170	1,115	–	806	1,824	4,192	17,943
The Netherlands	1,213	1,409	–	2,270	3,436	2,643	17,314
Cyprus	913	1,587	–	557	598	508	8,552
Germany	200	1,622	–	1,038	1,125	986	8,629
France	734	663	–	305	635	598	5,111
UAE	341	353	–	255	367	985	4,030
Total	**19,427**	**36,504**	–	**24,299**	**30,931**	**40,001**	**2,88,634**

Source: DIPP, Ministry of Commerce and Industry, Government of India.

The cumulative accumulation of FDI during 2000–2016 shows that India has FDI inflows worth US$2,88,634 million, out of which Mauritius contributed US$95,910 million, and Singapore was the second largest contributor, with the contribution of US$45,880 million.

Considering the sectoral share of India's FDI, it is seen that out of the total FDI inflows, 18% was attracted to the services sector during 2000–2016, which include banking, financial, insurance, non-banking, outsourcing, R&D and testing services, etc. Construction sector attracted US$24,188 million, accounting for 8% of the total FDI inflows in equity in the country. The sector-wise FDI inflows in equity are presented in Table 17.5.

Table 17.5 Sectoral Share of FDI Inflows in India During 2000–2016 (US$ Million)

Industries	*FDI*	*Share (%)*
Services sector	50,792	18
Telecommunications	18,382	6
Construction activities	24,188	8
Computer software and hardware	21,018	7
Chemicals	11,900	4
Drugs and pharmaceuticals	13,849	5
Power	10,476	4
Automobile industry	15,065	5
Hotel and tourism	9,227	3
Trading	11,872	4
Total	**2,88,634**	**64**

Source: DIPP, Ministry of Commerce and Industry, Government of India.

Closing Case: Investment Regimes in Nepal and Bhutan

Nepal and Bhutan are India's neighbour and constitute an integral part of South Asian Association for Regional Cooperation (SAARC). With the evolving investment regime in India, it is imperative that we understand the same in context of Nepal and Bhutan. A harmonisation of investment regime, though a distant reality, would definitely lead to more FDI inflows in South Asia.

Also, it is important to note that both Nepal and Bhutan are least developed countries (LDCs) and get preferential treatment by many developed and developing countries under the multilateral trading system.

Nepal

It was in the year 1987 that Nepal enacted its Investment and Industrial Enterprise Act. This act was instrumental in developing an institutional framework for investment. It focused on joint ventures as a preferred mode of investment and attracted FDI inflows to the medium and large-scale industries.

Nepal's Ministry of Industry has a Foreign Investment Promotion Division (FIPD) that is mandated to grant approval for the new projects. A 100% foreign equity was allowed in such large-scale industries, which export 90% of their total industrial production. Also, 50% foreign equity was allowed in medium-scale industries.[22]

Some of the sectors which are open through either equity or joint ventures (JVs) include the following:

1. Agro-based industries
2. Manufacturing
3. Tourism
4. Services
5. Mineral-based industries

Foreign investments are not allowed in the sectors including cottage industries, real estate, and those related to defence.

Some of the characteristics of the investment regime in Nepal include the following:

1. It provides incentives for export-related industries.
2. Such incentives could be relaxations or exemptions in taxation.
3. Process patent have been protected in case of IPR.
4. Product patents are yet to comply to the international commitments.
5. Institutional framework for investment need to be strengthened in terms of protection of investor's rights.

Bhutan

Bhutan is another South Asian country, which is continuously improving its investment climate. The country has a unique concept of maximising gross national happiness, which actually

22. Ramesh, C. and Weiss, J., 'Foreign investment in Nepal in the 1980s: A cost benefit evaluation', *The Journal of Development Studies*, 31(3), 1995.

guides its development interventions. Tourism is a major sector attracting FDI to Bhutan largely through JVs.

The Royal Government of Bhutan has adopted FDI policy in 2010.

The policy outlines that the FDI calls for encouraging FDI to contribute to the following:[23]

1. Investments in services that promote Brand Bhutan
2. Development of green and sustainable economy
3. Promotion of socially responsible and ecologically sound industries
4. Creation of a knowledge society
5. Promotion of culturally and spiritually sensitive industries

Some of the key features of this policy are listed below:

1. It provides for the protection of IPRs, as it is a member of World Intellectual Property Organisation (WIPO) and is also a signatory to Paris Convention, Madrid Agreement and Berne Convention.
2. It provides the guarantee to the foreign investors in terms of equal treatment.
3. It calls for carrying out nationalisation or expropriation in a non-discriminatory manner.
4. The Policy also provides incentives related to taxation.

Table 1 gives an account of the FDI inflows in Nepal and Bhutan as compared to some other South Asian economies including India.

Table 1 FDI Inflows in Select South Asian Countries (US$ million)

Countries	*1990*	*2000*	*2005*	*2008*	*2009*	*2010*	*2011*
Afghanistan	–	0.0	271.0	94.0	76.0	211.0	83.0
Bangladesh	3.0	579.0	845.0	1,086.0	700.0	913.0	1,136.0
Bhutan	2.0	0.0	9.0	7.0	18.0	16.0	14.0
Nepal	6.0	0.0	2.0	1.0	39.0	87.0	95.0
India	237.0	3,588.0	7,622.0	43,406.0	35,596.0	24,159.0	31,554.0

Source: World Investment Report 2012, UNCTAD.

Some of the potential sectors for attracting foreign investment to Bhutan include power projects, hydropower, construction, communication, airports infrastructure, etc. In case of Nepal, the potential sectors include tourism, services, hydroelectric power generation, manufacturing, pharmaceuticals, transport, communications, financial services, etc.

Source: This case is written by the authors based on inputs from the following sources:

1. FDI Policy 2010 document, Ministry of Economic Affairs, Royal Government of Bhutan, http://www.dit.gov.bt/sites/default/files/FDI%20POLICY%202010(new).pdf
2. C. Ramesh and J. Weiss, 'Foreign investment in Nepal in the 1980s: A cost benefit evaluation', *The Journal of Development Studies*, 31(3), 1995.

23. FDI Policy 2010 document, Ministry of Economic Affairs, Royal Government of Bhutan, http://www.dit.gov.bt/sites/default/files/FDI%20POLICY%202010(new).pdf

CASE QUESTIONS

1. Find out the most recent developments in the FDI regime in Nepal.
2. Examine Bhutan FDI Policy 2010 in detail and find out its major provisions.

REVIEW QUESTIONS

1. What do you mean by FDI?
2. Why is FDI important?
3. What are the various types of FDI?
4. What is the theory of market imperfection?
5. How does international production theory explain FDI flows?
6. Discuss the OLI Model of FDI.
7. In the developing world, which countries attract more FDI? Discuss.
8. Discuss the regional inflow of FDI.
9. What is the role of Foreign Investment Implementation Authority in India?
10. Highlight the sectors where 100% automatic FDI is allowed in India.
11. What are the major sources of FDI in India?
12. Outline the sector that attracts more FDI in India?

SUGGESTED READINGS

'Benchmark Definition of Foreign Direct Investment (FDI)', 2008, 4th ed., Organisation for Economic Co-operation and Development (OECD).

Circulars on Industrial Policy, Department of Industrial Policy and Promotion (DIPP), Government of India, New Delhi.

Daniels, J.D., Radebaugh, Lee, H., Sullivan, Daniel P., and Salwan, Prashant, 2009, *International Business: Environments and Operation*, 12th ed., Dorling Kindersley (India).

FDI in India and its Growth Linkages, 2009, NCAER, New Delhi.

'Handbook of Industrial Policy and Statistics (various issues)', Office of Economic Adviser, Ministry of Commerce and Industry, Government of India, New Delhi.

Hill, C.W.L. and Jain, A.K., 2009, *International Business: Competing in the Global Marketplace*, Tata McGraw-Hill Education, New Delhi.

Paul, J., 2012, *International Business*, PHI Learning, Delhi.

World Investment Report, 2014, UNCTAD, Geneva.

18

TRENDS IN GLOBAL TRADE AND ECONOMIC INTEGRATION

Learning Outcomes

After reading this chapter, you will

- Understand the basic concepts of multilateralism and regional integration
- Comprehend the various levels of economic integration including FTA, customs union, common market, etc.
- Develop an understanding of the trade blocs like EU, SAARC, ASEAN and others

Opening Case: IOR-ARC—Integrating the Boundaries of the Indian Ocean!

Indian Ocean Rim Association for Regional Cooperation (IOR-ARC) is an international organisation, which is unique in nature. It promotes cooperation among the coastal states situated along the Indian Ocean. The cooperation among the states encompasses countries from Southeast Asia, Indian subcontinent, Southern and Eastern Africa, Arabian peninsula and Australia.

This region is the most diverse region, which came together for both political and economic cooperation. The countries of the region came together in 1995 in Mauritius to discuss regarding the economic cooperation among them. Consequently, a Working Group was formed, which included stakeholders from the government, private sector and academics. The Working Group met in Mauritius again in the same year. In 1996, the Charter was finalised by the working group in the very next year, and IORA was formally launched.

Currently, 20 countries are the member states of the association, which include Australia, Bangladesh, Comoros, India, Indonesia, Iran, Kenya, Madagascar, Malaysia, Mauritius, Mozambique, Oman, Seychelles, Singapore, South Africa, Sri Lanka, Tanzania, Thailand, United Arab Emirates (UAE) and Yemen. The charter is known as the *Charter of the Indian Ocean Rim Association for Regional Co-operation.*

The fundamental principles of the charter speak about working towards facilitating and promoting economic cooperation between the member states. The priority areas are identified in the charter. These priority areas for cooperation include maritime safety and security, trade and investment facilitation, fisheries management, disaster risk management, science and technology cooperation, tourism and cultural exchanges. To achieve the proposed objective, the charter has also spelt out the action plan and policy guidelines. These guidelines are related to trade and energy cooperation, among others.

A key aspect of this organisation is the promotion of trade through sea transport. Thus, the organisation helps in integrating the countries beyond boundaries. This is an initiative for intercontinental cooperation as it includes countries from three major continents in the world including Asia, Africa and Australia. IOR-ARC is also planning to have a preferential trade agreement (PTA). The feasibility study for PTA is underway.

The region of IOR-ARC has more than 2 billion people, constituting more than one-third of the world and produces about 8% of the world production. The trade integration of the member countries would be largely beneficial to the vast population. The most important aspect is the trade through sea transport, which has a lower cost of transport eventually, leading to reduction in the trade cost.

Intraregional trade within IORA is 24% of its global trade, which has been increasing as well. The increase in intraregional trade would require close cooperation in certain area such as fisheries. Fisheries and marine resources have vital importance in the cooperation model of IOR-ARC.

Source: This case is written by the authors based on inputs from the following sources:

1. IORA Website; Department of Foreign Affairs, Government of Australia, https://www.dfat.gov.au/geo/indian-ocean/iora.html
2. IDSA, http://www.idsa-india.org/an-may-6.html
3. Ministry of External Affairs, India, http://mea.gov.in/Images/pdf/bengaluru-communique-infocus.pdf

18.1 DIRECTION OF WORLD TRADE

With an unprecedented growth and increasing liberalisation, international trade is now a major determinant of the global economic growth. Since 1970, the global trade has increased more than twenty-fold. This phenomenal increase in trade has also helped in increasing the level of productivity across the sectors. When we study the magnitude of global trade, it is important for us to know the trend of this trade and its direction in order to identify the major economies, which have gained from the trade liberalisation process. In addition, we need to look at economies which are least developed, but have performed well after having integrated with the multilateral trading system.

During the post-World War II period, colonialism started to disintegrate, and several newly independent countries took to democratic forms of government. India was among one such country. The period also saw the rise in regional building efforts at continental and sub-regional levels. Global trade became one of the important sources of such an integration process.[1] This process led to the growth of world economy after the World War II. During the first two decades

1. http://www.theworldeconomy.org/advances/advances2.html

of the post-World War II period, developed countries dominated the trade flows. This is also evident from Table 18.1 that trade openness had increased during this period.[2]

Table 18.1 Trade Openness (1948–1990)

Region	*1948*	*1958*	*1968*	*1979*	*1990*
World	22	22	22	35	34
Western Europe	35	33	34	48	46
North America	11	9	10	19	19
Asia	25	26	21	27	29
Latin America	30	30	21	27	28
Africa	50	58	37	56	53

Source: Nigel Grimwade (2000).

The international trade flows are typically divided into two parts, *viz.* imports and exports. Over the years, there is an evidence of significant change in the direction of trade in terms of both exports and imports. After the World War II, the trend of exports and imports indicates that European countries and the United States were dominating the world trade flows. In fact, these countries were the industrialised economies, where production of manufacturing items and heavy machineries were high. Consequently, the exports of goods from these countries increased by multiple times.

On the other hand, developing countries and LDCs were having raw materials such as minerals, agricultural produce and cotton for textiles. These items were exported to the industrialised countries and the products manufactured from these items were sent to the markets in the developing countries and LDCs. Thus, the terms of trade have been in the favour of industrialised countries.

Just after the World War II, several changes occurred in the world economy. These changes were based on multilateralism. General Agreement on Tariffs and Trade (GATT) became an important institution for multilateral agreements on trade. In 1995, World Trade Organisation (WTO) came into being and started negotiation among the developed countries, developing countries and LDCs for rule-making on international trade (see Chapters 14, 19 and 20 for more details on WTO). These systems systematically talked about reduction in trade barriers for international trade based on the principles of the trading system like most favoured nation (MFN) treatment (see Chapter 19 for more information on MFN and other WTO principles). This also resulted in increase in the export potential of developing nations.

In addition, the composition of exports and imports of these nations have also diversified after gaining WTO membership. During the past twenty years, several poor countries gained from trade liberalisation. Also, the practice of import substitution among the developing economies was replaced by a new regime of economic liberalisation.

Services sector trade became an important instrument for transfer of technological know-how. These developments have considerably impacted the direction of trade flows. Countries

2. Nigel Grimwade (2000), International Trade: New Patterns of Trade, Production and Investment, London: Routledge, http://www.unc.edu/~toatley/poli140/Chapter_2.pdf

like China, Taiwan, South Korea and Japan also became major players in the global trade network. In fact, China is now replacing the United States as a major player in the global trade. Table 18.2 provides statistics about the evolving export trend from 1948 through 2015, while Table 18.3 provides for import trend during the same period.

Table 18.2 Direction of Exports after World War II

World	*1948*	*1953*	*1963*	*1973*	*1983*	*1993*	*2003*	*2012*	*2013*	*2014*	*2015*
	Values (US$ billion)										
	59	**84**	**157**	**579**	**1,838**	**3,677**	**7,380**	**17,930**	**18,948**	**18,995**	**16,482**
	Share (%)										
World	100.0	100.0	100.0	100.0	100.0	100.0	100.0	100.0	100.0	100.0	100.0
North America	28.1	24.8	19.9	17.3	16.8	18.0	15.8	13.2	12.8	13.1	13.9
United States	21.7	18.8	14.9	12.3	11.2	12.6	9.8	8.6	8.3	8.5	9.1
Canada	5.5	5.2	4.3	4.6	4.2	3.9	3.7	2.5	2.4	2.5	2.5
Mexico	0.9	0.7	0.6	0.4	1.4	1.4	2.2	2.1	2.0	2.1	2.3
South and Central America	11.3	9.7	6.4	4.3	4.4	3.0	3.0	4.2	3.9	3.6	3.3
Brazil	2.0	1.8	0.9	1.1	1.2	1.0	1.0	1.4	1.3	1.2	1.2
Argentina	2.8	1.3	0.9	0.6	0.4	0.4	0.4	0.5	0.4	0.4	0.3
Europe	35.1	39.4	47.8	50.9	43.5	45.3	45.9	35.6	35.8	35.8	36.1
Germany	1.4	5.3	9.3	11.7	9.2	10.3	10.2	7.8	7.6	7.9	8.1
France	3.4	4.8	5.2	6.3	5.2	6.0	5.3	3.2	3.1	3.1	3.1
Italy	1.8	1.8	3.2	3.8	4.0	4.6	4.1	2.8	2.7	2.8	2.8
United Kingdom	11.3	9.0	7.8	5.1	5.0	4.9	4.1	2.6	2.9	2.7	2.8
Commonwealth of Independent States (CIS)	–	–	–	–	–	1.5	2.6	4.5	4.1	3.9	3.0
Africa	7.3	6.5	5.7	4.8	4.5	2.5	2.4	3.5	3.2	2.9	2.4
South Africa	2.0	1.6	1.5	1.0	1.0	0.7	0.5	0.5	0.5	0.5	0.5
Middle East	2.0	2.7	3.2	4.1	6.8	3.5	4.1	7.5	7.1	6.8	5.1
Asia	14.0	13.4	12.5	14.9	19.1	26.1	26.1	31.5	33.2	33.9	36.2
China	0.9	1.2	1.3	1.0	1.2	2.5	5.9	11.4	11.7	12.3	13.8
Japan	0.4	1.5	3.5	6.4	8.0	9.9	6.4	4.5	3.8	3.6	3.8
India	2.2	1.3	1.0	0.5	0.5	0.6	0.8	1.6	1.7	1.7	1.6
Australia and New Zealand	3.7	3.2	2.4	2.1	1.4	1.4	1.2	1.6	–	–	–
EU	–	–	24.5	37.0	31.3	37.4	42.3	32.4	32.1	32.4	32.7
GATT/WTO Members	63.4	69.6	75.0	84.1	78.4	89.3	94.3	96.6	–	–	–

Source: WTO.

Table 18.3 Direction of Imports after World War II

	1948	*1953*	*1963*	*1973*	*1983*	*1993*	*2003*	*2012*	*2013*	*2014*	*2015*
	Values (US$ billion)										
World	**62**	**85**	**164**	**594**	**1,882**	**3,787**	**7,696**	**18,188**	**19,011**	**19,104**	**16,725**
	Share (%)										
World	100.0	100.0	100.0	100.0	100.0	100.0	100.0	100.0	100.0	100.0	100.0
North America	18.5	20.5	16.1	17.2	18.5	21.4	22.4	17.6	16.8	17.3	18.8
United States	13.0	13.9	11.4	12.3	14.3	15.9	16.9	12.8	12.3	12.6	13.8
Canada	4.4	5.5	3.9	4.2	3.4	3.7	3.2	2.6	2.5	2.5	2.6
Mexico	1.0	0.9	0.8	0.6	0.7	1.8	2.3	2.1	2.1	2.2	2.4
South America and Central America	10.4	8.3	6.0	4.4	3.8	3.3	2.5	4.1	4.1	3.9	3.7
Brazil	1.8	1.6	0.9	1.2	0.9	0.7	0.7	1.3	1.3	1.3	1.1
Argentina	2.5	0.9	0.6	0.4	0.2	0.4	0.2	0.4	0.4	0.3	0.4
Europe	45.3	43.7	52.0	53.3	44.2	44.6	45.0	35.9	35.4	35.6	35.3
Germany	2.2	4.5	8.0	9.2	8.1	9.0	7.9	6.4	6.2	6.3	6.3
France	5.5	4.9	5.3	6.4	5.6	5.7	5.2	3.7	3.6	3.5	3.4
Italy	2.5	2.8	4.6	4.7	4.2	3.9	3.9	2.7	2.5	2.5	2.4
United Kingdom	13.4	11.0	8.5	6.5	5.3	5.5	5.2	3.8	3.5	3.6	3.7
CIS	–	–	–	–	–	1.2	1.7	3.1	3.0	2.6	2.1
Africa	8.1	7.0	5.2	3.9	4.6	2.6	2.2	3.4	3.3	3.4	3.3
South Africa	2.5	1.5	1.1	0.9	0.8	0.5	0.5	0.7	0.7	0.6	0.6
Middle East	1.8	2.1	2.3	2.7	6.2	3.3	2.8	4.1	4.0	4.1	4.2
Asia	13.9	15.1	14.1	14.9	18.5	23.6	23.5	31.8	33.4	33.1	32.5
China	0.6	1.6	0.9	0.9	1.1	2.7	5.4	10.0	10.3	10.3	10.1
Japan	1.1	2.8	4.1	6.5	6.7	6.4	5.0	4.9	4.4	4.3	3.9
India	2.3	1.4	1.5	0.5	0.7	0.6	0.9	2.7	2.4	2.4	2.3
Australia and New Zealand	2.9	2.3	2.2	1.6	1.4	1.5	1.4	1.6	–	–	–
EU	–	–	–	–	–	–	41.8	32.6	31.6	32.1	31.8
GATT/WTO Members	58.6	66.9	75.3	85.5	81.3	88.7	94.8	97.6	–	–	–

Source: WTO.

18.2 MULTILATERALISM AND THE MULTILATERAL TRADING SYSTEM

Multilateralism is a concept emerged with the emergence of Bretton Woods institutions (see Chapter 14 for more details on World Bank, a Bretton Woods institution). The concept got more intensified when conclusion of several agreements took place during Uruguay Rounds of negotiations in 1994. These negotiations established a multilateral trading system, which aimed at reducing tariff, non-tariff barriers and protectionism. The round concluded agreements pertaining to trade in both goods and services.

The negotiations in Uruguay Round largely focused on trade liberalisation through elimination of quota system and also through reduction of tariff rates. It also covered other trade-related aspects like intellectual property rights (IPRs), trademarks and copyrights, etc. The Uruguay Round increased binding commitments. The developed economies increased their shares of bindings in the total tariff lines from 78% before the round to 99% after the negotiations. In case of developing countries, it increased from 21% to 73% (see Table 18.4).

Table 18.4 Binding Commitments before and after the Uruguay Round

Percentages of tariffs bound before and after the 1986–1994 Doha Round		
	Before	***After***
Developed countries	78	99
Developing countries	21	73
Transition economies	73	98

Source: WTO.

The role of WTO gradually increased in the world. Many countries including China and Russia too joined the WTO over the years. WTO now has 164 members as of 29 July 2016 with the latest addition of Afghanistan. It controls more than 97% of the world trade.

Multilateralism has its own way, but owing to difficult and time taking stances of multilateral negotiations, countries have reverted to bilateral and regional agreements as well. In fact, Article XXIV of the GATT provides for free trade agreements. There is, however, a significant discourse on whether these regional trade agreements (RTAs) are building blocks of multilateralism or deters multilateral rule-making.

However, post the World War II, there has been a significant increase in the number of regional trade agreements (RTAs) or formation of regional blocs. Moreover, since the last decade of the 20th century, the world has also been witnessing an increase in the number of preferential/free trade agreements on a bilateral level. It, therefore, becomes important to first understand the various levels of economic integration.

18.3 LEVELS OF ECONOMIC INTEGRATION

Economic integration is defined as the process of harmonisation of policies between the countries and also adopting liberal trade policies. This process is generally achieved through systematic reduction or elimination of tariff and non-tariff barriers based on the global minimum commitments, regional arrangements and bilateral agreements, etc. The process of economic integration has been significantly affecting the global economy.

The level of economic integration is defined by the type of trade negotiations. There can be a preferential trade agreement (PTA) or a free trade agreement (FTA) among countries. For example, in South Asia, the member countries entered into South Asian PTA (or SAPTA) in 1993 and later signed South Asian FTA (SAFTA) agreement in 2004. In some areas, by the formation of customs union (CU), countries are shaping their integration process (see Figure 18.1 depicting various levels of economic integration). Some agreements are also taking place between one regional groupings. For example, EFTA (Comprising Iceland, Liechtenstein, Norway and Switzerland) signed an FTA with 6-member Gulf Cooperation Council (GCC) on 22 June 2009. However, the countries must aspire to adhere to the global minimum commitments as a part of the multilateral rule-making system.

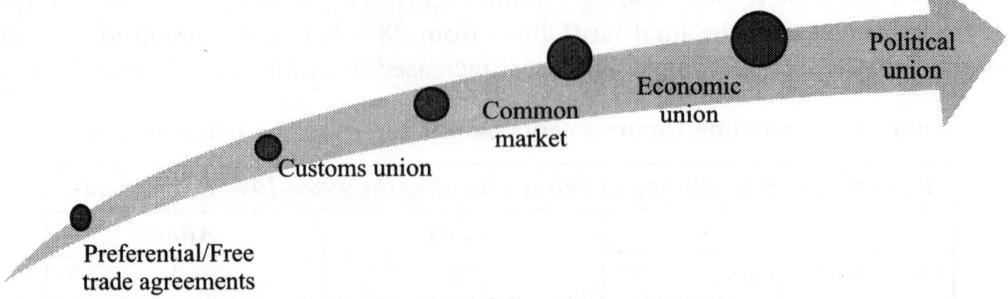

Figure 18.1 Levels of economic integration.

The various levels of economic integration are as follows:

Free trade agreement (FTA)

The countries can also enter into preferential trade agreements (PTAs) by providing tariff concessions for each other on specified commodities. Though some of the earlier agreements were PTAs, but in recent years, the basic level of integration starts with a free trade agreement (FTA) or a comprehensive economic partnership agreement (CEPA) or a comprehensive economic cooperation agreement (CECA).

Today, FTA may not necessarily be confined to an agreement on trade in goods also; some of them may be more comprehensive and also include services, IPR, investments, etc. just to be called *CEPA* or *CECA*. In fact, *FTA* is a process of elimination of tariff barriers and non-tariff measures for specified commodities by the contracting parties. Under such agreement, each member country is obliged to reduce trade barriers and helps in attaining seamless trade flows.

In such agreements, member countries generally prepare a negative list of commodities, which is kept out of the purview of the FTA. Some countries also follow positive list approach, specifying only those commodities which are allowed to be under the purview of FTA. For instance, Pakistan has followed a positive list approach towards India for a considerable duration under South Asian Free Trade Agreement (SAFTA). Such an approach has been a deterrent to the enhanced trade flows.

A better approach, however, is to follow the negative list approach and to it pruning over the years. This will allow more commodities coming under the purview of FTA and will, thus, support the process of liberalisation. India has signed several such agreements and is also negotiating several others. Over the years, India's PTA negotiations have become more robust in terms of methodological sophistication and stakeholder consultations, and have focused on comprehensive economic goals.[3]

3. Faisal Ahmed and P.C. Jena (2012), *India's Experiences on Preferential Trade Agreements (PTAs)*, Published by CUTS International, ISBN: 978-81-8257-162-4, March 2012.

For instance, some of the PTAs/FTAs/CECA/CEPA already signed by India include the following:

1. India–Sri Lanka FTA (1999)
2. India–Afghanistan PTA (2003)
3. India–MERCOSUR PTA (2003)
4. India–Chile PTA (2005)
5. India–ASEAN FTA (2009)
6. India–Republic of Korea CEPA (2009)
7. India–Japan CEPA (2011)
8. India–Malaysia CECA (2011)

Customs union

The next level of integration is the formation of a customs union.

The basic characteristics of a customs union include the following:

1. ***Single point of entry:*** For instance, if we take the example of Belarus–Kazakhstan–Russia Customs Union (BKRCU), a commodity which has reached Russia would be said to have reached Belarus and Kazakhstan as well (see Box 18.1 on BKRCU).
2. ***Common external tariff (CET):*** A customs union imposes a CET on its external trading partners. For instance, the Gulf Cooperation Council (GCC) countries imposed a CET of 5% when they formed a customs union.

A customs union implies a free trade plus common external tariff (CET).

Box 18.1 Belarus-Kazakhstan-Russia Customs Union

Five of the CIS countries, namely, Belarus, Kazakhstan, Kyrgyz Republic, Russia and Tajikistan entered into an agreement to form the Eurasian Economic Community (EurAsEC) in 2000. EurAsEC has further deepened this integration with three of its members—Belarus, Kazakhstan and Russia (BKR), forming a Customs Union. Recently, India agreed to start negotiations for a Comprehensive Economic Cooperation Agreement (CECA) with BKRCU. This is deemed to facilitate easier investments by Indian entrepreneurs in this customs union territory.

In fact, India already has an investment promotion agreement with each of these three countries, but on a bilateral basis. However, the level of mutual investment is inadequate. These economies having investor-friendly climate are capable of developing efficient regional value chains. Also, the companies from both sides can explore mutual cooperation through strategic alliances and JVs in sectors such as oil and petrochemicals, minerals, timber, pharmaceuticals, consumer goods, transport, construction, minerals, fertilisers, civil nuclear energy, infrastructure development, etc.

Source: Faisal Ahmed, 'India and Eurasia: Looking forward to CECA', Diplomatist, Special Report on India Eurasia 2013.

Common market

A common market implies a customs union with free movement of factors of production such as labour and capital. The common market for Eastern and Southern Africa (COMESA) is an example of such kind of integration (also see Box 18.2). Other example of a common market is Gulf Cooperation Council (GCC).

Box 18.2 Common Market for Eastern and Southern Africa (COMESA)

COMESA is a free trade area in Eastern and Southern Africa. It was formed in 1994 and comprises 20 member countries, some of which are Djibouti, Egypt, Kenya, Madagascar, Malawi, Mauritius, Sudan, Zambia, Zimbabwe, etc.

The COMESA Treaty strongly advocated strategies for the development of the region through creation of a common market. Its mission is to achieve a sustainable development process through trade liberalisation and customs cooperation.

Since its inception, intraregional FDI increased from 1% during 2003–2005 to 8% during 2009–2011. Similarly, the trade within COMESA increased significantly. For example, intra-COMESA exports increased by more than five-fold during 2000–2010; whereas, the intraregional imports increased by about six-fold.

COMESA has been actively contributing to African integration through its efforts at sub-regional level. It, however, faces some of the issue of sub-regional connectivity within its territorial extent in terms of high transportation cost.

Source: COMESA.

Economic union

An economic union is a common market with common monetary and fiscal policy along with the existence of a common currency. This type of integration is achieved in case of the European Union (EU), which is an economic union (see Box 18.3). On the other hand, some regional trade blocs such as the Association of Southeast Asian Nations (ASEAN) and COMESA are gradually progressing towards becoming an economic union.

Box 18.3 EU as Economic Union

Economic and Monetary Union (EMU) of Europe is a major step in creating economic union in the region. The European Union (EU) has formed a common monetary unit in this direction called *Euro*.

In fact, the decision to form an economic union within the region was advocated during the meeting of European Council (EC) in Maastricht in December 1991.

The Maastricht Treaty was signed in February 1992 and came into force in November 1993. This treaty created the european union. Together, 18 member countries, with Latvia joining in January 2014, of the 28-member EU share a common currency.

Moreover, the European Central Bank (ECB) was created to look after the common monetary policy of the region.

Source: European Union, http://europa.eu/about-eu/countries/index_en.htm

Political union

This is the highest level of integration. It is defined as a common government, with the presence of common economic and monetary policy.

18.4 REGIONAL INTEGRATION

Regional integration has now become a global phenomenon. It may be defined as a process of integration under which a group of countries within a geographical region enter into mutual cooperation for trade and socio-economic development. It is called as *regional trade agreement (RTAs)* or more commonly as *trade blocs*. It is, thus, also referred to as *regional cooperation.*

Regional cooperation has emerged concurrently with the emergence of globalisation. Most of the regional cooperation initiatives have been inclined towards a regional FTA, and ultimately the formation of an economic union. A significant example is the European Union. Also, the African Union integration process has the ambition to develop a common market.

Regional arrangements and FTAs are negotiated under the WTO agreements. Article XXIV of the GATT provides for the same. However, the article stipulates that the purpose of such agreements, however, should be to enhance trade flows among the member countries. It should not be aimed at increasing trade barriers for the other members.[4] The GATT/WTO, as of 1 July 2016, received around 635 notifications of RTAs. Out of these, 423 RTAs are in force.[5]

Moreover, India has an evolving trade relation with the regional blocs or regions as such (see Figure 18.2 for India's trade with the region as of 2014–2015). The subsequent section discusses about some of the major trade blocs across the world and India's trade with them.

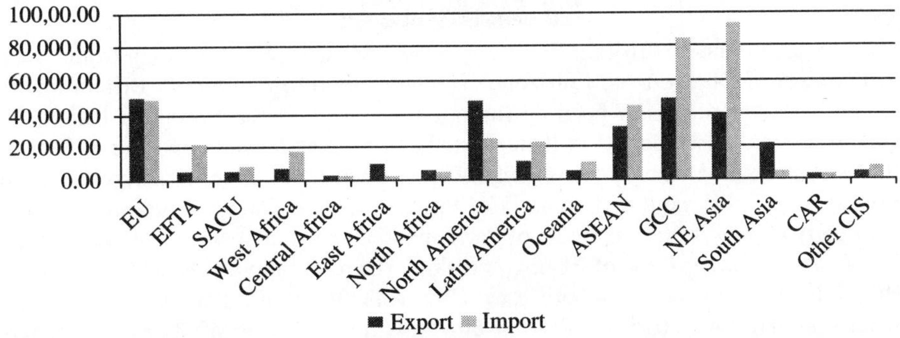

Figure 18.2 India's trade with the world (region-wise), 2014–2015 (in US$ million).
Source: Based on data from Export Import Data Bank, Department of Commerce, Government of India.

European Union

The European Union (EU) is a regional economic cooperation initiative among 28 member countries in Europe. The history of its formation dates back to the period just after the World War II. The war had left Europe in a volatile situation.

After the war, the European Coal and Steel Community started working towards uniting the European countries economically and politically. The genesis of the EU rests with the Treaty of Rome in 1957, through which a European Economic Community (EEC) or a common market was created. Its founding members were Belgium, France, Germany, Italy, Luxembourg and The Netherlands.

4. Understanding on the Interpretation of Article XXIV of the General Agreement on Tariffs and Trade 1994, http://www.wto.org/english/docs_e/legal_e/10-24_e.htm
5. Regional Trade Agreement, WTO, http://www.wto.org/english/tratop_e/region_e/region_e.htm

In 1973, three more countries joined the EU. These countries are Denmark, Ireland and the United Kingdom. In February 1992, the Maastricht Treaty was signed and it came into force in 1993, leading to the creation of European Union (EU). In 1993, the EU was able to establish a single or common market among the member countries through free flow of products as well as factors of production. Formally, the EU became an economic union, with over 200 agreed laws on monetary and fiscal policies.

After the establishment of the European Parliament in 1979, the EU had become an example of politically integrated area with common commitments. However, the European Parliament has limited legislative power as compared to the power vested with the national Parliaments of the member states. In 1995, Austria, Finland and Sweden joined the EU, making the union an effective organisation both in Central and Eastern Europe. It became a full-fledged economic union with the introduction of common currency—the Euro—in 1999.

The story of regional integration in EU is one of successful example of regional integration. However, it is noteworthy to present a recent event, popularly known as 'BREXIT'. The UK, which was posed with a question whether it should remain in the EU or exit it, went for a referendum. On 23 June 2016, the UK got 52% votes in favour of exiting from the EU (referred to as 'BREXIT') (see Box 18.4).

Box 18.4 BREXIT

Brexit is a term which refers to "Britain Exit", and it has been derived by analogy from 'Grexit' that refers to withdrawal of Greece from Eurozone. The term, therefore, refers to Britain's withdrawal from Eurozone Union. Britain has been an important member of the European Union. Since the inception of Britain in the EU, people in Britain had been supporting and opposing it. Several times, referendum took place on Britain's EU membership. However, in 2016, a different kind of wave started in political establishment of Britain. The Prime Minister, David Cameroon under pressure from his own party members and Members of Parliament, and also, due to rise of far right in politics announced referendum on the issue of EU membership. The referendum was held on 23rd June 2016 with the British having two choices—vote "Leave" or vote "Remain". The result of the referendum was announced on 24th June 2016, with 51.9% citizen voting in favour of "Leave"; whereas 48.1% voting in favour of "Remain". The outcome of the referendum was clear.

Next is to see the impact on the world economy after this referendum. As per statistics, the EU is the destination of half of exports from the UK. This is a result of free trade linkages between Britain and rest of the countries in the EU. The benefits are enjoyed by the UK under economic union of the EU. Under the Lisbon Treaty, a country leaving the European Union has 2 years to negotiate a withdrawal agreement. During this period, Britain will have to negotiate free trade agreement as well with major trading partner in the EU to offset the negative impacts on trade to reduce tariffs on its export. The estimates of impact of Brexit on the GDP of Britain indicate that there will be a decrease in GDP by the 2.2% to 9%. The Centre for Economic Performance at the London School of Economics estimates that Britain's leaving the EU and joining the European Free Trade Association (EFTA) will reduce British's GDP by at least 2.2% in its optimistic scenario, and between 6.3% and 9.5% in its pessimistic one.

The impact of Brexit was felt not only on the UK but also on its trading partners globally. The reaction of the referendum received negative impact on world market. During the Asian trading day, Pound plunged against the Dollar by over 10% to US$1.32, a 30-year low. When Europe's markets opened, the main stock indices followed the lead set overnight in Asia and fell by around 10%. Moreover, Brexit would hurt the world economy in other ways, which include its financial integration with the economy like China. But a significant impact would be the spillover effects across Europe. If such waves spread in the EU, then the world economy will definitely see a weaker Europe, leading to impact the economy of developing world such as China and India. In fact, the future depends on the kind of trade deals that would happen between Britain and other EU countries in a post-Brexit era.

Source: 'The Economic Impact of Brexit', *Woodford*, https://woodfordfunds.com/economic-impact-brexit-report/; and, 'Why Brexit Grin News for the World Economy', *The Economist*, 24th June 2016; http://www.economist.com/news/finance-and-economics/21701292-uncertainty-abounds-expect-global-chilling-effect-investment-why-brexit

The intraregional trade in the EU has grown significantly and establishes a strong trade linkage among them. Moreover, EU's global trade has also evolved over the years and its global exports accounted for US$5,803.3 billion in 2012, while its global imports stood at US$5,937.6 billion as of 2012. Exports of EU with the world increased to US$6,154.7 billion in 2014 and imports mounted to US$6,137.0 billion in 2014. However, exports and imports in 2015 decreased to US$5,387.3 billion and US$5,316.1 billion, respectively, in 2015 (see Figure 18.3). Also, Figure 18.4 depicts the annual growth (year on year) of exports and imports in the EU depicting negative growth in EU's global trade in 2015.

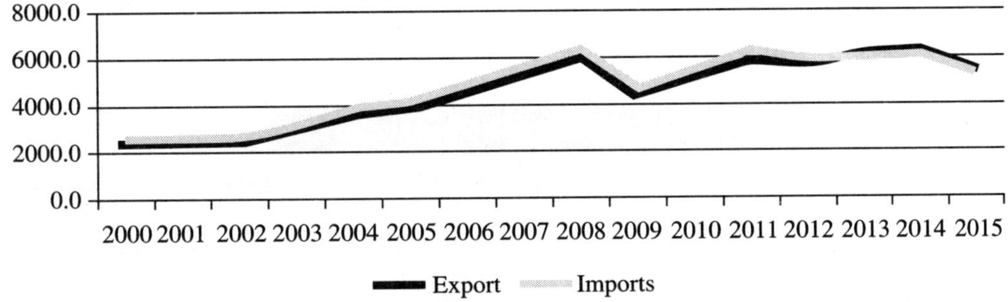

Figure 18.3 European Union's global trade (in US$ billion).
Source: WTO.

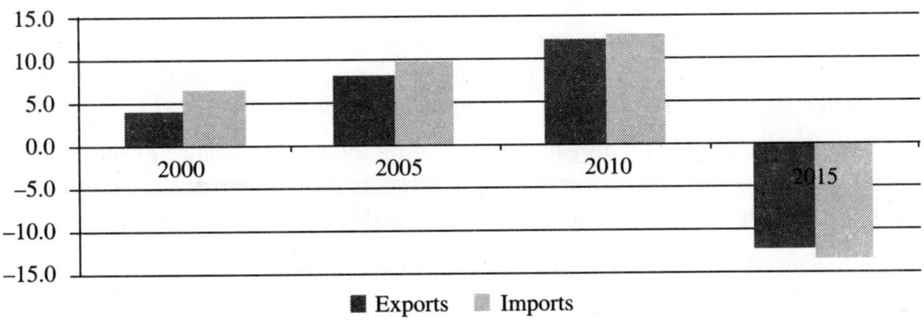

Figure 18.4 Annual growth of exports and imports in EU (%).
Source: WTO.

The trade and economic relations between India and the European Union have been evolutionary, since it first happened in 1962 when India established diplomatic relations with the EEC. India and EU adopted an ambitious Joint Action Plan (JAP) in 2005 as a framework for mutual cooperation. JAP aimed at building future strategic partnership in political and economic cooperation, trade and investment and other areas of mutual interest. A review of JAP was held during the 9th EU-India Summit in 2008 at Marseilles, France.

The 12th EU-India Summit was held in February 2012 in New Delhi and deliberated on bilateral, regional and global issues. Some of the key areas of cooperation between India and EU are industrial policy, science and technology, finance and monetary affairs, climate change, information and communication technology (ICT), transport, space technology, pharmaceuticals, development cooperation, etc.

The 13th India-EU summit was held in Brussels on 30 March 2016. It reaffirmed the commitment to strengthen India-EU strategic partnership on shared values and principles. The process of EU-India Broad-based Trade and Investment Agreement (BTIA) negotiations was reviewed. The summit mainly focused on growth and jobs through fostering trade and economic cooperation.

South Asian Association for Regional Cooperation (SAARC)

The *South Asian Association for Regional Cooperation (SAARC)* is a regional organisation of South Asian countries, which comprises India, Pakistan, Sri Lanka, Afghanistan, Bangladesh, Bhutan, Nepal and Maldives (see Box 18.5 on the Maldives). It was established in 1985. Afghanistan joined SAARC in 2007.[6]

Box 18.5 Maldives No Longer an LDC

In December 2004, the United Nations General Assembly (UNGA) requested the Committee for Development Policy (CDP) to monitor the development progress of the Maldives. This is a system of monitoring for highlighting the economic progress of a country based on which countries graduate from one category to another, for example, from least developed country (LDC) to lower middle income. This process took place in Maldives as well.

The CDP findings suggested that the country was able to meet the graduation criteria from LDC to middle income economy during two successive triennial reviews, i.e., 2001 and 2004 reviews. It, thus, recommended the graduation of Maldives accordingly.

The recommendation was accepted and Maldives has graduated from the LDC category to lower middle income country on 1 January 2011. The per capita income of the country was five times more than the graduation threshold. The average per capita income was $5,473 during 2008–2010.

This South Asian country faces the threat of submerging under sea because of the rising sea level caused by climate change. It is, however, taking adaptation and mitigation measures to combat the same. It desires to become a carbon-neutral country by 2019.

Source: United Nations (UN), Based on http://www.un.org/en/development/desa/policy/cdp/ldc_documents/maldives_monitoring_report_2012.pdf

6. India-EU Joint Statement on 13th India-EU Summit Brussels, http://www.mea.gov.in/bilateral-documents.htm?dtl/26576/IndiaEU+Joint+Statement+on+the+13th+IndiaEU+Summit+Brussels

With its 8 member states, SAARC's main objective is to promote peace, stability and progress. In a broad sense, the SAARC Charter defines its objectives as to promote welfare, improve living standard, generate economic growth and progress, strengthen mutual trust and mutual reliance, strengthen cooperation with the other developing nations and maintain peace in the region, etc. To meet these objectives, the SAARC Secretariat was established in 1987 in Kathmandu, Nepal. It is headed by a Secretary General appointed by the Council of Ministers of SAARC. It also periodically organises Ministerial Summits. The 17th SAARC Summit was held in November 2011 in the Maldives and the 18th Summit was hosted by Nepal in Kathmandu in November 2014.

SAARC also aims at creating a common market. To this effect, SAARC countries had came into agreement in trade in goods in the year 1993. The agreement is popularly known as *South Asian Preferential Trading Agreement* (*SAPTA*). This agreement was replaced by *South Asian Free Trade Area Agreement (SAFTA)* in 2004. As per the SAFTA agreement, the tariff lines have been reduced periodically by the member countries. In 2012, based on the working group on reduction in the Sensitive Lists under SAFTA, countries reduced significantly the number of commodities listed in their respective sensitive lists.

Maldives has reduced the list of commodities in its sensitive list from 681 tariff lines to 152 tariff lines for Least Developed Member States (LDMS). In SAARC, the countries under LDCs are Nepal, Bangladesh, Bhutan and Afghanistan. India has also reduced its tariff lines from 480 to 25 tariff lines for LDMS, which was 95% reduction in tariff lines. This is likely to impact regional trade, which is still hovering around 5% of SAARC's global trade.[7] SAFTA, however, is scheduled to get fully operational by 2016, and then the intraregional SAARC trade would also get a boost.

Moreover, SAARC's global merchandise trade has also evolved over the years and its global exports accounts for US$354.6 billion, while its global imports stands at US$602 billion as of 2012. In 2015, exports and imports from SAARC were US$ billion and US$ billion, respectively (see Figure 18.5).

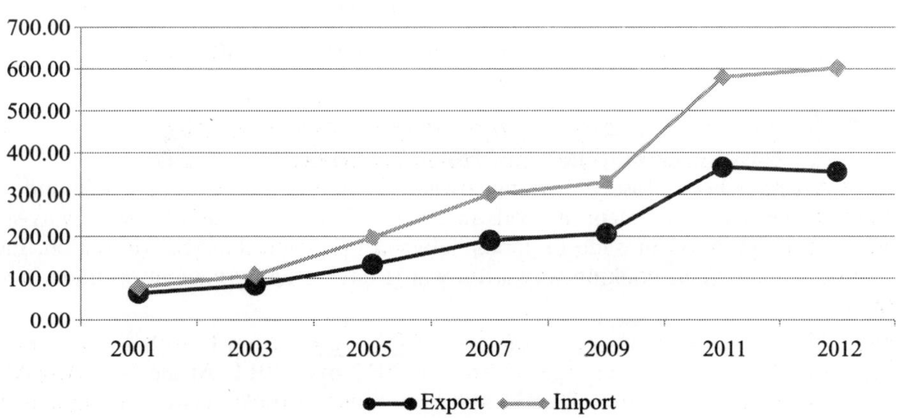

Figure 18.5 SAARC's global trade (US$ billion).

Source: World Bank.

7. M. Absar Alam (2014), 'Process of Cooperation and Integration in South Asia: Issues in Trade and Transport Facilitation', *Vikalpa—The Journal of Decision Makers* (*Journal of IIM-A*), Vol. 39, No. 1, pp. 87–102.

Association of Southeast Asian Nations (ASEAN)

The Association of Southeast Asian Nations (ASEAN) is a regional agreement among Southeast Asian countries, which was established in 1967 in Bangkok, Thailand. The initial signatories of the ASEAN Declaration were Indonesia, Malaysia, the Philippines, Singapore and Thailand. It was later joined by other Southeast Asian countries, including Brunei Darussalam, Vietnam, Lao PDR, Myanmar and Cambodia. Presently, ASEAN comprises 10 member states.

ASEAN has its own Charter, which serves as the founding principle for the group. The group has also adopted the blueprint for ASEAN Economic Community (AEC) proposed to be formed by 2015 with the following characteristics:[8]

1. Formation of a single market and production base
2. Developing a highly competitive economic region
3. Developing a region of equitable economic development
4. Working towards full integration with the global economy

Since its inception, the intraregional trade has been growing significantly. ASEAN's global trade is also growing (see Figure 18.6). Moreover, Box 18.6 highlights India–ASEAN FTA engagements.

Figure 18.6 ASEAN's global trade (US$ in billion).
Source: WTO.

Box 18.6 India–ASEAN FTA in Goods and Services

India and ASEAN have been closely working towards economic cooperation. India and ASEAN signed the initial free trade agreement in goods in 2003 in Bali. The final agreement was signed in 2009. Looking at the progress in trade in goods between India and the ASEAN region, India and ASEAN member countries are looking forward towards having an agreement on trade in services and investment.

Notably, bilateral trade volume between India and ASEAN grew from US$68.4 billion in 2011 to US$71.6 billion in 2012. This is a change of 4.6% in 2012 over 2011. At the 10th ASEAN–India Summit in November 2012, a target of US$100 billion bilateral trade between India and ASEAN was set to be achieved by 2015. With the progress in having agreement for services trade and investment, trade in goods are likely to grow at higher rates, as it will also improve digital connectivity between India and the Southeast Asian countries.

Source: Ministry of External Affairs, Government of India.

8. ASEAN Economic Community, http://www.asean.org/communities/asean-economic-community.

MERCOSUR

MERCOSUR is a regional economic block and common market of South American countries. It is basically a political and economic agreement among the member countries, which comprises Argentina, Brazil, Paraguay and Uruguay. The main objective of this organisation is to create a common market within the region, which can help in promoting free movement of goods, services, capital and people. In other words, it aims at increasing trade flows and the mobility of factors of production. Thus, this region has been focusing on eliminating the trade barriers. As per the 1991 Treaty of Asunción, free flow of trade among member countries was the main goal. Venezuela is also the member of this regional block and admitted in 2012. Figure 18.7 depicts the blocs' global trade scenario.

Figure 18.7 MERCOSUR's global trade (in US$ billion).
Source: World Bank.

Gulf Cooperation Council (GCC)

Gulf Cooperation Council (GCC) is a regional group of six West Asian countries, constituting the Arabian Peninsula. This group was established in 1981 in Riyadh, the capital of Saudi Arabia. This is a political and economic regional congregation. The member countries consist of Bahrain, Kuwait, Oman, Qatar, Saudi Arabia and the United Arab Emirates (UAE). The GCC Charter spells out the main objectives of the council. These objectives include carrying out coordination, integration and cooperation between the member countries, deepen and strengthen relations, formulate regulations to govern economic and financial affairs and promote scientific as well as technological progress of the region. GCC is headquartered in Riyadh and the member countries are rich in natural resources, predominantly oil and natural gas.

Bay of Bengal Initiative for Multi-Sectoral Technical and Economic Cooperation (BIMSTEC)

The Bay of Bengal Initiative for Multi-Sectoral Technical and Economic Cooperation (BIMSTEC) is a regional congregation, which includes member countries from both South Asian and Southeast Asian regions. The present members of BIMSTEC are India, Thailand, Myanmar, Sri Lanka, Bangladesh, Bhutan and Nepal. It was formed in June 1997 in Bangkok with the initiative of Thailand. Initially, the grouping was called *BIST-EC,* as the acronym of Bangladesh,

India, Sri Lanka and Thailand Economic Cooperation. Later, Myanmar, and Bhutan and Nepal became part of the group in 1998 and 2003, respectively. Now, this congregation is known as *BIMSTEC*. The first BIMSTEC summit was held in 2004 and the latest summit was held in 2014 in Myanmar. The group aims at cooperation in the areas of trade, investment, transport, trade facilitation, fisheries, energy security, information technology and tourism.

Closing Case: RCEP—Redefining Integration

Regional Comprehensive Economic Partnership (RCEP) is a partnership arrangement between the Southeast Asian countries under the aegis of ASEAN and three countries from East Asia, including China, South Korea and Japan. Besides, it also includes India (from South Asia), and Australia and New Zealand (from Oceania).

RCEP, is thus, a trade agreement being negotiated by ASEAN (including its 10 member countries), China, India, Japan, Korea, Australia and New Zealand, that is, in other words, ASEAN+6. It was formally launched during the ASEAN Summit in Cambodia in 2012 and is scheduled to be negotiated by 2015. As per ITC Geneva, RCEP's global merchandise exports stands at US$4.88 trillion, while its global imports account for US$4.65 trillion as of 2013. RCEP's total services export account for US$904 billion, while its services import stood at US$1.04 trillion in 2012.

It is believed that RCEP is emerging as a well-defined model of regional integration in Asia. Its impact on global welfare is also deemed to be high, given its wide coverage. The main feature of RCEP is the negotiation module, which includes free trade arrangements in goods and services as well as agreement on investments. It addresses the issues of technical cooperation, competition and dispute settlement as well. In fact, this negotiation is quite comprehensive in nature. Exhibit 1 shows the IMF projection for ASEAN+5.

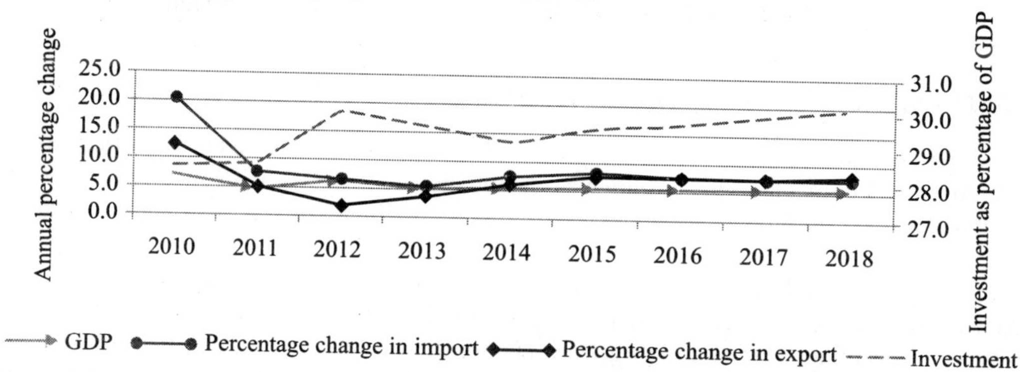

Exhibit 1 IMF projection for ASEAN+5.
Source: World Economic Outlook, IMF.

The evolving trend of trade between ASEAN and other countries like China, India, Japan and Korea created a new debate in the arena of policy-making. Advocates of regional cooperation programmes are now keenly arguing for an RCEP model. It is also argued that RCEP is an important and essential process of Asian integration. Dr. Ganeshan Wignaraja from Asian Development Institute says that RCEP needs more attention, as it has the potential to create the world's largest trading block. He argues that the proposal of RCEP is to reconcile the long-standing proposals into a large region covering three largest economies, *viz.* China, Japan and India in Asia.

More importantly, the RCEP block represents more than 45% of the world's population and also 30% of the world's GDP. The process of integration through RCEP has a potential to redefine the regional integration process. As per the IMF World Economic Outlook, the overall investment is projected to increase in the region. Also, exports and imports of ASEAN+5 are likely to grow over 7% annually.

Source: This case is written by the authors based on inputs from the following sources:

1. Working Paper from ADBI, http://www.adbi.org/files/2013.12.02.wp449.regional.economic.partnership.asia.pdf
2. World Economic Outlook, IMF.
3. Ganeshan Wignaraja, http://www.eastasiaforum.org/2013/05/15/why-the-rcep-matters-for-asia-and-the-world/

CASE QUESTIONS

1. What is RCEP? Study about Trans-Pacific Partnership (TPP) and compare and contrast the two.
2. How do you think RCEP could benefit India?

REVIEW QUESTIONS

1. What is IOR-ARC?
2. Why is international trade considered a major determinant of global economic growth?
3. What were the aims of the Uruguay Round of negotiations?
4. Discuss the different levels of economic integration.
5. Define customs union and common market.
6. What do you mean by regional integration?
7. Trace the evolution of the european union.
8. What do you understand by SAFTA?
9. Outline the roadmap of the ASEAN Economic Community.
10. Write a short note on MERCOSUR.

SUGGESTED READINGS

Ahmed, Faisal and Biswas, Anutosh, 2011, 'Grassroots Reachout of India's Foreign Trade Policy—Evidence from Indian States', Monograph, CUTS International, Jaipur.

Hill, C.W.L. and Jain, A.K., 2009, *International Business: Competing in the Global Marketplace*, Tata McGraw-Hill Education, New Delhi.

Rouis, Mustapha and Tabor, Steven R., 2012, 'Regional Economic Integration in the Middle East and North Africa: Beyond Trade Reform', World Bank, Washington DC.

'The Future of Trade: The Challenges of Convergence', 2013, Report of the Panel on Defining the Future of Trade convened by WTO Director-General Pascal Lamy, WTO, Geneva.

VanGrasstek, Craig, 2013, *The History and Future of the World Trade Organization*, WTO, Geneva.

World Investment Report, 2014, UNCTAD, Geneva.

'World Trade Report: Factors Shaping the Future of World Trade', 2013, WTO, Geneva.

19

THE WTO REGIME

Learning Outcomes

After reading this chapter, you will

- Become familiar with the WTO regime and its principles
- Develop fair understanding about GATT, GATS, TRIPS, TRIMs, Trade Policy Review Mechanism (TPRM) and dispute settlement system in the WTO
- Appreciate the workings of the WTO in respect of its major thrust areas like trade capacity building, Aid for Trade and others

Opening Case: Russia's Accession to the WTO—Wait and Watch!

Russia, a major player in the world economy, was not a WTO member till few years back! After 18 years of negotiation for accession to the WTO, Russia became the 156th member of this international organisation on 22 August 2012. As of 29 July 2016, i.e., the date of accession of Afghanistan, WTO has 164 members.

By 2011, Russia had already taken necessary steps to align its trade policy framework with that of the WTO requirements. It recognised the various WTO principles of most favoured nation (MFN), national treatment, freer trade, etc. to strengthen its candidature for accession. It had also fulfilled almost all the requirements for negotiating trade in services agreement. The case of Russia's accession was placed in the 2011 WTO Ministerial Conference in Geneva and was approved therein along with the approval for two other economies, namely, Samoa and Montenegro.[1]

The trade policy of Russia is an example of openness and gradual liberalisation. Its applied tariff is 13.3% for agricultural goods and 9.4% for non-agricultural goods. Table 1 shows the tariff profile of Russia.

The accession to WTO was seen as a major breakthrough in the trade policy framework of Russia and was deemed to be beneficial. However, some reports have pointed out that the

1. Eighth WTO Ministerial Conference, http://www.wto.org/english/thewto_e/minist_e/min11_e/min11_e.htm

Table 1 Tariff Profile of Russia

WTO accession	22 August 2012	
Trade policy review	–	
GPA accession	Observer	
Tariffs and duty free imports		
Tariff binding coverage (%)	100	
MFN tariffs	Final bound	Applied 2012
Simple average of import duties		
All goods	7.8	10.0
Agricultural goods [Agreement on Agricutlure (AOA)]	11.2	13.3
Non-agricultural goods	7.2	9.4
Non ad-valorem duties		
(Percentage of total tariff lines)	9.1	12.7
MFN duty-free imports (%, 2011)		
in agricultural goods (AOA)		9.0
in non-agricultural goods		32.6
Services sectors with GATS commitments		122
Contribution to WTO budget (%, 2014)		2.162

Source: WTO Tariff Profiles.

post-accession period did not yield much benefit to Russia, as its exports declined by 3.8%, while its imports increased by 4.4% in the first half of 2013.[2]

However, many argue that Russia has to wait for at least 3 to 5 years to reap the benefits of WTO membership, and that trying to gauge the benefits in just one year of accession would be too early. In line with this argument, the World Bank already estimated that the WTO membership could add an additional US$65 billion to Russia's GDP in the first three years, and US$220 billion within a decade.[3]

Russia has also started taking keen interest in managing its trade policy and utilising the disputes settlement mechanism of the WTO. On 6 January 2014, Russia complained against the EU and requested for consultation regarding anti-dumping measures imposed by EU on several products like ammonium nitrate and steel products imported from Russia.[4]

Source: This case is written by the authors based on inputs from the following sources:

1. 'Eighth WTO Ministerial Conference', http://www.wto.org/english/thewto_e/minist_e/min11_e/min11_e.htm
2. Russia files dispute against the European Union over anti-dumping measures, 6 January 2014, http://www.wto.org/english/news_e/news14_e/ds474rfc_06jan14_e.htm
3. 'Russia's first year in WTO: Short-term pain to get long-term gain?', 22 August 2013, http://rt.com/business/russia-wto-first-year-turnover-794/

---

2. 'Russia's first year in WTO: short-term pain to get long-term gain?' 22 August 2013, http://rt.com/business/russia-wto-first-year-turnover-794/
3. *Ibid.*
4. Russia files dispute against the European Union over anti-dumping measures, 6 January 2014, http://www.wto.org/english/news_e/news14_e/ds474rfc_06jan14_e.htm

19.1 GENERAL AGREEMENT ON TARIFFS AND TRADE (GATT)

The World War II had serious economic and social repercussions. After the end of the war, the international community started making efforts to realise the idea of multilateralism. Therefore, a general agreement on trade was also required due to the difficulties faced by nations in regulating international trade.

As mentioned in Chapter 14, in the post-war era, a need was felt to regulate and institutionalise the frameworks of international trade and economic agreements. The General Agreement on Tariffs and Trade (GATT) was signed in 1947 by 23 contracting parties. It came into effect on 1 January 1948. There was a proposal to establish International Trade Organisation (ITO) also; however, due to lack of consensus among the countries, it could not be established. In fact, the Charter of the ITO was agreed upon at the United Nations Conference on Trade and Employment in Havana in March 1948, but it failed owing to the US stand in 1950 that it was not ready for Congressional ratification.[5]

Several rounds of GATT negotiations were held, with an urge to strengthen the multilateral trading system. The famous Uruguay Round of GATT was the last one, as it resulted in the formation of World Trade Organisation (WTO).

In the first round of GATT negotiations, 45,000 tariff concessions were made that affected US$10 billion, or about one-fifth of the world trade.[6] The initial agreement was called *protocol of provisional application.* It was envisaged that this protocol would be replaced by international trade charter, which was later agreed as ITO but failed to be concluded. After a long period of trade negotiations, GATT remained an important pillar of international trading system. During 1947 to 1994, i.e., from the first round of the GATT negotiations to the Uruguay Round, 8 rounds of negotiations took place between the GATT member countries. Table 19.1 presents the outcomes of various rounds of GATT. These negotiations were mainly known as *tariff negotiations.*

Table 19.1 Round-wise Outcome of GATT

Year	*Name*	*Outcome*	*Number of Countries*
1947	Geneva Round	45,000 tariff concession	23
1949	Annecy Round	5,000 tariff concession	13
1950–1951	Torquay Round	8,700 tariff concession (25% reduction in tariff from the level of 1948)	38
1955–1956	Geneva Round	Tariff reduction amounting US$2.5 billion	26
1961–1962	Dillon Round	Tariff concessions worth U$4.9 billion of world trade	26
1963–1967	Kennedy Round	Measures taken to reduce tariffs and decision on anti-dumping measures	62
1973–1979	Tokyo Round	Decision regarding tariffs, non-tariff measures, frame-work agreements	102
1986–1994	Uruguay Round	Measures regarding tariff and non-tariff barriers and also intellectual property right-related law. It created the WTO	123

Source: WTO.

5. http://www.une.edu.ve/~cpittol/Archivo/GATT_History.htm
6. *Ibid.*

During the first round of negotiations, the module of agreement on tariffs was based on bilateral negotiation. The GATT member states concluded their bilateral agreements with each member countries. These bilateral agreements continued.

Generally, it is believed that the Tokyo Round was the first round, which tried to reform the international trading system. The round lasted for 6 years in which about 102 countries participated for global rule-making for an international trading system.[7] The Tokyo Round started in 1973 and ended in 1979. The round continued with previous GATT efforts for tariff reduction. This resulted in a reduction in the general tariff on industrial products as well as in a cut in the customs duty. The average tariff on industrial products was envisaged to be 4.7%. It was negotiated that the tariff reduction would be carried out in a phased manner in the next eight years.

The Tokyo Round was partially successful. It had to struggle to make full negotiations among the member countries on several issues. The agricultural trade and its associated problems were the core areas where Tokyo Round failed to materialise. It also reached close to the negotiating agreement on safeguards. Notwithstanding, the round successfully negotiated an agreement on non-tariff barriers. It also came up with the new codes for trade, which were partially accepted by GATT members.

These codes of the Tokyo Round are enlisted as follows:[8]

1. Subsidies and countervailing measures, which interpreted Articles VI, XVI and XXIII of GATT
2. Technical barriers to trade, also called the *Standards Code*
3. Procedures of import licensing
4. Government procurement
5. Customs valuation, which interpreted Article VII
6. Anti-dumping related to Article VI of GATT
7. Bovine Meat Arrangement
8. International Dairy Arrangement
9. Trade in Civil Aircraft

19.2 THE URUGUAY ROUND AND THE MARRAKESH DECLARATION

The Uruguay Round (1986–1994) was an important round of GATT negotiations, as it led to the formation of WTO and stressed on multilateral rule-making on many significant trade issues. It took around seven years to be concluded. The time taken for the negotiation was almost twice of the original proposed schedule. A total of 123 countries participated in this round. The negotiation covered a range of issues in trade and almost covered all the commodities, which were under global trade. The negotiation was the largest ever in the history of trade negotiations.

The main goals of the round were to reduce agricultural subsidy, eliminate restrictions on foreign investments and open services trade. With these major issues, the Uruguay Round started in 1986 in Punta del Este, Uruguay. Later, the meetings under this round took place at Geneva,

7. http://news.bbc.co.uk/2/hi/europe/country_profiles/2430089.stm
8. http://www.wto.org/English/thewto_e/whatis_e/tif_e/fact4_e.htm#rounds

Brussels, Washington, Tokyo and in Marrakesh, where 20 agreements were signed known as *Marrakesh Declaration*. Originally, there were 15 agenda proposed for the negotiation in 1986 (see Box 19.1). This agenda is also known as the *1986 agenda*.

Box 19.1 The 15 Original Uruguay Round Subjects

Tariffs	Tokyo Round codes
Non-tariff barriers	Anti-dumping
Natural resource products	Subsidies
Textiles and clothing	Intellectual property
Agriculture	Investment measures
Tropical products	Dispute settlement
GATT articles	The GATT system
Services	

Source: WTO.

To negotiate on the original agenda, the representatives of member countries met in Uruguay in 1986. The meeting accepted the negotiating agenda. After two years in 1988, member countries met in Montreal, Canada, but failed to reach any concrete outcome. The member states again met in Geneva in the April 1989. The meeting was a mid-term review of the progress of Uruguay Round of negotiations. The review was completed with some early packages for agreement, which included issues like market access for tropical products, streamlining dispute settlement system and the trade policy review mechanism.

The negotiation continued and another ministerial meeting was held in Brussels in 1990. The Director General of GATT in 1991, Arthur Dunkel, presented the first draft of legal document in the ministerial meeting in Geneva. The agreement known as the *Dunkel Draft* covered all the areas, which were identified in 1986, i.e., 15-point agenda.

After a year of differences between the developed and developing countries, a major breakthrough came in 1992, when the US and EU settled their respective differences on agriculture. During the subsequent two years, major issues were resolved and significant portion of agreement was accepted by the countries like Canada, Japan, US and also the EU.

Some of the important agreements were related to the issues like market access, negotiation on tariffs and negotiation on services, etc. In 1994, at Marrakesh, 123 countries signed the final agreement on trade. This deal was the breakthrough in the area of multilateralism. The major part of the world came under the umbrella of one organisation for the minimum global commitments.

The agreement in Marrakesh led to the foundation of WTO. It replaced GATT as an international governing body for international trade. In fact, GATT was not an organisation. However, the creation of WTO was envisaged as an organisation. Interestingly, a major part of the legal texts of GATT, however, continues to be an integral part of WTO for rule-making in trade in goods. GATT still exists. Some parts of GATT have been updated in 1994 and also in 1997. Table 19.2 depicts the outcomes of various meetings under the Uruguay Round.

Table 19.2 Uruguay Round Meetings and Outcomes

Place	*Year*	*Outcome*
Uruguay	1986	Ministerial meeting of GATT
Montreal	1988	Ministerial mid-term review; ministers agreed on a package of early results, including some concessions on market access for tropical products, streamlining dispute settlement system and TPRM
Geneva	1989	Mid-term review completed
Brussels	1990	Closing ministerial meeting ends in deadlock
Geneva	1991	First draft of the final act completed
Washington	1992	The US and EU settled most of their differences on agriculture through a deal popularly known as *Blair House Accord*
Tokyo	1993	Quad (US, EU, Japan and Canada) achieved market access breakthrough at G7 summit
Geneva	1993	Most negotiations end (some market access talks remained)
Marrakesh	1994	Agreements signed
Geneva	1995	WTO created, agreements took effect

Source: WTO.

Marrakesh Declaration

Marrakesh Declaration was the integral part of the Uruguay Round of negotiations. The declaration led to the creation of WTO. The declaration was one of the important events in the history of world trade. It focused not only on goods, but also on trade in services, dispute settlement mechanism, trade policy review mechanism, etc.

The declaration was made on 15 April 1994 in which 123 countries were the participating governments of the declaration. In addition, EU was also the participating organisation in this declaration. The Marrakesh Declaration noted that the participating member states were committed towards determining a successful world trading system.

Some of the outcomes listed out in the declaration included the following:

1. Conclusion of Uruguay Round of negotiation
2. Transition from GATT to WTO
3. Encouraging cooperation among WTO, IMF and World Bank
4. Adoption of a decision on trade and environment by the ministers

19.3 AIMS, OBJECTIVES AND FUNCTIONS OF WTO

The formation of WTO brought out an important change in the global trading system. This change was the formation of an organisation, which also had some of the elements that were present in the GATT arrangement. In fact, WTO provided a strong institutional framework. The Marrakesh Agreement on establishing WTO clearly points out that WTO is envisaged to provide the common institutional framework for the conduct of trade relations among its member countries. As per the agreements, the functions of WTO are to facilitate, implement and administer the legal arrangements related to trade between the member states.

From the Preamble of the Marrakesh Agreement establishing the WTO, the following objectives of the multilateral trading system and the WTO may be derived:[9]

1. To raise living standards of the people
2. To ensure full employment
3. To achieve higher growth of income
4. To internationalise trade and production of goods and services through sustainable means
5. To facilitate sustainable development of the world through expansion of trade
6. To alleviate poverty by increasing the income levels
7. To enhance the participation of developing and least developed countries (LDCs) in the international trade
8. To help in reducing the tariff and non-tariff barriers to trade
9. To eliminate discriminatory treatment
10. To develop an integrated and a strong multilateral trading system, taking cues from the experiences of trade negotiations in the past

The Article III of the Marrakesh Agreement on establishing WTO sets out the following functions of WTO:[10]

1. To facilitate the implementation, administration and operation of the multilateral and plurilateral trade agreements
2. To provide the forum for negotiations among its members on their multilateral trade relations
3. To administer the understanding on rules and procedures governing the settlement of disputes set out under the Marrakesh Agreement
4. To administer the Trade Policy Review Mechanism (TPRM)
5. To cooperate with the IMF, IBRD (an integral part of the World Bank Group) and its affiliated agencies

19.4 PRINCIPLES OF THE TRADING SYSTEM (WTO)

WTO establishes a trading framework for the world. It calls for a trading system that is non-discriminatory, freer, predictable, more competitive, and more beneficial for less developed countries.[11] The trading system has five main principles under which policies are designed to govern and facilitate the world trade flows. These five principles are as follows:[12]

1. ***Principle of non-discrimination:*** The presence of non-discriminatory trading regimes is one of the core principles of the multilateral trading system and the WTO.

9. Marrakesh Agreement establishing the World Trade Organisation, http://www.wto.org/english/res_e/booksp_e/analytic_index_e/wto_agree_01_e.htm#p
10. http://www.wto.org/english/docs_e/legal_e/04-wto_e.htm
11. Principles of the Trading System, http://www.wto.org/english/thewto_e/whatis_e/tif_e/fact2_e.htm
12. *Ibid.*

The main essence of the principle is derived from the original GATT agreement. This implies that the member countries would not discriminate with each other. There are two main instruments for non-discriminatory policy framework:

(i) *Most favoured nation (MFN):* The MFN principle implies that a country cannot discriminate among its trading partners. Every country has to grant MFN to all its trading partners alike. If a country grants any of its trading partners a special favour such as a lower customs duty for one of their products, then it has to do the same for all other WTO members. Article I of GATT, Article II of GATS and Article IV of the TRIPS Agreements also advocate for the same. Some exceptions to MFN rule are the preferential trade agreement (PTAs), regional trade agreements (RTAs), etc. However, exceptions apart, a case in point could be the non-compliance of this rule by Pakistan in case of not granting MFN to India (see Box 19.2).

Box 19.2 MFN Status: India and Pakistan

As part of the WTO agreement, India granted MFN status to Pakistan in 1996 like it did to all the WTO member countries. However, Pakistan also granted MFN status to many of its trading partners, but not to India. This is actually a violation of the WTO principles by Pakistan. India believes that in order to strengthen bilateral, regional and multilateral cooperation, Pakistan should abide by the rules of global trade.

Since 2011, there has been a serious discussion between both the countries on issues pertaining to bilateral trade, including MFN, but there is no concrete outcome. Pakistan, in its characteristic style, has many a times moved ahead to grant MFN to India but has pulled back without any obvious reason.

In September 2013, there was a news regarding the grant of MFN status by Pakistan, but its Prime Minister said in March 2014 that this decision has been postponed. However, just a month later, i.e., in April 2014, its Commerce Minister asserted that Pakistan was not at all considering granting of the MFN status to India. But with the government under Prime Minister Narendra Modi, the focus on region building on South Asia is high and such issues like MFN can reach a pragmatic solution.

(ii) *National treatment:* It implies that a country should not discriminate between its domestic products and foreign (imported) products. The foreign products should get a national treatment, once it enters into the domestic market. It applies to all goods, services, etc. The principle helps in ensuring that a country does not use tax and domestic regulations against the foreign products, with an agenda aimed at protecting its domestic industries. *Protectionism* is a discriminatory practice and it hampers competition as well, and could deprive the domestic consumers from availing the benefits of liberalisation. This principle is brought out in Article III of GATT, Article XVII of GATS and Article III of the TRIPS Agreement.

2. ***Principle of binding and enforceable commitments:*** When a country accedes to the WTO, it makes binding commitments for agricultural and non-agricultural goods. It is the bound rate or the maximum tariff rate negotiated and fixed by the country. This principle implies that a country cannot exceed these bound rates without negotiating with its trading partners.

3. ***Principle of transparency:*** This principle requires all member countries to publish their trade regulations and bring transparency in notifying these regulations to all the members as to well as to the WTO Secretariat in Geneva. Moreover, the countries must participate with transparency in the Trade Policy Review Mechanism (TPRM) through which the trade-related laws and regulations of a member country are reviewed periodically.
4. ***Principle of single undertaking:*** Since all WTO agreements are held together as a single undertaking, the member countries must adhere to all of them. They cannot be selective in choosing which agreement to join. They have to join all WTO agreements as a single package.
5. ***Principle of safety valves:*** WTO also provides for safety valves in which, under certain circumstances, the countries are allowed to restrict trade. For instance, under the Agreement on Safeguards, a country can restrict temporarily those products whose surging imports could cause serious injury to a specific domestic industry.

19.5 GENERAL AGREEMENT ON TARIFFS AND TRADE (GATT)

The *General Agreement on Tariffs and Trade (GATT)* was a legal arrangement between the member states, as discussed in the beginning of this chapter. The arrangement came into effect in 1948. After becoming a part of the WTO regime in 1995, GATT agreements deal with the tariff liberalisation and trading regimes in trade in goods. The final round of GATT was the Uruguay Round discussed earlier in this chapter.

19.6 GENERAL AGREEMENT ON TRADE IN SERVICES (GATS)

The *General Agreement on Trade in Services (GATS)* is the agreement under WTO, which governs the international trade in services. The agreement was negotiated during Uruguay Round. Recognising the growth and prospects of trade in services, the agreement envisaged to liberalise markets for services trade. Today, the services sector accounts for about a quarter of the world trade. It also provides opportunities for economic growth and employment. For instance, in India, more than 55% of GDP is now coming from the services sector, wherein exports of services, particularly IT services, play a dominant role. Services sector has also emerged as a major employer. In this context, GATS is not only important for the developed world but also has a vital impact on the developing world, particularly for the countries with large human capital.

The GATS agreement has three major elements in its main text, which are listed below:

1. General obligations of the contracting parties
2. Rules for specific sectors in its annexure
3. Country specific commitments for market access

Some of the characteristics of the GATS agreement include the following:

1. Article II of GATS highlights the need for MFN status among the member states in all the services meant for trade (see Box 19.3 for a case filed by Panama against Argentina in the WTO for violation of GATS rules, including Article II).

2. Article III highlights the binding commitments towards transparent regime for trade in services.
3. Article IV spells out the increasing role and participation of developing countries.
4. GATS is envisaged to facilitate the participation of developing countries in services trade.
5. It has a special provision in Article V for economic integration and points out that GATS will not prevent member countries from such process.
6. Under GATS, market access is based on the principle of non-discrimination. Article XVI of GATS has a detailed provision on market access.
7. It provides for MFN and national treatment clauses.
8. It also covers the modes of cross-border trade in services.
9. It covers all the services involved in trade.
10. It advocates transparent regulatory regime for services trade.
11. It calls for an unrestricted international payments system.
12. Commitments by individual countries are bound and negotiated.
13. It solicits progressive liberalisation.

Modes of services

Based on the territorial presence of the supplier and the consumer at the time of the transaction, Paragraph 2 of Article I of the GATS Agreement enlists four modes of services trade, which are as follows:[13]

1. ***Mode 1—Cross-border trade:*** It includes services supplied from the territory of one member country into the territory of any other member country. For example, if a consumer residing in India receives services from abroad like consultancy services, tele-medical advice, distance learning or architectural drawings, etc., then such services can be classified under Mode 1.
2. ***Mode 2—Consumption abroad:*** It includes services supplied in the territory of one member country to the service consumer of any other member country. For example, if a person belonging to India goes to the US as a student, patient or as a tourist, and avails the services in the country, then such services can be classified as Mode 2.
3. ***Mode 3—Commercial presence:*** It includes services supplied by a service supplier of one member country, through its commercial presence in the territory of any other member country. For example, if a service is offered in India by an India-based subsidiary of a foreign bank or a foreign construction company, then such a service can be classified as Mode 3.
4. ***Mode 4—Presence of natural person:*** It includes services supplied by one member country through the presence of a natural person in the territory of any other member country. For example, if an American national provides a service within India as an independent consultant or as an employee of a consulting firm, hospital, etc., then such services would be classified as Mode 4.

13. GATS Training Module, Chapter 1: Basic Purpose and Concepts, 1.3 Definition of Services Trade and Modes of Supply, http://www.wto.org/english/tratop_e/serv_e/cbt_course_e/c1s3p1_e.htm#boxa

Box 19.3 Panama-Argentina—Financial Services Dispute

Several disputes related to trade in goods and services have been highlighted by the various governments. In 2012, Panama, a southernmost country in Central America situated on the isthmus, complained against Argentina, the Latin American nation. Panama alleged that various measures taken by Argentina, as listed in its Regulations to the Income/Profit Tax Law, Decree 1344/98, as amended by Decree 1037/00, applied exclusively to only certain countries.

Panama argued that this measure was inconsistent with the articles of GATS and GATT including

1. Articles II (on MFN treatment), XI, XVI and XVII of the GATS
2. Articles I:1, III:2, III:4 and XI:1 of GATT

Panama requested consultations with Argentina in the WTO. Australia, China, Ecuador, European Union, Guatemala, Honduras, India, United States, Brazil, Singapore and Oman joined the dispute as a third party.

The case history is as follows:

1. 12 December 2012: Panama requested consultations with Argentina.
2. 21 December 2012: The European Union requested to join the consultations.
3. 28 December 2012: The United States requested to join the consultations.
4. 13 May 2013: Panama requested the establishment of a WTO Panel.
5. 25 June 2013: The WTO dispute settlement body (DSB) established a panel.
6. 30 October 2013: Panama requested the WTO Director General (DG) to compose the panel.
7. 11 November 2013: The DG composed the panel.

Note: See more about how DSB works in a later section of this chapter.

Source: Dispute DS453, Argentina—Measures Relating to Trade in Goods and Services, WTO Dispute Settlement, http://www.wto.org/english/tratop_e/dispu_e/cases_e/ds453_e.htm

19.7 TRADE-RELATED ASPECTS OF INTELLECTUAL PROPERTY RIGHTS (TRIPS)

Intellectual property refers to the creations of mind—inventions, literary and artistic works, and symbols, names, images, and designs used in businesses, trade and commerce. It is divided into the following two categories:

1. ***Industrial property:*** It includes patents, trademarks, designs and geographic indications (GI).
2. ***Copyright:*** It includes literary and artistic works such as novels, poems, films, musical works, artistic works such as drawings, paintings, photographs and sculptures, and architectural designs.[14]

In order to protect intellectual property, there are rights associated with them as provided by the international agreements, including the WTO. *Intellectual property rights (IPRs)* are the

14. World Intellectual Property Organisation (WIPO).

rights given to a person for the use of intellect or for the creations of mind. The one who is creator can get an exclusive right over the use of his/her creation for a specified time.[15] IPRs can be claimed not only by the individuals but also by the firms. It was felt that to encourage more such innovations, there should be a legal system to protect the intellectual property. Thus, the agreement on trade-related aspects of intellectual property rights (TRIPS) was negotiated during the Uruguay Round of GATT. This agreement, therefore, for the first time, introduced the rules related to intellectual property aspects into the multilateral trading system.[16] In other words, we can say that this agreement brought intellectual property law into the framework of GATT/WTO.

This agreement also covers five broad issues, which include the following:[17]

1. Application of trading principles and other IPR-related international agreements
2. Providing adequate protection to IPRs
3. Enforcing IPRs adequately in the member countries
4. Settling disputes on IPR issues in the WTO
5. Special transitional arrangements when the new system is being introduced

As far as India is concerned, it has a strong IPR regime. It is also a signatory to the international agreements on IPRs like Paris Convention for the Protection of Industrial Property 1883, Berne Convention on Copyrights 1886, and TRIPS of WTO.

Some of the major areas that are covered under TRIPS include copyrights, trademarks, geographical indications (GI), industrial designs and trade secrets, and are discussed as follows:

1. ***Copyright:*** TRIPS Agreement ensures that copyrights would be protected through TRIPS under the Berne Convention. This convention protects the literary and artistic works of individual, which was agreed on 9 September 1886, and revised and amended several times. This right protects against the unauthorised reproduction of such works. For instance, a performer has the right to prevent unauthorised recording and broadcast of live performances, while music producers have the right to prevent any unauthorised reproduction of their recording for a specified period, i.e., 50 years.[18]
2. ***Trademark:*** A *trademark* is defined as a word, sign, logo or label used to mark the intellectual property of a particular firm or an individual. It can be used for goods and services and are known as *trademark* and *service mark*, respectively. In India, the Trade Marks Registry, which registers trademarks, was established in the year 1940. It administers the Trade Marks Act, 1999.
3. ***Geographical indication (GI):*** A GI identifies a product's special characteristics based on its place of origin—a country or a particular place/region therein. It reflects an assurance of uniqueness and quality as a distinctive attribute of a geographical location. GIs are covered under Paris Convention for the Protection of Industrial Property and also under Articles XXII to XXIV TRIPS Agreement. The Geographical Indications of Goods (Registration and Protection) Act was enacted by India in 1999 and came into force in 2003. Some GIs registered in India are given in Table 19.3.

15. http://www.wto.org/english/tratop_e/trips_e/intel1_e.htm
16. *Ibid.*
17. WTO, http://www.wto.org/english/thewto_e/whatis_e/tif_e/agrm7_e.htm
18. *Ibid.*

Table 19.3 Examples of Some GIs Registered in India

Products	*Description*	*State of Registration*
Bangalore Blue Grapes	Agricultural	Karnataka
Villianur Terracotta Works	Handicraft	Pondicherry
Naga Mircha	Agricultural	Nagaland
Darjeeling Tea (word and logo)	Agricultural	West Bengal
Kalanamak Rice	Agricultural	Uttar Pradesh
Patan Patola	Handicraft	Gujarat
Orissa Pattachitra (logo)	Textile	Orissa
Bastar Dhokra (logo)	Handicraft	Chhattisgarh
Kaipad Rice	Agriculture	Kerala
Firozabad Glass	Handicraft	Uttar Pradesh
Nagpur Orange	Agriculture	Maharashtra
Moirang Phee	Textile	Manipur
Kangra Paintings	Handicraft	Himachal Pradesh
Lucknow Zardozi	Handicraft	Uttar Pradesh
Banaras Brocades and Sarees (logo)	Handicraft	Uttar Pradesh
Chettinad Kottan	Handicraft	Tamil Nadu
Bhagalpur Silk	Handicraft	Bihar
Dhaniakhali Saree	Handicraft	West Bengal
Kashmir Pashmina	Handicraft	Jammu and Kashmir
Mangalagiri Sarees and Fabrics	Handicraft	Andhra Pradesh
Kota Doria (logo)	Handicraft	Rajasthan
Nashik Grapes	Agricultural	Maharashtra

Source: Compiled from GI Registry, DIPP, Ministry of Commerce and Industry, Government of India, http://ipindia.nic.in/girindia/

4. ***Industrial design:*** *Industrial designs* refer to the creativity in appearance of a product in terms of its design during the process of industrial production. The design should be novel and original, and therefore, the owner of the design can get IPRs for it. The essential purpose of design law is to promote and protect the design element of industrial production. In India, the industrial designs are regulated by the New Designs Act, 2000 and the subsequent Designs (Amendment) Rules, 2008.[19] The TRIPS Agreement also protects industrial design for at least 10 years.
5. ***Patent:*** *Patent* is an intellectual property right, which is granted on a unique and distinctive invention in lieu of its public disclosure. Once a product or process is patented, it prohibits others from making, selling or distributing it without permission.

19. http://www.ipindia.nic.in/

A patent right is an important area of IPR. The TRIPS Agreement protects patent rights to an invention for at least 20 years.

WTO has the TRIPS Council to look after the developments and disputes in the area of intellectual property. This council consists of all the WTO members. It works closely with the member countries and cooperates in the areas such as technical assistance, review of implementation programme, etc. It also notifies the information shared by the member countries on TRIPS-related laws. It also monitors the operations of the agreement, as stated in the Article LXVIII of TRIPS.

Some of the disputes under TRIPS are given in Table 19.4.

Table 19.4 Some Disputes under TRIPS

Complainant	*Dispute*	*Respondent*	*Year*
Indonesia	Certain Measures Concerning Trademarks, GIs and Other Plain Packaging Requirements Applicable to Tobacco Products and Packaging	Australia	2013
Cuba	Certain Measures Concerning Trademarks, GIs and Other Plain Packaging Requirements Applicable to Tobacco Products and Packaging	Australia	2013
Brazil	Seizure of Generic Drugs in Transit	EU	2010
China	Measures Affecting the Protection and Enforcement of IPRs	US	2007
Brazil	US Patents Code	US	2001

Source: WTO.

19.8 TRADE-RELATED INVESTMENT MEASURES (TRIMs)

There are certain investment measures that can restrict or distort trade. The TRIMs agreement, therefore, states that no member country shall apply any investment measure that is prohibited under Articles III and XI of the GATT. Article III provides for the national treatment, while Article XI pertains to quantitative restrictions.

This agreement, which was negotiated during the Uruguay Round, applies only to the measures affecting trade in goods. Some of the examples of restrictive or trade distortive measures include local content requirements or trade balancing requirements. Therefore, it implies that a WTO member country cannot apply any trade-related investment measure that discriminates against foreign products or creates non-tariff barriers like quota.

The TRIMs agreement applies to the domestic policies of member countries of WTO, with the aim to discourage measures that distort trade and discriminate against the foreign investors. Three main areas are specified as the scope of WTO on trade and investment. These areas include analytical work by working group on trade and investment, overseeing TRIMs-related activities and facilitating investment in services.

The agreement comprises nine articles. Article II of the agreement clearly states that no member country will apply any investment measures, which are not consistent with the provision of the Article III and Article IX of GATT 1994. It simply implies that the MFN and national treatment clauses would also be applicable. Article IV of the agreement, however, has special provisions for the developing countries, which can temporarily deviate from the provisions for national treatment under TRIMs. Also, Article VI of the agreement deals with ensuring a transparent regime. Table 19.5 gives a list of some disputes related to TRIMs.

Table 19.5 List of Some TRIMS Related Disputes in the WTO

Complainant	*Dispute*	*Respondent*	*Year*
Japan	Certain Measures Concerning Taxation and Charges	Brazil	2015
EU	Certain Measures Concerning Taxation and Charges	Brazil	2013
Japan	Recycling Fee on Motor Vehicles	Russia	2013
Argentina	Certain Measures on the Importation and Marketing of Bio-diesel and Measures Supporting the Biodiesel Industry	EU	2013
USA	Certain Measures Relating to Solar Cells and Solar Modules	India	2013
Mexico	Measures Affecting the Importation of Goods	Argentina	2012
EU	Measures Relating to the Feed-in Tariff Programme	Canada	2011
Mexico	Certain Measures Granting Refunds, Reductions or Exemptions from Taxes and Other Payments	China	2007

Source: WTO.

The member countries should notify their policies under TRIMs. A committee on trade-related investment has been formed as per the provisions of Article VII of this agreement. Its main function is to monitor the operations and implementation of this agreement.

19.9 TRADE POLICY REVIEW MECHANISM (TPRM)

Trade Policy Review Mechanism (TPRM) was introduced in GATT in 1989 during Uruguay Round of negotiations. The mechanism has become an integral part of the WTO. We know that WTO also has a task of monitoring and reviewing the trade policies and its implementation in the member countries. Through TPRM, WTO keeps an eye on the national trade policies of the member states.

TPRM periodically reviews the national trade policies and practices of all the member countries to ascertain its compliance with the WTO rules. Under the Uruguay agreements, TPRM was established, with a view to help in improving the compliance to multilateral rules and to ensure the adherence by member states to the commitments under WTO.

There is a separate trade policy review division in WTO. The core responsibility of the division is to support WTO members by providing analytical work on trade policy of member states. There is also a Trade Policy Review Body (TPRB). The body elects its chairperson from its member representatives on an annual basis.

Depending on its share in the world trade, the trade policy of a member country may be reviewed under one of the three different cycles:

1. Every two years for the four largest trading entities, including the EU as one entity
2. Every four years for the next sixteen economies
3. Every six years for other members

There is a provision for longer interval in case of LDCs.[20]

The objectives of TPRM are as follows:[21]

1. To increase transparency and understanding of the trade policies of member countries through regular monitoring (see Box 19.4 for an example of first trade policy review of Myanmar, which was released in March 2014)
2. To improve the quality of public and intergovernmental discourses
3. To enable a multilateral assessment of its impact on the global trading system

Box 19.4 First Trade Policy Review of Myanmar

WTO released the first trade policy review of Myanmar in March, 2014. Myanmar is a WTO member since 1995. The current trade policy reviews of Myanmar highlights the recent economic reforms that took place in the country.

The concluding remark by the Chairperson mentions that this review helps in understanding the Myanmar's trade and investment policies in detail. The current engagement of Myanmar with the Trade Policy Review Body (TPRB) indicates that the country is keenly interested in renewing its integration process with the multilateral trading system. This step is taken after a long time, since the military rule in the country.

Myanmar has expressed commitment towards multilateral trading system. However, after reviewing the trade policies of Myanmar, some improvement areas (as suggested) include improving investment climate, improving business environment, simplifying customs procedures, liberalising tariffs and focusing on privatisation process.

Source: Trade Policy Review document of Myanmar, WTO.

19.10 DISPUTE SETTLEMENT SYSTEM

Dispute settlement is a vital area of WTO intervention. It is a central pillar of the multilateral trading system. The settlement of trade dispute under WTO has been a unique arrangement at global level, which is imperative to ensure a stable global trading regime. This system was integral to GATT as well, but not robust enough. In 1988, during the mid-term Ministerial Review Meeting, this system was streamlined.

Settling dispute under WTO is the responsibility of dispute settlement body (DSB). The DSB comprises of all the WTO member countries. It has the authority to set up an experts' panel on the disputes. When a dispute between the governments arises in the WTO, DSB sets up an experts' panel. The panel reviews the dispute and has a right to accept or reject the case. However, the dispute settlement in the WTO works through a three-tier process, which is described below:[22]

1. ***Consultation:*** It is the first level. In this level that lasts up to 60 days, countries in dispute enter into mutual consultations, with an urge to arrive at a settlement on

20. Trade Policy Review Mechanism, WTO, http://www.wto.org/english/tratop_e/tpr_e/tprm_e.htm
21. *Ibid.*
22. Understanding the WTO: Settling Disputes, Dispute Settlement Body, WTO http://www.wto.org/english/thewto_e/whatis_e/tif_e/disp1_e.htm

their own. In this process, countries in dispute may request the WTO Director General to mediate.

2. ***Panel:*** If, however, the consultations fail, the complainant (the country which has complained) can request the appointment of a panel. It may take up to 45 days for a panel to be appointed, and then, almost six months for the panel to give its ruling. The steps involved in this process can be summarised as follows:
   - (i) *Before the first hearing:* The sides submit their arguments of the case in writing to the panel.
   - (ii) *First hearing:* The complainants (i.e., the complaining country or countries), the respondents (i.e., the country or countries against whom the complaint has been filed) and the third party (countries having an interest in the dispute) present their case at the hearing.
   - (iii) *Rebuttals:* The countries in dispute submit written rebuttals and present oral arguments at the second hearing of the panel.
   - (iv) *Experts:* If any scientific or technical matter is raised by any of the disputing parties, the panel may seek the advice of experts or appoint an expert review committee to prepare an advisory report for the panel.
   - (v) *First draft:* Then, the first draft of the panel report containing facts and arguments is submitted to the disputing parties. The parties are given two weeks to comment on this draft report, which does not include findings and conclusions.
   - (vi) *Interim report:* After this, the panel submits an interim report including its findings and conclusions.
   - (vii) *Review:* The disputing parties get a maximum of two weeks for reviewing the interim report. The panel may, during this intervening time, hold additional meetings with the parties in dispute, if needed.
   - (viii) *Final report:* The panel then submits the final report to the disputing parties. Three weeks later, the final report is circulated to all WTO member countries.
   - (ix) *Ruling:* The final report becomes a ruling of the DSB within 60 days unless it is rejected by the WTO members through a consensus.

3. ***Appellate body:*** After the ruling of the panel, the disputing parties can appeal against this ruling. For the appeal to be made, the following pre-conditions are necessary:
   - (i) It is based on any legal interpretation.
   - (ii) It does not call for re-examination of the existing evidence.
   - (iii) It does not seek examination of any new issue.

The appeal is heard by three members of a permanent seven-member Appellate Body set up by the DSB.

The permanent members of the Appellate body are internationally recognised experts in the field of law and international trade, and are not affiliated with any government. They are appointed for a four-year term. The appeal can uphold, modify or reverse the panel's rulings. The DSB should accept or reject the report of the Appellate Body within 30 days.

The party which is found guilty of violation of WTO agreements or principles has to abide by the decision within 30 days or agree for compensation like tariff reduction, etc. Failing this, the complaining side may seek permission from DSB to retaliate by suspending concessions, etc. Importantly, the retaliation should be in the same sector as the dispute so as to reduce its spillover effects for the other sectors or countries.

Some instances of WTO disputes are given in Table 19.6, which gives an account of some of the cases filed by India as a complainant. Also, Table 19.7 shows some of the cases against India in the WTO filed by the other members.

Table 19.6 India in the WTO as Complainant: Select Cases

Name of the Case	*Month and Year*	*Case Against*
Measures Concerning Non-immigrant Visa	March, 2016	US
Countervailing Measures on Certain Hot-Rolled Carbon Steel Flat Products from India	April, 2012	US
Safeguard Measures on Imports of Cotton Yarn	February, 2012	Turkey
Seizure of Generic Drugs in Transit	May, 2010	EU and The Netherlands
Expiry Reviews of Anti-dumping and Countervailing Duties Imposed on Imports of PET from India	December, 2008	EU
Customs Bond Directive for Merchandise Subject to Anti-Dumping/Countervailing Duties	April, 2009	US
Anti-Dumping Duties on Certain Flat Rolled Iron or Non-Alloy Steel Products from India	October, 2004	European Communities (EC)

Source: WTO.

Table 19.7 India in the WTO as Respondent: Select Cases

Name of the Case	*Month and Year*	*Case Filed by*
Anti-dumping Duties on USB Flash Drives from the Separate Customs Territory of Taiwan, Penghu, Kinmen and Matsu	September, 2015	Chinese Taipei
Certain Measures Relating to Solar Cells and Solar Modules	February, 2013	US
Measures Concerning the Importation of Certain Agricultural Products	February, 2013	US
Certain Taxes and Other Measures on Imported Wines and Spirits	September, 2008	EU
Additional and Extra-Additional Duties on Imports	November, 2008	US
Measures Affecting the Importation and Sale of Wines and Spirits	July, 2008	EU
Anti-Dumping Measure on Batteries	February, 2010	Bangladesh

Source: WTO.

19.11 THRUST AREAS OF THE WTO

We know that WTO is an institutional arrangement, which governs the global trading system. Thus, to deal with the rules of trade and their adherence by the member countries is a major thrust area. Therefore, WTO deals with almost all the related matters of trading system. The major thrust areas of WTO are given as follows:

1. Trade negotiations (outcomes of some Ministerial Conferences have been discussed later in this chapter)
2. Implementation and monitoring of trade policies under WTO (as discussed under TPRM section in this chapter)
3. Settlement of dispute between the parties (discussed as a part of DSB earlier in this chapter)
4. Trade capacity building
5. Aid for Trade (AfT)

The last two thrust areas, including capacity building of countries for trade negotiations and AfT are discussed as follows:

Trade capacity building

Capacity building is an important thrust area of WTO. WTO actively involves itself in the capacity building of developing countries and LDCs, which enhances the preparedness of these countries in multilateral trade negotiations. The main aim of global trading regime under WTO is to facilitate sustainable development and poverty alleviation. However, there are several countries, particularly LDCs, which are not able to integrate their trade policy with their national development goals. It is, therefore, essential that these countries should be guided in terms of building capacity so as to improve their trade flows and also attain gains from trade (see Box 19.5 for an example). In fact, capacity building is one of the core elements of the Doha Development Agenda.

Box 19.5 Trade Capacity Building through CAFTA-DR in Africa

The United States supported a trade capacity building programme through the Dominican Republic-Central America-United States Free Trade Agreement (CAFTA-DR). This Sanitary and Phytosanitary (SPS) Trade Capacity Building programme was funded by the United States Agency for International Development (USAID) and implemented by the United States Department of Agriculture. It provided technical assistance to the public and private sector companies in six African countries, namely, Guatemala, Honduras, El Salvador, Nicaragua, Costa Rica and the Dominican Republic to expand their agricultural trade through compliance with US and international standards.

This case emphasises the importance of trade capacity building to ensure an integrated SPS regulatory framework for the region. Through this programme, 4,300 people across 1,000 public and private sector firms have been trained in processes like adoption of harmonised regulations, and certification procedures. The programme has created employment as well, and has generated export revenue accounting for US$100 million since 2006, with the positive impacts on employment creation. This has helped in enhancing their participation in international and has created a level playing field for them as well.

Source: Based on CS Ref. no. 223, Members' implementation-related reports and case studies, WTO, http://www.wto.org/english/tratop_e/tradfa_e/casestudies_reports_e.htm

WTO provides assistance to the countries in various ways for capacity development. Capacity building by WTO is undertaken in the following areas:

1. ***Development of human capital:*** WTO provides technical capacity building of government officials for trade negotiation. A country needs experts such as economists, lawyers and negotiators. The presence of such experts is essential to derive gains from trade negotiations. It trains the officials, including those from Commerce or Trade Ministries of member countries and also their official negotiators to build their capacity for multilateral trade negotiations. It also undertakes short-term courses for technical training.
2. ***Institutional capacity:*** WTO also provides technical assistance to the developing countries and LDCs to build institutional capacity. This helps in building the institutional framework for policy planning and economic reforms.
3. ***Strengthening infrastructure:*** This refers to strengthening the physical capacity for facilitating trade. In other words, it implies building a trade-related infrastructure like those related to transportation, customs procedures, advanced warehousing, global value chains, etc.

Aid for Trade

Aid for Trade (AfT), an instrument of global development cooperation, is also an important part of capacity building by WTO. AfT initiative under WTO was launched during the sixth WTO Ministerial Conference in Hong Kong in 2005. The declaration of the Ministerial Conference clearly highlights that AfT should aim at helping the developing countries, particularly the LDCs.

Paragraph 57 of the declaration further explains that AfT should also aim at strengthening the supply side capacity, which may include the development of trade-related infrastructure. The ninth WTO Ministerial Conference held in Bali, Indonesia in 2013 re-affirmed the need for this initiative by WTO. Thus, in order to facilitate AfT in the developing countries and LDCs, WTO is closely working with some multilateral donors such as Asian Development Bank, African Development Bank, IMF and the World Bank. Also, see Box 19.6 for an example of streamlining AfT with African Peer Review Mechanism (APRM).

Box 19.6 Streamlining Aid for Trade with APRM

WTO mainstreamed AfT into TPRM in its six pilot trade policy reviews of the countries, which include: China, US, Belize, Honduras, Malawi, and the joint review of Benin, Burkina Faso and Mali. It was a successful experience especially for middle-income developing countries and LDCs, and so, the AfT analysis in the TPRM process has been extended to the other projects as well. It has helped the beneficiary countries in enhancing the internal coordination on AfT priorities, developing national AfT strategies and also in collaborating with the regional institutions.

Source: Based on WTO Aid for Trade Case Studies, WTO.

Closing Case: Best Practices in Aid for Trade (AfT)

In 2007, a Global Review of Aid for Trade was established as a multilateral forum to explore the trade and development issues, especially in the global South (which constitutes more than 150 developing and least developed countries of the world). The Fourth Global Review of Aid for

Trade was held on 8–10 July 2013 at WTO headquarters in Geneva under the theme 'Connecting to value chains'. The aim of this review was to seek a judicious use of global development assistance for connecting the firms and business organisations in developing country and LDCs to the global value chains.

Some of the issues of concern and the way ahead that emanated from this review included the following:[23]

1. There is a need to engage the private sector especially in the areas like infrastructure deficits, which could provide them important business opportunities.
2. Services sector should be focused on to add value.
3. Skills and capacity development shall continue to play a pivotal role.
4. AfT could play a role in reducing investor risk.
5. AfT resources can leverage investments.
6. Border management and transport services have a critical role and should be focused.
7. Access to trade finance is a key concern.

Some of the examples of AfT initiatives being undertaken globally as submitted to the WTO by the stakeholders include the following:[24]

1. ***Cocoa Livelihood Rehabilitation Project:*** The Solomon Islands, a least developed country in the Asia and the Pacific region, was the beneficiary of an AusAid-funded Cocoa Livelihood Rehabilitation Project (CLIP). This programme aimed at increasing the productive capacity of cocoa through different ways, which are listed as under:

   (i) Training and capacity building
   (ii) Distributing cocoa equipment and tools
   (iii) Providing logistical assistance to remote farms

   This project boosted cocoa exports to 5,481 metric tones in 2010 as compared to the 400 metric tones annual export volume average of 2003–2009.
2. ***Cotton-4 Project:*** Brazil helped the C-4 countries (Benin, Burkina Faso, Chad and Mali) in increasing their profitability of the cotton supply chain.
3. ***B2B Project in Uganda:*** Denmark supported a business-to-business (B2B) project in Uganda. It was based on a three-year partnership between Ugandan African Organic and the Danish company, Solhjulet. It provided comprehensive training and information exchange necessary to build capacity of the Ugandan company. As a result, the production by African Organic increased. This company now exports at least 2 tonnes of fruit and vegetables to Denmark every week.
4. ***Ethical Fashion Programme:*** The International Trade Centre (ITC), Geneva implemented an Ethical Fashion Programme in Kenya and Uganda. The programme promoted trade in sustainable fashion products by international companies and

23. Based on Aid-for-Trade Review, http://www.wto.org/english/tratop_e/devel_e/a4t_e/global_review13_e.htm
24. Based on Part V: International Organisations Reports, Aid-for-Trade, Members' implementation-related reports and case studies, WTO, http://www.wto.org/english/tratop_e/tradfa_e/casestudies_reports_e.htm

microproducers in marginalised communities in the LDCs. Because of this programme, the microproducers, especially women, in Kenya and Uganda were able to get access to the global value chains, and thus, were able to enhance their livelihood.

Source: This case is written by the authors based on inputs from the following sources:

1. Aid-for-Trade Review, WTO, http://www.wto.org/english/tratop_e/devel_e/a4t_e/global_review13_e.htm
2. Part V: International Organisations Reports, Aid-for-Trade, Members' implementation-related reports and case studies, WTO, http://www.wto.org/english/tratop_e/tradfa_e/casestudies_reports_e.htm

CASE QUESTIONS

1. What is Aid for Trade? Examine the relevance of Aid for Trade for LDCs.
2. What is Cotton-4? What are their issues?

REVIEW QUESTIONS

1. What is GATT? Explain.
2. Outline the outcomes of the various rounds of GATT negotiations in terms of tariff concessions.
3. What are the codes of Tokyo Round of GATT negotiation?
4. Highlight the goals and the subjects of the Uruguay Round.
5. Highlights the Uruguay Round's meetings and outcomes.
6. What are the aims and objectives of the WTO?
7. Describe the principles of the trading system.
8. What are Mode 1, Mode 2, Mode 3 and Mode 4 in services?
9. What are the thrust areas of WTO? Explain each one of them.
10. What is TRIPS? What are the major areas covered under TRIPS?

SUGGESTED READINGS

A Handbook on Accession to the WTO, 2008, WTO, Geneva.

A Handbook on the GATS Agreement, 2005, WTO, Geneva.

A Handbook on the WTO Dispute Settlement System, 2004, WTO, Geneva.

Daniels, J.D., Radebaugh, Lee H., Sullivan, Daniel P., and Salwan, Prashant, 2009, *International Business: Environments and Operation*, 12th ed., Dorling Kindersley (India).

Hill, C.W.L. and Jain, A.K., 2009, *International Business: Competing in the Global Marketplace*, Tata McGraw-Hill Education, New Delhi.

Reinalda, B., 2013, *Handbook of International Organization*, Routledge.

VanGrasstek, Craig, 2013, *The History and Future of the World Trade Organization*, WTO, Geneva.

WTO website: www.wto.org.

20

MAJOR PROVISIONS UNDER WTO

Learning Outcomes

After reading this chapter, you will

- Understand the WTO provisions related to agriculture, sanitary and phytosanitary (SPS) measures, and rules of origin (ROO)
- Appreciate the meaning and importance of tariff and non-tariff barriers, and the provisions related to least developed countries (LDCs) in the WTO
- Comprehend the agreements related to anti-dumping, subsidies and countervailing measures in the WTO

Opening Case: India Challenges EU's Ban on Indian Mangoes on SPS Issue

From 1 May 2014, the European Union (EU) has temporarily banned import of mangoes from India. This decision was taken in the light of sanitary and phytosanitary test findings of Alphonso (a type of mango produced in India). The test found some fruit-flies randomly in Indian products, and that were considered to be new to the EU. In addition to the ban on Alphonso, EU has also banned the import of some vegetables including brinjal, taro plant and bitter gourd for the same reason. The ban is likely to last upto December 2015.

In an official statement, the reason that the officials of EU cited for this was the presence of pests in the fruits and vegetables during random sample testing. The ban was proposed by the EU Standing Committee on Plant Health. Importantly, a total of 207 consignments were found to be contaminated, as reported by the committee. This is a significant issue of phytosanitary certification.

The EU is a major destination for Indian mangoes. The major importer in the EU is UK. Statistics reveal that UK imports about 8% of India's global mango exports. More than 50% of mangoes are exported to the world (see Table 1). India has protested against this unilateral ban. It has asked EU to lift the ban. In addition, India has also threatened moving to the WTO's dispute settlement body on this issue (to know more about WTO dispute settlement system, see Chapter 19).

Table 1 India's Mango Exports

Country	2009–2010		2010–2011		2011–2012		Percentage Growth in Quantity on Previous Year	Percentage Share in 2011–2012
	Quantity	Value	Quantity	Value	Quantity	Value		
UAE	25,608.15	10,382.97	25,725.00	10,066.87	22,013.88	10,736.68	–14.43	51.19
Bangladesh	33,549.90	3,295.82	23,049.69	1,859.43	27,599.48	4,058.91	19.74	19.35
UK	2,958.65	1,746.88	2,723.54	1,453.81	2,532.42	1,641.64	–7.02	7.83
Total export	74,460.63	20,053.96	59,220.78	16,292.13	63,441.27	20,974.29	7.13	100

Source: APEDA, Government of India.

This kind of issue has also emerged earlier. In 2008, EU complained against India in WTO regarding discriminatory taxes used by India on imported bottles of wine from EU. In 2010, India requested consultations with the European Union and The Netherlands regarding the repeated seizures on patent infringement of generic drugs originating in India, but transiting through ports and airports in The Netherlands to third country destinations.

A similar issue was raised by India in 2008. On 4 December 2008, India complained against EU's, certain measures, imposing definitive anti-dumping and countervailing duties on polyethylene terephthalate (PET). Earlier in 1998, India had also requested consultation with EU on the issue of violation of sanitary and phytosanitary agreement through the use of import duty by EU against the rice imported from India.

On the current issue in question, India has also threatened EU for bringing this issue to the WTO. India's Commerce and Industry Minister strongly expressed his discontent with this move.

Source: This case is written by the authors based on inputs from the following sources:

1. *Indian Express*, http://indianexpress.com/article/cities/pune/eu-doors-shut-export-quality-alphonso-finds-way-to-pune-homes/
2. WTO
3. *Times of India*, http://timesofindia.indiatimes.com/business/india-business/India-threatens-to-drag-European-Union-to-WTO-over-mango-ban/articleshow/34539881.cms

20.1 AGREEMENT ON AGRICULTURE (AoA)

The Agreement on Agriculture (AoA) is a multilateral treaty under the aegis of WTO. It was negotiated during the Uruguay Round of GATT. In fact, agriculture has been one of the core areas of negotiations under WTO. Even Uruguay Round also began with an aim to liberalise markets for agricultural trade. During the GATT's rounds of negotiation prior to the Uruguay Round, agriculture-related issues dominated the deliberations, and therefore, the issue of liberalisation of agricultural trade was largely missed out. However, the Uruguay Round gave a new thrust to this issue by bringing it on table, and as a result, AoA emerged.

The original GATT also contained specific mention about agriculture sector. However, some loopholes were inbuilt in this agreement. For example, Article XI:2(c) of GATT permitted quantitative restrictions on agricultural products. On the other hand, subsidies were also envisaged to be especially treated in Article XVI of GATT. It also allowed using non-tariff barriers (NTBs) such as subsidies.

This created opportunities for countries to follow restrictive regimes in agricultural market at domestic level—a phenomenon which also potentially led to trade distortions. Export subsidies became a favourite instrument in the Western countries. For example, in the United States (US), the Agricultural Adjustment Act advocated the use of quantitative restrictions on imports, and similarly, some European countries also followed the practice of export subsidies.

With this background, Uruguay Round started negotiating on the agricultural trade liberalisation. The first draft of the agreement advocated the following:

1. Reduction of tariff barriers
2. Limitation on agricultural subsidies
3. Reform in export subsidies
4. Improved market access

The main objectives of the agreement are two-fold, which are listed below:

1. To carry out reforms in the trading regimes of member countries in relation to agricultural sector
2. To formulate policies for greater market access for agricultural products

With an aim to remove quantitative measures, which distort agricultural trade, AoA proposed three central ideas which are also known as the *pillars* of this agreement. Thus, the three key pillars of AoA are as follows:

1. ***Export subsidies:*** Export subsidies have been an important part of the agreement. The agreement exclusively highlights the need for elimination of export subsidies that are prevailing in the developed countries. Article 3 of the agreement provides that the member countries shall not give export subsidies, whereas Article 9 brings out the specific commitments on this pillar. As per the agreement, WTO members were required to cut both the quantum of money and volume of subsidies that the member countries spent on export subsidy. The reduction was supposed to be carried out over the base year, i.e., 1986–1990. The base level was, thus, the average of the quantum and volume of export subsidies by the member countries during 1986–1990.

In 1995, it was agreed that the developed countries would be required to reduce the value of export subsidies by 36% within six years. In case of developing countries, the same was required to be reduced by 24% over 10 years. It was also agreed that the developed countries would reduce the quantities of subsidised exports by 21% over the six years, while for the developing countries, this target was 14% over 10 years (see Table 20.1). As per the agreement, least developed countries (LDCs) were not supposed to make commitments to reduce tariffs or subsidies.

2. ***Market access concessions:*** Market access concessions in this agreement deals with the reduction in tariff imposed on agricultural imports. The member countries are bound to reduce tariffs so as to provide barrier-free access to their market. This is another important pillar of the agreement.

Table 20.1 Tariff, Domestic Support and Exports Targets under AoA

	Developed countries 6 years: 1995–2000	*Developing countries 10 years: 1995–2004*
Tariffs		
Average cut for all agricultural products	–36%	–24%
Minimum cut per product	–15%	–10%
Domestic support		
Total Agreegate Measurement of Support (AMS) cuts for sector (base period: 1986–1988)	–20%	–13%
Exports		
Value of subsidies	–36%	–24%
Subsidised quantities (base period: 1986–1990)	–21%	–14%

Source: WTO.

3. ***Domestic support:*** Another important pillar is the domestic support. Domestic support is expressed in terms of total Aggregate Measurement of Support (AMS) and Annual and Final Bound Commitment Levels. As per the agreement, *AMS* is defined as the annual level of support provided in the favour of agricultural producers. This binding commitment implies that the member countries would be bound to reduce agricultural-related support provided for the domestic producers.

However, Article 6(2) of the agreement has a provision for exemption of developing countries and LDCs if their development programmes depend on such measures. A significant level of support was provided for the agricultural sector as domestic support measures. Thus, the agreement, based on the AMS, concluded that the developed countries would reduce these supports by 20% over the next six years starting from 1995, while the developing countries would cut 13% over the next 10 years from 1995.

Subsidies: Amber, blue and green box

Not all types of agricultural subsidy in the WTO are prohibited. Therefore, they have been classified into three types and are generally identified by boxes. These boxes have been given the colours of traffic light, as follows:[1]

1. ***Amber box:*** The amber box, as per Article 6 of the AoA, implies those supports which are deemed to distort trade. They are, therefore, subject to reduction commitments. On a de minimis basis, the minimal supports are allowed. This is 10% of the agricultural production in case of developing countries, and 5% for the developed countries. It includes measures to support prices or subsidies directly related to the production quantities.

1. Domestic Support in Agriculture, WTO, http://www.wto.org/english/tratop_e/agric_e/agboxes_e.htm

2. ***Blue box:*** The blue box implies those permitted supports which are linked to production, but subject to production limits. They are, therefore, deemed to be minimally trade-distorting. It is described in Article 6(5) of the agreement.
3. ***Green box:*** The green box implies those domestic supports which do not distort trade, or at the most, have minimal distortion. They are, therefore, permitted without any limits, as per Annexure 2 of the AoA. It includes those subsidies which are funded by the government and do not involve price support. However, if it is government-funded, it should not be through charging higher prices to the consumers. They may include direct income support for farmers, those related to environmental protection and development programmes.

Moreover, in general, there are only three boxes—green, amber and red box, wherein red refers to those subsidies that are forbidden. But in case of agriculture, there is no red box.

The process of market liberalisation of agricultural sector has continued over the years. However, the differences between the developed and developing countries remain a major issue in the WTO negotiations. During the negotiations on the Doha Development Agenda (DDA), the developing countries fought to protect their respective interests. However, the issue of developing countries was addressed in the WTO. Mechanism such as Special Safeguard Mechanism (SSM) and treatment of Special Products (SPs) were proposed to address the concerns of developing countries. Since 2008, the member countries have been negotiating on the four major issues related to agriculture, which are also a part of the DDA.

These four issues include the following:

1. Export subsidies
2. Import quota
3. Food security measures
4. List of general services under green box (see Box 20.1)

Box 20.1 List of General Services: Bali Round

The Bali Round of WTO Ministerial Conference was held in Bali, Indonesia from 3–6 December 2013. The Ministerial decision of 7 December 2013 noted that the following programmes could be considered in the list of General Services Programmes in Annexure 2, Paragraph 2 of the Agreement on Agriculture (AoA):

1. Land rehabilitation
2. Soil conservation and resource management
3. Drought management and flood control
4. Rural employment programmes
5. Issuance of property titles
6. Farmer settlement programmes

The General Services Programmes support rural livelihood, food security and poverty alleviation, with a particular reference to the developing countries.

Source: WT/MIN(13)/37, WT/L/912, 11 December 2013, http://wto.org/english/thewto_e/minist_e/mc9_e/desci37_e.htm

During the 2013 Ministerial Conference of WTO in Bali, the member countries again started negotiating on agriculture-related issues. In March 2013, prior to the Bali Conference, member countries started the negotiation on this issue. The draft proposal was circulated in November 2013. On account of food security, the Bali package concluded that the developing countries would ensure that such programmes would not be misused. The negotiation on these is likely to continue. The Bali package decided to set up an interim mechanism. An agreement for permanent solution is likely to be concluded during the 11th Ministerial Conference.[2]

In December 2015, member countries concluded the 10th Ministerial Conference in Nairobi, Kenya. The WTO secured a number of trade-related initiatives during the conference. The negotiation is called 'Nairobi Package'. The Nairobi Package contains a series of six ministerial decisions on agriculture, cotton and issues related to LDCs. These include a commitment to abolish export subsidies for farm exports, which Director-General Roberto Azevêdo hailed as the 'most significant outcome on agriculture' in the organisation's 20-year history.[3]

There were decisions on public stockholding for food security purposes as well, which is a special safeguard mechanism for developing countries. The countries also revived their commitments for preferential treatment for LDCs in the service sector.

20.2 SANITARY AND PHYTOSANITARY MEASURES (SPS)

The Uruguay Round of negotiations also came with an agreement on the sanitary and phytosanitary (SPS) measures, known as the *Agreement on the Application of Sanitary and Phytosanitary Measures*. It came into force on 1 January 1995, and is related to the application of food safety and regulations pertaining to animal and plant health. The provision of SPS-related measures has also been a part of the Agreement on Agriculture (AoA). Article 14 of AoA points out that member countries are required to give effect to the Agreement on Application of SPS-related Measures. Article 20(b) of GATT 1994 clearly states that the contracting parties can enforce measures to protect human, animal or plant life or health.

The member countries have a right to ensure health protection through appropriate measures, and therefore, this agreement aims to ensure that these measures are not imposed unnecessarily. Thus, the agreement has allowed member countries to set their own safety standards subject to the need and necessity of such measures based on rationale. Therefore, the agreement encourages member countries to use internationally recognised standards for SPS measures.

Sanitary and phytosanitary has been defined in terms of health of human, plant and animal. As per the Annexure A of the agreement, the measures are applied to protect human, animal and plant life from spreading of diseases that could possibly come from an exporting country, particularly from products like food, beverages, etc.

The agreement clearly states that sanitary or phytosanitary measures include relevant laws, decrees, regulations, requirements and procedures, including, inter alia, end product criteria; processes and production methods; testing, inspection, certification and approval procedures; quarantine treatments, including relevant requirements associated with the transport of animals or plants, or with the materials necessary for their survival during transport; provisions on relevant

2. http://wto.org/english/thewto_e/minist_e/mc9_e/desci38_e.htm
3. https://www.wto.org/english/news_e/news15_e/mc10_19dec15_e.htm

statistical methods, sampling procedures and methods of risk assessment; and packaging and labelling requirements directly related to food safety.[4]

It is found that most of such measures are used through bilateral protocols. Therefore, the issue that the agreement on SPS addresses is the harmonisation of safety standards under SPS. Therefore, there are some recognised international organisations, which are closely working for harmonisation process of SPS measures across the member countries of WTO. Some of important international institutions are Food and Agriculture Organisation (FAO), World Health Organisation (WHO), World Organisation for Animal Health (OIE), International Plant Protection Convention (IPPC), etc.

Key provisions under SPS

The provisions of SPS Agreement state the right to adopt SPS measures in view of the protection of health of human, animal and plant, as mentioned in Article 2. Article 3 of the agreement, however, speaks about the necessity of harmonisation of SPS regimes. In order to adopt international standards, Article 3 also indicates that the members would be playing full part in the international organisations like the Codex Alimentarius Commission, the International Office of Epizootics, etc.

Similarly, Article 5 discusses the level of SPS measures, which can be used by the member countries. In addition, the SPS Agreement also recognises that the spread of pest and diseases is determined by the geography, rather than the political boundary. Under Article 6, the agreement recognises the concept of pest and disease-free areas, which can be determined by the factors like geography, ecosystems, epidemiological surveillance and the effectiveness of sanitary or phytosanitary controls.[5]

For efficient implementation of the agreement, Article 12 has established a Committee on Sanitary and Phytosanitary Measures. The main objective of the committee is to carry out implementation of the provisions of the agreement and it also assists in the process of harmonisation. The SPS committee is open to all the members of WTO.

The role of SPS committee includes the following:

1. Develop procedures and guidelines for the implementation of agreement.
2. Monitor the use of international standards in SPS measures.
3. Ensure compliance with the agreement.

In order to ensure safety, every country adopts such measures. Thus, as per the agreement, the measures can take any form, but has some scientific reasons for application. This makes the agreement unique and has features which are not considered as restrictive, though restrictions, are imposed.

Thus, the main features of the agreement with regard to SPS measures are as follows:

1. SPS measures are used to protect health of human being, animal and plant. Therefore, these are regarded as the measures for protection, not as an approach for protectionism.

4. Article 12–14, Agreement on the Application of Sanitary and Phytosanitary Measures, WTO, http://www.wto.org/english/docs_e/legal_e/15sps_02_e.htm#annA
5. Article 1–11, Agreement on the Application of Sanitary and Phytosanitary Measures, WTO, http://www.wto.org/english/docs_e/legal_e/15sps_01_e.htm#articleVI

2. The agreement allows the use of SPS measures, but subject to the fulfilment of scientific justification.
3. There is a need for harmonising SPS measures through multilateral cooperation in accordance with the international standards.
4. The measures are also considered to be varying in nature on products which are the same, but having different geographical origins.
5. There should be a transparent mechanism for the use of SPS measures.

Technical barriers to trade (TBT) and SPS

During the Tokyo Round of GATT's negotiation, an Agreement on Technical Barriers to Trade (TBT) was signed among the member countries. TBT pertains to the issues of labelling, safety regulations and quality requirements. The agreement is closely related to the safety standards, dealing with the technical requirements. This agreement has a close relation with the agreement on SPS. However, the SPS measures have the potential to be used as one of the methods or approaches to restrict trade.

The most important thing is that both the agreements address restrictions on trade using the right to protect health of human, animal and also plants. But the notable difference between these two agreements is that the TBT measures are applied in accordance with the technical procedures, which are different from the SPS measures, as defined by the SPS Agreement. As per the WTO, Box 20.2 presents some of the measures through which SPS and TBT measures could be differentiated.

Box 20.2 Differences between SPS and TBT Measures

SPS measures typically deal with

1. Additives, contaminants, toxic substances, residues of veterinary drugs or pesticides in food or drink
2. Processing methods having implications for food safety
3. Labelling requirements associated with food safety
4. Certification on food safety, animal or plant health
5. Plant and animal quarantine
6. Declaring areas free from pests or diseases
7. Preventing diseases or pests spreading to or in a country

TBT measures typically deals with:

1. Labelling of composition or quality of food, drink and drugs
2. Textiles and garments labelling
3. Quality requirements for fresh food
4. Volume, shape and appearance of packaging
5. Packaging and labelling for dangerous chemicals and toxic substances, pesticides and fertilisers
6. Regulations for electrical appliances, cordless phones, radio equipment, etc.
7. Testing vehicles and accessories
8. Regulations for ships and ship equipment
9. Safety regulations for toys

Source: WTO, http://www.wto.org/english/tratop_e/sps_e/sps_agreement_cbt_e/c1s4p1_e.htm

Implementation issues of SPS Agreement

The implementation of the agreement, particularly in the developing countries and LDCs, is not easy (see Box 20.3). One of the important challenges is to practically differentiate between the TBT and SPS Agreements. Generally, the small countries, which are producing limited products to their trading partners, are facing more difficulties. These measures have a potential to be used as non-tariff barriers, which can significantly deter trade flows of small countries.

Box 20.3 Measures Related to Import of Agricultural Products by India

The United States requested consultations with India on the issue related to prohibitive measures that India imposed on the imports of agricultural products from US due the concerns related to Avian Influenza. This request was made on 6 March 2012.

US claimed that the measures used by India were inconsistent with the WTO provisions, particularly with respect to Articles I and XI of GATT 1994 and also Articles 2.2, 2.3, 3.1, 5.1, 5.2, 5.5, 5.6, 5.7, 6.1, 6.2, 7, and Annexure B of the SPS Agreement.

The failure of consultation resulted in the request for establishment of a panel in May 2012. China, Colombia, Ecuador, EU, Guatemala, Japan and Vietnam reserved their rights as the third party. The panel is still in progress.

On 18 February 2013, the WTO Director-General composed the panel. Given the complexity of the dispute, it was informed that the panel expected to issue the final report no sooner than June 2014.

After the Panel report, on 26 January 2015, India filed an appeal and challenged several key findings of the Panel. Then, on 4 June 2015, the Appellate Body issued its Report and stated with reference to the Articles 2.2, 5.1, and 5.2 of the SPS Agreement. As per the WTO "The Appellate Body agreed with the Panel that its finding, that India's AI measures are inconsistent with Articles 5.1 and 5.2 because they are not based on a risk assessment raised a presumption that those measures are also inconsistent with Article 2.2". As per the WTO, "India informed the DSB that it had issued a notification that came into effect on 8 July 2016, allowing the importation of poultry and poultry products from countries, zones/compartments free from avian influenza virus, and providing for the process for recognition of such areas. On 22 September 2016, India informed the DSB that it had adopted additional measures to address concerns bilaterally expressed by the United States in respect of the measures notified on 18 July 2016".

Source: DISPUTE DS430, Dispute Settlement Body (DSB), WTO.

The difficulties and differences arising in the implementation of the agreement resulted in the measures taken by the WTO to facilitate its implementation. This included provision of two years as transition time in case of developing economies and five years in case of LDCs.

20.3 AGREEMENT ON TEXTILES AND CLOTHING (ATC)

The Agreement on Textiles and Clothing (ATC) was terminated on 1 January 2005. This agreement was to integrate the trading regimes of textiles and clothing with the multilateral trading system under WTO. Before this agreement, Multifibre Arrangement (MFA) existed under GATT. However, the contracting parties of GATT used restrictive policies and measures such as quota, which was outside the purview of GATT.

Also, voluntary export restraints (VERs) were used significantly by the developed countries on the import of textiles products. Considering this, the member countries looked for new arrangements, dealing especially with the trade in textiles and clothing. As a result, the Agreement on Textiles and Clothing (ATC) came into existence. It replaced the agreement, i.e., MFA.

Up to 2004, ATC restricted itself to the core of the agreement and its implementation programme. On 1 January 2005, the ATC and the restrictions brought out under ATC were terminated. Now, the trade in textiles and clothing is governed through the general rules and disciplines of the current multilateral trading system under WTO. The trade in textiles and clothing is now no longer subject to any restrictive policy such as quotas or any other special measures.

Key provisions of ATC

The agreement consists of nine articles and are annexure. Article 1 of the agreement mentions that trade in textiles and clothing sector among the member countries will be integrated into GATT 1994 through facilitating industrial reforms and competition in the industry. The products, which were supposed to be covered under ATC, were presented in Annexure 1 of the agreement.

The list covers all the products, which were under MFA or under MFA-type quotas. Further, the measures, which were under GATT prior to GATT 1994, were to be notified and governed by the ATC, as provided in Article 2 of the agreement.

Article 2 also stipulates the process of integration of products by the members into the new global rule under WTO. The period of integration was 10 years under the various stages, *viz.*

1. In 1995 (integration of 16% of the products imported in 1990 by the member countries)
2. In 1998 (integration of next 17% of the products)
3. In 2002 (further, 18% of the products included for integration)
4. In 2005 (when all the remaining products were supposed to be integrated)

Article 3 of the agreement is dealt with the quantitative restrictions, which were not listed in the MFA. Special transitional safeguard mechanism was also proposed in ATC. As per Article 6 of the agreement, the mechanism was set up to protect member countries during the transition period from those products which were not integrated with the GATT.

20.4 RULES OF ORIGIN (ROO or RoO)

The *rules of origin (RoO)* are considered as a criterion used to determine the source (i.e., the country of origin) of a product. ROO become an important instrument because duties and restrictions in many cases depend on the source of import. They also pave the way for preferential and non-preferential treatment of a product originating from a particular country.

Generally, determining the origin of a product is not an easy task, especially in a scenario where raw materials could be sourced across the world by different manufacturers. In view of the difficulties associated with the problems in defining the country of origin of a product, an agreement on rules of origin (ROO) was concluded during Uruguay Round.

As defined in Article 1 of the agreement,

ROO are those laws, regulations and administrative determinations of general application applied to determine the country of origin of goods except those related to the granting of tariff preferences.[6]

ROO are of following two types:

1. ***Preferential rules of origin:*** Preferential ROO are the part of FTA or PTA (signed on a bilateral or regional level) and are, thus, related to the granting of tariff preferences. Preferential ROOs are, however, not covered as part of the agreement on ROO.
2. ***Non-preferential rules of origin:*** Non-preferential ROO are used to determine the country of origin of a product in respect of instruments such as MFN clause, anti-dumping, quota restrictions, etc. The agreement covers only non-preferential ROOs.

ROOs are used for the following purposes:[7]

1. Determining whether an imported product would receive MFN treatment or preferential treatment (see principle of non-discrimination in Chapter 19 to know more about MFN treatment)
2. Implementing commercial policy instruments like anti-dumping duties and safeguard measures
3. Analysing trade statistics
4. Application of labelling and marking requirements
5. Government procurement

The agreement aims at harmonising non-preferential ROO among the WTO member countries. It is envisaged to increase the level of transparency, uniformity and impartiality in ROO-related laws, regulations and their implementation. In fact, the problem arises because there is a huge variation in ROO, as practiced by the different countries. All WTO members recognise the idea of substantial transformation as a criterion for determining ROO, yet there are three other criteria used by different countries for determining the same, which are as follows:[8]

1. Change of tariff classification
2. Ad valorem percentage criterion
3. Manufacturing or processing operation criterion

Provision of the agreement

The agreement is composed of four parts, with the definition and coverage of ROO under Part I. Disciplines of members are envisaged in Part II, while Part III presents the procedural arrangements for notification, review and consultation. Part IV gives a detailed presentation on the rules for harmonisation of ROO.

Harmonisation is an important task stipulated under the ROO agreement. Article 9 brings out the objectives and principles of harmonisation process (see Box 20.4). As per the article, the

6. Technical Information on Rules of Origin, WTO, http://www.wto.org/english/tratop_e/roi_e/roi_info_e.htm
7. *Ibid.*
8. *Ibid.*

Box 20.4 Principles of Harmonised Rules of Origin (HRO)

1. Rules should be equally applied for all purposes set out in the agreement.
2. The country of origin of a particular good is determined to be (a) either the country where the good has been wholly obtained, or (b) the country where the last substantial transformation has been carried (in case of more than one country involved in the production of goods).
3. The HRO shall be objective, understandable and predictable.
4. It should not be used as an instrument to pursue trade objectives directly or indirectly such as restrictive trade policies, which can create significant trade distortions.
5. The implementation of rules should be impartial, uniform and consistent, and it should be designed coherently.
6. Positive standards shall be used for HRO.

Source: Rules of Origin Handbook, World Customs Organisation; WTO; http://www.wcoomd.org/en/topics/origin/overview/~/media/D6C8E98EE67B472FA02B06BD2209DC99.ashx

main objective of the harmonisation process is to provide certainty in the conduct of international trade flows.[9] To attain this objective, the article sets out some principles. These principles are important for cooperation and coordination for the stipulated work programme for harmonisation process. The principles indicate that the rules of origin would be applied equally for all purposes.

Thus, the institutional framework for ROO includes the following:

1. WTO Committee on Rules of Origin
2. World Customs Organisation (WCO) Technical Committee
3. Harmonisation Work Programme (HWP)

However, there are differences among WTO members on the harmonisation of the rules of origin. On 26 September 2013, the Committee on Rules of Origin reported that the differences among the WTO member countries continued on whether or not to work towards completing negotiations for harmonising non-preferential ROO.[10]

On 10 April 2014, the committee agreed on steps to implement the decision on preferential ROO for LDCs considering the country's productive capacities, as agreed during the 2013 Bali Ministerial.[11]

20.5 PROVISIONS FOR LDCs

As per the United Nations, *least developed countries (LDCs)* are those countries which are deemed highly disadvantaged in their development process, for structural, historical and also geographical reasons.[12] They are highly vulnerable to the external financial crises and to the spread of communicable diseases as well. The LDCs continue to face some of the most rudimentary developmental challenges like poverty, unemployment and even lack of infrastructural facilities

9. http://www.wto.org/english/docs_e/legal_e/22-roo_e.htm
10. World Trade Organisation.
11. http://www.wto.org/english/news_e/news14_e/roi_10apr14_e.htm
12. Least Developed Countries (LDC), UNCTAD, http://unctad.org/en/Pages/ALDC/Least%20Developed%20Countries/LDCs.aspx

to support the basic amenities like education and health.[13] It is estimated that more than 75% of the population in LDCs live in poverty.

As of now, there are 48 LDCs in the world. Of this 34 are WTO members and 8 others are negotiating membership. The LDCs account for less than 2% of the world's GDP and contribute to approximately 1% of the world's trade. The United Nations has organised some conferences to deliberate on the challenges and prospects for LDCs in 1981, 1990, 2001 and 2011. The last one in 2011 is referred to as the *Fourth United Nations Conference on the Least Developed Countries*, which was held in Turkey and adopted the Istanbul Programme of Action (IPoA) for LDCs for the decade of 2011–2020.[14]

In order to accommodate concerns and development needs of LDCs, the WTO agreements have a preferential treatment for these countries. Broadly, some of such special provisions pertain to the following:

1. More time period allowed for implementation of agreements and commitments as compared to other countries
2. Getting extended duty-free quota-free (DFQF) treatment as per the provisions of WTO's Hong Kong Ministerial Declaration
3. Exemptions in duration of implementation of certain commitments such as tariff reduction
4. Measures to improve their trade competitiveness of LDCs and also provisions to safeguard their interests
5. Availing special and differential treatment in terms of market access (see Table 20.2)

Table 20.2 LDC Market Access by Developed Countries (2012)

Preference Granting Developed Country	*Duty-free Coverage and Exclusions (%)*	*Number Dutiable Lines (National Tariff Lines)*
Australia	100.0	None
Canada	98.6	105
European Union	98.3	162
Japan	97.8	202
New Zealand	100.0	None
Norway	99.9	2
Switzerland	100.0	None
United States	82.5	1873

Source: WTO Secretariat, IDB applied tariff schedules for the year 2012 and as compiled by Odari Hari in 'Duty-Free and Quota-Free Market Access for LDCs', 11 November 2013, http://unctad.org/meetings/en/Presentation/aldc2013_wtoBali_Odari2_en.pdf

13. 'Prospects of intra-regional investment in LDCs: A Case of Asia and the Pacific', Paper presented by Faisal Ahmed, as invited speaker, at ARTNeT Conference on empirical and policy issues of integration in Asia and the Pacific, organised by United Nations ESCAP in collaboration with ADB, IPS and IDRC Canada at Colombo from 1–2 November 2012.
14. Least Developed Countries (LDCs), UNCTAD, http://unctad.org/en/Pages/ALDC/Least%20Developed%20Countries/LDCs.aspx

6. Receiving trade capacity building to develop better negotiating stances at WTO to negotiate and handle disputes, etc.

The Doha Declaration, which emerged from the 2001 WTO Ministerial Conference in Doha, Qatar, also called upon member countries to provide special and differential treatment to LDCs. The 9th WTO Ministerial Conference held at Bali, Indonesia in 2013 also considered such provisions (see Box 20.5 for details about LDC package at Bali 2013). It reaffirmed the need for special treatment. The conference agreed upon the work programme for LDCs. It highlighted the development process and the issues faced by LDCs. The agreement on trade facilitation during the Bali Round sets out the special treatment and special provisions for LDCs which are highlighted in Box 20.5.

Box 20.5 LDC Package at WTO Bali Round 2013

The LDC package at Bali Round 2013 constituted the following:

1. ***Services waiver:*** LDCs have been looking forward to a preferential treatment for their services and services suppliers to both the developed and developing countries. With such a preferential treatment, the participation of LDCs in global services trade would increase manifold, as they get better market access. LDCs global export in services, estimated to be US$22.6 billion in 2012, is merely a two-fold increase from its 2002 statistics.
2. ***Duty-free quota-free (DFQF) market access:*** The issue of DFQF has garnered a lot of multilateral attention. It has been implemented by many countries and the decision of the Ministerial asserts that those countries which have not given DFQF market access to at least 97% of LDC products, should strive to work on it.
3. ***Rules of origin (ROO):*** The decision on ROO shall be helpful for LDC exports to qualify for preferential market access.
4. ***Cotton-4 issues:*** The Cotton-4 countries (Benin, Burkina Faso, Chad and Mali) of West Africa sought reduction in cotton subsidies in the United States. In fact, the US subsidised its cotton production, which caused oversupply and reduced the market price for cotton. The group called for granting DFQF access to cotton exports from LDCs to developed countries and also to those developing countries which volunteered for it. India also gave its support to the group's concerns. The WTO member countries agreed on a draft decision pertaining to trade and development aspects of the cotton issue.

Source: Based on Briefing note: Decisions for least-developed countries, 9th WTO Ministerial Conference, Bali, 2013 http://www.wto.org/english/thewto_e/minist_e/mc9_e/brief_ldc_e.htm

20.6 TARIFF AND NON-TARIFF BARRIERS

The WTO calls for eliminating all forms of trade barriers. Thus, both tariff and non-tariff barriers too have to be eliminated to enable the global trade to flow more freely and predictably.

Tariff barriers

Tariffs are the customs duties levied on merchandise imports. In fact, when a commodity is imported, an imposition of tariff on that commodity tends to give a price advantage to the locally-produced goods. Thus, tariffs become a source of revenue for the government also. An important outcome of the Uruguay Round was the commitments made by the member countries to reduce tariffs to bind their customs duty rates to a level, which are difficult to be raised.[15]

Following are the three types of tariff duty:

1. ***Specific:*** It is levied on the units of commodity. Just as a hypothetical example, it could be ₹55 levied on an imported chair or ₹200 levied on a barrel of oil, etc.
2. ***Ad valorem:*** It is levied as a percentage of the value of the commodity. Just as a hypothetical example, it could be 8% of the value of a commodity. If the commodity is priced at ₹200, then ad valorem duty would be ₹16.
3. ***Compound:*** It is levied both as specific and ad valorem duty. For instance, if a fabric is valued at ₹500, and the specific duty to be levied is ₹40 and ad valorem is 3%, then the compound duty levied on the commodity would be ₹40 plus 3% of ₹500, i.e., ₹55.

Table 20.3 gives details of average applied MFN tariffs imposed by some countries, including India for agricultural as well as non-agricultural (industrial) commodities.

Table 20.3 Average Applied MFN Tariff

	Agricultural	*Non-agricultural*	*Total*
India	33.44	10.20	13.50
EU	12.20	4.20	5.30
Afghanistan	7.10	5.70	5.90
Haiti	8.20	4.20	4.80
Myanmar	8.60	5.10	5.60
Russia	8.40	11.60	7.90
UAE	4.70	5.46	4.60
Timor-Leste	2.50	2.50	2.50
South Africa	8.40	7.40	7.60
Sri Lanka	23.30	7.30	9.50
United States	3.50	5.10	3.20

Source: Tariff Profiles 2015, WTO.

Non-Tariff Barriers

Non-tariff barriers (NTBs) are the non-price-related trade barriers. They include restrictions related to trade procedures, standards and regulations, packaging and labelling conditions, quantitative restrictions (quota), and occupational safety and health regulations, fixed minimum import price, buy national policies, import bans, etc. Though, some NTBs could have a legal justification, as interpreted under multilateral agreements, yet most of them could not be justified at a multilateral level, as they are country-specific requirements.

India also imposes NTBs on imports of various commodities, while other countries impose

15. Tariffs, WTO, http://www.wto.org/english/tratop_e/tariffs_e/tariffs_e.htm

NTBs of various kinds on Indian exports destined to their countries. For an example, some select NTBs imposed by other countries when they import from India are enlisted in Table 20.4.

Table 20.4 Examples of Some Select NTBs Imposed on Indian Exports

HS Code	*Commodity*	*Type*	*Country*	*Details*
280000	Chemicals	Customs	Syria	Fixed commission of 5% of the value of the total import
280000	Chemicals	Documentation	UAE	Attestation of documents by UAE which is costly/time-consuming
280000	Chemicals	Regulations	UAE	Enquiries through middlemen, wherein product specifications are vague
284400	Nuclear material	Certification	Armenia	Authorisation issued by the government
290000	Agro chemicals	Certification	Armenia	Registration, permission for importation
290000	Chemicals	Certification	Colombia	Strict registration procedures
80300	Bananas	Subsidy	Colombia	Export subsidies
80450	Mangoes	Standards	New Zealand	High food safety standards and bio-security issue
80600	Grapes	Standards	European Commission (EC)	Non-harmonised maximum residual level (MRL) in EC (Germany has more stringent standards)
80600	Grapes	Standards	New Zealand	High food safety standards and bio-security issue
80610	Fresh Grapes	Standards	Japan	No infestation as per the survey data of 3 years
80720	Papayas	Standards	New Zealand	High food safety standards and bio-security issue
81090	Pomegranates	Standards	New Zealand	High food safety standards and bio-security issue
90000	Spices	Standards	European Commission (EC)	New regulations imposed for determination of contaminations in spices; cost prohibitive and creates undue delay
90100	Coffee	Subsidy	Colombia	Export subsidies
90100	Coffee	Certification	Ukraine	Compulsory certification, i.e., (i) certificate of acceptance of foreign certification by Derzh Standard or (ii) conformance certificate by Ukrainian agency
90200	Tea	Public procurement	Egypt	Public sector procurement restricted to Kenya and other African countries

HS Code	Commodity	Type	Country	Details
90200	Tea	Import restriction	Iran	(i) Importers can import 1.5 kg at 4% if they purchase 1 kg of tea domestically, (ii) Import of tea in packets < 10 kg banned
90200	Tea	Certification	Iran	Registration with Iranian Health Authorities with a one-time registration fee of US$6,000, compliance with Plant Master File quality requirement Good Manufacturing Practice (GMP)/ Hazard Analysis and Critical Control Points (HACCP)

Source: Department of Commerce, Ministry of Commerce and Industry, Government of India.

20.7 ANTI-DUMPING AGREEMENT

The anti-dumping agreement was also the result of Uruguay Round of negotiations. *Dumping* is a measure that enables a company to sell its products in a foreign market at a price lower than what it normally charges in its domestic market. But the WTO does not regulate the dumping activities carried out by a company. It, in fact, focuses on how governments can or cannot react to dumping, thereby it disciplines anti-dumping actions taken by the countries, which are facing the problem of dumping in their territory. The WTO provisions related to how to discipline countries on their anti-dumping measures is known as the *Anti-dumping Agreement.*[16]

Anti-dumping measures are used by many countries as a measure aimed towards defending their domestic industry. As per WTO agreements, a country can take anti-dumping measures if it sees that there is a material injury to the competing domestic industry. Thus, for taking measures against dumping, a country should be able to precisely ascertain the differences in the price of the dumped product as compared to its price in the product's home country.[17] Dumping, in fact, is a trade-distorting measure.

Article VI of the GATT 1994 made provisions for the measures that can be taken by the governments against dumping. The Anti-dumping Agreement is the expansion of the same provision. Article 1 of this agreement highlights the principle of the agreement by saying that such measures would be used only under the circumstances provided for in Article VI. Article 2 of the agreement stipulates the process of determination of dumping. There are various processes of calculating the degree of dumping of a particular product. The article clearly says that a product is being dumped if the export price of the product exported from one country to another is less than the comparable price.[18]

Article 3 provides for the determination of the level of injury during the course of dumping. In case of emergence of disputes, Article 16 of the agreement establishes Committee on Anti-

16. Anti-dumping, WTO, http://www.wto.org/english/tratop_e/adp_e/adp_e.htm
17. Anti-dumping, subsidies, safeguards: contingencies, etc., http://www.wto.org/english/thewto_e/whatis_e/tif_e/agrm8_e.htm
18. WTO Agreement on Implementation of Article VI of the General Agreement on Tariffs and Trade 1994.

Dumping Practices to settle disputes. Also, as per Article 18, all the member countries are required to notify their anti-dumping law. See Table 20.5 for examples of few anti-dumping measures in force by India. Most of the anti-dumping measures taken by India are against dumping by the Chinese companies.

Table 20.5 Few Examples of Definitive Anti-dumping Measures in Force by India (as of 31 December 2013)

Country/ Customs Territory	*Product, Investigation ID Number*	*Measure(s)*	*Date of Original Imposition; Publication Reference*	*Date(s) of Extension; Publication Reference(s)*
Australia	Carbon Black 14-21-2008-1/6	Duties	28.1.2010 6/2010	26.4.2013 9/2013
Belarus	Acrylic fibre-VIII 14-05-2003-1/1	Duties	30.12.2004 117/2004	30.8.2010 85/2010
China	1-phenyl-3-methyl-5-pyrazolone 14-11-2004-1/1	Duties	10.1.2006 1/2006	24.8.2011 80/2011
China	Barium carbonate 14-18-2009-1/1	Duties	7.2.2011 6/2011	
European Union (except France)	Caustic soda-IV 14-39-2002-2/3	Duties	27.3.2003 168/2003	13.5.2009 48/2009
Hong Kong, China	Digital Versatile Disc Recordable (DVD-R) 14-17-2007-3/3	Duties	23.7.2008 8/2009	29.8.2013 19/2013
Indonesia	Cathode ray television picture tube-II 14-15-2008-1/1	Duties	9.12.2009 135/2009	
Indonesia	Melamine 14-35-2010-2/4	Duties	8.10.2012 48/2012	
Japan	Acrylic fibre-II 32-01-1997-1/4	Duties	17.11.1998 08/1999	30.8.2010 85/2010
Malaysia	Nylon filament yarn 14-05-2005-5/6	Duties	29.3.2006 85/2006	13.1.2012 3/2012
Malaysia	Polyvinyl chloride (PVC) (suspension grade) 14-08-2006-6/8	Duties	23.1.2008 11/2008	6.12.2012 52/2012
Norway	Caustic soda 14-01-2010-2/3	Duties	23.8.2011 79/2011	
Pakistan	Soda ash 14-17-2010-5/7	Duties	3.7.2012 34/2012	
Russian Federation	Hexamine-I 12-01-2000-1/2	Duties	28.6.2001 31/2002	6.8.2012 38/2012

Country/ Customs Territory	Product, Investigation ID Number	Measure(s)	Date of Original Imposition; Publication Reference	Date(s) of Extension; Publication Reference(s)
Saudi Arabia	Caustic Soda-I 56-01-1999-4/5	Duties	26.12.2000 69/2001	26.11.2012 49/2012
Switzerland	Vitamin-A Palmitate-II 14-11-2005-2/2	Duties	28.3.2007 112/2007	13.11.2013 30/2013
United States	Caustic soda-I 56-01-1999-5/5	Duties	26.12.2000 69/2001	26.11.2012 49/2012

Source: Compiled from Anti-Dumping Notifications, website of WTO.

20.8 SUBSIDIES AND COUNTERVAILING MEASURES

The Agreement on Subsidies and Countervailing Measures provides for disciplining the use of subsidies, and also for regulating the actions taken by countries to counter the effects of subsidies. For both purposes, a country can use the WTO's dispute settlement system.[19] If, however, a country carries out its own investigation and take prohibitive or retaliatory measures like charging extra duty, such measures are known as *countervailing measures*.

Subsidies can be categorised under the following two heads:[20]

1. ***Prohibited subsidies:*** These are the subsidies which are prohibited owing to their trade-distorting nature. They can be such type of subsidies that require recipients to meet certain export targets or compel them to use indigenous goods instead of the imported ones.
2. ***Actionable subsidies:*** These are the subsidies which are permitted only when they do not negatively impact the interests of a country.

Subsidies and countervailing duties are generally very difficult to be identified differently from the dumping measures. Therefore, some countries may have a common regulatory framework to deal with the dumping and countervailing measures. However, in WTO, subsidies and countervailing measures are dealt separately through an agreement on the same. Thus, a major difference between dumping and subsidies is that dumping is an action initiated by a company, however, in case of subsidy, it is a government initiative.

The Agreement on Subsidies and Countervailing Measures is composed of 11 parts and 32 articles. Part I of the agreement presents general definition of the concept related to subsidies and countervailing measures. Part II deals with the prohibition of subsidy when it has a significant impact on the trade distortion. Part V of the agreement deals with the countervailing measures. Moreover, the agreement provides special and differential treatments for the developing countries and LDCs.

The detailed provisions are made in Part VIII of the agreement. In case of the economies in transition process, Part IX has provisions for the existing programmes that are underway. Part X

19. Anti-dumping, subsidies, safeguards: contingencies, etc, http://www.wto.org/english/thewto_e/whatis_e/tif_e/agrm8_e.htm
20. *Ibid.*

states the mechanism for dispute settlement as per the Articles XXII and XXIII of GATT 1994 under WTO. In the final part of the agreement (Part XI), final provisions are listed which were envisaged to be applied for a period of five years starting from 1995.

Some key features of the agreement are as follows:

1. It clearly defines the term *subsidy*, which was not defined earlier.
2. It has established three categories of subsidies, including prohibited, actionable and non-actionable.
3. It has set out disciplines for the use of countervailing measures.
4. It has recognised the role of subsidy in the process of development.
5. It has special provisions for developing countries and LDCs, with per capita income less than US$1,000.

Moreover, a country may also restrict import of a particular product on a temporary basis if it feels that its domestic industry is getting threatened or injured. This would imply that the country has taken safeguard measures. This is provided under Article XIX of GATT.

Closing Case: US Imposes Countervailing Duty on Shrimps from India

The United States (US) has imposed countervailing duty (CVD) on shrimps from India in January 2013. The imposition of CVD has been a very serious issue. India had already called for consultation with the US on this matter way back in 1996. More important is India's export of shrimps to US, which was subjected to enhanced bond requirement (EBR) from August 2004 to March 2009.

This issue in the US was undertaken when Coalition of Gulf Shrimp Industries (COGSI), USA asked the government about the subsidies given to their shrimp industry by some countries like China, Thailand, Vietnam, Ecuador, Indonesia, Malaysia and India. This made shrimps from these countries more competitive and cheaper in the US market.

Against this backdrop, the US has been in the process to impose the CVD. As a result of this, it is expected that India's exports of shrimps to the US will decrease significantly. Most importantly, the US has already been using anti-dumping measures on shrimps imports from India since 2004. Any CVD imposed on India's imports of shrimp would be an additional measure.

Against the use of anti-dumping measures by the US, India had complained in the WTO and requested for consultation with the US in 2008. In 2009, the decision was taken in favour of India, and the US customs had to abide by the decision. However, the recent move was unexpected, as in January 2013, the US Department of Commerce published its initiation of the CVD investigations pertaining to certain frozen warm water shrimp from India.

Statistics indicate that India's seafood exports, including frozen shrimp stood at US$3.5 billion in 2012–2013. In May 2013, US decided to impose a 5.91% CVD on Indian shrimp besides the imports from the other countries, at different rates, as the shrimp industries in these countries allegedly enjoyed government subsidies and other benefits. But in September 2013, the United States International Trade Commission (USITC) lifted the CVD.

India is the largest exporter of shrimps to the US. As per the Marine Products Export Development Authority (MPEDA—an export promotion council for marine products in India), in 2013, Indian exports of shrimps to the US stood at 94,000 tonnes or US$1 billion, i.e., about half of India's global shrimp exports. India is the eighth largest exporter of food items to the US.

The shrimps' export is the part of marine exports from India. As per the MPEDA, during 2012–2013, India's exports of marine products reached an all-time high of ₹18,856 crore and in terms of volume of exports, it was 9,28,215 tonnes. Over the previous year, seafood exports has recorded a growth of 7.68% in quantity, 13.61% in rupee and 0.1% growth in US$ earnings, respectively.

As per the MPEDA, the markets for seafood include Southeast Asia, European Union (EU), US and China, etc. Southeast Asia is the largest buyer of Indian marine products, having a share of 23.12% followed by EU, with a share of 22.14%, and USA, with a share of 21.29%. Rest parts of the exports go to Japan (10.61%), China (7.67%), the Middle East (5.96%) and other countries.

Source: This case is written by the authors based on inputs from the following sources:

1. PBI, http://pib.nic.in/newsite/erelease.aspx?relid=92958
2. The Hindu, http://www.thehindubusinessline.com/industry-and-economy/agri-biz/us-panel-lifts-countervailing-duty-on-indian-shrimps/article5154357.ece
3. The Hindu Business Line, US panel lifts countervailing duty on Indian shrimps, http://www.thehindubusinessline.com/industry-and-economy/agri-biz/us-panel-lifts-countervailing-duty-on-indian-shrimps/article5154357.ece

CASE QUESTIONS

1. Examine the prospects of India's shrimp export. Do you foresee any further trade dispute on this issue?
2. Discuss the role of MPEDA in export promotion of shrimps.

REVIEW QUESTIONS

1. What are the objectives of the Agreement on Agriculture (AoA)?
2. Outline the key pillars of AoA.
3. Define sanitary and phytosanitary (SPS) measures.
4. Outline the features of SPS agreement of WTO.
5. What is the difference between TBT and SPS?
6. What do you mean by rules of origin (ROO)?
7. What are the types of ROO?
8. What are the categories of subsidies (box)?
9. Write a short note on the LDC package at Bali Round 2013.
10. Define anti-dumping measures and why it is used?

SUGGESTED READINGS

A Handbook on the WTO Dispute Settlement System, 2004, WTO, Geneva.

A Handbook on the WTO TRIPS Agreement, 2012, WTO, Geneva.

Daniels, J.D., Radebaugh, Lee H., Sullivan, Daniel P., and Salwan, Prashant, 2009, *International Business: Environments and Operation*, 12th ed., Dorling Kindersley (India).

Mehta, Pradeep S. (Ed.), 2012, *Evolution of Competition Laws and Their Enforcement: A Political Economy Perspective*, Routledge Publications in association with Consumer Unity and Trust Society (CUTS International), Jaipur.

WTO website: www.wto.org.

21

CROSS-CUTTING ISSUES IN INTERNATIONAL ENVIRONMENT

Learning Outcomes

After reading this chapter, you will

- Understand the various cross-cutting issues influencing the international business environment
- Learn the relation between the trade and climate change, and the trade and food security
- Acquire an introductory knowledge about the trade and geopolitics, and the contemporary issues related to it in the global business environment

Opening Case: India's Solar Power Policy and Dispute with the United States

The United States (US) has recently filed a complaint in the WTO against India's stand on domestic sourcing for its solar power programme. This actually is seen by the US as an action that discriminates against the American exports. In other words, the US sees it as a violation of the WTO principle of non-discrimination.

On 11 January 2010, the Government of India launched an ambitious Jawaharlal Nehru National Solar Mission with an aim to make India a global leader in solar energy. It target to deploy 20,000 MW of grid connected solar power by 2022.

The mission aims at reducing the cost of solar power generation in the country through the following four important means:[1]

1. Long-term policy
2. Large-scale deployment goals
3. Aggressive research and development
4. Domestic production of critical raw materials, components and products

1. Ministry of New and Renewable Energy, Government of India, http://www.mnre.gov.in/solar-mission/jnnsm/introduction-2/

According to the Government of India rules, half of the solar components has to come from the local sources. So, it maintains a local content requirement to fulfil the requirements of its solar policy. For instance, thin film solar technologies are also expected to be the sources from India for this project, but US is also an exporter of this technology to India.

As a matter of fact, India is developing its renewable energy programme to help in cutting down its carbon emissions, as desired by the multilateral conventions on climate change like the United Nations Framework Convention on Climate Change. The role of US in this case has been questioned by the experts. India is trying to build its renewable energy capacity, and therefore, justifies its stand in this case. The consultations as part of WTO dispute settlement system failed in March 2014 and in July 2014, WTO established a Panel for hearing this case.

Source: This case is written by the authors based on inputs from the following sources:

1. US Tries to Stop India's Solar Policy While Pushing Fight Against Climate Change, 28 March 2014, http://www.huffingtonpost.com/2014/03/28/india-us-solar-wto_n_ 5031345.html
2. Ministry of New and Renewable Energy, Government of India, http://www.mnre.gov.in/solar-mission/jnnsm/introduction-2/

21.1 CROSS-CUTTING ISSUES

In the contemporary world order, the study of international trade also requires an analysis of various cross-cutting issues, which affect the international business environment to a large extent. The aim of these cross-cutting issues is sustainability and sustainable business practices. It is, therefore, imperative that the managers of today need to be aware of such issues so that they can make informed decisions.

This chapter discusses four such factors, which come at the intersection of trade and other related disciplines (or areas). These include the following:

1. Trade and climate change
2. Trade and food security
3. Trade and finance
4. Trade and geopolitics

21.2 TRADE AND CLIMATE CHANGE

The interface with environmental issues and climate change is a major cross-cutting issue, affecting the global business environment. It acquires significance because of the global urge for environment-friendly and sustainable business practices. These issues which come at the nexus of trade, business and climate change include border measures, environmental regulations, standards and carbon labelling, etc. With the increase in trade and investment activities and the consequent industrialisation, carbon emissions have been seen a major concern globally.

Some of such cross-cutting issues that come at the intersection of trade and climate change, as envisaged during the 2011 Climate Conference in Durban include the following:

1. ***Unilateral trade measures:*** Sometimes, the developed countries impose restrictions on goods and services emanating from the developing countries on grounds for

ensuring environmental protection, etc. These measures can be tariff or non-tariff, or fiscal or non-fiscal trade measures, including countervailing measures.[2]

Emerging economies like India and China opposed such unilateral measures, as such measures violate the principle of common but differentiated responsibilities, as provided in Article 3(1) of the United Nations Framework Convention on Climate Change (UNFCCC).

2. ***Transfer of technology:*** The issue of technology transfer in context of climate change and climate protection came up during the Earth Summit in Rio. The focus of summit was on low-carbon technology, whose transfer is, however, obstructed because of the restrictive IPR regimes.

IPR in technology transfer constitutes many issues like compulsory licensing, etc., which have created a divide between the developed and developing world. Also, there is a cost associate with the dissemination of environmentally sound technologies, as the firms in the developing countries may not afford the cost of such patented technologies. Also, the use of technology in production process for products, which produces greenhouse gas emissions, is a major concern.

The challenge of technology transfer, as it applies in the context of climate change, has been addressed through the following two factors:[3]

(i) *Push factors:* It implies technology transfer by the governments of developed countries.

(ii) *Pull factors:* It implies conditions in the developing countries favourable to attract technology through trade and investments.

3. ***Carbon labelling:*** Another issue is of carbon labelling. It is a process in which the amount of emission generated during the process of production of a particular commodity is measured and this information is also communicated to the consumers. Though this process is beneficial and helpful in creating the incentives for production, but for the manufacturers in the least developed countries, its cost of compliance could be very high.[4]

It is, therefore, imperative for the corporate executives and managers to understand such type of complexities in the negotiations for adaptation and mitigation measures of climate change, as carbon labelling applies to the products and commodities of their company.

21.3 TRADE AND FOOD SECURITY

Food security is a major global concern, especially in the developing and least developed countries. The 2013 Bali Round of WTO also focused on this issue. Liberalisation has helped in developing agricultural trade and in securing agricultural markets. Trade can help in balancing

---

2. Faisal Ahmed, 'It's not Climate versus Trade'/'The international trade climate change interface is emerging as a 'new issue'', *The Economic Times*, 27 March 2012.
3. Patrick Low, Gabrielle Marceau, Julia Reinaud (2011). 'The interface between the trade and climate change regimes: scoping the issues', Staff Working Paper ERSD-2011-1, Economic Research and Statistics Division, World Trade Organisation, http://www.wto.org/english/res_e/reser_e/ersd201101_e.pdf
4. *op. cit.*, 2.

a country's food deficit with another country's surplus. This can also help in managing the food price inflation and food security in an economy.

In fact, food security issue already came up during the Uruguay Round and has been on agenda since then through Doha Round to the 2013 Bali Ministerial. The Agreement on Agriculture (AoA) in 1994 provided for the pertinent issues like market access, subsidies, etc.

Food markets are becoming more balanced and less price volatile, and in the year 2013, the world food import bill was estimated to decline by 3% to reach US$1.15 trillion.[5] Figure 21.1 gives an account of the global food price index.

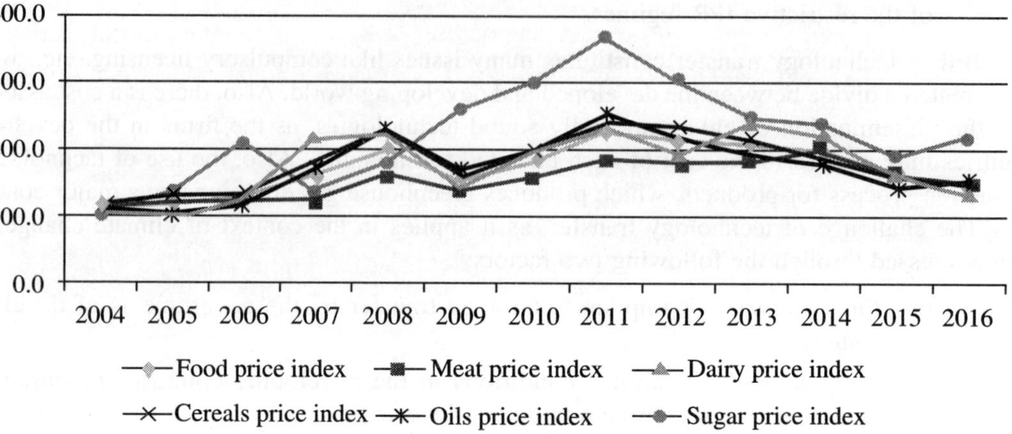

Figure 21.1 Global food price index (Base 2002–2004 = 100).
Source: FAO.

Some of the pertinent issues, which come at the confluence of trade policy and food security are discussed as follows:

1. ***Removing limits on public stockholding:*** This is a part of the G-33 proposal for food security and food aid. As per the provisions of the Agreement on Agriculture in WTO, the developing countries are restricted from providing domestic price support to their small farmers above 10% of the total value of production on a *de minimis* basis.

In fact, this 10% is the amount of domestic support that is allowed even though they distort trade. It may include government services like food security, direct income support and direct payments to the farmers that do not stimulate production, among others. They are actually measures with the minimal impact on trade. However, the purchase of food grain by the government has to be made at the current market price.

The issue was put on agenda during the Bali Round of the WTO Ministerial meeting in 2013, and yielded some good result. India, which was working to ensure food security for 820 million people to entitle them to 5 kg of food grain per person per month, at a very nominal rate took the issue seriously and gathered multilateral support at Bali. This is because such a food security bill in India will require huge purchases by the government.

5. FAO Food Outlook, November 2013.

In fact, many developing countries, including India and China were looking forward to an amendment, which would allow them to make unlimited purchases at government-set prices, and not necessarily at market prices. But since this amendment was not possible during Bali Round, they worked towards a short-term solution so that the developing countries got a temporary breather of four years. However, the developing countries are looking forward to a permanent solution for food security.

2. ***Subsidies:*** Many rich countries have been spending billions of dollars every year to support their agriculture sector. Such subsidies can be trade-distorting. The subsidy to farmers in the rich countries negatively impacts the ability of the farmers in the developing and least developed countries to compete in the international markets.
3. ***Export restrictions:*** Food export restrictions are prohibited as a part of the multilateral trading system.

21.4 TRADE AND FINANCE

Paragraph 36 of the Doha Ministerial Declaration and Paragraph 42 of the Hong Kong Ministerial Declaration of the WTO provide for the issues which come at the intersection of trade and finance. Trade financing is a significant issue, as the global financial crisis has brought volatility in the market and weakened the financial institutional frameworks.

The WTO has set up a Working Group on Trade, Debt and Finance, as proposed under its Seattle Ministerial Conference, which brought on agenda several issues pertaining to liberalisation, and market access; financial markets, trade financing and collaboration with international financial institutions; and domestic policy reforms.[6]

Some of the issues pertinent in this context are discussed below:

1. ***Managing volatility in exchange rate:*** In order to forecast the global demand, it is important that there is a stable exchange rate regime. Countries resort to hedging instruments to manage the exchange risk exposures. (For a detail on managing foreign exchange risk, refer to Chapter 22.)
2. ***Managing efficient sources of financing:*** An efficient and reliable source of long-term and short-term financing is much desired. This is critical in the context because many developing and least developed countries are heavily dependent on the international sources of finance like FDI and official development assistance (ODA). Loans may be required by the countries in case of balance of payments' problems.

21.5 TRADE AND GEOPOLITICS

Rudolph Kjellen, a Swedish political scientist coined the term *geopolitics* in 1899. It is the spatial analysis of a state (implying 'country') in terms of geography, polity and economy. It is generally a study of state behaviour.

6. Working Group on Trade, Debt and Finance, WTO, http://www.wto.org/english/tratop_e/devel_e/wgtdf_e.htm

Various theories have contributed to the discourse on geopolitics. Some of these include the following:

1. ***Organic State Theory:*** It was proposed by Fredrick Ratzel in the late nineteenth century, and emphasised that a state is like a living organism. It needs space and resources. This implies that a state grows organically, and therefore, it is natural for it to expand. Such assertions explain the rise of imperialism and colonialism.
2. ***Kjellen's Theory:*** In 1899, Rudolph Kjellen, who was a student of Ratzel, defined geopolitics as the theory of the state as a geographic organism and argued that it is engaged in a struggle for survival.
3. ***Heartland Theory:*** A landmark theory came in 1904 propounded by a British geographer, Sir Halford J. Mackinder.[7] He divided the world into following two regions:
   (i) *The World Island:* It was the continental landmass. The core of the World Island was referred to as the Heartland, which was supposedly a resource-rich region.
   (ii) *Periphery:* It constituted of the peripheral states surrounding the World Island.

Right from the World War I (1914–1918) and the Treaty of Versailles (1919) to the Great Depression (1929–1933) and the World War II (1939–1945), the geopolitical discourses have drastically evolved. From an act of asserting power and supremacy to an act of accepting global economic interdependence, the geopolitical discourses have evolved significantly over the years.

Today, most of the issues, which have a geographical and political relevance, have shaped up as an issue of the global geopolitical concern. Some of such issues could be the challenges of energy security, food security in WTO, North-South divide in climate change negotiations, Middle East turmoil and peace processes, and many others.

Even trade cannot be delinked from geopolitics now. There are several issues which come at the intersection of trade policy and geopolitics. For instance, oil resource in the Middle East is a trade and geopolitical issue. Ahmed (2010) identifies 11 enablers of geopolitics, i.e., the factors that lead to geopolitics.[8] Some of these factors are as follows:[9]

1. Geographical characteristics and location
2. Presence of oil, gas and other resources
3. Formation of international Economic Integration Agreements
4. Dynamic changes in foreign trade policy
5. Enhancement of international trading position of a country

Some contemporary issues in trade and geopolitics are mentioned below:

1. Competing claims by China, Vietnam, Philippines and other ASEAN countries over hydrocarbon resources and exclusive economic zone (EEZ) in the South China Sea

---

7. Halford J. Mackinder (1904), 'The geographical pivot of history', *The Geographical Journal*, Vol. 23, pp. 421–437.
8. Faisal Ahmed (2010), 'From Resource to Trade Diplomacy-Revealing the Hierarchical Nature of Geopolitics', *Romanian Economic Journal*, Vol. 13, No. 1, pp. 3–33.
9. *Ibid.*

2. Failure and revival of Iran–Pakistan–India (IPI) gas pipeline
3. Turkmenistan–Afghanistan–Pakistan–India (TAPI) gas pipeline
4. Geopolitics of water sharing in the Nile river
5. Trans-Pacific Partnership and China
6. Geopolitics of resource sharing in the Arctic region
7. Geopolitics of oil and gas cartels
8. US sanctions and Rupee-Rial arrangement

Closing Case: ONGC Videsh Limited in South China Sea Geopolitics

ONGC Videsh Limited (OVL—an Indian public sector enterprise) got a contract from Vietnam for oil exploration of an oil block, which was a part of the exclusive economic zone (EEZ) of Vietnam in the South China Sea.

OVL, incorporated as Hydrocarbons India Private Limited on 5 March 1965, is a Miniratna enterprise under the aegis of the Ministry of Petroleum and Natural Gas, Government of India. It is a wholly-owned subsidiary, and is the overseas arm of the Oil and Natural Gas Corporation Limited (ONGC). The main business of OVL is to prospect for oil and gas acreages outside India, and it includes exploration, development and production of oil and gas. The company has interests in 16 countries and contributes to 12% of oil and 7% of natural gas production of India. It has carried out exploration at various sites globally.

In case of its engagement in the South China Sea, OVL got a surprise when the same oil block was again put for bid by the Chinese National Offshore Oil Corporation (CNOOC), who claimed it to be in an area of China's sovereignty. By doing so, China also contested India's presence in the South China Sea.

In fact, the whole discussion reflects now on two provisions, i.e., EEZ and the United Nations Convention on the Law of the Sea (UNCLOS). The *UNCLOS*, established in 1982, is a convention which regulates the territorial rights related to water. EEZ (mentioned earlier) is supposed to extend up to 200 nautical miles (1 nautical mile = 1.852 km) from the extent of the territorial sea.

China, being a signatory to UNCLOS, asserts its claims on the resources in the South China Sea, and the same is done by some of the other ASEAN countries (like the Philippines, Vietnam, etc.) also.

Owing to China's intervention, earlier OVL withdrew from the block, but has again entered and is engaged in the exploration in Vietnam's EEZ along with Petro-Vietnam, the state-owned oil company of Vietnam.

The two countries—India and Vietnam are looking forward to a higher degree of cooperation in expanding their exploration's projects.

Source: This case is written by the authors based on inputs from the following source:

1. 'Easing geo-economic tensions in the South China Sea', by Faisal Ahmed, *The Financial Express*, 14 November 2012, p. 9, http://www.financialexpress.com/news/easing-geoeconomic-tensions-in-the-south-china-sea/1030957

CASE QUESTIONS

1. What is EEZ? What are the resources found in India's EEZ?
2. Do you foresee an amicable solution to the South China Sea geopolitics? Justify.

REVIEW QUESTIONS

1. Why is climate change considered as an important issue?
2. Transfer of technology is an issue. Give reason.
3. What is carbon labelling?
4. How much domestic support is allowed to small farmers in the developing countries?
5. Why is food security a critical issue at global level?
6. Highlight the issues related to trade and finance.
7. What is geopolitics?
8. Define the Organic State Theory of geopolitics.
9. Outline the factors affecting geopolitics.
10. What are the contemporary issues in trade and geopolitics?

SUGGESTED READINGS

Dodds, Klaus, 2007, *Geopolitics: A Very Short Introduction*, Oxford University Press, New York.

Low, Patrick, Marceau, Gabrielle, and Reinaud, Julia, 2011. 'The Interface Between the Trade and Climate Change Regimes: Scoping the Issues', Staff Working Paper ERSD-2011-1, Economic Research and Statistics Division, World Trade Organization, Geneva.

'Trade and Climate Change', A report by the United Nations Environment Programme and the World Trade Organization, 2009, WTO.

'Trade Reforms and Food Security: Conceptualising the Linkages', 2003, Food and Agricultural Organisation (FAO), Rome.

22

FOREIGN EXCHANGE RISK AND EXPOSURES

Learning Outcomes

After reading this chapter, you will

- Understand the global cash flow techniques like transfer pricing, etc.
- Comprehend the various types of exchange rate exposures
- Examine the exchange rate mitigation strategies

Opening Case: Tax Havens!

The British Virgin Islands is a tax haven. As per UNCTAD, in 2013, it got more FDI than India and Brazil taken together, accounting for US$92 billion. The FDI inflow in the United States was US$159 billion; in China, it was US$127 billion; in Russia, it was US$94 billion; in Brazil, it was US$63 billion, while in India, it was US$28 billion.[1]

It is true that the FDI for most of the countries mainly consists of equity investments in cross-border businesses, but for this Caribbean island, cash is moved through the treasury accounts of large firms in and out of the country.

There can be another case in point about Mauritius with respect to India. A major chunk of FDI inflows into India comes from Mauritius. The cumulative FDI inflows into India from Mauritius from April 2000 to January 2014 stand at US$77,779 million, accounting for 37% of the total FDI inflows.[2]

In fact, India and Mauritius signed a tax treaty in 1983, which exempted Mauritius-based investors from capital gains taxes in India. In other words, there is a bilateral Double Taxation Avoidance Agreement, and above all, Mauritius is a tax haven.

1. 'Top tax haven got more investment in 2013 than India and Brazil: UN', by Tom Miles, 28 January 2014, http://www.reuters.com/article/2014/01/28/us-tax-havens-idUSBREA0R1KF20140128
2. Department of Industrial Policy and Promotion, Ministry of Commerce and Industry, Government of India, http://dipp.nic.in/English/Publications/FDI_Statistics/2014/india_FDI_January 2014.pdf

By the end of the year 2010, thousands of holding companies controlled more than US$400 billion in assets. Many private companies now have subsidiaries in Mauritius also.[3] However, owing to such flow of funds, as provided by the 1983 treaty, India suffers huge problems of tax avoidance by the companies, which route their financing through Mauritius. Therefore, there is a need to review the 1983 treaty in light of contemporary development and regulations affecting the multilateral investments.

Even the issue has been on agenda in G20 Leader's meeting in St. Petersburg, in 2013. On the issue of tax evasion or avoidance by the large multinational corporations, many countries have joined the Multilateral Convention on Mutual Administrative Assistance in Tax Matters. India and China, along with 54 others, including the US, UK and Russia, are also a part of this campaign.[4]

Source: This case is written by the authors based on inputs from the following sources:

1. 'Top tax haven got more investment in 2013 than India and Brazil: UN', by Tom Miles, 28 January 2014, http://www.reuters.com/article/2014/01/28/us-tax-havens-idUSBREA0R1KF20140128
2. Department of Industrial Policy and Promotion, Ministry of Commerce and Industry, Government of India, http://dipp.nic.in/English/Publications/FDI_Statistics/2014/india_FDI_January 2014.pdf
3. 'Island Tax Haven Roils India's Ways' by Megha Bahree and Deborah Ball, 29 August 2012, http://online.wsj.com/news/articles/SB10000872396390444327204577615924257597492
4. Faisal Ahmed and M. Absar Alam, 'G20: Restoring growth in a stable external environment', Diplomatist, Vol. 5, No. 10, October 2013.

22.1 GLOBAL CASH FLOW

In international financial management and foreign exchange management, managing the global cash flow is a critical concern. There are several techniques of doing so. Some of the strategies and techniques used in this context include the following:

1. ***Transfer pricing:*** It is a fund positioning technique. It is, in fact, an internal price set among the subsidiaries of a multinational company. For instance, it can be the price at which a Korean subsidiary can purchase hardware from an Indian subsidiary of an MNC. Thus, it is simply the price at which the various divisions or subsidiaries of an MNC can do transactions with each other.
2. ***Tax haven:*** A *tax haven* is a geographical entity, generally a country, which levies low tax. Such countries make the business environment conducive and provide favourable conditions for the businesses. The countries utilise the benefits of tax haven by opening one of its subsidiaries in a tax haven country and following the mechanism of transfer pricing through tax haven. Some of the tax havens of the world include Cayman Islands, The Bahamas, Mauritius, Monaco, Bermuda, etc.
3. ***Multilateral netting:*** This is the process of determining the funds owed by a subsidiary to another subsidiary. This is because whenever the different foreign subsidiaries of a

3. 'Island Tax Haven Roils India's Ways' by Megha Bahree and Deborah Ball, 29 August 2012, http://online.wsj.com/news/articles/SB10000872396390444327204577615924257597492
4. 'G20: Restoring growth in a stable external environment', by Faisal Ahmed and M. Absar Alam, Diplomatist, Vol. 5, No. 10, October 2013.

multinational company enter into a transaction with each other, they may owe funds to each other. Multilateral netting helps the parent company in ensuring an early and quick settlement of funds among its various subsidiaries.

22.2 FOREIGN EXCHANGE EXPOSURE

Foreign exchange exposure is the possibility of a gain or loss that a company faces due to the fluctuations or uncertain changes in the exchange rate of currencies. This is generally caused by an adverse movement in the foreign exchange rates, which the export or import businesses face. With the introduction of the floating exchange rate mechanism, firms felt exposure to the foreign exchange risks, and started looking at ways to manage the associated risks. Several currency crises like the East Asia crisis and Argentinean Peso crisis paved the way for better management of foreign exchange risks.

Foreign exchange exposure can be of following three types:

1. ***Transaction exposure:*** This is a type of exchange rate risk when the company has already entered into a contract which solicits a foreign currency-related transaction. This is because, within the time gap till the contract is settled, there exist possibilities of exchange rate fluctuations.

Some of the key characteristics of transaction exposure are listed below:

(i) It measures cash gains or losses.
(ii) If the companies deal in more number of currencies, then there will be a possibility of a greater transaction exposure.
(iii) Such a volatility can be hedged through the instruments like currency swaps.
(iv) It can be found in transactions such as sale or purchase of those goods on credit which are denominated in foreign currency.
(v) It can happen for both multinational companies as well as those domestic companies which are engaged in the foreign exchange transactions.
(vi) Transaction exposure may be a gain or loss in short-term cash flows caused due to exchange rate fluctuations.

2. ***Translation exposure:*** Translation exposure happens when, in case of a multinational company, the financial statements of its foreign subsidiary are translated into the home currency of the parent company. Because of this translation, which is a necessity owing to the accounting standards, there can be translation gains or losses. Such gains or losses are known as *translation exposure*.

Some of the key characteristics of translation exposure include the following:

(i) It is also known as *accounting exposure*, as a consolidated financial statement of all foreign subsidiaries of a holding company is to be prepared.
(ii) It measures accounting gains or losses.
(iii) It may not affect a firm's cash flows.
(iv) It is associated with the companies that list foreign assets on their balance sheets.
(v) It is retrospective and short-term in nature.

(vi) If there are more assets and liabilities denominated in a foreign currency, the translation exposure would be higher.

(vii) It may have a considerable impact on a firm's stock price.

3. ***Economic exposure:*** It is the possibility of change in the present value of all future cash inflows, as caused by the unpredictable exchange rate fluctuations. In fact, the fluctuations in currency and the changes in price level together can have a considerable impact on a firm's cost and revenue.

Some of the characteristics of economic exposure include the following:

(i) It denotes a change in the expected long-term cash flows, and is, thus, long-term in nature.

(ii) It depicts a real exchange gain or loss.

(iii) It is also known as *operating exposure* and can have an impact on a firm's market share and cash flows.

22.3 MANAGING RISKS

Firms can use several foreign exchange hedging strategies to manage the risks associated with the exchange rate fluctuations.

Some of the techniques are discussed below:

1. ***Forward contract:*** It is a contract between two parties entering into a transaction to buy or sell an asset at a specified futures date, but on a price agreed at the time of inception of the contract.
2. ***Futures contract:*** A *futures contract* is a refined version of forward contract. It is a standardised contract and all the specification (such as delivery date, quantity, quality, and price) is fixed by the exchanges. Futures contract eliminates the risk of default. Exchanges take the guarantee of settlement of contracts, and thus, act as an intermediary between the buyer and the seller.
3. ***Options:*** An option gives holder the right, but not the obligation to buy or sell the specified amount of the underlying asset at a predetermined price known as *strike* or *exercise price*. Options are of two types—call options and put options. A *call option* gives the buyer the right, but not the obligation, to buy an underlying asset, whereas, a put option gives the buyer the right, but not the obligation, to sell an asset at a pre-determined price.
4. ***Currency swaps:*** *Swaps* are tailor-made agreements between the two parties to exchange net of cash flows in the future according to a pre-arranged formula. Swaps are, by and large, the most heavily traded contracts in the world.

Closing Case: Forex Risk for MSMEs

Fluctuations in the foreign exchange rate can have a huge impact on the micro, small and medium enterprises (MSMEs). MSME, which is a major employer in India after agriculture sector, contributes nearly 8% of the country's gross domestic product (GDP), 45% of the manufacturing output and 40% of the exports.

They produce a variety of products and services, and contribute to strengthening the national, regional and even the global value chain.[5] Enterprises with an investment in plant and machinery of up to ₹25 lakh are classified as microenterprises, while those with an investment up to ₹5 crore are classified as small enterprises, and up to ₹10 crore investment, the enterprises are classified as medium enterprises.[6]

Given their growing impact at a global arena, it is imperative to determine and manage the risk and exposures related to foreign exchange transactions. Some of the key factors that need to be assessed in order to ascertain the level of foreign exchange exposure faced by the SMEs include the following:[7]

1. Identifying the currencies in which the SME does its transactions
2. Assessing the cash flow status of the firm—whether it is good or bad
3. Feasibility of entering into a price variance clause

In fact, MSMEs have to be careful about the foreign exchange risk because it would not only impact the business but can also be a risk for the investor. An appreciation of rupee would negatively impact the exporters, while a depreciation of the currency will benefit the exporter.

The loans in foreign currencies received by the firms including small and medium enterprise lead to exchange rate risks caused due to the fluctuations in the value of the currency. Various risk mitigation strategies like hedging, swaps, etc. can be used to manage the exchange rate fluctuations.

Given the fact that since 2013, rupee has witnessed a high fluctuation with respect to the US Dollar, it has affected MSMEs to a large extent. But there has been a sigh of relief. Though the rupee breached the level of 69 per US Dollar mark in August 2013, it opened at ₹59.94 per US Dollar on 3 April 2014.

Yet, MSMEs need to enhance their preparedness to tackle the risk associated with any such foreign exchange fluctuations in future.

Source: This case is written by the authors based on inputs from the following sources:

1. http://www.indiamart.com/company/5414953/sme-corporate-services.html
2. Government looks to boost exports by MSME sector, 1 September 2013, http://www.livemint.com/Industry/HOulviYZuvEya7rOYCwkqK/Government-looks-to-boost-exports-by-MSME-sector.html
3. Ministry of Micro, Small and Medium Enterprises http://msme.gov.in/Web/Portal/New-Default.aspx)

CASE QUESTIONS

1. Discuss the role of MSMEs in Indian economy.
2. Explain the factors by which we can assess the level of foreign exchange exposures faced by SMEs in India.

5. Ministry of Micro, Small and Medium Enterprises, http://msme.gov.in/Web/Portal/New-Default.aspx
6. Government looks to boost exports by MSME sector, 1 September 2013, http://www.livemint.com/Industry/HOulviYZuvEya7rOYCwkqK/Government-looks-to-boost-exports-by-MSME-sector.html
7. http://www.indiamart.com/company/5414953/sme-corporate-services.html

REVIEW QUESTIONS

1. What is transfer pricing?
2. What is a tax haven?
3. What is multilateral netting?
4. What do you mean by foreign exchange exposure?
5. Define transaction exposure.
6. What are the characteristics of transaction exposure?
7. Define translation exposure.
8. What are the characteristics of translation exposure?
9. Define economic exposure.
10. Highlight some of the techniques of managing risk.

SUGGESTED READINGS

Daniels, J.D., Radebaugh, Lee H., Sullivan, Daniel P., and Salwan, Prashant, 2009, *International Business: Environments and Operation*, 12th ed., Dorling Kindersley (India).

Hill, C.W.L. and Jain, A.K., 2009, *International Business: Competing in the Global Marketplace*, Tata McGraw-Hill Education, New Delhi.

Rugman, A.M. and Hodgetts, R.M., 2004, *International Business*, Pearson Education, Delhi.

23

COUNTRY RISK AND POLITICAL RISK ANALYSIS

Learning Outcomes

After reading this chapter, you will

- Understand the meaning and importance of country and political risk analysis
- Appreciate how such an analysis could be beneficial for the multinational enterprises

Opening Case: Syrian Political Unrest and Country Analysis

The recent civil unrest in Syria has weakened the economy from a growth rate of more than 5% in 2007 to the negative growth rate of –25% in 2012. Amid conflicts, considering the prospects of peace, the World Bank has forecasted that the country is likely to attain positive economic growth by 2015. Analysts produce several scenarios. It has been highlighted that despite the fact that Syria has limited production of crude oil, the crisis has a significant impact at oil prices.

The less control by the Government of Syria over its widespread region has resulted in an increase in the civil casualty. In fact, 40% people of its population are homeless and a bulk of them are refugees in other countries and at least 1,50,000 people died during the conflict. The continuous crisis and its devastating results are leading Syria towards an economic crisis. The crisis coupled with deindustrialisation and rising debt is affecting the Syrian economic outlook.

In this scenario, crude oil production in the country has decreased drastically. The production of crude oil prior to the conflict was 3,80,000 barrels per day, which decreased to 20,000 barrels per day—a decrease of about 95% in the production of crude oil. The oil and gas exports of the country accounted for a major part of export earnings, which has now reduced significantly.

In addition to the oil sector, the industrial and agricultural sectors have also been affected by the recent ongoing conflict in the country. Around 75% of the industries are not operating now in Aleppo, a major Syrian city. This is a serious matter, as it is leading to deindustrialisation. The Damascus Securities Exchange (DSE) has lost its global value since the start of the civil unrest. It is estimated that the stock exchange has lost 86% of its value. The result of economic slowdown is the increasing inflation in the country. Inflation has been increasing at a higher rate, creating a situation of stagflation.

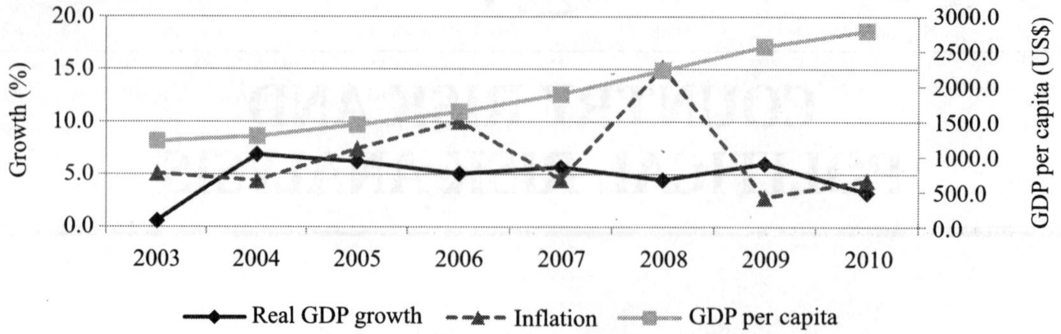

Exhibit 1 Pre-crisis economic scenario.
Source: World Bank.

Although some optimism is apparent from the point of view of the World Bank in Exhibit 1, yet the country's economic scenario poses a major risk for business communities in the country. The country risk is associated with both economic performance of the country and also the political scenario of the country. The current situation highlights that Syrian economy is moving towards a serious economic crisis due to the political scenario. The assessment of political risks and country risks entails a major loss in the industrial sector as well as in the oil sector. In addition, the investment in infrastructure sector will also have a high risk while assessing return on investment.

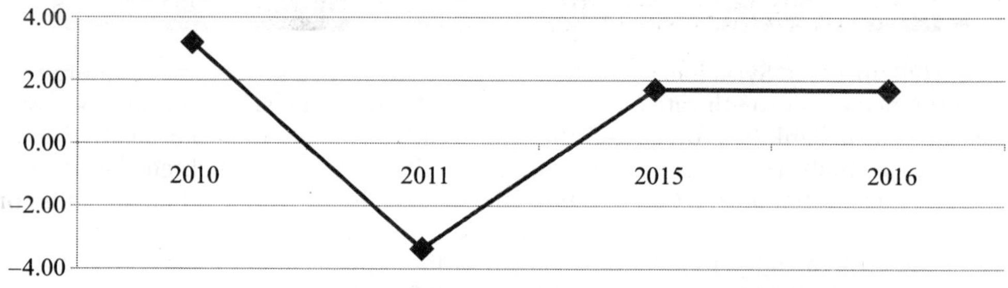

Exhibit 2 Syria's GDP growth forecast in 2010 US$ (%).
Source: Central Bank of Syria.

Also, the Doing Business Report 2013 ranked the country 147th among 185 economies. Its overall score decreased by 7 compared to the previous year, reflecting lower scores in 8 out of 10 indicators. In 2014, this rank again slipped to 165th, which is a matter of concern both for Syria as well as its trade and investment partners.

Source: This case is written by the authors based on inputs from the following sources:

1. World Bank Country and region specific forecasts and data.
2. CNBC, http://www.cnbc.com/id/100994327
3. The Economist, http://www.economist.com/blogs/newsbook/2011/04/unrest_syria
4. http://carnegieendowment.org/sada/2013/11/19/losing-syria-s-economic-future/gu5j)

23.1 RISK ANALYSIS

Country risk analysis and political risk analysis are the important tools to understand the current economic scenario and forecast the future economic situation. Country risk analysis examines the overall macroeconomic performance of a country and also the planning and policy framework of its government. The concepts are widely used by business houses, public sector, etc. to formulate strategies. For example, if a firm intends to do business in Africa, then it needs to formulate strategies for the same. To do the same, the firm would need a holistic view of African countries, which would include assessment of both the economic and political situations in these countries. In order to make such assessments, the concepts of country risk analysis and political risk analysis are employed.

23.2 COUNTRY RISK ANALYSIS

Conceptually, the *country risk analysis* is a process of environmental scanning of macroeconomic indicators of a country, coupled with the examination of policies and frameworks of the same country for both long and short-term periods.

We know that every country has its own economic system and the policy framework (see Chapter 4 on Economic Systems). For example, India has a Planning Commission as a major institution for formulating long-term as well as short-term policy planning. It also formulates the five-year plans for the country (see Chapter 5 to know more about five year plans). In case, a foreign firm intends to do business in India, it will have to scan the emerging economic opportunities through examination of macroeconomic indicators and their performance (see Chapter 6 to know more about macroeconomic indicators). In addition, to understand the future scenario, the firm would also undertake a holistic view of planning and targets that are being set up under these plans.

Considering the above contextual aspects of country risk analysis, it may be construed that it consists of some theoretical formulations. These theoretical formulations are related to country's economic performance at domestic level, its international or global economic expansion and its long-term policies set out to achieve the economic goals. With domestic performance, the analysts may choose indicators from the national income accounting and its trends. This is again based on the objective of the analyst while carrying out the country risk analysis. The analysts may choose the indicators that fulfil the requirements as per the set objectives.

Coming to the aspects of international performance, some important risks are analysed. The external economic performance relates to the performance of the economy at the current and capital account. It is also closely related to the rate of interest and exchange rate scenario. In order to avoid the exchange rate risk, analysts look at the related indicators. Exchange rate has significant impacts on both the current account and the capital account balance (see Chapter 22 to know more about foreign exchange risks). It also affects investment.

On account of the government planning, it is important for an analyst to do a detailed analysis of the policies. In order to do this exercise, the framework includes examination of sectoral strategies. This exercise again requires objectivity in analysis. The *objectivity* means identification of sectors that are strategically important for a firm. For instance, if a firm wants to make investment in infrastructure sector, then the firm will do an analysis of the programmes and plans in infrastructure while doing the country analysis.

23.2.1 Evaluation and Diagnosis of Risk

With the above framework, the process of country risk analysis, thus, includes four major aspects, *viz.* economic performance, current and future policies and strategies, legal frameworks, and institutional frameworks. These aspects of country risk analysis are discussed as follows:

1. ***Economic performance:*** Economic performance is based on the macroeconomic indicators of a country. Generally, the data on macroeconomic performance is published by the countries through their respective agencies. In addition, data on macroeconomic indicators are also published by the multilateral institutions such as the IMF, the World Bank and the UN. The data published by the multilateral institutions are very important in the context of comparative analysis of more than one country.

Government agencies as well as firms extensively use the data published by multilateral institutions. In addition, there are also some social indicators, which may be useful to examine the risk of doing business in a country. Social indicators, such as demographic structure, poverty, employment, education, health, etc. are vital for an economy. The countries doing well on these indicators are also expected to have good economic performance and also better business prospects.

2. ***Planning and strategies:*** The government, as an entity, also works in a systematic manner. It has its own structure and framework. The government of a country formulates policies to attain the long-term as well as short-term objectives. These strategies are being formulated as per the present performance and future need.

For instance, we would like to cite an example of recent policies on transport development in India. The Government of India has formulated National Transport Development Policy Committee (NTDPC) under the Chairmanship of a noted economist, Dr. Rakesh Mohan. The committee has submitted the report to the Government of India. The report has formulated policies and strategies for the development of transport sector in the country for 2032. Now, suppose if a firm wants to make an investment in India in the infrastructure sector in the logistics industry, it will need to examine the current policies and strategies of the transport sector in the country as well as the future strategies, which are documented in the reports of the committee.

3. ***Legal framework:*** Mere formulation of strategies and policies will not be the solution for attaining both long-term and short-term economic and social goals of a country. In order to achieve a set goal for a particular sector, the government not only formulates policies but also gives a legal status to these policies. The legal status of policies is called an *act*. For each sector, the government has a legal framework with the provision of acts. In case of India, the government has planned to pursue a liberalised economic policy as well as has also found space to pursue a socially significant policy such as those related to food security. Also, the Government of India has formulated policies to attract FDI in multibrand retail sector, which is deemed good for the industry, and has also enacted act to pursue the policy further. Similarly, through food security ordinance, the Government of India has also enacted a new subsidy policy.

With the purpose of country risk analysis, these policies are very important. Investors have to examine the nature of the economy through these legal frameworks (read Chapter 12 to know about India's legal framework governing businesses). In addition, the case of New Land Acquisition Act also has an imperative role for the infrastructure development. Thus, for country risk analysis, these elements are taken care off.

4. ***Institutional framework:*** To do a country risk analysis, an examination of the role of institutions is also important. Institutions, which are also the regulators, play an imperative role in bringing out the economic policies in practice. For example, when we carry out country analysis, we need to examine the set of institutional frameworks for various sectors such as industries, corporate sectors, infrastructure, financial markets and money markets, etc. With a focus on infrastructure, particularly shipping industry, the foreign firms need to examine the institutional mechanism before coming for business in India. In this regard, institutions like Tariff Authority of Major Ports (TAMP) is an institution, which is playing a pivotal role in developing a competitive port sector.

23.3 POLITICAL RISK ANALYSIS

Political risk analysis is another important tool for understanding the risks associated with a country while doing the business. *Political risk* is defined as a risk, which is political, strategic or geopolitical in nature that arises due to civil war, civil unrest, geopolitical disorder, regional contentions, disputes, etc. These unrests cause political instability in a country. Therefore, a foreign firm or government agency looks forward to a stable government or political system in the country, where it intends to do business. With this background, it becomes very important for an analyst to value the political risk.

The development of the concept of political risk has evolved over the period of time. The phases of theoretical development of political risk analysis have also been affected by the development of global policies and the global political scenario. The multinational firms also try to mitigate the political risks associated with their respective businesses in different countries.

Mitigating political risk has now become easier with the strengthening of the multilateral trading system. With the development of multilateral institutions, particularly Bretton Wood Institutions and GATT/WTO, the global businesses can now easily get pre-requisite information needed for making political risk analyses (see Chapter 14 to know more about international organisations).

In fact, political risk is related to the political instability in a country or the region. In addition, this risk is also associated with the kind of political regime. We have seen in the recent past that Myanmar was ruled under dictatorship of Military Junta and in Afghanistan, the regime was not recognised by the international community. Thus, if there is a continuous and frequent change, or an internationally unacceptable regime in any country, then it makes the business environment unpredictable for the foreign companies. Then, there exist political risks for the corporations as well as for the governments when they plan to do business with such countries. It affects the investment flows to a large extent.

23.3.1 Importance of Political Risk Analysis

Companies doing business at global level always face issues related to a country's political scenario. For example, as per The American Chamber of Commerce in Egypt, the revolution in the country in 2011 and the coup in 2013 led to the disruption of internal political security. This resulted in an increase in the political risks for the firms doing business in Egypt. There are 950 members of the American Chamber of Commerce in Egypt engaged in business in Egypt as well as in America. Some Egyptian companies are doing business in America, which is also one of the members of the chamber. The current political unrest caused major problems for the industries in their operation. The issues like energy shortages are yet to be solved. Energy is an important ingredient of industries.[1] There is an increasing uncertainty in Egypt for the business communities desiring for investment.

This highlights the importance of political risk analysis. A business firm requires to analyse the risk of investment in a country before making an investment. The associated risk also includes political risk and its valuation. The analysis of such risks is very tactical, as the existence of complex relation between economics and politics makes it an exhaustive and a carefully crafted task. The analysis also tries to formulate strategies to mitigate or manage the political risks.

23.3.2 Valuing Political Risk

Before designing adequate strategies to tackle the political risk, it is important for the corporations to do work on the following two aspects:

1. Assess the type of risks
2. Valuing the risk

The assessment of political risk broadly embraces the identification of possible dangers to the political situation of a country. The methodologies that are accepted in corporate strategies to assess the political risk analysis include event tree analysis, subjective analysis and statistical modelling, etc.[2] Event tree analysis is based on the negative events that occur in a country. Generally, the analysts, based on periodical events, can assess the political risks and also carry out the valuation of risks. In addition, a macro-level analysis as well as a micro-level analysis can also be used while doing the country and political risk analyses.

Macro-level analysis can be carried out through the identification of major political risks, for example, identification of political stability. Generally, the political instability in a country is caused by several parameters such as frequency of change in the government, events like civil unrest, insurgencies, inter-state or inter-country conflicts, etc. Some of the economic factors such as inflation, slow growth and industrial downturn may also be included into these analyses. It is also related to the internal governance. For example, corruption in a country also leads to inflation as well as economic slowdown. These can be a political risk arising out of the criticism of the policies of the government and the resultant political crisis and unrest.

In the process of subjective analysis of political risks in a country, several subjective factors are considered such as people's perception of private sector, role of households,

1. http://www.economist.com/blogs/schumpeter/2014/04/investment-egypt
2. Lemens, P.L. and Rodney J. Simmons (1998), 'System Safety and Risk Management', NIOSH Instructional Module, A Guide for Engineering Educators (Cincinnati, OH: National Institute for Occupational Safety and Health): IX-3: IX-7.

economic policies and perception about the government, etc. These subjective factors have a potential impact on a country's political scenario. After assessing the potential political risks, the valuation process anlyses that how these risks potentially impact the economic stability, including growth process, monetary policies, financial institutions, etc. These are also assessed in terms of government's fiscal measures.

Some of the research organisations carrying out country and political risk analysis include:

1. Business Monitor International (BMI)
2. Country Risk Solutions
3. Economist Intelligence Unit (EIU)
4. Eurasia Group
5. Maplecroft
6. Oxford Analytica

Closing Case: India's Business in Afghanistan

After the breakdown of Taliban's regime and the US intervention in Afghanistan, the country has been continuously in a period characterised by reconstruction and economic transition. During the period of reconstruction of Afghanistan since 2001, India has been playing a vital role. In the context of India's historical ties with Afghanistan, business prospects for Indian firms have increased after 2001.

Table 1 India's Trade with Afghanistan (US$ million)

	2005–06	*2006–07*	*2007–08*	*2008–09*	*2009–10*	*2010–11*	*2011–12*	*2012–13*
Export	142.67	182.11	249.21	394.23	463.55	411.78	510.90	472.56
Import	58.42	34.37	109.97	126.24	125.19	146.03	128.06	115.80
Total trade	201.09	216.48	359.18	520.47	588.74	557.81	638.96	588.36

Source: Export Import Data Bank, Department of Commerce, Government of India.

As per the recent statistics, India's trade with Afghanistan has increased more than three-fold since 2001 due to the increasing presence of Indian companies in the country. More than hundred companies have invested in the countries' businesses. The investment pattern indicates that the share of services sector is high.

According to a report published by the South and South-West Asia division of UNESCAP, Afghanistan is emerging from its long period of conflicts with strong economic performance. The report Doing Business with Afghanistan suggests that there exist various opportunities in the sectors such as mineral resources, agriculture, food processing industry, carpets, construction sector and communication sector, etc. As per the report, the country's economic scenario is positive.

The report highlights that between 2002 and 2009, Afghanistan's average per capita GDP increased by more than 75% in real terms. In addition, the real GDP growth in 2012 has been 12% owing to good agricultural harvest.

However, in 2014, the withdrawal proposal of foreign troops caused apprehensions among the investors. Amid this scenario, it was expected that the major companies from India may slash their investments in the country. It was expected that the Afghan Iron and Steel Consortium, led by Steel Authority of India Limited (SAIL) may bring down the initial outlay to US$1.5 billion.

Source: This case is written by the authors based on inputs from the following sources:

1. Doing Business with Afghanistan, UNESCAP, 2013, http://sswa.unescap.org/pdf/Doing-Business-with-Afghanistan-Report_Hires.pdf
2. DNA News, 20, November 2013, Indian companies may slash the biggest investment plan in Afghanistan, http://www.dnaindia.com/money/report-indian-companies-may-slash-the-biggest-investment-plan-in-afghanistan-1922171

CASE QUESTIONS

1. Examine the role of SAIL in Afghanistan.
2. What are the prospects for Indian businesses in Afghanistan?

REVIEW QUESTIONS

1. What do you mean by country risk analysis?
2. What are the areas that country risk analysis covers?
3. Discuss the aspects used to evaluate and diagnose a country risk.
4. Define political risk analysis.
5. What are the two important aspects for doing political risk analysis?
6. Discuss the importance of political risk analysis.

SUGGESTED READINGS

Cullen, John B. and Parboteeah, K.P., 2010, *International Business: Strategy and the Multinational Company*, Routledge, New York.

Doing Business Report 2014, World Bank and IFC.

Hill, C.W.L. and Jain, A.K., 2009, *International Business: Competing in the Global Marketplace*, Tata McGraw-Hill Education, New Delhi.

Rugman, A.M. and Hodgetts, R.M., 2004, *International Business*, Pearson Education, Delhi.

Sundaram, A.K. and Black, J.S., 1995, *The International Business Environment: Text and Cases*, PHI Learning, Delhi.

24

DOING BUSINESS IN SELECT MARKETS

Learning Outcomes

After reading this chapter, you will

- Understand the significance of Doing Business Report of the World Bank in assessment of the business environment
- Appreciate the key macroeconomic indicators of emerging markets and the ease of doing business in those markets
- Comprehend the doing business scenario in BRICS, ASEAN and ECOWAS regions

Opening Case: Doing Business in Afghanistan

Afghanistan has been a country with a long history of conflicts. The election held in 2014 was the second subsequent election in Afghanistan. With the new government, Afghanistan is likely to experience transition in both political framework and its economic policies. As far as the economic transition is concerned, the same is likely to continue with the current economic progress.

Afghanistan has been performing better on macroeconomic indicators. Its performance has been of one of the strongest nations among the least developed countries (LDCs) and land-locked countries. The robust economic performance can be understood by the fact that inflation has been low and the financials of the Government of Afghanistan has also been positive. This is also a result of the improvement in its business environment.

The per capita income, on an average, grew by more than 75% between 2002 and 2009. The GDP growth in 2012 was 12% and per capita income in the year 2012 was estimated to be US$680. The net international reserve was US$6.35 billion, which was enough to finance imports for seven months (see Exhibit 1).

The country is now embracing new economic reforms for better business environment. Its policy development during contemporary times has been laying the foundation for private sector development. The Afghanistan National Development Strategy (ANDS) in the country has been focusing primarily on the private sector which has led to the economic progress and development. Such development is catalysing improvements in the business environment of the country.

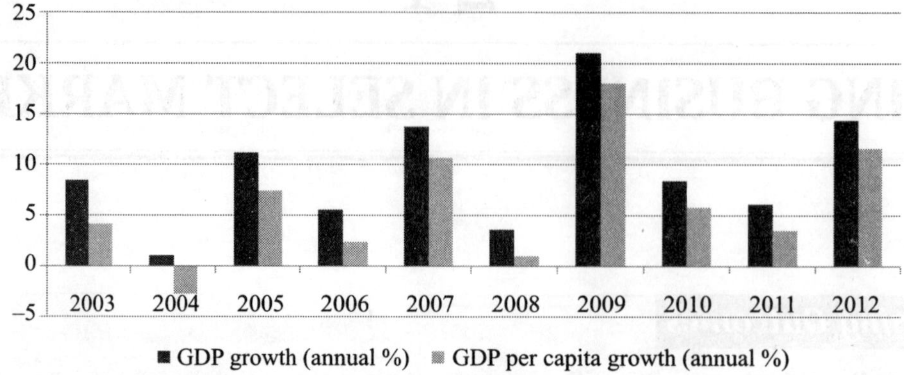

Exhibit 1 Afghanistan's economic progress.
Source: World Bank.

The progress of Afghanistan's economy can be traced by the fact that in 2012, there were as many as 17 commercial banks including public banks, private banks and branches of foreign banks. The increase in the assets of banking sector has also been spectacular. It increased from less than US\$300 million in 2004 to more than US\$4 billion in December 2011.

In addition, the roles of private sector have also been increasing at a faster rate. The share of private investment increased from 1.3% of GDP in 2003 to 8.6% in 2011. More than 30% of these investments are a part of FDI in the country. Some of the sectors are performing very well. These sectors include construction and food processing industries. Construction sector has been the highest receiver of the private investment, with a share of 38.1%. Almost 20% of the investment is received from the services sector.

There exist sectoral opportunities for business in Afghanistan. These sectors include mineral resources, construction sector, food processing industry, etc. Afghanistan has extensive deposits of minerals, and precious and semiprecious stones, and is also endowed with the deposits of copper, gold, and high quality emerald and ruby stones. Afghanistan's Hajigak field, for which seven Indian steel and mining companies, led by Steel Authority of India Limited (SAIL) placed their bid in 2011, has an estimated 1.8 billion metric tons of ores.[1] As per the ranking of the World Bank's Doing Business Report, the overall rank has improved in 2014 as compared to 2013.

This improvement has been evident due to the reforms carried out by Afghanistan. Some of the reforms which are undertaken by the country doing 2007–2014 are as follows:[2]

1. ***Starting a business:*** Afghanistan made starting a business easier by reducing the time and cost to obtain a business licence, and also eliminated the inspection of the premises of newly registered companies. It simplified business start-up through taking

1. Indo-Afghan engagements: less economics and more geo-economics, by Faisal Ahmed, *The Financial Express*, 6 October 2011, http://www.financialexpress.com/story-print/856394
2. Doing Business Report 2014, World Bank and IFC.

company registration out of the commercial courts. The business environment further improved as the country established a new company registry that acts as a one-stop shop (ACBR) combining company registration, tax registration, and publication in the Official Gazette, while charging the flat registration fees.

2. ***Getting credit:*** On account of getting credit, Afghanistan strengthened its secured transactions system through the implementation of a unified collateral registry. The new law also allows out of court enforcement.
3. ***Registering property:*** Afghanistan reduced the property transfer taxes by 3% of the property value, resulting in easing the registration of property.

Source: This case is written by the authors based on inputs from the following sources:

1. UNESCAP, Doing Business in Afghanistan, http://sswa.unescap.org/pdf/Doing-Business-with-Afghanistan-Report_Hires.pdf
2. Doing Business Report 2014, World Bank and IFC.
3. Indo-Afghan engagements: less economics and more geo-economics, by Faisal Ahmed, *The Financial Express*, 6 October 2011, http://www.financialexpress.com/story-print/856394

24.1 EMERGING MARKETS SCENARIO

This chapter deals with the business environment in various regions and select countries in the world. It, thus, deals with the current macroeconomic situation and tries to understand the business scenario through the lens of these indicators. While discussing the current business scenario of select markets, the chapter also highlights the rankings on various parameters on doing business, which is a research project of the World Bank, covering analysis of business regulations and their enforcement across 189 countries in the world. The main objective of this project is to highlight the business environment in each country on certain parameters, which are important for doing business in a country. It also provides ranking of countries on each parameter.[3] Some other organisations also periodically produce such indicators. However, the study of doing business by the World Bank includes new methodology and approach to define the business environment in a country.[4]

The economic progress of developing Asia and Latin America as well as some countries from Africa have become the centre of economic activities. The economic performance of emerging markets and developing economies across the globe has been highlighted in Table 24.1. Overall, the GDP of these economies has been growing more than 5% annually during 2000–2016.

In emerging and developing markets, investment as percentage of GDP increased from 23% in 2000 to 32% in 2015. The emerging market direct investment was US$148 billion in 2000 and US$520 billion in 2011. However, it accounted for US$487 billion in 2012 and US$471 in 2013. The emerging markets and developing countries are contributing more than two-third of the world GDP. The IMF projection suggested that the GDP growth in developing economies of the emerging markets will be above 4.1% during 2016.[5]

3. http://www.doingbusiness.org/~/media/GIAWB/Doing%20Business/Documents/Annual-Reports/English/DB04-FullReport.pdf
4. http://www.doingbusiness.org/methodology/methodology-note
5. World Economic Outlook, 2014.

Table 24.1 Emerging Markets and Developing Economies Scenario

Subject Descriptor	*Units*	*2000*	*2005*	*2010*	*2011*	*2012*	*2013*	*2014*	*2015*
GDP constant prices	Percent change	5.7	7.3	7.5	6.3	5.3	4.9	4.6	4.0
Investment	Percent of GDP	23.7	26.7	31.4	31.7	31.7	31.5	31.7	31.5
Volume of imports of goods	Percent change	13.2	11.0	14.9	10.0	5.4	4.8	3.0	0.4
Volume of exports of goods	Percent change	13.4	10.9	13.8	6.9	4.2	4.3	3.1	1.5
Direct investment, net	US$ billion	–147.4	–268.2	–453.4	–534.4	–486.6	–470.7	n/a	n/a

Source: IMF World Economic Outlook, 2016.

It is also projected that the growth prospects in the emerging market economies from Latin America are likely to be robust. Some economies are projected to grow at higher economic growth. It is also estimated that the emerging markets are likely to contribute a large part of the world GDP. The IMF estimates suggest that the emerging market will have a potential to overtake industrial economies in future. Emerging market economies will contribute one-third of the growth in world economy over the next few years. The economies like China and India will account for more than 35% of such growth.[6]

Moreover, IMF forecast brings out the fact that the global investors are now moving toward the emerging markets. This is also the result of new economic reforms, which are being carried out in the emerging markets to attract the foreign investment. At present, these markets are attracting almost 50% of the foreign direct investment (FDI) global inflows and also account for 25% of the FDI outflows. Africa and the Middle East are the regions where these investments are likely to be directed in the future.[7] Brazil, in Latin American region and also the Southeast Asian countries are moving towards creating a new policy framework for attracting investment. The next section highlights regional analysis of doing business and business prospects.

24.2 REGIONAL COMPARISON OF DOING BUSINESS

Regional performance of the world economy in the year 2014 is presented in Table 24.2. The performance of the economies across region typically highlights that how the regions are moving towards a better business environment. Growth prospects of a region create opportunities for more business. The IMF has also forecasted for the future years (see Figure 24.1).

As per the IMF, the growth prospects of the world economy were only 3.1% in 2015. Thus, during 2015, the economies across the developed regions were experiencing a slow-down but on recovery path. In 2015, the story of advanced economies was also the same which experienced GDP growth of 1.8% in 2015. As per the World Bank, the GDP in North America grew at the rate of 2.5% in 2014 over the previous year. The same in case of Europe and Central Asia had been 1.4%. Asia and Africa had seen major growth prospects in 2014 and the projection as per IMF is depicted in Figure 24.1 for regions across the world.

6. http://www.ey.com/Publication/vwLUAssets/Tracking_global_trends/$FILE/Tracking%20global%20trends.pdf
7. *Ibid.*

Table 24.2 Region-wise Data on Macroeconomic Indicators, 2012

Country	*GDP Growth (Annual Percentage)*	*GDP per Capita Growth (Annual Percentage)*	*FDI (Percentage of GDP)*	*OFDI (Percentage of GDP)*	*Gross Capital Formation (Percentage of GDP)*
East Asia and Pacific	3.6	2.88	2.8	2.2	28.7
Europe and Central Asia	1.4	1.16	1.8	2.5	19.7
Latin America and the Caribbean	1.3	0.24	3.5	1.0	21.5
Middle East and North Africa	2.5	0.55	1.5	1.1	26.7
North America	2.4	1.6	1.0	2.2	20.2
South Asia	6.9	5.46	1.5	0.4	29.6
Sub-Saharan Africa	4.4	1.57	2.7	0.8	21.9
World	2.5	1.3	2.0	2.0	22.4

Source: World Development Indicator (WDI), World Bank.

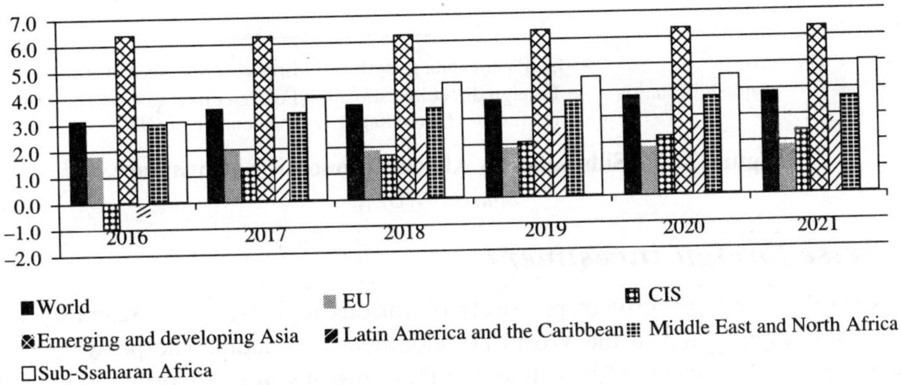

Figure 24.1 GDP growth projections.

Source: World Economic Outlook, IMF.

As per the IMF World Economic Outlook, some signs of improvement are now visible on the map of world's economic order. It is found that the Euro area has now been gradually coming out of the crisis. Notably, the world has been experiencing an economic growth of below 3% during recent years. The recent growth prospects across the region have been one of the important factors that are shaping the prospects of business across the globe.

IMF projections suggest that in the Middle East and North America (MENA) region, the growth is projected to increase moderately. In case of Sub-Saharan Africa, the growth is expected to increase from 4.9% in 2013 to 5% in 2014–2015. In Africa, commodity-related projects in the region are expected to support a higher growth. Acceleration in the economic progress is also likely to catalyse regional growth in Latin America. The IMF has estimated that the regional growth of Latin America is likely to rise from 2% in 2014 to 3% in 2015.[8]

8. World Economic Outlook.

Africa's growth story is redefining the world's economic progress. Six of the ten fastest growing economies in the world are from Africa. It is expected that the continent's economic growth will continue at 5%. Some countries are recording faster growth individually. The factors which are catalysing the growth of African economies are the faster movement for economic reforms. Another important factor which is significantly impacting the rising growth story of Sub-Saharan African region is its agriculture sector (see Figure 24.2 on macroeconomic indicators of Sub-Saharan Africa). The agriculture sector feeds 65% of the population in the region. Thus, the importance of the sector is immense. The countries in the region made investment in the region, which derived a higher agricultural growth.[9]

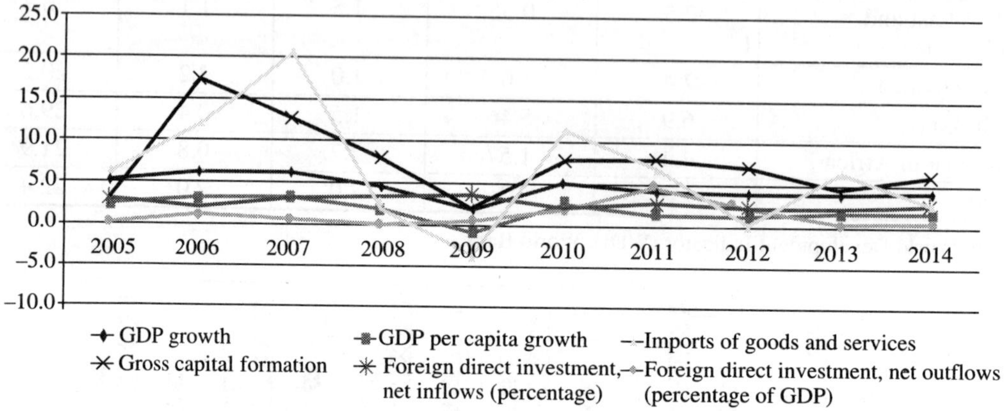

Figure 24.2 Sub-Saharan Africa's economic performance.

Source: WDI.

Region-wise foreign investment

We have seen the trend and growth prospects of various regions, as estimated by the IMF as well as the trend highlighted in the World Development Indicators. The prospects of business are also related to the prospects of investment in these regions. It is important to understand that how the regions are attracting investment from the foreigners. The FDI trend would also define future prospects of FDI. Region-wise, the current trend is presented in Figure 24.3.

The trend suggests that the net FDI inflow has been increasing since 2000. In the Asia and the Pacific region, the FDI inflow increased from US$163.58 billion in 2000 to US$179.91 billion in 2005. After 2005, the increase has been significant. The increase in the FDI inflow between 2005 and 2010 was more than two-fold in case of Asia and the Pacific. The regional performance of the FDI inflows indicates that Asia, Africa and Latin America are likely to be the major markets.

As per the World Investment Report 2013, net FDI flows to developing countries decreased in 2012 as compared to 2011 owing to an increase in their net outflow of investments. The FDI inflow in absolute term has been increasing. The FDI inflows to the developing and transition economies increased by 18% in the first half of 2013. As per the World Investment Report 2016, FDI recovery was strong in 2015 as the FDI inflows to developed countries nearly doubled in 2015 compared to 2014, rising from US$522 billion in 2014 to US$962 billion in 2015.

9. http://forumblog.org/2014/05/four-overlooked-factors-economic-success-forum-africa-2014/

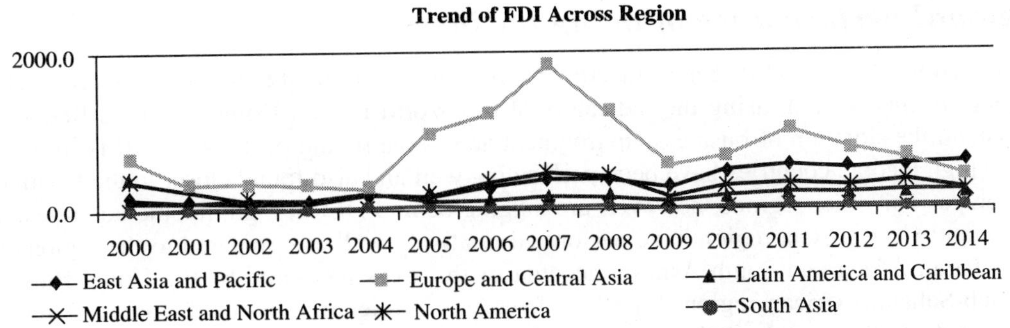

Figure 24.3 Region-wise trend of foreign investment (US$ billion).
Source: World Development Indicator (WDI), World Bank.

FDI inflows to developing world, excluding developing countries in Caribbean region, increased to US$765 billion and rose by 9% over 2014, while FDI inflows in transition economies decreased by 38% in 2015 over 2014. After a slight decline in 2012, FDI inflows to Latin America and the Caribbean increased by 35% in the first half of 2013, reaching to US$165 billion. FDI inflows in 2015 in Latin America and the Caribbean was estimated to be US$168 billion experiencing a decrease of US$ 2 billion over 2014 when it was estimated to be US$170 billion. In the developing Asia, the economies are gradually on the recovery path. However, the attraction of FDI inflows was weak. During the first half of 2013, the total inflows in the developing Asia amounted to US$192 billion. This was lower than the total FDI received during the same period in the year 2012. However, the fast moving economy of Asia, i.e., China is now recovering from it and the FDI is increasing.[10]

As per the World Investment Report 2016, the overall FDI inflows to developing and transition economies registered a modest rise (6%). This increase, however, belies a much more complex picture, as a large increase in FDI to some Asian economies offsets significant declines in nearly every developing region and in transition economies. Developing Asia registered FDI inflows of US$541 billion in 2015 compared to US$468 billion in 2014.

Asia and the Pacific (developed and developing) are the largest recipient of the World FDI inflow accounting for 54% in 2015. Asia Pacific Economic Cooperation (APEC) is the grouping which received US$669 billion in 2015. It received FDI inflows of US$954 billion in 2014.[11] Other regions are also expediting mixed performance on account of the net FDI inflows. In case of West Asia, FDI inflows dropped by 19% in the first half of 2013 compared to the first half of 2012. Moreover, the political instability in West Asia is also a cause of concern for the business environment. The case of Syria and Turkey, and also the case of North African countries like Egypt have significantly been impacting the business environment of the region. In 2015, owing to Egypt's political stability, some recovery was seen in North Africa, which received FDI inflows of US$12.7 billion in 2015 compared to US$11.6 billion in 2014. In West Asia, the FDI situation more or less remained stagnant in 2015. The region received US$42.4 billion in 2015 compared to US$43.3 billion in 2014. The FDI to transition economies in South-Eastern Europe and the Commonwealth of Independent States (CIS) has decreased in 2015, and in case of Africa, the FDI has also decreased slightly over the period.

10. World Investment Reports, various issues.
11. World Investment Report, 2016, UNCTAD.

Regional performance of doing business

We have now understood that how macroeconomic indicators define the business prospects in a region. In this section, using the indicators of the World Bank's Doing Business Report, we understand the situation of business environment across the region of the world. It is found that OECD high income countries have been performing well and also found closer to the frontier on an average. The other regions, however, are lagging behind OECD high income countries. The Europe and Central Asia region have performed relatively well as compared to the regions like Sub-Saharan Africa and South Asia on account of the areas measured by the Doing Business. The Sub-Saharan African region is farthest from the frontier in most of the areas. Almost in 6 areas out of 10 areas, the Sub-Saharan African region has performed the worst. These areas include starting a business, getting electricity, paying taxes, trading across borders, protecting investors and resolving insolvency.

The regional performance of various regions, thus, varies significantly. East Asia and the Pacific in some cases perform equally to OECD high income countries. For instance, in case of number of procedures required to get electricity, East Asia and the Pacific has same number of procedure, as in the case of OECD region. Moreover, Europe and Central Asia have also performed similar to the OECD region in several areas. However, the collective average on the performance of the Europe and Central Asia region, on dealing with the construction permits, has more number of procedures than any other regions, even more than that of the Sub-Saharan Africa. The performance of the Middle East and North Africa has been diversified and less consistent. At some parameters, the region has performed closer to the frontier and in some cases, it has performed worse than the Sub-Saharan Africa.

As evident from Table 24.3, the least documents are required in Europe and Central Asian region, whereas Latin America and the Caribbean region has the highest member of procedure. OECD high income countries have performed well on almost all the variables. In case of South Asian region, procedures to get start the business and time delays are slightly better than that of Sub-Saharan Africa, and Latin America and the Caribbean region. However, as compared to the region like East Asia and the Pacific and Europe and Central Asia, South Asia has been performing poor.

Table 24.3 Starting a Business Across Regions in the World

Region	*Starting a Business*			
	Procedures (Number)	*Time (Days)*	*Cost (Percentage of Income Per Capita)*	*Paid-in Minimum Capital (Percentage of Income Per Capita)*
East Asia and Pacific	7.0	25.9	23.0	9.8
Europe and Central Asia	4.7	10.0	4.8	3.8
Latin America and the Caribbean	8.3	29.4	31.0	2.8
Middle East and North Africa	8.2	18.8	25.8	37.7
OECD high income	4.7	8.3	3.2	9.6
South Asia	7.9	15.7	14.0	0.2
Sub-Saharan Africa	8.0	26.8	53.4	45.1

Source: Doing Business Report 2016, World Bank and IFC.

Table 24.4 highlights the number of procedures and time delays as well as the cost of getting construction permits in various regions of the world. The most efficient countries are in the OECD high income region, and Latin American and the Caribbean region in case of lesser number of procedures in getting construction permits. Europe and Central Asian regions are the worst performers. However, in case of time delays, Latin America and the Caribbean region takes the highest number of days. South Asian region is close to European and Central Asian region. In case of cost per capita to get construction permits, South Asia has the highest cost and even higher than that of the Sub-Saharan region.

Table 24.4 Construction Permits Across Regions of the World

Region	*Construction Permits*		
	Procedures (Number)	*Time (Days)*	*Cost (Percentage of Warehouse Value)*
East Asia and Pacific	14.7	134.6	1.8
Europe and Central Asia	15.9	176.3	4.4
Latin America and the Caribbean	14.1	178.1	2.6
Middle East and North Africa	14.8	139.7	3.1
OECD high income	12.4	152.1	1.7
South Asia	15.1	194.6	14.7
Sub-Saharan Africa	14.4	162.2	6.6

Source: Doing Business Report 2016, World Bank and the IFC.

Figure 24.4 presents the number of procedure and documents required to complete various formalities, as per the indices of doing business.

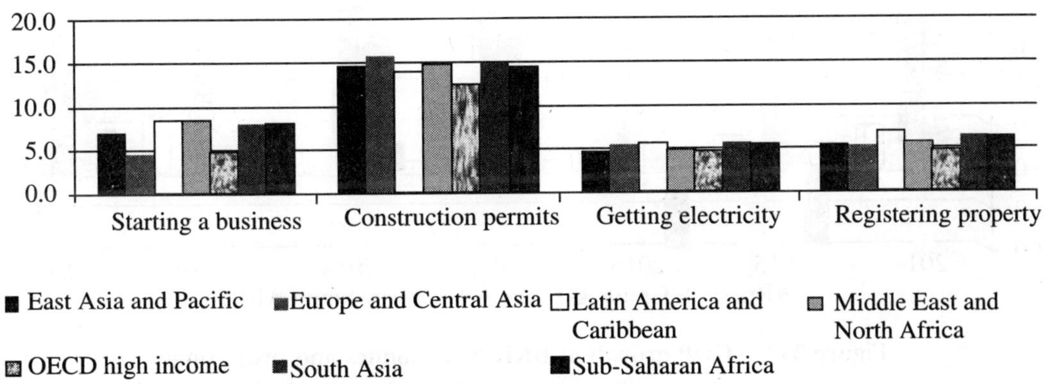

Figure 24.4 Number of procedures and documents required in various regions.
Source: Doing Business Report 2014, World Bank and IFC.

Figure 24.5 depicts the time required for completing the various activities across the region in terms of doing business.

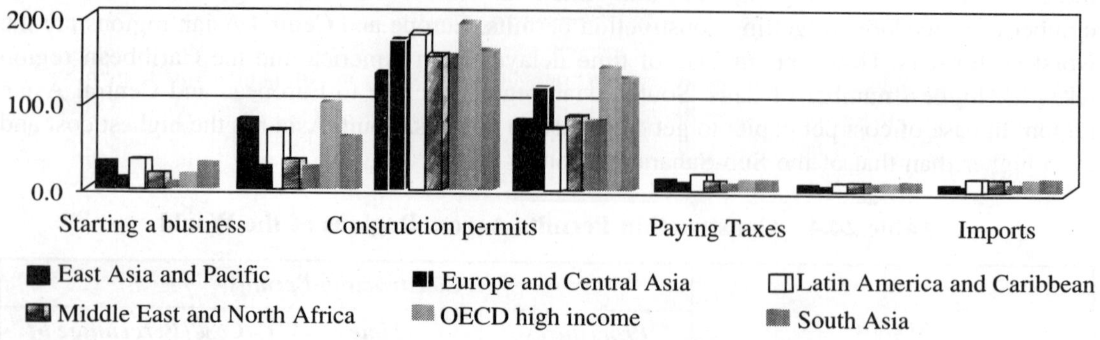

Figure 24.5 Time required for completing various activities across regions.

Source: Doing Business Report 2014, World Bank and IFC.

24.3 DOING BUSINESS IN BRICS, ASEAN, ECOWAS

Among the emerging economies, Brazil, Russia, India, China and South Africa (BRICS), and ASEAN markets are considered to be the rising economies. The markets of these economies are likely to perform well in the coming years.

BRICS

Jim O'Neill coined the term BRIC in 2001. Later, it was joined by South Africa in 2011 and became BRICS. Figure 24.6 depicts the growth rate of BRICS economies over the years, and Figure 24.7 shows the total investments as percentage of GDP in BRICS.

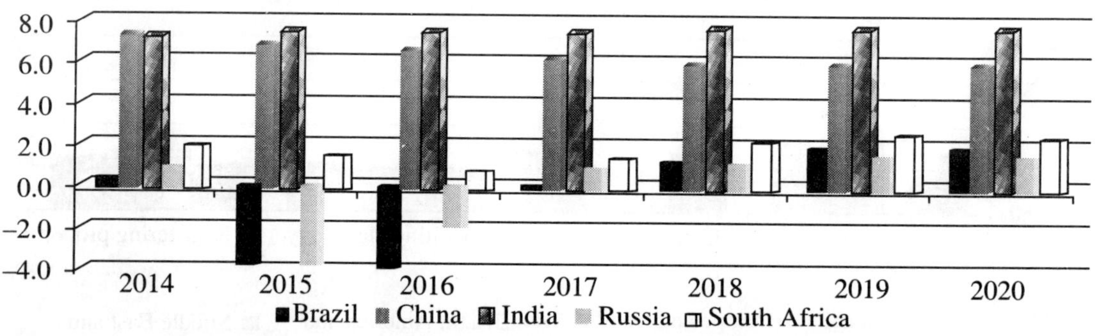

Figure 24.6 GDP growth of BRICS economies and projections.

Source: World Economic Outlook, IMF.

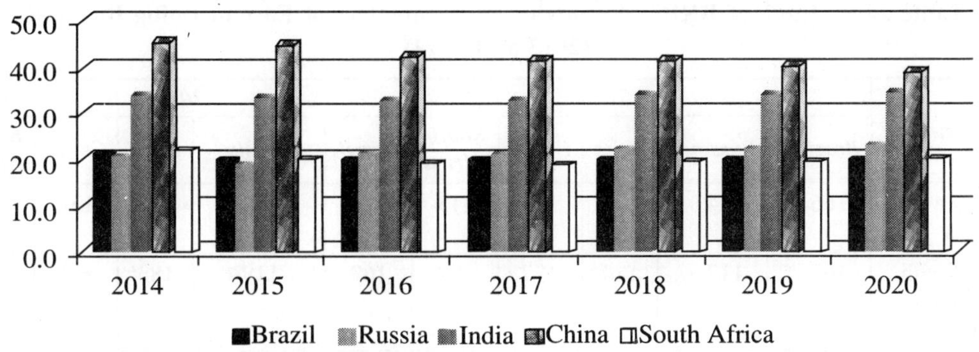

Figure 24.7 Total investment as percentage of GDP in BRICS.
Source: World Economic Outlook, IMF.

BRICS and Doing Business

Among BRICS nations, South Africa had the highest ranking in 2013. It was ranked 41st among 189 nations in 2014, and also 41st in 2013. But in 2016, South Africa ranked 73rd among 189 countries. So, the ranking of South Africa changed drastically indicating restrictions on doing business. On the other hand, ranking of Russian Federation went up from 111 in 2013 to 96 in 2014 and 51st in 2016. The rank of Russian Federation went up due to the measures undertaken by the government in terms of starting a business and major reforms in the areas of dealing with construction. In fact, on account of starting a business, Russia ranked 88th in 2014. Brazil's ranking has further gone up in 2014 as compared to 2013. It was ranked 118 in 2013, and in 2014, it was ranked 116 which remained in 2016 also (see Figure 24.8).

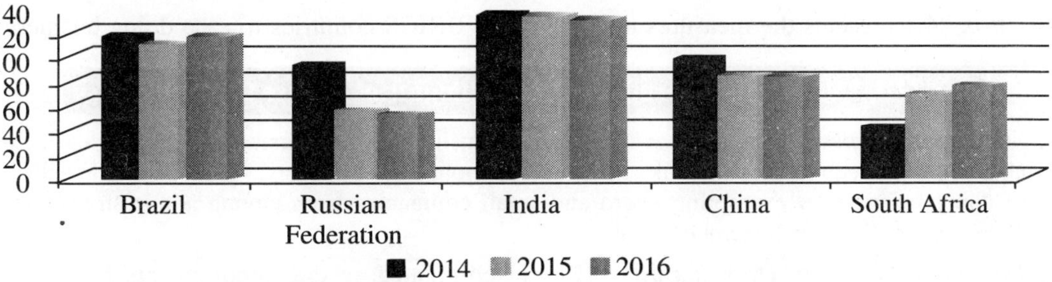

Figure 24.8 BRICS ranking on ease of doing business (2013 and 2014).
Source: Doing Business Report 2014, World Bank and IFC.

The case of China is also improving. It was ranked 99th in 2013, and improved to 92nd in 2014 and 84th in 2016. However, the improvement in India is little slow in the year 2015. In fact, India's rank remained at 130th in 2016 as compared to 131st in 2013. It was ranked 134th in 2014. Except dealing with the construction permits and paying taxes, India's rank on other variables slipped down. Table 24.5 presents the performance of BRICS economies on various parameters of ease of doing business.

Table 24.5 Rank of BRICS Countries on Parameters of Ease of Doing Business (2013 and 2014)

Indicators	*2015*					*2016*				
	Brazil	*Russia*	*India*	*China*	*South Africa*	*Brazil*	*Russia*	*India*	*China*	*South Africa*
Starting a business	166	34	164	127	113	174	41	155	136	120
Dealing with construction permits	167	117	184	177	82	169	119	183	176	90
Getting electricity	23	53	99	86	168	22	29	70	92	168
Registering property	125	8	138	41	97	130	8	138	43	101
Getting credit	90	61	36	71	52	97	42	42	79	59
Paying taxes	177	50	156	133	19	178	47	157	132	20
Trading across borders	148	169	133	96	130	145	170	133	96	130
Enforcing contracts	45	5	178	7	117	45	5	178	7	119
Resolving insolvency	55	44	136	53	38	62	51	136	55	41

Source: Doing Business Report 2016. World Bank and IFC.

Box 24.1 presents the measures undertaken by BRICS countries to ease doing business.

Box 24.1 Measures Undertaken by BRICS Countries to Ease Doing Business

1. ***Starting a business:*** On account of starting a business, Russia made the process easier by abolishing the requirement of bank signature card notarised. Similarly, China also reduced cost of doing business by exempting micro and small companies from paying administrative fees from January 2012 to December 2014.
2. ***Dealing with construction permits:*** Russia eliminated several requirements for project approvals from government agencies and also reduced the time required to register a new building. India, in the same way, reduced the time required to obtain a building permit by establishing strict time limits, and China also simplified the process of obtaining construction permits by streamlining and centralising the preconstruction approvals.
3. ***Getting credit:*** China improved its credit information system and introduced credit information industry regulations.
4. ***Registering property:*** Russia streamlined the procedures and also implemented effective time limits for processing transfer applications. Brazil on the other hand, made transferring property difficult, as it introduced a new certificate of good standing on labour debts.

5. ***Trading across borders:*** Russia introduced an electronic system for submitting export and import documents, which also reduced the number of physical inspections. South Africa reduced both the time and number of documents through modernisation of customs process.
6. ***Getting electricity:*** Only Russia has taken initiatives recently in this category. It has made it easier.
7. ***Enforcing contracts:*** Brazil implemented an electronic system for filing initial complaints at the São Paulo civil district court in the area of enforcing contracts. China also amended its civil procedure code to streamline and speed up all court proceedings.
8. ***Paying taxes:*** South Africa made paying taxes easier for companies by replacing the secondary tax on companies with a dividend tax borne by the shareholders. India is on the verge of introducing Goods and Services Tax (GST). However, simplification of tax is still to be done in BRICS region.

Source: Doing Business Report 2014, World Bank and IFC.

Association of Southeast Asian Nations (ASEAN)

ASEAN is a regional trade block representing Southeast Asia. Its economic growth is depicted in Figure 24.9, and Figure 24.10 depicts the total investment as the percentage of GDP.

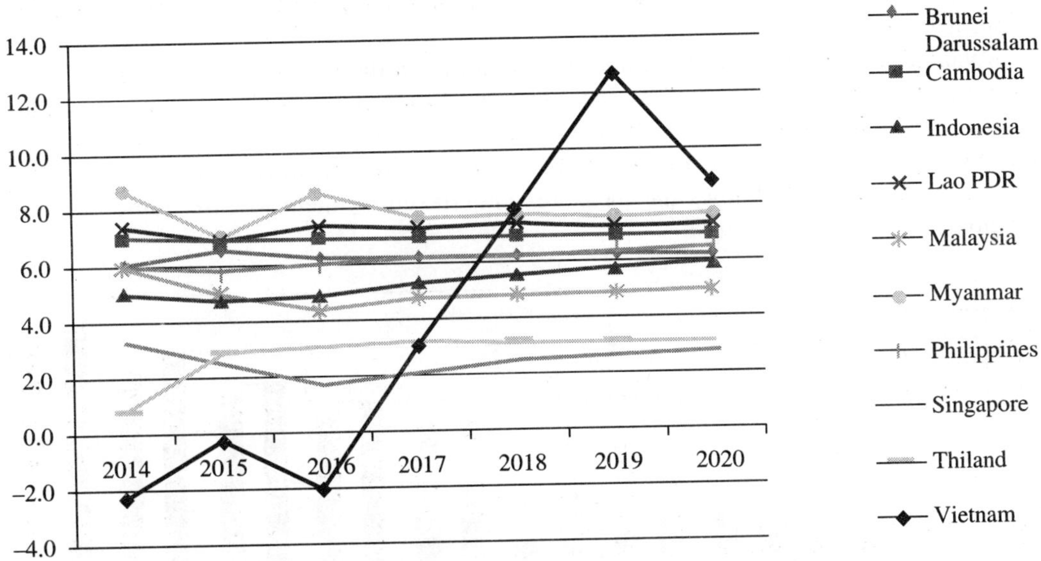

Figure 24.9 Economic growth of ASEAN: Performance and projections.
Source: World Economic Outlook, IMF.

Doing Business and ASEAN

Doing business provides information on the performance of the member countries of ASEAN on account of various parameters considered under the ranking of doing business. The overall final ranking of the member countries indicates that the region has been a well-performing area.

As per the survey report of US Chamber of Commerce, Indonesia, Vietnam, Thailand and Myanmar are the most attractive countries for new business expansion.[12] Singapore has been

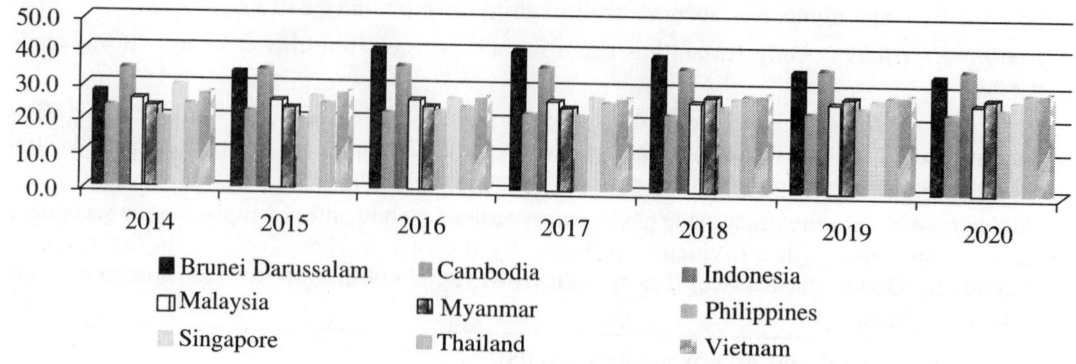

Figure 24.10 Total investment as percentage of GDP in ASEAN.
Source: World Economic Outlook, IMF.

continuously providing the most business-friendly regulatory environments for local entrepreneurs globally. Other countries like Thailand, Indonesia and Malaysia have continued to ease business-related measures.

Myanmar has been one of the important countries in the region, which has recently been transformed both politically as well as economically. In terms of starting a business, Myanmar had 167th position in the world in 2016. Myanmar made improvement on account of ease of doing business in recent years. Figure 24.11 depicts the doing business ranking of ASEAN countries, while Box 24.2 shows the measures undertaken by them to ease doing business in the region.

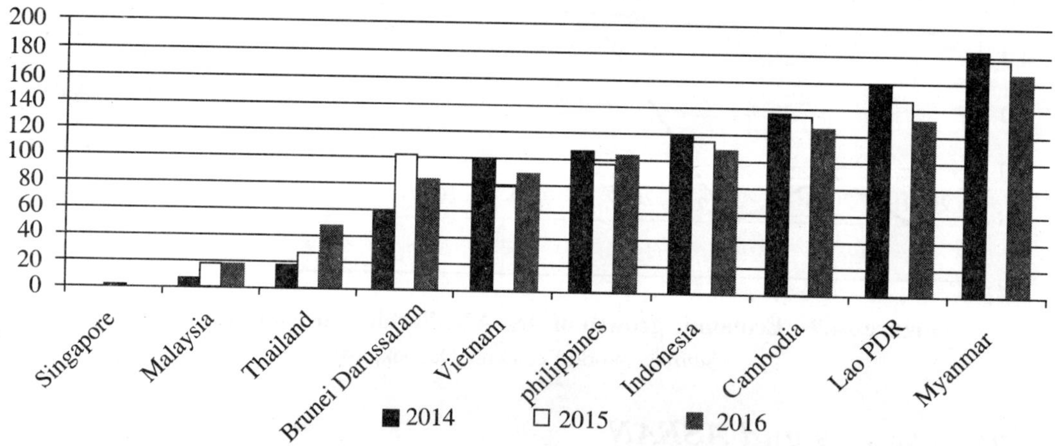

Figure 24.11 Ranking of ASEAN countries on ease of doing business in 2013 and 2014.
Source: Doing Business Report 2014, World Bank and IFC.

12. https://www.uschamber.com/sites/default/files/legacy/international/files/ASEAN%20Survey%202014.pdf

Box 24.2 Measures Undertaken by ASEAN Countries to Ease Doing Business

1. ***Starting a business:*** The progress has been made by Indonesia, Lao PDR, Malaysia, Thailand and Vietnam. Indonesia simplified application process by allowing simultaneous acquisition of both a general trading licence and a business registration certificate. Similarly, Lao PDR allowed tax registration at the time of incorporation of business entity. Malaysia reduced the registration fee and Thailand also made starting business easier by allowing the registrar at the Department of Business Development to receive the company's work regulations. In Vietnam, one can also use own self-printed value added tax invoices to start a business. On the other hand, Cambodia made it difficult by introducing a requirement for a company name check at the Department of Intellectual Property, which also increased the cost.
2. ***Dealing with construction permits:*** Dealing with the construction permits was made easier by creating a one-stop shop for preconstruction approvals in Brunei and Malaysia. The Philippines made dealing with construction permits easier by eliminating the requirement to obtain a health certificate.
3. ***Getting credit:*** Brunei Darussalam established a public credit registry and Cambodia established its first private credit bureau, which was also done by Indonesia. The Philippines started to distribute both positive and negative information and enacted a data privacy act that guarantees borrowers' right to access their data. Singapore guaranteed credit information by a law through which borrowers' right to inspect their own data has been established. Similarly, Vietnam improved its credit information system through setting up a legal framework for the establishment of private credit bureaus.
4. ***Registering property:*** Malaysia reduced the number of days it took to register property transfers, and also Singapore introduced an online procedure for property transfers.
5. ***Trading across borders:*** Lao PDR reduced the time to export and import by implementing the Automated System for Customs Data (ASYCUDA), an electronic data interchange system at the Thanaleng–Friendship Bridge border crossing.
6. ***Getting electricity:*** Brunei Darussalam established a one-stop shop and reduced the time required to obtain an excavation permit. Indonesia eliminated the requirement for new customers applying for an electricity connection to show a neighbour's electricity bill, as a way to help in determining their address. Malaysia increased the efficiency of internal processes at the utility and improved its communication and dialogue with contractors.
7. ***Protecting investors:*** Vietnam strengthened investor protections by introducing greater disclosure requirements for publicly held companies in cases of related-party transactions.
8. ***Paying taxes:*** Brunei Darussalam reduced the profit tax rate. Lao PDR reduced the corporate income tax rate, though it also introduced a new property transfer tax. Myanmar reduced the corporate income tax rate. The Philippines introduced an electronic filing and payment system for social security contributions. Thailand reduced employers' social security contribution rate and Vietnam increased employers' social security contribution rate. On the other hand, Cambodia introduced a new tax on immovable property. In addition, Malaysia and Vietnam introduced a minimum wage policy. Vietnam abolished priority rules for redundancy dismissals or layoffs and increased the minimum wage.

Source: Doing Business Report 2014 and 2013.

Economic Community of West African States (ECOWAS)

ECOWAS is a regional bloc representing West Africa. Table 24.6 shows the growth of ECOWAS and Table 24.7 presents the total investment as percentage of GDP.

Table 24.6 GDP Growth in ECOWAS Region: Performance and Projections

Country	*2014*	*2015*	*2016*	*2017*	*2018*	*2019*	*2020*
Benin	6.5	5.2	5.0	5.2	5.4	5.4	5.6
Burkina Faso	4.0	4.0	5.0	5.7	6.0	6.0	6.0
Cape Verde	1.8	1.8	2.9	3.5	4.3	4.4	4.4
Côte d'Ivoire	7.9	8.6	8.5	8.0	7.6	7.3	7.1
The Gambia	–0.2	4.4	2.3	3.3	4.8	5.2	5.5
Ghana	4.0	3.5	4.5	7.7	5.9	6.2	5.4
Guinea	1.1	0.1	4.1	5.4	5.8	6.6	6.3
Guinea-Bissau	2.5	4.8	4.8	5.0	5.0	5.0	5.0
Mali	7.5	6.1	5.0	5.2	4.8	4.5	4.5
Niger	7.1	4.0	4.9	6.9	7.8	6.6	7.6
Nigeria	6.3	2.7	2.3	3.5	3.9	3.7	3.9
Senegal	4.3	6.5	6.6	6.8	7.0	7.1	7.1
Sierra Leone	4.6	–21.5	5.3	–0.7	5.2	8.7	5.6
Togo	5.4	5.3	5.2	5.2	5.4	5.4	5.4

Source: World Economic Outlook, IMF.

Table 24.7 Total Investment as Percentage of GDP in ECOWAS

Country	*2014*	*2015*	*2016*	*2017*	*2018*	*2019*	*2020*
Benin	25.0	27.8	28.0	27.6	27.8	27.9	27.9
Burkina Faso	19.8	14.2	13.2	15.5	16.7	16.9	17.4
Cabo Verde	37.4	40.7	42.4	43.9	45.4	47.1	47.8
Côte d'Ivoire	16.8	18.2	19.4	20.2	20.4	20.6	21.0
The Gambia	25.2	19.8	22.3	28.4	23.4	22.8	21.8
Ghana	24.8	23.9	24.0	24.4	25.7	28.6	29.3
Guinea	9.3	10.2	20.6	33.7	41.5	56.8	59.6
Guinea-Bissau	10.8	11.2	10.8	11.9	12.0	13.0	13.2
Mali	27.8	24.0	25.5	24.5	24.5	23.9	22.8
Niger	40.2	42.1	40.3	40.5	39.4	37.9	33.9
Nigeria	15.8	14.5	13.6	13.2	12.9	13.0	13.0
Senegal	25.1	25.3	26.4	27.1	27.2	26.4	28.3
Sierra Leone	13.5	16.3	15.4	15.5	16.1	16.1	17.1
Togo	23.5	24.2	25.6	24.3	23.8	24.1	24.1

Source: World Economic Outlook, IMF.

Figure 24.12 depicts the ease of doing business ranking of ECOWAS countries.

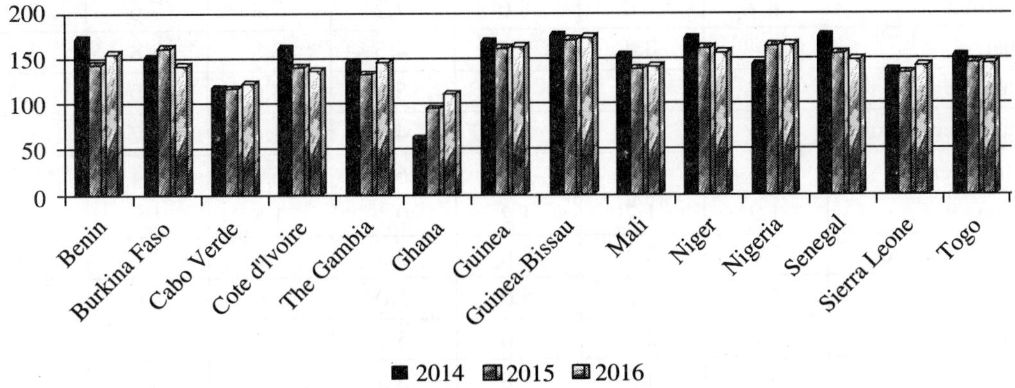

Figure 24.12 Ease of doing business: Ranking of countries from ECOWAS, 2014, 2015 and 2016.

Source: Doing Business Report 2014, World Bank and IFC.

Doing Business in Asia and the Pacific Region

The Asia and the Pacific region remains the most dynamic region of the global economy. Economies of the South and Southeast Asia are expected to grow at faster rates. Table 24.8 below indicates the current and projected economic growth in Asia Pacific countries.

Table 24.8 GDP Growth in Select Countries of Asia and the Pacific

Country	*2014*	*2015*	*2016*	*2017*	*2018*	*2019*	*2020*
Bangladesh	6.3	6.4	6.6	6.9	7.0	7.0	6.7
Bhutan	6.4	7.7	8.4	8.6	11.2	7.6	6.5
Brunei Darussalam	–2.3	–0.2	–2.0	3.0	7.9	12.8	8.9
Cambodia	7.1	6.9	7.0	7.0	7.0	6.9	6.9
China	7.3	6.9	6.5	6.2	6.0	6.0	6.0
Fiji	5.3	4.3	2.5	3.9	3.9	3.6	3.6
India	7.2	7.3	7.5	7.5	7.6	7.7	7.7
Indonesia	5.0	4.8	4.9	5.3	5.5	5.8	6.0
Kiribati	2.4	4.2	2.7	2.5	2.6	2.5	2.2
Lao PDR	7.4	7.0	7.4	7.4	7.4	7.3	7.3
Malaysia	6.0	5.0	4.4	4.8	4.8	4.9	5.0
Maldives	6.5	1.9	3.5	3.9	4.6	4.7	4.8
Marshall Islands	1.0	1.6	1.8	1.8	1.6	1.6	1.3
Micronesia	–3.4	–0.2	1.1	0.7	0.7	0.8	0.5
Mongolia	7.9	2.3	0.4	2.5	5.7	7.9	10.5

Country	*2014*	*2015*	*2016*	*2017*	*2018*	*2019*	*2020*
Myanmar	8.7	7.0	8.6	7.7	7.8	7.6	7.7
Nepal	5.4	3.4	0.5	4.5	3.8	3.8	3.8
Palau	4.2	9.4	2.0	5.0	4.0	3.0	3.0
Papua New Guinea	8.5	9.0	3.1	4.4	1.4	3.2	3.2
Philippines	6.1	5.8	6.0	6.2	6.3	6.4	6.5
Samoa	1.2	1.7	1.2	–0.1	1.8	1.9	1.9
Solomon Islands	2.0	3.3	3.0	3.3	3.0	3.0	3.0
Sri Lanka	4.5	5.2	5.0	5.0	5.0	5.0	5.0
Thailand	0.8	2.8	3.0	3.2	3.1	3.1	3.1
Timor-Leste	5.5	4.3	5.0	5.5	6.0	6.5	5.5
Tonga	2.0	2.6	2.8	2.6	2.8	2.7	2.1
Tuvalu	2.2	2.6	3.9	1.9	2.0	1.8	1.6
Vanuatu	2.3	–0.8	4.5	4.0	3.8	2.7	2.5
Vietnam	6.0	6.7	6.3	6.2	6.2	6.2	6.2

Source: World Economic Outlook, IMF.

It is assumed that the domestic consumption in countries like Indonesia, Malaysia and other pacific nations is likely to lead economic growth. India can attract foreign investment but domestic consumption is likely to play a pivotal role in determining the trajectory of growth. Table 24.9 presents the investment scenario in Asia and the Pacific region.

Table 24.9 Current and Future Investment as Percentage of GDP in Select Countries of Asia Pacific

Country	*2014*	*2015*	*2016*	*2017*	*2018*	*2019*	*2020*
Bangladesh	28.8	29.0	29.8	31.8	33.1	33.6	33.8
Bhutan	55.4	56.0	56.3	55.9	56.1	56.1	56.0
Brunei Darussalam	27.4	33.6	40.2	38.0	38.4	34.9	33.5
Cambodia	23.2	22.5	22.7	22.7	23.0	23.0	23.0
China	45.9	43.3	41.8	40.8	40.1	39.2	38.1
Fiji	17.6	18.6	19.3	19.2	19.2	20.2	21.2
India	34.1	33.3	32.8	32.8	33.2	33.6	34.1
Indonesia	34.6	34.6	35.1	35.4	35.7	36.1	36.5
Malaysia	25.0	25.1	25.7	25.6	25.5	25.6	25.9
Maldives	20.0	20.0	20.0	20.0	20.0	20.0	20.0
Mongolia	35.2	26.2	29.9	36.6	40.4	40.4	39.3
Myanmar	23.5	23.8	24.3	25.2	27.0	27.3	27.7

Country	*2014*	*2015*	*2016*	*2017*	*2018*	*2019*	*2020*
Nepal	28.7	28.9	21.2	24.8	26.2	26.1	24.4
Palau	27.3	22.5	24.0	33.7	26.1	24.0	22.2
Papua New Guinea	20.2	8.1	8.1	8.1	8.0	8.0	8.0
Philippines	20.9	20.9	22.5	23.1	23.7	24.3	24.8
Solomon Islands	19.3	19.7	23.4	22.9	21.3	20.9	20.7
Sri Lanka	27.4	27.9	30.9	30.5	30.4	30.3	30.1
Thailand	24.1	24.1	25.5	26.5	27.3	27.9	28.4
Timor-Leste	16.5	22.3	38.3	50.7	50.3	55.8	59.3
Vanuatu	27.0	51.2	40.7	39.5	35.5	33.3	31.5
Vietnam	26.8	27.6	26.1	27.4	28.0	28.6	28.9

Source: World Economic Outlook, IMF.

In East Asia and the Pacific, China stands out with the biggest improvement in doing business and Singapore leads the world ranking. Countries like Malaysia, Brunei Darussalam and Indonesia made starting a business easier in 2016. In addition, several countries adopted tax-related reforms. Table 24.10 shows the reforms undertaken by select countries in Asia Pacific, as presented in the World Bank's Doing Business Report 2016.

Table 24.10 Reforms in Select Countries in Asia Pacific in 2016

Countries	*Reforms in 2016*
Brunei Darussalam	Made starting a business easier by improving online procedures and simplifying registration and post-registration requirements in 2016 and made paying taxes easier and less costly for companies by merging contributions for the Employee Provident Fund and the Supplemental Pension Fund and increasing the capital allowance for industrial buildings.
Cambodia	Made starting a business easier by simplifying company name checks, streamlining tax registration and eliminating the requirement to publish information on the new company's incorporation in the official gazette and reduced the average frequency and duration of power outages experienced by a customer over the course of a year in Phnom Penh by increasing power generation capacity.
China and Hong Kong	Made paying taxes less costly for companies in Shanghai by reducing the social security contribution rate, and Hong Kong SAR, China made paying taxes easier and less costly for companies by simplifying compliance with the mandatory provident fund obligations and increasing the allowance for profit tax. At the same time, it increased the maximum contribution to the mandatory provident fund and reduced the property tax waiver. It also made starting a business easy by eliminating the requirement of company seal and also made easier access to credit by using collateral registry.

Countries	*Reforms in 2016*
Indonesia	Made starting a business in Jakarta easier by reducing the time needed to register with the Ministry of Manpower and improvement in access of credit by enabling searches of the collateral registry by the debtor's name and made tax paying easier and less costly by implementing online system for paying social security contributions, etc.
Lao PDR	Improved access to credit information by eliminating the threshold for the minimum size of loans to be included in the credit registry's database and by expanding borrower coverage.
Malaysia	Made paying taxes easier and less costly for companies by making electronic filing mandatory and reducing the property tax rate. At the same time, it also increased the capital gains tax.
Myanmar	Made starting a business easier by eliminating the minimum capital requirement for local companies and streamlining incorporation procedures and facilitated the process to obtain a new electricity connection in Myanmar by reducing delays through fewer approvals.
Vietnam	Made starting a business easier by reducing the time required to get the company seal engraved and registered and guaranteed borrowers' right to inspect their credit data while the new credit bureau expanded borrower coverage, improving the credit information system.

Source: Doing Business Report 2016, the World Bank and IFC.

Southeast Asia and the Pacific are considered as one of the fastest growing region in the world. It is believed that business is likely to strive in the countries situated in Southeast Asia and the Pacific. In addition, developing and emerging economies of Asia and the Pacific have started major economic reforms which are also reflecting in doing the business indicators. Table 24.11 sums up doing business indicators for Southeast Asia and the Pacific.

Table 24.11 Doing Business Ranking of Countries from South, Southeast Asia and Pacific

Economy	*Rank in 2014*	*Rank in 2015*	*Rank in 2016*
Singapore	1	1	1
Hong Kong SAR, China	2	5	5
Taiwan, China	16	11	11
Malaysia	6	17	18
Thailand	18	46	49
Bhutan	141	70	71
Tonga	57	74	78
Brunei Darussalam	59	105	84
China	96	83	84
Fiji	62	86	88
Vietnam	99	93	90

Economy	*Rank in 2014*	*Rank in 2015*	*Rank in 2016*
Vanuatu	74	96	94
Nepal	105	94	99
Philippines	108	97	103
Sri Lanka	85	113	107
Indonesia	120	120	109
Solomon Islands	97	109	112
Cambodia	137	133	127
Maldives	95	125	128
India	134	134	130
Lao PDR	159	139	134
Palau	100	131	136
Marshall Islands	114	137	140
Papua New Guinea	113	141	145
Micronesia, Fed. Sts.	156	146	148
Kiribati	122	143	149
Myanmar	182	177	167
Timor-Leste	172	167	173
Bangladesh	130	172	174

Source: Doing Business Reports of 2014, 2015 and 2016

Closing Case: Reforms, Growth and Business Climate

India embarked on economic reform agenda in 1991. The result of economic reforms was encouraging. At one time, India's economic growth approached double digit growth during the later part of the post-reform period as compared to the lower rate of economic growth during the pre-reform period. The robust economic progress was hampered by economic crisis during 2008. Later in the years 2009 and 2010, the economy recovered from the international financial turmoil. However, the ongoing slowdown in Europe led to further deceleration in India's economic progress. Experts generally consider that India's slow economic progress is not only the result of global economic slowdown but also the result of slow pace of economic reforms.

The progress of economic reforms was halted after having quick progress in economic reforms during 1991–2000. Later the economic reform agenda, which include major policies like goods and services tax (GST), privatisation, lowering subsidies, reforms in labour laws, and banking sector reforms, are now on halt. The most important example is the effort towards attracting foreign investment in multibrand retail industry.

In an interview, the former Finance Minister pointed that we should not have lifted the foot that have been kept on the accelerator of growth. We should have pressed on with growth, pressed on with reforms even while we were continuing our flagship programmes.

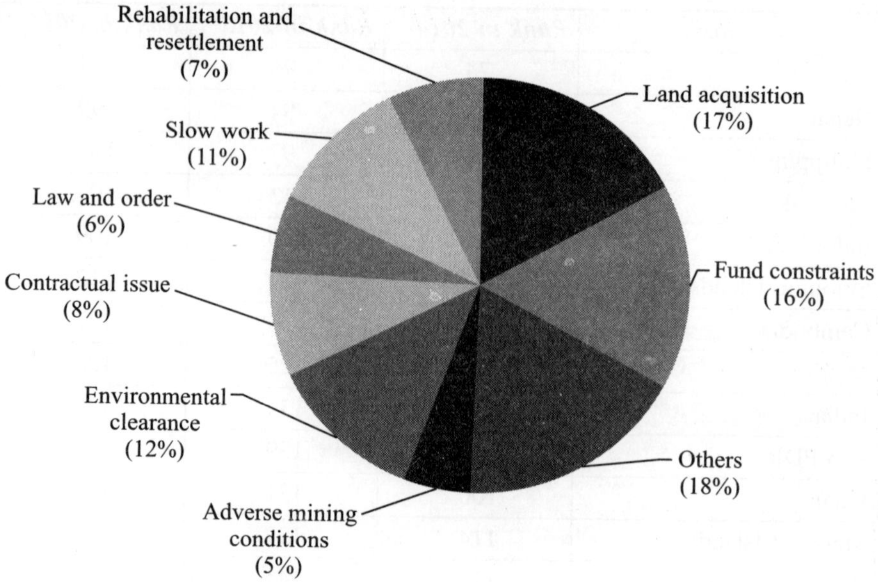

Exhibit 1 Reasons for the time and cost overruns: Case of 408 projects.
Source: Rediff.Com and Business Standard

The Government of India carries out reforms for making doing business easy. Reforms are destined to improve business environment of the country and also to attract international business.

However, the process of growth in investment slowed down in 2012–2013. It is believed that the delay in clearance of the projects in various sectors contributed to this slow process of investment in the economy, and as a result, caused slow economic growth. Economic Survey of India, 2013–2014 quotes a study by the Centre for Monitoring Indian Economy (CMIE), which highlights that the delay in projects contributed significantly to the slowdown in the economy. With the new government headed by Prime Minister Narendra Modi, the business community is hopeful of an improved business climate.

Source: This case is written by the authors based on inputs from the following sources:

1. *Business Standard*, http://www.business-standard.com/article/news-cm/india-no-policy-space-to-ease-the-slowdown-in-capital-inflows-moody-s-global-macro-outlook-for-2014-15-114050800577_1.html
2. *Business Standard*, http://www.business-standard.com/article/pti-stories/upa-should-have-continued-with-economic-reforms-chidambaram-114043001622_1.html
3. Economic Survey of India, http://indiabudget.nic.in/budget2013-2014/es2012-13/echap-01.pdf
4. Rediff.com, http://www.rediff.com/money/report/nib-likely-to-be-toothless-in-cutting-project-delays/20121016.htm)

CASE QUESTIONS

1. What is GST? How will it be beneficial?
2. How can reforms make India's business environment conducive?

REVIEW QUESTIONS

1. Highlight the macroeconomic performance of the emerging markets.
2. Discuss the trend of foreign investment in the emerging and developing markets.
3. Why are investors attracted towards the emerging markets?
4. Discuss the economic performance of Sub-Saharan Africa.
5. Why is business environment not conducive in Syria and Egypt?
6. Discuss the doing business parameters of BRICS.
7. Write a note on the doing business environment of ASEAN.
8. What is ECOWAS? How conducive is to do business in ECOWAS countries?
9. Discuss the ranking of various regions in the world on account of doing business, 2014.
10. Examine the doing business environment in India.

SUGGESTED READINGS

Doing Business Report 2014, World Bank and IFC.

Global Competitiveness Report 2013–2014, World Economic Forum, Geneva.

Mathur, Sajal and Dasgupta, M. (Eds.), 2013, 'BRICS: Trade Policies, Institutions and Areas of Deepening Cooperation', Centre for WTO Studies, IIFT, New Delhi.

'Sustaining the Momentum: Vigilance and Reforms', Asia and Pacific Regional Economic Outlook, April 2014, International Monetary Fund (IMF), Washington DC.

INDEX

1986 agenda, 376

Absolute poverty, 119
Accounting exposure, 425
Acquisitions, 326
Actionable subsidies, 412
Additional Central Assistance (ACA), 71
Agents of an economic system, 55
Agflation, 117
Agreement on Agriculture (AoA), 395
Agreement on Textiles and Clothing (ATC), 402
Agreement on the application of sanitary and phytosanitary measures, 399
Aid for trade, 391
Aims, objectives and functions of WTO, 377
Allianz's microinsurance initiative, 281
Amber box, 397
AMS, 397
Analytical research, 45
Anti-dumping agreement, 410
Appellate body, 388
Association of Southeast Asian Nations (ASEAN), 368
Automatic route, 334
Autonomous, 110
Autonomous investment, 112
Average tax rate, 175

B2B project in Uganda, 392
Backward vertical FDI, 334
Balance in current account, 219
Balance in merchandise trade account, 218
Balance of payments, 217
Bank of England base rate (BOEBR), 204
Bank rate, 204
Bay of Bengal Initiative for Multi-Sectoral Technical and Economic Cooperation (BIMSTEC), 369
Bharat Nirman, 180
BIMARU states, 139
Blue box, 398
Board for Industrial and Financial Reconstruction (BFIR), 257
Book keeping system, 98
Boom, 118
BRICS, 446
  and doing business, 447
Broad money, 199
Bullionism, 61
Burden of taxation, 177
Business call to action, 280
Business cycle, 117
Business environment, 2
Business research, 45

Call market, 242
Call option, 426
Capital account balance, 219
Capital expenditure, 163
Capital flows, 163
Capitalism, 61
Capital market, 235, 236, 243
Capital receipts, 163
Carbon labelling, 417
Cash investments, 236
Cash Reserve Ratio (CRR), 202
Centralised, 328

Centrally Sponsored Schemes (CSS), 71
Central Plan Scheme Monitoring System (CPSMS), 71
Central Sector Schemes (CS), 71
Cisco networking academy programme in LDCs, 280
Climate change, 39
Cocoa Livelihood Rehabilitation Project, 392
Command and control economy, 66
Common external tariff (CET), 361
Common market, 361, 365
Communist system, 63
Companies Act, 1956 and 2013, 260
Comparative overview of economic systems, 68
Competition Act, 2002, 261
Components of balance of payments, 217
Constant and current price, 98
Consultation, 387
Consumer, 259
Consumerism, 28
Consumer Protection Act, 1986, 258
Consumption in economics, 109
Convention on Contracts for the International Sale of Goods (CISG), 272
Copyright, 382, 383
Corporate securities market, 243
Corporate social responsibility, 25
Cost push inflation, 116
Cotton-4 Project, 392
Country risk analysis, 431
Country-specific variables, 336
Cross-border investment, 334
Cross-cutting issues, 416
Currency swaps, 426
Customs duties, 168
Customs union, 361

Data scanning and quantitative analysis, 46
Decentralised, 328
Declarations, 294
Deflation, 117
Demand for money, 198
Demand pull inflation, 115
Demographic environment, 7
Demography, 7
Descriptive research, 45
Digital opportunity initiative, 280
Direct Benefit Transfer (DBT), 24, 71
Direct cash transfer scheme, 181
Direct exporting, 325
Direct investment, 332
Direction of world trade, 355
Discount rate, 204
Dispute Settlement System (DSB), 387
Doing Business and ASEAN, 450
Doing business in BRICS, ASEAN, ECOWAS, 446
Doing business report, 45
Dunkel draft, 376

Early phase of economic planning, 79
Eclectic theory or OLI model, 335
Economic and Social Council (ECOSOC), 284
Economic Community of West African States (ECOWAS), 451
Economic conditions, 4
Economic environment, 3
Economic exposure, 426
Economic factors, 48
Economic integration, 359
Economic performance, 432
Economic policies, 4
Economic reforms, 91
Economic system, 4, 54
Economic union, 362
Effect of taxation, 177
Emerging markets scenario, 439
Environmental analysis, 44
Environmental scanning, 44
Ericsson in Haiti, 280
Errors and omission, 219
Ethical fashion programme, 392
Ethnocentric, 328
European union, 363
Evaluation and diagnosis of risk, 432
Evolution of economic ideas, 56
Exchange rate, 197
Excise duties, 167
Expenditure approach, 98
Exploratory research, 45
Exporting, 325
Export Promotion Councils (EPCs), 50

Factor endowment theory, 311
Factors of PEST analysis, 48
FDI policies, 5
FDI through automatic route, 333
FDI through government route, 333
Features of Indian planning, 77
Final consumption expenditure, 99
Finance Commission, 190
Financial Markets Committee (FMC), 208
Financial stability, 197
Fiscal deficit, 172, 173
Fiscal instruments, 175
Fiscal measures, 113
Fiscal policy, 5, 160
Fisher index, 115
Five year plans, 77
Food security programme, 180
Foreign Direct Investment (FDI), 326, 331
Foreign exchange exposure, 425
Foreign Exchange Management Act (FEMA), 263
Foreign Exchange Regulation Act, 155
Foreign exchange reserves, 219
Forward contract, 426
Forward vertical FDI, 334
Franchisee, 325
Free Trade Agreement (FTA), 360
Fundamental conventions, 294
Futures contract, 426

General Agreement on Tariffs and Trade (GATT), 298, 374, 380
General Agreement on Trade in Services (GATS), 380
General assembly, 283
General council, 300
Geocentric, 328
Geographical indication (GI), 383
Gilt edged market, 243
Gini coefficient, 123
GIPC International IP Index 2014, 269
Global, 328
Global business environment, 18
Global cash flow, 424
Global warming, 39
Gold, 296
Goods Council, 300
Government route, 334
Governance conventions, 294
Gravity model, 315
Greenfield investment, 333
Green revolution, 85
Gross capital formation, 99
Gross Domestic Product (GDP), 101
Gross fixed capital formation, 99
Gross investment, 112
Gross National Product (GNP), 101
Growth, 35
Guiding principle of tax policies, 175
Gulf Cooperation Council (GCC), 369

Heartland theory, 420
Heckscher–Ohlin (HO) model, 311
High Yielding Varieties Programme (HYVP), 86
Hilton-Young Commission, 206
Horizontal investment, 334
HO theory, 311
Hyperinflation, 117

Idea of inclusive growth, 31
Impact of land reform, 85
Importance of political risk analysis, 433
Incidence of taxation, 177
Inclusive growth, 31
Inclusiveness, 31
Income approach, 100
Income per person in a country, 106
Indian solar loan programme, 281
Indirect exporting, 325
Indirect taxes, 167
Induced investment, 112
Industrial design, 384
Industrial policies, 4, 5
Industrial Policy Post-2015, 155
Industrial Policy Resolution, 1948, 131
Industrial Policy Resolution, 1956, 132
Industrial Policy Resolution, 1991, 155
Industrial Policy Statement, 1973, 138
Industrial Policy Statement, 1980, 139
Industrial Policy Statement, 1991, 140
Industrial property, 382
Industries under Schedule A and Schedule B, 134
Inequality, 121
Inflation, 113

Inflation in general price level, 98
Institutional economists, 60
Institutional frameworks, 208
Instruments of monetary policy, 201
Instruments of money market, 242
Integrated childhood development scheme, 180
Intellectual property, 382
Intellectual property rights (IPRs), 382
Intellectual Property (TRIPS) Council, 300
Intensive Agricultural District Programme (IADP), 86
International Bank for Reconstruction and Development (IBRD), 297
International Centre for Settlement of Investment Disputes (ICSID), 297
International Court of Justice (ICJ), 285
International Development Association (IDA), 297
International Finance Corporation (IFC), 297
Internationalisation, 324
International Monetary Fund (IMF), 295
International organisation, 281
International production theory, 335
Intra-Industry Trade (IIT) Model, 314
Investment, 90, 112
  expenditure, 99
  policy, 5
  through government route, 334
Invisible transactions, 218
Inward and outward (FDI), 333
Issue department, 207

Janata Party government, 138
Joint ventures, 326

Kalyan, 87
Key indicators of balance of payments, 225
Kjellen's theory, 420

Land reforms, 84
Land tenure system, 84
Laspeyres' index, 114
Least Developed Countries (LDCs), 405
Legal environment, 9
Legal framework, 256, 432
Legal procedure, 256
Leontief paradox, 312
Lerma Rojo, 87
Levels of economic integration, 359
Licence Raj, 139
Licensee, 325
Licensing agreement, 325
Licensor, 325
Liquidity Adjustment Facility (LAF), 209
Lok Sabha, 256
Lorenz curve, 122

Mahalwari system, 84
Mahatma Gandhi National Rural Employment Guarantee Act (MNREGA), 180
Major impacts of the green revolution, 88
Managing risks, 426
Marginal tax rate, 175
Market economy, 64
Market information and trend, 46
Market intelligence, 50
Market strength and its segmentation, 47
Marrakesh declaration, 376, 377
Marshall–Edgeworth index, 114
Marxism, 63
Measurement of inequality, 122
Measurement of inflation, 114
Measuring income at constant prices, 98
Measuring income at current prices, 98
Members of the UN, 283
Mercantilism, 60
MERCOSUR, 369
Mergers, 326
Mid-day meal scheme, 180
Ministerial conference, 300, 301
Mixed economy, 66
Modes of entry into a foreign market, 324
Modes of services, 381
Monetary measures, 113
Monetary policies, 5, 196
Monetary policy strategy group, 209
Money aggregates in India, 199
Money market, 235, 236, 237
Monopolies and Restrictive Trade Practices (MRTP) Act, 1969, 261
Monopolies Inquiry Commission, 1964, 137
Most Favoured Nation (MFN), 379

Multidomestic, 328
Multilateral Investment Guarantee Agency (MIGA), 297
Multilateralism and the multilateral trading system, 358
Multilateral netting, 424
Multinational Corporations (MNCs), 327

Narrow money, 199
Natco pharma, 270
National income accounting, 97
National Rural Health Mission (NRHM), 180
National Rural Livelihood Mission (NRLM), 180
National treatment, 379
NCHMobiApp, 254
Net Domestic Product (NDP), 101
Net investment, 112
Net national product (NNP), 101
New agricultural strategy, 86
New trade theory, 312
Non-economic environment, 3
Non-Tariff Barriers (NTBs), 407, 408

Objectives of fiscal policy, 174
Objectives of monetary policies, 196
Objectives of planning, 78
Objectivity, 431
Official bank rate, 204
Official cash rate, 204
Open market operation, 204
Opportunity cost, 309
Option, 426
Organic state theory, 420
Organisational structure of World Bank group, 298
Organised retailing, 30
Organised sector of the market, 237
Output approach, 100
Overnight rate, 204

Paasche index, 114
Panel, 388
Patent, 384
Periphery, 420
Personal income tax, 165
PEST analysis, 48
Pillars, 396
Planned economy, 66
Planning and strategies, 432
Planning Commission of India, 73
Policies of government expenditures, 161
Policies of revenue collection, 161
Political environment, 8
Political factors, 48
Political risk analysis, 433
Political union, 362
Polycentric, 328
Porter's diamond, 326
Portfolio investment, 332
Poverty, 35, 119
  and economic environment, 121
  lines, 120
Pravasi Bharatiya Divas, 1
Predatory pricing, 262
Predictive research, 45
Pre-independence period, 75
Pre-policy consultation meetings, 209
Price index, 114
Primary deficit, 174
Primary market, 237
Principle of comity, 271
Principle of international jurisdiction, 271
Principle of sovereignty and sovereign immunity, 271
Principle of the act of state doctrine, 271
Principles of international law, 271
Principles of the Trading System (WTO), 378
Production approach, 100
Progressive taxation, 176
Progress of India's capital market, 244
Prohibited subsidies, 412
Proportional taxation, 176
Protectionism, 61, 379
Protocol of provisional application, 374
Public debt, 177
Public expenditures, 170
Public policy, 23
Public revenue, 162
Public sector, 89
Pull factors, 417
Push factors, 417
P.V.18, 87

Quotas, 296

Rajya Sabha, 256
Rangarajan Committee, 124
Ready forward contract, 243
Real investment, 112
Rebasing, 98
Recent developments in stock exchanges, 246
Recent trends in monetary policy, 209
Recession, 118
Recovery stage, 118
Regional comparison of doing business, 440
Regional Comprehensive Economic Partnership (RCEP), 370
Regional cooperation, 363
Regional integration, 363
Regional performance of doing business, 444
Regional trade agreement (RTAs), 363
Region-wise foreign investment, 442
Regressive taxation, 176
Relative poverty, 119
Repo rate, 204, 209
Research process, 46
Reserve Bank of India, 205
Restrictive trade practices, 259
Revealed Comparative Advantage (RCA), 313
Revenue deficit, 173
Revenue expenditure, 163
Reverse repo rate, 209
Right of first refusal, 322
Risk analysis, 431
Role of capital market in India, 243
Rules of origin, 403
Ryotwari (or Raiyatwari) system, 84

Sanitary and Phytosanitary Measures (SPS), 399
Sarv Siksha Abhiyan (SSA), 180
Savings, 111
Schutz index, 123
Scope of international trade law, 272
Secondary market, 237
Secretariat, 284
Securities and Exchange Board of India (SEBI), 251
Security council, 284
Service mark, 383
Services council, 300
Sick Industrial Companies Act (Special Provisions), 1985, 256
Sick industrial units, 256
Single point of entry, 361
Social factors, 49
Social indicators, 119
Socialist system, 63
Socio-cultural environment, 6
Socio-economic indicators, 119
Sonara-64, 87
Sources of international law, 270
South Asian Association for Regional Cooperation (SAARC), 366
South Asian Free Trade Area agreement (SAFTA), 367
Special Drawing Rights (SDRs), 296
Specialised committees, 300
Stages of business cycle, 118
Stagflation, 117
Standard presentation of BoP in India, 221
Standards code, 375
Statistical tools, 46
Statutory Liquidity Ratio (SLR), 203
Strategic analysis, 47
Strategic management, 2
Strike or exercise price, 426
Structure of Indian capital market, 243
Structure of Indian financial system, 235
Structure of organised banking system, 237
Structure of the UN, 283
Subsidies and countervailing measures, 412
Sustainable development, 37
SWOT analysis, 47

Tariff barriers, 407
Tariff negotiations, 374
Tax haven, 424
Tax revenues, 163
Technical Advisory Committee (TAC) on Monetary Policy, 209
Technical barriers to trade (TBT), 401
Technological environment, 9
Theories of FDI, 334
Theory of absolute advantage, 307
Theory of comparative advantage, 309
Theory of market imperfection, 335

The Uruguay Round and the Marrakesh Declaration, 375
The World Island, 420
Thrust Areas of the WTO, 389
Total domestic income, 99
Total stock of money, 199
Trade, 35
Trade and climate change, 416
Trade and finance, 419
Trade and food security, 417
Trade and geopolitics, 419
Trade blocs, 363
Trade Complementarity Index (TCI), 314
Trademark, 383
Trade policy, 5
Trade Policy Review Mechanism (TPRM), 386
Trade-Related Aspects of Intellectual Property Rights (TRIPS), 382
Trade-Related Investment Measures (TRIMs), 385
Transaction exposure, 425
Transfer of technology, 417
Transfer pricing, 424
Translation exposure, 425
Treasury bill, 242
Triple Bottom Line (TBL), 25
Trusteeship council, 284
Trust territories, 284
Turnkey projects, 325
Types of deficits, 173
Types of FDI, 333
Types of inflation, 115
Types of research, 45

UNCTAD XIII, 286
Unemployment rate, 123
Unilateral trade measures, 416
United Nations Commission on International Trade Law (UNCITRAL), 273
United Nations Conference on Trade and Development (UNCTAD), 285
United Nations Industrial Development Organisation (UNIDO), 157
Universal climate agreement, 39, 50
Unorganised money market, 237
Uruguay round meetings and outcomes, 377

Value-added approach, 100
Valuing political risk, 434
Vertical investment, 334
Vidhan Parishad, 256
Vidhan Sabha, 256

World Bank, 296
World Bank Group (WBG), 296
World Economic Forum (WEF), 15
World Trade Organisation (WTO), 298
WTO Ministerial, 301

Zamindari system, 84

